BEFORE BRASÍLIA

Before Brasília

FRONTIER LIFE IN CENTRAL BRAZIL

Mary C. Karasch

University of New Mexico Press • Albuquerque

© 2016 by the University of New Mexico Press
All rights reserved.
Published 2016
Printed in the United States of America

Library of Congress Cataloging-in-Publication Data

First Paperback Edition, 2021
Paperback ISBN: 978-0-8263-6332-9

Names: Karasch, Mary C., 1943– author.
Title: Before Brasília : frontier life in central Brazil / Mary C. Karasch.
Other titles: Frontier life in central Brazil
Description: [First edition] | Albuquerque : University of New Mexico Press, [2016] | Includes bibliographical references and index.
Identifiers: LCCN 2016002826 (print) | LCCN 2016016528 (ebook) | ISBN 9780826357625 (cloth : alk. paper) | ISBN 9780826357632 (electronic)
Subjects: LCSH: Goiás (Brazil : State)—History—19th century. | Goiás (Brazil : State)—History—18th century. | Tocantins (Brazil)—History—19th century. | Tocantins (Brazil)—History—20th century. | Frontier and pioneer life—Brazil—History. | Brazil—History—1763–1822. | Brazil—History—Empire, 1822–1889.
Classification: LCC F2651.G63 K47 2016 (print) | LCC F2651.G63 (ebook) | DDC 981/.73—dc23
LC record available at https://lccn.loc.gov/2016002826

Cover illustration from Gloria Kaiser and Robert Wagner, *Thomas Ender*.
Courtesy of the Library of Congress, Washington, DC.
Designed by Lisa Tremaine
Composed in Minion Pro and ITC New Baskerville

To

my sister Jean A. Hall,
brothers Robert John Karasch Jr. and Richard A. Karasch,

and their families

Contents

List of Illustrations	ix
Acknowledgments	xiii
Introduction	xvii

PART ONE: CONTACTS AND CONQUESTS

Chapter 1. Into the "Heart of Brazil": Landscapes of Contact and Decimation	3
Chapter 2. The Indigenous Nations of Central Brazil	33
Chapter 3. *Bandeiras* and *Entradas*: The Invaders of Central Brazil	63
Chapter 4. Indigenous Warfare and Peacemaking	95

PART TWO: COLONIAL SOCIETY: WHITES, *PARDOS*, AND BLACKS

Chapter 5. "Good Order": Structures of Empire	129
Chapter 6. The White Propertied Elites of the Captaincy of Goiás	159
Chapter 7. "Masters of the Dance": Enslaved Africans and *Crioulos*	185

PART THREE: POINTS OF CONTACT AND CULTURE CHANGE

Chapter 8. People of the Holy Spirit: Christians and Their Sacred Spaces	215
Chapter 9. Shadows in the Night: Women and Gender Relations	247
Chapter 10. Defenders of the Conquest and Useful Vassals: The Free People of Color	273
Conclusion: Reflections on Frontiers/Borderlands of Central Brazil	299
Appendix A. Indigenous Nations of Central Brazil	305
Appendix B. Censuses	311
Appendix C. Colonial Churches and Lay Brotherhoods in the Captaincy of Goiás	326
Glossary	329
Notes	331
Bibliography	387
Index	407

Illustrations

Figures

1.	Tocantins River and boatmen	8
2.	Interior of an Apinaje house	39
3.	Xavante and Apinaje baskets	40
4.	Karajá and Apiaká portraits	47
5.	Xerente chief Chiotay	53
6.	Captive women and children	66
7.	Bororo family in the 1820s	75
8.	Apinaje warrior	97
9.	Porekamekrã anchor-axe	100
10.	Karajá warrior	107
11.	Xavante horn	110
12.	Xerente leader Xuathe	114
13.	Vila Boa de Goiás in 1803	130
14.	Inhabitants of Goiás	160
15.	King of Congo in a *congada* in the 1980s	186
16.	Religious procession before Saint Ann's Church	216
17.	Church of Our Lady of the Rosary in Natividade	220
18.	The mission of São José de Mossâmedes	231
19.	Officer and woman in white	248
20.	Baby-carrying sling from Cocal Grande	252
21.	Snakeskin boots, gun case, and hat	283

Maps

1.	Brazil, showing Goiás, Tocantins, and neighboring states	4
2.	Rivers and mountains	6
3.	Indigenous nations	34
4.	*Entradas* and *bandeiras*	64
5.	Colonial trade routes and towns	140

Chart

1. Decline in annual income of the *quinto*, 1752–1805 — 135

Tables

1. Annual income from the *quinto*, 1752–1805 — 138
2. Value of trade, 1804 — 143
3. Men with gold from the captaincy of Goiás, 1750–1824 — 165
4. Locations of gold mines, 1826 — 171
5. Retail businesses in the captaincy of Goiás, 1783 — 175
6. Plantations, mills, and slaves, 1783 — 177
7. Bureaucrats in São Félix, 1783 — 183
8. Africans sold in the captaincy of Goiás, 1810–1824 — 197
9. Number of slaves by occupational category, 1783 — 203
10. Population and deaths among the Kayapó of Maria I by age and sex, 1781–1783 — 236
11. Inhabitants of Pedro III do Carretão, 1824 — 242
12. Number of married couples by color, 1783 — 262
13. Percentage married by color and sex in the captaincy of Goiás, 1804 — 263
14. Percentage married by color, sex, and legal status in Goiás, 1825 — 265
15. Marital status by color in Cavalcante, 1828 — 266
16. Marriages of free people of color in Vila Boa and Meia Ponte, 1796–1816 — 267
17. Manumitted slaves in the captaincy of Goiás, 1792–1824 — 275
18. Forms of manumission by number and gender, 1790s — 278
19. Number of *pardo* men in the auxiliary infantry regiment, 1789 — 287
20. *Pardo* occupations in five communities, 1820s — 291
21. Occupations of black militiamen, 1820s — 295
A.1. Indigenous nations of central Brazil — 305
B.1. Whites in the Comarca of the South, 1779–1832 — 311
B.2. Whites in the Comarca of the North, 1779–1832 — 312
B.3. Whites in the captaincy of Goiás, 1779–1832 — 312
B.4. Whites and slaves by sex, 1804 — 313

B.5.	Whites and slaves by sex, 1825	314
B.6.	Whites and slaves by sex, 1832	315
B.7.	Enslaved population in the south, 1736–1750	316
B.8.	Enslaved population in the north, 1736–1749	316
B.9.	Enslaved population of the captaincy of Goiás, 1782–1832	317
B.10.	Enslaved Africans, blacks of Brazil, and *pardos*, 1832	318
B.11.	Blacks in the Comarca of the South, 1779–1832	319
B.12.	Blacks in the Comarca of the North, 1779–1832	320
B.13.	Indians, 1832	321
B.14.	Free people of color, 1804	322
B.15.	Free people of color, 1825	323
B.16.	Free people of color, 1832	324
B.17.	Population of the captaincy of Goiás, 1779–1832	325
C.1.	Colonial churches and lay brotherhoods in the captaincy of Goiás	326

Acknowledgments

My decision to study the history of Central Brazil was made in part so that I could return to the region where I had lived in the late 1970s. What I did not realize is that this decision would lead to new friendships and many debts of gratitude to those who have assisted me with my research. Especially helpful in first orienting me to the local sources were Frei Simão Dorvi, Dalísia Doles, and Luis Palacin. The warm hospitality of Professor Doles before her death in 2000 made me feel at home in Goiânia. I will always remember our trip together with Heliane Prudente Nunes to explore the Pireneus mountains, the town of Pirenópolis, and the *fazenda* Babylonia. Luis Palacin kindly received me at the Jesuit residence in Goiânia and gave me an orientation to the colonial documents that he had helped to sort and organize. Unfortunately, he too has died (1998), and Frei Simão has retired to Italy. I was privileged to know these three "pioneers" in the development of the study of the history of Goiás. Also very helpful to me on colonial sources were Marivone Chaim and Janaína Amado, and I am especially grateful for their assistance with sources in Portugal. Before his death in 2005, Paulo Bertran not only shared with me his numerous publications, but also told me about essential sources in Brazil.

When I taught at the Federal University of Goiás (UFG) in 1993, the then head of the history department, Dr. José Antônio de C. R. de Souza, and his Goiano-born wife, Waldinice Nascimento, shared many documents and insights with me in Goiânia. Their warm friendship and continuous support have greatly facilitated my research. In the 1990s I also met Dona Lena Castello Branco Faria de Freitas and Dona Gilka Fereira Salles, whose company I enjoyed when Dona Lena hosted a tea at her fazenda near Trinidade. My former students Professor Cristina C. P. Moraes, who has taught at UFG, and Professor Maria de Fatima Oliveira have also enriched my visits to Goiânia, and Fatima has also taken me to Anápolis to meet her students and colleagues at the state university of Goiás (UEG). David and Angela McCreery, whom I first met when they lived in Goiânia, have shared research trips and tourism, in particular our "voyage" across the backlands from Recife to Araguaina in 2000. David McCreery has also been my most significant North American collaborator and coauthor on the history of Goiás. In 2004 the anthropologist James Dow, my former Oakland University colleague, accompanied me on a trip by car to the Ilha do Bananal, where we did a riverine trip with a Javaé guide. All of these friends have made traveling to and living in Central Brazil so meaningful.

John Monteiro, who tragically died in an auto accident in 2013, told me about an ethnographic collection on the Brazilian Indian in Vienna, Austria. Based on our conversation at the American Historical Association in January 2013, I went to Vienna in May and secured permission to view the collection. The artifacts had been collected by Johann E. Pohl in Central Brazil, and some have now been published in the catalogue *Beyond Brazil*, edited by Claudia Augustat. I am deeply grateful to her for the opportunity to view the original artifacts and to receive permission to publish images of some of them in this book.

Another debt of gratitude is owed to the many archivists and librarians who have personally assisted me in Portugal, Brazil, and Washington, DC, in particular those who confront enormous odds in preserving the past in Goiás and Tocantins. In Portugal I am especially indebted to the staffs of the Archivo Histórico Ultramarino, the Biblioteca Nacional, the Biblioteca da Ajuda, and the Arquivo National da Torre do Tombo for their assistance in locating sources on the captaincy of Goiás. Professor Dauril Alden gave me an invaluable orientation on how to do research at the Torre do Tombo. Since I intended to include the military in my book, I also went to the military archive, but it had only a small number of documents on Goiás. More importantly, staff there referred me to the Gabinete de Estudos Arqueológicos de Engenharia Militar (GEAEM), where I located many maps for Central Brazil. Larissa Brown kindly told me about the documentation on Goiás at the archive of the Tribunal de Contas and also passed her Xeroxes of Goiás documents on to me.

In Brazil I actually began my research on this project at the Biblioteca Nacional in Rio de Janeiro, where the manuscript collection holds many treasures from Goiás. Over the years I have also received much help from the staffs of the Arquivo Nacional, the Museu do Indio, the archives of the Curia Metropolitana of Rio de Janeiro, the Casa Oswaldo Cruz, and the Instituto Histórico e Geographico do Brasil. From Rio I then moved on to Brasília, where my former student Vera Ferreira at the University of Brasília oriented me to the resources of the Libraries of Congress, and I located many reports of the provincial governors of Goiás at the Library of the Senate. I also worked in the libraries of the Ministries of Agriculture and Transportation. The library of the National Foundation of the Indian (FUNAI) was also important, as well as interesting, since many indigenous visitors stopped there when they came to Brasília. In Goiânia it has been a pleasure to do research at the state archive

(AHG) and the Sociedade Goiana de Cultura, Instituto de Pesquisas e Estudos Históricos do Brasil-Central (SGC), where Dona Carmen Lisita and Antônio César Caldas Pinheiro have made me feel so welcome. Before the archive of the curia was moved to the SGC, I was given permission to work in the library with uncatalogued documents then held at the cathedral of Goiânia. José Mendonça Teles also welcomed me to SGC and to the Instituto Histórico e Geographico de Goiás. In the City of Goiás the Museu das Bandeiras, the Educational Library (Biblioteca da Fundação Educacional da Cidade de Goiás [BFEG], which then held the archive of Frei Simão), and the Orfenato de São José, which holds parish registries, were also most helpful. In contrast, in the state of Tocantins Professor Odair Giraldin and I mostly confronted the lack of colonial documentation as we visited notarial and parish archives. I would also like to thank him for arranging a visit to the new archive of indigenous recordings in Carolina, Maranhão, and for taking me to visit the Apinaje reserve in 2007. It was a pleasure to meet the descendants of the Apinaje who had played an important historical role in the eighteenth century. David McCreery and I made a special visit to Natividade to check out the new library at the Associação Cultural da Natividade, but we found only fragments of colonial documents. Simone da Ascuna was especially helpful to us on this visit and shared with us her photographs of the feast of the Divine Holy Spirit (Divino Espirito Santo), which I was fortunate to witness with a research team, including Professor Giraldin, from the Federal University of Tocantins in 2004.

In the United States, the Hispanic Division of the Library of Congress, under the leadership of Dr. Georgette Dorn, has consistently aided me in finding sources on Goiás as well as facilitating my access to the CDs of the Projeto Resgate on Goiás. The Inter-Library Loan Department of Kresge Library at Oakland University located rare books on Goiás, while the Oliveira Lima Library at Catholic University in Washington, DC, enabled me to find still others. Without the collaboration of the professional staffs of all these libraries and archives, as well as those at the Instituto Histórico e Geográfico and the Biblioteca Mario de Andrade of São Paulo, I could not have undertaken research that often seemed impossible.

At the end of my research trips, I was able to consult the William John Burchell Papers at the Kew Archives in London and the Johann E. Pohl Ethnographic Collection at the Museum für Völkerkunde in Vienna, Austria, where Claudia Augustat was especially helpful.

I would also like to thank Maria Beatriz Nizza da Silva, not only for her hospitality in Lisbon, but also for including me in her conferences on colonial history in Lisbon and sharing her many publications on Luso-Brazilian women and colonial society. She has also placed my initial studies on Goiás in her edited collections. I also thank Edith Couturier and Asunción Lavrin, whose friendship and stimulating discussions on colonial Latin American history, as well as their many publications on women's history in Hispanic America, have been essential to my understanding of gender in the colonial period in Latin America. Before his death in 2010, A. J. R. Russell-Wood also aided me in doing research on colonial Brazil, and I have missed his mentorship. The reviewers Alida C. Metcalf and David McCreery provided useful suggestions for revisions, which have contributed to making this a much improved book.

I am especially grateful to those who have helped fund my numerous research trips. The National Endowment for the Humanities Fellowship of 1986–1987 launched the major archival research in Brazil. A summer research fellowship from Oakland University in 1988, which was followed by a sabbatical grant, enabled me to continue the archival research in Brazil and Portugal. After that, Oakland University continued to support my research with travel grants to do additional research. The Fulbright-Hays Senior Scholar Award made it possible for me to return to Goiás in the fall semester of 1993, and a Fulbright research and teaching award took me to the University of Brasília for the first time in 1977–1978.

My sister Jean A. Hall and her son Michael D. Hall provided essential technical and computer support, and Michael assisted me in photographing manuscripts and artifacts in London and Vienna. Sasha Ramayya was indispensable in the final preparation of the manuscript, for which I am most grateful.

If I have failed to name and properly thank anyone here, please be assured that it is due only to my faulty memory after so many years of research. It is a truism that no one does research alone, and an entire community of scholars, students, librarians, and archivists have made possible this lengthy project, not to mention the people of the region. All of them have my deepest gratitude. I continue to be especially grateful to Thomas Skidmore, who started me off as a "Brazilianist" so many years ago, and he was still mentoring me when I joined him in conversation at Brown University in April 2006.

Introduction

The genesis of *Before Brasília* came in a seminar in African history that I did as a graduate student at the University of Wisconsin with Professor Jan Vansina in which we studied poorly documented regions of Africa, and my paper focused on the history of Darfur. His seminar planted the idea of choosing a region of Brazil that needed research, that is, West Central Brazil, then Central Brazil. A second influential reason for this choice was a trip that I made in 1969 to São Miguel de Araguaia and a Karajá beach encampment on the Araguaia River. My "first contact" with the Karajá was a typically superficial tourist visit in which we talked briefly with a few of the Karajá, took photographs, and enjoyed swimming in the clean blue river. Other memories of the 1969 visit to Goiás are of the many *flagelados* (flagellated ones), as they were then called, who were poor families with wrinkled, sun-damaged skin being transported about the state in open trucks. I also saw gangs of agricultural workers in the fields, evoking images of plantation slave labor. Since illegal slavery then occurred in the interior of Brazil, I have often wondered if some of them were actually enslaved.

After a long trip by bus and train through Goiás and Mato Grosso to Corumbá on the border with Bolivia and back to Rio de Janeiro, I completed my research for the dissertation, wrote the first draft of *Slave Life in Rio de Janeiro*, and began teaching at Oakland University. In the 1970s I began to show Adrian Cowell's film *The Tribe That Hides from Man*, to my classes.[1] This documentary demonstrated how Orlando and Claudio Villas Boas tried to make contact with the Kreen-Akarore, who refused to accept pacification with the expedition, thus leading the filmmakers to speculate about their fear of contact. The visual images of the lengthy pacification process fascinated me, as they did my students. After years of refusing pacification, the Kreen-Akarore (also Kranhacãrore or Kren-akarôre) eventually made contact in 1973; we now know that among their ancestors were the Kayapó/Panará, who had once lived in Goiás.[2]

These types of experiences foreshadowed my future interest in Central Brazil, but even more important was the Fulbright-Hays award for eighteen months of research and teaching at the University of Brasília (1977–1978), where I came to love the beauty of the *cerrado* (savanna) and its many flowering plants and trees. For the first time, I also had the opportunity to meet many of the people of the interior, especially those living in the satellite cities of

Brasília. They had brought their culture and folklore to the modern capital, and I could listen to their music and observe the religious and cultural traditions that I had only read about in Rio de Janeiro. One of my students, Catarina Helena Knychala, took me to the satellite city of Sobradinho to meet a weaver, Dona Ana Helena de Morais, who introduced me to the handwoven coverlet tradition of the region. Living in Brasília and discovering popular culture that had died out elsewhere in Brazil, I was curious about how and why such practices had been preserved in the Brazilian interior. What also intrigued me was the incongruity of Oscar Niemeyer's glass buildings and the colonial-style coverlets woven on a coarse wooden loom.[3]

While exploring the region and getting to know its people, I traveled with Vera Blinn Reber in July 1978 to the *Cidade de* (city of) Goiás (also known as Goiás Velho, or Old Goiás). While touring the Museu das Bandeiras, which houses the archive, I saw the types of documents on enslaved Africans that I had not located for the city of Rio de Janeiro. These included tax records that a local scholar was organizing. In the museum, they had also preserved chains once used on slaves and an African-style sculpture from the black church of Santa Efigênia in Niquelândia. On that same trip I also met the Italian missionary Frei Simão Dorvi, who showed me the parish registers and other church documents that he had collected on his trips throughout the region. The survival of so many church records, including those on the black brotherhoods, also convinced me to study Central Brazil.

Finally, while teaching at the University of Brasília, I learned about late-1970s contacts with isolated indigenous populations through my student Diana Cléa Garcia da Motta, who missed classes to participate in pacification expeditions; obviously, she gave me many insights into gift-giving techniques as used in the late 1970s. She also studied historical contacts with the Xavante, which introduced me to their history. I first met two of the Xavante when they came to Brasília to sell their baskets. While researching at the university library, I learned about an indigenous woman, Dona Damiana da Cunha, who had led pacification expeditions to contact her people, the Kayapó, and bring them to settle in the mission of São José de Mossâmedes. At the urging of David Sweet, I wrote a small biography of her based on the sources that I could then locate in Brasília.[4] This biography then posed one of many questions: Why would an indigenous woman lead a pacification expedition? Furthermore, why would a Portuguese governor entrust such a mission to a Kayapó woman? As Robert Darnton demonstrates in *The Great Cat Massacre*, what is most "opaque" and difficult to comprehend about a foreign culture are the "points of entry" into penetrating that "alien culture."[5] In this case, Dona Damiana da Cunha's role in contacting the Kayapó is central to deciphering how this frontier society operated; that is, the indigenous of both sexes were significant historical actors who shaped this region's history. The governor's decision to give the expedition to her—and not her second husband—should soon make sense to contemporary readers of *Before Brasília*.

Meanwhile, however, I had to set Central Brazil aside to complete *Slave Life in Rio de Janeiro*, which was finally published in 1987. As the work on that manuscript ended, I began research in Rio de Janeiro and Lisbon on Central Brazil with the aid of a National Endowment for the Humanities fellowship for 1986 and 1987. After much initial research was completed, I participated in an ethnohistorical meeting in 1991 in São Paulo, for which I wrote "Catequese e cativeiro: Politica indigenista em Goiás, 1780–1889," which was included in the *História dos índios no Brasil*, edited by Manuela Carneiro da Cunha.[6] There I met the anthropologist and ethnohistorian Odair Giraldin and later went to visit him in Porto Nacional, while I was on a second Fulbright grant at the Federal University of Goiás in 1993. As the author of an ethnohistory of the Kayapó, he has been especially helpful as an informant on the indigenous populations of Goiás and Tocantins.[7] The hospitality of Professor Giraldin and his first wife, Deusamy, in Porto National in the 1990s contributed to my growing interest in researching the colonial history of the north, now the Amazonian state of Tocantins. Together Professor Giraldin and I have explored the region and searched for lost documents, especially those of Natividade, one of the historic cities of Central Brazil.[8] We also visited the Apinaje on their reserve in 2007. Finally, Professor John Monteiro's invitation to participate in an ethnohistorical panel in conjunction with the XXIII National Symposium of History in Londrina, Paraná, in 2005 led to the conceptualization and writing of chapter 4.

There are still many others who have influenced the writing of this book, who will be noted elsewhere; here I would like to stress that this is a book that has taken decades to bring to its current shape and form, and it draws on many sources and experiences for its insights and analysis, including residence and travel in Central Brazil. In the midst of my other publication, editorial, and teaching responsibilities, the region and its people have continued to hold my affection and interest. It is my hope that *Before Brasília* will introduce readers to the dynamic history of the region in which Brasília was constructed, for Central Brazil was occupied long before Brasília was built between 1957 and 1960.

Methodologies

The diversity of my experiences and research in Brazil, Portugal, Vienna, and the United States have also affected my search for a way to conceptualize or contextualize the history of Central Brazil. When I began the archival research for this book in 1986, I thought that I would be writing about African slavery in Goiás, but I have long since broadened the study. In particular, I came under the influence of North American frontier studies, which seemed to be an especially useful methodology, although North American examples did not seem to be entirely applicable to the book that I was writing.[9] Then I turned to recent works on the African diaspora, in particular creolization debates, which also seemed relevant but incomplete, because many did not include relationships with the indigenous population.[10] As I have also published on black and indigenous women in Brazil, a gender-based analysis also seemed appropriate for this male-dominated frontier, and I have tried to integrate women into this book.[11] The latest trends in Atlantic history have also shaped this study, as I have tried to understand the region with reference to the Atlantic World.[12] Recent cultural history studies, especially those concerned with identity formation, led me to question word usage, and since then I have been especially sensitive to color terminology, elite discourse, and the constructions of identity.[13] Due to the influence of my former colleague Richard Tucker, an environmental historian, I have included the impact of human settlement and war on the environment of the region. A collaborative book project organized by Dona Lena Castello Branco Ferreira de Freitas and Dr. Joffre Marcondes de Rezende of the Academia Goiana de Medicina, the first medical history of the region, published in 1999, also facilitated an understanding of the disease environment.[14]

The last important influence on the writing of this book was the Borderlands project of Professors Cynthia Radding and Danna Levin-Rojo. Participation in their two conferences, which are to lead to a publication on the *Borderlands of the Iberian World* by Oxford University Press in 2018, enabled me to make final revisions in the light of the most recent research by international scholars.

In writing *Before Brasília*, I have been seeking, in the words of the anthropologist José Ribamar Bessa Freire, the one theory or string that holds the strand of pearls together as a book.[15] Instead, readers will see reflected here many interwoven strands of pearls, especially methodologies linked to those in frontiers, borderlands, enslavement, and ethnohistory, and the results of research conducted over decades. But if there is only one constant theme it is that of enslavement—of indigenous captives and enslaved Africans and their descendants, because this was a frontier shaped by slavery as *bandeira* (expedition) leaders kidnapped Indians, and subsequent bandeiras did the same throughout the colonial period. Enslavement of the owners of the land then led to the evolution of a slaving frontier with all its dislocations, as slavery spread its tentacles throughout Central Brazil; even resistance to enslavement led to greater warfare and a culture of violence that decimated indigenous populations.[16] The introduction of enslaved Africans led to still more slavery and resistance, with Africans joining in the warfare in communities of escaped slaves (*quilombos*). Thus a central theme is the evolution of frontier violence and enslavement that ultimately led to the consolidation of white rule over a majority population of color, both free and enslaved. Therefore, the violence on this frontier did not lead to peaceful occupation and a more equitable society but instead to marked social inequality, originally based on slave labor but later on control of rich pastoral and agricultural lands in the nineteenth century.

In other words, this is a broad history of one *sertão* (backlands; pl., *sertões*) and its peoples, whose history cannot be easily categorized, from first contact ca. 1590s to the 1830s. Most documentation, however, is from the late eighteenth century, beginning ca. 1775, due to the number of surviving documents, including censuses, and ending about 1835, shortly after the important census of 1832. The region this book covers is the Portuguese administrative unit known as the captaincy of Goiás, largely the modern states of Goiás in the south and Tocantins to its north. Its focus is on the evolution of a freeborn society of color on a violent frontier located between two great rivers: the Araguaia River to the west and the Tocantins River to the east, which flow north from Central Brazil to the delta of the Amazon River.

A major contribution of *Before Brasília* is simply definitional and perhaps encyclopedic; that is, it locates and describes the peoples of the region in a period of alleged economic decadence attributed to the decline of gold mining in the late colonial period. To do so, this book depends heavily on a variety of written Luso-Brazilian sources that are scattered in archives and libraries in Europe, Brazil, and the United States. Literate evidence is often incomplete due to the loss of documents, especially in the move of the state archive from the City of Goiás to Goiânia, when documents literally flew off the back of the truck. Part of the colonial history of the former mining town of Natividade in Tocantins is missing because a judge took its eighteenth-century documents home to her residence in Goiânia. Many of the documents collected by Frei Simão Dorvi have been held in precarious locations without security since 1986.

Also missing for the colonial period, however, are testimonies by the conquered and enslaved, since most people were then illiterate, but I have attempted to include their voices whenever possible. Many times we can only guess at what they thought or feared through their actions rather than their words. Especially in the case of the indigenous populations, past events may be obscured by myths or reflected in rituals, but not even the white residents of mining towns recorded their history, nor did missionaries, who were generally absent from Central Brazil from the expulsion of the Jesuits in 1759 to the arrival of the Italian Capuchins in the 1840s. Therefore, the late colonial history of Central Brazil must be written largely from fragmented elite sources until more oral traditions are collected and preserved.

On the other hand, one notable strength of sources for the region results from the number of Luso-Brazilian and foreign explorers who visited Goiás, including artists. In the 1790s the *pardo* (mulatto) explorer of the Tocantins and Araguaia Rivers was Tomás de Sousa Vila Real, who left a diary of his trip. The Austrian Johann Emanuel Pohl and the French Auguste de Saint-Hilaire supplement the documentary record with vivid descriptions of the indigenous people that they met and the "strange customs" of the place. Pohl collected indigenous artifacts that are now housed in Vienna, while Francis de Castelnau's expedition made invaluable portraits of the indigenous of the region in the 1840s. Even a British botanist, John Burchell, collected plants in the region and left drawings of what he saw there. Visual images from the late colonial period are especially useful, but incomplete. They rarely include the people of African descent. But above all, this book is deeply indebted to the detailed descriptions of a Portuguese military officer, Raimundo José da Cunha Matos, who had also served in Africa.[17]

Other sources include contemporary popular religious rituals and festivals that may preserve some of the past; therefore, they will also be integrated into this book wherever possible. For example, how people once organized themselves may be most evident in the *congada*, a theatrical dance performed on the eve of Pentecost in May or June. Since rituals often reflect local societal values, the dancers were clearly divided by distinct groups: the Congos, led by their king, who was dressed in blue; the *caboclos*, or mestizo Brazilians, dressed in green, whose queen processed first; and the Tapuias, who were costumed as Indians. How long the congada has been danced in Goiás is uncertain, but it points to one local vision of the society that was created in the City of Goiás.[18] Another elaborate festival, once common throughout Brazil, is still celebrated in Goiás and Tocantins. The festival of the "Divine Holy Spirit" begins on Pentecost Sunday and gives a leading role as "Emperor" to local white elites, such as ranchers, but includes people of all colors, who participate in the procession carrying red banners and drums, afterward enjoying foods distributed to the people. I was fortunate to assist at one Festa do Divino in Natividade with Professor Giraldin and a research team from the Federal University of Tocantins.[19]

Before Brasília is divided into three parts. The first explores the initial encounters with the land (chapter 1), defines the indigenous peoples as they were contacted (chapter 2), records the invading expeditions that sought gold and indigenous captives to enslave (chapter 3), and chronicles the warfare that erupted as a consequence (chapter 4). Part 2 focuses on the colonial order that the Portuguese tried to establish within their structures of empire (chapter 5) and the evolution of local propertied elites (chapter 6) along with enslaved African communities (chapter 7). All these people could not live isolated from each other, however, and part 3 clarifies the role of the Catholic Church and its missions that brought diverse groups together for Christianization (chapter 8); describes gender relations, including concubinage and marriage (chapter 9); and examines the emergence of the free/freed men and women of color and the ways in which they grew in numbers and significance in local society. Thus another theme of this multifaceted book is the escape from legal enslavement by 1835, when two-thirds of the men and women of color of African descent were no longer legally enslaved. The indigenous, however, continued to be taken as war captives, since Goiás was one of the locations in Brazil where Indian slavery was legalized in the early nineteenth century.[20]

Finally, to return to the frontier themes stressed in North American historiography, this frontier did not lead to social equality or to the complete abolition of slavery, nor did it close by 1835. Social distances continued to widen in the nineteenth century as the land-rich cattle barons/*coroneis* strengthened their political and economic power while contesting indigenous nations for land.[21] Elite privilege and wealth continue to the present, leading the rural poor to flee the countryside and migrate to the cities, where many now live in urban slums, or to reserves, if indigenous by birth. By the early twenty-first century, the state of Goiás has become one of the richest agricultural states of Brazil, while Tocantins state has experienced the expansion of the soybean frontier; both states support the growth of great agribusinesses, often at the cost of fragile and rare ecosystems and small farmers. Contemporary transformations are eliminating free-flowing rivers, virgin rainforests and savannas, and traditional ways of life. This book is an attempt to capture a moment in time and a way of life long before Brasília was built. My hope is that readers will come to share my own love for a beautiful region and its people in spite of its often violent past. But then violence has usually been a characteristic of frontier regions, and late colonial Goiás was no exception.

PART ONE

Contacts and Conquests

CHAPTER 1

Into the "Heart of Brazil"

Landscapes of Contact and Decimation

Writing to the count of Oeiras (marquês de Pombal) in 1760, Governor João Manoel de Mello (1759–1770) described the captaincy of Goiás as the "heart of Brazil."[1] Indeed, this remote region must have seemed to him to be the very center of Brazil because of the rigors of his journey there to assume his post as governor. Many eighteenth-century sources permit insight into how governors and other outsiders reached the "heart of Brazil" and constructed their landscapes of difficult terrain and harsh climate.[2] One objective of this chapter, therefore, is to recover what they reported about their journeys and the environment they encountered in Central Brazil. We will first survey general characteristics of this vast region, followed by more specific locations for contacts and encounters, such as the rivers. The next part of this chapter will describe late colonial visions of the climate, forests, mountains, and savannas, where indigenous peoples lived and challenged invaders. Since malaria seems to have increased in virulence in the eighteenth century, the disease environment will be a particular focus at the end of this chapter, since it seems to have played a significant role in population migrations and indigenous mortality. Before we take the reader into the "heart of Brazil," however, we need to define the region of West Central Brazil (later Central Brazil).

The region of Brazil that is the subject of this book is the captaincy of Goiás in the late colonial period (map 1). Since *captaincy*, a Portuguese administrative term, holds no meaning for contemporary readers, it may be easier to relate the region to the modern city of Brasília, which has been the capital of Brazil since 1960, although in the eighteenth century there was no town of Brasília, which was carved out of the cerrado (savanna) of the central plateau of Brazil in the late 1950s. In fact, the capital of the captaincy of Goiás was Vila Boa de Goiás, which was founded in the 1720s as a mining town and then served as a Portuguese administrative center in the 1730s. Renamed the City of

MAP 1
BRAZIL
Showing
GOIÁS, TOCANTINS,
and Neighboring States

Study Area: The Captaincy of Goias

Goiás in the nineteenth century, it served as the capital of the province and state of Goiás until the 1930s, when Goiânia was constructed. The name *Goiás* derives from the indigenous people who formerly inhabited the region, the Goiá (also Goyá) or Goiases (Guaiazes), who used to live at the headwaters of the Vermelho River. According to Estevão-Maria Gallais, the name *Goiases* in their own language signified "flowers of the fields." In the seventeenth and eighteenth centuries, their encounters with Paulista bandeiras (expeditions) led to their enslavement and destruction as a culturally distinct people. Taking their women as captives, gold miners built the new town of Vila Boa de Goiás on the banks of the Vermelho River.[3]

The Goiá also gave their name to the Portuguese administrative unit, the captaincy of Goiás, which was divided into two large territories known as *comarcas* that then comprised one million square kilometers in Central Brazil. The captaincy was a country-sized region that now includes the state of Goiás in the south (the former Comarca do Sul) and the northern state of Tocantins (the Comarca do Norte), which was separated from the state of Goiás in 1989. Furthermore, parts of Maranhão; Minas Gerais (the Triângulo Mineiro); Mato Grosso, including the region of the Rio das Mortes (River of the Dying); and Mato Grosso do Sul were once governed from Vila Boa.[4]

Since the captaincy was so centrally located, many other captaincies surrounded it. To the north was the Amazonian state of Pará and its neighbor to the east, Maranhão. In the northeast, Piauí, Pernambuco, and Bahia also shared borders with Goiás. To the southeast, Goiás had economic and trade relations with Rio de Janeiro, the capital of the viceroyalty of Brazil after 1763; but the viceroy resident in Rio had little real administrative authority over the distant captaincy. In some ways, Goiás was like a separate colony in itself since its governors were directly responsible to Portuguese bureaucrats resident in Lisbon. The reason was gold. In the late eighteenth century, Goiás was the fifth-wealthiest captaincy in Brazil, and Portugal imposed bureaucratic controls to try and secure that gold (see chapter 5). In contrast, many of the captaincy's closest cultural and economic ties were with the neighboring captaincy of São Paulo to the south, to which Goiás was subject until 1748. The other nearby captaincy that was especially significant to Goiás was the mining state of Minas Gerais, through which significant trade passed via Paracatú. To the west was the captaincy of Mato Grosso, which provided foodstuffs to the mines of Goiás and refuge to the indigenous peoples and enslaved Africans who fled Goiás.

Thus Central Brazil was not totally isolated, and it was firmly integrated into the Atlantic economy of the late eighteenth and early nineteenth centuries. From Portugal, manufactured goods, sea salt, wine, and animals were brought to Belém do Pará at the delta of the Amazon River; to Salvador, the capital of Bahia; and to Rio de Janeiro. Enslaved Africans were also imported and conducted along with these commodities to the gold mines. In return, the captaincy produced and exported gold, cattle, sugar, *aguardente* (distilled sugarcane), cotton, tobacco, marmalade, coffee, deer skins, and shoe

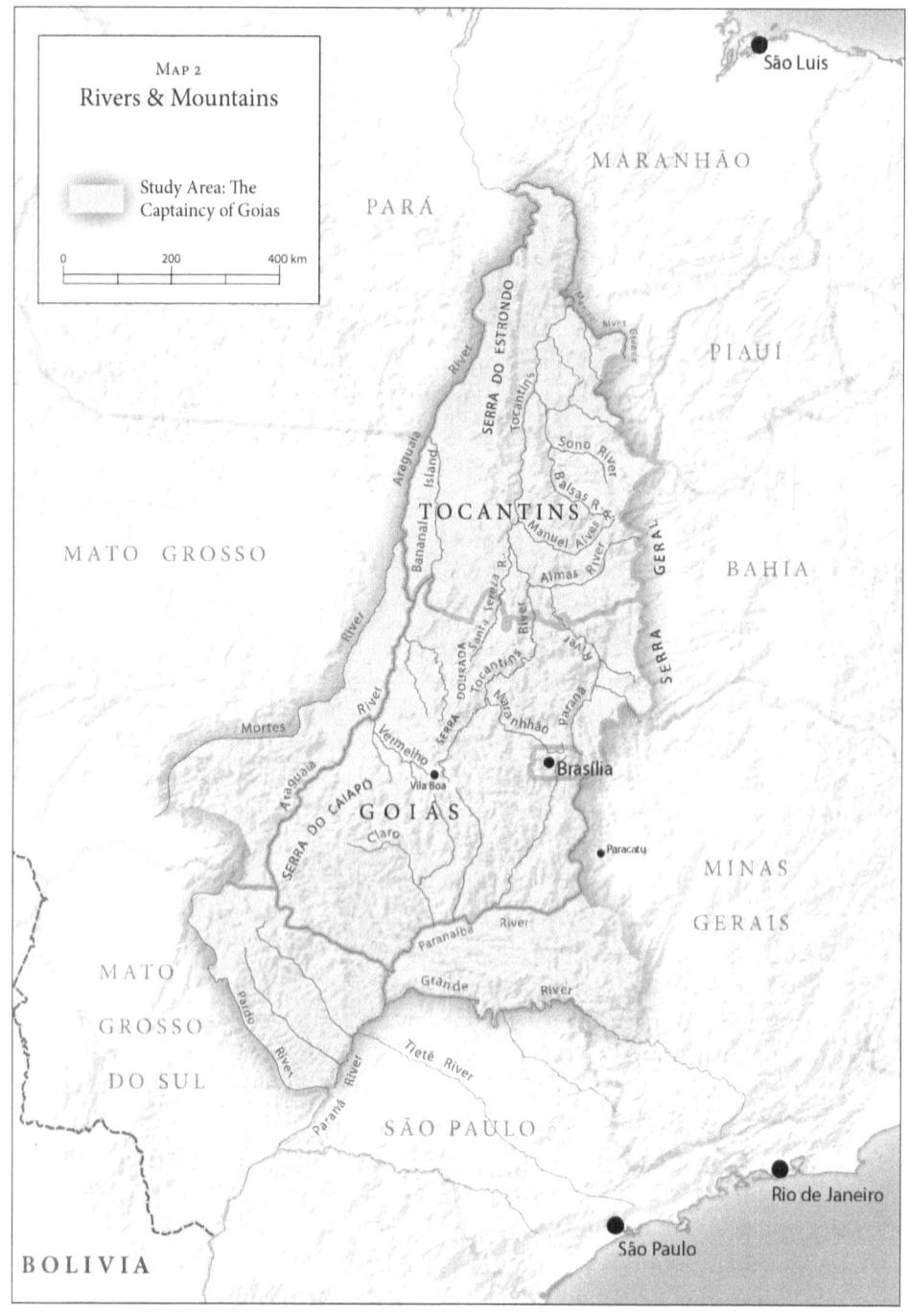

MAP 2
Rivers & Mountains

Study Area: The Captaincy of Goias

leather.⁵ Even indigenous slaves were traded from Goiás to other captaincies. Such trade presupposes physical environments that permitted the movement of goods and people (map 2). Basically, our journey into the heart of Brazil will begin in the north, then move to the northeast, proceed to the southeast and south, and end with the far west. In the course of this journey, we will identify some of the indigenous nations that outsiders encountered, as well as many of the dangers, especially from diseases, that outsiders and local inhabitants confronted.

The North: The Amazon Region

The port of Belém do Pará at the delta of the Amazon River was the city of significant religious and economic influence over the northern part of the captaincy, what is now the state of Tocantins. Merchants resident in Belém financed and organized essential trade networks that stretched far south into Central Brazil, at least to the mining towns of Pontal, Porto Real (now Porto Nacional), Natividade, and São Félix. Since the seventeenth century, Franciscan and Jesuit priests had also led canoe expeditions down the Tocantins River to contact the many peoples who once lived along it and named it the Peraupeba (also Paraopeba) River. Slave ships, arriving directly from Africa or from São Luis, Maranhão, anchored in Belém and unloaded newly imported Africans who had traveled for months from Portuguese Guiné or from Congo and Angola, while indigenous women and children captured in Goiás were transported north to be sold in the city.⁶ Those descending the Tocantins River to the mines of Goiás began a journey in Belém that could require an entire year to return to the port via the Tocantins River. At least one segment of the trip from Porto Real to Belém could take more than six months, as the English botanist William John Burchell learned when he arrived in Porto Real in November 1828. He had to wait for "the proper season" to begin his journey to Pará. Because of this, he did not reach Belém until June 1829.⁷

Late eighteenth-century traders also left Belém when it was possible to take advantage of the higher water levels on the Tocantins River, which were due to the intense rains of the rainy season. In 1791, for example, Tomás de Sousa Vila Real embarked from Belém on 5 February and traveled to Carmo, where he rested briefly before continuing on to Vila Boa, which he reached on 21 April 1791. The crew on such a long-distance trip could be indigenous men, such as the Apinaje, who hired on in order to return to their villages with iron wares

Figure 1. A view of the Maranhão Serra with the Tocantins River and boats in the foreground as travelers begin to cross the river. Source: Kaiser and Wagner, Thomas Ender. Courtesy of the Library of Congress, Washington, DC.

purchased in Belém, or men of any color who were skilled paddlers. A single woman might accompany the crew to cook for the men. Before the era of steamships, they voyaged in one of the long river canoes (*ubás* or *ajôjos*) with a covered section that protected the cargo from the sun and rain. They usually made the trip with minimal food provisions because the river was so rich in wildlife that they could hunt and fish to sustain themselves on the long journey.[8]

In contrast to the ease of finding food, the Tocantins River trip was difficult due to the length of the river, which begins in the central plateau over 1,600 miles to the south. As of 1806, the river was navigable from near Belém until the Uruú River. Clear and tourmaline green in sections, the river appears like a thin silvery ribbon as it meanders north toward the Amazon's delta, but its waters also hide sharp "rocky falls, rapids, and whirlpools" around which travelers had to portage. Especially dangerous were the falls at Lageado and Pilões, north of Porto Nacional. The river's narrow width farther south meant that potential enemies could assault and kill travelers as they journeyed south or portaged at the rapids. On the other hand, people could easily swim across the river or build rafts to cross it; thus the Tocantins River was not a significant barrier to population movements.[9]

As they traveled south from Belém, the canoers would encounter the town of Cametá and then small towns and villages located along the banks of the Tocantins River, which have now disappeared due to the Tucuruí dam. According to Francisco de Paulo Ribeiro, they passed the following locations before reaching Porto Real: the place of Cuxúará, the Mangabeiras, Baião, the vila of Paramerim, the Pederneiras, and the register at Alcobaça near what is now the city of Marabá. At Alcobaça, the Portuguese had established a military outpost to intimidate the Apinaje and other nations, as well as fugitive slaves, who threatened to disrupt passage on the long river. In fact, among the few known people to travel the length of the Tocantins River were three fugitive slaves who fled the mines of Goiás in 1723 and made their way up the entire length of the river to Belém.[10]

Other points of reference for Luso-Brazilian traders were the *registros* (registers or checkpoints): Arrôios on the Ponta do Arapari Tapéra and the register at São João das Duas Barras (now São João do Araguaia) at the confluence of the Araguaia and the Tocantins Rivers. At São João the captaincy of Pará ended and that of Goiás began. Merchants then had the choice of continuing south on the Tocantins River to São Pedro de Alcântara (now Carolina) on the east bank of the river in Maranhão (after 1810) or proceeding south on the Araguaia River. A third choice was to go overland from São João das Duas Barras to Carolina and from there by land to Pontal (after 1738) or nearby Porto Real (after 1800).[11]

A few travelers who chose the Araguaia route, such as Tomás de Sousa Vila Real in the 1790s, encountered a beautiful blue river, filled with "cristaline" waters, which was broad and shallow.[12] In the dry season its waters notably retreated, exposing wide sandy beaches, where the Karajá went to camp in temporary shelters and contemporary tourists continue the tradition; when the rains began, the rising river drove the Karajá inland to their more permanent villages. If merchants traveled on the Araguaia, however, they would not find Luso-Brazilian settlements because much of the river was still under the control of the Karajá and Javaé; their villages were located along the banks of the Araguaia River or on Bananal Island (also Ilha de Sant'Ana), one of the largest riverine islands in the world. South of the island another tributary, the Crixás River, recalled the Quirixás (Crixás), who have disappeared as a distinct ethnic group.[13] When canoers reached the Vermelho River at its confluence with the Araguaia, they could travel directly on this tributary of the Araguaia until Vila Boa, but only if the rains had raised the water level in the rock-filled river. Otherwise, low water would force them to transport goods overland to Vila Boa or wait for months until the waters returned—Vila Real had to wait for eight months. Other tributaries of the Araguaia River were the Mortes River to the west, and in the southwest the Claro and Pilões Rivers, which were rich in diamonds. The headwaters of the Araguaia River were in the Serra dos Caiapó, near which the Kayapó built their large villages and attacked invaders. In spite of indigenous resistance, those who engaged in the contraband gold trade often elected the Araguaia route, where they apparently established trade relations with indigenous peoples, such as the Karajá, who traded with Belém.[14]

In contrast, at the confluence of the two rivers at São João, most merchants chose the Tocantins River route to voyage south, which was a shorter three- or four-month trip. At this juncture, the path of the Tocantins River curved to the east and then south. The land in between the two rivers is nicknamed the parrot's beak (O Bico de Papagaio, or simply the Bico). The indigenous people who then controlled both the Araguaia and Tocantins Rivers at the Bico were the Apinaje.

To the east, the first significant tributary of the Tocantins River, just south of Carolina, is the Manuel Alves Grande River, where some Xavante once lived along its banks. Near its headwaters to the east, part of this river parallels the Balsas River of Maranhão, from which the peoples of Maranhão crossed between the rivers to enter Goiás, or conversely, the Xavante left their homes in Goiás to raid cattle ranches between the Balsas and Paranaíba Rivers in Maranhão. To the south of the Xavante, the Krahô claimed lands along a second tributary, the Manuel Alves Pequeno River. Where the Sono (also Sonho, Somno) River joins the Tocantins River (now at Pedro Affonso), the boatmen would encounter "an abundance of forests and fields" along the Sono, as well as the Xerente, who lived on both banks of the Tocantins River. In 1813 Captain Francisco José Pinto de Magalhães described the Sono River as "healthy" and in a "very agreeable situation," with "good airs." Those who had once lived south of the Sono River were the Acoroá (Akroá).[15]

Such late colonial descriptions clarify that the eastern tributaries of the Tocantins River between São João and Porto Real were still dominated by indigenous nations in the early nineteenth century. According to Colonel Sebastião Gomes da Silva Berford, who visited the region of Maranhão and Goiás in 1809–1810, there were more than nine nations of "gentiles" between the arraial of the prince regent in Maranhão and Porto Real, including the Timbira da Matta, Canella fina, Bou, Copinharó, Timbira do Campo, Tapacoa,

Caraou [Krahô], and others. He also reported that at the confluence of the Manoel Alves Grande and the Tocantins Rivers the "force" of the Xerente, Temembó, and Caraou was "great." They were then attacking the Mirador ranch, which was owned by Elias Ferreira de Barros, who shipped beef to Pará with the aid of an Indian fugitive from Pará.[16]

Because of such hostilities, travelers did not find Luso-Brazilian settlements or places to purchase foodstuffs within the captaincy of Goiás until they reached the mining town of Pontal, founded in 1738. Pontal is not actually on the Tocantins River and no longer survives as a town, but after 1800 travelers could stop at the river port of Porto Real (now Porto Nacional). This might be as far as the long canoes would journey, since goods could be unloaded and taken overland to the mining towns in the north, such as Carmo and Natividade. Otherwise, they would remain on the river to travel to São Félix, the site of the second foundry house, that is, if the river were safe enough for travel and if it were deep enough to permit the passage of canoes. Otherwise, mule teams followed a land route from Natividade to São Félix via the Estrada do Norte that linked the mining towns to the river routes.[17]

South of Porto Real and Pontal, the Tocantins River changed names; colonial sources referred to it as the Maranhão River, and we will follow colonial usage in denominating the most southern part of the Tocantins River as the Maranhão River. Near here travelers would find many small but prosperous mining towns, such as São José do Tocantins (Niquelândia) and Traíras (Trahiras). São Félix was also located near the river. West of the Maranhão River, canoemen could journey on yet another tributary of the Tocantins, the Almas River, to other mining towns, such as Meia Ponte (Pirenópolis); on the Almas River they faced attacks from the Canoeiro. On modern maps the Maranhão River extends all the way to its headwaters in what is now the federal district of Brasília.[18]

To the south of Natividade and Porto Real was yet another eastern tributary of the Tocantins River; it is also the third one named Manuel Alves. This was the Manoel Alves de Natividade, which flowed south of Natividade to join the eastern bank of the Tocantins River. Its headwaters were to the east, almost to the border with Maranhão, and north of the mission of Duro (now Dianópolis). The indigenous peoples who lived along this Manuel Alves River and at Duro were the Akroá and Xacriabá. Just south of the confluence of the Manuel Alves and the Tocantins River was a tributary that entered the Tocantins River from the west and just north of the town of Peixe. This was the Santa Teresa River, which began in the Serra Dourada and flowed north to join the Tocantins River.[19]

A significant tributary of the Tocantins River in this more southern region was the Paranã, whose headwaters are also near Brasília and Formosa. Not to be confused with the Paraná River of the River Plate system, this Paranã River begins in the central plateau, meanders north and northwest through a fertile valley with herds of grazing cattle, and empties into the Tocantins River. Located between it and the Maranhão River is the Chapada dos Veadeiros. A notable falls of the Paranã that appears in colonial sources was the Parantinga, as Captain Pinto de Magalhães reported. Above the confluence of these tributaries, the Tocantins River notably widened in size, permitting more riverboat travel to the north.[20]

The Northeast

The Maranhão River was far from the captaincy of Maranhão, which was one of the captaincies from which so many people traveled to Goiás, including the Jesuits before 1759. The routes were difficult, however, because they had to cross the mountain range that ran from the north to the south through the *serras* of Tabatinga, Marcela, and Canastra. Merchants journeyed via the official roads through the mountains and entered the captaincy at the checkpoints of Duro, Taguatinga, and São Domingos, while *contrabandistas* (smugglers) followed secret trails through the mountains, as did many indigenous warriors.

One important overland route to Goiás began in São Luis, the capital of the captaincy of Maranhão. Portuguese merchants and *sertanejos* (men of the backlands), who traded in manufactured goods, foodstuffs, and enslaved Africans, began their journey at the port of São Luis. They then followed the old Jesuit road to the former mission of Aldeas Altas, located near Caxias in eastern Maranhão, which was the site of all the trade between São Luis and the captaincy of Piauí and the towns of Natividade and São Félix in Goiás. Here they could buy horses for their journey to Goiás. Colonel Sebastião Berford, for example, recorded his trip from São Luis to the Tocantins River in 1809–1810. He left São Luis on 29 September 1809 and traveled on or near the Itapicuru River to Aldeas Altas, which he identified as Caxias. From there he rode to Pastos Bons, where he found good pasture for his horses. The men then followed an overland route with stops at ranches that ran parallel to the Balsas River until they came to the Mirador ranch on the Manuel Alves Grande River near its confluence with the Tocantins River. The entire journey took a little over two months, and he arrived in Vila Boa on 2 or 3 December 1809.

Conversely, Pinto de Magalhães made the trip from Porto Real do Pontal to the "City of Maranhão" in eighteen to nineteen days.[21]

After reaching the captaincy, other travelers continued on to mining towns such as Pontal, Carmo, and Natividade to exchange their goods and slaves for gold that they then conducted back to São Luis via the same overland route. If they were fortunate, they avoided Xerente, Xavante, and Krahô raids on their convoys in the region of Pastos Bons or along the Manoel Alves Grande River.[22]

A second route from São Luis followed the rivers. After leaving São Luis, merchants traveled a short distance to the Mearim River and canoed it as far as possible, depending on water levels. Between the Mearim and Tocantins Rivers they apparently had to tote their goods (and canoes?) to the Farinha River, a tributary of the Tocantins. But after reaching the Tocantins River, they were easily able to descend to the mining towns of Goiás.[23]

Reflecting the strength of the Maranhão trade, yet a third route began at the Itapicuru River, where it emptied into the ocean, and traders followed that river until Caxias, from whence they transported goods to the Parnaíba River, which divides the captaincies of Maranhão and Piauí. They then voyaged south on the Parnaíba to join the road to Pastos Bons, which wound its way west all the way to the Tocantins River. According to one report, traders could cross the sertão between the Parnaíba and Tocantins Rivers in fifteen days in 1800. The indigenous peoples of the region of the Parnaíba and the headwaters of the Itapicuru were the Timbira, while the Acruá (Akroá) occupied the Sono, Manuel Alves Grande, Balsas, and Tocantins Rivers and extended their territory to the south of the Timbira. Both of these nations contested the north with the Capajús, the Almanajós, the Gamelas, and others.[24]

Since there were many navigable rivers in Maranhão, it is understandable why it was possible for merchants, bandeiras, and Jesuit priests to travel to Goiás in search of gold, captives, and converts. The major obstacle to their progress was usually indigenous resistance, but as soon as each nation was "pacified" and settled in a mission village, their territory was opened up to outsiders. Those who resisted, however, were attacked and pushed westward into Goiás, or they were driven west by epidemic diseases or drought conditions in the great sertão of the Northeast. The Xerente, for example, had once roamed freely in the arid regions to the east of the Tocantins River.[25] Entire villages, or only shattered survivors of warfare and epidemic diseases, also journeyed into the captaincy to find refuge along the Tocantins River or its tributaries, where they could plant their crops and find a reliable source of water.

To the east of Maranhão was the captaincy of Piauí, which was notable for its large cattle ranches and Jesuit missions in the early eighteenth century. The gold of Goiás also attracted merchants based in its port city of Parnaíba. Although some of these merchants journeyed into the captaincy of Maranhão and to Aldeas Altas, others traveled via the old Jesuit route that linked their missions to Oeiras in Piauí and then across the sertão to Barreiras in western Bahia. From there travelers crossed through the mountains to the registers of Taguatinga and Duro and ultimately to the mines of Goiás. A second route took a total of fifteen days to make the trip: three days from the first passage of the Preto River to the second crossing in its headwaters, two days from the second passage of the Rio Preto to Duro, four days from Duro to São Félix, and six days from there to Vila Boa. All across the sertão to Duro, travelers faced raids from the Akroá, especially if there was a lack of water in the dry season.[26]

Cowboys also conducted cattle and horses to and from Goiás, especially in drought periods in the arid sertão of the Northeast, or driven by their thirst, cattle ran away from the ranches of Piauí and Bahia to seek water to the west along the tributaries of the Tocantins River.[27] Some cattle and horses that went wild, if they escaped Krahô raids, even made it to the banks of the Tocantins River. Of course, people also fled the droughts in southern Piauí to find water in Goiás along its great rivers. The Gueguê, who had lived in a Jesuit mission in the district of Oeiras, Piauí, also crossed over to the Duro region and lived briefly in a mission there.[28]

The Jesuits who journeyed to the northern missions at Duro, Natividade, and Pontal also followed one of the river routes linked with the ports of Belém, São Luis, and Parnaíba.[29] Through their missions and ranches they also contributed to the establishment of official trade routes used to reach the gold mines. Although many contraband trails obviously escaped Portuguese notice and documentation, the river routes were of particular significance to mission efforts in Pará, Maranhão, and Piauí.

Linked with these routes were those of the captaincy of Pernambuco, which provided yet another way to get to the goldfields of northern Goiás via the semiarid sertão of Pernambuco and southern Piauí and the lush tropical south of Maranhão. The final section of the trip between Oeiras and São Pedro de Alcântara (Carolina) is remarkably beautiful for its flat tablelands (*chapadas*) covered in green vegetation, *buriti* palm trees along the creeks and rivers, and green pastures for cattle. Near Carolina the tall Chapada do Chapeu dominates the landscape with its high tableland in the form of a broad-brimmed hat. Wherever there were rivers and creeks, strands of buriti palm trees proclaimed the existence of water. People, animals, and birds looked for buritis to find water in the dry season. The rolling hills and rough terrain must have made travel very difficult in the past. Other routes were more southerly and stretched to the Goiano registers of Duro, Taguatinga, or São Domingos and from these checkpoints to Natividade and other mining towns in the captaincy of Goiás.[30]

Of all the northeastern routes, the most common one to Goiás began in Salvador, the capital of the captaincy of Bahia. Arriving there from Portugal were new governors, soldiers, bureaucrats, merchants, and priests, and from West and Central Africa many enslaved Africans, known in Brazil as Guiné, Mina, Congo, or Angola. Additional merchants and slaves came from the islands off the coast of Africa, such as Cape Verde, the Azores, and São Tomé. Merchants resident in Salvador organized great *comboios* (convoys) to conduct trade goods, horses, and slaves to Goiás. Typically, the mule teams, which were followed by new Africans walking on foot, left the city of Salvador and made their way to Cachoeira, inland from the coast. From there they set off across the semiarid and mountainous terrain of the sertão of Bahia until they reached the banks of the São Francisco River. After crossing the river they went on to Barreiras in western Bahia and then across the border of the two captaincies to the register of Duro, from whence they continued on to Natividade and São Félix and from the latter town to Vila Boa. The whole journey from Salvador to Vila Boa, as Governor Luis da Cunha Menezes (1778–1783) reported in 1778, had taken him only thirty-seven days of "march."[31] Contrabandistas in gold, who knew the routes through the mountains, must have been able to do the trip more quickly, since they usually traveled in small groups with pack animals that carried their Bahian purchases back to Goiás. Other small traders brought salt into the captaincy from the São Francisco River valley, for which they traded gold and other goods.[32]

A second Bahian route also crossed the sertão of Bahia and entered Goiás via the registers of Taguatinga or São Domingos. The closest mining towns there were Arraias and Cavalcante, and it was only a short distance from the latter to São Félix to join the road to Vila Boa. A third Bahian route entered the captaincy of Goiás via São Domingos or the register of Lagoa Feia and continued on to Meia Ponte (Pirenópolis). This route also connected the cattle ranchers and traders with Couros (now Formosa) and the Paraná River traders.[33] Overall, the Bahian routes probably carried the largest number of travelers to the northern mining towns—and the most contraband gold.

The Southeast and West

In contrast, the southern mining towns and the capital of Vila Boa were more closely linked with the captaincy and port of Rio de Janeiro and the captaincy of São Paulo. The Luso-Brazilian merchants who did not follow the northeastern or Tocantins routes instead traveled from Rio de Janeiro, especially after 1763. From the port of Rio, European manufactured goods and enslaved Africans were conducted via the Estrada Real through the hinterland of Rio de Janeiro, the forested mountains of Minas Gerais, and Vila Rica (now Ouro Preto), then the capital of the captaincy of Minas Gerais. From the mining town of Vila Rica, the mule teams and slaves proceeded inland to Paracatú (formerly part of the captaincy of Goiás, but now in Minas Gerais) and then on to Santa Cruz in southern Goiás, Meia Ponte (Pirenópolis), and finally Vila Boa.[34] In 1755 the new governor of Goiás, the Conde de São Miguel (1755–1759), left Rio de Janeiro on 17 June and recorded the length of his trip. It took him fourteen days to reach Vila Rica, presumably via the Estrada Real. His men rested there, and they bought horses for the rest of the journey. Leaving Vila Rica on 8 July, he took twenty-five days to reach Paracatú, arriving there on 2 August. After again resting his men and animals, he departed for Meia Ponte on 5 August, reaching there after fifteen days. Dom Marcos de Noronha (1749–1755), who was leaving office as governor, met him in Meia Ponte, where they discussed the affairs of the captaincy. After nine days the Conde de São Miguel left for Vila Boa, which he reached on the twenty-eighth, and he assumed the governorship on 31 August 1755. In his long trip, what he had feared the most was crossing the São Francisco River, which was then "pestiferous."[35] Notably, his journey to Goiás to assume the governorship took place during the dry season in the captaincy. This was also the route by which Portuguese military officers in the dragoons conducted the king's gold back to Rio de Janeiro for export to Lisbon.[36]

In the early nineteenth century, Padre Luiz Antônio da Silva e Sousa filled in details about some of the southern route from Vila Boa to the Paraná River in the south. He reported that the southern road ran from Vila Boa to Meia Ponte, Bonfim, Santa Cruz, and then to the three former Jesuit missions of Rio das Pedras, Pissarrão, and Santa Anna. Near Santa Anna was the register of Rio das Velhas. From there the road continued on to the former mission of Lenhoso, and ten leagues later it reached the Rio Grande. Overall, he calculated the total distance from the capital to the Rio Grande as 127 leagues.[37]

There was also a second route to the gold mines of Minas Gerais from Paratí on the coast south of Rio de Janeiro, but it is uncertain how common it was as a direct route to the mines of Goiás in the late eighteenth century. Far more significant for travel to Goiás were the riverine routes of southern Brazil. The difficulties of mountain travel and the high transport costs of the Rio de Janeiro, Minas Gerais, to Vila Boa route led others to prefer the alternate route from the small town of São Paulo to Vila Boa. Merchants and bandeiras from São Paulo traveled via the Tietê and Paranaíba Rivers, while others went by land via Desemboque and Santa Cruz with mule teams loaded with salt, iron wares, and foodstuffs to exchange for gold. In 1817 João Caetano da Silva of Meia Ponte discovered a new river route between the captaincy of Goiás and São Paulo that went via the River of the Bois until reaching the Grande, Pardo, and Jaguari-Mirim Rivers. On the way he located an unidentified Indian village with thatch-roofed houses and fields of rice, manioc, and corn in Camapuã, a traditional Kayapó territory. Eventually he met a Portuguese-speaking captain by the name of Manuel, who had once served as a soldier in the mission of Maria I before he had deserted the mission and made his way to Camapuã.[38]

Another important southern route also went by river, although this route seems to have been more commonly used before the mid-eighteenth century. It was possible to land in Buenos Aires, Argentina, and travel north on the Paraná River to the Paraguay River to Mato Grosso in western Brazil. In the colonial period, the famous monsoon expeditions took five to seven months to reach the gold mines of Cuiabá, Mato Grosso.[39] Presumably some journeyed on to Vila Boa, but merchants usually spent months or years in Cuiabá before transferring to Vila Boa. Silver from Potosí (now in Bolivia), quinine, and Paraguayan mate (tea) entered Goiás via this route, and Goiano gold flowed west to Cuiabá and Vila Bela. In the far western outpost of Vila Bela, merchants joined the trade of the Amazon River system and could even journey via the Guaporé and Madeira Rivers and the Jesuit missions of the Moxos in what is now Bolivia. Although merchants could travel the entire distance from Belém via the Amazon and Madeira Rivers to Upper Peru (Bolivia) and from Bolivia to Cuiabá, Mato Grosso, and from there to Vila Boa, most of the travel and trade involving Goiás followed only the route between Cuiabá and Vila Boa.[40] Between 1759 and 1821 the Portuguese required the governor of Goiás to send gold to the governor of Mato Grosso to defray the costs of defending Portugal's western frontier.[41] Thus mule teams regularly plodded west to Cuiabá, returning with trade goods and cattle for Goiás.

As early as 1750, traders and sertanejos could make the trip between Vila Boa and Cuiabá in twenty-five days across a barren landscape without sufficient food resources; therefore, they had to carry foodstuffs for themselves or face hunger on the road. One remarkable but unnamed Indian from Mato Grosso traveled to the Tocantins River and then to the Mearim River in Maranhão with only a month of daily travel, more or less. Cattlemen also conducted their animals to Goiás from eastern Mato Grosso to exchange for gold. In the 1790s, merchants from Cuiabá journeyed to the Fazenda do Leda at the falls of the Vermelho River, which were about eight days away from Vila Boa, to acquire trade goods there. If they did not find them, then they made "great journeys by land" to Minas Gerais or São Paulo. Mule teams laden with foodstuffs and herds of cattle were tempting targets to Kayapó raiders along the road to Cuiabá, as well as along the road to São Paulo that ran through Kayapó lands.[42]

The preceding survey of colonial routes and methods of travel to the captaincy includes only the most important ones that can be documented from late colonial sources. Given Portuguese complaints about contraband gold on hidden trails, there were many others, as well as indigenous trade networks that were unknown to the Portuguese. This framework of known routes into the heart of Brazil, however, provides only a brief introduction to the diverse physical and disease environments the travelers encountered as they journeyed within the captaincy of Goiás in the late colonial period.

In the Time of the Waters

New visitors to the captaincy of Goiás usually commented on the unusual climate they encountered there. There were two distinct seasons: the dry season and the rainy season, which was then called "the season of the waters."[43] The dry season lasted from April or May to September or October and even included low temperatures at night in July, especially at higher elevations, but cold spells in July could even afflict the indigenous peoples in their villages as far north as the Bico. Whenever it was cold, six hundred to seven hundred Porecamecrãs, both male and female, squeezed together with their feet around burning fires to keep warm in their village at Cocal Grande on the Maranhão River. The Kayapó at the mission of São José de Mossâmedes also suffered from the cold.[44] High winds and dry storms from May to July could destroy trees and harm people in the north, but overland travel and warfare took place in the dry season, when it was possible to walk or ride for long distances, although heat and thirst with blowing dust and insects caused discomfort. Since creeks and streams often dried up, people could even travel along dry riverbeds. On occasion, severe droughts assailed the captaincy and caused widespread food shortages, forcing people and animals to migrate in search of food and water. At the end of a normal dry season, ranchers and farmers, as well as the Kayapó, burned their lands to bring up new grass for pastures and to prepare the land for planting fields. Smoke from the controlled fires greeted travelers as they passed through agricultural and pastoral lands and warned bandeiras of nearby Kayapó villages ripe for destruction. In turn, indigenous raiding parties struck the slaves and *roceiros* (small farmers) at work in the fields and the mines. The Canoeiro commonly raided for food in the dry season and then retreated to their mountain refuges for safety.[45]

The rainy season brought relief from war and interrupted trade and raiding because few could travel in the time of the waters, especially in the north, where the rains began earlier and lasted longer. Portuguese governors and European visitors alike were astounded by the intensity of the rains that fell in sheets of water and by the daily downpours that lasted for six or more months, generally from the end of September (in 1760) until April or May. Since it rained every day, streets became streams of water, while each night dangerous lightning strikes of remarkable intensity and frequency alarmed visitors. In "the time of the waters" in 1760, "there was not a day without thunderstorms in Vila Boa." But in any season of the year, thunder boomed like "gross artillery" over the mountains.[46] Lakes, bogs, and swamps formed where there had not been any before. Although indigenous families constructed well-thatched houses that stood up to the daily downpours, local settlers suffered in their leaky mud-and-wattle houses. If they were built too close to a river, however, even solid houses were flood damaged or swept away, as happened in Vila Boa when it flooded. Since mining towns were usually located in mountain valleys along a stream that held placer gold, flooding was an annual problem. If the rains lasted too long, inhabitants and travelers had difficulty finding food in flooded landscapes, and nutritional diseases, such as pellagra and beriberi, debilitated the people.[47]

But that was not the only danger that the rainy season brought. The flooding also led to the formation of pools of stagnant water, where mosquitoes bred. Epidemics of fevers soon followed. In the 1730s on the Maranhão River, the Arraial do Maranhão was depopulated and abandoned due to a great epidemic. To save their lives, people fled to the nearby mining town of Água Quente. The gold mines of the Maranhão River had attracted as many as twelve thousand miners, including thousands of newly enslaved Africans. According to José de Sousa Azevedo Pizarro e Araújo, so much greed had led to "grave illnesses and successive deaths, in which there were days of counting 50 dead corpses." To explain why so many died, Manuel Aires de Casal wrote that the epidemic was due to the "putrefying of the bogs, occasioned by the overflowing of the Maranhão." The epidemic subsided only after the arrival of a herd of cattle from São Paulo.[48] The introduction of so many new people who worked in water, especially new Africans who carried malarial parasites in their bodies, combined with mosquito vectors and flooding, must have provided optimal conditions for an epidemic of malaria. Furthermore, mining practices of digging holes in the ground and abandoning them afterward meant that they filled up with water during the rainy season. Raimundo José da Cunha Matos, who had lived in Africa and was familiar with fevers there, correctly observed that "putrid waters" in which mosquitoes bred, left by "excavations," were the "cause of the most cruel sicknesses." Miners and their slaves continued to contract and die of fevers along the Maranhão River in the eighteenth and nineteenth centuries.[49]

Other eighteenth-century sources are even more suggestive about the existence of malaria in the captaincy. As early as 1735, Agostinho Barboza, who visited the "mines of the Tocantins," reported that in every house he entered he found one or more sick persons with "aleytas" (*maleitas*?) and others with "sezões." According to James Wells, "sezões [*sic*]" and "maletas [*sic*]" were remittent and intermittent fevers, nineteenth-century names for malaria. In fact, *sezõens* was and is a popular term for malaria in Brazil. Correspondence from 1779 and 1780 identifies the *presídio* of Nova-Beira, a small fort that the Portuguese built on Bananal Island in the Araguaia River, as "pestiferous" and "very infested with Sezoens and other diseases." Two years later yet another observer linked the rainy season, flooded lands, vapors, and "cezoens [*sic*]." He reported that merchants traveled during the dry season because the time of the waters made the trips difficult. With the torrential rains, rivers rose, their current became more rapid, and fields and roads were soon inundated, making river crossings impossible. The flooding also produced "many vapors" that infected and corrupted the air and "caused severe malignants [fevers], cezoens, and other dangerous sicknesses" that attacked those who traveled at that time in the "vast sertões."[50]

An indigenous nation also made the connection between mosquitoes and a bad place to live. When the Portuguese governor Tristão da Cunha Menezes (1783–1800) schemed to move a group of Xavante to Salinas on the east bank of the Araguaia River, they refused to obey him because of the mosquitoes that plagued Salinas in the 1780s. A decade later, when Tomás de Sousa Vila Real traveled along the Araguaia River in the 1790s, he recorded the sicknesses of his men and the death of one of them from "maleitas," which was probably malaria.[51]

Early nineteenth-century descriptions of malaria are more common, being enriched by travelers' observations as well as those of Cunha Matos, who led troops into the north in the 1820s. Such individuals agreed that the north had more sickness than the south, perhaps because the rains lasted longer. In 1828 Governor Miguel Lino de Moraes noted that the north was "so sickly, principally of sezões, in which every year many people die." The soldiers who accompanied Cunha Matos became sick with sezões on his expedition to Cavalcante and Porto Real (Porto Nacional). On the banks of the Almas River, a southern tributary of the Tocantins River, he reported that "the people are prostrated by malignant sezões, and bilious fevers," while Porto Real and Cavalcante were also suffering from epidemics in 1824. Notably, he referred to "tertian fevers," which was a common term for malaria in the past. He also used the appropriate treatment for these fevers, that is, *quina* (quinine), which he gave to his soldiers and took himself to preserve his health. Elsewhere in the north, Cunha Matos called attention to the intermittent fevers of the Bezerra River, near Arraias, which was "one of the most unhealthy [rivers] of the universe." Its endemic sicknesses were "sezões and other pernicious fevers." But he regarded all the valley of the Paraná River as unhealthy, as did many other travelers and local people. Annual flooding of the Paraná River that left many pools of stagnant water helps to explain why mosquitoes and fevers flourished there.[52]

The European traveler Johann E. Pohl also regarded the north as an insalubrious region "from Água Quente above until the environs of São João da Palma." There, during the dry season, he reported, "the putrid fever rages with such fury that it kills entire families" and few travelers "escape the attacks of that sickness." Furthermore, the principal cause of this evil was in the "stagnant water that the inhabitants are obliged to drink." Although people could have become sick from contaminated water or died of typhoid fever, it is probable that they were suffering from subsequent attacks of malarial parasites. Yet another foreigner who connected low country, swamps, marshes, and treatment of fevers with quinine was the American George Gardner, who traveled to Arraias in the 1830s. He reported that the diseases of that district were very similar to those in the north: "In the low country, which during the rainy season, is full of marshes and swamps, intermittent fevers are prevalent, and are often fatal to those coming from upland districts." People seldom died of the disease itself but rather of its effects. The principal organ affected was the spleen, which became so enlarged it filled the whole abdominal cavity, but the liver was less rarely affected. One of the Indians with Gardner, who became his servant, almost died from a "tertian ague," but he recovered after receiving treatment (with quinine?). Gardner also noted that many of the fevers lost their intermittent character and assumed "a malignant remittent nature." In the district of Natividade "intermittent and malignant fevers," especially at the beginning and toward the end of the rainy season," were the principal diseases, while in the district of Água Quente intermittent fevers killed "about fifty Indians" each day.[53]

In addition to the focus on fevers, late colonial sources also reported on what seems to have been a high incidence of "apoplexy," which then as now generally suggests a stroke, but it may also have been one more way in which contemporary observers described cerebral malaria. Pohl, for example, associated "nervous apoplexies" with the rainy season, with the "violent evaporation of the soil." Daily, he added, there were "cases of these unexpected deaths. The person leaves the house with health and is returned [to the house] dead." Why were nervous apoplexies related to the rainy season? Did the stress of that season contribute to strokes? On the other hand, cerebral malaria may lead to convulsions, delirium, and coma. One of the governors, João Manoel de Menezes (1800–1804), suffered from a "nervous sickness" that worsened over five months. He had contracted his illness with some paralysis after traveling on the Tocantins and Araguaia Rivers; notably, others on his expedition had also died on that trip, which may point to malaria.[54]

From such descriptions of "nervous apoplexies" and fevers, it seems that malaria was a serious threat to local people and to outside visitors. It also affected indigenous peoples when Portuguese officials transferred them from their original homes, forcing them to settle near a pestiferous river. As early as 1806, Francisco José Rodrigues Barata reported on the negative impact on indigenous communities of coerced resettlement from healthy locations to Christian missions, although the relocations continued throughout the nineteenth century. In the 1850s, for example, "violent epidemics" with "inflammation of the liver" killed many Indians.[55] In contrast, some free blacks and fugitive slaves deliberately chose to live where fevers were common, because no one else claimed those lands; they did not die from the fevers, possibly due to some genetic resistance to one or more malarial parasites. Enslaved Africans with such resistance also survived in many of the mining camps along mosquito-infested rivers. Blacks living in communities attacked by fevers included those in Santo Antônio on the Paraná River before they moved to Couros (Formosa) and those who lived near Salinas and extracted salt for their use.[56]

Although the north was the most dangerous region for fevers, the south did not escape them. Cunha Matos reported meeting many sick people along the rivers of the south. There is also evidence of malaria in Vila Boa, along the Vermelho, Araguaia, and Paranaíba Rivers. The traveler Auguste de Saint-Hilaire found that Vila Boa was unhealthy because of its location along a river where "the water does not appear healthy" and the heat was "almost always suffocating during the dry season." Therefore the people lacked "health, vigor, and energy." Pohl also concluded that whites, who had weak constitutions, were declining in numbers in Vila Boa, but *mulatos* and blacks were "robust and healthy."[57]

There is less evidence of the unhealthiness of the Araguaia River until official contact in 1775, after which the Karajá and Javaé began to suffer from many illnesses. Already in 1778 Manoel Gomes Rebello reported that Nova Beira was "very infested with Sezoens [sezões]." In contrast, Vila Real reported in the 1790s that "the river, and the airs" of the Araguaia River appeared "healthy" since he did not experience any disease in May. After presídios were constructed along the Araguaia River in the nineteenth century, soldiers stationed in the north came down with fevers. Mission Indians living along the river also died of diseases. In 1857 Ernesto Vallée blamed their deaths on "the choice of improper places contrary to the customs and resources of the Indians." Furthermore, the Indians were victims of "violent epidemics" characterized by "inflammation of the liver." Why they died of fevers is clarified by Cunha Matos, who called attention to the lakes along the banks of the Araguaia River and at Nova Beira on Bananal Island as a cause of "great sicknesses" because the lakes were shallow, with "miasmas so malignant that they infect the atmosphere." Although he used the European concept of miasmas, it seems likely that "clouds" of mosquitoes were breeding in the shallow lakes, afterward transmitting malarial parasites.[58]

If malaria existed along other rivers of the south, it is not surprising to find that intermittent fevers were epidemic along the Paranaíba River in the far south, where the river had a reputation for insalubriousness. Such fevers may have protected the quilombo that sheltered a community of fugitive slaves who settled on an island in the Grande River, an alternate name for the Paranaíba River. But there are also other rivers known as Rio Grande, such as the southern part of the Araguaia River that was called the Rio Grande in the eighteenth century. Or the dangerous Rio Grande may have been the river at the modern border between Goiás and São Paulo.[59]

Plateaus, *Chapadas*, and Mountains

To escape fevers, some of the inhabitants of Goiás deliberately chose to live away from the dangerous rivers and in the more elevated regions of the captaincy. The mining town of Meia Ponte (Pirenópolis) had a reputation for being "very healthy," which helped attract residents and may explain its growth in population in contrast to fever-plagued towns. Governors of Goiás went there to rest either on their long journeys to Vila Boa or to recover their health after visiting a fever region. To the east, the great central plateau (*planalto central*) was famous for its healthiness, and in the nineteenth century imperial bureaucrats planned to build a new capital of Brazil there because of its salubrious reputation. Near the future Brasília were two towns: Santa Luzia (now Luziânia, south of Brasília) and Couros (now Formosa) to the northeast of the capital city. Santa Luzia was founded in the 1740s and became one of the richest mining towns in this region, while Couros was settled by blacks (*crioulos*) from the Paraná River region about the middle of the eighteenth century. They moved to Couros from the village of Santo Antônio to escape the "intermittent fevers" of the Paraná River; the local people named the black settlement Couros after the houses they made out of animal skins. In contrast to their experience along the Paraná River, they prospered in Couros, particularly from the trade in animals and hides, some of which were traded to Bahia via the register of Lagôa Fêia. All those who wanted to avoid the fevers of the Paraná River valley, including traders from Paracatú, thenceforth journeyed to Couros to trade with those from the Paraná River. Thus the founding and early development of the future town of Formosa was related to the unhealthy disease environment of the Paraná River.[60]

Another healthy place was Caldas Novas, to the southeast of contemporary Goiânia, where its hot springs, located in low mountains, attracted clients from all over the Brazilian interior to obtain healing, especially of skin diseases and leprosy. Some even traveled from São Paulo to be healed in its waters.[61]

On the central plateau, the savanna (cerrado) flourished, and one insect plague was not the mosquito but the *carrapato*, a large tick that feeds on cattle and people. Although ants and termites were troublesome, they were not significant health threats to people. The cerrado supported herds of cattle that roamed among the short, thorny trees and termite mounds in search of food. Here the hot dry season often lingered and extended, especially into Bahia, Piauí, and Pernambuco. Indigenous men hunted deer and flocks of *emas* (South American rheas, ostrich-like birds), while women gathered the nourishing fruits and nuts of the cerrado, such as *cajú* (cashew). Colorful *ipé* trees with yellow flowers and toucans and macaws brightened the landscape, while small flowers decorated the savanna. Along the trails, long-legged *seriemas* (gray-brown birds) darted away from passing hunters. Also hunting were pairs of long-legged wolf-*guarás*, pumas, and spotted cats, including the great jaguar. Along the rivers anacondas and poisonous snakes, *jacarés* (caimans), river otters, and stingrays that hid in the sandy beaches of the Araguaia were other potential threats. In spite of its natural wealth in flora and fauna that are unique to this part of Brazil, settlers did not choose to live in great numbers in the savanna because they had not found a lot of gold there, although some ranchers raised cattle for export to Bahia.[62]

Nor did Luso-Brazilians choose to live in the *matas* (forests) of the captaincy. Colonial sources make frequent references to matas as boundary markers for *sesmarias* (land grants), but they rarely describe the type of forest that bordered a small farm or ranch. From traveler descriptions, we can sense that the captaincy still had impressive strands of tall trees, especially in the north, where hunting was good for both people and jaguars, suggesting that there was a healthy ecosystem that supported the large cats. Elsewhere, low trees grew so close together that they formed "a thicket," which obstructed travel. But even near Vila Boa and the mission of Maria I, there were strands of deep woods that sheltered wild animals, providing food to indigenous hunters. Luso-Brazilians who were skilled hunters also entered the forests to find food, but even though they themselves hunted, they perceived the Indians as living like *feras* (wild animals) in the matas. To eliminate those they defined as "savages," local settlers set fire to the forests to drive them off the land. Descriptions of such acts document that indigenous communities built some of their villages in the midst of forests, in part to protect themselves from discovery by outsiders. The Timbira da Matta in the north were among those who chose to live in the forests "for their defense."[63]

Other peoples lived in the mountains, which were of "modest altitude," often little more than low hills. The highest mountains were the centrally located Pireneus range, at the foot of which the mining town of Meia Ponte (now Pirenópolis) was constructed in the 1720s on the Almas River.[64] Also significant were the mountains of the Serra Dourada, between the Santa Teresa and Tocantins Rivers, where the Canoeiro built their villages high in the mountains. Near them were hidden quilombos, in which fugitive blacks had hid out successfully since the first half of the eighteenth century. The most famous of the quilombos, occupied at least since the early nineteenth century and to the present, was Kalunga, located in difficult-of-access terrain in the Chapada dos Veadeiros. During the peak period of gold mining, most mountains near the gold-mining towns sheltered fugitive slaves.[65] Because of the threat from quilombo dwellers, Luso-Brazilians did not seek out the mountains unless gold was there. Both the Serra Dourada behind Vila Boa and the mountains near Natividade held camps of miners, who tunneled into the mountains after rich gold veins, but most people in Goiás were not mountain dwellers unless forced to be so. In fact, people may have avoided one mountainous region between Arraias and [Santa Maria] Taguatinga because of the large vampire bats. Each night swarms of the bats left their caves on the sides of the mountains to attack cattle, sucking their blood.[66]

Besides the Pireneus and the Serra Dourada, some of the most significant mountainous regions were the mountain ranges (serras) in the east of the captaincy that separated the captaincies of Maranhão, Piauí, and Bahia from the captaincy of Goiás and sheltered all those who sought refuge from Luso-Brazilian rule: fugitive slaves, indigenous peoples, bandits, smugglers, and military deserters. They often supported themselves by raiding convoys that journeyed via official roads or by trading in contraband goods that evaded official taxes on gold and cattle. A sparsely populated region was the Chapada das Mangabeiras of southern Maranhão and Piauí, which was a watershed. Rivers to the east of the chapada ran north and east through Maranhão and Piauí; rivers to its west flowed into the Tocantins River.[67] Another obstacle to travel were the mountains of the Serra Geral de Goiás and the Espigão Mestre, which divided the Tocantins River basin from the São Francisco River basin to the east and also obstructed river trade, although not official trade via the roads through the mountains. Governor José de Almeida de Vasconcelos (1772–1778) compared this mountain range to an "inaccessible wall" with some breaks in it that served as "doors" to the mines of Goiás. At the entrances of the mountain passes, the Portuguese placed their tax contractors to inspect trade goods at the checkpoints of Duro, Taguatinga, and São Domingos.[68]

To the west of the Serra Geral is the Chapada dos Veadeiros, named for the deer that may still be found in the beautiful national park located north of Brasília, with waterfalls, a cave system, and river rapids. Its "sea of serras," such as Mocambo, was a notable refuge for fugitive slaves and Indians.[69] To the north of this region are still other serras named Passa Três, Dourada, Cana Brava, Xavantes, Javaés, Estrondo, and Cordilheiras. Of this list, the one most cited in colonial sources is the Serra Dourada, due to its proximity to Vila Boa. The Serra do Estrondo, which lies between the Tocantins and Araguaia Rivers, now appears on contemporary maps of the state of Tocantins, but it was generally not so identified on colonial maps. One early nineteenth-century map, for example, identified the mountainous region between the Araguaia and Tocantins Rivers as simply the "Cordillera Grande."[70]

In the far south of Goiás is the mountainous region of the headwaters of the Araguaia River in an area that borders Mato Grosso. This mountainous area separates the basins of the Araguaia and Paranaíba Rivers and includes the serras of Dourada, Divisões, Rio Claro, and Caiapó. Many rivers run parallel to each other from the Serra do Caiapó to the Paranaíba River. In the eighteenth century the Kayapó built their many villages from the Serra Dourada, east of the Araguaia River, to the sertões south of the Pardo River, a tributary of the right bank of the Paraná River (also the Rio Grande). Because of Kayapó warfare and raiding, Luso-Brazilian settlement was limited except for diamond-mining camps along the Claro and Pilões Rivers.[71]

The disease associated with the semiarid cerrado or even drier regions to the east in Bahia and southern Piauí was Chagas disease, one of the few endemic health hazards of American origin that was unknown to Europeans. Chagas is transmitted by triatomines, insects that live in thatched roofs. Symptoms include fever, edemas, and enlargement of the lymph nodes, and in the chronic form of the illness, the heart becomes greatly enlarged. In the digestive form of the disease, megaesophagus makes it difficult to swallow and megacolon leads to chronic constipation. Some possible indications of Chagas disease in eighteenth-century Goiás are frequent references to heart problems or sicknesses of the chest. In 1810, for example, Antônio de Souza Telles e Menezes petitioned the Crown for a doctor for Vila Boa because of the many deaths there due to sicknesses of the chest. The illnesses had killed the leading men without anyone knowing the cause of their deaths. In Piauí and Maranhão near Goiás, the travelers Johann B. von Spix and Carl Friedrich P. von Martius encountered people afflicted by "engasgue" (choking), which is a common symptom of Chagas.[72]

Another condition that was especially common in Goiás was goiter. In fact, it was one of the most characteristic conditions of the region and usually impressed outsiders with the enormity of the disfigurement. According to

Auguste de Saint-Hilaire, goiter was a particular problem in Vila Boa, where "almost all the inhabitants of the city and its environs have bócio [goiter]." Pohl also observed "many cases of papo," another name for goiter, and it even afflicted animals. In the 1830s, Gardner found that it was very common in Natividade, Arraias, and Conceição, but the people reported that it had become prevalent among them only in the last twenty years and even related it to changes in salt use. Goiter, of course, may be prevented by consuming iodized salt. Without gold to attract the trade in marine salt, goiter increasingly plagued the people of the region in the nineteenth century, although it did not noticeably affect outsiders unless they remained in the captaincy for a long period of time.[73]

Epidemic Diseases

Also invading along the trade routes in all regions of the captaincy were the deadly pathogens of the coast. Unknown to the indigenous populations before the arrival of Europeans and Africans, two of the most deadly invaders were smallpox and measles. The dates of their arrival in Goiás are unknown, but high mortality rates typical of first contact seem to have occurred as late as the eighteenth century. Apparently the captaincy did not experience many recorded epidemics, but both diseases were particularly lethal to the indigenous populations when they did strike. Writing in 1811, Governor Fernando Delgado Freire de Castilho (1809–1820) reported that "bexigas," a common term for smallpox, was "very rare"; furthermore, in 1812 Custodio Pereira da Veiga claimed that the captaincy had not known the disease for forty years. The traveler Pohl (1819) also noted that *variola* was "rare, but when it appears it devastates terribly, especially among the Indians."[74]

As compared to the coast, there are several possible explanations for the smaller number of documented cases of smallpox epidemics in the captaincy. Smallpox is a viral disease that depends on urban population densities where people meet face to face on a frequent basis, but in Goiás many people lived on isolated ranches and mines or in hidden indigenous villages. When epidemics entered the captaincy via the trade routes, people saved their lives by moving away from those who were sick. The government also established checkpoints in the early nineteenth century to prevent the entry or exit of infected individuals, as it did during an outbreak of smallpox in Meia Ponte. Another reason is that the captaincy's black slaves utilized methods of self-inoculation (learned in Africa?) to protect themselves and their children from the high mortality of the disease. In addition, the government introduced European vaccination methods after 1804. On 1 December 1805, 620 people were vaccinated in five different towns, although the total number vaccinated is not known because "many vaccinated themselves."[75]

There were, however, three significant outbreaks of smallpox that afflicted the people of Goiás. The first struck in 1771, the second during the administration of Governor Freire de Castilho (1809–1820), and the third in 1873–1874. In 1771 an epidemic of "variola" spread throughout the captaincy, probably killing many of the indigenous people, such as the Kayapó. Thereafter, government officials believed that the captaincy was free of the disease, but in 1816 an epidemic of "bexigas" struck Meia Ponte, where it caused "great harm." The government's vaccination program was blamed for the epidemic, but this epidemic may have been linked to the one in the north that had spread from Maranhão or possibly to the one in the south that had struck the Kayapó in 1811. To prevent the further spread of the disease to other towns, the government posted guards at the Almas River, Ouro Fino, and Mato Grosso.[76]

At the same time, there was also an outbreak of smallpox among the indigenous nations living along the Tocantins and Araguaia Rivers. Possibly deliberately introduced to the Indians, it had apparently come from Caxias and/or Pastos Bons, Maranhão, where it killed so many Canela that "no one" knew "how many had died." Those Canela who fled the epidemic in Caxias then spread the disease to the Apinaje in 1817. According to Colonel Francisco de Paula Ribeiro, this contagion caused "horrible harm." Smallpox progressed so rapidly among the indigenous peoples that it had already spread three hundred leagues away to the west of the Tocantins River by October 1817. Those who suffered from high fevers tried to alleviate their pains by putting stones on their heads or "burying themselves in the rivers." They named the painful illness "Pira de Cupê," or "sarna of the Christians." Smallpox caused sickness and death in Central Brazil into the 1820s. In the same period, according to Cunha Matos, sick slaves with "bexigas" were being taken to Cuiabá, which undoubtedly spread the disease farther west into Mato Grosso.[77]

The third notable epidemic of smallpox, in 1873, also followed the trade routes. That epidemic was blamed on the riverboat crews who traveled to and from Pará.[78]

The other virulent epidemic disease that had a catastrophic impact on the indigenous peoples of the Americas is measles. There are few references to *sarampo* (measles) in the colonial sources consulted, although it too struck in epidemics that afflicted all groups in the captaincy, especially the indigenous nations, such as the Apinaje and Kayapó. In 1753 an especially deadly measles outbreak among the Akroá and Xacriabá in Duro was linked to soldiers in a nearby presídio. Other documented measles epidemics among the indigenous population took place in the north of the captaincy, as well as among the Kayapó in the south. According to Saint-Hilaire, "almost all were attacked by the sarampo some years ago, and in the delirium of the fever, they went to bathe in the cold water. More than eighty died." Other documentation on the disease comes from the mission villages of the nineteenth century, when the people died of measles shortly after being settled in a mission. As late as the 1880s, Dr. Vírgilio M. de Mello Franco reported that the "sarampão rages with frequency in the province."[79]

Although smallpox and measles would generally not be dangerous to outsiders from the coast if they had had the diseases as a child, they were more likely to encounter other serious health problems the longer they remained in the captaincy. Three great dangers to them were filariasis, leprosy, and syphilis. Filariasis is a disease caused by an invading parasite transmitted by mosquitoes that live in the lymphatic vessels. As the parasite multiplies, the legs, scrotum in men, and breasts swell to enormous size. One of the notable characteristics of the disease is the elephantine appearance of a sick person's legs, hence the name of elephantiasis. Since the disease incapacitated people for work due to the enormity of the disfigurement, they had to support themselves by begging; Saint-Hilaire observed it among the beggars of Meia Ponte.[80]

Leprosy, now known as Hansen's disease, seems to have been endemic in the interior of Brazil, although outsiders would not have contracted it unless they had close and prolonged contact with those suffering from the disease. We can trace its incidence via terms such as the "evil of St. Lazarus," Greek elephantiasis, or "evil of morféia," but the best documentation of leprosy comes from the lists of patients treated at Caldas Novas for leprosy in the 1830s. Patients from nearby provinces, as well as Goiás, went for treatment there and exhibited classic symptoms of Hansen's disease. Both Saint-Hilaire and Cunha Matos also described cases of "morféia." As late as the 1880s, Mello Franco reported that "morféia is frequent, as well as sarna and other skin diseases." Since there often were severe food shortages in the mines, where enslaved Africans were fed only corn and popcorn, pellagra must have afflicted them with severe dermatitis, since pellagra is common in those with corn-based diets. Patients who recovered their health after being fed a better diet in Caldas Novas or at the hospital of São Pedro de Alcântara in the City of Goiás may have been suffering from a nutritional disease rather than leprosy.[81]

Frequently confused with leprosy in the nineteenth century, particularly in its advanced stages, was the venereal disease syphilis. Patients with syphilis were also treated at Caldas Novas, where one unfortunate patient from Cavalcante was described as having both elephantiasis and syphilis. Travelers, such as Pohl, were surprised to find that syphilis was so common in Goiás, especially in the district of Natividade. He also reported that the Portuguese transmitted the disease to the indigenous populations, such as the Kayapó. Given the prevalence of prostitution in the towns and sexual abuse of indigenous and African women, syphilis must have afflicted women and men who had many sexual partners. Cunha Matos tried to warn his men to avoid "amorous adventures" because the women of the towns had incurable venereal sicknesses, but the young soldiers ignored his warnings and had to be treated for syphilis at the military hospital in Vila Boa.[82]

Unfortunately for the outsiders and especially for the residents of the captaincy of Goiás, these were not the only serious health problems that people developed.[83] Clearly, malaria was the great killer in some locations, but syphilis, leprosy, and Chagas disease were also significant threats to good health. The healthiest people were isolated indigenous populations, but as soon as contact took place, they began to die of foreign diseases. In fact, entire villages could be wiped out in an epidemic of smallpox or measles. The Luso-Brazilian policy of congregating indigenous populations in state-administered mission villages in regions outside their traditional lands also contributed to indigenous mortality, especially when the Portuguese coerced settlement along pestiferous rivers. In sharp contrast, late colonial sources often recorded populous indigenous nations that numbered in the thousands and that lived in healthy locations, as opposed to later narratives of catastrophic depopulation and disappearance as a people. Outsiders' journeys into the captaincy of Goiás, or within it, would be especially problematic to the survival of indigenous populations, and their dangerous pathogens most likely killed more indigenous people than any bandeira. While the intruders too might die of malaria or catch Chagas disease, most complained about the great distances they had to travel on perilous rivers or across hot, dusty savannas to get to the gold mines. Although a few left good landscape descriptions, most perceived the captaincy of Goiás as a dangerous place with deadly fevers and even more treacherous inhabitants. Having safely arrived, the outsiders would now have to confront the original inhabitants of the land, who did not want to leave their homelands unless forced to do so.

CHAPTER 2

The Indigenous Nations of Central Brazil

By the 1770s the original inhabitants of the land had had a long, often negative, experience of contact, conquest, and captivity in the region; yet many had survived as autonomous nations or as mission Indians.[1] Although the indigenous population may have numbered more than fifty thousand, with perhaps an additional eighty thousand resident between the Tocantins River and Pastos Bons, Maranhão, we will focus here on twelve nations that played a significant role in the history of the region: the Akroá, Xacriabá, Apinaje, Krahô, Karajá, Javaé, Tapirapé, Araés, Xavante, Xerente, Canoeiro, and Kayapó do Sul.[2] Our goal is to identify and describe each nation in the late colonial period and assess their response to warfare and enslavement. When possible, smaller groups will be included, such as the Goiá, who have disappeared as unique ethnic groups. A longer list of indigenous peoples, derived from sources consulted for this book, is in appendix A.

Before describing specific nations, we must clarify several problems in reconstructing the identities and history of the indigenous peoples of the captaincy of Goiás. First, few comprehensive oral traditions of any indigenous population extend back to the colonial period, although some past events have been mythologized into their religious traditions. Not even the Xavante, who have written their own history, narrate events of the eighteenth and early nineteenth centuries.[3] Therefore, we must rely on outsider sources to try and document a little about the original inhabitants of the land under Portuguese colonial rule. Whenever possible, their voices and perspectives will be included, but in most cases only their actions, such as attacks and raids, can be retrieved from Luso-Brazilian sources.

Second, foreign missionaries were absent from this frontier after the Jesuit expulsion of 1759 until the arrival of the Italian Capuchins in the 1840s. Consequently, missionary correspondence and reports, which are so

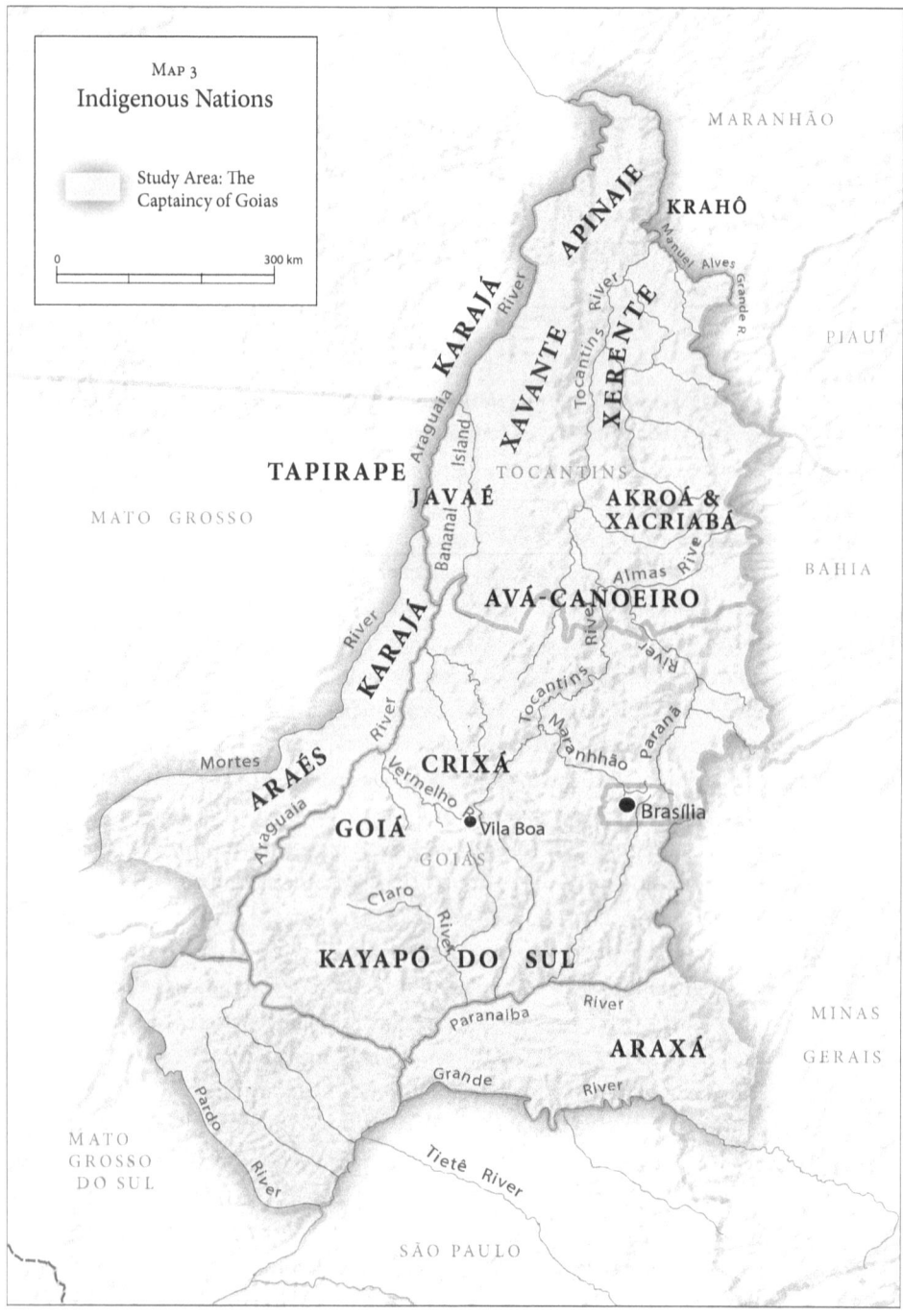

MAP 3
Indigenous Nations

Study Area: The Captaincy of Goias

important to the study of other frontier societies, do not exist for that period. Although European travelers provided information, on the whole we must rely on written records produced by those who conquered, governed, and enslaved indigenous peoples of the region. While some might argue that it is best not to use biased imperial sources, if we exclude them, we will miss valuable insights into indigenous resistance or fail to document the history of their relations with Luso-Brazilians and Africans. Furthermore, such documentation may help indigenous peoples to secure lands based on historical occupation of specific territories.

Finally, we can establish little about indigenous peoples' sociopolitical organization except for brief references to chiefs, villages, housing styles, gardens, and warfare; even less survives about their belief systems unless within a mission context. Where possible, we will integrate this information, but the lack of appropriate sources does not always permit a more complete ethnohistorical analysis or detailed studies of self-constructed identities. We will utilize the Portuguese construct of "nation," which appears so frequently in colonial documentation, but there is no intent to suggest that indigenous nations formed nation-states, although some peoples, such as the Kayapó and Karajá, created polities that were strong enough to control their own territories for centuries. Fortunately, the anthropologist Curt Nimuendajú lived in the north of this region in the 1920s and 1930s, and subsequent anthropologists have conducted significant fieldwork on the peoples living there. More than two centuries have passed, however, since the nations of Goiás lived in the savannas and along the rivers of Central Brazil, and this chapter will try to reflect insights into the lives of those who lived more than two centuries ago rather than the experiences of their twenty-first-century descendants.

Akroá and Xacriabá: Warriors and Mission Indians

The Akroá (alternately, Acroá, Acoroá, Coroá, Coroados) are a Gê-speaking Timbira people who used to live to the east of the captaincy of Goiás. They were then divided into three nations: the Akroá-Assú, who were the most populous; the Akroá-Mirim, who later joined the Xavante; and the Pânaca of Piauí. Historically, the Akroá were famous warriors who roamed a large territory to the east of the Tocantins River, including the captaincies of Goiás, Maranhão, Piauí, and Pernambuco, until some settled in missions in Goiás. The Xacriabá (Chacriabás, Jacaribás, Chikriabá, or Chyquiriabás), who speak a Central Gê (also Jê) language, are an Akwen people related to the Xerente and Xavante. They too had lived to the east of the Tocantins River in the south of Piauí and at least as far east as the São Francisco River in Bahia and had been in contact with Luso-Brazilians since the seventeenth century. Traditionally, they were enemies of the Akroá.[4]

The first contact of the Akroá with bandeiras (armed expeditions) probably occurred at the Gurguéia River in the south of Piauí in 1698. For decades afterward they were continually fighting invading settlers and bandeiras in the south of Piauí, but by the 1730s they had moved into the Tocantins River region, where their attacks threatened to disrupt gold mining and trade in the north of Goiás. Also threatening were neighbors of the Akroá, the Gueguê (Gueguêz, Guenguen), who occupied riverine lands to the east of the Tocantins River along the Gurguéia and Parnaíba Rivers. They especially concerned Luso-Brazilians because they attracted fugitive blacks and mission Indians to join them in the fight against their enemies.[5]

As usual, therefore, the colonial government organized bandeiras against both the Akroá and Gueguê. Captain-mor Antônio Gomes Leite subdued the Gueguê, and a Pernambucan *sertanista* (frontiersman), Lieutenant Colonel Wenceslau Gomes da Silva, settled the Akroá and Xacriabá in missions, where he proceeded to treat them as captives under his military rule.[6] As early as 1747, a Portuguese *provisão* refers to the need to settle "a great number" of them in an *aldeia* with Jesuit missionaries; this same source reveals that the Akroá then lived in the neighborhoods of Natividade and Remedios. But it was not until 1751 that the Xacriabá went to live in the aldeia dedicated to São Francisco Xavier, which was located to the north of the Manuel Alves Grande River. According to Gomes da Silva, he had settled the Xacriabá at that aldeia and deliberately separated them from their enemies, the "Acoroas." A map of the mission of São Francisco Xavier reveals that they then lived in horseshoe-shaped villages; the aldeia of the Akroá had 286 houses, while that of the Xacriabá was larger, with 396 houses.[7]

As of 1753, the Jesuits had formally created the mission of São Francisco Xavier, uniting the two aldeias of the Akroá and Xacriabá. Unfortunately, a great measles epidemic decimated them and led many to flee the mission, blaming "whites for the death of their brothers"; but many did not travel far, as their corpses littered the roads to the interior. Not too surprisingly, given their past history of conflict, the Akroá moved to another aldeia named São José do Duro (popularly known as Formiga), located two leagues from São Francisco Xavier. In 1754 Formiga had 398 Akroá led by two captains: Pedro and

Lourenço. Also transferred to Duro were the "Gueguê from the banks of the Gurguéia River. Since most Gueguê disappear from Goiano sources, those who had lived in Duro may have returned to Piauí.[8]

After the expulsion of the Jesuits and several years of revolt, the Akroá and Xacriabá might have been expected to abandon the aldeias of São Francisco Xavier and São Jose do Duro, and some clearly did so, but others returned to the mission sites.[9] Some Akroá took up residence again in São José do Duro, while their warriors entered the employ of the Portuguese as *pedestres* (paid foot soldiers). When Raimundo José da Cunha Matos visited São José do Duro in 1823, he found only 49 Akroá men still resident there because the Portuguese had transferred some of them to a new aldeia, São José de Mossâmedes, created in 1755 for the Kayapó. Other Akroá continued to inhabit Duro and were counted by Cunha Matos in the 1820s, along with six Aricobés, six Kayapós, and six Tupinambás, who spoke the *língua geral* (Tupi). In all, 203 Indians lived in Duro in 1823. Fifteen years later the Akroá were working as hired canoemen in the Tocantins River trade to Belém, exchanging their services for money to buy axes and iron tools.[10]

The aldeia of São Francisco Xavier was soon abandoned as well, and the Xacriabá were sent south to another aldeia. Presenting themselves to the governor, they laid "at his feet bows, arrows and lances" and asked him for "pardon of their frequent insults." Their years in the mission had apparently had mixed results. When the governor met them in 1775, they still did not use clothing, and the governor had them covered so that they could enter the church for the baptism of their "innocents." The governor noted that their cacique (chief) or *mayoral* (great chief) had lived with them near the Duro checkpoint from 1743 to 1748, presumably in São Francisco Xavier. Therefore he understood some Portuguese and was able to ask the governor to be the godfather of his only son, whom he left in the governor's company to be educated.[11]

Either this group or another of the Xacriabá continued on south to the aldeia of Santa Ana do Rio das Velhas, which is now in the state of Minas Gerais. Previously this aldeia had housed the Bororo, Macro-Gê speakers from Mato Grosso, until they were moved to the aldeia of Lanhoso. Descendants of the Bororo informed Auguste de Saint-Hilaire that the aldeia of Santana had actually been founded by the Jesuits for coastal Indians. To these, Colonel Antônio Pires de Campos had added some Karajá and Tapirapé. The people of this mission had then mixed with the Bororo and in 1775 were replaced by the Xacriabá. According to Saint-Hilaire, the Xacriabá lived in the sertões (backlands) of the Paranã River and had spread all the way to the São Francisco River and to the northern part of Minas Gerais, which suggests that the Xacriabá had once been an extensive nation, but only a small number of them actually lived in Santa Ana in the 1780s. By the time Saint-Hilaire visited them in 1819, most no longer spoke their original language, and only one woman would give him a vocabulary list. Apparently, those who remained in Goiás assimilated to Luso-Brazilian culture, while others with a Xacriabá identity lived in Bahia.[12]

Apinaje: Canoe Raiders and Allies

A people who have not disappeared but who continue to live on their own reserve in the north of the modern state of Tocantins are the Apinaje (Apinayé, Apinajé). In 1782 the "Panajé," a name that is similar to other names used for them in the late colonial period, such as Pinajé, occupied the east bank of the Tocantins. By the early nineteenth century, the Apinaje had five aldeias near the Santo Antônio Falls on the Araguaia River. They were then described as a tall and handsome people, whose women were especially admired by Luso-Brasilians. They speak a Gê language of the Timbira family, related to that of the Northern Kayapó. According to Padre Silva e Souza in 1812, they moved around by land, which suggests similarities to other Gê populations, but unlike other Gê, they made ubás (hollowed-out canoes) with which they traveled on the rivers. In the eighteenth century they used their ubás to raid north to Cametá on the Tocantins River and to travel all the way to Belém, Pará, to trade their goods for metal tools.[13]

According to Curt Nimuendajú in the 1930s, the "Apinayé," the name they call themselves, "consider themselves an offshoot of the Timbira living east of the Tocantins, more specifically of the Krikatí (Caracaty) now residing at the headwaters of the Rio Pindaré." Nimuendajú and other sources consulted do not establish when the Apinaje arrived at the two great rivers. Jesuits who traveled south of Pará to the region beyond the juncture of the Araguaia and Tocantins Rivers did not leave descriptions of them, perhaps because they had to flee war canoes on the rivers. In Nimuendajú's view, the "first demonstrable contact" of the Apinaje with "civilization" occurred in 1774, when Antônio Luiz Tavares Lisboa was attacked at the rapids at Três Barras by a "large crowd" that encircled him, but the expedition's guns prevailed against bows and arrows (see chapter 4).[14]

The Indigenous Nations of Central Brazil 39

Figure 2. This illustration of the interior of an Apinaje great house shows furnishings of a hammock and baskets. Source: Castelnau, Expédition. Courtesy of the Catholic University of America, Oliveira Lima Library, Washington, DC.

Because of the danger from the Apinaje and from *quilombolas* (fugitive slaves), the Portuguese established a small fort at Alcobaça, to the north of modern Marabá, in 1780. Why the Apinaje threatened local settlers is documented in a letter by Hilário de Morais Betancourt, who had a sugar plantation on the Tocantins River. Writing to the governor of Pará in 1790, he reported that Maria, a black woman who had been with the Apinaje (as a captive?), informed him that they were a "nation" who were not at peace with any "gentiles." They did not have a *principal* (chief), and the head of each family governed only the people who did not owe obedience to anyone else. Furthermore, they were a numerous people with more women than men. She further explained why the Apinaje worried local settlers—they stole their tools. Like the Karajá, they also built *barracas* (thatch-roofed shelters) on the beaches at the mouth of the Araguaia River at a place called Muruxituba, where they laid down their "Bandeiras" (flags), some for food, and others for their hostilities.[15] Figure 2 reveals that their more permanent houses were large and able to accommodate more than one family in the 1840s.

Another source from 1793 asserts that the Apinaje were "much stronger" than the Karajá and more industrious since they farmed and planted large fields of manioc. In the 1790s they inhabited both banks of the Araguaia River and interacted with the Karajá, trading and dancing with them, even though they lived about a month apart in terms of travel on the Araguaia River. In fact, Nimuendajú notes that the Xambioá Karajá may have taught the Apinaje how to make ubás, which suggests that the two nations exchanged ideas and material culture as they interacted with each other, although it is uncertain if they were then political allies.[16]

The Apinaje also lived peacefully with troops stationed at a presídio (small garrison) at São João das Duas Barras (now São João do Araguaia), which is at the juncture of the Araguaia and Tocantins Rivers. But the peace did not last, because some soldiers from the presídio either raided or totally destroyed their fields in 1812. In retaliation, the Apinaje killed them. So many deaths quickly led to a Luso-Brazilian artillery attack against one or more of their villages. Angry and vengeful, the survivors joined in coalition with the Xavante and Karajá to attack and destroy the presídio of Santa Maria do Araguaia in 1813.[17]

At the time of their revolt, the Apinaje were a "populous" nation with many men able to fight as warriors under sixteen chiefs. In spite of warfare and

Figure 3. Xavante and Apinaje baskets. On the left are Xavante baskets, which are similar to the one I purchased from a Xavante in the 1970s. The Apinaje baskets are on the right. The Johann E. Pohl Ethnographic Collection. Courtesy of the Museum für Völkerkunde, Vienna, Austria.

encroaching Luso-Brazilian settlement, they remained a strong nation until 1817, when they were struck by smallpox. The epidemic also afflicted the Timbira and had spread from Caxias in Maranhão via fugitive "Capiecran" (Ram-Ko'kamekra) to the Apinaje. It is unknown how many died. Apparently demoralized by the disease, they agreed to make peace with Plácido Moreira de Carvalho in 1818. As opposed to the five villages listed by Silva e Souza, they then had only three. Shortly thereafter, Pohl described them as "industrious," making a "diversity of objects" for their own use, raising cattle, and domesticating beasts and birds, such as emas and parrots. He admired their baskets, trumpets, and *pilões de pau* (wooden pestles). Besides this, they were peaceful and lived in harmony. From time to time they also helped travelers carry their baggage over the stones at the waterfall on the Maranhão River.[18]

Once again, peace did not last because some of the Apinaje entered the political conflicts of Goiás and Pará, even fighting against Portuguese attempts to regain control of the interior after the declaration of Brazilian independence in 1822. Over two hundred warriors allied with a Luso-Brazilian force led by José Dias de Mattos, a rancher from Maranhão, until the Apinaje revolted against the commandant in Carolina in 1824 and fled their aldeias on the Tocantins River. By November 1824 at least one group of the "Pinagé" had asked for peace.[19]

When Cunha Matos met up with the Apinaje in 1824, he counted four aldeias, with a total population of 4,200, that were then at peace: Bom Jardim under Captain Jozê Conumo, which was not far from Carolina, with 1,000 inhabitants; Santo Antônio, led by Captain Francisco Pecobo, which was five leagues further north, with 1,300; Araguaya, under Captain Marcelino Juxum, with 1,400; and the Santo Antônio of Captain Veluco, with 500. There were two additional aldeias: one in Carolina, of the Afotigé nation, with 120 persons led by Captain Francisco Juhocrit, and another named Concordia, which was nearby. One of the villages near Carolina also included a fugitive black slave, who had fled from Cametá on the Tocantins River ten years earlier. Joaquim Angola had adopted Apinaje customs, including the use of a disc in his lower lip.[20]

While the Apinaje lived at peace with the Luso-Brazilians, their warriors also served as soldiers in forces sent against other hostile nations, including expeditions that attempted to subdue the Canoeiro and the Xerente. Some also entered Christian missions, but they seem to have been especially resistant to Christianization, even as late as the 1930s, when Nimuendajú visited them and concluded that missionary influence was "quite imperceptible."[21] Thus, at the end of the colonial period, the Apinaje were still autonomous, although they were willing to assist Luso-Brazilians in waging wars against their mutual enemies.

Krahô: Cattle Raiders and Herdsmen

To the south of the Apinaje at Carolina were those who lived on the east bank of the Tocantins River, the Krahô (also Caraôs, Macamekrans, or Mãkamekra), a people who speak an eastern Timbira dialect of the Gê language family. In Pastos Bons, Maranhão, the Krahô were known as the Macamekrans, while those who traveled on the Tocantins River referred to them as Temembós and Pépuxis. According to Major Francisco de Paula Ribeiro, the same one who led royalist forces against the Krahô and who lived among them, they were one of the powerful branches of the Timbira family. According to traditions and some historical sources, they had migrated to the Tocantins River after living in Maranhão. Major Ribeiro also placed them in the region of Maranhão of the Balsas, Mearim and Grajaú Rivers, where cattle were "abundant," sometime before they made peace in 1809. In Maranhão they had been noted for "horrible devastations" and cattle raiding, but after they were reduced to peace in 1809 they no longer attacked local settlers, who then feared only the Xavante, who were also the enemies of the Krahô.[22]

What changed their lives was typical frontier violence. Either the Krahô or the Xavante struck a fazenda and killed its owners in 1808. A retaliatory assault against a Macamekrans village was so severe that the survivors decided to make peace, and after 1809 the Macamekrans lived peacefully in their villages. Major Ribeiro reported that they were governed by a mayoral called Apúicrît, who had supported the peace process and who had become a strong ally of Captain José Pinto de Magalhães. Apúicrît praised his ally for generously giving them all the prisoners he made—most likely to be sold as slaves. In return, he was gifted with a pistol and clothes, which he wore only when his allies came to visit him. Otherwise he did not use clothing nor did his people. After the mayoral's death, the Macamekrans no longer kept the peace that he had enforced, in part because their protector Magalhães traveled to Pará in 1813 and stayed away for two years. His absence left them vulnerable to slave raiders.[23]

Another people, the Põrekamekra (Porecamecrã), occupied the west bank of the Tocantins River from about 1808 to 1819, according to Pohl, who met them, but Ribeiro placed them on the east bank, north of the Farinha River.

Pohl described them as being a yellow-brown in color with unclothed bodies painted in red and black streaks. Unlike others, they did not perforate their lips, but only the lobes of their ears. They lived on a high bank of the Maranhão overlooking the broad river, and on the east bank there was a beautiful mountain range. A large grove of palm trees added to the beauty of the landscape and gave their village its name of Cocal Grande; it had a large square that included Carvalho's residence and open porches.[24]

This idyllic life and landscape were soon shattered by enslavement. In 1814 the mulato bandeira leader Alferes Antônio Moreira da Silva offered to make peace with one of the Pōrekamekra villages. Led by their chief, Cocrît, they traveled to São Pedro de Alcântara (now Carolina), bearing "green twigs in token of peace." They settled near there, forming a community of four hundred to five hundred, plus children. But soon their chief was taken captive, and they were abused and enslaved. The survivors of this catastrophe took refuge among the Krahô and merged with them. A second village of the Pōrekamekra also suffered at the hands of this mulato's bandeira. Apparently the chief Cocrît persuaded them to meet the bandeira, but the expedition slapped them in chains and at least 130 of them were branded and sold to Pará in 1815. The severely weakened survivors among the Macamekrans and the Pōrekamekra joined and enlarged Krahô villages.

Therefore, the Krahô were still a large group of over three thousand in 1815. When Major Ribeiro visited them in 1815–1816, he reported that they had returned to their "brutal condition," meaning that they were following traditional customs that he objected to, such as not wearing clothing, but he thought their method of cooking food in holes in the dirt, with the meat covered in moistened earth and hot stones, made it "more agreeable and savory" than his own. Unlike other nations in the region, the Krahô did not prepare manioc meal (*farinha de páo*) or cultivate cotton and tobacco.[25]

After Magalhães returned from Pará, he continued his alliance with the Krahô and even took a Krahô woman as his mistress until he sold her. Together, he and the Krahô attacked other nations in order to enslave captives and sell them in Pará and Piauí. Until he was "poisoned by his own people," the Krahô chief Apúicrît turned over all his captives to Magalhães. In 1823 the Krahô joined the Apinaje in fighting against Major Ribeiro's royalist forces. Two years later Cunha Matos estimated that there were two hundred Krahô warriors living in three villages.[26]

The Krahô were not rewarded for their services to the independence cause, however, because settlers forced them to abandon their lands. One reason is that they were so successful at cattle raising that local authorities forced them off Maranhão's good pasture lands. In 1849 three hundred of the Krahô entered the Christian aldeia of Pedro Affonso on the east bank of the Farinha River, in the parish of Porto Imperial (Porto Nacional). Soon after settling in the aldeia, they were devastated by an epidemic; but afterward the survivors remained as allies of the Luso-Brazilians and as cattle raisers—and raiders, according to local ranchers. Another group of the Krahô settled in the aldeia of Boa Vista do Tocantins in 1841, where they were joined by the Apinaje and Gradaú (Northern Kayapó) and continued to raise cattle. Curt Nimuendajú, who lived among them in the 1930s, concluded that "the influence of the mission on tribal custom seems to have been extraordinarily slight"; but their experiences in the missions had led them to mix with blacks and to choose black chiefs. They have endured to the present on their reserve named Kraolândia in the north of the state of Tocantins.[27]

Karajá, Javaé, and Xambioá: River Dwellers of the Araguaia

To the south of the Apinaje—a month's journey on the Araguaia River—lived the Karajá (Carajá, Carajai, Carajahi, Carajaúna, Carajaputanga, or Carajaupivana) and related peoples, the Javaé and Xambioá (Chambioá), or Karajá of the north. The Karajá speak one of the Macro-Gê languages, although the women have their own way of speaking and the men another, masculine speech. Their villages extended up and down the Araguaia River, while some were clustered on Bananal Island, the largest fluvial island in the world. The Karajá are among the most stable indigenous peoples of the region, with more than one thousand years of occupation along the Araguaia River. Unlike their enemies the Xavante, they have no history of continuous migration from east to west, but they do have a historical memory of a migration from the north in the remote past.[28]

The Karajá were in contact with Luso-Brazilians from at least the early seventeenth century, and possibly earlier in the sixteenth century. At least six Carajaúna were captured in the sertão of the Paraúpava River sometime between 1608 and 1613, and the inventory of Lourenço Gomes Ruxaque recorded Carajáuna captives as "negros," or slaves, in São Paulo as early as 1611. Thereafter the Karajá had to be wary of slave-raiding expeditions, most of which originated in São Paulo.[29] A different bandeira, led by Bartolomeu Barreiros de Ataíde, penetrated south from Belém via the Tocantins River to its confluence with the Araguaia and ascended the Araguaia. In 1644 this expedition recorded the presence of three tribes of Carajás on the Araguaia, as well as those Ataíde reduced: the Carajais, Carajáupivanas, and Carajáputangas. The Jesuits followed up on this expedition, and Padre Manuel Nunes reached "the island of the Carajás," Bananal Island, in 1659.[30]

The violence of their response to the invaders gave them a bellicose reputation, and they continued to merit this reputation as they violently resisted future Luso-Brazilian efforts to penetrate their lands. This in combination with the attraction of gold mines elsewhere in the captaincy led expeditions to prefer to travel on the Tocantins River and avoid the Karajá. In 1755, however, Antônio Pires de Campos attacked the principal village of the Karajá, taking captives that he led away in chains. This destructive bandeira was then followed by the official bandeira of 1775, led by Lieutenant José Pinto da Fonseca, who made peace with the Karajá with the aid of Xuanam-piá, a Karajá war captive, who served as his interpreter (see chapter 4).[31]

From the official correspondence regarding this expedition we learn a little about the Karajá in 1775. First, they were reluctant to deal with the bandeira because they believed that the expedition "had come to their lands to kill them, and conduct them to our lands, and make them our slaves." Pinto da Fonseca stressed their fear of the bandeira, yet Mayoral Abuênonâ finally agreed to meet them. He did not say why, but the lieutenant observed that the rains had been scarce and good hunting and water were hard for his bandeira to find. He also reported on their interest in acquiring tools and weapons to protect themselves from the Xavante, who were raiding their fields for food and stealing their women.

Pinto da Fonseca's narrative also reveals some characteristics of gender relations on this violent frontier. Since women were so often targeted for capture by bandeiras or enemy nations, their husbands hid them from the view of the expedition's men, either under mats in their canoes or isolated in their villages. Only after he had established a kinship relationship with the mayoral's sister was Pinto da Fonseca able to meet other women and give them gifts. Even so, some women were still so fearful of the bandeira that he never saw them.

With reference to Karajá material culture and lifestyle, what stands out was their use of canoes. There is no doubt that they were "canoe Indians," in contrast to the Xavante and other Gê populations who did not make and use canoes. In fact, one of the prized gifts the governor sent to the Karajá was an iron tool used to make canoes (*enxó*). At the time of the 1775 bandeira, the Karajá had not yet acquired firearms, and their weapons were bows, arrows, and lances. At present, Karajá women are famous potters whose clay sculptures of women and animals are sold as popular art in Brazil, but there is only one reference in Pinto da Fonseca's narrative to a clay object, a pipe that was used for smoking tobacco. Since the pipe was a symbol of peace among them, they smoked it with Pinto da Fonseca in the direction of the place "where the sun is born." They wore crowns of feathers, which Castelnau illustrated, but little else; the lieutenant made no mention of body paint, although the Xambioá Karajá decorated each cheek with a circle.

Pinto da Fonseca's narrative also documents that the Karajá lived a settled agricultural lifestyle. Perhaps more than eight thousand people lived on Bananal Island or along the banks of the Araguaia River, although this number seems high for the number of villages that Pinto da Fonseca counted. He reported that there were six large villages on the island. In contrast, the Javaé lived in only one large aldeia, which was three days away by canoe travel. The villages and their fields were located inland away from the beach, most likely to give more security from flooding during the rainy season or from armed war canoes. The Karajá also established more temporary structures on the sandy beaches of the Araguaia River during the dry season. The barraca of mats that sheltered the mayoral from the hot sun during the negotiations may have been typical. Besides living by agriculture, the Karajá also hunted deer and went fishing—one man was treated for a piranha bite. Their various activities must have supported a growing and prosperous population at the time of contact with the bandeira of 1775, at least until foreign diseases struck.

At that time little was recorded about their religious or spiritual beliefs and customs since the lieutenant and the priest who accompanied the expedition were focused on Christianization, and they spent too little time among the Karajá to learn much about their belief system. Possibly reflecting pre-Christian beliefs is the idea that the sun is born in the east. Pinto da Fonseca was convinced that the Karajá knew nothing of the Christian God, and the Javaé mayoral even asked if a paper was "God." On the other hand, the Karajá mayoral Abuênonâ knew Portuguese and could even write his letter in the Portuguese language. Perhaps he had had some exposure to Jesuit missions or Catholic priests elsewhere in Goiás or Pará.

Gift giving and reciprocal relations were also important to the Karajá. After Pinto da Fonseca treated a piranha bite, the man's relatives came to rub his face to thank him. When the peace agreement and alliance were made, the Karajá sent their own feathered crowns and lances as gifts to the governor. They also

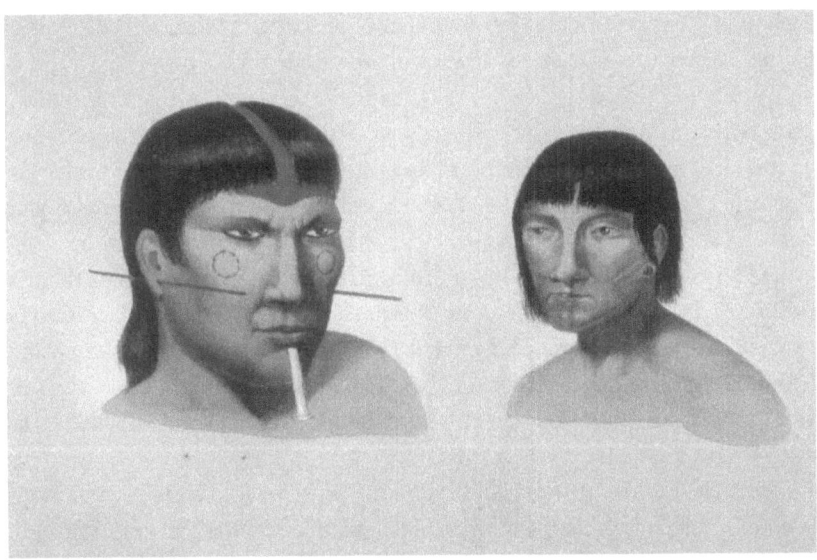

Figure 4. Pictured on the left is a Karajá warrior. On the right is a portrait of one of the Apiaká people of Mato Grosso, who were notable for the beauty of their body decoration in the nineteenth century. Source: Castelnau, Expédition. Courtesy of the Catholic University of America, Oliveira Lima Library, Washington, DC.

shared information with Pinto da Fonseca about the other peoples who lived near them: the Araés, Tapirapez, Comacariz, Jandariz, Lauecrayues, Janquirage, Tapucura, and Sirinquique. Their list suggests that the Araguaia River had formerly sheltered ethnically diverse populations.[32]

In the 1790s Tomás de Sousa Vila Real identified the principals among the Karajá. The "Principal chefe" of all was Auribedu. Apparently, six others also held the rank of principal: Aranabedu, Tuida, Baturi, J[?]aribedú, Quatibedú, and S[?]educurabedú=Tuixaua=mirim. Among the Carajahi were four principals: Tuida, Briuera, Aricabedu, and J[?]aina. What is of interest about Vila Real's list is that all ten principals used indigenous names. By the 1820s, Cunha Matos provides information on three Karajá villages and their leaders, two of which had Portuguese names: Lapa, the aldeia of Captain Bento, which was on the right bank of the Araguaia River; and Almeida, an aldeia on the left bank, which was also known by its principal's name, Francisco. Of particular interest is that Almeida had a large cemetery. To the north was the third aldeia of the Karajá, which was called Semancelhe, and its principal was José Maria. According to Cunha Matos, these were the three aldeias that had been "conquered" in 1774 (actually 1775). Yet another aldeia in Karajá territory was Salinas, where the Karajá used to visit in order to request ironwares.[33]

The image that emerges from these sources, therefore, is that of a settled, prosperous, and artistic people, where women played important roles and men were skilled hunters, fishermen, and warriors. They lived in villages under the rule of a mayoral, or principal chief. In time of peace they performed war dances, but at least before they made peace, they fought so well that they prevented Luso-Brazilians from conquest and settlement until after 1775. Although previous bandeiras had left legacies of bitterness, the Karajá had successfully defended most of their people from both the Portuguese and the Xavante and had lived autonomous lives, free of Portuguese colonial rule. But the events of 1775 brought them into contact with Luso-Brazilians, and this bandeira introduced many changes into their lives.

After their agreement to join in alliance with the Portuguese, the Karajá permitted the founding of a mission aldeia named Nova Beira and a presídio, São Pedro do Sul, which were built on Bananal Island. In the 1770s they were trading directly with merchants of Pará, which suggests that they had items to trade that Luso-Brazilian merchants desired and that they had acquired a taste for iron tools and European weapons. They also traveled on the Tocantins River, and in 1786 five ubás full of Karajá reached the site of an *engenho* on the Tocantins in Pará. By about 1813 they were using firearms and gunpowder, with which they attacked the presídio of Santa Maria do Araguaia in 1813. Portuguese governors had also arbitrarily moved them from their riverine homeland to new missions in the captaincy. About eight hundred Karajá and Javaé were sent to live in São José de Mossâmedes with the Kayapó, while another one thousand Javaé were transferred to the aldeia of Carretão to live with their old enemies, the Xavante. In turn, 180 Xavante were ordered to settle in a new aldeia at Salinas, which was in Karajá territory.[34]

By the time the French explorer Francis Castelnau reached the Xambioá Karajá further north in the 1840s, he found them to be a large nation, with a village of 1,500 people as well as fields in which they raised cotton for their women to make hammocks, although they still did not wear clothing. They invited the expedition into their capital village and entertained them with dances that included straw masks. Overall, Castelnau's visit suggests that the Xambioá to the north had not experienced the same degree of settler intrusions as those to the south on Bananal Island.[35]

Two other nations that lived along the Araguaia River, but to its west, were the Tapirapé and Araés.[36] The Tapirapé, a name that means "tapir's trail," are a

Tupi-speaking nation who settled along the river that is now called the Tapirapé River. Sometime in the remote past they had descended the Tocantins River from the north and established their villages along that river. The Jesuits may have contacted them as early as 1656 (see chapter 3), and bandeiras definitely attacked them. In 1756–1757, João de Godói Pinto da Silveira led an expedition to the "peaceful" Tapirapé, where he assaulted them and took a hundred prisoners to Vila Boa. Unfortunately, "the greater part of them" died of disease. In spite of this tragedy, the Tapirapé survived, and some entered missions in the nineteenth century—yet on the whole, they were not commonly described in late colonial documents.

In contrast, the Araés were famous in the bandeira chronicles of the seventeenth century. In the late sixteenth century the Araés lived in the sertão of the Paraúpava (see chapter 3). Bandeiras from São Paulo especially sought out the Araés due to their golden jewelry and legendary mountain of gold, but they also enslaved them. In the 1680s one of the most brutal of the Indian slavers was the first Antônio Pires de Campos, who massacred them at the Rio das Mortes (River of the Dying), also located west of the Araguaia River, and took the survivors as captives to Cuiabá. As of 1775 they were recorded as one of the nations "who drink in the [Araguaia] river," but when Silva e Souza wrote in 1812, he reported that he had had no notice of this nation, which suggests that they may have migrated elsewhere by that date.

Xavante and Xerente: A Divided People

The enemies of the riverine peoples were the invading Xavante (Chavante), who had once lived to the east of the Tocantins River. They are an Akuên people, hence Akwe-Xavante, who speak a Central Gê language. Their own term for themselves is *Auwe*, which means "people." According to their own oral traditions, their first contact with non-Indians was "at the sea." One tradition even suggests that they had come from Rio de Janeiro. By 1751 some had crossed the Tocantins River and were listed on a map to the east and northeast of Bananal Island. During the governorship of Dom Marcos de Noronha (1749–1755), they had already acquired a reputation for their violent resistance to local miners and settlers, and they were still waging war against Luso-Brazilians in Crixás and Tesouras in 1762. One illustration of a Xavante from around 1750 is that of a warrior with a feathered crown who holds a bow and arrows in his hands. Thus their image in the captaincy's sources is that of indomitable warriors who struck Luso-Brazilian settlements in the region between the Tocantins and Araguaia Rivers.[37]

Although they were among the most feared of the indigenous nations of the captaincy of Goiás, there is little detailed information about them before the arrival of the 1788 expedition that settled the Xavante at Carretão (see chapter 8). When the bandeira met Xavante warriors, they were riding horses in the sertão of Amaro Leite. A Kayapó chief who was with the bandeira as an interpreter convinced the Xavante to negotiate, and a small group went to Vila Boa to visit the governor, who issued orders for their aldeia in Carretão. Because they were so numerous, he wanted to send some to Salinas, while the other half were to be settled at Carretão. But the Xavante refused to go to Salinas, so perhaps as many as three thousand Xavante marched together to Carretão.[38] After a six-month journey, the "Xavante de Quá" arrived in Pedro III in Carretão on 7 January 1788 with their elderly, blind, and crippled and an "infinite" number of children, some of whom they carried, with others on their shoulders. With their mayoral Arientomô-laxê-qui in front, they entered dancing to the sound of maracas, trumpets, war boxes, and loud cries. After their official reception, the priest from Pilar baptized 412 children. Some children were not baptized because their families were in the forests, hiding from an epidemic that had attacked them. More than one hundred Xavante died in the epidemic, but they all were baptized "in their last moments." Only after the epidemic ended did the Xavante return to the aldeia and begin work on the fields that the governor had set aside for them. Also settling at Carretão were fourteen non-Xavante who had lived among them: freedpersons, captives, and some whites. The large number of Xavante recorded in 1788, however, did not remain at Carretão; only 227 Indians were still there in 1819 when Pohl visited the remnants of the aldeia.[39]

Another group of Xavante were living on the east bank of the Tocantins River between the Farinha and Manuel Alves Grande Rivers in 1814, when they were forced to move south of the Manuel Alves Grande. A year later Ribeiro placed those who had fled Carretão between the juncture of the Manuel Alves Grande River at the Tocantins River and Porto Real do Pontal, and they lived on both banks of the Tocantins River as far west as the right bank of the Araguaia River. Pohl met up with a group of them in 1819, and he also located them on both banks of the Maranhão River from Porto Real (Nacional) to São Pedro de Alcântara (Carolina), with a much larger territory extending to the east in Maranhão to Pastos Bons. Around Duro and Formiga, he reported, they were called Xerentes. In the past the Xavante, Xerente, and Acroá-Mirim had been three different peoples, but they were then united because the Xavante had conquered and incorporated the other two nations. The three distinct peoples had once lived in the region of Duro, including the Jesuit missions. According to Silva e Souza, the "Coroa [Akroá], and Coroamerim [Akroá-Mirim]" lived by hunting, fishing, and robbery. They went about on the land and crossed rivers on *balsas* (rafts). At that time, he did not regard them as very warlike. By Pohl's time they lived in three villages on the west bank of the Maranhão River: the first was called Baliza, the second, Aldeia Grande, and the third was far inland near the rivers that flow to the Araguaia River.[40]

The Xavante whom Pohl met impressed him with their vigor and force and their beautiful women. Like the Apinaje, they used their women to lure Luso-Brazilians into an ambush. They were of medium height with rounded faces and copper-colored bodies that they painted in red and black with *jenipapo* and *urucu* and then covered with palm oil to protect their body painting and deter mosquito bites; those in mourning painted their bodies all black. Although they used no clothing, they tied a white cord around the neck with two strings, from which a bird feather dangled. Around their wrists and ankles they wrapped black cords. Pohl also saw one man who had wrapped a cord of palm fibers around his body. On men these cords on the wrists and ankles were the insignia of the warriors. They also used sticks in their ears.[41]

The chief or cacique of each aldeia was called captain, and he had supreme authority over his aldeia. When major decisions were to be made, the captains of all the aldeias "acted in common"—in other words, they had to agree to go to war or to make peace. The "ancients" also came together in a council. In time of war, all young men between the ages of fifteen and thirty were obliged to do war service. As we will see in subsequent chapters, Xavante warriors were very skilled in time of war.[42]

Contrary to Portuguese discourse on the Xavante as nomadic vagabonds, or worse still as feras (wild animals), they lived a settled life in their large, round houses made of palm fronds. Their homes were so well constructed—by women in recent times—that they even protected the Xavante from the heavy rains of the rainy season. They "diligently" cultivated their fields of corn, manioc, tobacco, and sugarcane along the banks of the Tocantins River. The men also hunted, with the meat being roasted on stones, and caught fish with arrows, while women collected firewood and gathered foodstuffs and went for water. Both sexes were skilled swimmers, and they were able to cross rivers with the help of rafts bound together with lianas.

Although Pohl was in Xavante territory for too short a time to learn much about their religion, he did note that there were still "light vestiges" of what their ancestors had learned at the Jesuit missions. They believed in a supreme being to whom they prayed when they had accidents or were sick. But they also took the sick to a *furna* (cavern or grotto), where the relatives of sick persons danced around them, or they cured the sick with herbal medicines. They also danced during their festivals, especially after the harvest season, and they got drunk on palm wine. They were "rigidly monogamous," although widows could remarry. Burials were occasions for great lamentation, and the body was placed in a hole in the ground in a crouching position. At a man's side, they placed his bow and arrow and some provisions, and they crossed slats of wood over his head to form a cavern, over which they placed dirt. While the rest of his belongings were being burned, the people present remembered the achievements of the dead person. The mourning period then lasted eight to thirty days for his relatives, who blackened their bodies and wore a feather hung from a cord on their shoulders.

Pohl's vivid description of the Xavante in 1819 suggests a peaceful lifestyle with only a hint of the wars and political divisions that afflicted them. In that same period, more cattlemen were invading the Tocantins River region, putting pressure on the Xavante, their "irreconcilable enemies" the Krahô, and the Canoeiro. Because of the difficulties they experienced living so near Luso-Brazilians, there occurred a separation among them sometime between the 1810s and 1840s. The Auwe people split into separate nations now known as the Xavante (or Akwe-Xavante) and Xerente. According to contemporary sources, the cause of the division was over resistance or willingness to live with whites, but the Xerente had had a separate identity as early as 1782, and they had already established their own villages before the nineteenth century. In any case, the Xerente remained to live among whites along the east bank of the Tocantins River, while those Xavante who rejected living with whites moved west, eventually settling in the Mortes River region of eastern Mato Grosso, where their descendants still live on reserves. Thus the Xavante abandoned Goiás, but the Xerente became one of the most significant indigenous nations of the modern state of Tocantins, where they have their own reserve.[43]

According to Nimuendajú, the Xavante and Xerente are "essentially one in speech and custom" and their "history must be considered jointly." Like the Xavante, the Xerente of the Tocantins River region speak a Central Gê language and have a tradition of living east of the Tocantins River; according to Nimuendajú, they had once roamed in dry, drought-stricken areas as far as the São Francisco River. As of 1819 they lived in seven villages, one of which was

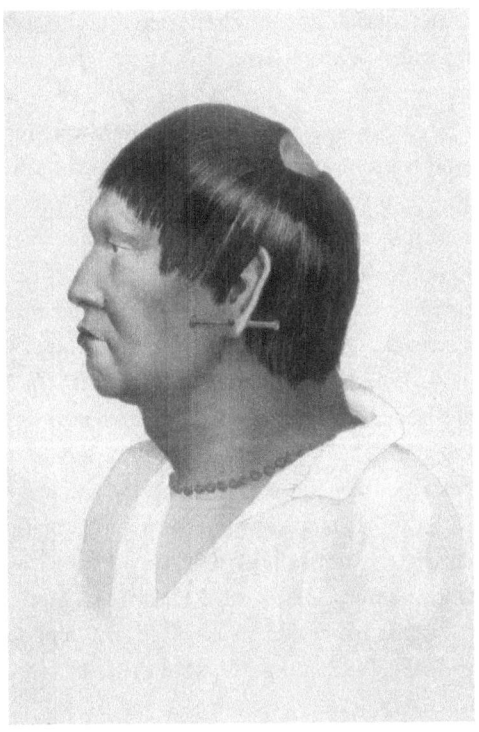

Figure 5. Chiotay was a Xerente chief, pictured here at age eighty. Source: Castelnau, Expédition. Courtesy of the Catholic University of America, Oliveira Lima Library, Washington, DC.

on the Balsas River; their territory also extended to Pastos Bons in Maranhão. In historical sources they were often linked with the Xavante and lived together with them in the same mission aldeias until the Xavante moved west of the Araguaia River. For example, Governor Miguel Lino de Moraes sent twenty-five Cherentes to join the Chavantes in Carretão in 1829 because they had "homogeneity in language and customs" to the Chavante who lived there.[44]

In the eighteenth century the Xerente lived with the Xavante on the banks of the Sono and Manuel Alves Grande Rivers, which are tributaries of the Tocantins River; their territory extended to the foothills of the Mangabeira to the east and near the creeks that flow into the Sono River, which is where Frei Ganges found them in 1851. As early as 1782, Colonel João Manoel de Braun reported that the "Xerentediquá" occupied the west bank of the Tocantins River. Another early use of the name *Xerente* is from the time of Governor Fernando Delgado Freire de Castilho (1809–1820), when some Cherentes of the Sertão do Duro were given food; they then returned to their own lands. Silva e Souza also identified them separately from the Xavante as "Cherentes" and

"Cherentes de qua" and reported that they lived above the falls of the small lake on the Araguaia River and their territory extended to the sertão of Duro between the Preto and Maranhão Rivers, where they had seven villages. He described them as "valiant and hardworking," but in his view the Chavantes, who used bows and arrows and lived between the Araguaia and Tocantins Rivers, were "cruel and robbers." On the other hand, José Vieira Couto de Magalhães reported that the Xerente had villages on both sides of the Tocantins River, from which they attacked travelers on the Tocantins River as well as the inhabitants of the north of Goiás and Maranhão. According to Pohl, they also raided the aldeia of Duro, capturing and enslaving baptized children.[45]

Although some sources suggest that the Xerente were more peaceful than the Xavante, others reported quite warlike behavior, or else they were confusing the Xerente with the Xavante. For example, two Xerente were actually described as "Chavante" when they initiated a peaceful contact on 13 April 1824 with the "great captain" on the sugar plantation of Lieutenant Severino Ferreira da Crus, two leagues from Porto Real. One of them was Captain Francisco, whose Xerente name was Xuathe (also Xuaté), and his aldeia was "in the place denominated gurgulho [sic]." He had come seeking peace and alliance with the military and Cunha Matos in order to secure their help against his enemies (see chapter 4).[46]

The director of the aldeia of Graciosa, which was established for the Xerente, identified the enemies of the Xerente. According to Estevão Joaquim Pires, the Noroguajés were "the same Cherentes nation, who do not want peace." This nation, he wrote in 1824, was "the greatest that there is in this region and the most traitorous." When they were in Pastos Bons, Maranhão, they had taken gifts from ranchers but then had abandoned peaceful relations and killed and robbed, taking women to their villages. Pires had received this information on the identity of the Noroguagé from the Christian women who lived among them. Significantly, Pires placed the Xerente in Pastos Bons before they migrated to the Tocantins River, where they lived in 1824; the other possibility is that he was actually describing the Xavante, who, according to tradition, were the faction that did not want peace. By 1824 the Noroguagé were living on the Gorgulho beach. Pires also used the term *Xerente* for those living on the Gorgulho and asked for more troops to defend the aldeia of Graciosa from the nations along the Sono River because they intended to eliminate the aldeia. About 130 years later, in the 1950s, the anthropologist David Maybury-Lewis encountered the Xerente on the Gorgulho River.[47]

Although these documents reveal little about the customs of the Xerente, they are especially valuable for identifying the leadership of those Xerente who chose to travel from the aldeia of the Gorgulho to settle at Graciosa under the protection of Cunha Matos. The documents refer to a Xerente named Pacifico who accompanied the Xerente captain Francisco Xuathe. Pacifico was the one who had brought together the twelve captains and four hundred warriors who settled at Graciosa, but the sources are unclear about his title and position. Captain Francisco Xuathe brought his aldeia (elsewhere *maloca*, or "big house"), which was subject to him, to Graciosa, while Captain João was a "Christian" who spoke Portuguese and wanted to go to Cavalcante. Attached to the correspondence of 1824 is a list of eleven captains (excluding Pacifico): Francisco Xuate, João Icomoth (or Ieomoth?), Seremeohe (or Seremeehe?), Axumaran, Seremituen, Etxumaran (?), Cune, Xitumine, Oremetiopre (?), Acornith (?), and Coth.[48]

One of the reasons these captains chose to seek the assistance of Cunha Matos was to secure the protection of his troops, but when he left the north in 1825, the Xerente quickly abandoned Graciosa and returned to raiding ranches. Only twenty-five agreed to be settled in Carretão among the Xavante. The positive image of the Xerente of Silva e Souza's time does not appear in Luso-Brazilian sources of the 1830s, when new bandeiras were plotted against them, as well as against the Xavante. Luiz Gonzaga de Camargo Fleury (governor, 1837–1839) referred to the Cherentes in 1837 as "this dissembling, traitorous, cruel, and barbarous nation," words the Portuguese had applied to the Xavante in the eighteenth century. It was not the first time, he argued, that they had had a pretext to make peace, "being their principal intent to probe our forces, and dispositions, to acquire knowledge of the land, and to make us suppose that there was nothing to fear, and for this we remain unprepared."[49]

The Canoeiro: The Tupi-Speaking Canoe Nation

In the nineteenth century the Canoeiros were the most demonized people of all in official correspondence.[50] Little was then known about them, since they refused to make peace with Christians and other indigenous nations and were enemies of the Xavante. Perhaps the reason is that they spoke a language that was not one of the Gê languages, but some of them knew prayers in Latin and some Portuguese, indicating that they may have lived with Christians at some point in their history. Originally the name may have been used by the Portuguese for any canoe Indians who attacked them as they invaded their lands and mined for gold along or near the Tocantins and Maranhão Rivers. In the past, many authors have speculated about their true identity, such as Cunha Matos in the 1820s and Couto de Magalhães in the 1860s. Couto de Magalhães, who had lived among the Araguaia populations, took down vocabulary words and concluded that they spoke Tupi. Writing in 1924, Paul Rivet used these word lists to assert that the language spoken by the Canoeiros was a very pure Tupí-Guaraní dialect, while in the 1930s Nimuendajú reported that they were a Tupi group. More recent studies have established that the Avá-Canoeiro, as they are now known, are linguistically related to the Tupi of the southern Tocantins River and the Tapirapé.[51]

Although Cunha Matos regarded the Canoeiro as similar in culture to the Payaguás of Paraguay and Mato Grosso, there is no evidence to support a Paraguayan connection. Since they had once lived in the mountains near the Jesuit mission of Duro, it is more probable that they had had some contact with the Jesuits in or near Duro rather than in Paraguay sometime before 1759.

Perhaps they had been among those attracted by the Jesuits to Duro or another mission, were angered at treatment there or enslavement by local settlers, and thereafter took up arms against all Luso-Brazilians. After the Jesuit expulsion from Duro, the Canoeiro invaded their former cattle ranches in the "sertões agrestes" of Amaro Leite.[52]

What is most likely is that the Canoeiro were the Tupi-speaking inhabitants of the Southern Tocantins River region that antedated Portuguese penetration of Central Brazil; that is, they had lived along the Tocantins River from pre-contact times.[53] During the gold rush of the 1720s and thereafter, they were driven off their homelands and even massacred, but by the late colonial period they were still a large nation who were formidable foes of all those who lived in the captaincy. Although the term "Canoers" is inexact, their descendants self-identify as ãwã, while FUNAI lists them as Avá-Canoeiro. But in the eighteenth century they were a mysterious people who were poorly documented in Luso-Brazilian sources, except in regard to their numerous attacks on ranches and towns and resistance to pacification.[54]

The search for the Canoeiro begins with the basic question: where did they live? According to the anthropologist Dulce Pedroso, the Canoeiro preferred to establish themselves in gallery forests on the banks of the Tocantins River and its tributaries. In contrast to much larger Gê villages, they built small villages with thatch-roofed houses and raised corn on fields cleared from fertile lands along the rivers. Their descendants, the contemporary Avá-Canoeiro, live by planting manioc and corn, hunting, and fishing. The sense from disparate sources is that the late colonial Canoeiro occupied desirable riverine lands in demand along an expanding agropastoral frontier. As the bandeiras and settlers forced them off these lands, they fought back, but they also retreated to more isolated lands at the headwaters of rivers, to the mountains, or to islands in the Tocantins River. As they adapted to less fertile lands, they relied less on planting fields and more on hunting and fishing. Constant migration to escape their enemies forced them to change their traditional way of life and abandon agriculture, and without reliable sources of food, they turned to raiding to feed their families.[55]

In the nineteenth century the Canoeiro raided and fought in a larger region than in the eighteenth century. According to Pedroso, their traditional territory was the southern Tocantins (or Maranhão) River. Additional locations include mountains to the "left" of the Maranhão River, islands in that river, the neighborhood of the fazenda Corriola, the region of the towns of Amaro Leite and Descoberto da Piedade (actual Porangatu), the region of the Paranã River, and all the land between the Preto and Santa Tereza Rivers. Their villages were also found on the Almas and Cana-Brava Rivers and near the Vila da Palma, but in the nineteenth century their raids were even more extensive, from Carmo and Pontal in the north to the Claro River in the far south. According to Pedroso, the "left bank" of the Maranhão River was more densely occupied by the Canoeiro than the right bank.[56]

Such a vast distribution suggested to Pedroso that the Caneiro had been a large nation who had fought invaders from 1770 to 1860 and afterward. The scale of the violence over more than a century is suggested by local traditions recorded by Pedroso and documentation of their assaults on the following towns: Peixe, Palma (Paranã), Descoberto (Porangatú), Amaro Leite (Mara Rosa), Pilar, Crixás, Traíras, São José do Tocantins, Cavalcante, Cocal, São Félix, and Água Quente. At least through their attacks, we can trace their migrations and dislocations throughout the captaincy.[57]

Unfortunately, Portuguese sources reveal little about Caneiro culture or customs. More often what we encounter in outsider records are negative stereotypes forged in frontier warfare (see chapter 4). According to Silva e Souza, with reference to the Canoeiro of the period of the governorship of Tristão da Cunha Menezes (1783–1800), they had depopulated "a great part of the ranches of the vicinity of the Maranhão River." They were then a "very cruel and bellicose nation," who did not know how to flee. In combat, they resisted to the death, furiously investing their women and fierce dogs with the same qualities. They went about in canoes on the Tocantins, Paranã, and Manoel Alves Rivers and to the Barra da Palma, where they caused much damage. Their principal aldeia was located among the mountains at the side of Duro, where they were based. Besides the bow and arrow, they used lances, toothed on the ends, of more than twenty *palmos* (hand spans) in length. He concluded by citing their love of horse meat, which was their "most savory food."[58]

In 1824, Cunha Matos, who fought against the Canoeiro, added some additional insights into their way of life in the 1820s. He reported that they all went about nude because they considered clothing to be "superfluous." Although they were monogamous, he called attention to the existence of a general house (*vivenda*) of prostitutes, who were not permitted to communicate with "other honest women under the most severe penalties." All the aldeias were governed by caciques or captains, some of whom were "so barbarous that for the lightest motive they impose the death penalty." Of particular interest is that he accused them of maintaining a commerce in slaves, which may be true since the merchants of Pará bought slaves from diverse nations between Pontal and the juncture of the Araguaia with the Tocantins River by exchanging them for gunpowder, arms, aguardente, and tobacco. Finally, he noted the difficulty of making peace with them—they responded with showers of arrows—and their practice of leaving the lowlands and retreating to their mountains and villages until they would attack again at the beginning of the dry season.[59]

Such descriptions, however, do not usually appear in eighteenth-century sources. Invading bandeiras and gold miners were the ones who slaughtered unnamed nations, and the many Luso-Brazilian massacres after the 1720s undoubtedly led to fierce Canoeiro resistance. In 1773 an official bandeira organized by Governor D. José de Almeida Vasconcelos (1772–1778) traveled to the west bank of the Tocantins River in the direction of Pontal and on to the Almas River, where they battled a group they called the Xavantes de canoa, which was a name used for the Canoeiro to distinguish them from the Xavante, who did not use canoes. In 1789 more Canoeiro were killed, and many of their villages located on islands in the Tocantins River were destroyed in 1796. Although José Luis Pereira tried to contact and make peace with the Canoeiro in 1803, instead he "made great slaughter among them," in part because he was assisted by their enemies the Xavante from Carretão. After capturing fifty of the Canoeiro, he took his captives to Porto Real to be sent along with other captives to Belém.[60]

The next large bandeira that tried to conquer the Canoeiro was the infamous bandeira of 1819, which was organized by Joaquim Theotonio Segurado (see chapter 3). When the bandeira actually confronted the Canoeiro, they found them living in a village of thatch-roofed houses on the Almas River, where they cultivated corn. When the bandeira proposed peace to the

Canoeiro, they refused; the troops shot the bearded chief, who spoke some Portuguese, and massacred all but six children and one old woman. As late as 1830 the Canoeiro were still angry about "the atrocities" committed against their village.[61]

The mutual warfare and raiding continued. The next expeditions sent against the Canoeiro were those of 1823–1825, organized by Cunha Matos. He justified his bandeira by noting that the Canoeiro were "the most barbarous of the universe, whose cruelty exceeded that of the bugres and Botocudos." Although they were not cannibals, they killed with war clubs and arrows and, along with the Xavante, had attacked more than eight hundred cattle ranches and plantations spread over four hundred leagues, including the towns of Amaro Leite, Descoberto da Piedade, São Félix, Palma, Carmo, and Chapada, and as far as the presídio at Duro. Around São Félix and Amaro Leite in particular, the Canoeiro had "ruined" three hundred ranches and mining camps. Whenever the government sent patrols against them, they continued attacking. After one such attack, the surviving interpreter, an Indian woman, reported that the Canoeiro were tinted black from the fruit of the "Ginipapeiro."[62]

In the 1840s Castelnau recorded that the Canoeiro then lived along both banks of the Tocantins River, from Peixe in the north to ten leagues to the south of Amaro Leite on the left bank and São José do Tocantins on the right bank of the river. Their boundary with the Xavante coincided with the road that ran from Porto Imperial (Nacional) to the City of Goiás and passed by Peixe, Descoberto, Amaro Leite, and Pilar. On the left bank of the Tocantins they covered all the sertão of the Paranã, while a plateau separated them from the Xerente living in Bahia.[63]

Never pacified, the Canoeiro continued their resistance throughout the nineteenth century, and some kept fighting until the 1980s, when several were found hiding in caves from their enemies. Nearly extinct, only small groups of Avá-Canoeiro remain in Central Brazil, reminders of this once-large nation that was noted for the courage and ferocity of their resistance to enslavement and settlement in Christian missions.[64]

The Kayapó of the South (Panará) and the North (Mebengokre)

In the south of the captaincy, the people who once roamed a large part of the region near the capital of Vila Boa and to the west and south of it were part of the nation the Portuguese called the Bilreiros and later the "Caiapó." A Gê-speaking population, the Kayapó are most closely related linguistically to the Apinaje and the Suyá of eastern Mato Grosso. According to some sources, the name used for the Southern Kayapó (Kayapó do Sul) was of Tupi origin and means "monkey," but Jézus Marco de Ataídes and David L. Mead both argue that "Caiapó" means "carrier of fire" for the firebrands they used in warfare. The Northern Kayapó, however, self-defined themselves as Mebengokre, or the "people of the space in or among the waters."[65]

The Kayapó who first met the invading bandeiras of the seventeenth century in Goiás and Mato Grosso were the Southern Kayapó. Although settlers drove them from Goiás, their descendants, the Kreen-Akarore or Panará, now live in southern Amazonia in a forested area known as the Peixoto de Azevedo.[66] Yet their modern names rarely appear in seventeenth-, eighteenth-, or nineteenth-century sources. To determine who was a "Caiapó" in those centuries is extremely complex because their enemies gave them other names or referred to diverse peoples as the Caiapó nation. Among the names that Luso-Brazilians used for them in the seventeenth century was Bilreiros, for their war clubs (see chapters 3–4).[67]

In the case of the Northern Kayapó, one large group mentioned in the sources consulted is a people known as the Nhyrykwaye, who used to live between the Araguaia and Tocantins Rivers in the far north. According to one oral tradition, cited by the anthropologist Terry Turner, these Kayapó were attacked by whites and after a battle in which they suffered heavy losses, they crossed the Araguaia River to escape them. In fact, the first documented reference to the Nhyrykwaye occurs in an 1810 narrative by Luso-Brazilian slave hunters, who assaulted them in the area between the rivers in 1810. By the 1820s Cunha Matos clarifies that the Kayapó, who were called Gradaús by the Karajá, still occupied the cerrado between the Tocantins and Araguaia Rivers to the north of Santa Maria on the Araguaia River, about fifty kilometers south of Conceição. Twenty years later Castelnau also placed the Gradaús in that area, but by the time of the arrival of Capuchin missionaries in 1859 they were living to the west of the Araguaia River.[68]

In contrast, most of the Caiapó who appear in eighteenth-century sources were the Kayapó do Sul, who lived in large villages to the east of the Araguaia River and in the region of the Claro and Pilões rivers, the Serra do Caiapó, and the hilly country of Caiapônia in western Goiás. They also controlled the east bank of the Pardo River, a tributary of the Paraná River, and raided along the roads to São Paulo and Cuiabá. Paulista bandeiras attacked them in the seventeenth and early eighteenth centuries, enslaving war captives. In 1741 the bandeira of Antônio Pires de Campos took Kayapó heads as war trophies and enslaved a reputed eight thousand Kayapó. Those who survived fled to near

Vila Boa, where they embarked on revenge raids and warfare for almost forty years. With the help of 120 Bororo from Mato Grosso, who were traditional enemies of the Kayapó, Antônio Pires de Campos destroyed an entire Kayapó village in 1742.[69]

Thus one image of the Kayapó that emerges from the bandeira chronicles is that of raiders and warriors who resisted the bandeiras whenever they attacked their populous villages. On the other hand, two bandeira leaders provide a glimpse of peaceful villages, each with its own chief, where there were wide roads and cultivated fields of corn (hard and soft for roasting), sweet potatoes, manioc (bitter and sweet), yams, pumpkins, squashes, and peanuts stored in gourds. After men cleared the forests (with stone tools or stolen axes), women cared for the crops. While women provided garden crops to feed their families, men hunted and fished or acquired other foodstuffs by raiding ranches and mule teams. In 1828 Antônio Pires de Campos accused them of cannibalism before describing their weapons and plundering of other nations (see chapter 4). Thirty-two years later João Godói Pinto da Silveira added some additional insights but did not describe cannibalism. He reported that they wore no clothing and painted themselves with urucu. The men cut their hair "from the forehead to the crown of the head in a pyramidal fashion," and the women wore it long. Not only did they dance, leaping from one place to another, but they also had a "game of strength" in which they practiced carrying the body of a sick or dead person by toting logs of buriti wood, some of which were of great size and weight that the Bororo could not lift. In fact, Pinto da Silveira counted two hundred logs in one village alone. As for political leadership, he reported that they "have no chiefs with absolute power" and if a chief failed "to administer well," then people would join other leaders. Furthermore, they did not adore idols or have superstitions.[70]

In the 1780s a group of the Kayapó visited Vila Boa and camped near the governor's palace.[71] Each morning they went out to hunt and gather food in nearby forests. They were so successful that they were able to leave gifts of animals, birds, honey, and wax as gifts for one resident of the town. Soon after these Kayapó went to live in the aldeia of Maria I, which the governor had set aside for them about fifty miles from Vila Boa on the Fartura River. Two chiefs, Angraí-oxá and Xaquenau, led their people there. They were soon joined by more Kayapó under the chiefs Cunã-puaxi and Pupuarê, until there may have been as many as 2,400 inhabitants living in the four hamlets that made up the aldeia.[72] The inhabitants, however, did not long remain at Maria I. Within twenty years most of the Kayapó had either abandoned the aldeia or died of deadly diseases that ravaged the mission population. After further negative experiences of coerced labor, those who fled quickly resumed raiding and attacking settlers and mule teams in the southern Araguaia region. By 1813 there were so few still living in Maria I that they were relocated to São José de Mossâmedes. The population of the two aldeias combined then numbered only 267; by 1824 only 124 Kayapó remained, and these either fled or were moved against their will and resettled in Mato Grosso in 1833–1834.[73]

While the Kayapó resided at Maria I or São José, they served the state as soldiers in the pedestres. Thus the Southern Kayapó who remained in the missions in Goiás lived under the protection of the governors and as soldiers and allies. Their women intermarried with the mulato and black troops stationed in the aldeias. In contrast to the mission Kayapó, most Southern Kayapó did not abandon their traditional lands and large villages, nor did they relinquish raiding and warfare. Throughout much of the nineteenth century, they continued to resist the Luso-Brazilians who invaded their lands in Camapuã, at the headwaters of the Araguaia River, and in the Triangulo Mineiro. Many of those warriors who were most forceful in opposing encroaching settlers were the very mission Kayapó expelled against their will from São José de Mossâmedes. Other Panará found refuge in the Peixoto de Azevedo, where they lived autonomous lives, but the Kayapó do Sul no longer survive as a distinct ethnic group in Goiás.[74]

This survey of the major nations of the captaincy of Goiás is notably incomplete because it excludes the peoples who did not come to the attention of invading Luso-Brazilians and therefore were able to remain autonomous, nor does it take into account those who were decimated by diseases, enslaved and traded to other captaincies, or massacred; thus we know little about them. Sometimes only their names were recorded. Still others passed through the captaincy of Goiás and did not remain long enough to capture official attention before they moved on to Mato Grosso or other captaincies. Many Gê-speaking populations are nomadic or seminomadic, so that by the time official scribes had recorded their existence, they had migrated, changed their names, or died. Some of the lost peoples are so recorded in appendix A. Subsequent chapters will trace the further relationships of the indigenous nations in the captaincy as they resisted or accommodated to those who invaded their lands or changed cultures and even languages as they had to deal with these newcomers. Thenceforth their history would be linked with that of Luso-Brazilians and Africans as they all competed to control the land between and along the rivers.

CHAPTER 3

Bandeiras and Entradas

The Invaders of Central Brazil

When Portuguese governors of the captaincy of Goiás organized expeditions (bandeiras) in the late colonial period, the indigenous peoples of Goiás had already confronted almost two centuries of bandeira incursions. Since the captaincy was so centrally located, the bandeiras had struck from all directions: from São Paulo in the south; Pará and Maranhão in the north; Piauí, Pernambuco, and Bahia in the northeast; Minas Gerais in the southeast; and even from the west, Mato Grosso. Beginning with those from São Paulo, we will briefly survey the more significant expeditions that hunted and enslaved indigenous peoples, explored the great rivers in search of gold, and "conquered" the Karajá, Kayapó, and Xavante. One of the constants in these centuries was the expansion of the slaving frontier as more and more nations fell captive to the bandeiras. Those who raided quilombos to re-enslave fugitive blacks will be described in chapter 7.

In the invasions of Central Brazil, there were at least four types of expeditions that penetrated indigenous lands. The first type of expedition is the most difficult to document since these were more similar to predatory gangs of adventurers and corsairs, traversing Central Brazil by canoe and on foot with the goals of enslaving indigenous peoples and runaway Africans and discovering gold and emeralds. If they received official authorization for their bandeiras, they expected to be rewarded for their services to the Crown with rights to vast lands via a *sesmaria* (land grant) and to high offices with annual incomes, but they also acquired still more wealth by ignoring royal instructions about fighting "just wars" and took as many captives as possible, including women and children. While other types of bandeiras were somewhat regulated by Crown and Council, this type owed loyalty only to its leader and to other members of the bandeira. Unlike the solitary individualists of the North American frontier, these were highly mobile "small armies" that

64 CHAPTER 3

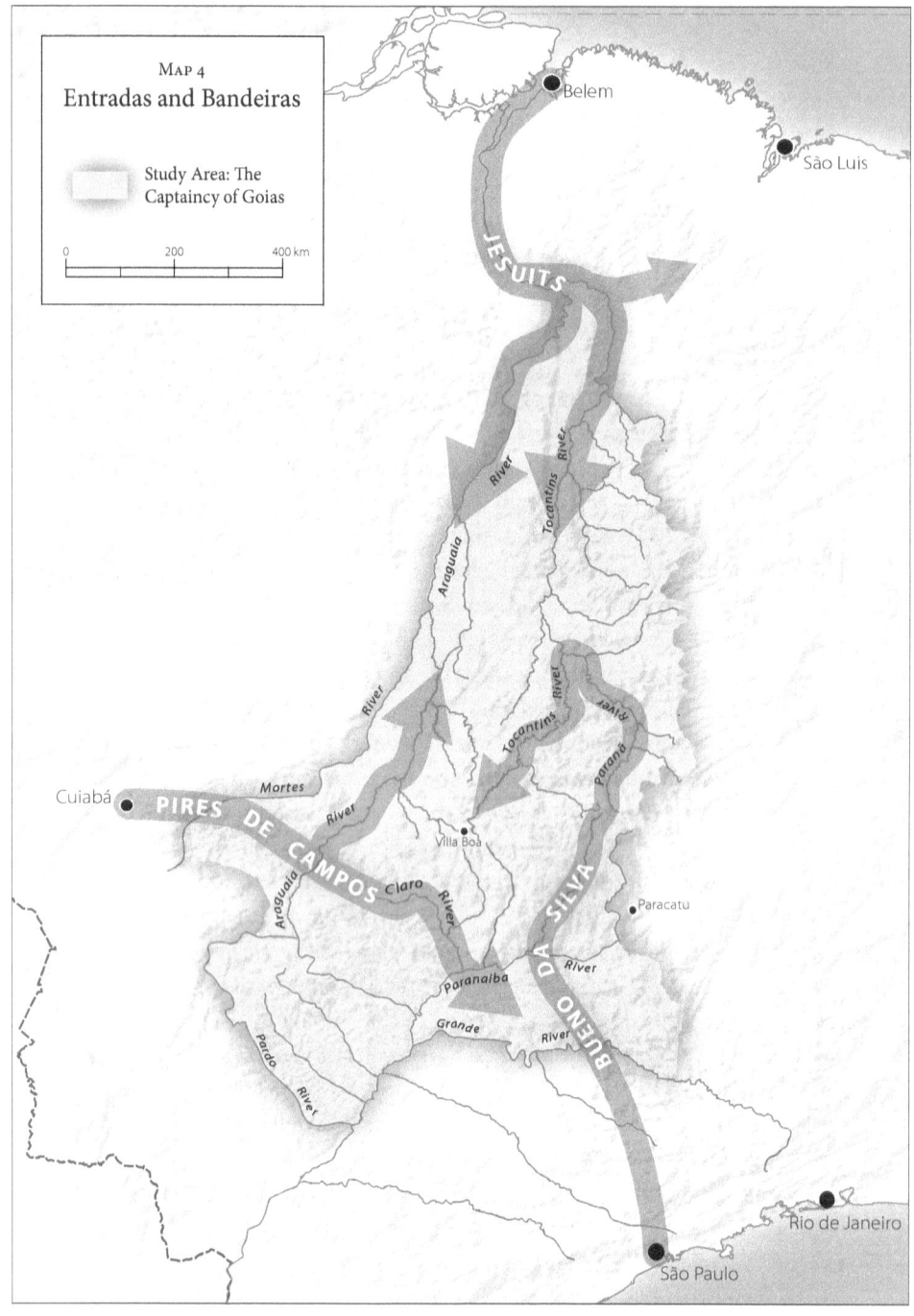

MAP 4
Entradas and Bandeiras

Study Area: The Captaincy of Goias

0   200   400 km

included members' relatives, servants, and slaves; they were led by a "chief" or sertanista (backlander or frontiersman) who knew how to live in the "wilderness" of the sertão. While official and municipal bandeiras usually included Luso-Brazilian officers, these roving gangs often followed a mestizo or mulato leader. Such bandeiras could be multiethnic expeditions in which there were few whites; they might even speak not Portuguese but the língua geral (Tupi). In the captaincy of Goiás, most of those who accompanied the bandeiras were actually men of color and indigenous men; indigenous women served in support roles, although one remarkable woman led pacification expeditions between 1808 and 1830.

The second type of bandeira was organized and partially funded by the Portuguese colonial government, if only in supplying regular troops. A governor of São Paulo or Goiás had the responsibility of finding the men and resources to achieve Portuguese objectives of defending the captaincy from its enemies, discovering and protecting gold mines, and enslaving or settling war captives in Christian missions. Henceforth we will refer to these expeditions as state-funded bandeiras. They were usually led by one or more Portuguese officers or skilled sertanistas who were knowledgeable about indigenous customs and languages. These official expeditions also included a chaplain, notary, interpreter, and indigenous auxiliaries. Since they required government approval and delivery of the royal share of captives, we can trace the largest of them in the documentary record.[1]

The third type of bandeira often escaped Portuguese notice. These were the locally recruited expeditions formed by a city council to protect its town or to attack nearby indigenous communities and quilombos in order to acquire captives. Funding usually came from the slaveholders in each town, who donated gold for the enterprise, while farmers and local ranchers provided provisions. In return, they expected to suppress any threats and acquire new captives, thus bringing "peace" to their parish and labor for their households. City council documents permit some insight into these local bandeiras, which were usually smaller than the large state-funded bandeiras, although they might include regular troops, or at least paid foot soldiers (pedestres) and local militias.

Finally, the fourth type of expedition was the Jesuit expedition or *entrada* (literally entry/entrance), which necessarily had to be armed as it traveled on the Tocantins River due to the number of enemy nations along the river. Until 1759 Jesuits made entradas from Belém do Pará or neighboring Maranhão and Piauí. Although the priests might have been unarmed, Luso-Brazilian soldiers and "civilized" Indians defended them on their voyages south on the Tocantins

River to make contact with non-Christian peoples. Jesuit goals were to locate "gentile nations" in order to convert them to Christianity and save their souls, but the military officers who accompanied them often had less altruistic motives of enslavement and gold prospecting. Although Jesuits penetrated the north of the captaincy of Goiás and established missions in Pontal, Natividade, and Duro, they could no longer send entradas into Goiás after 1759, when they were forcibly expelled by the Portuguese government. Some bandeiras even participated in the expulsion of the Jesuits.

Thus, between 1760 and the 1840s, priests rarely led mission entradas. If they participated in an expedition, they accompanied the bandeira as its chaplain and shared in the division of captives. Yet there were at least three priests who actually led bandeiras. One, a Padre Pôsso (also Passos), was a rich mine owner in Pilar, who sold what he had to lead a bandeira in 1759 to discover the riches of the Araés and Bananal Island in the Araguaia River. He also fought against the Xavante and died near Pontal. Padre José Simões da Mata of Vila

Figure 6. Indian hunters with long rifles lead two mothers roped together. One child clings to its mother, while another sits on the shoulders of its mother with two older children behind her. This iconic image of indigenous captivity in Brazil evokes the victims of the slavers who attacked indigenous villages, killing the men and leading the women and children into slavery. Source: Debret, Voyage pittoresque. Courtesy of the Library of Congress, Washington, DC.

Boa commanded another bandeira in 1772. The third priest had been sent as a missionary to convert the Krahô; instead, he led slaving expeditions against them until he fled to Pará with his captives in 1815.[2]

Our survey of bandeiras for the colonial period will begin in the south with the predatory Paulista enslavers of the 1590s and describe noted bandeira leaders of the seventeenth century who enslaved Indians in Goiás. The next section will examine the efforts of Portuguese governors and their state-funded bandeiras to discover gold, as well as *corsairs* who actually found it in diverse locations. Third, we will briefly describe the Jesuit entradas on the Tocantins River and the secular bandeiras that sought Jesuit gold in the north. The final section will conclude with the state-funded pacification expeditions of the late colonial period, including those that were not successful, such as those sent against the Canoeiro. A particular focus of this chapter will be on the increasingly negative impact of slave raiding with the expansion of the slaving frontier.[3] Therefore, this chapter will take a more chronological approach than other chapters, since all three types of bandeiras were active in Central Brazil throughout the colonial period—only the Jesuit entradas ended by 1760. Furthermore, the bandeira tradition linked with enslavement continued long after independence and inspired local elites and city councils in the nineteenth century.

The Slaving Frontier of the Paraúpava

The search for captives in Central Brazil actually began in the late 1500s, when bandeiras from São Paulo voyaged up the rivers, hunting Indians to enslave. One of the bandeiras that may have reached Goiano lands between 1590 and 1593 left São Paulo under the leadership of Antônio de Macedo and Domingos Luís Grau; it is uncertain exactly where that bandeira went, possibly to as far as the sertão of the Paraúpava of the Araguaia and Tocantins Rivers. Another bandeira, led by Sebastião Marinho, probably reached an area to the northeast of the future Vila Boa in 1592, while a bandeira of 1596 traveled to the sertão of the Tocantins River. With João Pereira de Sousa Botafogo at its head, this bandeira included Antônio Zouro, a sertanista from São Paulo. Although they may have reached the Tocantins River valley, little is known about this bandeira or the people it enslaved, but sources suggest that the peoples of this region, such as the Araés, were among the first targets of the bandeiras of the 1590s.[4]

By the early seventeenth century, the governor of the southern captaincies, D. Luís de Sousa Henriques, encouraged the formation of bandeiras to hunt for indigenous captives and gold. The most prominent of his bandeiras was that of 1613–1614, led by André Fernandes of Parnaíba. At least thirty whites participated in this bandeira, which journeyed to the sertão of the Paraúpava, where they pursued the Apuatiaras (Kayapó).[5] They did not return to São Paulo until early in 1615 because they had reputedly traveled to Pará on the Tocantins River. Near the juncture of that river with the Araguaia, this bandeira contacted a people known as the Caatingas, who lived in seven large villages east of the Tocantins River. Somehow they convinced three thousand of them to embark for São Paulo in three hundred canoes, but the Caatingas revolted and fled back to their homeland and the bandeira had to return via the Araguaia River without thousands of captives.[6]

In that same year of 1615 a second important bandeira was organized, led by the Paulista Antônio Pedroso de Alvarenga. One of its objectives was to conquer the Apuatiaras, but the governor was also encouraging Paulistas to look for mines in the sertão of the Paraúpava. Alvarenga's bandeira, accompanied by "diverse Carijós," who were captives, left São Paulo in July 1615 and traveled more than three hundred leagues, passing by an aldeia of the Gualachos (Kaingang) before reaching the sertão of the Paraúpava in April 1616. Due to the extent of their explorations, Alvarenga's bandeira did not return to São Paulo until 1618.[7]

An offshoot of one of the Paraúpava bandeiras may have reached the Araguaia River in 1613. Pêro Domingues, who spent nineteen months in the sertão, apparently explored the Araguaia River. A possible participant in one of the bandeiras between 1613 and 1618 was Antônio Rodrigues Vilares, who hunted the Araés in the sertão of the Paraúpava, but the bandeira from São Paulo that actually reached the "celebrated Araés" was commanded by Sorocabano Manuel Correia, who was "ambitious" to find gold.[8]

Prior discoveries of large numbers of Indians to enslave and rumors of gold among the Araés led to the formation of still more bandeiras. Paulistas continued to organize bandeiras and to penetrate the sertão of Central Brazil, moving up from the south. The Paulista bandeira that went to the north of Goiás in pursuit of "wild gentiles" was that of Francisco Lopes Benavides, a Paulista sertanista who led a "great bandeira" of 1664–1665. Accompanying him were two brothers, Bartolomeu and Paulo Bueno. It is uncertain exactly where this bandeira went or how far north it traveled.[9]

In less than a century, therefore, bandeiras had explored and enslaved the populations of the Araguaia-Tocantins Rivers. As they contacted the Araés, Karajá, Kayapó, and other peoples whose names have disappeared in historical sources, they established the predatory bandeira tradition of slaving on the frontier of Goiás. But as each new population was devastated by the invaders, the bandeiras had to raid farther and farther north, going as far as Pará on the Tocantins River. In the process, however, each bandeira gained further knowledge of the routes into the interior to secure even more indigenous captives. Those who were successful at Indian slaving soon built powerful reputations to intimidate their enemies into submission.

Bartolomeu Bueno da Silva, Father and Son

By the 1680s, one of the most feared bandeira leaders was Bartolomeu Bueno da Silva, the first Anhangüera, who was a famous sertanista from Parnaíba, São Paulo. His young son, also named Bartolomeu Bueno da Silva (the "boy," or the second Anhangüera), began to accompany him into the backlands from at least the age of twelve. Together they searched for the legendary mountain range of the *martírios* (martyrdoms). This legend had been brought back by earlier adventurers who had explored the land of the Araés. Allegedly, Antônio Pires de Campos, the elder, had found a mountain of gold in the land of the Araés; in 1682–1683 the first Bueno da Silva joined with him to conquer the Araés and find their gold. Together their large bandeira took many captives among the Karajá and Araés, many of whom were taken to Cuiabá by Pires de Campos. The search for the gold of the martírios, the mountain of gold, or the gold of the Araés would soon lead to the formation of still more bandeiras and the eventual discovery of gold in the 1720s.[10]

At that time, Bueno's son, Bartolomeu Bueno, the second Anhangüera, was living in Parnaíba, São Paulo. Then a father with married daughters, he decided to pursue his father's earlier explorations with the help of his sons-in-law. One of his partners was the famous bandeira leader Bartolomeu Pais de Abreu, who helped him organize the bandeira of 1722. With official authorization from the governor of São Paulo, Dom Rodrigo César de Meneses (1721–1728), the bandeira of 152 armed men with thirty-nine horses entered the sertão in July 1722. This number included twenty Indians from the royal aldeias, who were to carry supplies, and three religious: two Benedictines and one Franciscan. Besides the Portuguese, the whites included five or six Paulistas and one Bahian. There were also thirty-five slaves, including *negros*, most likely *negros da terra* (Indians), of whom they lost twenty-five. The bandeira was away from São Paulo for over three years, and in all that time they found only thirty-two *oitavas* of gold, at the cost of forty lives.[11]

The bandeira initially followed a route to Goiás that later became the road to the mines, but after crossing numerous rivers, they got lost in the sertão of eastern Goiás while trying to connect to the road to Cuiabá. They crossed a great forest and the sertão of the Paranã River, where they found feral cattle that may have wandered there from Bahia. In the midst of their own wanderings, they attacked and occupied a village of the Quirixá (Crixá) for three months. Since Bueno seemed unable to find gold, dissension soon broke out among the men, leading to desertions. Along with fourteen Indians and a mulato, José Peixoto da Silva Braga, the Portuguese Francisco Carvalho de Lordelo and his brother José Alves de Lordelo abandoned the expedition and built rafts on which they traveled via the Tocantins River to Belém do Pará. Upon their arrival in Belém in 1725, however, he and his men were detained until the authorities determined the motive for their voyage on the Tocantins River.[12]

While Silva Braga was exploring the Tocantins River, Bueno's men, now reduced to about seventy, were starving, which suggests that they had gotten lost in a sterile landscape before they reached the Tocantins River; yet they did not follow the river north but instead traveled west and south to Ferreiro on the Vermelho River. They were looking for a place previously described by Manuel Peres Cañamares, and in Ferreiro they found five locations where gold could be mined. They returned to São Paulo in 1725 with a little gold (thirty-two oitavas) and the news of the potential mines, which led to the formation of Bueno's second bandeira.[13]

A year later in May, Bueno da Silva, now more than fifty years old, journeyed back to the Vermelho River to begin work on the mines. This time it took the expedition only six months to reach the site of the future Vila Boa. They captured two elderly Goiá, who showed them the place of Ferreiro, where they established the first mining camp. According to Luiz Antônio da Silva e Souza, the second Bueno da Silva had stood at that very place forty years earlier with his father. He then founded other camps with his colleagues on the Vermelho River, where they discovered more gold. His own method of locating gold, however, was not the most ethical: his strategy was to seize the Goiá women who wore gold as pendants on their necks. He then made their men show him where they had found the *folhetas* (leaves) of gold that adorned the women. This time he returned to São Paulo with eight thousand oitavas of gold.[14]

For delivering so much wealth to the Crown, Bueno da Silva received the title of regent captain-mor, sesmarias (land grants) and the right to collect the tax at river crossings (*passagens*) for a period of three lifetimes. He lost control of this tax in 1733 and was unable to pay his debts due to the expenses he had incurred on his bandeiras. He was typical of many bandeira leaders in bearing all or part of the costs of the expedition himself. He died in 1740 without receiving appropriate rewards, in his view, for the great wealth he had delivered to the Portuguese Crown. His son continued to protest this injustice and followed in his father's line of work, joining the bandeira of Antônio Pires de Campos that attacked the Kayapó in 1748.[15]

Pai Pirá and the Boy

Besides the two Anhangüeras, two other significant bandeira leaders of Goiás were a father and son, both named Antônio Pires de Campos, who were originally based near Itú, São Paulo. Their fazenda was in Itaici, about twenty kilometers away, where they held six hundred administered Indians, apparently the war captives that they had brought back from the sertão. The elder Pires de Campos had spent years in the sertões of Mato Grosso and Goiás. While still a boy with his father, Manuel de Campos Bicudo, he had also participated in the bandeiras of the two Anhangüeras in Mato Grosso and Goiás.[16]

According to the first Pires de Campos, his father had gone on an expedition in pursuit of the "gentiles." Upon his return, he met with the father of the first Anhangüera, who had traveled to the location where there were two large villages of the Araés. But the bandeira was unable to profit from those they enslaved due to "the plague, which almost finished all of them." According to Jézus Marco de Ataídes, Manuel de Campos Bicudo made twenty-four entradas into the sertão.[17]

About 1716, his son, the first Antônio Pires de Campos, traveled via the Cuiabá River in order to hunt the Aripoconé or Coxiponé in Mato Grosso. Since he did not have great success, he returned to São Paulo, before settling in Cuiabá, Mato Grosso, from whence he launched bandeiras for many years. He also participated in the conquest of the Paiaguá of Mato Grosso in 1733. As an elderly man of eighty-seven in 1746, Pires de Campos once again lived in São Paulo, where he died in his nineties. It would be his son, the second Antônio Pires de Campos, who would move from Cuiabá to Goiás in order to conquer the Kayapó, who raided both captaincies.[18]

Bandeiras to the Kayapó and the Araguaia River

These early bandeiras clearly discovered routes to the indigenous villages of the Maranhão, Tocantins, and Araguaia Rivers and uncovered enough sources of slaves to attract future expeditions. In their efforts to reach these rivers, however, they encountered fierce resistance from a people they named the Bilreiros for their war clubs; they later called them the "Caiapó nation."[19] Although some of the bandeiras that explored the sertão of the Paraúpava most likely contacted the Kayapó as early as the 1590s, the better documented Paulista bandeira that made contact with the Kayapó was that of Belchior Dias Carneiro, who led a bandeira of five hundred men to the sertão of the Bilreiros in 1607, where he met some of the Bilreiros and traded a large knife for a "piece" (Indian slave) known as a Guaguaroba. While this contact was apparently peaceful, perhaps because they traded knives for captives, five years later Garcia Rodrigues seized captives among the Bilreiros in order to enslave them.[20]

A year later, in 1608, a second Paulista bandeira also went in pursuit of the Bilreiros, but it ended up exploring as far as the Pará River, near the delta of the Amazon River. Led by the Spaniard Martim Rodrigues Tenório de Aguilar, the expedition included the sertanista Diogo Martins, the Paulistas Salvador de Lima and Antônio Nunes, and Lourenço Gomes Ruxaque, who died in the sertão of the Bilreiros. His inventory of 1611 recorded three "indios Carajaúna" (Karajá) among other Indians in his estate. Although the expedition had searched for the "Bilheiros," Ruxaque had actually returned with Karajá captives, suggesting that they had also traveled to the Araguaia River.[21]

Obviously the early bandeiras had not been successful in destroying the Bilreiros, because Governor Luís de Mascarenhas (1739–1748) issued instructions from Vila Boa as to how they were to fight the Kayapó in the captaincy of Goiás. In January 1742 he recommended that all the Indians who were captured in battle be put to the sword, without distinction of sex. The only ones to be spared were children ten years of age and younger. The survivors were to be taken to Vila Boa and divided up after the king's *quinto* had been taken from among the captives. Thus the Portuguese Crown shared in the profits of enslaving war captives, while the rest of the captives were distributed among those who had captured them.[22]

The governor originally gave Antônio de Lemos e Faria, a sertanista of São Paulo, the task of fighting the Kayapó. In March 1742 Captain Lemos e Faria, with two companies of twenty soldiers, attacked Kayapó warriors and took two heads as trophies to convince the governor of his victory. In May 1742 Governor Mascarenhas also appointed Bento Pais de Oliveira, Anhangüera's son-in-law, as a corporal in the bandeira sent against the Kayapó in 1742. Oliveira was also a sertanista from São Paulo, and he owned gold mines in Goiás. Besides fighting the Kayapó, he was also instructed to look for new sources of gold, especially in the rivers that flowed into the Grande and Turvo Rivers. Apparently his efforts did not yield many war captives, but with the aid of José de Godói Pereira and other Paulistas he explored tributaries of the Tocantins River, such as the Sono (Somno) and the two Manuel Alves rivers, Grande and Pequeno.[23]

Since these bandeira leaders were more interested in finding gold than in fighting the Kayapó, the governor turned to a known "savage-killer" for help against the Kayapó. Between 1739 and 1751, the Paulista Antônio Pires de Campos was the most important figure in the wars against the Kayapó. In contrast to his father, who died in his nineties, he was nicknamed "the boy." To his indigenous enemies he was "Pai Pirá" (Father Fish) and a feared leader, who "conquered by iron and fire" and "vanquished by terror." According to Aires de Casal, he was the "cacique" (chief) of "a horde of Bororos" who lived between the Parnaíba and Grande Rivers. In 1741 the "boy" was living in Cuiabá, where his father had also been based when not exploring the sertão. The following year he and the governor reached an agreement that he should wage war on the Kayapó, as well as on the Guaicurú, Paiaguá, and all Indians who "infested" the mines of Goiás and Cuiabá. For his services he was to receive an *arroba* of gold, contributed by the miners of Vila Boa. Each one was to give a half *pataca* of gold for every slave he owned. A total of 4,357 oitavas and 5 grams of gold were collected, with the excess being used on the works of the Church of Santa Ana.[24]

After the expedition was organized in 1742 by the governor of São Paulo, Pires de Campos, with about one hundred Bororo and a *terço* (third) of 150 to 200 archers, left on his first official war campaign against the Kayapó. One reason the Bororo fought with him was due to the European weapons they acquired to fight the Kayapó, their traditional enemies.[25] In their very first battle, the bandeira defeated the Kayapó and took prisoners. They apparently attacked them in the Claro River region, which was a traditional homeland of the Kayapó. It was also rich in diamonds, and Pires de Campos had been instructed to explore and find diamond-rich rivers. According to Alencastre, this expedition traveled over 150 leagues and took one thousand captives. Pires de Campos also invaded a Kayapó village, causing the death of at least sixteen Kayapó and taking thirty-two captives. From that time he spread more terror until the bandeira reached Camapuã in Mato Grosso, where his bandeira destroyed the largest Kayapó village.[26]

In the view of Alencastre, the "barbarities" practiced by João Godói and Pires de Campos reached the "ultimate excess." They burned entire villages to the ground and took as captives only those adults who could walk a long distance. Those who could not keep up with the bandeira were abandoned or put to the sword. Since the notices of these "atrocities" had reached the most remote Kayapó, the governor feared that they would avenge them. Therefore, Governor Mascarenhas created companies of "adventurers," composed of *bastardos* (mestizos) and freed blacks, to police the places where the Kayapó were most likely to attack.[27]

In the 1740s, for the first time, according to Alencastre, the government adopted practices that would be used against "Indian corsairs." Thenceforth this would be the model for the formation of bandeiras: first the governor chose a "skilled and experienced chief," such as Pires de Campos, who gathered a force of men of "confidence." Then they collected funds for the expedition, using a tax on slaves that every mine owner had to pay. Farmers and ranchers had to contribute their share as well, apparently in food and cattle to provision the bandeira. To this well-armed and well-supplied force, the governor added a third force, the terço of Indians, who were the enemy of the nation to be conquered. Each bandeira was also to take along a chaplain, a rule evaded by many bandeiras.[28] All future bandeiras did not faithfully follow this model, however, since they usually lacked sufficient funding, provisions, and archers.

Nonetheless, the bandeira was expected to fight the enemy, and they were to be subject to the "laws of war," which meant they were to kill those they encountered until they gave up alive or ceased resisting. Those the bandeira took alive as captives were to be subject to "war justice." Of the prisoners, they were to select those needed for the payment of the expenses incurred by the Royal Treasury. From the remaining portion, they were to deduct the king's share (the quinto); the rest of the captives were to go to the captain general, the corporal and other officers, the *vedor* (fiscal inspector) and treasury official (*provedor-mor*), and the auditor of the people of war. They were also to take three *peças* (prime slaves, usually young adult males) for the minister of the government. The rest were to be distributed among the soldiers and other bandeira participants. This allocation of war captives clearly reveals that the king and his royal officials regulated the division of captives and shared in the profits of Indian warfare and enslavement.[29]

Another instruction of the governor to Pires de Campos concerned mission aldeias. In spite of his reputation for brutality, Pires de Campos was expected to establish mission villages, which were to serve as centers of Christianization and civilization for those he reduced to mission life. According to Padre Silva e Souza, the Jesuits first served in his aldeias. Furthermore, the aldeias were

Figure 7. This Bororo family of Mato Grosso in the 1820s recalls those Bororo families who were enslaved in the captaincy of Goiás and coerced into leaving their homelands to serve the bandeira leader Antônio Pires de Campos in Goiás. Source: Expedição Langsdorff. Courtesy of the Library of Congress, Washington, DC.

designed to control the Kayapó. To stop Kayapó raids even further, Pires de Campos brought Bororo warriors and their families to settle in the missions and guard them. The six missions under his authority were Rio das Pedras, which was established for the Bororo in 1746 on the road to São Paulo; Piçarão (or Pissarrão), between the Velhas and Parnaíba Rivers; Santa Ana, which was seven leagues from Piçarão; Guarinos, which was three leagues from the town of Pilar; Rio das Velhas, which was also inhabited by the Bororo until 1775; and Lanhoso, where the Bororo lived after 1775.[30]

After the "success" of his first bandeira, which led to a period of peace from Kayapó raids around Vila Boa, Pires de Campos returned to Cuiabá. But the interlude without warfare was brief because the Kayapó, having recovered from the violence of his first campaign, took up arms again, avenging the losses that Pires de Campos had inflicted on them. As the violence escalated, the governor of Goiás turned to Pires de Campos for help. In March 1746 the king ordered the captain general of São Paulo to arrange with Pires de Campos to "disinfest" the road to the mines of Vila Boa. At the end of the year, he was asked to move his Bororo allies in order to guard the São Paulo road from their base in the aldeia of Rio das Pedras. A year later Governor Mascarenhas reported that the Bororo were preventing the Kayapó from raiding mule teams on the road to the mines, but the Kayapó had shifted their attacks to those who lived away from the road. Pires de Campos then received permission to return to Cuiabá to "persuade" more of the Bororo to move to Goiás. In November 1747 he returned from Cuiabá accompanied by "bastardos" and the Bororo, but these Bororo were being sent into Kayapó lands against their will. He also settled 120 Bororo from Cuiabá at Santa Ana of Rio das Velhas.[31]

Since the Kayapó were still at war in the captaincy, Pires de Campos and the governor made a new agreement in 1748. After Pires de Campos had reduced the Kayapó to "impotency," he was to receive the honor of the Order of Christ, fifty thousand *réis* annually, and the office of notary for the general superintendent of the mines of Goiás for all of his life. With the governor's authorization, Pires de Campos began new efforts in 1748 to keep the road free of the Kayapó. He led a violent and determined campaign against them, using the strategy of staffing aldeias with Bororo warriors within lands claimed by the Kayapó. From these aldeias he and the Bororo warriors launched their attacks on the Kayapó, but they had limited success because they could not stop further Kayapó attacks. Therefore Pires de Campos went back to Mato Grosso to acquire more "allies" from a Bororo village in 1748. He then forcibly transferred them to the aldeia of Lanhoso on the Goiás road. Two years later, in 1750, he had enough men to resume striking the Kayapó in the Claro River region.[32]

In the midst of his third campaign of war against the Kayapó, Pires de Campos and his Bororo warriors marched north to the Araguaia River in search of allies to fight the Kayapó. Rather than allies, they found enemies. A slaver from Cuiabá named João Leme had taken more than two hundred captives among Tupi speakers of the Araguaia River. When Pires de Campos reached the village that Leme had slaved, an angry people ambushed the bandeira, and in the midst of the fighting an arrow struck Pires de Campos on the right breast below the shoulder. Although he was wounded, he subsequently led an attack on a village of the Curumaré (Karajá). At first he pretended to be friendly to them, but then he and his men assaulted their principal village, killing many, including children, and taking prisoners that they led away in chains. On their journey from the village, Pires de Campos ordered some prisoners tied to trees and whipped "to make them understand captivity." Although many Karajá had escaped, Pires de Campos treated the others as chattel property, exchanging some for cattle and horses and selling others for oitavas of gold. One of his captives was a young girl who would return to her people over twenty years later as an interpreter.[33]

Although Pires de Campos profited from taking captives, he would ultimately lose his life. While he was recuperating from his wound, the governor asked him and his allies to protect the quinto from a bandeira of "fugitive men" who wanted to steal the gold on the road to Vila Rica (Ouro Preto). Even with a festering wound, Pires de Campos agreed, but he only managed to reach Paracatú in Minas Gerais. Although his companions tried to treat his high fever, he died of the infection in 1751, after which his Bororo allies conducted a month of chiefly funeral rites for him. At that time he held the rank of colonel and had led three significant campaigns against the Kayapó, in 1742, 1748, and 1751, plus numerous small entradas.[34]

After his brother's death, Lieutenant Manoel de Campos Bicudo, a Paulista sertanista, briefly assumed his responsibilities, but upon the request of the Bororo, the Paulista João de Godói Pinto da Silveira took over their leadership. According to his patent of 1740, Pinto da Silveira had been a cavalry captain in the auxiliary regiment of the mines of Goiás. With his father, he had explored the lands between Vila Boa and Traíras on the west bank of the Maranhão River and discovered gold mines at Papuan (later named Pilar), where he was named *guarda-mor* in 1742. With Pires de Campos, he had learned how to become an Indian fighter, and he too fought the Kayapó into the 1760s, for which he received the reward of the habit of Christ, fifty thousand *réis de tença*, and the office of notary of the *ouvidoria* of Vila Boa in property. In 1763 he worked in that enterprise as a captain-mor.[35]

Pinto da Silveira is most famous for his explorations of numerous parts of Goiás, Mato Grosso, and Minas Gerais. He traced the course of the Parnaíba River, from which he crossed to Meia Ponte, explored the captaincy of Mato Grosso, traveled along the Araguaia and Mortes Rivers to the confluence of the Araguaia and Tocantins Rivers, and from there followed unknown lands to the west, trying to find the celebrated gold of the martírios. In 1756–1757 Pinto da Silveira also led a bandeira to the villages of the "peaceful" Tapirapé, where he assaulted them, taking a hundred prisoners to Vila Boa in a fruitless effort to settle them in a mission aldeia; instead, "the greater part of them" died of disease. In contrast, Pinto da Silveira had a long life, dying in Pilar on 20 March 1776.[36]

While Pinto da Silveira fought the Kayapó and enslaved the Tapirapé, Colonel Amaro Leite Moreira from Parnaíba, São Paulo, went in pursuit of the

Araés, who had been famous for their gold for more than a century.[37] Amaro Leite had already founded the gold mining settlement of Lavrinhas in Goiás when he organized a bandeira of four hundred men with Captain João da Veiga Bueno and Baltazar Gomes Alarcão about 1739. This bandeira sought to locate the blue hills reported by Pires de Campos and a village of the Araés where women wore leaves of gold, but the places where the bandeira actually found gold were on the banks of the Bonito, Vermelho, Grande, and Caiapó Rivers. At the Claro River the expedition constructed canoes and voyaged to the Araguaia, exploring the river in search of the blue hills and the principal villages of the Araés, located on the west bank of the Araguaia River south of the Mortes River in the 1740s.[38]

The expedition actually reached the juncture of the Araguaia River with the Mortes River, where it enters an arm of Bananal Island, and they remained there for one or two winter seasons. After crossing the island, they disembarked on the east bank of the Araguaia and continued overland, reaching the Paraúpava River, from whence they went on to Vila Boa. Since they had encountered many threatening "vestiges" of the "gentiles," they did not go farther, but they had explored a rich sertão that Luso-Brazilians would come to call the "sertão do Amaro Leite." Although Amaro Leite also founded a mining camp on the Mortes River, he found little gold there and died a poor man.[39]

Thus bandeira leaders like Amaro Leito, Pinto da Silveira, and Pires de Campos expanded a slaving frontier in the eighteenth century that led to further warfare, gold discoveries, and enslavement and that stretched all the way to the Tapirapé living north of Bananal Island on the Araguaia River and the Araés west of it. But the indigenous peoples who lived along that river also faced a serious threat from expeditions traveling south from Belém on the Tocantins River. Increasingly, they would be caught between bandeiras, some invading from the south but others from the north.

Entradas and *Bandeiras* in the North

The northern expeditions are generally less well known than the Paulista bandeiras, unless they involved Paulistas, who had traveled from São Paulo to Pará. Others were associated with the bandeiras of Pará or Maranhão. In particular, the northern expeditions included Jesuit entradas, as well as bandeiras from Belém or nearby captaincies that penetrated south via the Tocantins River. An early entrada by a missionary on the Tocantins River was actually made by a Franciscan, Cristovão Severin de Lisboa, who entered the sertões of the Tocantins River in 1625. Following a brief period of Franciscan missionary activities, Jesuit priests voyaged south in search of Indians to take back to Pará and settle in missions there. According to Serafim Leite, Padre Luís Figueira led the first Jesuit expedition in 1636, but it actually went to the Xingu River, to the west of the Araguaia River.[40]

Almost twenty years later, at the end of 1653, a larger entrada led by Padres Antônio Vieira, Francisco Veloso, Antônio Ribeiro, and Manoel de Souza traveled in canoes on the Tocantins River in search of a "multitude of people," almost all of whom spoke the língua geral (Tupi). The great bandeira, whose chief military officer was Captain Gaspar Gonçalves Cardoso, had sixteen canoes and over three hundred persons, including the captain, eight officers, two hundred "Indian archers and paddlers," forty cavalrymen, and up to sixty in service of the others (slaves?). The objectives of the Jesuits were to penetrate the sertões and bring the Indians to Christ and save their souls. In particular, they intended to persuade the Poquiguará to settle in a mission village near Belém. But the captain had other, secret instructions from the governor of Pará. They left on St. Lucy's Day (13 December) in 1653, and by 23 December they had reached the Itaboca Falls on the Tocantins River, near which they celebrated Masses for Christmas. Near that time they met a group of indigenous women who came in a canoe with a Christian pilot. Vieira reported that the women knew who the king of Portugal was and gave his name. As for the river itself, Vieira described the "poetry" of the beach with its fresh breezes, as well as the river's many turtles. But the beautiful river that Vieira eulogized hid the reality of Indian enslavement, as Captain Cardoso collected eight hundred Indians to deliver in Pará so that the governor could pay his debts. When Vieira realized that Cardoso was badly treating the Indians, he left the expedition and returned to Pará.[41]

In contrast, the entrada of Padre João de Sotomaior, the founder of the Jesuit *colégio* (secondary school) in Belém, had less religious motivations; its stated objective was to discover gold. On 11 February 1656 Sotomaior left Belém with an armed expedition whose captain was Pedro da Costa. In three canoes, there were 32 whites with miners and the pilot (other sources say 40 Portuguese), along with 190 (or 200) Indians. They passed the falls on the Tocantins River and reached the end of their journey on 4 April, just before Holy Week. There the priest had a church built of *pau-a-pique* construction, where he celebrated Mass during Holy Week. On this expedition many became sick, including Padre Sotomaior, who died, and they lost most of the Indians due to "hunger and excessive work."

The entrada reduced five hundred people of the Pacajá nation (of the Pacajá and Tocantins Rivers) and many of the Pirapés (Tapirapés) from the west bank of the Araguaia River. Apparently this entrada had largely explored lands west of the Tocantins River, where they failed to discover gold.[42]

As opposed to Sotomaior's well-armed expedition, the entrada of Padre Francisco Veloso was notable for not seeking military aid. He argued that Christian doctrine was "not to be preached at the cost [prejudice, harm] of arms." For three months in 1655 he traveled with Padre Tomé Ribeiro on the Tocantins River and passed south of the falls. According to John Hemming, they took only a hundred Indian paddlers and a Portuguese surgeon, with "no military escort." They contacted the Grajaú, Karajá, Cátinga (also Caatinga), and Tupinambá. When Veloso returned to Belém, he brought 1,200 Tupinambá with him, which suggests that he may have been in Maranhão for part of the time or that significant numbers of the Tupinambá had once lived along or near the Tocantins River, south of Itaboca. According to Rita Heloísa de Almeida, survivors of wars against the "Topinambás" elsewhere in Brazil had been sent to Tocantins River missions in the seventeenth century.[43]

Another heavily armed expedition traveled down the Tocantins and Araguaia Rivers in 1659. Headed by a captain of the infantry, Paulo Martins Garro, with 45 Portuguese soldiers as an escort, it also included 450 Indian archers and paddlers. Its missionary was Padre Manuel Nunes, who was the superior of the Jesuit house and missions in Pará and who spoke the língua geral with facility. They encountered a very warlike and valorous nation known as the Inheiguarás (also Neiguarás). Reputedly, this group used to kill "Christians" who passed through their lands. In spite of their fierce reputation, the bandeira pursued the Inheiguarás for a distance about fifty leagues from the Tocantins River, where they captured 240 of them and divided them up as slaves. After a month of travel on the Tocantins River, Padre Nunes spent two months among the Poquiguirá (also Poquins), living in ten villages that were about a month's walk from the river. He then dispatched one thousand of the Poquiguirá to Pará. Continuing on his journey, Padre Nunes reached the site of the Tupinambá, where three years before the Jesuits had baptized 1,200 Indians and taken them to Pará. The missionary met yet another thousand, who sought him out. From descriptions of the landscape, it is likely that Padre Nunes had reached Bananal Island. Overall, he had journeyed five hundred leagues to the south and reduced the two nations of the Tupinambá and Poquiguirá in six months. For the Inheiguarás, however, the expedition had brought enslavement and exile to Pará.[44]

In 1661 Padre Vieira wrote to the camara of Pará about the Guassú River, "which discovery there is to be made by [traveling on] the Tocantins River." When one entered it via the arm of the Araguaia River, there were "various nations," which were said to have "many slaves," and the Pirapés (Tapirapés).[45] Another entrada, which ventured even farther south of the Tapirapé in 1658, was that of Padre Tomé Ribeiro, who, along with Ricardo Carew, headed a "great expedition" via river into Karajá territory. The expedition members tried to catechize the Karajá, but they resisted, killing some Christian Indians who were with them. These brief descriptions clarify that the Jesuits had penetrated the Araguaia River region and contacted both the Tapirapé and Karajá by the late 1650s.[46]

Ten years later, in 1668, Padre Gaspar Misch with Brother João de Almeida made an entrada to the Tocantins, reaching the Poquis, who were then in rebellion. This entrada was followed in 1671 by a large expedition led by Padre Gonçalo de Veras and Brother Sebastião Teixeira; the troops were commanded by Sergeant-mor Francisco Valadares. Seventy canoes with numerous Christian Indians traveled on the Tocantins River to the sertões of Goiás. The objective of this entrada was to verify the information they had received from the Aruaquis that their aldeias "had been invaded by the Portuguese of Brazil, which is what they call the Paulistas of São Paulo." In fact, Paulista sertanistas had been slaving in fifteen Aruaquis villages. When the expedition reached the Araguaia River, thirty Aruaquis armed with bows came to join them. Another one hundred followed some days later, along with thirty Caatingas, who lived at the juncture of the Tocantins and Araguaia Rivers. Including their slaves, this expedition was one of the largest to travel to the villages of the Karajá on the Araguaia River.[47]

Due to the Jesuit voyages down the Tocantins River, there evolved not only a broader geographical knowledge of the Araguaia-Tocantins Rivers but also a popular belief that the Jesuits had discovered gold mines in the region, from which they were secretly extracting great wealth, particularly at the fabled "mines of the martírios." When he was in Belém and gave a sermon, Padre Vieira tried to disabuse the people of such ideas, but he was unsuccessful in convincing them that the Jesuits were not concealing any gold mines. Thereafter rumors of Jesuit mines fueled the formation of more gold-seeking bandeiras in the north of the captaincy.[48]

While the Jesuits were voyaging on the two rivers, more secular bandeiras were also active on the Tocantins River. In 1669 a sertanista from the north, Gonçalo Pires, led an expedition to the banks of the Tocantins River. Although he did not find rich gold mines, he discovered Brazil nuts. Yet another sertanista in 1669 was Sergeant-mor João de Almeida Freire, who also penetrated the Tocantins River. His expedition pursued the Poquizes, some of whom he brought back as captives.[49]

Five years later, in 1674, a Portuguese sertanista based in Belém, Francisco da Mota Falcão, further explored the Tocantins River. The governor sent him to reach an understanding with the Paulista Corporal Sebastião Pais de Barros and Pascoal Pais de Araujo, a sertanista from São Paulo, who had been searching for gold and raiding for slaves among the Guajará and Arauqueres, possibly near the confluence of the Tocantins and Araguaia Rivers. Corporal Pais de Barros had led a great bandeira to the Tocantins River between 1670 and 1674, which included two hundred whites, two hundred *mamelucos* (mestizos), four hundred Indians, and Bartolomeu Bueno da Silva (senior). When they reached the place where the two rivers joined, Padre Antônio Raposo went to find them and verify that they were returning to São Paulo, apparently with their captives. According to Padre Raposo, the bandeira had fought violently with the Aroaquins and Bilreiros (Kayapó). During one of the battles, Pais de Barros had been killed and Bueno da Silva wounded. As a result, one thousand Arauqueres accompanied Padre Raposo to the aldeias of Pará. According to Serafim Leite, references to Jesuits on the Tocantins River thenceforth ceased; yet there was one more entrada on that river, by Manuel da Mota and Jerônimo da Gama to the Jaguari and Tocaíuna Indians in 1721–1722.[50]

After 1700, bandeiras turned to even more intensive gold prospecting in the north. Manuel da Costa Romero, a Portuguese from Belém, tried to discover gold on the Tocantins River between 1719 and 1721 and again in 1725, without "practical results." Therefore, in 1731 the governor of Pará sent João Pacheco do Couto, a Portuguese sergeant-mor, and the sertanista Francisco Ferraz Cardoso to search for gold. They traveled down the Tocantins River and to the headwaters of the Manuel Alves River, where they located rich deposits of gold in Natividade and São Félix. Also finding gold in the neighborhood of Natividade in 1734 was Manuel Ferraz de Araujo, a Paulista sertanista, and Manuel Rodrigues Tomás, who had served in Anhangüera's bandeira of 1722. In addition, Tomás discovered gold in Meia Ponte (1731), Água Quente (1732), and Tocantins and Traíras (1735). Near Natividade, Antônio Sanches, a sertanista of Goiás, located gold in Pontal near the left bank of the Tocantins River in 1738. Thus, by 1740 there had been three significant gold discoveries in the north, at Pontal, Natividade, and São Félix.[51]

The excitement of the gold discoveries in the north as well as in the south of the captaincy did not mean, however, that bandeiras would abandon another source of wealth: Indian slaving. With so much gold on Indian lands, the new motivation to organize bandeiras was to drive away or enslave all those who resisted the seizure of their lands for mining. Therefore, Governor D. Luiz de Mascarenhas (1739–1748) approved a bandeira to find new mines and fight the Pindarê. In 1740 João Pereira Brandão, José Monteiro Guimarães, Diogo Lopes de Miranda, and Balthazar Gonçalves Lima left Natividade under the conduct of the sertanista Jacinto de Sampaio Soares, with other companions and slaves in a bandeira of 150 armed men. According to their petition, they went to discover new mines, but they ended up pacifying the Gamela of the Mearim River region in Maranhão. Their petition reveals that they traveled to the Tocantins, Sono, and Manuel Alves Rivers and from there explored the headwaters of the Guamá, Gurupí, Turi, Pindaré, and other rivers before arriving at the Mearim and Grajaú. In that region they encountered and fought with various "gentiles," with deaths on both sides. They also made canoes on the banks of the Mearim River and descended in them to meet the Acurúa (Akroá?), Timbira, and Gamela, with whom they fought many battles. Finally, they pacified six or seven villages of the Gamela, where the Jesuit priest Antônio Machado served. Overall, they were gone for seven years and apparently did not find much gold but instead encountered a very fertile country between the Tocantins and Itapicuru Rivers. The sense from their petition is that this bandeira principally operated in Maranhão, where they faced continuous indigenous resistance. They also asked for permission to station their "slaves" in two missions and requested that they be paid like regular troops.[52]

Additional northern bandeiras were concerned with the conquest and pacification of the Akroá and Xacriabá in the 1750s. As more and more mines were discovered in the north, these nations threatened the new mining economy. Therefore, Governor D. Marcos de Noronha (1749–1755) gave the task of conquering them to two brothers, Manoel Alves and Gabriel Alves, who failed to subdue them, as well as to Antônio Gomes Leite. A Pernambucan sertanista, Lieutenant Colonel Wenceslau Gomes da Silva, completed the conquest, and he was appointed to administer the missions. After Gomes da Silva settled the Xacriabá at the aldeia of São Francisco Xavier, he housed them in his *senzalas* (slave barracks). Four years later, in 1755, about 250 Akroá went to live in a nearby aldeia named São José do Duro. Although Jesuit priests served in the aldeias, Gomes da Silva treated them as he did his captives and soldiers, with a strict military discipline, including punishments. At the same time, he was allegedly misappropriating royal funds sent to him for the missions, keeping them instead for his own use on his fazenda. Although he was arrested, he did not stand trial in Lisbon because he died in transit to Portugal. Apparently, Gomes da Silva was the only bandeira leader of this region to be punished for misusing mission funds.[53]

Official Pacification Bandeiras[54]

By 1774 official bandeiras sent to the Araguaia and Tocantins Rivers had objectives other than seizing indigenous captives or finding gold. This period was different due to the greater financial investment of the governors of Goiás and royal officials in Lisbon, who increased funding for official bandeiras charged with contact, pacification, and settlement of "hostile nations" in mission aldeias. Now the objective was to buy peace on the frontier—and locate new sources of gold to revive a declining mining economy. After that the indigenous nations were to be conquered through gift giving and diplomatic negotiations rather than enslavement and warfare. They were also to be "civilized" and Christianized, transforming them into peaceful vassals of the Crown who would willingly work for Luso-Brazilians. The three most significant of these official bandeiras were those sent against the Karajá in 1774, the Kayapó in 1780, and the Xavante in 1788. These three bandeiras reveal that by the 1770s Luso-Brazilians still relied greatly on indigenous interpreters and experienced sertanistas to accomplish their goals of pacification and Christianization.

The "Conquest" of the Karajá

The first of these three bandeiras, and the model for subsequent ones, was formed by Governor D. José de Vasconcelos in 1774 to conquer and pacify the Karajá and their allies the Javaé. The objectives of this bandeira, funded by the town of Traíras, were to make peace in order to free up the Araguaia River for Luso-Brazilian trade and to find new sources of gold. The governor gave command of an expedition of one hundred men to Lieutenant José Pinto da Fonseca and instructed him to avoid all violence and use only peaceful means. For an interpreter, he took with him a former captive of Pires de Campos, who was reunited with her relatives. Thus the Karajá woman Xuanam-piá would play a critical role in convincing the Karajá to make peace.[55]

In July 1775 the bandeira arrived at Bananal Island and set up camp. Initially the Karajá refused to meet them, saying that "we had come to their lands to kill them, and conduct them to our lands, and make them our slaves." Pinto da Fonseca tried to persuade them otherwise and tempted them with tools. The next day their mayoral, Abuênonâ, came to meet Pinto da Fonseca at his campsite, and he gave the Karajá more gifts of ironware. Apparently the mayoral was most interested in obtaining Portuguese military aid against his enemies the Xavante, who were raiding Karajá fields for food and kidnapping their women. Later Abuênonâ received Pinto da Fonseca at his beach camp, presenting him with a clay pipe for smoking, which was a symbol of peace. Together they smoked in the direction of the place "where the sun is born."

After this ceremony Xuanam-piá met with her relatives, and she told them what had happened to those who had been captured or killed by the Pires de Campos bandeira, including the son of the mayoral's sister. Although Xuanam-piá tried to persuade the Karajá of the new bandeira's good intentions, they were still distrustful. They sent a Bororo slave to talk to Pinto da Fonseca, and the slave convinced the mayoral to speak to Pinto da Fonseca, who assured them that "the time of barbarity" was already over and "the bad men" who had "scandalized" them were gone. He assured them that he did not intend to enslave them but instead came in friendship so that they would live in peace with whites as vassals of the Crown. They would also receive iron tools and protection from their enemies the Xavante.

After the negotiation of an agreement, the new peace led to a period of mutual visiting, with music. Every day the Karajá went to the beach to hear the bandeira's men play their instruments, sing, and dance, but they continued to hide their women from the bandeira, and the women feared to approach Pinto da Fonseca to receive their gifts from the governor. Only after Pinto da Fonseca won the mayoral's sister to his side via a mutual adoption agreement did the women accept their gifts. Afterward Pinto da Fonseca claimed Bananal Island for church and state. In contrast to past bandeira devastations, this so-called conquest had been achieved not through warfare but through negotiation, music, and gift-giving, in part mediated by women. As a reward for making peace with the Karajá and their neighbors the Javaé, Pinto da Fonseca received a promotion to the post of captain of the dragoons.

The "Conquest" of the Kayapó

While the Karajá were at peace, as of 1775 the Kayapó continued their hit-and-run raids in both Mato Grosso and Goiás. In 1778, more than a quarter century after the death of Pires de Campos, a new governor, D. Luiz da Cunha Menezes (1778–1783), decided to end the chronic state of warfare by also giving gifts in order to persuade the Kayapó to stop fighting and raiding local settlers. Two years later he sent a bandeira of fifty men led by Corporal José Luis Pereira, including three Kayapó interpreters, to contact the Kayapó. The expedition was instructed to travel to the Claro River, one of the traditional homelands of the Kayapó, and to make contact with them. They were to give the Kayapó gifts of iron tools and other trade goods in the name of Queen Maria I. As usual, other Indians (thirty-six Bororo and twelve Akroá) accompanied the bandeira. Thus all but two members of this expedition were indigenous. In five months, they succeeded in persuading only thirty-six of the thousands of Kayapó to return with them to meet their "great captain."[56]

The Kayapó who entered Vila Boa with the expedition of 1780 were led by Romexi, an old man who had come in place of Angraí-oxá, their principal chief, in order to verify Pereira's promises. Accompanying Romexi were six warriors, women, and children. The governor welcomed the group with musket and cannon fire, and he received the envoys at his headquarters in full dress uniform and with all his staff. He assured Romexi and his people of the full protection of the Portuguese government, as long as the Kayapó would cease their hostilities toward the vassals of Her Majesty. The ceremonies concluded with a Te Deum, or hymn of thanksgiving, in the main church, after which the Kayapó enjoyed a series of parties in their honor. With these festivities, the conquest and submission of the Kayapó as loyal vassals of the Crown was complete, or so the governor believed.[57]

Their reception in Vila Boa had been so positive that Romexi sent the six warriors to bring more people from their home village. In May 1781 a group of more than two hundred Kayapó, led by their principal chief, Angraí-oxá, and another chief, Xaquenau, entered Vila Boa and camped near the governor's palace. The new era of friendly relations was confirmed by the baptism of 113 Kayapó children and one elderly woman in her fifties, who insisted on being baptized. Two of the children baptized were Damiana and her brother Manoel da Cunha, possibly the grandchildren of Angraí-oxá. They were both named in honor of the governor and went to live in his household. The rest of the Kayapó were then settled in the new aldeia of Maria Primeira, along with those subject to the chiefs Cunã-puaxi and Pupuarê, until possibly as many as 2,400 lived in the four hamlets that made up the aldeia. As usual, the Kayapó did not remain there long, and most came to live in another aldeia, São José de Mossâmedes.

It is uncertain when Dona Damiana da Cunha became one of the leaders of São José, as the "captain-mor of the Indians," a title often given to bandeira leaders. Her brother Manoel da Cunha would serve as the interim director of the aldeia (1827–1832), a position occupied by Luso-Brazilian men in other aldeias. Sometime in the 1790s Dona Damiana married her first husband, at age fourteen. In popular belief, José Luis Pereira was a Portuguese soldier of the royal dragoons; in reality he was a sergeant of the pedestres and first director of Maria I. In any case, this marriage between a young girl from a chiefly family and a bandeira leader undoubtedly strengthened the Portuguese-Kayapó alliance. After her marriage, Dona Damiana may have traveled with Pereira on some of his bandeiras, since indigenous women did accompany their husbands on such expeditions. Somehow she learned the skills needed to lead an expedition of contact, gift-giving, and pacification, and she embarked on her first trip to the Araguaia River, returning to São José de Mossâmedes with about seventy Kayapó in 1808. According to Cunha Matos, she used to travel as a Kayapó woman, painting her body red and black rather than wearing clothing.[58]

Thus began a series of the most unusual pacification expeditions commissioned by a Portuguese governor—they would be led by a Kayapó woman. Dona Damiana's second expedition was an official state-sponsored expedition whose objective was to pacify the Kayapó. In 1819 Governor Fernando Delgado Freire de Castilho (1809–1820) delegated Dona Damiana to lead the expedition to contact her people and make an "impression" on them. Before she left on the three-month trip, Saint-Hilaire met her, and she told him that she intended to bring back not only the Kayapó who had fled from São José but also a good number of her compatriots, who were still "savages." She confessed that in the "savage state" her people had "no idea of God" and that it was for this reason that she had requested permission to go after them. But the expedition of 1819 was not a great success. She could convince only another seventy Kayapó to join her at São José. Since the autonomous Kayapó continued to raid the road to Mato Grosso, in 1821 the authorities dispatched Dona Damiana at the head of a third expedition, which returned with "a great quantity" of her people (in reality it was only thirty-five). In the following year hostilities resumed, and government forces indiscriminately slaughtered the Kayapó in their villages.[59]

Although Dona Damiana had been widowed by 1823, she continued to have the confidence of the new provincial presidents (governors). In 1828 President Miguel Lino de Moraes sent her to make yet another effort to secure peace with the Kayapó. For seven months she tracked her fugitive people to the Camapuã River and the upper Araguaia, and in 1829 she brought back one hundred Kayapó, including two chiefs. At that time some Kayapó may have been more willing to seek protection in Goiás because of the pressure of bandeiras from Mato Grosso that were driving the Kayapó away from Cuiabá and back to the area of the Araguaia and Claro Rivers in Goiás. For the last time, Dona Damiana accepted the task of returning to a war zone. In 1830 Lino de Moraes instructed her to attract the Kayapó as "our brothers, sons of Brazil," who would always be treated as "free men." She was not to force them to leave their villages but to invite them to come to speak with him in the capital, where they would be treated well and given gifts of iron tools—on the condition that they respected the people of the province and did not rob or kill. If they persisted in their rebellion, he would send men to the forest to castigate them because "crimes are deserving of punishment."[60]

This time Dona Damiana left São José with her second husband, the soldier Manuel Pereira da Cruz, along with her niece Luiza and Luiza's husband, José Antônio, who had accompanied her on previous trips. For eight to nine months they traveled to the upper Araguaia and a swampy region, which may have been the Pantanal. Reputedly, Dona Damiana followed her people to Camapuã and as far west as the Serra do Tombador near the road to Cuiabá. On this trip she suffered greatly from hunger and a virulent fever (malaria?). Shortly after she returned to São José on 12 January 1831, she died. In all, Dona Damiana had led at least five expeditions in a futile attempt to save her people and keep her aldeia from dying out. Although her second husband and a niece went with her on at least one trip, she was the one who had been appointed to lead the expeditions of contact and pacification. Furthermore, she was the one who received the pension for these services. Therefore Lino de Moraes denied a remuneration request from her second husband.[61]

In the history of *bandeirantes* and sertanistas, Dona Damiana may be the only indigenous woman to have the distinction of having led four state-funded expeditions. She was in the employ of both the Portuguese colonial power and the provincial government of Goiás. Her objectives, however, were not to enslave the Kayapó but rather to find her own people and take them back to the mission that she and her brother led so that they might know God and live under Luso-Brazilian protection. Her prestige and skilled leadership had held the aldeia of São José together, but after her death her brother Manoel da Cunha, who was "gravely ill," encouraged the Kayapó to flee the aldeia, even though he was its interim director. For his resistance and alleged corruption, he was sent to Vila

Boa, where he died in jail. The few remaining Kayapó were moved to Arinos, Mato Grosso, in 1833 and 1834. Embittered by their treatment and the loss of lands they had occupied since the 1780s, the Kayapó took up arms once again in the Claro River region. Thereafter bandeiras would attack the Kayapó throughout the nineteenth century in both Goiás and Mato Grosso.[62]

The "Conquest" of the Xavante

In the same year that he organized the Karajá expedition, Governor D. José de Vasconcelos required the propertied men of Traíras to contribute gold for another bandeira, whose objectives were to reduce the Xavante to peace and stop their attacks on towns and neighborhoods of the Tocantins River, Crixás, and Amaro Leite, which had led to the flight of African slaves to join them. Besides preventing these escapes, the governor also wanted the bandeira to explore the area between the Tocantins and Araguaia Rivers in order to discover new gold mines. Although seventy-one men contributed to the bandeira in 1774 and a captive boy served as interpreter, it failed in its objectives. The Xavante would not make peace and invaded lands near Crixás, killing twelve Portuguese.[63]

The next attempt to organize a bandeira against the Xavante occurred ten years later, in 1784. Governor Tristão da Cunha Menezes ordered Lieutenant of Dragoons José Rodrigues Freire to raise a force of armed men to help the people of Crixás. The governor instructed him to "reduce them to peace, by the efficacious and suave way of persuasion, or by force to make them regret their rebellion." Freire soon gathered a bandeira of eighty-five "men of war," most of whom came from Vila Boa, plus thirteen others conscripted to conduct the baggage and munitions. But Freire was unable to complete his task due to illness; therefore Lieutenant Miguel de Arruda e Sá took over command. When the small expedition met up with the Xavante, they rejected the Portuguese peace proposals, so the bandeira took some of them prisoner with the help of the Kayapó who were with them. The lieutenant returned to Vila Boa with his captives: one "valiant" man, four women, and some children. Shortly thereafter, the governor freed the prisoners and gave his own name of Tristão da Cunha to the Xavante man. After some months, the Xavante Tristão da Cunha was permitted to return home, a journey of three months.[64]

Upon reaching his homeland, the Xavante Tristão da Cunha secured an agreement from his people and returned with his brother and some women to give to the governor in order to assure him that they accepted peace and would come "to render him obedience." Meanwhile, the governor ordered some men to prepare fields and plant crops where the Xavante were to be settled at the site of Carretão, which was named Pedro Terceiro (III). In anticipation of their arrival, Lieutenant Manuel José de Almeida and the Xavante Tristão da Cunha marched with a small military escort and Kayapó and Akroá interpreters to meet the Xavante in the sertão of Amaro Leite. After meeting a group of warriors who were riding horses, da Cunha took them to the lieutenant, who persuaded them to find more Xavante to bring to him. Some days later, Xavante warriors appeared, planning to capture the lieutenant and his men. Before they could do so, a Kayapó chief spoke, threatening the Xavante "that all the power of the whites accompanied by the Kayapó, and other nations, Acrôas, Chacreabás [Xacriabás], Carajás, and Javâes, would fall on them, and would castigate their rebellion once and for all." After hearing his speech, the Xavante responded that they were persuaded and they would enable their nation to enter in the future summer. But first thirty-eight warriors traveled to Vila Boa to meet with the governor.[65]

Although the governor tried to settle some of the Xavante in Salinas, the Xavante refused to live there; instead, they marched all together, perhaps three thousand strong, to take possession of the aldeia of Pedro III do Carretão. It took the Xavante six months to reach Carretão because they could not walk more than half a league a day due to the great number of elderly, infirm, and children, some of whom they carried, with others on their shoulders. In this way, a great "multitude" of the Xavante, led by their mayoral, arrived at the aldeia of Carretão on 7 January 1788. Dancing to the sound of maracas, trumpets, war boxes, and loud cries, the Xavante entered Carretão. The vicar of Crixás and military officers received them, while Pinto da Fonseca gave them a welcoming speech. On 13 January 1788 the mayoral Arientomô-laxê-qui of the Xavante de Quá signed an oath of fidelity, swearing to be a "faithful vassal of the Queen of Portugal, Maria I," and "to have perpetual peace, union, and eternal alliance with the whites." Afterward the mayoral and the principal chiefs traveled to Vila Boa, where the governor received them with grand ceremonies designed to impress them. He also presented them with iron tools.[66]

After the official ceremonies, the vicar of Pilar baptized 412 children, but these were not all the children. Others were being hidden in the forests. When an epidemic had struck Carretão, killing one hundred Xavante, many had fled to save their lives. As soon as the epidemic abated, the Xavante returned to the aldeia and began to work in their fields. The alleged "conquest" of the Xavante was now complete, or so the governor believed. It had been accomplished not through warfare but through negotiations mediated by a Kayapó chief and a Xavante warrior. But the peace did not last, and the Xavante returned to their homelands and resumed fighting against Luso-Brazilians in the north.[67]

The alleged "success" of Portuguese governors in organizing dramatic "conquests" of the Karajá, Kayapó, and Xavante in the 1770s and 1780s led them to form new bandeiras to negotiate peace agreements with other enemy nations. As of 1811, if such nations did not make peace and attacked local settlers, the bandeiras had official permission to wage offensive war and make captives of those who resisted. One of the bandeira leaders of the early nineteenth century who fought such wars was the mulato Antônio Moreira da Silva, who had participated in Indian conquest and enslavement in southern Maranhão. By 1816, however, he had moved with his family to the west bank of the Tocantins River, where he founded a small settlement. Among the many nations that he had fought against on both sides of the Tocantins River were the Porekamekrã Timbira. After one of their villages made peace with him in 1814, the Porekamekrã had settled near Moreira da Silva, who soon abused and enslaved them. Another village did not trust him and hid their families from the bandeira, but some Krahô warriors who were with him convinced them to come out of hiding, and many were immediately taken prisoner, branded, and dispatched to Pará. At the time of independence, Moreira da Silva turned his bandeira skills to fighting in the independence cause against a royalist force led by Captain Francisco de Paula Ribeiro, whom he defeated. In 1825 he was officially recognized by the governor of Goiás as a "commander." Subject to him were six indigenous villages: four of the Apinaje with 4,200 people and another with only 120 Afotigé, as well as one named Concordia. Although he was a feared and "cruel" bandeira leader, he had congregated "a vast number of Indians," who lived briefly in peace with Luso-Brazilians.[68]

Even with government support, not all bandeiras were successful at conquest and enslavement, especially when they confronted the Canoeiro, a nation that resisted peace overtures and pacification attempts. One bandeira sent against the Canoeiro in the 1770s was that of Francisco Martins dos Reys, who was authorized to go to Amaro Leite, a town near the Canoeiro, to convoke local men to participate in the bandeira. They were instructed to encounter "sylvan Indians" and to examine small rivers, streams, mountains, and tablelands for gold. It is uncertain what the outcome of this bandeira was, but it obviously failed, since the Canoeiro continued to occupy lands in the high sertão of Amaro Leite.[69]

In 1773 Governor Dom José de Almeida Vasconcelos (1772–1778) organized yet another expedition. The bandeira of Pilar traveled to the west bank of the

Tocantins River in the direction of Pontal and on to the Almas River, where they had a "furious encounter" with "Xavantes de canoa" (another name for the Canoeiro, which distinguished them from the Xavante, who did not use canoes). The battle resulted in the death of the commander Captain Maximiano, who was betrayed by a "domestic Indian" who was with the bandeira. A year later, in 1774, Manoel Antunes Guimaraens received permission to organize a bandeira, including his slaves, to go to a place named the Corriola, on the other side of the Maranhão River. He requested that they all be armed in case they met "gentiles" or quilombolas there. In that same year, Athanazio Leite was ordered to attract "without violence" a nation of "sylvan Indians." Here the source refers to a bandeira from Meia Ponte as well as one from the Julgado do Tocantins, sent in the dry season to explore the sertão between the Maranhão and Araguaia Rivers. In 1789 a fourteen-boat expedition slaughtered many Canoeiro, after which the survivors continued to attack local settlers, and in 1796 another bandeira destroyed many of their villages located on islands in the Tocantins River. The cruel violence of these bandeiras against the Canoeiro clearly contributed to their resistance.[70]

A more significant bandeira of 206 men, including Xavante recruits from Carretão, was organized to fight the Canoeiro in 1803. It was led by Dona Damiana's husband, Sergeant José Luis Pereira of the pedestres. After finding evidence of the Canoeiro at the juncture of the Tocantins and São Valerio Rivers, his bandeira sought out the Canoeiro for two months. Just when he was within reach of overtaking them, fifty-two of his Xavante recruits fled with their provisions. Nonetheless, Pereira and his remaining force attacked the Canoeiro, capturing fifty of them. The bandeira took their prisoners to Porto Real do Pontal, which they reached after a journey of four months. Lieutenant Miguel da Arruda e Sá was waiting for them to take the prisoners along with other captives to Belém. Of the original 206 men in this bandeira, Pereira turned over to the lieutenant only 66; all the rest had fled or deserted, because "none" of the recruits had gone of their own free will. Once more a bandeira had failed to conquer and pacify the Canoeiro.[71]

In 1819 a Canoeiro attack on the town of Amaro Leite was the cause of the formation of one of the most infamous expeditions sent against them. The *ouvidor* (superior magistrate) Joaquim Theotonio Segurado organized the bandeira, which was reluctantly permitted by the governor of Goiás, who believed that the murdered inhabitants of Amaro Leite had provoked the Canoeiro by their "imprudent conduct." The bandeira's ambitious objective was to drive the Canoeiro from the Tocantins region. Although they did not want to do so, the people of each district raised food, money, and men for the campaign. The expedition began "well" and with much enthusiasm, but soon many of the young men, "tormented by hunger," deserted it. Those who remained were badly led by the brother-in-law of Segurado, an aged and infirm commander of the presídio near Vila da Palma.

For about three months, the bandeira searched for the Canoeiro, until they found a trail leading to a village on the Almas River, which had a large field of corn. Encircling the village, the bandeira proposed peace to the Canoeiro, who firmly refused it. While besieging the village, they called upon a boy of ten who had been enslaved there two years earlier to abandon the Canoeiro and join them instead. But the Canoeiro killed the child in front of them. Among them lived a bearded Canoeiro man, elsewhere described as a chief, who had been baptized ten years before and who had lived in São Paulo (as a captive?). According to Pohl, he was "very obstinate, not wanting to hear [anyone] speak of negotiations." In response, Major Joaquim Pereira, the commander of the expedition, cried out, "Then you will all die!" The chief shouted back, "And you, too!" The troops immediately shot him and opened fire on the thatch-roofed houses, which they also set on fire. Using swords and muskets, they slaughtered "without compassion" all who tried to flee. Only six children and one old woman were taken prisoner, but two escaped to carry news of the massacre to other Canoeiro villages and to the men who had been away on a raiding party. Eleven years later, in 1830, the Canoeiro were still angry about "the atrocities" committed against them by the 1819 bandeira, and Segurado had failed to drive them from the Tocantins River region.[72]

The mutual warfare and raiding continued unabated. The next bandeiras to oppose the Canoeiro were those of 1823–1825, organized by Raimundo José da Cunha Matos. In forming his first expedition, he stressed his intention of destroying, civilizing, or subjugating them to prevent further raiding.[73] Soon after his arrival in July 1823, he began collecting weapons for one hundred men, including bows and arrows for archers, and he sent a soldier of the pedestres to Carretão to recruit Xavante warriors for the bandeira. By January 1824 he was in Cavalcante and writing of a frontier that had exploded into brutal warfare. Not only the Canoeiro but also the Xavante were attacking ranches and plantations over an area of four hundred leagues, including the districts of Amaro Leite, Discuberto da Piedade, São Félix, Palma, Carmo, and Chapada, sometimes as far east as the presídio of Duro. But Cunha Matos focused his anger not on his allies the Xavante but on the Canoeiro, accusing them of killing all those who came to make peace with them unless they were well armed.

Cunha Matos was having so little success against the Canoeiro that he asked provincial authorities to send one hundred Kayapó in the company of Dona Damiana da Cunha to Amaro Leite to help against the Canoeiro. While Cunha Matos was trying to set up the bandeira, Joaquim Pereira, who had participated in the 1819 massacre, went to São João da Palma. In 1824 he wrote to Cunha Matos that the Canoeiro were playing their *buzinas* (horns) in the Pontal of the Paratinga and to the southeast of the same. He then went to talk to an Indian woman on Bananal Island, who told him about three aldeias near one another and also close to the one burned in 1819. Based on that information, Pereira intended to send troops to both sides of the Maranhão River so that the Canoeiro who "infested" the region would not remain there, and if they retreated, he would follow them. He requested that more troops be sent to join him, but it is uncertain what the results of this expedition were. In May 1825, almost two years after he had started collecting weapons, Cunha Matos had still not defeated the Canoeiro, who were still at war with local settlers. He left for Rio de Janeiro in 1825 without achieving the conquest of the Canoeiro.[74] Canoeiro attacks continued throughout the nineteenth century, since they refused to accept gifts or settle in Christian missions. As late as the 1880s, the Canoeiro continued to exact vengeance on local settlers who organized local bandeiras to commit "atrocities" against them.[75]

In conclusion, the era of the great pacification bandeiras was clearly over by the 1830s, although nineteenth-century governors of Goiás would look back to them and to the so-called successes of the 1770s and 1780s in hopes of persuading hostile nations to make peace via negotiated gift-giving. Nineteenth-century governors tended to stress the glories of those bandeiras rather than the era of Indian slaving of the sixteenth and seventeenth centuries or the theft of indigenous lands during the gold rush of the eighteenth century, when bandeiras cleared mines of indigenous peoples, who resisted the seizure of their traditional homelands. The bandeira tradition persisted to the end of the twentieth century, if we count the police patrol that tracked down the last Avá-Canoeiro, hiding in caves north of Brasília in the 1980s. In any case, the bandeiras of contact, gift-giving, and pacification resurfaced with the 1940s contact of the Xavante and the 1970s contact of the Kreen-Akarore. The people who hid from the pacification team of Orlando and Claudio Villas Boas were the Panará, descendants of the Southern Kayapó, and their initial reluctance to make contact was likely due to their centuries of experience of the predatory bandeiras that had traumatized their ancestors since the sixteenth century.[76]

CHAPTER 4

Indigenous Warfare and Peacemaking

In Portuguese discourse of the eighteenth century, governors praised their conquests, by which they brought pagan enemies to be vassals of the Crown and loyal Christians.¹ The language of conquest evoked medieval and early modern European imagery of the Crusades, in which Christians prevailed over gentiles and Moors; ritual *cavalhadas*, still performed in Pirenópolis, reinforced a Luso-Brazilian view of war as a noble crusade against the enemies of Christendom. This self-image of the Luso-Brazilians was even internalized by their indigenous enemies, who called them "Christians."² The other side of violent warfare, however, was peacemaking and alliance building. Although Portuguese governors tried to stop attacks on mining towns and ranches by making peace with and settling enemy nations in Christian missions, those who actually negotiated peace agreements were not necessarily Christians but rather indigenous men and women. Since peacemaking had been a characteristic of their interethnic relations, we can also document their initiatives to pursue peace, such as that of a Xerente captain who voyaged south on the Tocantins River to meet a military officer in Porto Real (Nacional).

This chapter will, therefore, take up the themes of indigenous warfare in resistance to the Christians, as well as interethnic warfare, coalition building, and peacemaking in the captaincy of Goiás. We will describe how indigenous nations fought the invaders of their lands and document alliances they made with each other as well as with the governors of Goiás. Even before the entry of Luso-Brazilians into Central Brazil, indigenous nations had been at war with each other. Invading bandeiras, as we have seen in chapter 3, took advantage of such wars to ally with a nation against their mutual enemies. The bandeira narratives, therefore, sometimes reveal who was fighting whom upon the arrival of the Luso-Brazilians and who became enemies and allies of the Portuguese—and of each other. Indigenous peoples to be discussed include the

Apinaje, Krahô, Karajá, Xavante, Xerente, Canoeiro, and Kayapó of the late colonial period. Although many other nations fought and made peace with Luso-Brazilians, less documentation survives on their resistance strategies or methods of warfare and diplomacy.

Apinaje

Perhaps the Apinaje were among those unnamed peoples who attacked Jesuit expeditions on the Tocantins River in the seventeenth century. Even much later in 1760, the bishop of Pará reported on the difficulties that a religious of São Bento had in traveling from the mines of São Félix on the Tocantins River. The problem with this route, he complained, was that the river was bordered by "very tall trees." On both of its banks lived "nations of bellicose Indians," who hid "in its bushes like wild animals in order to ambush them."[3] Although some traditions suggest that the Apinaje lived at peace with their neighbors and traded with others, such as the Xambioá Karajá, there is also evidence that they raided all the way to the Luso-Brazilian port of Cametá on the Tocantins River in search of iron tools and beads. According to traditions collected by Curt Nimuendajú in the 1930s, the Apinaje also raided the Kupe-rob (Cupelobos) of Vermelho Lake and farther downstream. Allegedly, their enemies were the Xavante, although Nimuendajú could find no traditions about Xavante attacks on their villages. On the other hand, four hundred Apinaje assisted Raimundo José da Cunha Matos in an expedition against the Xavante and Xerente. The traditions stress, however, that their ancient enemies were the Kradaú-ya (Gradahú), that is, the Northern Kayapó. A fourth people they sometimes had conflicts with were the Xambioá Karajá, but they also lived in peace with them at other times.[4]

According to Nimuendajú, the only cause of warfare among the Apinaje was "blood-revenge." He reported that they did not engage in wars of conquest, nor did they raid for slaves or form expeditions to capture women, although they sometimes kidnapped a woman to serve as the village "wanton." In contrast, colonial sources document that they attacked both Luso-Brazilians and their traditional enemies along the Tocantins River in order to acquire tools. In fact, the Apinaje and Timbira were characterized as being "corsairs" in the 1780s, while Tomás de Sousa Vila Real called them "killers." But his informants were biased, since they were the Karajá.[5] The Apinaje also assaulted quilombolas (fugitive slaves) at Pederneiras on the Tocantins River in the late colonial

Figure 8. An Apinaje warrior holds a bow and arrow. Source: Castelnau, Expédition. Courtesy of the Catholic University of America, Oliveira Lima Library, Washington, DC.

period, again in search of iron tools. Perhaps they were the "gentiles" of the eighteenth century who attacked fugitive slaves in the Tocantins River region. When these Indians captured fugitive slaves, they cut off their heads and left them impaled on posts on the banks of the river. Yet the Apinaje did not take trophy heads; at most they cut off a slain enemy's arm.[6]

These descriptions suggest that the Apinaje were indeed raiders and that warfare was more characteristic of their society in the late colonial period than in the twentieth century, when they had a more peaceful reputation. For war they carried *maças* (clubs) made of wood, and for hunting, bows and arrows "without poison." According to Colonel João Vasco Manuel de Braun, all the nations were "valorous and inclined to war." This same 1780s source recorded that what ordinarily motivated them to fight one another was defense of their stone quarries (*pedreiras*), which they exploited for *pedras de fogo* (fire stones) due to their lack of axes and other tools. At that time, the colonel noted, they did not have peace or commerce with whites. If they captured a white man during combat, they did not kill him; on the contrary, they treated him well and gave him a wife, according to their customs.[7]

For more specifics on Apinaje warfare we must turn to Nimuendajú, who reported that all the warriors used to fight only to repel hostile attacks on their settlement. One tradition recalls that they used pitfalls to protect their villages. Otherwise, only small groups or individuals engaged in warfare by sneaking into enemy villages or camps in order to ambush their opponents. Only when they and their enemies were equal in number did they fight a pitched battle. Their weapons were bows and arrows, lances, and clubs of the round, sword, and paddle types. They also carried an anchor-axe into battle, which was suspended from a warrior's shoulder until he needed it to crush the skull or neck of an opponent. In revenge murder cases, a captive's skull would also be crushed with an anchor-axe.[8]

Unfortunately, such detailed descriptions of weapons do not survive in late colonial narratives. Perhaps the Apinaje were the unknown peoples of the Tocantins River who practiced "deceptions," feigning weakness, but then, suddenly coming face-to-face with the opposing troops, they loosed their arrows, "shooting like the ancient Persians." The best colonial description of Apinaje war tactics is from 1774, when a large crowd of them encircled the canoes of Antônio Luiz Tavares Lisboa on the Tocantins River. At the rapids of Três Barras, Lisboa saw "formed regiments" on the beach to the left, while three canoes brought more warriors to strengthen the circle around him. Apparently the Apinaje organized their warriors in groups or squadrons, since a fugitive slave named Joaquim Angola headed one of these squadrons, while the rest were led by Apinaje captains. At this time, they unleashed arrows from bows until forced to retreat by men with firearms. But even after encountering guns, they attacked again on the next day, shooting with bows and arrows from the shore and from the water in two ubás (hollowed-out canoes).[9]

After making peace with Luso-Brazilians, the Apinaje had an interlude of peace that lasted until 1812, when soldiers from a presídio (small fort or garrison) raided or destroyed their fields. In revenge, the Apinaje killed them. The Austrian traveler Johann E. Pohl explains how: they had their women and girls pretend to attract the soldiers for a sexual encounter; instead, they lured them into an ambush, where the waiting men clubbed them to death. In retaliation, Luso-Brazilians used artillery against one or more Apinaje villages. In turn, the Apinaje joined with the coalition of nations, including the Karajá, Xavante, and Xerente, in destroying the presídio of Santa Maria do Araguaia in 1813.[10] Thus this series of events documents Nimuendajú's emphasis on blood revenge. When the Apinaje were again mistreated in São Pedro de Alcântara (Carolina), Maranhão, in 1824, they revolted against the local commandant Antônio

Moreira da Silva and fled their aldeias on the Tocantins River. In the 1820s some of them allied with Raimundo José da Cunha Matos until he left for Rio de Janeiro in 1825. They also contributed to the cause of independence by fighting with a Luso-Brazilian proindependence force against Portuguese royalists in the 1820s.[11]

Porekamekrã and Krahô

Among the best late colonial descriptions that survive of how a people made war along the Tocantins River is one from Pohl, who visited the village of Cocal Grande on the west bank of the Maranhão River in 1819. Resident there was a merchant from Meia Ponte, Plácido Moreira de Carvalho, who had lived in Europe before returning to Brazil and settling among the Porekamekrã. Therefore, Pohl had an informant who bridged Luso-Brazilian and indigenous worlds and provided him with more accurate information on warfare than usual—or misled him entirely, if, in fact, he observed a Xerente war game.[12]

Upon first contact, the Porekamekrã had lived much farther south. As cattlemen invaded their lands, they were pushed farther and farther north, until they lived more than ten leagues from Cocal Grande. In 1808 Francisco José Pinto de Magalhães met them, convincing them to ally with and obey him; in return he agreed to protect them. After he left for Pará on business, those who inhabited both sides of the Tocantins River began to fight over fruit. In particular, the Macamecrã (Krahô), who lived on the east bank, lacked palm fruit, which the Porekamekrã had in abundance in their village on the west bank. Without permission from the Porekamekrã, the Macamecrã started gathering palm fruit on the west bank of the river, which the Porekamekrã objected to as theft. The ensuing war was "bloody," but Magalhães, who returned from Pará in 1810 and founded São Pedro de Alcântara that same year, succeeded in making peace between the two groups with the help of a Macamecrã woman, who played the role of ambassador and peace negotiator. For this reason, Plácido Carvalho, who had come with Magalhães from Pará, was able to settle with the Porekamekrã at Cocal. Nine years later Pohl spent about three days at Cocal.[13]

The following description of diplomacy and warfare in Cocal is based on Pohl's personal observations.[14] According to Pohl, the Porekamekrã chose their military chief from among themselves and called him "captain." In declaring war or making peace, he was assisted by a council of elders. The captain also acted as a supreme judge, exercising all the functions of public

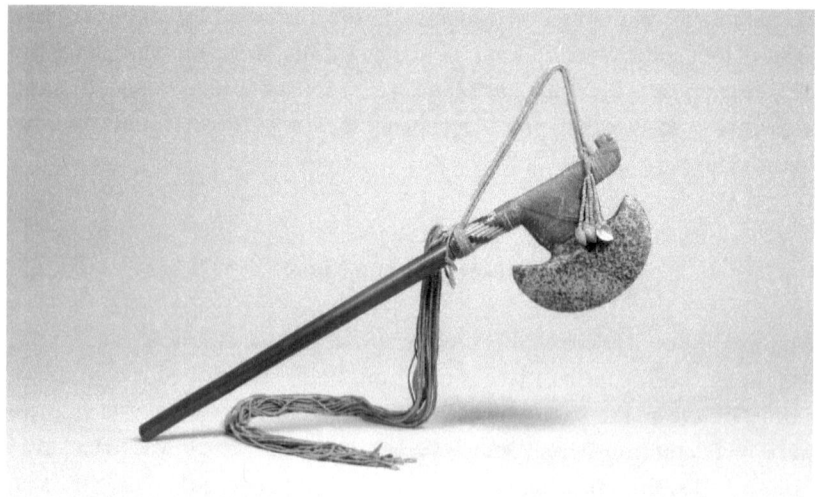

Figure 9. This Porekamekrã anchor-axe was collected by Johann E. Pohl in 1819. Courtesy of the Museum für Völkerkunde, Vienna, Austria.

authority, and his people owed him "unconditional obedience." The captain at the time of Pohl's visit was Captain Romão, who was "much praised for his love of peace." Pohl described him as forty years old, with "amiable features." The insignia of his authority was a granite anchor-axe in the form of a half moon with attached cords made of red cotton; the axe was hung on a cord over his shoulder. In war, this axe was used to split the heads of their enemies.[15]

In order to demonstrate how the Porekamekrã made war, Captain Romão and his warriors reenacted the whole process of diplomacy and violence for the European visitor. Traditionally, diplomacy was the initial step to try to prevent the outbreak of war. First an ambassador from an enemy people entered the aldeia. An unarmed, "robust man," he leaped before their "dwelling place" and declared them to be at war. With "harsh cries," he planted his feet firmly on the ground, keeping them apart. An envoy for "our tribe" and the ambassador approached each other and gestured and argued heatedly about the cause of the war. After further back-and-forth responses, each one tried to grab the other and throw him to the ground. In this reenacted drama, the ambassador who had declared the war was always the victor. Next, second, third, fourth, and fifth ambassadors arrived, which suggests that traditionally the groups made more than one attempt to resolve conflicts. If none of these efforts were successful in achieving peaceful results, the envoy of "our tribe" returned, running, to the forest, which was the sign that diplomacy had failed. The horns sounded from all sides, and the muffled howling noise frightened Pohl because this was the signal that blood would flow. For the Austrian, "the most terrible and the strangest" was this "dreadful noise," which even impressed the Portuguese when they fought the Porekamekrã for the first time.

After the "dreadful" horns, then the troops of "our Indians" appeared. With solemn steps in cadence, they left the forest, each one carrying a bow in one hand and a horn in the other. On each shoulder they had a sheaf of arrows of bamboo with points of raw cane or with barbs, some with points of sharpened bones. Some also brought *tacapes* (clubs) of hard wood, about one meter in length; with this weapon a warrior could crush the head of his enemy, or he could use it as a deadly projectile, when forcefully thrown.[16]

From the opposite side of the forest, a second "division" went out in files, representing the enemy, until a little afterward they halted. Both sides had blackened their faces and painted their bodies in various ways in order to assume "a terrifying and martial appearance." Those who were to be attacked soon caught sight of their adversaries, responded quickly, and confronted them. Then they loosed their arrows "with great agility," in such a way that the arrows flew over their heads without wounding them; they shot with "unquiet movement," rocking the body back and forth. They were so used to this movement that they could not shoot an arrow from a rigid position. After each shot, they played their horns, which the elderly, women, and children accompanied with loud cries in order to give courage to the men. During combat, a woman followed behind her husband, holding a sheaf of arrows, so that he could easily put a hand over his shoulder to receive a new arrow. Women and the elderly also retrieved the bodies of the dead and those who were wounded, because it was "considered an ignominy to fall dead or alive into the hands of the enemy."

Next came the body-to-body combat. The *clavas* (clubs) flew in all directions, and in spite of every precaution and skill in this simulated combat, there were broken heads and wounds as the warriors grabbed, fought back, and wrestled each other on the ground. In the midst of "the ardor of combat," it appeared to Captain Romão that the "game" had begun to be "serious," and he ordered a stop to the mock combat for fear it would end in bloodshed and the destruction of the village. In such a case, fires set by burning arrows would level their thatch-roofed dwellings. According to tradition, the vanquished tribe, which had experienced the greatest mortality, asked the victor for peace, which under certain conditions was conceded; for this purpose the elders were convened in council. But rarely did this peace last long, for the least pretext, a dispute over palm fruit or something similar, would lead to a renewal of hostilities.

Pohl's vivid description provides some idea of the weapons and tactics used by the Porekamekrã and suggests their skills in battle that left their enemies with burned homes and dead warriors. Unfortunately, their warriors could not protect them against treachery. When Magalhães returned to Cocal Grande in 1815 after an absence of two years, he found it in ruin and disorder. The commandant of a bandeira from Maranhão, Antônio Moreira da Silva, had attacked them, as well as other nations living along the Tocantins River. In May 1815 Moreira da Silva had offered peace to the larger of their two villages. According to Francisco de Paula Ribeiro, the Porekamekrã had performed a ceremony of alliance with the lieutenant on the banks of the Tocantins River. The men and women had formed two columns and paraded without weapons or small children under ten before Ribeiro and other observers, who embraced them in peace. Afterward they danced all night and again the next day, leaving before sunset because there was not enough to eat due to the "miserable state" of São Pedro de Alcântara. The Porekamekrã were led by their principal or mayoral, known as Cocrît, a man of fifty, of medium stature, who was respected among them and was of an "un-savage conduct." Because of this ceremony, some aligned with and trusted Moreira da Silva. Apparently they now believed that they were vassals and allies of the Portuguese Crown.[17]

Others of the Porekamekrã, who lived in a second village, did not trust the bandeira of Moreira da Silva. When they heard that some of his men were nearby, they hid their families in the forests. With the bandeira were some Krahô warriors, who convinced them to come out from their hiding places because the *cúpéz* (from *cupins*, termites), their name for whites, "did not want more of them than peace, and friendship, to give them good iron wares, and to establish them in lands famous [for their fertility] as thus had happened to the Krahô themselves." Another who persuaded them was the mayoral Cocrît, "a man among them of great reputation," who accompanied the Krahô and wore a cap that "we had given him." Trusting the mayoral and his compatriots, 364 people came out of hiding but were immediately taken prisoner and robbed by the Krahô and laughed at by "our Bandeira." Then they raped the young "virgins" and divided the children among themselves. The dead were left in the fields, where their bones were still visible in 1815. Ribeiro personally saw 164 of the survivors as shackled captives, who were "sad and depressed" when they entered São Pedro de Alcântara on 27 July 1815. In the afternoon of that same day, 130 of them were branded on the right wrist with a large O, which was the sign of their captivity. A few days later João Apollinario embarked with them for Pará. Those who were older were forced into private service and thenceforth suffered "insupportable hunger."[18]

When parents looked at their children so enslaved, "the tenderness with which they observed them at that moment" was so impressive to Ribeiro that he never forgot it—or the "unjust tyranny" of that betrayal of a people who had agreed to make peace and had trusted in "the Royal Word" when they had tried to establish themselves as vassals of the "most amiable Majesty." Another episode of Krahô violence against the Porekamekrã also touched Ribeiro. He personally observed the tears of one Porekamekrã woman who was obliged to watch their treatment of her baby. While they held her by the arms to restrain her, other Krahô put her baby son in a tree to serve as target practice for their arrows.[19]

Led by their principal Cocrît, the Porekamekrã from the first village then traveled to São Pedro de Alcântara, bearing "green twigs in token of peace." They were settled near there in a community of four hundred to five hundred inhabitants, plus children. But soon their chief was seized, and they too were abused and enslaved. Some refugees from this catastrophe then joined a Krahô village, while others fled. Once again, however, Magalhães, with Carvalho's help, returned some of them to peace, which is how Pohl allegedly found them in Cocal in 1819.[20]

Also among the victims of Moreira da Silva were some of the Krahô, who were then called Craós or Macamecrans. In 1813 the Macamecrã had more than three thousand people, who were governed by a chief or cacique with seven *cabos* of war. Six years later, when Pohl met some Macamecrã upon arriving in São Pedro de Alcântara, they were armed with bows and arrows. Wearing no clothes, but only red and black paint on their thin bodies, some had blackened their faces. Their captain wore blue cotton trousers, a shirt, and a cap, while his wife wore a tattered blue skirt and a blouse. Both stood indifferently and with their hands crossed.[21]

During the period when cattle ranching expanded in southern Maranhão between the Paranaíba and Tocantins Rivers, the Krahô, in exchange for peace, had helped the "whites" fight and enslave their Timbira and Akuên neighbors, taking their former territories. Thus both cattlemen and Krahô warriors had pushed the Timbira and Akuên west into the captaincy of Goiás. But once the cattlemen had consolidated their control over their lands, they no longer needed the Krahô as allies and turned against them, driving them to settle in the mission of Pedro Affonso at the falls of the Sono River in 1848.[22]

Before their removal to the Tocantins River, the Krahô had lived in Pastos Bons, Maranhão, where they had commonly raided local settlers for cattle. Having acquired a taste for beef, they demanded gifts of it when they lived on the Tocantins River at Carolina. Their enemies, the Xavante, may have attacked a ranch in 1808, but the Krahô were blamed for the act and Luso-Brazilians took vengeance on a Krahô village, taking seventy prisoners that they sold to São Luis, Maranhão. Therefore, the Krahô agreed to make peace in 1809. Their great chief or mayoral was Apúicrît, and he supported the peace process and forged an alliance with the merchant Magalhães, who protected them until he went to Pará for two years in 1813.[23]

After Magalhães returned from Pará in 1815, he resumed his alliance with the Krahô, and together they attacked other nations in order to enslave and sell the captives in Pará. At that time, Krahô motivations for war were to acquire captives to sell as part of the trade in indigenous captives with Maranhão and Pará. According to Nimuendajú, the Cakamekra, Porekamekrã, and Augutgé were especially victimized by "false proposals of peace and mendacious promises, made through interpreters," but ended up as slaves on cotton and rice plantations in Maranhão. If they were sent to Pará, indigenous captives sold there for fifty to sixty *mil-réis* each in 1815. Cunha Matos clarifies that it was customary for the merchants of Pará to buy "Indians" who lived between Pontal and the confluence of the Araguaia River with the Tocantins in exchange for gunpowder, arms, aguardente (sugarcane liquor), and tobacco.[24]

In contrast, some of the Krahô who had lived in Pastos Bons, Maranhão, joined with four other nations from the banks of the Tocantins River and the headwaters of the Grajahú, Turi, and Gurupí Rivers in Maranhão to protest against "the ambition of the powerful who practiced 'horrible atrocities,' depriving them of their liberty and treating them as slaves of Ethiopia and robbing them of their lands."[25] On 7 March 1821 the "princes" of five "United Indian Nations" asked the king to restore the liberty of their persons and property and commerce, to demarcate lands, and to enable them to build a "majestic temple" dedicated to St. John the Baptist. In support of their petition, they reminded the king of their service to the Portuguese when they had embarked in 1614 and were hospitably received in their nine villages. They had also marched, they recalled, via land to Itapicuru and burned sugar plantations without the help of Africans, and in 1644 they had participated in the expulsion of the Dutch until the last battle with them on the island of Maranhão.

Further supporting their petition, the procurator Manoel de Araujo testified that they had left their aldeias and marched a distance of three hundred leagues to Pará. In particular, they sought to baptize a son of the Christian principal Manoel Nunes Roballo of the "Carahó" (Krahô) nation. Instead of baptism, however, they had received "firearms, fire, and the plague of bexigas [smallpox] that [someone] traitorously knew [how] to introduce to them, of which many died." The children of the petitioners were also sold through the backlands of Pará and from Aldeias Altas, Pastos Bons, and Mearim, from which many went to Belém, where they were made "captives as slaves of Guiné." Another document clarifies that Manoel Nunes Roballo, "Christian," was the principal (or head chief) of the five "United Nations" and that he had been pacified by Captain and Commandant Francisco Alves dos Santos, of the District of Pastos Bons. In addition to the Krahô, the other four nations were the Canella fina, Copinheiro (Cupinharóz or Purécamekrans), Timbira, and Gabião (Gavião).

After a long process, the petition of the five nations finally resulted in a royal decision to demarcate their lands in 1822. A year later, in 1823, the Krahô were allied with Luso-Brazilian forces in Goiás and fought against the pro-Portuguese royalist army of Major Ribeiro. In spite of bad treatment by settlers in Maranhão or Goiás, the Krahô ended the late colonial period as strong allies of the Luso-Brazilians, who no longer fought them, especially after the arrival of a missionary, Friar Rafael Taggia, in 1845.[26]

Karajá and Javaé

In contrast to the descriptions of warfare in the northern Tocantins River region, there are few from the Araguaia River for the late colonial period. Although Jesuits and later sources commonly noted fierce resistance from the Karajá and other populations living on the banks of the Araguaia, they reveal little about how or why they fought. The Xavante were among their enemies because they commonly raided Karajá fields for food in the dry season, and if they could, they kidnapped Karajá women. When the Karajá raided or went to war, they also took captives and kept them as slaves. For example, the mayoral of the Karajá had one Bororo as a slave in the 1770s, but we cannot document enslavement as a motivation for war.[27]

Besides their Xavante enemies, there was also hostility between the Karajá and Apinaje. When Vila Real visited the Karajá and apparently allied with one of their principal chiefs, he personally observed one of their attacks on the Apinaje. On 8 February 1793 the Karajá who accompanied Vila Real approached the right bank of the river and an Apinaje village. As soon as they saw their canoes, the Apinaje ran and hid, but the Karajá seized a woman with two small girls. The next day they encountered two canoes of the Apinaje. When they went ashore, they found no one, so they carried off everything, including the canoes. While Vila Real was resting, the "principal do meio" (João?) arrived with five canoes. He told him that he was "very content," saying that he had taken them from the Pinage (Apinaje).[28]

Such raids undoubtedly led to retaliation from the Apinaje. In fact, the principal chief of the Karajá traveled all the way to Pará in 1792 in order to ask the governor for help in resisting the attacks of the Apinaje. The Karajá were so concerned about the Apinaje that they even asked for permission to travel to Alcobaça to settle near the Portuguese fort. Apparently it was on this visit to Pará that João, the principal from the "Aldeya do Meyo," received arms from the governor, D. Francisco. Perhaps it was on this occasion that the Karajá learned how to use guns, for by 1813 they were being accused of stealing *espingardas* (rifles) and gunpowder. Vila Real also gave João three axes, two scythes, and two knives.[29]

The best description of Karajá warriors comes from Lieutenant José Pinto da Fonseca, who observed the ritual meeting of the Karajá and Javaé on Bananal Island in 1775. When the Javaé pulled up in their canoes, they wore feathers on their heads and carried lances in their hands. Like the Porekamekrã, they also played "disagreeable" horns and gave loud shouts, which were answered by the Karajá. The Javaé then took up a battle formation with their weapons in their hands. The two nations met each other with further shouts, forming a large circle. Next a warrior from each nation went to fight within the circle. Afterward they went out of the circle and formed a line, running in pairs, and greeted everyone with more loud cries and sounds of their horns. In contrast, the symbol of peace among them was a pipe that they smoked in the direction of the place "where the sun is born."[30]

After they allied with the Portuguese and signed a formal document accepting the status of vassals, the Karajá agreed to the establishment of a mission and garrison on Bananal Island. Perhaps due to the garrison there, they soon grew fearful of losing their lands. Apparently the Karajá initiated the coalition with the Xerente and Xavante by traveling to Pontal to convince the Xerente to join with them in a war against the presídio of Santa Maria do Araguaia. Their justification for the destruction of the presídio was that "the whites had taken their lands and wanted to enslave them."[31]

Figure 10. A Karajá warrior, depicted with a large war club. Source: Castelnau, Expédition. Courtesy of the Catholic University of America, Oliveira Lima Library, Washington, DC.

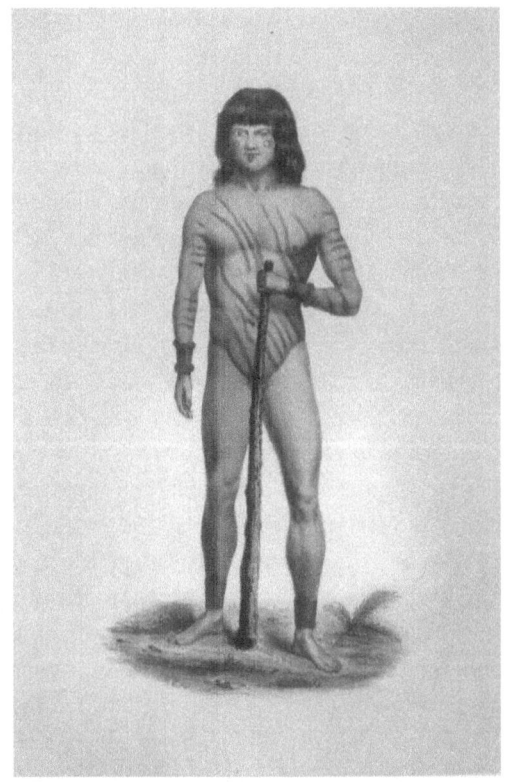

Xavante and Xerente

In contrast to the few detailed descriptions of Karajá warfare, the Xavante and Xerente were memorialized in the chronicles of Goiás for the ferocity of their warfare and continuous assaults on mining towns and ranches in the late colonial period, although members of both nations accepted settlement in missions. In the first half of the eighteenth century, the Xavante were described as "less barbarous gentiles," since they did not live by raiding, but there are references to them stealing food crops in Crixás, Tesouras, and Santo Antônio dos Morrinhos (Amaro Leite). After 1762 they caused "continuous problems" for the people of Pilar, Traíras, São Félix, and Natividade, as they pillaged *roças* (small farms with food crops) and cattle ranches, taking children and blacks to their villages.[32] They, too, were willing to make peace with Luso-Brazilians, as well as with other indigenous nations, but after their experiences in the missions, they became bitter enemies of the Luso-Brazilians. Angered by their "gross treatment" in the aldeia of Carretão, the Xavante returned to their old customs and no longer had confidence in any white man. According to Pohl, the Xavante ordinarily did not attack anyone, except in case of "great necessity," but they acted with "extreme cruelty against their persecutors." Before living in Carretão they had always fled whenever it was possible, but after being treated like slaves there, they had become "violent and vengeful," even against their own who had become Christians. No longer allies of the Luso-Brazilians, they had been transformed into "the most dangerous and courageous enemies." Thenceforth, as a rule, they assassinated all those they could easily capture in "cruel retaliation," which was clearly in reaction to a similar pattern of warfare on the part of Luso-Brazilians. Both sides were then making an effort to exterminate their enemies by any means possible. On the other hand, Pohl reported on the good treatment they gave Clemente, a rancher's son who was enslaved by them for three years and who served as Pohl's informant.[33]

A second cause of war, according to Pohl, was the desire of Luso-Brazilian men for Xavante women, which led to many conflicts with the Xavante. The Xavante also used the beauty of their women to lure Luso-Brazilian men into ambushes. Finally, many raided for iron. When they took an espingarda from a man after they had killed him, it was put on a stone and broken into pieces, which were then distributed. Each Xavante modeled his portion into a large knife that he used to make bows and arrows. They also molded the iron into lance points.[34]

Among the indigenous nations, the Xavante had many enemies. Historically, the Xavante who invaded and lived west of the Tocantins River were the ones who preyed on the Karajá and Javaé, but their objective was not to exterminate or conquer them but to steal their food in the dry season and to kidnap their women. There is no question that the Xavante kept slaves, since sources record that slaves of all colors lived among them, and male captives even received Xavante wives. In the 1780s the Xavante encouraged black slaves to run away from their Luso-Brazilian masters and join them and marry their women, but during most of the colonial period they killed blacks when they attacked mines and ranches. It is unlikely that warfare was conducted to acquire slaves, as in the case of the Krahô. More often they were simply raiding for food, especially in regions where food supplies were scarce, and many of their attacks were on cattle ranches and roças, where small farmers raised corn and manioc.[35]

Since the Xavante were often the aggressor nation, they incorporated others, as they did with the Akroá and Xerente when they lived in the Duro region.

Perhaps for these reasons, the Xerente were often at war with the Xavante in the 1820s, even though they had allied to destroy the presídio of Santa Maria do Araguaia in 1813. More probable is that there were conflicts over territory, because the Xavante who had fled Carretão settled along the Tocantins River once again, and those Xerente whose villages were located on both banks of the Tocantins River were being threatened by the Xavante. On the other hand, some Xavante and Xerente lived together at Carretão in the 1830s.[36]

In contrast, the Xavante remained implacable enemies of Luso-Brazilians and those of African descent. Although they respected whites, Pohl alleged that they despised blacks. Such antagonism may have been due to the violence of pardo and black militias who had fought against them or who had guarded them in the missions.[37] In the 1820s, according to Cunha Matos, the Xavante were "daily" crossing the Tocantins River on *jangadas* (rafts) and coming to kill and rob people and cattle near the mining towns of São Félix, Carmo, Chapada, and Amaro Leite.[38] One description that suggests the depth of their anger is from an 1830 newspaper account in the aftermath of one of their raids:

> The body of one [settler] was found blacked with whip marks, also a girl with an arrow through the back of her neck and sticking out her throat and another woman with an arrow entering the same place and coming out her mouth, and all of them naked. Another man was propped up by a lance through his shoulder that came out between his legs and was struck in the ground; in his right hand they put another lance, on his head a crown of colored feathers and hanging from his shoulder a bow and a quiver of arrows.[39]

Although he offers less detail than in his description of Porekamekrã warfare, Pohl also provides insights into how the Xavante conducted warfare. Their chief or cacique, he reported in 1819, was called "captain" and had supreme authority over the people of the village. When they made war, all the captains of the villages acted in common, and the elders were convoked for a council. All men between fifteen and thirty years of age were obliged to serve in war, and the insignia of the warriors were the cords they wore attached to their wrists and ankles. Their weapons were large bows and arrows, which were specially equipped with barbs for war, and clubs (tacapes) of a meter in length made of very hard wood. They called people together using a horn made from a small curved bottle gourd, painted black inside. In case of attack, they played it with "terrible loudness" in muffled, intermittent,

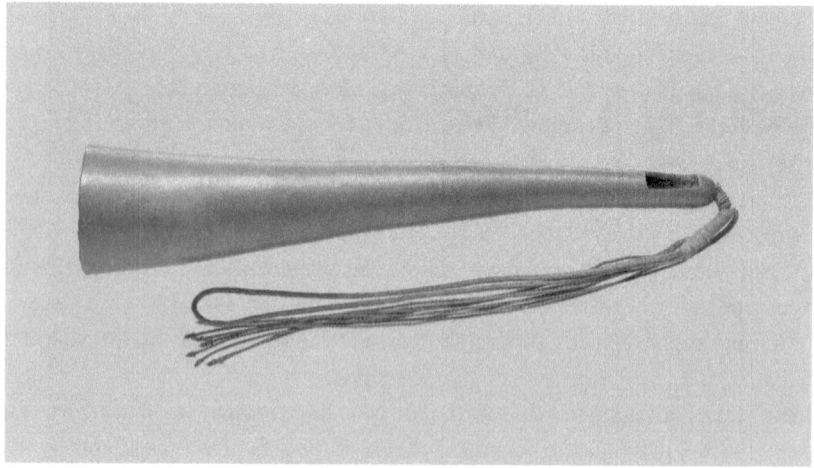

Figure 11. A Xavante horn, which was used in battle to produce a fearful sound. The Johann E. Pohl Ethnographic Collection. Courtesy of the Museum für Völkerkunde, Vienna, Austria.

and "penetrating" sounds. Since each warrior carried one of these instruments and blew it with each arrow he shot, we can only imagine the tumultuous noise that resulted, especially when the Xavante made sudden surprise attacks at night.[40]

One of the strategies that the Xavante utilized was to hide themselves from the Luso-Brazilians in the southern part of the Tocantins River so that their enemies would believe that they lived farther to the north. According to Pohl, "they judged . . . , with that subterfuge, that they could better hide their raids and attacks and afterward throw suspicion on other tribes." They also took advantage of administrative boundaries, where troop strength was less significant, by living in one captaincy, Goiás, but raiding cattle ranches for food in Maranhão and Piauí. As the nineteenth century progressed, they left Goiás and found refuge in the Mortes River region of Mato Grosso. Thus their territory for raiding and warfare in the eighteenth and nineteenth centuries extended from at least Pastos Bons, Maranhão, to eastern Mato Grosso.[41]

In contrast to their focus on warfare in the nineteenth century, the Xavante were more willing to make peace in the late colonial period. One of the best examples of peace making comes from the famous "conquest" of the Xavante organized by the governor of Goiás, Tristão da Cunha Menezes (1783–1800).

The objective of this conquest was to settle them in the mission of São Pedro do Carretão, which the governor had set aside for them in 1784 on land near Vila Boa, four months' travel from their traditional territory near the town of Pontal and the Tocantins River.[42]

The long process of pacification began in 1784 and was completed only when the Xavante entered Carretão in 1788 (see chapters 3 and 8). Soon after Governor Tristão da Cunha Meneses took office, he organized a bandeira led by Lieutenant Miguel de Arruda e Sá, who met the Xavante. With the help of the Kayapó, who were the Xavante's "irreconcilable enemies," the bandeira took some of them captive. One captive was a warrior who took the governor's name, Tristão da Cunha. After some months, the Xavante Tristão da Cunha was permitted to return to his own people to convince them to make peace. Meanwhile, the governor had Carretão prepared to receive the Xavante. In anticipation of their arrival, Lieutenant of Dragoons Manuel José de Almeida, who was accompanied by the Xavante Tristão da Cunha, marched with a small military escort and Kayapó and Akroá interpreters to contact the Xavante in the sertão of Amaro Leite. When many warriors appeared with plans to capture the lieutenant and his men, a Kayapó chief who was with the bandeira convinced the Xavante to consider peace. They then went to Vila Boa to meet the governor and arranged for the remainder of their people to travel to Vila Boa.[43]

While waiting for the Xavante to march there, the governor sent José de Mello e Castro to construct a tax register near Pontal. In October 1788 José de Mello learned of a large number of Xavante near Pontal and went to meet them. He was accompanied only by three unarmed men and an interpreter. When he saw the Xavante, he left the others behind and went alone with the translator to speak to them. He told them that he would show them "the utilities" [tools?] they could gain from friendship, but apparently he was not too convincing, since they listened to him with sullen expressions. Then their "cacique," or chief, spoke to them. After his persuasive speech, they erupted in shouts and played their "barbarous instruments" as a sign of peace and their acceptance of José de Mello's proposal. Having concluded the initial negotiations, they went to Pontal, where they were hospitably treated for three days. At first there were only 869 Xavante, but their number swelled to 2,500 to 3,000 as they journeyed toward Vila Boa, which took them four months.[44] Thus it was largely due to the intervention of indigenous men that the Xavante considered making peace. As usual, this peace would only be temporary, for they returned to warfare and with the help of the Xerente attacked the town of Pontal in 1788.[45]

In contrast to this period before 1835, much more is known about Xerente warfare in the later nineteenth century because of the research of Curt Nimuendajú, who interviewed the grandsons of those who had fought in the nineteenth century.[46] According to Nimuendajú, the enemies of the Xerente in the north and west were the Xavante, which Cunha Matos and his officers at Graciosa and Porto Real confirm for the 1820s. To their south, their enemies were the Canoeiro. Other enemies of the Xerente were the Macamecrã and the Apinaje. Although the Xavante frequently clashed with the Karajá due to Xavante raids, there is no evidence that the Xerente did so independently of the Xavante. The Xerente also lived in peace with the Northern Kayapó. On the other hand, Padre Jardim reported that their "mortal enemies" were the Kayapó of the south. Furthermore, they were often at war with Luso-Brazilians, as Pohl clarifies: "All the murders" of the boatmen on the Maranhão River, which were reported to him, "had without exception a single motive—retaliation for ignominy endured and revenge for deceived confidence and the kidnapping of their offspring." Thus, like other nations, the Xerente's motivations for war against Luso-Brazilians usually involved vengeance, although when they raided ranches, they were after their favorite food, horse meat. It was probably for this reason that they attacked ranches near Porto Imperial (Nacional). In the 1830s, near the mining town of Pontal, they killed the justice of the peace, his wife, and three slaves, and they took five other members of his family captive. In retaliation, the Luso-Brazilians went after them, retrieved thirteen "Christians," and seized nineteen Xerente children, whom they put in service to local residents in Porto Imperial.[47]

Their traditional weapons were hunting bows, arrows with unbarbed heads from the thigh bone of the ema, clubs (three feet in length), and long lances with a pointed head made from an ema femur. According to Nimuendajú, their "national weapon" was a staff-club with a "thickened butt somewhat curved in sabre fashion." Padre Jardim called it a clava and said it was four feet in length. On their backs they might also carry a dagger made of bamboo or the femur of a deer and a wooden handle ornamented with feathers. As a symbol of hostile intent to their enemy, they "impaled an arrow in a piece of burity rachis, which they put in the enemy's path." The other side then had the choice of war or peace. If they sought peace, in response they would shoot "an arrow with a broken-off head" toward their opponents.[48]

To prepare for war, according to Padre Jardim, they used simulated combat, especially carrying a heavy weight of wood. Any boy who could not do this could not marry. But in preparation for a real war, a messenger, wearing a double whistle of two bamboo tubes on his back (the sign of war), summoned the council of chiefs to make the decision for war or peace. Those who led the Xerente into war were three chiefs: the leader of the campaign, the leader in the attack, and a counselor. The mark of their status was a white forehead band with a pendant of falcon and macaw tail feathers; the warriors wore only two macaw feathers in their hair and only when at war—"never in peacetime." These warriors were divided into four companies by associations, which were each under two leaders. Their method of signaling was via bamboo whistles.

An attack usually began with the whistles, and then they shot arrows from ambush. This was followed by an assault with clubs and lances. Their strategy was to hold out and keep a good supply of arrows until the enemy no longer had any. Either the enemy then surrendered or they moved to the next phase, hand-to-hand combat. But when fighting Luso-Brazilians, the Xerente avoided any open fighting against men with firearms and horses. Padre Jardim also reported that they were "courageous" and openly attacked their enemies during the day.[49]

Cunha Matos was impressed with how they charged their enemy with bared teeth and roars like tigers designed to frighten them. Several of his soldiers regarded these and their body paint as more terrible than arrows. "From personal experience," Nimuendajú regarded "the demonic impression made on unseasoned troops by the unexpected sight of an Indian assault as the natives' most potent means of attack." They also used wind instruments made of curved gourds that they blew after every arrow shot. According to Pohl, its tone was "very penetrating and powerful," and during battle "they resound with terrific noise in jerky, dull tones."[50]

When an enemy tried to escape by hiding in his house, they set the house afire with arrows tipped with "a cross of little rods around which is wrapped and tied a tuft of rosinous pindahyba bast." Nimuendajú recorded one tradition in which the Xerente lured a group of horse soldiers into a path surrounded by dry bamboo, which they set on fire. While the terrified men and horses struggled to get out of the fiery bamboo, the Xerente escaped.[51]

After the Xerente won a battle, they killed all adults, which accounts in part for their "savage" reputation among Luso-Brazilians, who found the bodies of their friends and relatives disfigured by blows to the head from war clubs. They did not take trophies from dead bodies or cannibalize them, but a warrior who had slain an enemy marked himself with lines on both sides of his chest, which were rubbed with the ashes of a root; they believed that this practice would

Figure 12. A portrait of the Xerente leader Xuathe, who initiated contact and settlement of his people in the aldeia of Graciosa. Apparently, he is dressed in the clothing gifted to him in Porto Real. Source: Burchell, Brasil do primeiro reinado. Courtesy of the Library of Congress, Washington, DC.

magically protect them against arrows. Unlike the Canoeiro, they did not kill children but took some as captives.[52]

Although some of the ancestors of the Xerente probably lived at the missions in Duro in the mid-eighteenth century, their principal experience in a government-sponsored aldeia did not occur until the 1820s, when Cunha Matos settled a group of "Xerente" at the aldeia of Graciosa, which he founded for them on the Tocantins River in 1824. Of particular interest is that it was the Xerente rather than Cunha Matos who initiated their aldeia experience. On 13 April 1824, two "Chavante" came in peace to make contact with the "great captain" on the sugar plantation of Lieutenant Severino Ferreira da Crus, two leagues from Porto Real. One of them was Captain Francisco, whose other name was Xuathe (also Xuaté), and his aldeia was "in the place denominated gurgulho [sic]."[53]

When Commandant Pacifico Antônio Xavier de Barros met Xuathe in Porto Real, he was impressed with the spirit with which Xuathe spoke to him and with his strong memory. Before the interpreter arrived, they communicated by signs and with the words they already knew in each other's language. Then, with the interpreter's assistance, the commandant asked Xuathe why he had come there with only one other person rather than his usual companions. Xuathe replied that his only reason was to see the commandant because the merchants who traveled to Pará had given him "many notices" about him. In order to illustrate how long it had taken him to travel to Porto Real, Xuathe showed the commandant a stick on which he had made sixteen knife cuts to represent the number of nights that he had slept since he left his aldeia to reach Porto Real. He also explained that he had come to ask the commandant for help against the Xerentediquá, who resided on the banks of the Tocantins River below the Xerente and who had attacked them with firearms.[54] In the end, Xuathe and the commandant agreed that the people of Xuathe's aldeia would come and settle near Porto Real in the time when the *cigarras* (cicadas) sang, that is, August 1824.

The next phase of their visit included Xuathe's many queries about the weaponry at the garrison. Xavier de Barros showed him two mortars, some guns, cartridges, gunpowder, and lead. He also paraded his troops before the captain and explained how they were trained and how they fought wars. As Xavier de Barros admitted to Cunha Matos, he exaggerated what his weapons could do, obviously to impress Xuathe. After this tour, Xuathe informed the commandant that he "too wanted to be a soldier," so they gave him clothing, a cap, and shoes as well as a sickle, some knives, and an axe; he also received stone earrings. The two Xerente then went for a visit throughout the town, going from house to house, and the people also gave them gifts.

After returning to the garrison, they found soldiers who were singing Brazilian hymns and playing the viola, trumpet, horns, and war boxes. Responding to the music in Portuguese, Xuathe exclaimed, "beautiful, beautiful" and said that "when he [Xavier de Barros] went to his land ... he would cry much for me, and he would grow thin from saudades [longings]." To enable them to return safely to their own homes, Xavier de Barros arranged for them to travel in the same canoe with Corporal Felizardo Nazareth. Apparently they were to negotiate with other captains.

Before they left, Xuathe saw Xavier de Barros writing to Cunha Matos, and he directed him to tell Cunha Matos that he would like him to find a gun and a sword for his use and many sickles, axes, and hoes for his people. Although it is uncertain if Cunha Matos gave him all these gifts, he did establish the aldeia of Graciosa for Xuathe and his people on 3 July 1824. To attract even more people, Corporal Felizardo Nazareth was instructed to make peace with the Xerente in their villages and to bring them to Graciosa; he was also to threaten them that the expedition of Cunha Matos would attack them if they continued their "insults." The Xerente captains were also to go to talk with Cunha Matos, then in Cavalcante, in order to negotiate a "durable and sincere peace."

Having received his instructions, Corporal Nazareth prepared to leave Porto Real on 25 April 1824. He and Captain Xuathe went down to the beach, where a large crowd had gathered. After unpacking his bow and arrows on the *igarité* (canoe), Xuathe said good-bye to those who had come to see him off. Ascending the Tocantins River in the canoes, they reached the Gurgulho (also Gorgulho) beach on the twenty-eighth and rested until early the next morning, when a group of Indians appeared on the beach. Nazareth sent the interpreter to explain their peace mission, and he apparently convinced them of their peaceful intentions, since more than fifty men and some women approached them. Nazareth then saw a "maloca" (great house) of more than thirty Indians coming toward him in a single file, led by their captain, João. After exchanging greetings, Captain João asked to be dressed in pants and a shirt before his subjects. He also asked for an axe, which Nazareth gave him.

A group of eight captains led by Captain Francisco next arrived, which made a total of ten captains, with three more captains yet to come. All those present agreed that they wanted peace, not war. After the corporal spoke to them, Captain Francisco lectured them that they should be "constant" in what they promised. The last captain to arrive, at noon, was Acometh, who was described as the "great captain." He too expected to be dressed, as had been done for Captain João, and Corporal Nazareth gave him his own cape and then repeated what he had already told the other captains. After dining that night with Captain João, Nazareth met yet another captain the next day but could give him only manioc meal because he had run out of gifts. He did not see the thirteenth captain. As Nazareth was preparing to leave, Captain Francisco insisted that they all dance in honor of the "friendship contracted among us." But Corporal Nazareth remained apart, observing the dance with his soldiers, because he feared the Xerente would commit some treachery. There was no violence, however, and Nazareth returned to Porto Real on 6 May 1824. He was accompanied by a Xerente captain and his slave boy of the "Pinagé [Apinaje] nation."

Meanwhile, Cunha Matos, who had planned to meet the Xerente captains in Cavalcante, decided to go to Porto Real due to an outbreak of disease in

Cavalcante. While he waited for them in Porto Real, he received word that eight hundred men, armed with bows, were coming to meet him. Since he could not feed so many men, he sent Simão de Souza to ask that not all of them come to Porto Real, due to lack of food; therefore, only 117 were fed and gifted at his cost in the town. Afterward, Cunha Matos sent them on to the aldeia of Graciosa at a place called Tacuarussú, a river twelve leagues from Porto Real on the left bank of the Tocantins River, on 3 July 1824. Altogether, twelve captains, four hundred unarmed warriors, and a great number of women and children were those who initially settled at Graciosa. Their numbers soon rose to eight hundred, apparently under as many as seventeen captains. Other Xerente traveled from the Sono River, the Gorgulho do Carmo, and Pontal during the dry season. By October 1824 they were building their houses and working on their large houses and fields on the left bank of the Tocantins River.

In late August, however, the Noroguagé (Chavantes) and Inhajurupés struck the new aldeia. Furthermore, the Xerente's "irreconcilable enemies," the Xavante of the Sono River," threatened to assault the aldeia. Although the Xerente had sought out the protection of the Luso-Brazilians in 1824, few soldiers, only seventeen at most, were based at Graciosa in 1824 or 1825, nor were the Xerente given all the weapons they had expected to receive to defend themselves. They were so angry and fearful that they composed a unique threat. If they were not granted troops, the Xerente argued, they intended to go to Porto Real, Carmo, or Pontal, and resume attacking those towns. They also wanted the government to organize a bandeira to "disinfest" the Noroguagé. If this were all done, they proposed, then they would tell the Luso-Brazilians where there was gold.[55]

The director of the aldeia of Graciosa, Estevão Joaquim Pires, clarified who the enemies of the Xerente were. The Noroguajés were "the same Cherentes nation, who do not want peace." This nation, he continued, was "the greatest that there is in this region and the most traitorous." When they had lived in Pastos Bons, Maranhão, they had taken gifts from ranchers but then had abandoned peaceful relations and killed and robbed, taking women to their aldeias. This information on the identity of the Noroguagé he had received from the Christian women who lived among them. Significantly, Pires placed the Xerente in Pastos Bons before they migrated to the Tocantins River, where they lived in 1824; the other possibility is that he was actually describing the Xavante, who, according to tradition, were the faction that did not want peace. By 1824 the Noroguagé were living on the Gorgulho beach. Pires also used the term "Xerente" for those living on the Gorgulho and asked for more troops to defend Graciosa from the nations (the Xavante?) living beside the Sono River, because they intended to finish off the aldeia. About 130 years later, in the 1950s, the anthropologist David Maybury-Lewis encountered the Xerente on the Gorgulho River.[56]

After the establishment of Graciosa, the Noroguagé and Inhajurupés attacked the aldeia. Elsewhere Captain Francisco of the Xerente also asked for help against the Cherente-dequá, whom he described as "our allies," because they had attacked them with firearms. He also feared the Xavante of the Sono River region, who threatened to assault Graciosa. These threats and attacks plus the decision of Cunha Matos to move to Rio de Janeiro in 1825 led the Xerente to abandon Graciosa and return to raiding. By the 1830s the governor was treating them like the Xavante, and he organized a bandeira that he sent against them in 1836. After an initial, apparently peaceful encounter with them, the troops learned that the Xerente's peaceful gestures were intended only to allow their elderly, women, and children time to escape. The next day the Xerente appeared on a hill and shouted that they "would never want peace, raising a war cry." The bandeira then assaulted their village, capturing fourteen children. Therefore, many Xerente continued fighting until some agreed to enter mission aldeias in the nineteenth century.[57]

Canoeiro

Of all the nations of Central Brazil, the most feared by Luso-Brazilians in the eighteenth and nineteenth centuries, due to their skill in warfare (but not in peacemaking), were the people known as the Canoeiro. According to Frei Berthet, the Canoeiro were an "object of terror" to other Indians, who viewed them as "the most valiant warriors" as late as the 1880s. As canoe Indians, they attacked Luso-Brazilian expeditions traveling on the Tocantins River. When cattle ranchers tried to build ranches along the banks of the Tocantins, the Canoeiro drove them out in the late eighteenth century. Elsewhere, they raided ranches for horses and cattle. In the nineteenth century they prayed in Latin while attacking local towns on Sunday, while the Christians were at Mass. In one notable case at Amaro Leite, they responded in Latin to the Christian prayers, saying "ora pro nobis." In other cases they set fire to churches in order to obtain iron from nails. They caught the attention of chroniclers because their women participated in the fighting, as well as dogs trained for war. In battle, Cunha Matos reported, their women were "fiercer and more courageous than their husbands."[58]

Their enemies were everyone. Although their particular animosity was directed at Luso-Brazilians, they warred with every nation on the frontier. Apparently the Xavante were one of their traditional enemies, since Xavante warriors participated in at least two bandeiras sent against them, in 1803 and 1823–1825. Furthermore, they seem to have worked out a division of territory between themselves and the Xavante in the nineteenth century. The boundary line was the road that ran from Porto Imperial (Nacional) to the City of Goiás.[59] In the late colonial period they never entered into peace negotiations with Luso-Brazilians. Only a few of them ever spent time in a mission or Christian settlement, and they resisted all efforts to settle them in missions because they did not want to be "our slaves." Implacable resistance to whites and vengeance seemed to be their primary motivations during their ferocious campaigns against Luso-Brazilians, especially in the nineteenth century. Fugitive blacks, who lived among them, may have contributed to their ideology of resistance to enslavement.[60]

In Luso-Brazilian discourse, Canoeiro warfare was a narrative of atrocities and massacres. According to Silva e Souza, they were "a very cruel and bellicose nation, who did not know how to flee." In combat they resisted to the death, furiously investing their women and fierce dogs with the same qualities. After years of warfare, Dr. José Vieira Couto de Magalhães reported on their "profound hatred against the white race: they persecute it incessantly and give no quarter." They preferred to die rather than be settled among whites. Since they did not surrender or make peace when overwhelmed, as was traditional among Gê and Timbira populations, they also did not permit their enemies to surrender, since they took no captives. If they prevailed in combat, they killed everyone, including children; in contrast, other nations took captives, incorporating them as slaves or selling them to Luso-Brazilians. The Canoeiro's Luso-Brazilian enemies, however, admitted that they fought with "ferocious and indomitable courage."[61]

One of their principal opponents, Cunha Matos, calculated that there were one thousand Canoeiro *arcos* (bows), or warriors, who had raided four hundred properties in the 1820s, and his expedition with Xavante warriors failed to conquer them. One of the few Canoeiro leaders who appears in the sources consulted was the unnamed bearded chief shot in 1819 when a bandeira massacred his village.[62] Apparently the Canoeiro used classic guerrilla warfare tactics of surprise attacks after careful intelligence gathering. They chose their targets carefully, and if they struck, "destruction is certain, for they do so only after choosing an opportune occasion." To prevent an attack, they hid their canoes beneath the water, weighted down by heavy stones. They avoided confronting armed men with guns but struck ranches when least expected, setting fire to buildings and killing everyone. In the 1820s they commonly assaulted Luso-Brazilian settlements in the dry season and retreated to mountain hideouts during the rainy season.[63]

Sometime in the 1820s, one group of the Canoeiro left the Tocantins River region and migrated to the Araguaia River, where they hid themselves on Bananal Island. The second group remained around Cavalcante and Formosa, where they continued to fight settlers.[64] Over the years, and especially in the 1830s, the violence seems to have worsened. By the 1850s they had depopulated large sections to the north of the province of Goiás, where they had ruined the agropastoral economy. Unlike other nations that avoided towns, the Canoeiro were infamous for assaulting towns in the nineteenth century: Peixe, Palma (Paranã), Descoberto (Porangatu), Amaro Leite (Mara Rosa), Pilar, Crixás, Traíras, São José do Tocantins, Cavalcante, Cocal, and Água Quente. Furthermore, they completely burned down the colonial mining town of Tesouras, which had once yielded a fortune in gold. Due to the violence, the sertão of Amaro Leite was vacant of settlers and ranchers. Cattle ranches near São Félix, Cocal, Água Quente, and Amaro Leite had been reduced to ashes, unburied skeletons lay scattered in the ruins of ranch houses, and the rich mining towns of Crixás and Pilar had been decimated.[65] Thus the Canoeiro had not only been deadly in exacting vengeance in all these places, but they had also been so expert at warfare that they had prevailed in spite of Luso-Brazilian forces and weaponry.

The successes of the Canoeiro in warfare are even more notable considering that most accounts of their weapons stress that they fought with metal-tipped arrows and captured swords, daggers, and bayonets. In the late colonial period they had used bows and arrows and long lances, toothed on the end, of more than twenty palmos (palm widths) in length. According to Pohl, their lances of three meters had barbs (*farpas*), as did their arrows, which made it difficult to remove them from a victim's body. Putting resin on the tip, they shot flaming arrows that set fire to the thatched roofs of their enemies. Like the Gê, they also used wooden clubs, but they hurled them while attached to the end of cords. Although they used war dogs like the Spanish, descriptions do not reveal the size or breed. Apparently they played horns in battle like the other nations, since there is one reference to their buzinas.[66]

Obviously the Canoeiro were a remarkable example of resistance against overwhelming odds and a deliberate strategy of state-sponsored massacres in the nineteenth and twentieth centuries. Their success in preserving their autonomy through warfare in the face of Luso-Brazilian expansion was not due to superior weaponry but rather to effective organization and discipline, guerrilla tactics, and an ideology of nonenslavement. Possibly they had the example of outstanding leadership, but the sources are silent on the identities of their chiefs in the colonial period. Although they kept some of their lands through much of the nineteenth century, small groups struggled to survive and live autonomous lives in the twentieth century. In effect, they were never completely subjected to Luso-Brazilian rule, but neither did they prosper, as their enemies relentlessly massacred them, driving them almost to extinction.[67]

Kayapó do Sul

Thus far, the nations with the greatest reputations as fearless and cruel warriors were the Xavante and Canoeiro, but the Southern Kayapó were the third most warlike or "bellicose" nation. Unlike the Canoeiro, however, they were also famous for their willingness to make peace in the 1780s, after forty years of warfare. Thus we have two contradictory images of the Southern Kayapó in elite discourse: the "savage warrior" who raided and killed Luso-Brazilians v. the peaceful mission Indian, symbolized by Damiana da Cunha, the Kayapó woman from the mission of São José de Mossâmedes (chapter 3).[68]

Their motivations for warfare were innumerable. First, as the Bilreiros, they defended themselves against the bandeiras who enslaved them. In turn, they took captives (women and children) from smaller nations, expanding the slaving frontier. Then they resisted gold miners who seized their lands, especially around Vila Boa, which was followed by the invasion of cattlemen from the Triangulo Mineiro. In the eighteenth century they had to fight to save their villages from bandeiras that invaded them from three captaincies: Goiás, Minas Gerais, and Mato Grosso.

Their motive for war was not only self-defense but also "vengeance," as the anthropologist Odair Giraldin argues in describing Kayapó–Luso-Brazilian conflicts. In 1753 and 1755 the Kayapó invaded the arraial of Antas, killing about forty people. In retaliation, the "whites" attacked and captured six women and twenty-five children in 1756. A year later the Kayapó returned to

Antas and slaughtered nineteen black slaves, most likely to avenge their losses of the previous year. Therefore, whites retaliated in 1763, and a year later the Kayapó returned the violence. The whites then struck a Kayapó village, which was soon followed by a Kayapó siege of the rich mining town of Santa Luzia. Each time whites attacked, the Kayapó did not passively accept the violence but returned it with equal force and similar mortality.[69]

As the bandeiras pressured the Kayapó and as cattlemen invaded, the Kayapó often confronted a subsistence crisis, especially those who lived in the more arid and less fertile lands of eastern Mato Grosso along the road to Cuiabá or in the region south of the Paraná River. Because of Luso-Brazilian land grabs, the Kayapó faced hunger and had to raid for food, that is, cattle. Or they attacked the well-supplied convoys of mules that plied the road from Vila Boa to Cuiabá. Since the mule teams could not depend on hunting to feed their men, they had to carry their own food with them while on the road. Food-laden mules proved to be tempting targets to hungry Kayapó raiders on the road to Cuiabá, as well as on the road between Vila Boa and São Paulo. Kayapó warriors also sought other types of plunder, such as tools for their fields or weapons.[70]

Another motivation for warfare was injustice. When some Kayapó from one of the aldeias went to petition the governor, they were badly treated and put in irons. When other Kayapó learned of this injustice, they deserted their aldeia and returned to attacking the captaincy.[71] Yet another incident provoked further flight from an aldeia. In 1813 ten Kayapó from the mission were jailed: Captain Julio and his wife, Silveria; Feliciano; Antônio da Cunha and Joana; Antônio Baixo and Antonia; João and Maria da Silva; and Joaquim Moreira. According to official sources, the men had served as soldiers under Sergeant Luis Brás of the pedestres, and they had been assigned to the new presídio of Manoel Alves Grande. On their way there, they had traveled as far as the district of Porto Real in 1811, when they were accused of shouting loudly, shooting arrows at the other men with them, and clubbing them to death. Allegedly, Captain Julio had murdered his sergeant and the crioulo slave Manoel, while the other men killed Manoel and Bonifácio da Silva and Manoel Tavares. As a result, Captain Julio was condemned to death at the gallows and to have his hands and feet cut off; the other men were sentenced to whippings and the galleys. Even their wives received prison sentences of two years. The severity of the sentences angered their communities and led to further desertions after 1813.[72]

Finally, one period of warfare began after the Kayapó were forcibly removed from the aldeia of São José de Mossâmedes in the 1830s. Those who had lived with Dona Damiana da Cunha at the mission resented the decision to transfer them against their will to Arinos, Mato Grosso, after they and their ancestors had lived at São José since the eighteenth century. After an interlude, many Kayapó returned to warfare in the 1850s against the ranchers and farmers who were invading their lands, especially in the areas of the Claro and Bonito Rivers.[73]

Besides their numerous Luso-Brazilian enemies, the traditional enemy of the Kayapó was the Bororo nation. The reasons they sought vengeance against the Bororo are obvious. In 1742, with the help of 120 Bororo from Mato Grosso, the bandeira of Antônio Pires de Campos destroyed an entire Kayapó village. As his allies, the Bororo also participated in other bandeiras against the Kayapó. But the Kayapó were also the aggressor nation against smaller nations, such as the Goiá and Crixá, whom they raided for captives— that is, women and children. Along with the bandeiras, the Kayapó contributed to the disappearance of these two groups as autonomous nations.[74]

Other targets of the Kayapó were enslaved blacks, perhaps due to the role of black and pardo militias in fighting against them. Furthermore, they captured fugitive slaves who were hiding out in the captaincies of Goiás, Mato Grosso, and Minas Gerais, and they conducted them to the towns, presumably to trade for tools or other commodities. They also raided and destroyed quilombos, notably the quilombo on an island in the Grande River. Possibly one reason for their animosity toward quilombos is that they were largely occupied by single men, who often stole indigenous women—or persuaded them to join them.[75]

The tactics that the Kayapó used when they struck quilombos or Luso-Brazilian settlements were not always detailed in the sources consulted. But in the mid-eighteenth century around Vila Boa, the city council testified that the Kayapó were in their neighborhood, where they were assaulting scattered mining camps and small farms, including a miner and his forty slaves. According to the council, the Kayapó were "so sagacious and cunning" that after each attack they fled quickly, dispersing throughout the fields and forests. Furthermore, they varied the routes and river crossings by which they came to attack the environs of Vila Boa so that the people of Vila Boa never knew from whence they would come. According to Padre Jardim, they preferred to launch their assaults at night. They also used spies. The council accused the Kayapó of not having an occupation other than raiding. As a result, "there was no secure life in Vila Boa"; its inhabitants had to go about armed, and they also had to arm their slaves.[76]

In the late eighteenth century a resident of Minas Gerais recorded one of the Kayapó tactics, which had been used in the Rio das Velhas region of Minas

Gerais. According to the survivor, the Kayapó followed him and his men for some days without giving them the opportunity of being attacked. Meanwhile, they slyly watched them, waiting for them to build thatched huts in which to sleep. While they were all sleeping, the Kayapó set fire to the huts and killed the men as they fled the flames.[77]

This description of the use of fire in their war tactics is verified in other accounts. The citizens of the town of Mogi-Mirim in São Paulo stressed "the cruelty of the Indians" in order to obtain the governor's support for the formation of a bandeira against them. Although the citizens were biased, this report also has some useful insights into how the Kayapó fought. Typically they struck isolated farms and ranches throughout their territory, in this case, a small farm about thirty leagues from the town, where they killed four persons. Afterward they set fire to the houses, burning them down, as well as other buildings. The second attack on a fazenda came fifteen leagues closer to the town, but they did not cause much damage because it was the rainy season. One reason that they chose to strike in the rainy season is that mounted soldiers could not easily follow them if the paths were extremely muddy and the rivers were high. In 1772 a third attack came even closer to the town, at four leagues. Six were killed and their houses burned. From that town to the Grande River, a distance of nearly five hundred kilometers, the people lived in fear of the Kayapó. Therefore, the bandeira was instructed to attack them in their villages.[78]

Since the Kayapó commonly struck ranches, they also killed those who were working on the ranches, that is, the resident slaves. The captaincy of Goiás recorded numerous deaths of enslaved blacks at the hands of the Kayapó. In 1757, for example, the Kayapó killed not only a miner named Manoel da Costa Portella and his four slaves while they were at work on his mine, but also the guarda-mor of Vila Boa, Balthezar de Godoy Bueno e Gusmão, and his nineteen slaves. In these narratives of Kayapó violence, it usually seems that more enslaved Africans died than Luso-Brazilians.[79]

In spite of the frequency and number of assaults over a vast territory, there are few comparable descriptions of Kayapó weapons. Antônio Pires de Campos reported in 1728 that they used "very large bows and very long and thick arrows." Their clubs were four or five palms in length with a large head, which was thrown "a great distance," never missing a head. The club was the weapon that "they trust and value the most." To this description, João Godói Pinto da Silveira added more details on their weapons in 1760. He too called attention to their large bows and the length of their arrows, at twelve palms. He added a palm to the length of their clubs and noted that they were thick, but thicker toward the point. About the same period, in 1757, they were using the bow and arrow and a stick of "notable greatness in their hands, in order to kill, which is all its point." According to the city council of Vila Boa, they then ate parts of the body of those they slaughtered: the fatty part of the arms and the thighs of the legs as well as the eyes.[80] The petition of the city council was clearly biased, because they wanted to convince the governor to declare an offensive war against the Kayapó; cannibalism was one of the conditions for such a war. In contrast, most sources on the Kayapó fail to mention cannibalism, except for their biased enemy Pires de Campos, who claimed that "they esteem most among them who has killed the most, for no other reason than to eat those they kill, as they greatly enjoy human flesh."[81]

Rumors of cannibalism led Luso-Brazilians to fear Kayapó warriors, and they seemed to have manipulated that terror to their advantage. But what is notable over the centuries is that the Southern Kayapó resisted Luso-Brazilian invasion of their lands in three captaincies. They successfully fought pitched battles against men armed with firearms in the eighteenth century, but they more often turned to raiding for plunder and captives in the nineteenth century. Although some tried peace in the 1780s, they returned to warfare when they were expelled from São José in the 1830s because whites wanted their lands; they then lived briefly at peace before renewing hostilities in the 1850s. The ultimate survival strategy of some of the Kayapó was to disappear into the forests of Mato Grosso, to be recontacted in the late twentieth century as the Panará.[82]

This survey of indigenous warfare and peacemaking reveals some characteristics of warfare in Central Brazil. First, it was episodic, interrupted by periods of peace that usually did not last long. When Portuguese governors presumed that permanent "conquests" and pacification had taken place, they were misguided. Traditionally, negotiated peace agreements were only interludes in what seemed to be continuous warfare among traditional enemies. Sometimes people fought over resources, such as stone quarries or palm fruit; at other times thefts of women and foodstuffs led to war. Luso-Brazilian intrusions, beginning with the bandeiras of the 1590s, clearly provoked vengeance warfare, more enslavement and sale of war captives, and shifting patterns of alliances. Although some nations profited by allying with the Portuguese, such as the Krahô, others rarely did, such as the Canoeiro. Still others never had a chance to make a choice and disappeared as distinct ethnic groups because diseases destroyed them before Luso-Brazilians reached them. Second, warfare was pursued by most nations with a minimum number of weapons: bows, arrows, lances, war clubs, and fire. Only occasionally in the late colonial period did they acquire guns and gunpowder, in some cases as gifts or via trade in exchange for captives and other commodities. But they did not always use guns, in preference to traditional weapons, even when they served Luso-Brazilians. Third, since most peoples were not numerous enough to repel invaders, most of the villagers who were able helped in some way. Women fought or participated in support roles. Even African men, if they were skilled leaders, could become war chiefs. Finally, wars for vengeance often led to vicious violence on both sides, but there is little evidence of cannibalism as a significant motivation for war. In most cases, indigenous men raided ranches and mule teams for animals, especially in the dry season, and for women who could cultivate manioc and corn.

Clearly, abilities in warfare enabled the indigenous peoples of Central Brazil to survive and to contest the Portuguese for hegemony in the region. In the first half of the nineteenth century, they almost succeeded in driving settlers from vast portions of the north of the captaincy, from what is now the state of Tocantins. They were even strong enough to burn down entire towns. Their skills in warfare and hit-and-run raids were remarkably enduring over two centuries or more of intermittent warfare. But what is also remarkable from the documentary record, as opposed to Luso-Brazilian discourse, is that diplomacy and peacemaking were also pursued by the very warriors and their leaders who fought each other. Not only did they have diplomatic procedures for making peace among themselves, but they also mastered the protocols of making peace with their colonial enemies by accepting the protection of local military officers and a vassalage relationship to the distant Crown in Portugal. Chapter 5 will introduce the reader to those with whom they made peace.

PART TWO

Colonial Society
Whites, *Pardos*, and Blacks

CHAPTER 5

"Good Order"

Structures of Empire

As previous chapters reveal, Portuguese hegemony was not firmly planted in the heart of Brazil during the colonial period. This was still a violent frontier in which there had not been any resolution in favor of the dominance of the Portuguese Empire; indigenous peoples and Africans, as well as Luso-Brazilians, challenged Portuguese governors. In order to understand how Portugal established and maintained its rule over the region of Central Brazil, we intend to examine Portugal's imperial system that attempted to impose "good order" on the captaincy of Goiás and to sustain Portuguese dominance.[1] We will discuss four key areas: Portuguese administrative structures as they operated in Goiás, the mining economy and trade networks, the military and militias that defended the captaincy, and the religious organizations they used to win converts—in other words, all the imperial structures of power. Where possible, we will also describe key members of the governing elites who won wealth and political power from the governance of this frontier and its peoples. Some of these colonial elites will also be described in chapter 6.[2]

The first characteristic of Portuguese rule in the region was the naming of this administrative division of the Portuguese Empire. After 1748 the Portuguese called it the captaincy of Goiás, or simply Goiás, for the indigenous people who had formerly inhabited the banks of the Vermelho River, where the capital, Vila Boa de Goiás, was founded. The colonial captaincy was an immense region of one million square kilometers. In the eighteenth century, the Portuguese governors based in Vila Boa tried to conquer and govern what are now the states of Goiás and Tocantins; border areas of Pará and Maranhão; Paracatú, Araxá, Desemboque, and Rio das Velhas, which became part of Minas Gerais; and lands to the west and south of the Araguaia River that now belong to Mato Grosso and Mato Grosso do Sul. In effect, the captaincy of Goiás was larger in area than many sovereign European nations.[3]

Figure 13. A perspective of Vila Boa de Goiás in 1803, made from the height of the Chapel of Santa Barbara. The artist is Joaquim Cardozo Xavier, alferes of the militia infantry. Courtesy of the Biblioteca Mario de Andrade, São Paulo, Brazil.

The first fairly permanent Luso-Brazilian settlements in this vast region were mining camps. From the 1720s to 1748 the governor of the captaincy of São Paulo claimed the mining region, and Goiás was then subject to his authority.[4] Only in 1734 did the Portuguese send an ouvidor (superior magistrate) to impose bureaucratic controls on the unruly men of Vila Boa, which the Portuguese raised to *vila* (town) status in 1736–1739. Another objective was to develop efficient administrative structures to collect taxes and export the king's share of gold (the quinto) to Lisbon, since gold smugglers were evading Crown authorities. The Portuguese also tried to bring greater administrative order to the region by separating Goiás from the captaincy of São Paulo and creating the captaincy of Goiás in 1748. The expectation was that by basing the new governor in Vila Boa, he would be better able to intimidate smugglers and maintain royal authority in the region.[5]

The first Portuguese governor, Dom Marcos de Noronha, later the Conde dos Arcos, took office in Vila Boa in 1749 (to 1755). Thereafter the captaincy would be governed by a governor captain-general, who was to be responsible for the delivery of the quinto (from 1752 on) and for the defense of the captaincy and its gold from all those seeking to divert it into private hands. The governor's authority came directly from the king or queen of Portugal, and he corresponded regularly with the Overseas Council and other state councils in Lisbon rather than with the viceroys resident in Salvador and later Rio de Janeiro (after 1763). When Queen Maria I (1777–1816) and her son João VI (regent, 1792–1816) settled in Rio in 1808, correspondence from Goiás went directly to the court in Rio de Janeiro.[6] In the administrative system of the late colonial period, the governor of Goiás was the personal representative of the Crown in this remote part of the Portuguese Empire. His authority was equal to that of other governors in Brazil, but the gold of Goiás placed his captaincy among the five richest in Brazil in the 1770s, which gave him considerable influence—as long as the gold lasted.[7] Because of his responsibilities and access to gold, the governor was expected to be a nobleman "of quality" and honor and above corruption, who would serve his king and queen before moving on in royal service to more prestigious postings. Moreover, governors came alone, without wife or children but with ambitious retainers and faithful servants, who were much less honest. Their corruption alienated Goianos, even though they too enriched themselves from the gold of Goiás. However, the family and friends of the Goiano women that various governors took as mistresses clearly benefited from their proximity to the powerful men. One such mistress, the daughter of a carpenter, had two children by Governor Fernando Delgado Freire de Castilho (1809–1820). When she demanded that he marry her and take her and the children to Portugal, he committed suicide in Rio de Janeiro.[8]

One of the governor's principal and "noble" obligations was to see to the spread of Christianity to pagan nonbelievers and to provide funds for the Christian missions. In order to accomplish these duties, each governor organized armed expeditions (bandeiras) to conquer the "obstreperous" nations whose members refused to settle down in missions and work for the Portuguese. After forcibly implementing the expulsion of the Jesuits of 1759, the governors saw to the support of the new secular missions and took pride in their Christianization efforts, although most indigenous peoples fled the forced labor imposed on them in the missions. When not defending Vila Boa from Kayapó attacks, the governors also sent troops to destroy quilombos (communities of fugitive slaves) and return the former slaves to captivity, as well as to seize gold mines within their lands.[9]

Since so many Africans and indigenous peoples refused to work for them, the governors expended much effort in making economic proposals and needed reforms to resolve the labor shortages of a sparsely populated region.

They also enforced the king's justice when the gold of Goiás proved too tempting to men of lesser "quality."[10] What is remarkable about the governors of Goiás is that such high-born men, some of whom were capable administrators, lived in and governed a frontier outpost that was barely a town. Their "palace" (since 1751) in the very hot and unhealthy town of Vila Boa was small, with "dark and ugly" rooms, according to Saint-Hilaire, and hardly fitting for such a powerful man; they took "vacations" in the much healthier town of Meia Ponte (Pirenópolis) or at a nearby mission.[11]

Various sources help to explain why men of such stature endured the danger and isolation of Central Brazil. Wilhelm Ludwig von Eschwege, who visited Vila Boa in the 1820s, narrated the custom of miners in which they gained the "benevolence" of the Portuguese governor when he first visited a mining region. They preserved intact a vein of an "extraordinary concentration" of gold. They then invited each new governor to give the first *bateada*, or washing of gold in a pan.[12] Whether this custom was followed in all of the mining captaincies is uncertain, but there is no doubt that Portuguese governors, bureaucrats, military officers, and priests notably enriched themselves while serving in Goiás. One method by which a governor could acquire the gold of Goiás was to exchange a military patent for a small gift of gold dust. But only the Conde de São Miguel, who was governor from 1755 to 1759, was imprisoned for malfeasance in office, after he returned to Lisbon along with twenty-nine high functionaries, such as judges, intendants, and treasurers.[13] Obviously, much corruption went unreported and unpunished, which makes it difficult to document using official records.

Rivals to the governors in status and position were the intendants of the foundry houses, which were established in Vila Boa in 1752 and São Félix in the north in 1754 (until 1796, when it was moved to Cavalcante).[14] The intendants, appointed from Lisbon, were expected to be incorruptible and able to oversee the registering, assaying, and shipment of the quinto to Rio de Janeiro for transport to Lisbon. Each intendant supervised many men, including four *fiscais* (fiscal agents), a treasurer, a *fundidor* (smelter), two scribes to record receipts and expenditures, and slaves. With so many men having access to gold, it is understandable why the Portuguese complained of corruption at the foundry houses, in particular at São Félix. Official correspondence from Goiás also clarifies that the intendants were powerful men in their own right, who could challenge the governors, as Manuel Pinto Coelho did in 1805. Four years later, in 1809, the intendants were replaced with fiscais.[15]

In addition to the powerful governors and autonomous intendants of gold, judges were also powerful, especially if they served as an ouvidor of a comarca. But educated men trained in law at the University of Coimbra were few in number, and they were never sufficient to meet the demands for justice on a violent frontier.[16] Only those who committed serious crimes, such as murder, or significant tax evasion or fraud involving large sums of money were sent for trial at the high court (the Relação) in Salvador or Rio de Janeiro. While awaiting transport to the coast, criminals as well as the innocent languished in the great jail located on the ground floor of the Senado da Câmara (town council) building. Men died in jail before their cases were resolved. One of the principal judicial institutions was the *devassa*, or judicial inquiry, in which deponents gave testimony regarding a crime, which was then forwarded to Salvador, Rio de Janeiro, or Lisbon. Present were the notary to record the testimony and an ouvidor to preside at the hearing. Men and women of all social classes, including slaves, could tell what they knew about a crime.[17]

Such devassas took place wherever there were the appropriate officials, but most commonly in the capitals of the comarcas. In 1809 the capital of the Comarca of the South was Vila Boa and the capital of the Comarca of the North, created in 1809, was São João das Duas Barras. The ouvidor of the southern comarca, resident in Vila Boa, exercised both judicial and administrative functions, having the ability to arrest, sentence, and punish criminals. As a magistrate (*corregedor*), he was in charge of the police, but he also supervised the notaries, scribes, and justice officials. Moreover, he was the superintendent of mineral lands, president of the Tribunal of Ausentes, which was charged with the administration of the property of absentees, and superintendent of the property of the lay religious brotherhoods (*irmandades*). During the eighteenth century only one ouvidor served the entire captaincy of Goiás, a situation that changed only when Joaquim Theotonio Segurado assumed the position of ouvidor in the north in 1805.[18]

As of 1809, Vila Boa also had a *juíz de fóra* (municipal judge), who sat on the Senado da Câmara. Like so many public officials in Goiás, he also had other responsibilities, as *juíz dos órfãos* (judge of the orphans) and procurator of the Crown. More common were the *juízes ordinários* (ordinary judges); a juíz ordinário presided over the Senado da Câmara of Vila Boa in the eighteenth century.[19] There were two judges assigned to each of the *julgados*, the subdivision of a comarca. In the early nineteenth century the southern comarca had eight julgados, and presumably sixteen juízes ordinários. The southern julgados were Crixás, Pilar, Meia Ponte, Sant'Ana/Vila Boa, Santa Luzia, Santa Cruz, Araxá, and Desemboque. The northern comarca also had eight julgados but rarely sixteen judges. The julgados were São João das Duas Barras, Porto Real, Natividade, Barra do Palma, Arraias, São Félix, Cavalcante, and Traíras.[20] Although these judges were elected by the "good men," that is, men of property and status, of each julgado, they were often "ignorant of the law." They owed their position to their local political power, wealth, and family connections rather than a knowledge of the law acquired at the University of Coimbra in Portugal.

Judges detained prisoners or sentenced them to serve time for lesser crimes in local jails. In the nineteenth century the construction of a jail was a sign of a town's growth and development, and the presence of a jail became a ubiquitous argument advanced by petitioners to elevate a village's status to that of a vila (small town). The most famous jail of the eighteenth century, however, was the heavily barred lower half of the city council building in Vila Boa. While the meetings of the Senado da Câmara were held on the upper floor, the ground level confined prisoners, including slaves and fugitives who had lived in quilombos. Women were also sentenced to prison there. Before the baroque building once stood the *pelourinho* (pillory), which was a whipping post for criminals and slaves, as well as a symbol of vila status. The grandiose public building, constructed in 1763, visibly demonstrated the power of the town council not only in making laws but also in enforcing them and maintaining social control in the captaincy. Prisoners from all over the captaincy were housed there.[21]

The correspondence on justice, or rather the lack of it, in late colonial Goiás demonstrates that most judicial positions went unfilled, especially after the decadence of the mining economy set in, and most communities lacked even the minimum level of security—a jail—to protect their citizens from criminals. In contrast to other parts of Brazil, the magistracy was comparatively weak and ineffectual. Only a powerful military officer or wealthy miner or landowner backed by an armed force could protect local citizens from the lawless. Vigilante justice was the norm, rather than the king's justice as applied by trained lawyers, especially in the northern comarca.[22]

In contrast to the weak magistracy in late colonial Goiás, the financial arm of the state could be strong, imposing jail time, confiscation of properties, and even deportation from the captaincy for fiscal "crimes," such as nonpayment of the quinto and other taxes. The Tribunal of the Junta of the Royal Treasury and the Tribunal of Accounts in Lisbon exercised power over Goianos under the authority of the provedor-mor, the captaincy's chief financial officer. Given the significance of gold in Goiás, the governor served as the president of Vila Boa's Junta of the Treasury, established in 1761. Its other members included a

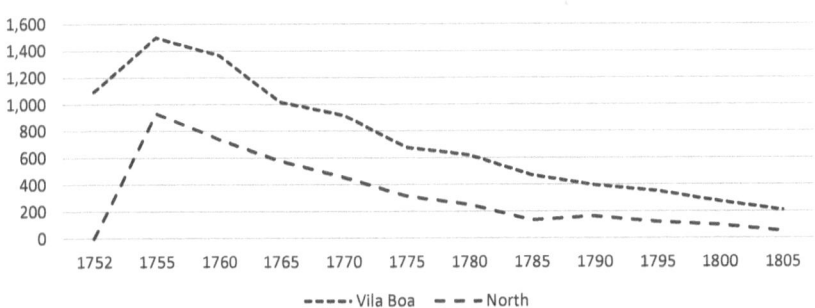

Decline in Annual Income of the Quinto, 1752-1805

----- Vila Boa — — — North

Source: Table 1, Annual income of the Quinto, 1752–1805. Prepared by Jean A. Hall

judge, the procurator of the Crown, a treasurer, and a scribe. Officials of the Junta of the Treasury in Vila Boa were feared, yet their "unjust" taxes were widely evaded.[23]

Goianos had to pay burdensome taxes. Gold miners were subject to the quinto, which claimed 10 or 20 percent of gold production.[24] They were required to send all their gold dust and bars to the foundry houses to be weighed and assayed and have the royal tax recorded. Merchants who received gold in exchange for merchandise were also expected to submit their gold to one of the houses. The problem they faced, however, was that adulterated and fool's gold (pyrites) circulated in the captaincy, and if they obeyed the law, they would not receive appropriate payment for their goods. Therefore, they avoided sending gold to a foundry house, where it might be confiscated as false gold.[25]

After the assayers determined whether the gold was real and recorded the amount delivered each year, the governor had the responsibility of organizing a troop of men to take the quinto to Rio de Janeiro.[26] At the beginning of the dry season, trusted military officers in the dragoons or even a bandeira leader, such as Antônio Pires de Campos, escorted a mule team loaded with bars of gold to Vila Rica, Minas Gerais, and then on to Rio de Janeiro. As table 1 reveals, the quinto declined after 1767, and fewer bars of gold were delivered to Rio de Janeiro. Chart 1, based on table 1, records the progressive decline in the quinto, whether in the northern or southern comarcas.

In contrast to the wealthy men who paid the quinto in order to obtain the Habit of Christ, most Goianos had to pay the hated taxes of the entradas and dízimos.[27] The entradas were the taxes imposed on merchants that had to be paid at registros (registers or checkpoints) when commodities and enslaved blacks were imported into the captaincy. Taxes were paid based on weight rather than value. Thus a merchant paid more to import necessities, such as salt, than luxury goods, such as jewelry or fine silks. Bribes to officers at the registers led to lower royal revenues, as military officers and merchants evaded the required taxes. The dízimo (tithe) was a tax imposed on the value of each year's crops and animals. Since it was collected by a tax contractor from both small farmers and wealthy landowners, it imposed great burdens on the agropastoral economy and led to rural revolts, resistance, and tax evasion in Goiás. It was also responsible for pushing small farmers and ranchers to migrate to frontier lands to escape the tax contractors, who did not always have a reputation for honesty. Those who remained in more settled areas often did not pay the dízimo but remained on the debtors' lists year after year. Apparently the fiscal authorities chose not to collect the taxes or could not collect them from many impoverished farmers and ranchers.

But these were not the only taxes, only the most onerous. For example, "transit tolls" were imposed at river crossings (the passagens).[28] Specific donations were also levied, in particular for the rebuilding of Lisbon after the earthquake of 1755.[29] What is obvious from a study of income obtained from the captaincy of Goiás in 1774 is that dízimos and entradas yielded significant income in gold for Portugal. In the period 1772–1774, the total income for the captaincy was 109:344$305 réis, of which the dízimo contributed 24:913$332 and the entradas yielded 12:120$000. In contrast, the quinto collected in Vila Boa amounted to 22:361$850, while the yield from São Félix was larger, at 30:559$266. In other words, the quinto accounted for less than half the income of the captaincy in the early 1770s. Obviously the Portuguese had means of capturing the gold of Goiás other than through the quinto. Needless to say, revenues then extracted from Goiás amounted to far more than expenditures in the captaincy. In that same period, Portugal spent only 57:084$187 réis in Goiás.[30] The captaincy of Goiás produced a substantial surplus for Portugal in the 1770s, which helps to explain the colonial government's concern about this remote region.

The Extractive Economy

Although we can easily describe colonial institutional structures by which the Portuguese governed the captaincy of Goiás in order to extract its wealth, it is more difficult to characterize its economy in the colonial period. Obviously, the Crown, the Overseas Council, the Royal Treasury, and other councils, such as the Tribunal of Accounts, imposed a colonial, state-directed economy on the region, or rather tried to do so. The region was just too vast for the state to dominate everything. The governor was the key person assigned to devise, suggest, and execute economic policies, which were ultimately set in Rio de Janeiro (after 1763) and Lisbon. The reports of the governors in the late colonial period are replete with elaborate plans to revive a decadent mining economy, and some were quite sophisticated in their analysis. They were also quite prophetic, since contemporary Goiás has fulfilled their hopes for agropastoral development. At that time, however, they were notably unsuccessful in transforming the economy of Goiás to their own purposes because of underlying structural weaknesses in the economy, as well as Goiano evasion of taxes, refusal to send gold to the foundry houses, and widespread contraband activities devoted to gold and cattle. Goiás was, therefore, a region in which there was "a pervasive culture of evasion," which led to a growing internal economy linked to neighboring captaincies in which the gold of Goiás slipped from the Crown's hands into Luso-Brazilian hands that were white, mulato, black, and indigenous. Everyone from the governor of Goiás to pious priests and enslaved Africans accumulated gold, hiding it in sacred statues and using it to buy letters of liberty, build churches, and give gifts (i.e., bribes), to local officials.[31] How much of the gold of Goiás circulated in Brazil is unknown; here we can only document what was delivered to Lisbon as the quinto (table 1).

The first colonial economy that Luso-Brazilians brought to Goiás was a raiding economy that prevailed in Central Brazil during the era of the great bandeiras from the 1590s to the discovery of gold in the 1720s.[32] For more than a century, raiders from São Paulo pillaged the indigenous peoples of the region, seizing their persons and their resources. Although indigenous nations, such as the Kayapó, also accumulated wealth in animals and foodstuffs as hit-and-run raiders, those who were especially adept at the raiding economy were the bandeiras from São Paulo. They were the true marauding "corsairs" who struck settled indigenous villages where the people lived by subsistence agriculture, trade, hunting, fishing, and cattle husbandry, burning houses and fields to the ground and taking away any survivors as slaves.

The second stage of the colonial economy began in the 1720s with the establishment of the mines and mining camps that grew into towns. Unlike the great silver mine of Potosí in Upper Peru (now Bolivia), there was no one mountain of silver but rather many locations of placer gold and some diamond mines worked by enslaved Africans. Therefore, there would be not one mining

Table I. Annual income from the *quinto*, 1752–1805 (in *réis*)

Year	Total	Year	Total	Year	Total
1752	1:094	1770	1:376	1788	529
1753	2:641	1771	1:268	1789	529
1754	2:249	1772	1:324	1790	558
1755	2:428	1773	1:013	1791	549
1756	2:029	1774	1:105	1792	546
1757	2:155	1775	991	1793	436
1758	2:159	1776	1:005	1794	485
1759	2:010	1777	955	1795	470
1760	2:102	1778	950	1796	421
1761	1:577	1779	811	1797	427
1762	1:822	1780	871	1798	398
1763	1:701	1781	658	1799	424
1764	1:544	1782	675	1800	370
1765	1:593	1783	652	1801	275
1766	1:329	1784	612	1802	280
1767	1:530	1785	606	1803	299
1768	1:438	1786	686	1804	339
1769	1:406	1787	631	1805	260

Source: Karasch, "Periphery of the Periphery?," table 3, 153.

core but many in the captaincy. Among the locations of the most profitable "old discoveries" were Traíras, Pilar, São José, São Félix, Arraias, Natividade, Pontal, Santa Cruz, Santa Luzia, Meia Ponte, Anta, Santa Rita, and Tesouras.[33]

Each of the locations where gold could be mined thenceforth served as a pole of development for a surrounding agropastoral economy designed to provide food to the miners. Typically in Goiás the economy was decentralized and undirected by the state, no matter what the governor desired. Capital and great wealth did not concentrate in one place nor remain in the region, since the Portuguese who made great fortunes left the remote and dangerous captaincy for coastal cities or Portugal. In contrast to the opulent and populous city of Potosí, Vila Boa and Natividade survived as small towns; others disappeared entirely, becoming uninhabited "ghost towns." As the colonial period ended, and as the mines dwindled in output (chart 1), Goianos increasingly focused on agriculture and ranching rather than mining. From then on the true wealth of Central Brazil would be based on the land rather than the mines.

Petitions for land grants (sesmarias), however, reveal that the agropastoral wealth of the region originated as soon as miners put their slaves to work raising foodstuffs to feed them. Exactly when this began is uncertain, since early reports from the mines focused on hunger and starvation as enslaved Africans died due to malnutrition—they were being fed only popcorn, which undoubtedly led to severe nutritional diseases. Other early reports stress that miners died when they had no slaves who could gather *guairoba*, a type of palm heart with a bitter taste.[34] Although food shortages were severe in the first years of mining, requests for sesmarias document the increasing presence of roças, or small plots of land specifically devoted to food crops to feed the slaves used in mining.[35] A second type of early sesmaria petition was for engenhos (sugar plantations), where sugarcane was cultivated for sugar, *rapadura* (raw brown sugar), and distilled sugarcane (aguardente, *cachaça*). Nearby engenhos supplied the miners with an alcoholic drink and sweeteners for quick energy.[36] Besides food crops and cachaça, agriculturalists also raised tobacco and cotton, at first to meet local needs but later for export to neighboring captaincies. In the nineteenth century some fazendas (large properties) in the south also added coffee to their cash crops. Slaveholders in the late colonial period typically employed some of their slaves in mining, others in the households, and still others in food production on roças, engenhos, and fazendas (chapter 7).

The mines also stimulated the emergence of large ranches, where cattle and horses were raised. Sesmaria petitions often stipulated which animals were being raised on the ranches.[37] In the late colonial period cattle were raised for beef and for shoe leather, which was exported to Belém. Cattle and hides were also exported from ranches to Bahia. In the north, the cattle frontier invaded Goiás from Maranhão, and its progression can be traced through narratives of frontier warfare and Indian thefts of cattle and horses. In the south and southwest of Goiás, the cattle frontier expanded in the 1830s due to migration from Minas Gerais and São Paulo. Here too the new people challenged the Kayapó, as well as older settlers and ranchers, for lands.[38]

Finally, the mines contributed to the growth of retail businesses and crafts in the towns, although both sectors would never be as dominant as on the coast. Each mining town usually evolved a complex of stores, shops, and market stalls for food and drink, as well as taverns. Furthermore, a prostitution quarter staffed by women of color met the demands of the sex trade. Although a wealthy man might own a store, all other retail trades included women, who earned gold by exchanging foodstuffs, cooked foods, and alcoholic drinks for gold dust. Officials also accused women of selling themselves for gold.[39]

The manufacturing sector of the economy did not extend much beyond a

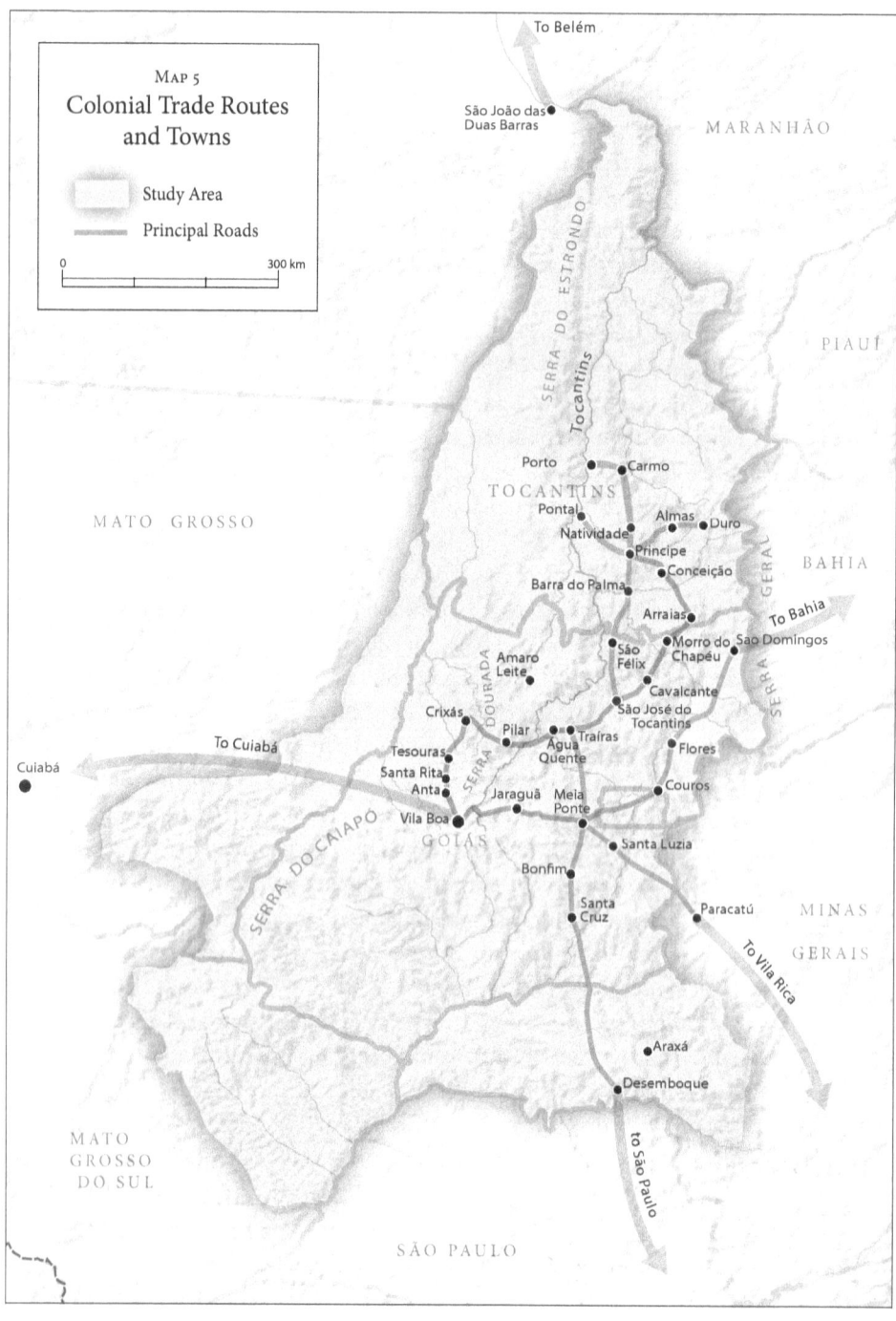

MAP 5
Colonial Trade Routes and Towns

cottage textile industry in which men, women, Indians, and slaves spun cotton and wove cloth. There was only one small textile factory in Vila Boa, which produced cotton cloth in the nineteenth century. Most cloth, however, was produced in the households; for example, Cunha Matos counted 1,581 looms in 1824. Otherwise, most industrial activities were limited to salting or drying beef and fish, tanning leather for export, making marmalades, processing tobacco and coffee, and distilling sugarcane.[40] The captaincy of Goiás imported most manufactured goods, especially luxury items and ironware, and was thus most reliant for its tools and weapons on long-distance traders.

Trading Posts in a Sea of Grass

In general, the staples of life, such as salt, cloth, and iron wares, had to be brought by merchants using long-distance trade routes from the coast. In the eighteenth century they organized large comboios (convoys or caravans) of pack animals, horses, and new Africans that transported dry goods, sea salt, and wet goods from coastal cities to Central Brazil to exchange for gold. There were many trade routes from the coast to the mining towns, extending from the east at Salvador, Bahia; to the far west, at Cuiabá and Vila Bela, Mato Grosso; as well as from the north, at Belém do Pará, and the northeast to Natividade and Pontal; and from the south at Rio de Janeiro or São Paulo to Vila Boa and Meia Ponte. Except in the case of luxury items, commodities did not travel entirely along these routes but usually moved along segments to reach interior towns from coastal ports.

As one eighteenth-century observer noted, gold was "the blood of the mines"; its circulation along the trade routes enabled the economy to flourish, as long as gold was plentiful. Without gold, however, the weakened body of trade declined in strength and dynamism, for gold dust, as well as Spanish dollars, served as the medium of exchange or currency in the interior of Central Brazil. Without gold, one could not buy a slave or a horse, pay one's debts, or even pay for a funeral.[41]

In the early eighteenth century this trade narrative begins in Salvador, Bahia, Brazil's first colonial capital and first significant port city in the first half of the eighteenth century. It was also the northern comarca's principal trading partner in 1804 (table 2). Here in Bahia were unloaded European textiles and Asian silks, enslaved Africans from West and Central Africa, silver from

Potosí via the Río de la Plata region, ritual objects from Africa and saint statues from Portugal, olive oil and wines from Portugal, and tools and weapons from Europe. These were loaded on horses and mules or on the heads of new Africans, who walked to Central Brazil. They traversed a well-worn road from Salvador to Cachoeira, across the sertão of Bahia to the São Francisco River, then to the towns of Barreiras and Duro, on to Natividade and São Félix, and from São Félix to Vila Boa. A second Bahian route crossed the backlands of Bahia via São Domingos, or Lagôa Feia, to Meia Ponte (now Pirenópolis) and Vila Boa. Goiano gold followed similar routes for the return trip to Salvador and for export to Lisbon. As the governor controlled the quinto trade, Portuguese merchants resident in Bahia and northern towns and Vila Boa organized the contraband and legal trades between Salvador and Goiás. They imported slaves, luxury goods, and dry goods and exported gold to Salvador. After the decline of the mines, cattle, tobacco, and cotton traveled along the old gold routes to Bahia.[42]

Continuing west from Vila Boa, merchants took trade goods by mule teams across eastern Mato Grosso through Kayapó lands to Cuiabá, the center of the gold-mining region of Mato Grosso. Since the captaincy of Mato Grosso was strategically important to the Portuguese after the Treaty of Madrid (1750), the governor of Goiás was required to send an annual subsidy of six to eight arrobas of gold to the governor of Mato Grosso between 1759 and 1780 to strengthen the military defenses of his border captaincy with Spanish-claimed territory. Merchants based in Vila Boa, however, also forwarded gold to the merchants of Cuiabá, as well as other trade goods that were "indispensable to the provisioning of the far west." In exchange, the merchants of Cuiabá returned salt, quinine used in treating fevers (malaria), and other "drugs of the sertão." Cattle were also driven from ranches in Mato Grosso to meet the demand for meat by miners in Goiás. Trade between Vila Boa and Mato Grosso stretched as far west as Vila Bela, whose merchants accessed the trade of the Amazon River via the Guaporé and Madeira Rivers and the Jesuit missions of the Moxos in what is now Bolivia. Apparently the gold of Goiás was smuggled into Spanish territories by the merchants of Mato Grosso, who engaged in contraband. Perhaps some of that gold bought the "Herva de Paraguai" (mate), which was sold in Desemboque in the south of the captaincy. In brief, one could travel overland from Salvador to Vila Bela and then by river to Belém do Pará, but it is uncertain whether any one merchant did so due to the time and distances involved, not to mention the hazards of deadly diseases and indigenous raiders. Most merchants usually

Table 2. Value of trade, 1804 (in *réis*)

Captaincy	Comarca of the South	Comarca of the North
Bahia	3:577$369	42:968$000
Pará	5:326$100	5:000$000
Rio de Janeiro	51:035$091	644$000
São. Francisco River	—	2:008$057
São Paulo	25:555$597	995$200
Total	85:494$157	51:615$257

Source: AHU, cod. 2109, Reflexoens economicas sobre as tabellas statisticas da capitania de Goyaz pertencentes ao anno de 1804 e feitas no de 1806; as printed in Karasch, "Periphery of the Periphery?," 160.

handled only one branch of that trip: Salvador to Vila Boa or Natividade, or Vila Boa to and from Cuiabá, or Cuiabá to and from Vila Bela.[43]

Another branch of the east–west trade routes went across the sertão of the northeastern captaincies of Maranhão, Piauí, and Pernambuco, where merchants exchanged cattle, horses, meats (salted/dried), tallow, salt, fish, leather, and rapadura for gold. The merchants from these captaincies traded principally with the mining towns of the northern comarca, in particular with Natividade. Both legal trades and contraband gold passed through Duro, as well as contraband gold via Bocaina, near the register of Santa Maria to the south. In particular, the trade from Pernambuco went via Duro, Taguatinga, and São Domingos. Through Duro were imported gunpowder, dry goods, agricultural implements, tobacco, salt of the earth, fish, cattle, wine, and dried beef. In the 1820s merchants were dealing in salt, and gold was no longer a significant commodity in official registers. The size of the northern comarca's trade to the São Francisco River was recognized by the governor of Goiás when he had the imports of the captaincy tabulated in 1804. They were more valuable than its trade with either Rio de Janeiro or São Paulo (table 2).[44]

How significant the northeastern routes were for the gold trade of the eighteenth century is uncertain, except that the Portuguese complained about the amount of contraband gold that exited the captaincy via the sertão. In the eighteenth century the mining towns of Goiás depended on the captaincy of Maranhão for Portuguese manufactures, foodstuffs, and enslaved Africans that were exchanged for gold, cattle, and horses. Almost all commerce of the port city of São Luis with Piauí and the towns of Natividade and São Félix went via the small town of Aldeas Altas, located near Caxias in eastern Maranhão. Another gold route from the mines of Goiás was northward via the Tocantins River. The merchants then traveled east to the Mearim River, which took them almost to São Luis. A second river route followed the Parnaíba River of Maranhão to the headwaters of the Itapicuru River and then via that river to the ocean at São Luis. Presumably, enslaved Africans and European trade goods followed the same river routes to the mining towns of Goiás.[45]

Related to the trade of the Tocantins River and the northeast was that of eastern Amazonia, dominated in the north by merchants resident in Belém do Pará. After 1782 they could legally outfit the riverboat expeditions that made annual trips down the Tocantins River to connect with the mining towns of the Maranhão River. They sent European manufactures, foodstuffs, and marine salt to exchange for gold and shoe leather. The opening of the Tocantins River route in the early 1780s apparently played a pivotal role in increasing the volume of contraband gold transported on the long river. The Portuguese had forbidden trade on the Tocantins between 1737 and 1782 in a vain attempt to stop the contraband gold trade. Indigenous attacks on river expeditions had also slowed trade on the Tocantins. With indigenous removals in the 1790s and government encouragement of trade to counteract mining declines, trade rebounded once again, and by 1804 trade with Pará was once more significant. By 1806 the ouvidor Joaquim Theotonio Segurado had organized a "company of commerce" in the town of Traíras to trade with Pará.[46]

To the west of the Tocantins River, the Araguaia River's trade was also linked to the port of Belém do Pará, but additionally to Cuiabá, Mato Grosso. In the 1790s Vila Real traveled on the Araguaia River and reported that merchants from Cuiabá transported trade goods destined for Vila Boa via the Fazenda do Leda, above the falls of the Vermelho River. In turn, Portuguese merchants in Vila Boa or Cuiabá sent goods via the Araguaia River—if the Karajá permitted them to do so. In fact, the Karajá traded directly with merchants based in Pará in order to obtain iron wares. Because so much of the Araguaia was still under indigenous control, this river was not as important for the legal trades dominated by Portuguese merchants. In the 1790s, however, Francisco de Souza Coutinho referred to the "poor Comboyeiros" who traded upriver to Belém, transporting sugar, leather, shoe leather, and tobacco, as well as bars of gold. In 1806 Segurado left gold off his list of commodities carried in ten canoes on the Araguaia River to Belém but included sugar, tobacco, *toucinho* (pork fat or bacon), and shoe leather.[47]

Belém-based merchants also participated in the slave trades of eastern Amazonia. They imported enslaved Africans into Belém and sent them down the Tocantins River to the mining towns. After the decline of the mines and the collapse of the trade in Africans, some may have turned to the trade in captive indigenous women and children from the Tocantins River region, who were branded and sold north as slaves to Belém. Captain Francisco José de Pinto Magalhães was only one of many who traded in Indian captives, sending them via river to Belém from Carolina. Others were sold to the cotton and rice plantations of Maranhão. How large or significant this trade in indigenous captives was is uncertain, although the entry of Africans into the captaincy can be documented from some entradas (chapter 7).[48]

In general, the merchants of the northern comarca traded with northeastern ports and Belém. Apparently much of this northern trade was independent of the trade conducted in the southern comarca. In contrast, Vila Boa looked not only to Salvador but also to the southeast, since the great majority of its imports came from Rio de Janeiro or São Paulo. After 1783 the legal quinto trade followed the road from Vila Boa to Meia Ponte and then south to Santa Cruz, Paracatú, Vila Rica (Ouro Prêto), and overland through Minas Gerais to the port of Rio de Janeiro. European goods loaded on mules and enslaved Africans followed the same route overland to Vila Boa. The merchants of Minas Gerais also sent *viveres* (live goods) raised in their own captaincy through the register at Desemboque for sale there or in Araxá. Peddlers also brought luxury European imports that they had purchased from merchants resident in Vila Rica and São João del Rei. By 1804 Rio de Janeiro provided the greatest volume of imported goods to the southern comarca, and such items as textiles, hats, wine, codfish, paper, gunpowder, and iron all followed the route via Minas Gerais to Vila Boa.[49]

Other important southern routes followed a river, and the men of São Paulo traded with the captaincy of Goiás via the Tietê and Paranaíba Rivers. Their journeys took less time and were less hazardous than the much longer Amazonian routes. Others traveled overland to Goiás with pack animals laden with salt, tools, and foodstuffs. Upon arrival in Vila Boa, they sold everything, including the mules and horses, and returned to São Paulo with gold. We suspect that much contraband gold, as well as other trade goods, followed the trade routes to and from São Paulo. Notably, many Paulistas returned with the gold of Goiás to build family fortunes in Santa Anna de Paraíba and elsewhere in São Paulo. Some measure of the relative significance of the São Paulo trade with the southern comarca comes from 1804. By then São Paulo was second to Rio de Janeiro in the value of imports into the southern comarca (table 2).⁵⁰

Two other important riverine routes of the south were the Paraná River, which connected Goiás to the trade of the Río de la Plata region, and to Spanish silver, and the Paraguay River, originating in Mato Grosso and connecting to the Paraná River system. In other words, the gold of Goiás was also traded west to Cuiabá and then south via the Paraguay River and into Spanish hands. Most likely this was the return route by which Spanish silver entered Goiás.⁵¹

The rivers of the interior of South America thus facilitated the trade of late colonial Brazil. Only one small leg of a vast interior trade network was under the effective authority of the Portuguese governor resident in Vila Boa: the collection and delivery of the quinto to Rio de Janeiro. As is obvious from its location, Central Brazil's remoteness from coastal cities made possible an extensive internal trade, including in contraband gold, that more closely resembled a free market responsive to the forces of supply and demand than a command economy dominated by Portuguese governors resident in Goiás, Mato Grosso, or Pará. Northern towns, such as Pontal and Natividade, were even freer of royal authority, and a free but hidden trade flourished in the north either via the Tocantins and Araguaia Rivers or across the sertão to Salvador. The interior of Brazil may have been more integrated into and linked with Spanish America than Portuguese authorities would have desired.

Merchant identities and their ties with coastal entrepôts are more difficult to determine than trade routes, in particular the names of those who were involved in gold contraband. According to the historian Luís Palacin, however, those responsible for the trade to the ports were one and the same; that is, the wealthiest merchants controlled both legitimate and contraband trades between Vila Boa and the coast, and they bribed guards and scribes at the checkpoints or the soldiers who guarded the quinto convoys to the coast. Much of the contraband was actually in gold dust, but they utilized bars of gold for more valuable trade. In official records, however, especially those of the Tribunal de Contas, those customarily accused of contraband were nonwhites (pardos, blacks, and mestizos), especially those involved in the sertão trade to Salvador.⁵² In any case, merchant identities were quite diverse.

The first type of merchant was the long-distance trader born in Portugal or the Azores who imported both dry goods and slaves to Vila Boa and Natividade. One of the wealthiest of these merchants, who was resident in Vila Boa, was João Botelho da Cunha, born in São Miguel in the Azores. He had been a businessman for forty years by 1765, when he submitted a petition to become a *familiar*, or agent of the Inquisition, in Vila Boa. In the petition he revealed that he and his brother João Antônio Botelho da Cunha did more than sixteen thousand *cruzados* of business. According to one testimony, his fortune was thirty thousand cruzados in size. He customarily traveled between Vila Boa and Bahia, and on one occasion he had brought a large convoy of 170 slaves and horses along with dry goods. Other merchants who traded in slaves and dry goods testified on his behalf, suggesting that the Bahian traders commonly dealt in both dry goods and slaves, which they exchanged for gold in Goiás.[53]

During the same period, Francisco José Barretto, a businessman, organized convoys of dry goods and slaves between Bahia and Natividade. Beginning in 1757, he had gold delivered to the foundry house in São Félix, which was fifty leagues distant from his home. At the time of his petition for a Habit of Christ, he was living in Natividade and maintained an extensive web of business and personal relationships with those he trusted to take gold on his behalf to São Félix. He did not deliver one large sum of gold to the foundry house, however, but rather small amounts that eventually added up to more than eight arrobas of gold in 1762 and 1763.[54]

The next merchant of significance, due to his educational background at the University of Coimbra, was Antônio de Souza Telles e Menezes. In the 1790s he was living in Vila Boa and held the title of captain-mor of the *ordenanças*. Moreover, he was professed in the Order of Christ, another indicator of his high social position in the Portuguese value system. He was a merchant with thirty-three years of experience in the mines, in recognition of which he had served as an administrator of the contract for the entradas for six years. Three of his letters document that he had brought salt-laden beasts from São Paulo to Vila Boa in 1794, as well as iron wares from the city of Rio de Janeiro. His career illustrates a number of characteristics of the merchants then resident in Vila Boa. They did not limit themselves to trade with a coastal port, but they also combined economic, military, and political roles; in this case Telles e Menezes served as a captain in the ordenanças as well as a tax contractor.[55] If typical of other merchants, he was probably involved in mining—as an investor in a mine and its enslaved labor force—and in landownership, both for wealth and food production. In some cases wealthy merchants acquired their vast properties through the bankruptcy of miners who were indebted to them for the purchase of slaves or imported goods.

The 1807 petition of yet another merchant, Lieutenant Manoel José Tavares da Cunha, for the Habit of Christ reveals his variety of roles as a merchant in the captaincy of Goiás (since 1775). Not only had he managed "a high degree of commerce" in dry goods in Goiás, but he had also worked in São Paulo. After residing in Goiás he went to Cuiabá, where he also did business. He bragged that he had sent "many arrobas" of gold to the foundry houses of Goiás and Mato Grosso. In 1776, at his own expense, he had equipped a convoy of forty horses and his own slaves to conduct weapons and foodstuffs to supply the garrison on Bananal Island in the Araguaia River, where José Pinto da Fonseca had pacified the Karajá in 1775. After his service to the military, he and his two partners (*socios*) received the contract for the entradas of 1782–1787, which reveals that he too had been a tax contractor. Furthermore, he acted as a lawyer in the causes of the Royal Treasury, administered the mail service, and served as *promotor* (attorney) in the Juizo da Provedoria Geral dos Auzentes and as guardian of the orphans of the comarca, thus also exercising bureaucratic and administrative roles. In the previous ten years he had resided in Pilar and Crixás, two of the wealthiest mining towns of Goiás.[56]

The São Paulo/Mato Grosso/Goiás connections of Tavares da Cunha were duplicated by another merchant, Antônio Navarro de Abreu, who petitioned for the Order of Christ in 1816. His petition is especially valuable because it clarifies that he dealt in both slaves and agricultural commodities. In 1816 he too held a military title, as a captain in the first cavalry militia regiment of Goiás, in which he had served for fifteen years; yet as the governor noted when he refused to support his petition for this high honor, the only military duty he did in Goiás was to walk in processions. Abreu claimed to be one of the best established (wealthiest?)] inhabitants of Goiás, with "a great establishment" in Mato Grosso, having sent "great caravans of trade goods and slaves" to other captaincies. In particular, he cited how he had furnished the Royal Treasury with supplies needed for the troops in Mato Grosso. Furthermore, under the previous governor he had been one of the first to transport goods to Pará as part of the first expedition funded by the Royal Treasury.[57] In other words, he had conducted both private and public business, and the governor concluded that his services were typical of most merchants in the captaincy and were not exceptional enough to merit the special recognition of the Order of Christ.

An examination of the multiple roles of merchants, including service to the Inquisition as a familiar and to the military in a provisioning capacity, suggests future lines of research into their roles in maintaining the flow of gold throughout the diverse trade routes of Central Brazil. But what is also notable is that the long-distance traders had plugged Central Brazil into the Atlantic economy of the late eighteenth century. Although the ability of the Portuguese to find new gold mines, or at least to collect the quinto, had declined, rising population statistics suggest that there were enough people still there to support the internal trade in the hands of these merchants. If they did not leave the region, Portuguese merchants began to trade in commodities produced by the agropastoral economy. By 1800 Portuguese officials were complaining about the contraband trade in cattle leaving the captaincy, suggesting that evasion of taxes at the registers was still significant, as it would be throughout the nineteenth century. The "culture of evasion" was being transferred from gold to contraband cattle.[58]

The question is this: if the population were increasing in numbers, especially the free population of color (chapter 10), then how were they supporting themselves? One answer is that they were planting foodstuffs, tobacco, cotton, and coffee trees and raising cattle and pigs. But Antônio Luis de Souza Leal argued that the true reasons for the decline of the quinto were not due to lack of gold but rather due to administrative inefficiency in Vila Boa and to the societies of black miners who kept the gold for themselves. As he reported, a society of sixty black freedmen organized themselves in two groups: forty who mined and twenty who raised foodstuffs to sustain them. Afterward they divided the gold equally among themselves, thus depriving the Crown of the quinto and permitting themselves to utilize gold for their own purposes, such as purchasing the freedom of family members and supporting black churches.[59]

Even though many Portuguese left the captaincy in the early nineteenth century, the internal economy did not completely collapse. Gold, tobacco, leather, cattle, cotton, coffee, and quince marmalades were moved via the old trade routes to neighboring captaincies, while Goianos continued to import salt and European luxury goods. In the nineteenth century the agropastoral economy would come to dominate the province of Goiás, as immigrants from nearby provinces contributed to the economic development of one of contemporary Brazil's most important agricultural regions.

Dragoons, *Pedestres*, and Militias

In most colonial empires, a local economy is critical to the financial support of military forces, or at least to the provisioning of the troops. As income from the quinto declined in the captaincy of Goiás, however, the Portuguese defended their empire using the minimum number of men and wherever possible the recently conquered and enslaved. Thus both indigenous men and those of African descent fought for the Portuguese with bows and arrows and antiquated weapons (arquebuses and muskets) in the frontier wars, and their women cultivated the food crops needed to provision the garrisons. When it came to the military, the Portuguese did empire "on the cheap."

The reason that the Portuguese employed the recently conquered and ex-slaves is that few soldiers and officers from Portugal served in the region. Their small numbers gave them an elevated social status, and those who lived for decades in the captaincy married local women and acquired property, slaves, and extended families of white and racially mixed children. Those who left the captaincy continued to serve in other parts of Portugal's empire, including Angola, where they probably exchanged the gold of Goiás for enslaved Africans. One military unit that employed men from Portugal as professional soldiers was the cavalry force, the company of mounted dragoons. The first company of dragoons arrived in Goiás in 1736. Composed of less than fifty men, it was headed by a captain and a lieutenant. As late as 1806, the dragoons had only seventy-six men, including a captain (absent), one lieutenant, one *alferes* (second lieutenant), one *furriel* (third sergeant), six corporals, one drummer, and five officers annexed to the company. Two years later, in 1808, only sixty remained. So few men had an extraordinary variety of responsibilities: to guard the Pilões and Claro Rivers, which were reputed to be rich in gold and diamonds; to protect the checkpoints and the intendant's safe where gold was safeguarded; to conduct the quinto to Rio de Janeiro; to lead bandeiras to conquer indigenous nations, discover new gold mines, and destroy quilombos; to patrol the roads in search of contraband; and to accompany the governor on his visits of inspection. Ill health and the demands of long trips led many dragoons to petition for permission to travel to Portugal, and their "vacations" from their duties contributed to further understaffing on the frontier.[60]

Because the dragoons focused on Portuguese concerns regarding gold and service to the Crown and governors, more prosaic and difficult matters of public safety and frontier warfare were left to less prestigious military units. Obviously of inferior status, in the Portuguese view, were the barefooted pedestres, a paid infantry troop (organized in 1743) that earned minimal salaries—if they were paid at all. Led by a captain, two alferes, a furriel, and two corporals (1777–1780), the pedestres based in Vila Boa were composed of mestizos, bastardos (illegitimate sons of indigenous women), and pardos, as well as mission Indians, such as the Akroá from Duro. In 1806 the pedestres numbered one hundred men, led by a captain, one alferes, one sergeant, one furriel, and six corporals. There was also a drummer. Mission Indians were also recruited from the aldeias of São

José de Mossâmedes and Maria I, and many of them were the Kayapó. Thus men of color and indigenous warriors did the difficult work of frontier forces, including manual labor, carrying provisions and weapons, and fighting with bows and arrows against their traditional enemies. They protected the missions and towns from enemy attacks and kept peace within the missions. Upon notice of impending threats, they were also sent on patrol to more remote regions of the captaincy to capture common criminals and hunt down and re-enslave fugitive slaves. In addition, some staffed garrisons in the north. Lists of the men who joined the pedestres document their few numbers in the eighteenth century, as well as their frequent desertions and low pay. Indigenous soldiers received half the salary of other men.[61]

Since the paid troops, that is, the dragoons and pedestres, were based in Vila Boa, and the region of their responsibility was immense, many of the military duties were actually performed by the unpaid militia units of the companies of ordenanças of white men, the auxiliary regiments of the terços (thirds) of pardos, and the black regiments of Henriques, named for Henrique Dias, the black hero of the war against the Dutch in the seventeenth century. There were also additional regiments (*agregados*) that were attached to the regular militia troops. In sharp contrast to the few Portuguese officers resident in the captaincy, the officers in the militias were numerous, and so too were their honorific titles. As Palacin observes, the ordenanças (the reserve white militias, who numbered 3,311 men in 1806) were "always affected by macrocefalismo, [a] great head without any body." The officers' patents were given to men who had no military experience, who were of advanced age, and who sought the elevated social status linked to a military title with the right to carry a *bengala* (large staff) in public processions in which rank and status were displayed. Portuguese governors, in particular Tristão da Cunha Menezes (1783–1800), used this hunger for social status to increase the delivery of gold to Vila Boa. He exchanged military patents for small gifts of gold—gold dust was preferred. Thus ambitious men could "buy" military patents during his governorship without ever fighting in one battle.[62]

Those who actually did the fighting were more likely to be the mulato men of the captaincy, often the sons of Portuguese officers and African women, who served under their own pardo officers in a terço dos pardos. The duties of these pardo regiments are well summed up in a petition to the Crown by the leading pardo officers then resident in the captaincy. In their petition they protested against their treatment by the city council of Vila Boa and recorded their services as "humble and faithful vassals" of the Crown in the bandeiras that conquered the Kayapó and Xavante. They also staffed the garrisons of the missions and defended the captaincy from its enemies. In spite of the exalted military titles granted to them in patents and signed by the king or queen in Portugal, the pardos actually provided many of the same services as the soldiers in the pedestres. Perhaps one status difference is that some of the pardos fought in cavalry units, but their much higher ranking than the pedestres is revealed by an episode that challenged color hierarchies in the captaincy. In the 1780s, when the post of governor fell vacant, the highest-ranking and most senior military officer, who held the oldest patent and who should have assumed his duties until the Crown appointed a new governor, was a mulato colonel. The white men on the Senado da Câmara loudly protested and refused to allow him to become the interim governor. In defending this violation of past practice, the members of the council justified their decision in these words: "By his quality [of being a mulato], he ought not to be admitted to the interim government." The Portuguese authorities in Lisbon agreed in 1790.[63]

Of less status than the pardo regiments was the third militia regiment known as the Henriques, which was originally created as a militia artillery regiment. Formed of ex-slaves and free black men, the Henriques performed duties similar to those of the pedestres and pardo regiments, that is, serving in bandeiras that attacked indigenous nations and quilombos, defending their families and slaves from indigenous attacks, and in general providing an additional force with which to defend the mining towns of the frontier. As one regimental list clarifies, they were Africans by birth or the sons of African parents in the mining town of São José do Tocantins in 1799. By the 1820s, however, other regimental lists document that those who belonged to the Henriques were largely Brazilian-born blacks (crioulos), who were miners, small farmers, artisans, and craftsmen. Many were also small slaveholders, owning one to three slaves. In 1789 the captaincy had seven companies of Henriques, but in the early nineteenth century, around 1812, their number had increased to at least twelve Henriques regiments headed by black officers. As the pardo and white men prized their titles, so too did the officers in the black regiments.[64]

The Portuguese depended on the men of color and local white men to guard and protect the captaincy of Goiás. They rewarded those who served them with military patents that raised their social status and might even have a salary attached. "Selling" patents also helped compensate men for risking their lives on a violent frontier. Serving as an officer might also give them access to remunerative bureaucratic positions, especially if they had been born in Portugal.

Since there were so few white men "of quality" throughout the captaincy, the Portuguese relied on militia soldiers and officers to perform the functions that troops of the line did on the coast. Hence, one of the major characteristics of the military (and the clergy) was that many of them also exercised political power, being noted for their involvement in affairs of state and use of public office to gain additional wealth. Even the indigenous caciques in the pedestres might secure additional authority over other chiefs due to their service to the Portuguese.

The Institutional Church

While it is understandable that military men would transfer leadership skills learned on the battlefield into political power, it is notable that the priests of Goiás were also politically powerful, with great personal wealth and even large families. After the Jesuit expulsion of 1759, secular priests from nearby mining towns were to replace the Jesuits, but after gold production declined, both Indian missions and small towns had difficulty finding a resident priest. Correspondence from Goiás reveals a neglected Catholic Church, unable to meet the religious needs of parishioners or to engage in significant missionary work among non-Christians.[65] As an institution, the Catholic Church was comparatively weak in late colonial Goiás, and the missionary enterprise was almost nonexistent until religious orders returned to the province in the 1840s. Italian Capuchins renewed a missionary effort among the indigenous in 1842, and they were followed by the French Dominicans in the 1880s.[66]

The captaincy of Goiás also had no resident bishop in the colonial period, nor was the captaincy subject to only one bishopric. At various times the people of Goiás fell under the religious authority of a bishop resident in Rio de Janeiro, Recife, or Belém. Although the prelacy of Goiás was created by Pope Bento XIV in 1745, the first bishop was not named until 1782, and Goiás would not have a resident bishop in Vila Boa until 1824. Officially, the first named bishop of Goiás was Dom Frei Vicente do Espirito Santo, a Portuguese Augustinian who was appointed bishop of Goiás in 1782, but his alleged ill health prevented his taking up his religious post. He died in Portugal in 1798 without ever visiting the captaincy. The second bishop was another Portuguese, Dom José Nicolau de Azevedo Coutinho Gentil, who was named to the prelacy of Cuiabá in 1783 and five years later to that of Goiás, but he refused to take up the post in Goiás and instead moved to Minas Gerais. The third bishop named for Goiás was a Bahian, Dom Vicente Alexandre de Tovar, who had actually served as a vicar in Pilar, Goiás, but he died suddenly near Paracatú without assuming his office in Vila Boa. The fourth named bishop, Dom Antônio Rodrigues de Aguiar, was born in Rio de Janeiro. Although he took possession of the prelacy in 1811, he did not leave for Goiás until 1818. Only five days into his trip from Rio, he died of a sudden fever.[67]

For another six years, there was no bishop for Vila Boa, and the fifth choice to be bishop initially seemed problematic to many because he was blind. This bishop from Bahia, however, was the one who built up the institutional church in the region, in spite of his disability. Although he lost his sight in 1821, Dom Francisco Ferreira Azevedo took up residence in Vila Boa on 21 October 1824 at the age of fifty-nine. His right-hand man, who handled his correspondence and assisted him in the administration of the prelacy, was the vicar general Luiz Antônio da Silva e Souza (until 1840). His second assistant and vicar general was José Joaquim Xavier de Barros. The blind bishop died at an advanced age in 1854, leaving behind a reputation as an eloquent orator, whose inspiring sermons were printed and distributed throughout the province. The long Portuguese neglect of the church in the late colonial period was ended by the blind Bahian, who reenergized the institution in the thirty years of his episcopate in Goiás.[68]

Although the power of the Portuguese Inquisition stretched to this remote region in the colonial period, those accused of heresy or grave sins against morality were sent all the way to Lisbon to be tried by the Holy Office. At most, investigations into suspect Jews (allegedly hiding in the region), African *feiticeiros* who practiced African healing traditions, and notorious cases of concubinage fell under the purview of pastoral visits authorized by the bishop of Rio de Janeiro. The agents of the Inquisition who denounced all types of immorality and heresy in Goiás were the familiars, who, according to their petitions to serve in that role, were prominent merchants in Vila Boa. Their victims were few, and the historian Luiz Mott did not find many cases from Goiás in his research on the Inquisition in Brazil. One of the more tragic cases he cites was that of a poor pardo who was transported to Lisbon to stand trial for wearing a *bentinho*, a type of amulet.[69]

In the absence of a bishop or Holy Office of the Inquisition, the highest ecclesiastical official resident in Vila Boa in 1804 was the vicar general, who was attached to the church of Santa Anna. He assumed some of the duties of a bishop, but he could not ordain priests. Young men who wanted to be ordained had to travel to Rio de Janeiro, another captaincy, or Europe. No more than thirty priests, who had studied in Coimbra, Portugal, served in Goiás. Of fifty priests ordained in 1782 in Rio de Janeiro, only one was assigned to Goiás. In the north the isolated parishes were under the authority of another vicar general, who was under the jurisdiction of the bishop of Pará. The first decree for a seminary in the City of Goiás was only issued in 1860, but it was not inaugurated until 1872.[70]

In general, eighteenth-century sources are not kind to the notorious priests who served in the captaincy, who were reputed to be more interested in the acquisition of gold than in saving souls. Notably, many priests disappeared in Goiás, especially those who had collected large donations in gold. On the other hand, conscientious priests, who followed their religious vocation by saying Masses and administering the sacraments, were overworked "circuit riders," who had to travel long distances to minister to isolated flocks. They often had short clerical careers in Goiás because they became incapacitated with malaria or died untimely deaths due to accidents or frontier warfare. Less religious priests neglected their sacramental obligations in order to supervise their numerous slaves and support their large households. Since many priests did not observe clerical celibacy, they lived openly with the mothers of their children, as well as their slave women. Moreover, they owned slaves who labored in the mines to support them all, since priests could not depend on clerical incomes. In fact, they were usually the largest slaveholders in many small towns.[71]

In addition to their clerical and familial responsibilities, priests also acted as merchants or at least as partners in commercial ventures. In 1816, for example, the vicar of the vara of Traíras, Manoel de Silva Álvares, petitioned for the Order of Christ for performing his clerical duties, as well as promoting a mercantile society between the captaincy of Goiás and Pará. Although he was one of the richest priests in the captaincy, his petition was denied because he had already received an exemption for the entradas, which he did not have to pay for ten years.[72] Other priests loaned money, took gold to the foundry houses, and even purchased slaves in Salvador on behalf of business partners or family members. Priests also held local political positions and undertook secular responsibilities for the governors of Goiás. Padre Silva e Souza was appointed a deputy to the Cortês in Lisbon to serve in the interim government of 1820. For his many services, he was recognized with the Order of Christ.[73] In the absence of a notary, priests worked as scribes and collected census data from the parish registers. They also taught Latin and other subjects to young boys. Such secular and familial responsibilities made it difficult to perform their clerical duties, and parishioners complained to Rio de Janeiro and Lisbon of local priests who did not say Mass or administer the sacraments. In fact, some parish pastors who were preoccupied with secular affairs hired poor priests to perform their sacramental duties.[74]

In other parts of the Americas, women who wanted to enter religious life could join a convent near their home, but there were no convents in Goiás in the colonial period. Elite white women who desired to become professed nuns, or at least to receive an education, had to travel to Salvador or Lisbon to enter a convent. By 1794, for example, Quiteria Rodrigues da Conceição had entered the convent of the Ursulines in Salvador. But the great majority of Goiano women could not afford such a journey; therefore, pious women (*beatas*) lived with family members or other beatas and engaged in charitable works or took an active role on the boards of local irmandades. Other women who did not become Catholic played important roles in Afro-Goiano religions as feiticeiras or worked as *curandeiras* within Indigenous healing traditions. Some simply became *rezedeiras*, who prayed for others in exchange for money.[75]

Since priests were often negligent or missing altogether, lay Catholics formed lay brotherhoods with female associates to meet the religious and social needs of the people who lived so far from coastal churches. The lay brotherhoods (irmandades) were essential to the construction of chapels and churches, where each brotherhood buried the dead. As society was divided by color into white, pardo, and black, so too were these brotherhoods. Whites formed the brotherhood devoted to the Blessed Sacrament, one of the most prestigious in the captaincy, while Portuguese military officers joined the brotherhood devoted to Saint Anthony. Pardo officers honored Our Lady of the Immaculate Conception, and blacks built churches dedicated to Our Lady of the Rosary or Our Lady of Mercies. They also constructed chapels in honor of the black saints Benedict and Efigênia.[76] The presence of these lay Catholic institutions in the mining towns helps to explain how many people remained Catholic in spite of the decline of the mines and a weak institutional church. As in the case of the military, the lay brotherhoods composed of lay Catholics of all colors ensured the continued practice of essential rituals that expressed religious values (chapter 8).

In conclusion, the Portuguese attempted to establish "good order" on the frontier of Goiás in order to capture the mineral wealth of Goiás and convert the gentiles to Christianity and a settled way of life working for local elites, but they never devoted sufficient resources in men or treasure to achieve their objectives. They also faced recalcitrant locals of all colors and ethnicities, who refused to work for them or deliver fortunes in gold to Lisbon. At times the governors complained bitterly about "lazy" Goianos, who refused to obey them, and about even more "obstreperous" Indians and Africans, who rebelled and fled their towns. As in the case of most colonial powers, Portugal had imposed the structures of empire to establish its hegemony and extract resources, but the imperial state did not achieve full control over Central Brazil in the colonial period. Indigenous nations and free people of color escaped the "good order" imposed by Lisbon, but not even local white elites bowed to Portuguese officials. In spite of Portugal's ideologies and efforts, Central Brazil was still an unruly frontier by the end of the colonial period in 1822.[77]

CHAPTER 6

The White Propertied Elites of the Captaincy of Goiás

The goal of most Luso-Brazilian men who traveled to the captaincy of Goiás was to get rich quickly by finding a fortune in gold.[1] By the 1770s the easy path to great wealth was more difficult, since the easily exploited gold had already been discovered. Fortune hunters were increasingly disappointed in their efforts to locate the amounts of gold similar to those found in the past, and ambitious men found themselves heavily in debt to Portuguese merchants or threatened with confiscation of property by Portuguese bureaucrats. Without rich gold mines, the "good men" of property diversified their economic activities and made good marriages with white women from local families. They also challenged Portuguese governors by avoiding taxes and engaging in contraband trade. Most of the time, however, the Goiano elite practiced "passive resistance" by refusing to obey the instructions of Portuguese governors, who complained about their "laziness" and lack of loyal obedience. Taking pride in their extended families of bandeirante heritage, local whites hung on tenaciously while the Portuguese abandoned the captaincy, especially after 1804, and they built new lives based on agropastoral activities and cattle contraband in the nineteenth century.[2]

The late colonial period was most difficult for the white elites of the captaincy, as they saw their enslaved Africans die and their fortunes based on gold mining and slave ownership slip away. Many families were left in poverty as Portuguese men returned to Portugal, taking their gold with them. This chapter will attempt to describe in general terms what happened to the propertied elites of Goiás during the period of so-called decadence.[3] We will begin with the census data on whites that document characteristics of their population decline and then describe the "good men" (and a few women) of the captaincy who formed the local propertied elites and whose interests often ran contrary

Figure 14. Inhabitants of Goiás. This picture depicts the long-horned cattle raised in Goiás, as well as the dress of the cowboys. The standing figure in the background wears a hat similar to the one shown in figure 21. Source: Rugendas, Viagem pitoresca. Courtesy of the Library of Congress, Washington, DC.

to those of their Portuguese rulers. After independence these white Goianos and their families would take the place of the Portuguese at the top of local society.

The first marker of high status in the captaincy was "quality." To govern in the Portuguese imperial system, a man needed to be not only white but also a person of "quality." Yet there were few men of quality resident in the captaincy, usually only the governor, high judges (the ouvidores da comarca), prominent officials, and some priests.[4] Tax contractors and intendants of gold at the foundry houses might also use their "quality" to secure their lucrative positions. Most white men, however, were of much less exalted position, and they used their whiteness to set themselves at the top of local society. The identifier *branco* (white man) was usually all a scribe indicated on censuses or other documents, but by the 1820s some scribes refined whiteness even further by calling those at the top of society *alvo*, in the sense of pure white. Thus those with the largest number of slaves and large estates could be recorded as alvo; those of middle status in slave ownership were branco.[5] What the scribes were probably recognizing were the status differences between the most important members of a community and whites of lesser wealth, who probably had some degree of racial mixture. Alvos and brancos were often married in the Catholic Church with legitimate children; their households were large, with many family members and agregados (household dependents); and they held the largest fortunes in slaves, mines, and large estates (fazendas, engenhos). Their wives and children often lived in a nearby town for protection against indigenous attacks. Many attempted to maintain the purity of their lineage and to remain white. Such a focus on lineage and color did lead to marriage within families and inbreeding, with genetically linked health problems that became more evident after the eighteenth century. Although close scrutiny of a family genealogy might reveal an African or indigenous woman as an ancestor, local elites were identified as white and treated as the white members of illustrious local families.[6]

Of the censuses of the eighteenth century, only one, in 1783, identifies those who headed households and controlled great wealth in slaves. Although we know little about how they accumulated their wealth, we can at least establish who the wealthiest men and women were in 1783 and where they lived. Additional sources provide other insights into these white elites. Unfortunately, the household lists do not always clarify a person's birthplace, that is, whether Portugal, the Azores, or Brazil. Before examining this census, however, we must turn to other censuses, beginning in 1779. Most of these censuses also provide few specifics on the national origins of the propertied elites and only clarify total numbers of men and women in the captaincy of Goiás, as well as providing some age data. When age data accompanies the statistics, it is evident that a small subset of elite men controlled the wealth of the captaincy.

The first census that counted the white population was the census of 1779 (tables B.1–B.3). In that year, those identified as "branco" numbered only 8,930 out of a total population of 54,489, or 16.4 percent. In the southern comarca, the julgado with the largest concentration of whites was Meia Ponte, with 1,809, actually more whites than the capital of Vila Boa (1,460). On the other hand, even fewer whites were registered in the northern julgados, especially in proportion to blacks. Only 679 whites maintained social control over 3,176 blacks in Traíras, while São Félix registered only 387 whites and Carmo had the least number of whites, at 84. Overall, the proportion of whites who lived in the northern comarca was only 13.3 percent, as opposed to 18.8 percent in the southern comarca. In terms of numbers, whites were a vulnerable group since they were greatly outnumbered by the enslaved and free people of color.

The next census was that of 1781. The total number of whites had risen slightly to 9,072, in part because the census takers registered more whites in Vila Boa, at 2,310, while Meia Ponte still had 1,809. The third-largest number of whites lived in the julgado of Traíras (955). In contrast to the census of 1779, which was less carefully done, the census takers found 6,220 blacks in Traíras. The low proportion of whites in relation to blacks was duplicated in São Félix, which had 387 whites and 2,645 blacks, and in Natividade, with only 690 whites to 3,536 blacks. The reality of whites being outnumbered was replicated in the captaincy as a whole. Of a total population of 58,829, only 9,072 were defined as branco in 1781, or 15.4 percent. In the following year, 1782, there was a slight decline in the total white population, which fell to 8,963, with the majority of whites living in the south of the captaincy. In fact, Vila Boa, with 2,289 whites, and Meia Ponte, with 1,840 whites, held almost half of the white population of the captaincy (46.1 percent). In the north, Traíras had the largest white population, 960, and Natividade was second at 677, while São Félix's white population had declined slightly, to 382.

The next census, of 1783, reveals that 8,898 whites remained in the captaincy and more than half lived in only three julgados: Vila Boa (2,289), Meia Ponte (1,727), and Traíras (967). The number in Natividade had declined to 628, with 625 in Santa Luzia. Six years later, in 1789, the total number of whites had grown to 9,079, yet over a period of ten years the white population had hardly increased in size. Ten years before the largest number of whites had lived in Vila Boa, at 2,293, and the second-largest concentration was in Meia Ponte, with 1,772. Traíras had 914 and São Félix, 385.

Two years later, in 1791, the census takers registered slight declines. There were 2,279 whites in Vila Boa, 1,766 in Meia Ponte, and 906 in Traíras, while the number in São Félix had risen slightly, to 400. But Natividade lost 20 whites from the 643 recorded in 1789. Overall, there were less than 9,000 whites in the captaincy (8,961). The following year the number of whites declined in Vila Boa to 2,233 and to 1,725 in Meia Ponte. In the north, Traíras still had 808 whites, while Natividade was second to it with 630 and those in São Félix numbered 362. Overall there were 9,172 whites in the captaincy, which marked an increase over 1791.

After this sequence of censuses there is a significant gap, since only fragments of the census for 1798 survive. The next detailed accounting of the population of the captaincy of Goiás dates from the census of 1804 (table B.4). This census also provides additional data on the white population by marital status and sex (see chapter 9). By 1804 the sexes were nearly balanced, at 3,508 males to 3,442 females, for a total of 6,950, which is significantly lower than the 9,172 whites documented in 1792. One of the julgados that had lost the most whites was Vila Boa, which then had only 1,219 whites. Males and females were also nearly equal in number in Vila Boa, at 610 males to 609 females, suggesting that by 1804 fewer single Portuguese males resided in the capital than had in the past. Meia Ponte also saw a drop in its white population, to 1,268, while there were only 79 whites remaining in Crixás. Clearly 1804 marked a low point in numbers for local whites.

The next census, of 1825, documents white flight from the north or an official inability to count those who lived in the north (table B.5). The total white population declined to only 1,355, with some julgados losing significant numbers of whites. São Félix then counted only 44 whites, while Traíras had dropped to 395 and Natividade to 157. As we will see in chapter 10, however, the freeborn and freed population of color had continued to grow, reaching 16,036 and far outnumbering local whites and slaves (table B.15). In the south, there were 2,527 whites in the City of Goiás, but even more whites lived in Meia Ponte, at 2,767, while Santa Cruz had also expanded, with 2,083 whites. There were even 1,113 whites in Santa Luzia. What these statistics suggest is that whites had left the north in the face of escalating warfare with indigenous nations and had settled in more southerly towns. But according to Paulo Bertran, the district of Traíras had lost whites due to the decline of the mines. Immigrants from the north of Portugal who had settled in Traíras moved to towns such as Jaraguá and Anicuns, where they could establish farms and fazendas on fertile soils.[7]

The final census of this period was conducted in 1832 (table B.6). This census documents the recovery of the white population from the low point of 1804. By 1832 the census takers were able to find 11,761 individuals who were white, almost all of whom lived in the south (10,001). The largest number of whites actually lived in Santa Cruz (3,330), followed by the City of Goiás (2,527) and Meia Ponte (2,441). As usual, Traíras had the largest white population farther north, but it then numbered only 517; second was Arraias at 415. All other julgados in the north had less than 300 whites. Most notably, only six whites continued to live in São Félix. White decline obviously continued in the north, where the total population numbered only 1,760. In contrast, the white population continued to grow in size in the south, in part fueled by migration from the provinces of Minas Gerais and São Paulo.

The above census figures locate the sections of the captaincy of Goiás where those defined as "white" lived. Even though the statistics might have been poorly collected and analyzed, they provide some sense of how few people were available in the captaincy to engage in slave control or to fight the indigenous populations, especially as the Portuguese left the captaincy. As chapters 7 and 10 will reveal, most people who lived in the captaincy were of African or indigenous descent; these two groups formed at least four-fifths of the population. Whites, therefore, were only a fifth or less of the population, and even fewer of them belonged to the privileged wealthy of the region. Of course, women and children, as well as impoverished men, were included in that fifth, so that only a small minority of white men enjoyed both high social status and wealth at the end of the colonial period.

Mine Owners

Among the wealthiest men in the captaincy were those who owned a hundred or more slaves, who were engaged in mining on a *lavra* (mine) under the supervision of an overseer or as an independent prospector (*faiscador*), who turned in a weekly amount of gold to his or her slaveholder.[8] Since so many enslaved Africans worked without direct supervision, even priests and women formed part of the group of wealthy mine owners. Those who were notably successful at acquiring the gold of Goiás can be traced through their petitions to the Portuguese Crown for the Order of Christ based on their ability to deliver eight arrobas of gold to the foundry houses of Vila Boa or São Félix. Table 3 lists a sample of the men who sent petitions to Lisbon based on their delivery of eight or more arrobas of gold. Most sought recognition from the Crown for the prestigious Order of Christ, although Ignacio Soares de Bulhões, then serving in the Provisional Junta of Goiás, requested the rank of noble (*foro de fidalgo*) in 1820. As the dates in table 3 reveal, it often took a petitioner years to receive official recognition. The case of Paulo José de Aquino, for example, dragged on until 1824. He had first sent gold to the foundry house of Vila Boa in 1761. While the mining of the gold often went quickly—requiring less than a year to acquire eight arrobas—the bureaucratic process took years.

Table 3 also documents the variety of elite occupations held by the petitioners. Three were military officers serving in the dragoons; others were

The White Propertied Elites of the Captaincy of Goiás   165

Table 3. Men with gold from the captaincy of Goiás, 1750–1824

Name	Birthplace[a]	Profession	Dates	Source
Amado, José de Oliveira	—	*Furriel*, dragoons	1759–1774	ANTT 320
Aquino, Paulo Jose de, heir of Thomas João Ruffo and Miguel da Costa Pereira	—	—	1761–1824	ANTT 324
Araujo, Bartholomeu Ferreira, son of Manoel Ferreira	Viana	Business	1770	AH 29
Barretto, Francisco José	—	*Comboieiro*[b]	1757–1766	AH 11
Bechiga, Manoel Ferreira	—	Business	1770–1778	ANTT 320
Bulhões, Ignacio Soares de	—	Junta Provisória	1823	RJAN
Campello, Manoel da Silva	Rio de Janeiro	Priest	1767–1773	ANTT 320, AH 29
Carvalho, Henrique Manoel de	Vila Real	Business	1773–1790	ANTT 321
Costa, Manoel Ribeiro da	Vizeu	Business	1769–1770	AH 29
Fonseca, José Pinto da	—	*Alferes*, dragoons	1773–1775	ANTT 320
Fonseca, José Ribeiro da	—	Treasurer	1762–1765	AH 6
Freire, José Rodrigues	Alvaro	Lieutenant, dragoons	1769–1780	ANTT 320
Leite, Francisco Xavier	—	Captain-mor	1752–1764	AH 6
Lisboa, Francisco and António da Silva (brothers)	Lisbon	Business	1754–1769	AH 4
Lisboa, José Pedroso	—	Notary, *fazenda*	1764–1780	ANTT 320
Mattos, Gregorio da Costa	Goiás	*Bacharel*	1776	AH 29
Miranda, João Machado de[c]	Lisbon	Business	1769	AH 29
Paiva, Manoel Joaquim de	—	Lives by his *fazendas*	1778	ANTT 320
Peixoto, António Luis	—	Lives by his *fazendas*	1772–1779	ANTT 320
Peixoto, João da Rocha	Guimarães	—	1768–1777	ANTT 320
Pinto, Manoel Cardozo	Baião	Business	1763–1779	AH 21
Rebello, Manoel Gomes	Baião	—	1769–1777	ANTT 320

Table 3 (continued)

Name	Birthplace	Profession	Dates	Source
Rebello, Simão da Silva, age 70	Lisbon	Business	1764–1769	AH 29
Reis, José Alves dos	Lisbon	Business	1770	AH 29
Silva, Belxior da	—	Business	1754–1773	AH 6
Souza, João Teixeira de, age 58	Amarante	Business	1763–1769	AH 29
Taques, Ignacio Joaquim	—	—	1750–1777	AH 25
Telles e Menezes, Antônio de Souza	—	—	1763–1773	AH 6
Vianna, Antônio Gonçalves, and Pedro Rodrigues Bandeira, partners, living in Bahia	Viana	Business	1779	AH 29

Sources: AHU = Arquivo Histórico Ultramarino, Goiás, no. 1002, caixa 4, 1736–1825; Goiás, caixa 6, 1740–1794; Goiás, no. 1003, caixa 11, 1750–1807; Goiás, caixa 21, 1760–1782; Goiás, caixa 25, 1765–1799; and Goiás, caixa 29, 1772–1799.

ANTT = Arquivo Nacional da Torre do Tombo, Ministerio do Reino, Conselho Ultramarino, Consultas, 1773–1780, maço 320; Consultas, 1805–1825, maço 324; and Consultas, 1781–1792, maço 321.

RJAN = Rio de Janeiro, Arquivo Nacional, IJJ9 535, Ministerio do Reino e Império, Goiás, Oficios de diversas autoridades, 1808–1829.

[a]All listed place-names are in Portugal, except for Rio de Janeiro and Goiás.
[b]Convoy owner, long-distance trader.
[c]And for his other son, Luiz Machado Teixeira, student, University of Coimbra.

Portuguese merchants and property owners who were living in Portugal upon the completion of the petition for the Order of Christ. The most notable merchant on this list was Francisco José Barretto, a long-distance trader from Bahia who dealt in dry goods and slaves, bringing them to Natividade. Apparently he also transported gold on behalf of mine owners from Natividade to the foundry house of São Félix. Notable among those on the list of those for whom he delivered gold between 1757 and 1763 were four priests: José da Gama Faustino, resident in Carmo of Natividade; Valentim Tavares of Paranagua; Manoel do Salvamento, vicar of Natividade; and the Reverend Doctor Visitor José dos Santos Pereyra, inhabitant of São Félix. He also twice placed gold to the account of "Senhor Bom Jezus do Bomfim" of Bahia. Unfortunately, his other business partners were not identified. In addition, two others from Pontal stand out: Serafim Ferreira da Costa, who sent more than fifteen *marcos* of gold to São Félix, and Manoel Francisco de Azevedo. The other property owners were largely based in Natividade, and most of them sent only one to five marcos of gold to São Félix.[9]

The documentation on these successful men who acquired so much gold, as well as the census data on the white population, raises important questions. In Portuguese discourse of that period, the 1780s and 1790s were regarded as significant periods of economic decadence in which the ability of the Portuguese to collect the quinto had seriously declined. Table 1 and chart 1 clearly illustrate that less and less of the gold of the captaincy was reaching Lisbon after 1780. By 1800 the situation was dire for the Portuguese. By 1798, declining revenue in the fifth-richest captaincy of Brazil led the Portuguese to do a year-by-year calculation of the captaincy's population between 1789 and 1792. Remarkably, the number of whites had remained relatively stable from 1779 to 1792, while slaves continued to be numerous (see chapter 7). So what had happened to the gold? Was mining still taking place in the 1780s? Did some whites still base their status and wealth on gold mines?

According to official correspondence as of 1788, the gold of Goiás had once come from the following "discoveries": Traíras, Pilar, São José [do Tocantins], São Félix, Arraias, Natividade, Pontal, Santa Cruz, Santa Luzia, Meia Ponte, Santa Rita, and Tesouras; by 1788, however, these mines were all "exhausted."[10] The "good men" of the Senado da Camara of 1788 probably included those who remembered when these mining towns had generated great wealth. Perhaps their ordering of the "discoveries" suggests a memory of those that had been the richest, but this list is incomplete. Portuguese discourse about decadence and exhausted mines hides the reality on the ground and at other mining towns. The problem is to document the persistence of mining, for which there are a number of official sources. Obviously, future archaeological research and historical studies should uncover other mining activities and sites. First of all, the household lists of 1783 register not only the number of whites resident in key mining towns but also the slaves that they owned and their place of employment, that is, the lavra, the house, or the field. Some also record those slaves who went prospecting on their own.[11]

In 1783 the census takers, usually parish priests or military officers, distinguished between those who owned slaves who worked on lavras and those who were faiscadores, who prospected for gold and returned a *jornal* on a weekly basis. In Pilar the census takers even recorded that fifty-seven slaves made twelve *vinténs* (one vintém = twenty réis) of gold as the jornal. Thus the household lists reveal that the whites who owned slaves who were still mining at lavras in 1783 lived in the following places: Água Quente, with 9 lavras; Amaro Leite, 1 lavra; Arraias, about 60 slaves in mining; Barra, 13 miners; Cachoeira, 4 lavras; Cavalcante, 400 slaves on lavras plus a gold "factory"; Cocal, 6 lavras; Crixás, 8 lavras; Pilar, 506 slaves; Santa Cruz, 7 lavras and 140 slaves; Santa Luzia, 616 slaves; Santa Rita, 2 lavras; São Félix, 45 slaves on lavras; and Traíras, 1,086 slaves who were engaged in mining.

In the mining town of Anta there were three large "Fabricas de Negros" in 1783. Apparently the scribe used this term to describe gold workings. Those with the most slaves were a lieutenant colonel and his relations with 130; Padre Pedro Monteiro de Araujo with 130; and Padre Paulo de Souza Pinto de Aguiar with 110. Two other men with military titles also had slaves: Lieutenant Francisco da Silva Braga possessed 50 and Alferes Silvestre Rodrigues Jardim, 40. Pedro Barbosa Leão also had 44 slaves.

As distinct from the slaves working on factories or lavras, whites also owned slave faiscadores: 10 of them in Arraias, which was no longer a major mining center in 1783; 40 in Carmo; 150 in Cavalcante; 83 in Chapada; 300 in Pilar; 147 in Santa Cruz; 240 in Santa Luzia; and 106 in São Félix. It is uncertain if these faiscadores worked all year round or only in the dry season, or if they were expected to do other occupations besides mining.

None of these official figures, however, document the true dimensions of the mining activities in the captaincy, since census takers often admitted their inability to record all of the enslaved. In Crixás, for example, it was very difficult to count the slave prospectors who worked in remote locations. But the figures do point to these still-significant locations of gold mining in 1783:

Cavalcante, Crixás, Pilar, Santa Cruz, Santa Luzia, and Traíras. Notably, Natividade was not on the list.

The 1783 accounting of enslaved blacks in mining also identified those who were the richest men in mining, to the extent that we can determine this based on slave ownership. Working sixty slaves each on three different lavras in Cavalcante were Captain Domingos Antônio Cardoso, Antônio Rodrigues Pereira and Domingos Pires, and Domingos Antônio Cardoso and partners (socios). Thus the Cavalcante ownership pattern was typical for this period, when those who mined at lavras formed business and/or family partnerships to work the mines with each person's slaves. In Crixás three of those with more than one hundred slaves were also partnerships: Antônio de Camargo Pimentel, with more than 100 slaves; Alferes Mathias de Crasto Aguiar, with 200; and Guarda Mor José Francisco de Carvalho, with 190 slaves.

The same partnerships were true on the lavras of Pilar: Antônio de Meirelles Lobo, 140 slaves; Captain Francisco Pereira do Lago, 95; and Captain João Carvalho de Araujo, 80. In Santa Luzia, 280 slaves were subject to Colonel João Pereira Guimarães and Captain Manuel Ribeiro da Silva plus two overseers. The next wealthiest were Captain José Pereira Lisboa and his overseer José Álvares, with 150 slaves. Of the many men involved in mining who were slaveholders in Traíras, the wealthiest were Lieutenant Colonel Agostinho Alvarez Cardozo, with 90 slaves, and Colonel Manoel Lopes Chagas, with 80. In contrast, fewer slaves worked on the lavras of São Félix. The two largest slaveholders who sent their slaves to mine as faiscadores were Manoel Ferreira Martins, with 40, and Padre Franco Alves Teixeira, with 37.

A second measure of continued gold mining in the 1780s comes from a document sent to Lisbon that recorded the *guias* (registry books) of bars of gold that were sent to Salvador in 1786. This list is especially interesting because comparative data is available for other parts of Brazil. By this measure, in order of importance, were: Goiás, 151 bars; São Félix, 140; Vila Bela (Mato Grosso), 62; Jacobina (Bahia), 54; Serro Frio (Minas Gerais), 47; Vila Rica (Minas Gerais), 28; Sabará (Minas Gerais), 20; Rio das Mortes (Minas Gerais), 9; and São Paulo, 2.[12]

A third measure of continued mining in the 1780s is from an undated document held at the Instituto Histórico e Geographico de Goiás. The unnamed author, who includes some of the slaveholders from the 1783 census, lists more than two thousand miners and the number of slaves that they held in each location. Unlike the 1783 census takers, however, he did not divide them by color, and some may have been pardos or blacks. This list of miners and their slaves adds additional names and locations for mining; confirms the continued significance of Pilar, Santa Luzia, and Traíras; and documents mining in Vila Boa and nearby Ouro Fino and Anta, as well as in Meia Ponte. The wealthiest slaveholders engaged in mining were Captain Manoel Ribeiro da Silva, with 250 slaves, and Captain José Pereira Lisboa, with 150, who were both of Santa Luzia, as well as Captain Mamedes Mendes Ribeiro and his partners, with 200 slaves in Cocal. The next-wealthiest each had 100 slaves: Reverend Pedro Monteiro de Araujo of Anta, Captain João Pereira Guimarens of Santa Luzia, and Antônio Barrozo Basto and partners of Água Quente.[13]

The ownership of slaves in mining was clearly a male-dominated activity in the 1780s, but two women appear on the list, with notably fewer slaves than the wealthiest men. Apparently they had inherited their properties from their deceased husbands. Dona Getrudes was a widow in Vila Boa with only thirty slaves, while the widow of Frota in Meia Ponte held forty.

These documents prepared during the period of decadence clarify that many wealthy men and a few women still devoted many of their slaves to work on the lavras, or they sent them out as independent prospectors. Even though many Portuguese slaveholders had left the captaincy, especially after 1804 and independence in 1822, mining continued in the province of Goiás. In 1826 José Rodrigues Jardim forwarded to the Court of Rio de Janeiro a list of places where gold still existed but was not being worked due to a lack of labor, that is, enslaved Africans. The objective of sending this list to Rio was to attract an English company to invest in Goiás. For our purposes, however, this list of potential gold-mining sites prepared by Padre Silva e Souza includes many of the locations of eighteenth-century gold mines. Clearly they had not yet been totally "exhausted."[14]

By the 1820s there were still individuals who went prospecting for gold, many of them free or freed pardos and blacks, as subsequent chapters illustrate; yet it is uncertain how many whites continued to mine at the above locations. Fortunately, there are still more census records from the 1820s that reveal a little about the number of white mine owners. These same census records also document the significant number of blacks and mulatos who continued to mine. Perhaps Padre Silva e Souza compiled his list of mining sites from those individuals who were still panning for gold in the 1820s.

At that time, Raimundo José da Cunha Matos had statistics collected on the population of many towns, especially those he visited during his northern campaigns against the Canoeiro.[15] One of his objectives was to determine which men lived where in order to call them up for military or militia service

Table 4. Locations of gold mines, 1826

City of Goiás and its environs	hill of Moquem, Pilar parish
parish of Anta	plus the *pedreira* (quarry) of the Carvalho
"very rich *pedreiro*" of Taveira	all the land in Crixá parish
rich hill of São José	Maranhão River
lavras of Tesouras	*lavras* of Água Quente
the Onça	Cocal
Ferreiro River	*sertão* of Amaro Leite
hill of Santo Antônio, Meia Ponte parish	rich *pedreira* of Cavalcante
mines of Jaraguá	Arraias
Peixe River	hill of the Chapéu
Santo Antônio, Montes Claros, Santa Luzia	Etaipabas, Paraná River
	lavras of Mattança, near Pontal
hill of Clemente, district of Santa Cruz	mineral lands of the Cajazeiras
lavras of Bonfim	in the parish of Conceição

Source: RJBN, I-47, 26, 21, manuscript section, Abaixo-assinado de José Rodrigues Jardim e outros a José Feliciano Fernandes Pinheiro, sobre as despesas da Companhia Inglesa exploradora de minas na província de Goiás, City of Goiás, 30 May 1826 (cópia). The *parecer* dated 30 May 1826 of Luis Antônio de Silva e Sousa accompanies this document with the list of mining sites.

in case of attacks on their communities. Thus we learn the name of each propertied head of household in some of these communities. They were classified by colors denoted A, B, and C. The As were obviously whites, since they occupied high-status occupations and headed large households, including slaves. The Bs were the racially mixed, usually defined in the censuses as pardos, while the Cs were crioulo blacks, who often served in the black militia force, the Henriques. The census takers also identified each head of household by age and marital status, listed the members of their households along with their slaves, and recorded the occupations of the male and female heads of households. Because these household lists recorded both color and occupation for the leading men of each mining town, we can use them to suggest an important transformation in elite ownership of property by the 1820s; that is, whites no longer owned a large number of slaves engaged in mining. Those who mined were middle-aged and even elderly blacks and pardos.

In the once rich mining town of Água Quente, a total of 708 persons remained, of whom 111 were still enslaved. Only 17 white men and 18 white women composed the small white elite. None of the whites were miners or owners of slave miners, but 8 men, only 1 of whom was above the age of thirty-five, were listed as pardos. Those who were still mining in the 1820s were free or freed blacks, many of whom were in their fifties and sixties, which suggests that they had been mining there for decades. In the 1780s and 1790s they had probably been counted among enslaved blacks, but by the 1820s they were property owners. The oldest black slaveholder was Catherina Nogueira, age eighty-one, a widow of property with one male slave. If she had been brought to the mines when she was in her twenties, she might have been in the mining region from the 1740s or 1750s. Overall, twenty-eight black men and two women were slaveholders in the 1820s. As opposed to the large number of slaves per master or partnership before the 1790s, those involved in mining controlled very few slaves. The largest number belonging to any one slaveholder was five. Lourenço Dias and his wife, Maria Ponsedonia, owned one male and four female slaves, which was hardly like the profile of slave ownership in eighteenth-century mining towns.

The noninvolvement of whites in mining is also documented for the mining town of Cocal. In the 1820s only four white men and seven white women remained of a total population of five hundred. João Nepumuceno Ribeiro, age thirty, was a corporal in the cavalry and a *traficante* (trader). Three white agregadas (household dependents) actually served a pardo soldier in the cavalry (Antônio da Silva Leite) and his mother, Maria de Souza, who had a plot of land for food crops. On the whole, there were only two crioulo men, Jacinto de Almeida, age forty-nine, and Malaquias Gomes, age twenty-four, who were miners. Cocal had already shifted from mining to food production on small plots of land (roças), and its predominantly black and pardo population now lived by agriculture rather than mining. None of the whites had any obvious links with mining.

In the far north, Porto Real and Pontal also had few engaged in mining in the 1820s. The first town was a river port, while Pontal had once been a center of gold mining in the north. In Porto Real, Manoel Ferreira da Crús, age fifty-two, crioulo, and Lucianno da Gama, age sixty-two, crioulo, were the only two miners resident in the city. In the traditional mining town of Pontal, there was only one miner so identified, and he was João Lopes, pardo, age fifty-eight. But there must have been more men involved in gold mining in the district of Pontal, since the town had a resident *ourives* (goldsmith or jeweler). He was José da Costa Amurim, age forty, who also owned four slaves. No whites were involved in mining in either town. Thus these fragmentary household lists suggest that by the 1820s the number of whites linked to mining had collapsed, especially in the north, while slave ownership by whites had also greatly declined.

Merchants and Businessmen

When gold had been more plentiful, businessmen had prospered. Table 3, based on those who sought honors in the captaincy of Goiás in the eighteenth century, reveals that long-distance merchants and local businessmen also captured the gold of Goiás in sufficient quantities to put eight arrobas of gold in the foundry houses. Although some may have had slaves who mined for them, it was also possible for them to acquire gold by receiving payment in gold dust for the commodities they sold in the general stores (*lojas*) of the captaincy. Being a *negociante* (merchant, businessman), especially one who dealt in long-distance trade, could bring a man wealth and status in the eighteenth century. Furthermore, the businessmen were usually of Portuguese ancestry, with commercial ties to Portuguese merchants resident in Lisbon or Porto in Portugal, or in Brazil at Belém, Salvador, Rio de Janeiro, or São Paulo. If not from Portugal, they may have been born in the Azores, Portuguese islands off the coast of West Africa. To some extent, the status values and income attached to being a negociante in the eighteenth century transferred to the early nineteenth century, since local whites continued to occupy these occupations in the 1820s, although pardos and a few blacks had entered business by the 1820s.

The petitions for honors of the eighteenth century reveal that twelve men had ties to business (table 3). At the time of their petitions, Henrique Manoel de Carvalho was a businessman from Vila Real in the comarca of Lamego; brothers Francisco and Antônio da Silva Lisboa were businessmen from Lisbon; Manoel Cardozo Pinto was from Bayao (Baião, Portugal); Antônio Gonçalvez Vianna and Pedro Rodrigues Bandeira were business partners from Viana (Portugal) in their forties, who both lived in Bahia; and José Mauricio Vianna's trading house was based in Rio de Janeiro. Still other businessmen born in Portugal were Bartholomeu Ferreira Araujo, the son of Manoel Ferreira, from Vila de Viana; Manoel Ribeiro da Costa, son of Joam Ribeyro, born in Vizeu, Portugal; João Machado de Miranda, son of a native of Lisbon, who did a large business; Simão da Silva Rebello, native of Lisbon, age seventy; José Alves dos Reis of Lisbon; and João Teixeira de Souza, native of Amarante, which is near Porto, Portugal, age fifty-eight. We might also add Francisco José Barretto to the list of businessmen because he was a *comboieiro*, who ran convoys of dry goods and slaves from Bahia to Natividade, but he was the only one so identified among this group of petitioners.

The census of 1783 also permits some insights into the number of whites who ran retail businesses in the towns and villages of the captaincy (table 5). In each town or mining camp, those who did business with miners and received gold dust in payment for their commodities set up small stores or shops (lojas), where the women of their households could be involved in sales. Others established taverns, where locally produced sugarcane drinks (cachaça) were sold by black women. We can trace the number of general stores in each community in 1783 because the census takers also recorded them, as well as the number of taverns. Even if a merchant was not officially listed for some towns, we can at least establish where the retail businesses were located. What often gave identity to a small settlement and attracted other people to live there was the presence of a retail section and local businessmen, who could supply the miners with tools, foodstuffs, and goods from the coast, as well as alcoholic drinks in the taverns. What is also evident from table 5 is that whites owned much of the retail sector of the local economy, with 1,416 white owners in Vila Boa and 340 in Anta.

As table 5 reveals, there was only one large commercial/retail center in Goiás in 1783, and that was Vila Boa. Unfortunately, data from Meia Ponte is missing, but it too may have had many stores and taverns. According to the accounting of 1783, Vila Boa had twenty-two stores that sold dry goods, twenty for wet goods (actually, warehouses of wet goods and houses of commission), and two *boticas*, where medicines could be purchased. Saint-Hilaire was impressed with the well-supplied stores that sold all types of goods imported from Rio de Janeiro.[16] Elsewhere general stores also sold medicines, since the captaincy generally lacked boticas in the eighteenth century. Second in number of stores was Santa Luzia, which was apparently a commercial center with its fourteen dry goods stores and one for wet goods.

The most numerous retail businesses, however, were the taverns: Vila Boa had sixty-three, apparently the most in any one town in the captaincy. According to Saint-Hilaire in 1819, a "prodigious" amount of cachaça was sold in Vila Boa.[17] Second to Vila Boa in number of taverns was Santa Luzia, with sixty *vendas* or taverns, third was São José do Tocantins with twenty-four, while Traíras had twenty-one and Cavalcante, eighteen. In the colonial period, taverns often did other business besides selling drinks. In towns such as Água Quente, which had only three dry goods stores, the fifteen taverns may have conducted other types of businesses. Small communities, such as Cachoeira and Ferreiro, had no stores but four and eight taverns, respectively.

In contrast to the 1783 accounting of the retail sector, the 1820s household lists reveal that there were few men or women identified as doing business in most towns. In Água Quente, Roza, pardo, age fifty-eight, was a negociante,

Table 5. Retail businesses in the captaincy of Goiás, 1783

Town	Whites	Dry goods	Wet goods	Taverns	Vendas[a]
Água Quente	48 men	3 *lojas*	—	15	—
Amaro Leite	27 men	—	2	11	—
Anta	340	3 *lojas*	1	5	6[b]
Arraias	64	3 *lojas*	—	14	—
Barra	24 men	1 *loja*	—	6	—
Cachoeira	5	—	—	4	—
Carmo	33	—	—	—	—
Cavalcante	72	6 or 7	2	18	—
Chapada	27	—	—	—	—
Cocal	76 men	4 *lojas*	—	14	—
Crixás	23	8 *lojas*	—	6[c]	—
Ferreiro	—	—	—	8	—
Ouro Fino	12	4	—	15	—
Pilar	32 couples	9	3	48[d]	—
Rio das Velhas	18	1[e]	—	—	—
Santa Cruz	57 couples	5	—	20	—
Santa Luzia	81 couples	14	1	60 *vendas* or taverns	
Santa Rita	5	1	—	9	—
São Felix	66 couples	1	—	—	—
São José do Tocantins	105	1	1	24	—
Traíras	72	5	2	21	—
Vila Boa	1,416	22	20	63	2[b]

Source: RJBN, manuscript section, cod. 16.3.2, Notícia Geral da Capitania de Goiás, 1783.
[a]A *venda* was a market stall or store where fruits and vegetables, as well as distilled sugarcane, were sold.
[b]The *botica* was an apothecary type of store where medicines were prepared and sold. 1 was in Anta and 2 were in Vila Boa.
[c]6 houses of commission for the *engenhos* of Pilar and "*tabernagens*."
[d]Taverns that received commissions from nearby *engenhos*.
[e]*Mercador* (cloth merchant).

along with João, crioulo, age thirty-five. The only white businessman was Joaquim José do Amaral, age thirty-nine. On the household lists of Porto Real, the only businessman was Francisco Rodrigues Nogueira, crioulo, age forty-eight, who did business with Pará. He also owned three slaves and had two agregados. Farther south in Santa Cruz, the two business men who were clearly white were the Portuguese, José Antônio Correia, age forty-eight, and Felippe Gomes Guimarães, age sixty-five, who had a house of business in Santa Cruz.

Of all the merchants and businessmen in the early nineteenth century, perhaps the most exceptional was Plácido Moreira de Carvalho, a merchant from Meia Ponte whose business clients were the indigenous nations of the Tocantins River. He had acquired an education and traveled widely, learning English and French. After living in England, he was in Portugal in 1810 when he was captured by Napoleon's troops, who were then occupying Portugal, and taken to Paris. After being ruined financially, he left France for Brazil, where he went to live among the Indians. Johann E. Pohl met him in the indigenous village of Cocal Grande in 1819 and reported that Carvalho's house, made of *barro* (clay) and palm fronds, was always filled with Indians. Apparently one reason for his success with those who lived in Cocal Grande was that he facilitated their trade with the merchants of the Tocantins River, bringing in goods then in demand by the indigenous communities. Carvalho himself also traveled on the Tocantins to Belém, presumably to bring trade goods back to Cocal Grande.[18]

Obviously Carvalho's trading post did not match the retail establishments of the rest of Goiás, nor is there evidence that he became wealthy from his trade with indigenous communities. But available household lists of 1783 or the 1820s document that most businessmen in former mining towns lost wealth in the late colonial period. In the 1780s most whites were involved in slave and mine ownership; by the 1820s most whites on the household lists surveyed were no longer in mining or business. They had clearly shifted to landownership of sugar plantations, ranches, or small farms. Although a minority held military titles, usually in the militias, and a few were skilled craftsmen, such as goldsmiths, all of these tendencies had already been there in the 1780s. Basically, the household lists for the 1820s suggest that mining was then unlikely to support a wealthy lifestyle, and business was also not an option for most whites because of the decline in available gold dust to pay for commodities imported from coastal ports. Therefore, control of land and people would be the key to future high social status and a higher standard of living.

Planters and Ranchers

Besides recording slaves on the mines and in the households, census takers in 1783 listed the number of slaves on engenhos (sugar plantations), *engenhocas* (small mills for sugar or manioc meal), and some ranches. Although historians usually view sugar plantations with more than one hundred slaves as characteristic of coastal Brazil, the captaincy also had many sugar plantations that

Table 6. Plantations, mills, and slaves, 1783

Julgado	Engenhos	Engenhocas	Slaves
Água Quente	2	—	—
Amaro Leite	2	—	—
Arraias	3	2	81
Cavalcante	5	9	250
Cocal	9	—	—
Meia Ponte	1	—	86
Muquém	—	1	—
Paranã, Ribeira do	8	—	80
Pilar	7	8[a]	428
Santa Cruz	4	—	94
Santa Luzia	14	3	453
Santa Rita	1	—	—
São José do Tocantins	10	—	—
Traíras	29[b]	—	1,112
Vila Boa	17	16	—

Source: RJBN, manuscript section, cod. 16.3.2, Notícia Geral da Capitania de Goiás, 1783.
[a]3 engenhocas were for manioc processing.
[b]21 engenhos were run by water and 8 by oxen.

produced sugar for the internal market, often in the form of rapadura (raw brown sugar in a brick form), molasses, and distilled sugarcane (aguardente or cachaça). Among the richest owners of engenhos in 1783 were the following men: Captain José Rodrigues Bragança, with two engenhos and 165 slaves in Traíras; Captain José da Costa Vieira of Santa Luzia, with 118 slaves; Captain Barnabé Moreira de Paiva, with two engenhos and 106 slaves in Traíras; Jacinto José Pinto dos Santos, with 101 slaves, also in Traíras; and Antônio Barradas Fontes, who owned the Engenho de São Lourenço with 100 slaves in Cavalcante. With so many slaves, these were exceptionally large establishments, and the enslaved Africans also labored at raising food crops, such as wheat, corn, manioc, and *azeite* (a vegetable oil), as well as cotton. More commonly, most slave owners had a few to forty slaves working on their engenhos or engenhocas (table 6).

Large numbers of slaves also continued to work on engenhos into the 1790s and 1820s. João Dias d'Aguiar, a captain of the Auxiliary Company, was one of the largest slaveholders, with two hundred slaves and a fine residence in Pilar. He possessed not only an engenho in 1791 but also good lands for farming, a lavra for gold, cattle, and uniformed slave musicians, who played the boxes, flutelike *pifanos*, clarinets, and trumpets. By 1801 the number of sugar engenhos had expanded further, which Governor D. João Manoel de Menezes (1800–1804) attributed to the arrival in Goiás of people from Minas Geraes and São Paulo. They were then cultivating many new lands that had previously been uncultivated.[19]

At least for the district around Cavalcante, we have some insight into its cattle ranches. In 1783 there were 106 ranches with cattle and horses on either side of the Paraná River that annually produced fifteen thousand crias (offspring). The scribe noted that their production would have been even greater if the cattle had not been eaten by jaguars, other cats ("tigres"), jacarés (caimans), and *sucuris* (large snakes) or troubled by bats. To care for the cattle, masters employed 280 slaves besides cowboys and other salaried employees. Natural predators, however, were not the only cause of cattle decline. The increase in the number of indigenous attacks led to the abandonment of many cattle ranches in the north. Where ranches survived in the north, ranchers often killed the cows and exported the males to nearby captaincies, such as Pernambuco and Minas Geraes. By 1828 only twenty-four cattle ranches had survived in the district of Cavalcante, but they were able to produce enough of a surplus to export cattle and hides to Bahia. Second in the number of ranches in the 1820s was Crixás, which had eighteen ranches that exported three hundred head of cattle.[20]

In 1828 more people in Cavalcante were earning their living from agriculture than from ranching. Small farmers then had 123 *lavouras* (farms), where they were cultivating a remarkable variety of food crops: wheat, manioc, corn, rice, beans, cotton, tobacco, coffee, and *mamona* (the castor-oil plant). There were also eight engenhos producing sugar, rapadura, and aguardente.[21]

In contrast to the wealthy who owned engenhos with a hundred or more slaves, some whites also had roças or other small plots of land for food production. In 1783 mines and roças were commonly linked together in patterns of slave ownership. Thus the wealthy mine owner who focused on gold mining usually employed some of his slaves in raising foodstuffs for all of them. The slaveholder's wealth, however, came from the ownership of the mine and its slaves rather than from ownership of roças—or from ownership of a large engenho where food crops were also raised. Whites were involved in this typical pattern, especially in the 1780s, but by the 1820s prominent whites (alvos) with more than thirty slaves were usually not listed with roças but rather as *lavradores* (farmers) in the sense of land holders. They also bore prominent military titles. In this way, the census takers distinguished them from those whites with roças and a few slaves or none at all, who were definitely not among the wealthy and privileged of the captaincy.[22]

In the district of Pilar in 1783 there were a large number of roças with *monjolos* (mills) in which they processed manioc meal. The roças sustained not only the district of Pilar but almost all of that of Crixás, where many of those who farmed had commission houses to sell their foodstuffs.[23] Such activities reveal that whites were also involved in the ownership of small farms and mills for manioc meal (*farinha*).

By the 1820s slaveholding whites of high status also combined farming with either an engenho or a ranch or both. In Pontal, for example, the commander general, Adjutant Tristão Pinto Cerqueira, had thirty-six slaves that he employed in farming and ranching, raising cattle and horses. The next-largest slaveholder, with thirty-four slaves, was Padre José da Franca Amaral, who owned both an engenho and fazenda in the district of Pontal in 1824. But most whites had fewer than twelve slaves, with some having none at all, suggesting the impoverishment of many whites in that district.[24]

Priests

After property ownership, especially of slaves, the next significant indicator of high status in the captaincy was the priesthood. But not all priests were of equal status and wealth, since many lived lives of poverty if they were dependent on unreliable clerical incomes. Nor were they always respected, since many pursued lives and loves to the contrary of community expectations and accumulated fortunes in land and gold, a hundred or more slaves, and numerous retainers and women in their households. Rather than devote themselves to their priestly duties, they spent their time administering their estates. Typical of this type of priest was the one described by Saint-Hilaire who had a sugar plantation near Conceição, where he was more preoccupied with making sugar than with religious conversion.[25]

Padre Monteiro de Araujo, with 130 slaves in Anta, was the wealthiest priest on the household lists of 1783 and the 1820s. Few secular slaveholders could rival his wealth in slaves. Second to him was Padre Paulo de Souza Pinto de Aguiar with 110 slaves, also of Anta. All other priests were notably below them in slave ownership—and they clearly held fewer slaves than the wealthiest secular men. The next-richest priests were Padre José Antônio de Araujo of

Traíras, with 45 slaves; Padre Francisco Alves Teixeira of São Félix, with 44 (37 in mining and 7 in the house); and Padre José da Franca Amaral of the district of Pontal with an engenho and 34 slaves in the 1820s. In Santa Rita in the district of Anta, Padre Francisco da Cruz Álvarez held 30 slaves, while in Barra Padre Fernando José da Motta employed 20 slaves in mining and food production on roças. All other priests had 8 or fewer slaves, which would put them in the category of modest or poor slaveholders. We do not know the size of the labor force of the following priests identified as having engenhos and mines in Vila Boa: Padre Francisco da Cruz Alves, who had an engenhoca; and with lavras, Padres João de Souza de Oliveira, Francisco Alves, Fernando José da Motta, Paulo de Souza Pinto e Aguiar, and Pedro Monteiro de Araujo. In any case, their clerical office and ownership of sugar plantations and mines would have placed them high in local society, especially if they came from prominent families.[26]

Military Officers

In spite of their status due to clerical orders and property and slave ownership, priests did not bear military titles, although there were priests who led bandeiras (see chapter 3). Those with military titles, even if only a lieutenant or captain, usually occupied the summit of local society or contested power to be the colonel. What are ubiquitous throughout the household lists are military titles for the wealthiest white men in each community. Some scribes, such as the one in Traíras, even rank-ordered the men with military titles in a type of hierarchy that paralleled slave ownership. For example, he listed the owners of lavras in this order: Colonel Manoel Lopes Chagas with eighty slaves; Colonel Mamedes Mendes Ribeiro with sixty; and Lieutenant Colonel Agostinho Álvarez Cardoso with ninety. They were then followed by three captains, a sergeant-mor, another captain, a lieutenant, and finally a second lieutenant with only twenty-four slaves. But the correspondence between the military hierarchy and numbers of slaves was not rigid, since the lower ranked sergeant had sixty slaves. In other cases, titles, such as guarda-mor, were also markers of those with the most wealth in mines, engenhos, ranches, and slaves.[27]

Therefore, a military title, the most prestigious of which were linked with Portuguese troops of the line, such as the mounted dragoons, gave additional status to a white man. Portuguese officers in the dragoons appear to have been the most prestigious in the captaincy, but ordinary soldiers in any of the military forces had no prestige at all and were commonly drafted against their will and treated badly. Most military titles were due to participation in local militias for whites, such as the ordenanças, and their responsibilities were to defend their communities against indigenous attacks. But if they lived in an area of the captaincy that was not at war, their only onerous responsibility was to march in religious processions, thus displaying their status and position in local society. Carrying bengalas (staffs), the elderly titled men also participated in some part of the rituals connected with the cavalhadas and Festas do Divino, but they saw no combat. Although their titles were largely honorific, they were clearly powerful men and wealthy slaveholders.[28]

Beginning with the petitions for honors, 1750–1824 (table 3), José de Oliveira Amado, a furriel in the dragoons, is first on the list; the next officers were an alferes (second lieutenant) of the dragoons, José Pinto da Fonseca, who had "conquered" the Karajá; and Lieutenant José Rodrigues Freire, also of the dragoons, who had contacted the Xavante and settled them at Carretão. He served in Goiás between 1765 and 1775; before then, he had fought in Uruguay in 1756. He had acquired some of his gold by leading bandeiras in which he discovered gold and captured fugitive blacks.[29] Captain-mor Francisco Xavier Leite also petitioned for the Order of Christ. All four men expected to secure the order because of their military service and delivery of eight arrobas of gold to the foundry house in Vila Boa.

This same pattern emerges when we turn to the 1783 lists of slaveholders. In Anta those with the most slaves working in the "Factories of Blacks" were an unnamed Lieutenant Colonel with 130, Lieutenant Francisco da Silva Braga with 50, and Alferes Silvestre Rodrigues Jardim with 40. Perhaps reflecting his lower status, Sergeant-mor Miguel Pereira de Amorim possessed only 36 slaves in Carmo, while Captain Domingos Antônio Cardoso had 60 slaves in Cavalcante. In Crixás Alferes Mathias de Crasto Aguiar and his associates held 200. Close behind him with 190 slaves was the guarda-mor José Francisco de Carvalho and partners. In Santa Luzia the most important mine owner was a colonel with 280 slaves, followed by a captain with 150. As usual, the correspondence between military ranking and number of slaves was not always exact; in Traíras Lieutenant Colonel Agostinho Álvarez Cardoso had 90 and Colonel Manoel Lopes Chagas owned 80.

By the 1820s, as in Traíras, ownership of engenhos, fazendas, and slaves often went hand in hand with a military title; thus Captain Barnabé Moreira de Paiva owned two engenhos and 106 slaves; Captain José Rodriguez Bragança held two engenhos and 165 slaves; Adjutant José da Silva Rocha had two engenhos and 87 slaves; and Alferes José Francisco Porto had one engenho and 43 slaves. Clearly, in the 1780s as well as in the 1820s, a high-ranking military title was one more marker of social position and wealth in Goiás. It also reflected the reality that many single men sent to serve in the military in the captaincy established families and helped found notable elite families, whose descendants still enjoy wealth and position in Goiás and Tocantins. On the whole, white men with high-ranking titles do not appear as poor men on household lists of the 1780s and 1820s, that is, without slaves.

Judges and Bureaucrats

The final marker of high status in Goiás was that of service as a judge or bureaucrat in the Portuguese government. In the colonial period these men owed their positions to the Crown, but they appear to have acquired their wealth in gold and slaves through corruption—if we are to believe the accusations of other Portuguese officials, who constantly complained about their ability to "acquire" the gold of Goiás. More honest men apparently did it by setting their slaves to mining; the dishonest ones accepted bribes and engaged in contraband trade to smuggle their new wealth out of the captaincy. Others simply stole the king's share at the foundry houses. Those in São Félix were especially skillful in siphoning gold into their own hands. There were many ways to accumulate wealth as a royal bureaucrat or judge in the late colonial period.[30]

Among those who petitioned for the Order of Christ, one of those who acquired gold was a treasurer, José Ribeiro da Fonçeca, and another, José Pedroso Lisboa, a notary of the fazenda. Significantly, both served in Goiás in positions with access to gold. A review of local bureaucrats and judges, however, reveals a greater variety of government offices that were combined with slave ownership. In 1783 the ordinary judge Antônio Rodriguez Pereira held sixty slaves, plus he also used another twelve in raising food crops in Cavalcante. The ordinary judge of Santa Luzia, João de Oliveira Rodriguez de Sá, was a more modest slaveholder with only twenty-two slaves. Two *licenciados* (degree holders) in Pilar in 1783 were Francisco Gomes Fição and André Vilella da Cunha e Roza. The first was part of a partnership with ninety-five slaves. Three men with the honorific title of doctor were also involved with engenhos and mines in Vila Boa: Dr. Ignacio José Álvares de Oliveira, Dr. José Pinto Ferreira, and the Goiano-born Dr. Gregorio da Costa Matos, who had

Table 7. Bureaucrats in São Félix, 1783

Position	Name	Number of slaves
Intendant	Unnamed	12
Judge of orphans	Félix de Moura Andrade	43
Fiscal	Captain José de Moura	48
Treasurer	Felipe Thomaz de Almeida	5
Scribe	Captain Manuel Luis Lisboa	7
Scribe	Adjutant João de Sant'Anna	2
Scribe	Captain Manoel Cabral Pinto	3
Assayer	Silverio Antônio de Mattos	6
#1 *fundidor*	João Ferreira Cortes	4
#2 *fundidor*	Ignacio da Silva Borges	1
Notary	João de Almeida Lara	1
Jailer	Manoel José Ribeiro	1
Lawyer	Bento de Brito Barros	15
Lawyer	Joaquim Nicolao	7

Source: RJBN, manuscript section, cod. 16.3.2, Notícia Geral da Capitania de Goiás, 1783.

studied law at the University of Coimbra. It is unlikely that they were medical doctors, since there were none in the captaincy, which had only surgeons attached to the military.[31]

Of all the household lists, the best profile of bureaucrats and slaveholding comes from São Félix, where most white males were listed with their occupations and slaves. Most obviously, the bureaucrats were linked with the foundry house of São Félix. Here slave ownership and political position did not necessarily go together, since the intendant clearly outranked the judge of orphans and the fiscal, with forty-three and forty-eight slaves respectively, while the intendant owned only twelve. Table 7 lists the men who held bureaucratic posts in São Félix along with the number of slaves that each one owned.

Such data was not provided for the foundry house of Vila Boa, but one presumes that similar individuals served the more important foundry house in the capital. Only one among many who made a career at the foundry house in Vila Boa was Dr. Gregório da Costa Matos, who worked there for twenty years. In 1786, at about fifty years of age, he was serving in the Junta de Justiça.[32]

In conclusion, the white male elites of the captaincy and province of Goiás in the 1780s and 1820s based their wealth and position at the top of the social structure on being "men of quality" and Christians who were white (or regarded as white); they also held a military or honorific title that recognized their high status and owned mines, large estates, and a hundred or more slaves. Many also added to their income by engaging in trade within the captaincy and nearby provinces. Their elevated social position in each district could even lead them to serve on the Senado da Camara, which was composed of the "good men" of each town, although their political power was always limited by the Portuguese colonial system. As members of the Senado, however, they could appeal directly to the Crown in Lisbon. Some also married in the Catholic Church and had white wives, or at least parda wives (chapter 9). As a consequence, their children were born legitimate and inherited their property. Many who were Portuguese by birth left the captaincy after the decline of the mines and independence, but their mistresses along with their mulato children remained in the province. In the nineteenth century their children would claim social position and property based on who their fathers and grandfathers had been. By the 1820s, as we will see in chapter 10, many of the racially mixed had moved into middle status positions, leaving behind both slavery and poverty. The small white elite, however, struggled to survive in isolation, especially in the north. Yet in spite of their material poverty and loss of slaves, they would build new wealth in the nineteenth century based on agriculture and ranching.

CHAPTER 7

"Masters of the Dance"

Enslaved Africans and Crioulos

On the feast days of Our Lady of the Rosary and St. Benedict, the "captives," wearing masks, used to dance with all kinds of amusements. The congadas of more recent times have continued the dancing tradition in the City of Goiás, but without the masks of the 1780s.[1] The use of masks and dancing on sacred occasions calls to mind that the third great population group in the captaincy of Goiás was not of indigenous or Portuguese descent but African, and they occupied an ambiguous position between the indigenous nations and their colonial rulers and enslavers. At times Africans formed a part of the colonial regime as enslaved miners and free blacks; at other times they revolted and created autonomous communities of fugitive slaves (quilombos). This chapter, therefore, will survey who the Africans were in terms of numbers and national identities; their coerced labor in the mines, fields, and households; and finally their resistance to enslavement in the form of slave revolts and flights to quilombos. Other points of contact will be examined in subsequent chapters. In effect, this chapter seeks to document that the captaincy of Goiás was most ethnically diverse, and historians cannot use a North American construction of white-Indian conflicts because Africans and their descendants also played pivotal roles. Without enslaved Africans and free/freed black men and women, the Portuguese could not have extracted the region's wealth in gold or defeated the indigenous nations who attacked the mines.

Early Arrivals and Gold Discoveries

The exact date of the arrival of the first Africans in the modern states of Tocantins and Goiás may never be known. At most, we can only point to possible times of entry into the captaincy of Goiás with the first missionary

Figure 15. The king of Congo, here dressed in blue and white with a golden crown, is remembered in a congada at the feast of Pentecost in the 1980s. Photograph courtesy of Mary C. Karasch.

expeditions and Paulista bandeiras, but the official narratives do not specify whether the "captives," "negros," or "slaves" were indeed Africans or indigenous captives. Even the use of the term "negro" can be misleading because in the early colonial period negros da terra (blacks of the land) were not blacks but indigenous peoples.[2] In 1612, for example, the São Paulo inventory of Martins Rodrigues, who died that year, listed "a black woman" (negra) of the Guoya (Goiá) nation, slave of Domingos Rodrigues of Paraúpava, along with three children, who were appraised at 22$000 réis. In 1611 another inventory identified two Carajaúna (Karajá) women as negras: one was elderly and the other was a "new black," or someone who was new to slavery. Both inventories were using negra in the sense of negro da terra, thus documenting Karajá enslavement as early as 1611–1612.[3]

In the seventeenth century, therefore, "captives" who accompanied bandeiras to Goiás were most likely to be indigenous men and women, since Africans imported into São Paulo were rare and expensive. When Gilka Salles examined inventories from São Paulo, she located fifty-three slaves, only four of whom were Africans, between 1610 and 1612. She also determined that one Guiné African was worth the price of four indigenous captives, thirty-two head of cattle, or twenty horses.⁴ Why the Africans were so costly was probably due to their scarcity and later to their reputed skills in mining. In contrast, indigenous captives were more common, since the bandeiras could enslave thousands. Consequently, the "captives" who accompanied Paulista bandeiras to Goiás as porters, servants, and guides were usually born in Brazil rather than in Africa.

All this changed, however, with the discovery of gold. In the 1720s Bartolomeu Bueno, the second Anhangüera, took 152 armed men on his bandeira, including 20 Indians and 35 slaves. Over the three years that he sought gold, between 1722 and 1725, he lost twenty-five slaves; and only ten of them returned to São Paulo with him.⁵ Bueno's second expedition to the Vermelho River, in 1726, possibly included some Africans, since his men intended to establish mining camps and pan for gold. After the Goiá revolted against them, they took Goiá men back to São Paulo as war captives.⁶ Apparently they kept some women to serve them in the future Vila Boa. Thus indigenous captives and a few Africans may have made up the early enslaved population of Vila Boa.

As the mining boom developed, more African men were brought to pan for or wash gold on or near the Vermelho River to its juncture with the Araguaia River. After that time Africans would be located in the centers of "gold washing" at Barra, Ferreiro, Anta, Ouro Fino, Santa Rita, and Pilar.⁷ That Africans were already resident in Goiás by 1726–1727 can be documented from two *bandos* (official proclamations). The first forbade Indians and blacks from selling gold as if it belonged to them. The second ordered the whipping of fugitive Africans who lived near other residents. Furthermore, anyone who did not denounce their flight would be fined.⁸ From the beginning, therefore, repressive regulations reveal that Africans were already finding gold on their own, running away, and resisting enslavement. As of 1729, the settlement of Santa Cruz on the road to São Paulo probably also had Africans resident there. The nearby Peixe River would later yield a fortune in alluvial gold.⁹

The next concentration of Africans came in the 1730s, when Manuel Rodrigues Tomás exploited rich sources of gold ore in the Pireneus mountain range and along the Almas River. He also founded Meia Ponte (now Pirenópolis) in 1731. The great amount of gold discovered there quickly attracted miners and their enslaved Africans. Only a year later a convoy from Bahia illegally imported "some slaves" and cattle to Meia Ponte. According to Luís Palacin, Meia Ponte soon rivaled Vila Boa, in part due to its location at the juncture of three trade routes: to São Paulo, to Rio de Janeiro via Minas Gerais, and to Bahia.¹⁰

The gold-rush fever quickly spread to nearby locations. In 1737, fugitive blacks who were panning for gold discovered some in the small stream of Jaraguá; the settlement of Jaraguá soon attracted a large population of black miners. There were also some blacks in Corumbá, which was initially settled in 1729. Along the Claro and Pilões Rivers in Kayapó territory, miners soon found diamonds, although indigenous attacks usually made it difficult to mine there.[11]

To the north of Meia Ponte and Jaraguá prospectors also discovered the "mines of the Tocantins." As of 1732 perhaps twelve thousand miners had reached the Maranhão River, where they secured abundant gold with only a few hours of work. According to Gilka Salles, these mines involved alluvial gold located in the riverbeds and along the riverbanks. Many Africans were then imported to the richest locations of alluvial gold, that is, the Arraial do Maranhão (1730), Água Quente (1732), Traíras (1735), São José do Tocantins (1735), and Cachoeira (1736).[12]

According to tradition, as narrated by Padre Luiz Antônio da Silva e Souza, the miners of the Maranhão River had diverted the river from its normal riverbed for at least a year. Thousands of slaves had once worked on the massive project or in washing gold, discovering "leaves of gold." But the river soon reclaimed its normal pathway, and a great epidemic that killed fifty people a day struck the Arraial do Maranhão, forcing the survivors to move to Água Quente in 1732. Still others left the Maranhão River and the settlement of São Sebastião on the left bank of the river to settle along the Ouro Fino River and on nearby mountains. Another mining town, São José do Tocantins, also grew in population. In general, the failure of the Maranhão River project led to the transfer of surviving Africans to other mining locations.[13]

To the west of these mines, and actually closer to the Araguaia River, were the mines discovered in Crixás in 1734. Although the mining town took its name from an indigenous people, the Crixá, most of its population came to be African, as many gold strikes were made along the Crixás River. By 1741 at least 2,736 slaves were taxed in Crixás (table B.7). As of 1762, one mining society alone had three hundred slaves, and by 1779 almost 80 percent of the population of Crixás was "black."[14]

Farther north in the captaincy, even more gold was located during the 1730s and 1740s. The great mines in and near Natividade were discovered in 1734, next came Traíras in 1735, then São Félix in 1734–1736, and Pontal and Porto Real in 1738. According to Salles, the second great center of gold productivity was the region of Traíras. Since the Tocantins River runs through the rugged rocks of this region, the river made it possible to mine during the dry season.

Near Traíras was São José do Tocantins, which also had many productive gold works after 1735.[15] The gold was so plentiful that 2,666 slaves were working there by 1741 (table B.8).

The 1740s brought even more discoveries of gold—and more Africans to the captaincy. One of the largest strikes was in Arraias in 1739. According to tradition, its first inhabitants were the gold miners of the Chapada dos Negros, which was the site of a quilombo. Shortly thereafter there were 3,169 slaves working in Arraias (table B.8). In 1740 gold was also found at Cavalcante and in 1741 at Papuã (now Pilar), and soon after at Conceição, by 1745.[16] The Luso-Brazilian settlement of Papuã began in 1741, when João Godói Pinto Silveira reached the mines of Papuã, which were then occupied by fugitive slaves who were apparently living in a quilombo and supporting themselves by mining gold. The gold rush that ensued took over their mines, and the new men built a church dedicated to Nossa Senhora do Pilar. Thereafter the mining town would be known as Pilar. Fugitive slaves who had been mining in the Córrego (creek) do Quilombo also led a bush captain to the rich mines of Tesouras in 1757.[17] What is obvious from the examples of Pilar and Tesouras is that fugitive slaves were sometimes the ones who actually discovered the gold that others exploited to enrich themselves.

The last three major discoveries of this period were in Cocal in 1751, Santa Luzia (now Luziânia) in 1746, and Carmo in 1747.[18] Thus, by the mid-eighteenth century, African miners were scattered throughout the center and northeast of the captaincy (map 5). Consequently, there would be a concentration of enslaved Africans, mostly males, in the mining cores, while the rest of the captaincy was still held by autonomous indigenous nations and fugitive slaves in quilombos.

Estimated Slave Population, 1730s–1740s

The initial period of enslavement in the captaincy does not permit many insights into the number of Africans who worked in the mines, much less their specific identities or cultural traditions. It is only with the *capitação*, or tax on slaves, imposed in the 1730s, that historians can begin to estimate the minimum number of Africans who mined in the region. The Portuguese, however, were able to count only twelve thousand to eighteen thousand slaves per year during the mining boom from 1736 to 1750. Undoubtedly many Africans were never counted due to the ease of tax evasion in that period, about which there were many complaints by Portuguese officials. Furthermore, the nature of mining along the rivers led to frequent changes of mine locations without official knowledge.[19]

Prior to 1750 it is uncertain how many Africans were imported into the captaincy or how they journeyed there, although it is probable that they accompanied mule teams from São Paulo or walked with convoys of dry goods and horses from Bahia, Minas Gerais, or Rio de Janeiro. Still others traveled via canoe down the Tocantins River from Belém. According to official sources, the first legal convoy of "negros" entered Goiás in 1752.[20] Obviously, most Africans had been brought to Goiás without being counted or having taxes levied on them, especially in the north.

One of the largest documented convoys of slaves brought from Salvador, Bahia, arrived in Meia Ponte (Pirenópolis) in 1755. After a journey of six months, the convoy of 260 slaves under the command of Sergeant-mor Antônio José de Campos brought the image of Our Lord of Bonfim to be installed in the church there. According to local tradition, the convoy's slaves obtained their freedom in compensation for the safe delivery of the statue.[21] Five years later, in 1760, the governor reported on the entry of convoys that had introduced only 770 slaves to the captaincy. The small scale of the legal slave trade to Goiás is also obvious in 1767, when 1,123 slaves were registered upon their entry into the captaincy: 464 passed through São João das Três Barras; 158 via Rio das Velhas; 114, Bosqueirão; 109, São Bartolomeu; 104, Estrema; and 80, Duro. In addition, Muquém reported 54, Cavalcante 29, São Marcos 7, and Taguatinga only 4.[22]

Consequently, by the 1770s governors of Goiás were complaining about the shortage of Africans, and official registries recorded only 1,208 new slaves entering the captaincy between 1791 and 1799.[23] Even fewer new Africans arrived in the captaincy between 1800 and 1804. In the early nineteenth century most Africans traveled in small numbers from coastal ports, usually bought on commission. Such was the case of Michaela Xavier de Aguirre, who gave 230 oitavas of gold to a "comboieiro of slaves," Captain Gaspar José Lisboa, to buy three *moleques* (young boys) of the Mina nation. He was to pay about 80$000 réis each in the slave market of Salvador, Bahia.[24]

Although it is difficult to document the total number of Africans imported in this early period, the head tax on slaves (the capitação) indicates a minimum number of enslaved blacks resident in the captaincy between 1736 and 1750. At that time, slaveholders had to pay a tax in gold for each one of their slaves, but not all did so. The capitação records for the 1730s, however, reveal the locations of slave miners who were taxed, and it is no surprise that the region of the capital registered the most taxed slaves. According to Palacin, the total number of slaves (and freedmen) in 1736 was 10,263, which included 4,021 in Santa Anna, 1,366 in Crixás, and 1,196 in São José, plus another 3,682 new arrivals.[25] Thus in one year alone almost 3,700 new slaves had been introduced to Goiás. A year later the total number of the enslaved had increased to 12,589, with a small drop to 12,498 in 1738. The next two years reveal for the south that there were 7,346 in 1739 but only 5,055 in 1740. Either there was significant tax evasion, which is highly probable, or masters shifted their slaves to the north. In 1741 the total rose to 15,321, most likely driven by the new gold strikes in Papuã (Pilar).

In spite of their limitations, the tax figures for 1740–1749 reveal shifts in the enslaved population and document the flexible migration patterns typical of miners and their enslaved Africans. Between 1741 and 1749 most of the taxed slaves lived in the intendency of Santa Anna, with 4,836 in 1748. Second in the size of its slave population in 1741 was Crixás (2,736), followed by Meia Ponte (1,336). In 1749, however, the new mines of Pilar had attracted 2,762 slaves, while Meia Ponte at 1,086 and Crixás at 1,432 had lost Africans. Additional slaves were moved to Santa Luzia (262) and Santa Cruz (206). By 1749 almost 11,000 slaves labored in the south (table B.7).

In the north of the captaincy, the largest numbers of Africans were living in São José do Tocantins (3,817) in 1742, followed by Arraias in 1741 (3,169). The development of the mines in Natividade more than doubled its slave population, from 730 in 1741 to 1,820 in 1749. But Raimundo José da Cunha Matos claimed that Natividade had once employed 40,000 slaves in mining.[26] The wealth of the mines of Natividade appears to have drawn slave labor away from Arraias, because only 229 slaves were counted there in 1749. The other Africans were working in São Félix (1,017). Overall, the north actually lost taxed slaves between 1741 and 1749. Almost 7,000 had been counted in 1741, most likely due to the gold rush in Arraias, but the total had declined to 6,264 by 1749. In great part this was due to northern resistance to payment of the capitação tax and resentment of the higher tax imposed in the north.[27] According to Salles, the sum total of the captaincy's slaves in 1749 was only 17,154, which is clearly too low (table B.7). A year later an estimate put the total enslaved population of the captaincy of Goiás at 20,000, although Governor D. Marcos de Noronha (1749–1755) officially recorded a decline of captives, to 14,437.[28]

The Enslaved Population after 1750

In 1750 the Portuguese abolished the hated capitação tax because of the difficulty of collecting it and shifted to a new system of collecting gold at foundry houses in Vila Boa and São Félix. Therefore historians are missing data on the number of enslaved Africans for almost thirty years (1750–1779), when apparently there were no official tallies of the captaincy's enslaved population. Only after a significant decline in the quinto did the Portuguese return to trying to determine the number of blacks in the captaincy who could mine gold. The first significant accounting of the captaincy's black population took place in 1779, but there was no differentiation between the number of black slaves and freedmen or free blacks (tables B.11–B.12). According to the census of 1779, there were 26,184 black males and 8,698 black females in the captaincy out of a total population of 54,489, excluding 1,219 newborns of unknown color.[29] In other words, almost two-thirds of the captaincy's population was then defined as black. In some julgados (judicial districts) the proportion of blacks rose to over 70 percent, as was the case in Crixás (79.9 percent), Cavalcante (75.9 percent), Carmo (75.6 percent), and Pontal (73.4 percent), which were all major mining centers (appendix B).

The accounting of the black population of 1779 and thereafter clarifies the government's efforts to determine the number of blacks, free, freed, and enslaved, who would be available to mine for gold. The more detailed census of 1783, however, also includes the captaincy's enslaved population and suggests important characteristics of its transformations (table B.11–12). Once again it is obvious that the institution of slavery—or at least of counted slaves—was most dominant in Vila Boa in 1782 and in all future census years. The reason is simply proximity to the census takers, who were parish priests and military officers. What is of particular interest is that the total of 4,689 slaves for 1783 is only slightly higher than the 4,461 slaves of 1742 and slightly less than the 4,720 in 1749—or the 4,432 registered in 1804 (table B.4). The figures for Santa Anna/Vila Boa are remarkably consistent over half a century. Only after 1804 did Vila Boa lose slaves, with the number of slaves declining to 3,073 in 1832 (table B.6).

Another center of slavery after 1779 was the julgado of Traíras. It was usually recorded as part of the Comarca of the North, except in 1804, when it was included in the southern comarca. The 1825 and 1832 census takers returned Traíras to the north, thus decreasing overall totals in the south but raising them in the north. Wherever Traíras fell in terms of administrative juggling, the numbers illustrate that it had the second largest enslaved population in most census years. It was at its highest in 1789 at 6,245, but its lowest number did not occur until 1832, at 1,441 (table B.9). Aside from these two largest julgados, which consistently registered the most slaves, the enslaved population in the other julgados surged and waned with shifts in the mining strikes.

The census of 1789 may have been among the more accurate of this fifty-year period, and census takers took more complete records by age. This was also a period of revived mining—as indicated by the quinto collection registered in Lisbon. It is in 1789 that a sizeable enslaved population was first documented in the captaincy, one that was larger than those officially recorded during the so-called mining boom of 1750. Although the captaincy was allegedly characterized by economic decadence, the figures for the enslaved population reveal the contrary. They suggest that the captaincy's economy was stronger than the Portuguese believed. Not only had the enslaved populations of the three julgados of Vila Boa, Traíras, and Meia Ponte soared in size, to 9,200, 6,245, and 4,777 slaves respectively, but the other julgados had also seen notable increases as well. In 1789 the fourth-largest julgado was Santa Luzia, whose enslaved population had jumped from 899 in 1783 to 2,960 in 1789. Fifth largest was São Félix, the site of a foundry house, where slaves numbered 2,707. Also with more than 2,000 slaves was Crixás, with 2,444, and Natividade, with 2,338, while Pilar had almost 2,000, at 1,967. Population growth in the far south was reflected in the more than 1,000 slaves (1,223) then resident in Santa Cruz (table B.9).

The transitory and irregular nature of census taking in a frontier region is then notable in the next census of 1792, which registered a slight upward trend, to 38,533 slaves, but also showed considerable movement between julgados, as miners uprooted their gangs of slaves and took them on to the next important strikes. Vila Boa and Traíras both experienced decreases in their slave population, to 8,568 and 5,328, respectively, while Meia Ponte had only 4,855 slaves. Pilar's slave population rose to fourth place, at 3,839, an increase of 1,872 slaves. In fifth place was São Félix, at 2,599, but Santa Luzia had dropped to 2,491 and sixth place. Most striking of all is that Rio das Velhas was apparently responsible for some of these dislocations, because its enslaved population soared from 277 in 1789 to 2,261 in 1792. The addition of 1,872 slaves in Pilar and 1,984 in Rio das Velhas indicates that a mining boom was underway in those two julgados (table B.9).

In contrast, the 1804 census documents economic decadence in the julgados, as most julgados experienced a decline in the number of slaves after the boom year of 1792, with some julgados losing 50 percent or more of their enslaved population between 1792 and 1804. By 1804 the Portuguese could find only 20,027 slaves (table B.9) in the captaincy of Goiás. What is also of interest, however, is the contrast in the number of slaves recorded in 1782 and 1804. If the 1782 census is accurate, and if we look only at the 1782 and 1804 censuses, it is obvious that most julgados actually saw large decreases in their enslaved population. Thus the number of slaves in Meia Ponte declined from 4,545 in 1782 to 2,282 in 1804. Santa Luzia also lost slaves, from 2,543 to 1,264, as did Pilar, from 3,772 to 1,575. Furthermore, Crixás's slave population dropped from 2,100 in 1782 to a low of 634 in 1804, suggesting that gold mining was collapsing there and that slaveholders were moving their enslaved Africans to other mining towns.

In the northern comarca, Traíras's enslaved population declined from 6,080 in 1782 to 2,807 in 1804, and São Félix's dropped from 2,681 in 1782 to 641 in both 1804 and 1825. Although one julgado in the north showed an increase— Cavalcante, from 921 slaves in 1782 to 1,209 in 1804—most lost slaves, such as Arraias, which went from 1,085 slaves in 1782 to 469 in 1804; and Natividade, which went from 3,398 to 1,529 in the same years (table B.9).

What the 1804 census suggests, therefore, is that there was a significant drop in recorded numbers between 1782 and 1804, especially in julgados such as Vila Boa and Crixás. Elite consensus on the decadence of gold mining and the loss of enslaved Africans is further confirmed by the two censuses of 1825 and 1832. Although Vila Boa still reported the most slaves, the new provincial government of Goiás could locate only 3,274 slaves in the capital in 1825. For the first time since 1782, Vila Boa's slaves numbered less than 4,000. The withdrawal of the Portuguese upon independence undoubtedly influenced the decline of slavery in the capital, as Portuguese officers and bureaucrats took their enslaved Africans with them or permitted them to purchase their freedom. Without replacements of new Africans for the aged African men who had died, Vila Boa continued to lose enslaved blacks, whose numbers fell to a low of 3,073 in 1832 (table B.9).

Meia Ponte also lost enslaved blacks, seeing their numbers decline from the 4,777 recorded in 1789 to 1,842 in 1825 and 1,800 in 1832. Santa Luzia maintained 741 slaves in 1825 and again in 1832, a number that was significantly lower than the figure of almost 3,000 (2,960) in 1789. Pilar reveals a similar pattern. The largest number of slaves recorded was 3,839 (1792), but only 1,033 remained in 1832. Overall, the number of slaves in the southern comarca had declined from 25,212 in 1792 to 8,412 in 1825 and 8,130 in 1832. The latter two figures were also lower than the documented 23,265 slaves of 1782. If we remove

Traíras and its 2,807 slaves from the 1804 count, however, the southern comarca would have had only 11,844 slaves in 1804. In spite of Goiano officials moving Traíras around, the census figures clearly document that the total number of enslaved blacks in the southern comarca fell to 8,412 in 1825 and 8,130 in 1832 (table B.9).

In contrast to the south, the northern comarca experienced even more significant declines in slave numbers, or at least in the ability of the new provincial government to obtain accurate numbers on them. In 1789 most slaves resided in Traíras (6,245), but by 1825 there were only 1,493, with 1,441 in 1832. Both figures were significantly lower than the 2,807 of 1804 or 6,080 of 1782, but they were the largest recorded for the two provincial censuses. No other julgados in the north had even a thousand documented slaves in 1825 or 1832. The highest number was 904 for Natividade in 1825, a figure that dropped slightly, to 879, in 1832. Arraias, however, had actually increased its slave population from 469 in 1804 to 765 in 1825 and 792 in 1832, while the slave population of the newly created capital of the comarca, Vila de São João, rose from 78 in 1825 to 228 in 1832. All others declined, as did the overall figures. In 1782, 14,925 slaves had been counted in the north; in 1789 the number was about the same, at 14,461, but in 1804 it fell to 5,376 (excluding 2,807 in Traíras). By 1825 there were only 4,963, and there were 5,131 in 1832. Together both comarcas had only 13,261 slaves in 1832, in sharp contrast to the 38,533 recorded in 1792. The drop in the enslaved population between 1792 and 1804 confirms the erosion of black slavery in the captaincy and its continued decline from 1825 to 1832. In particular, the number of those born in Africa decreased due to the deaths of the elderly men who had been imported in the eighteenth century.

African and *Crioulo* Nations

Numbers alone, however, reveal little about the enslaved Africans and their descendants who labored in the captaincy, and we must also examine a variety of other sources, including tax records and baptismal registries. In other parts of Brazil, tax records were burned at the time of abolition in 1888, but many survived in Goiás.[30] Particularly useful is the *meia-sisa*, or tax on the sale of manumitted and ladino slaves (Africans who had learned how to speak Portuguese and work in the house or fields). The meia-sisas clarify that the identities of the enslaved African population in the late colonial period varied from the northern comarca to the southern comarca. Table 8 reveals that the northern comarca had received a majority of its Africans from West Africa, who were usually identified as Mina, except for a minority of Nagô (Yoruba) and Guiné. Additional ethnic groups from West Africa further document the prevalence of West Africans in the north. In other words, two-thirds (66.7 percent) of the enslaved Africans in the north had originated in West Africa; an earlier sample from Arraias (1739–1800) documents a similar percentage (65 percent) of West Africans (Minas and Nagôs).[31]

The appearance of Guiné, however, raises questions. A regimental list of the black troops in the Henriques from São José do Tocantins gives an even more prominent place to the people of Guiné. According to the roster of black soldiers and their officers, which had been compiled sometime before 1799, only six soldiers were Guinés, but many of the other soldiers had at least one parent who was born in Guiné. All of the other African men were listed as Mina.[32] Were these Guiné among the Africans sold from Guinea-Bissau to Belém and Maranhão? In the eighteenth century Guinea-Bissau was the site of a Portuguese fort and trading factory that sent many enslaved Africans to Brazil. The Guiné were also apparently more common in Brazil in the eighteenth century than later, since the parents of the black troops of São José were more likely to have been born in Guiné than were the next generation.

The northern comarca also had enslaved Angolas, one Benguela, and two Mutecos from Congo North. The populations of Central Africa were clearly less well known to the scribes of the northern comarca, and most Africans were simply termed Angolas. In fact, in many parts of the north a single Angolan man often lived among Mina slaves or with indigenous communities; Joaquim Angola, for example, became a war chief among the Apinaje.[33]

In sharp contrast, the southern comarca, excluding Vila Boa, whose meia-sisas are not part of this sample, had a smaller percentage of West Africans than Central Africans (37.6 percent v. 62.4 percent). Angolas were far more significant in the south than in the north, and they frequently appear, along with Congos and Benguelas, in other types of documentation, such as inventories, manumissions, and parish registers. The southern comarca evidently received more of its slaves via the trade routes from Rio de Janeiro, and its enslaved Africans probably mirrored those imported into Rio de Janeiro. The Minas, however, had most likely traveled from Bahia to Vila Boa.

Another type of tax record that records ethnicity is a tax of 1$000 réis imposed on 469 slaves from the City of Goiás in 1837 and 1838. This sample of records regarding ethnicity also confirms the small number of Africans identified as Mina (8), Usá (Hausa) (1), and Caboré (4). The rest were from Central

Table 8. Africans sold in the captaincy of Goiás, 1810–1824

	West Africans			Central Africans		
	Mina	Nagô	Other[a]	Angola	Other[b]	Total
NORTH						
São João da Palma	1	—	—	2	—	3
Traíras	27	2	1 Mina[c]	9	—	39
Cavalcante	1	1	1 Nagano	3	1 Cabunda	7
Flores	2	—	1 Guiné	1 freedman	—	4
Arraias	2	—	—	2	—	4
Conceição	3	—	1 Busa	3	—	7
Natividade	10	—	1 Cobû	4	1 Benguela	16
Porto Real	7	1	4[d]	4	3[e]	19
Total, north	53	4	9	28	5	99
SOUTH						
Vila Boa	—	—	—	—	—	—
Meia Ponte	4	2	—	12	3[f]	21
Santa Luzia	2	1	—	7	2[g]	12
Santa Cruz	—	—	—	1	—	1
Bonfim	—	—	—	4	—	4
Pilar	5	—	—	7	1 Congo	13
Crixás	16	4	—	8	1 Banguella	29
Araxá	—	—	1 Guiné	—	5[h]	6
Desemboque	—	—	—	2	5[i]	7
Total, south	27	7	1	41	17	93
Sum total	80	11	10	69	22	192

Source: Mary Karasch, "Central Africans in Central Brazil, 1780–1835," in Heywood, *Central Africans*, tables 4.9–4.10, pp. 137–38. Table 8 has combined information from tables 4.9 and 4.10 in that article.
[a] Others in West Africa.
[b] Others in Central Africa.
[c] Mina Segode to do (Mina, all blind).
[d] Guiné, Sabarû, Tapa, and Ussá.
[e] 1 Canjongo and 2 Mutecos.
[f] 1 Congo, 1 Bonguela, and 1 Comunda.
[g] 1 Banguela and 1 Banguita.
[h] 2 Benguela, 1 Camundá, 1 Songa, and 1 Cassange.
[i] 3 Benguela, 1 Banguela, and 1 Mofumbe.

Africa, with 4 from Congo, 30 from Angola, 1 from Banguela, and 1 from Casange. There were also 22 Africans whose identity is uncertain or unknown. Only 15 percent of the 469 slaves were African. What is also of interest about this small sample of enslaved Africans is that the 37 female Africans outnumbered the 34 male Africans.[34]

These tax records point to vast regions in Africa and reveal little about specific individuals and their identities. To refine our understanding of the African population of Goiás further, there are still other sources, such as baptismal registries. Upon arrival in the mining towns of the captaincy, many, but not all, of the newly enslaved were baptized. Some had already been baptized in coastal ports or before departure from the Portuguese African colonies, and many masters simply ignored the baptism of their slaves.[35] Fortunately, there are baptismal registries that provide information on the identities of adult Africans and the mothers and infants who were baptized. Africans also enter the historical record as godparents. Four samples, from Santa Luzia, Vila Boa, Jaraguá, and Carmo, provide further insights into African ethnicities or nations in Goiás.

Fragments of baptismal registries survive for Santa Luzia for the period 1749 to 1754. They reveal that four Mina men were baptized in 1754, plus another man identified as MuCambique. Five children of Mina mothers were also baptized. So few individuals might suggest that there were no Central Africans resident in Santa Luzia, but two Angolan men served as godfathers and another Angola was the actual father of Vicencia, the legitimate child of Francisco Angola and Thereza Mina. Unfortunately, no nation was recorded for godmothers; they were all black freedwomen *(forras)*, except for Quiteria Pinta, who was still enslaved in 1754. Finally, two Bororo women and one infant were recorded as *administradas* in 1753.[36]

In contrast to the sparseness of data on slaves baptized in Santa Luzia, far more Africans and their children were baptized in the Church of St. Ann in Vila Boa and nearby chapels between 1794 and 1827, where there were 157 adult baptisms. In terms of national identities, there were 48 Minas, followed by 47 Angolas, and 19 Congos. More specific names linked to Central Africa were Robôllo (Libolo), Banguella, Cabinda, and Munjollo (Tio slaves). Overall, more than half of the Africans baptized at St. Ann's had come from Central Africa. In addition to the 48 Minas, the scribes listed only 3 Nagôs and 2 Buças for West Africa. Even 5 Africans had traveled all the way to Central Brazil from Mozambique in East Africa.[37]

This sample of adult baptisms not only registers the existence of Africans in

Vila Boa but also reveals shifts in ethnicity over time. Between 1794 and 1806, only two adult Angolas were baptized at St. Ann's, suggesting that few had been imported in that period or that Angolas had been baptized elsewhere. In contrast, fifteen Minas received the sacrament of baptism. Beginning in 1807, however, there were renewed baptisms of Angolas; overall, forty-five Angolas and nineteen Congos received baptism. Apparently the revival of the slave trade into Rio de Janeiro after the arrival of the Portuguese court in 1808 led to the introduction of more Central Africans, until the early 1820s; no adult Africans were baptized in 1821–1822. The situation had become so desperate for slaveholders that they petitioned the royal court in Rio de Janeiro to authorize the Royal Treasury to buy slaves for them in Africa.[38]

This sample also suggests that the trade in Mina slaves from Salvador to Vila Boa had collapsed. Between 1794 and 1813, twenty-seven Minas plus three Nagôs and two Buças were baptized in Vila Boa. Then, between 1814 and 1817, another twenty Minas were baptized, including twelve who belonged to one master, who may have had them purchased for him on the coast. After 1817, however, not one adult Mina was baptized until 1826, when a single Mina received baptism. Apparently the internal slave trade in Minas had declined, or Mina slaves no longer converted and accepted baptism. The first explanation is more likely, because there was also a sharp decline in the number of Mina parents of baptized children—only three men and two women were so identified after 1807. In contrast, eleven Mina fathers and two Mina mothers had baptized their children in 1794 and 1798.[39]

Yet another measure of the prevalence of Angolas and of the decline of Minas in Vila Boa comes from the baptisms of the children of unmarried African mothers. Between 1794 and 1805, Angolan mothers had 44 infants baptized—20 more than in the later period, 1806–1817. In contrast, Mina women had 31 infants baptized between 1794 and 1805, with a drop to only 13 from 1806 to 1817. Overall, 91 infants of Angolan mothers (64.5 percent) were baptized, versus 50 of Mina mothers (35.5 percent), for a total of 141 baptized infants of African mothers. In other words, this sample of mothers suggests that almost two-thirds of the African mothers resident in Vila Boa in the late colonial period were Angolas—a higher percentage than that for the adults baptized.[40]

Another sample of baptisms from Jaraguá is for a more limited time period, from 1824 to 1832. In this period only twelve "adult" Africans were baptized: nine males and three females. They were six Cabindas, three Angolas, and one Nagô; two others had no nation listed. Five of them were between twelve and fifteen years old, typical ages for Africans imported through Rio de Janeiro in the early nineteenth century.[41] Since so few adult Africans were baptized, we actually learn more about the baptized from the mothers, and on occasion the fathers. Of the fathers identified, only one was a Mina, and he was married to another Mina at the time of the baptism of the child. Furthermore, four mothers were from Angola and three from Congo; six others were crioulas. One widow was identified as of the Cobú nation.

What this small sample also reveals is that fourteen Africans were married to or living in a consensual union with a crioulo partner. Thus the Jaraguá baptisms suggest that the town's enslaved population was then in transition to a predominantly Brazilian-born population of color. As with the Africans, only two fathers were listed, and they were pardo or *cabra*; the other eleven were of unknown color, since only the mothers were recorded. There were twenty-eight infants baptized for crioula mothers, nine for cabras, nine for slave women, and one unknown. The total was fifty-eight Brazilian-born infants of color (48 percent).

The fourth sample of baptisms comes from the church of Nossa Senhora do Monte do Carmo for 1802 until 1812.[42] Unlike the separate book of slave baptisms in Vila Boa, these slave and forro (freed) baptisms were recorded along with baptisms of free people, as well as those of Indians. Unfortunately, the ethnic and national data are not as rich as for Vila Boa; most Africans were simply identified as Minas or Angolas, and others were crioulos. The limited data suggest that no adult Africans were baptized in this ten-year period, which may reflect the decline in the slave trade to the north, but eleven children of African mothers, most of whom were Minas, received baptism. In sharp contrast to the number of Angolan mothers in Vila Boa in a comparable period, only two Angolan mothers and one Lundû can be identified at Carmo. In the absence of Africans, local slaveholders were utilizing indigenous captives to labor for them. In the baptismal registry they were listed as children of the Kayapó or as adult Temembõ (Krahô). Overall, there were four indigenous children, eight of unknown age, and one whose nation was recorded illegibly. The most numerous "nation," however, were the crioulos. Thirteen were enslaved, another twelve were freedpersons, and four were probably free crioulos, for a total of twenty-nine. Two *pretos* (blacks) were also baptized. Those who were racially mixed infants were less numerous. There were only two mulatos, presumed to be free; nine pardos, of whom five were freed; and six cabras, four of whom enjoyed the freed status. One exceptional child was the legitimate infant boy of an indigenous father and a crioula mother (baptized in 1804).

Finally, the priests recorded twenty-one individuals simply as the infants of unmarried enslaved women. Therefore we know little about their color or nation. Overall, this sample records ninety-two baptisms, which is only a minimum number due to the number of illegible or missing pages. Its value, however, is that it also documents the decline of African slavery in the parish as well as an increase in the number of crioulos, who were largely of West African ancestry.

The Nations of Color

Enslaved crioulos (blacks born in Brazil) can also be traced via census data and tax records. Unlike the city of Rio de Janeiro, where the term *nation* was rarely used with color terms, "crioulo nation" was a more common usage in Goiás. If we understand *nation* in its archaic sense as "a foreign people," then why did slaveholders and scribes think of the enslaved as belonging to the crioulo nation?[43] Were such individuals still so linked to the cultures of their parents and grandparents that they followed a more African cultural and religious tradition? The links with African parents on the part of the crioulos in the Henriques regiment of São José do Tocantins are notable. They were clearly second-generation crioulos, whose parents had been identified as either Guiné or Mina. In contrast, their sons had been born in São José or elsewhere in Brazil.

Whatever the cultural context of the term *crioulo nation*, the meia-sisas of the early nineteenth century clarify that the great majority of Brazilian-born slaves who were sold were crioulos, that is, 627. Another 177 were listed as cabras. Many children who were sold were simply identified as cria (offspring), without color or nation indicated. The identity of a cabra in late colonial Goiás is uncertain. The baptismal registries for Vila Boa of the early nineteenth century recorded cabra infants of African mothers. Perhaps they were darker persons of color, as opposed to pardos. In São José do Tocantins, however, those known as cabras had come from Cape Verde via Bahia.[44] Since the tax records distinguished between cabras and other racially mixed individuals, such as mestizos, mulatos, and pardos, the scribes apparently had another identity in mind for those they defined as cabras. The third most numerous group were those termed mulato, of European and African ancestry, of whom 77 were identified, while another 11 were pardo, or someone who was racially mixed of brown color. Finally, 6 mestizos were openly sold, which may reflect the enslavement of indigenous captives in the captaincy.[45]

In general, the sources consulted suggest that between 1779 and 1832 a significant population transformation took place. In 1779 the Portuguese had recorded a high proportion of those defined as "black" in the captaincy, usually ranging between 60 and 70 percent of the population.[46] Presumably the majority of those blacks had been born in Africa. But with the decline of the mines, fewer Africans were imported into Goiás, and the population began to evolve in the direction of a Brazilian-born population that included crioulos and the racially mixed mulatos, pardos, cabras, and mestizos. By the time of the 1832 census, the new provincial government could find only 1,923 Africans (14.5 percent) in a total enslaved population of 13,261. The situation for slaveholders was most critical in the north, where only 10 percent of those enslaved were Africans; their descendants, the crioulos, comprised 89.9 percent. In all of the north there were only eight pardos recorded. Africans made up a slightly higher share of the enslaved, at 17.4 percent in the southern comarca, while crioulos constituted 62 percent and pardos 20.6 percent. Together, the Brazilian-born slaves (crioulos and pardos) far outnumbered Africans in the province. Crioulos totaled 9,652 (72.8 percent) and pardos 1,686 (12.7 percent) (table B.10).[47]

Work

At present, what gives identity to many people is their occupation, especially if they define themselves by their profession. Unfortunately, there are few good surviving descriptions of slave occupations in the captaincy in the eighteenth century, nor can we say much about their working conditions or treatment. At most we can determine where they worked at a particular point in time. Nonetheless, the Portuguese methods of categorizing enslaved Africans provide some insights into who they were and where they worked.

The census of 1783 is the only colonial census that attempted to locate enslaved blacks in their workplaces. The reason for this effort was to determine how many of them were available to mine gold, since the Portuguese were less and less successful in capturing the Crown's quinto. The 1783 household lists are also important because they demonstrate that slaveholders were employing their slaves in activities other than mining.[48] In the early period, from about the 1720s to the 1740s, most enslaved blacks had mined, but as the mining economy developed, petitions for sesmarias (land grants) reveal that some masters had engenhos (sugar plantations), ranches, and roças (small plots of land for food production), where their slaves were raising sugar, cattle, and foods such as corn and manioc.[49] Thenceforth, a certain percentage of Africans, especially the women, would be employed in activities outside the mines. For example, Pilar had more slaves working on roças and in households (1,528) than in mining (806) by 1783. In contrast, Santa Luzia, which apparently still had a mining boom, had only 38 slaves on roças as opposed to 856 in mining; but there were also 434 slaves working on engenhos, producing sugar and aguardente for the miners (table 9).

Another attempt to determine the number of mining slaves is undated but perhaps took place in the late 1780s. Not too surprisingly the mining town with the largest number of slaves was Santa Luzia at 580, followed by Traíras and

Table 9. Number of slaves by occupational category, 1783

	Mining	Household	Engenhos	Roças	Unknown[a]	Total
SOUTH						
Vila Boa	—	—	—	—	4,689	4,689
Anta	841	—	—	—	—	841
Santa Luzia	856	225	434	38	—	1,553
Santa Cruz	287	—	94	305[b]	—	686
Pilar	806	—	428	1,528[b]	—	2,762
Total, south	2,790	225	956	1,871	4,689	10,531
NORTH						
Traíras	1,086	—	—	—	1,064[c]	2,150
São Félix	189	233	10[d]	228	14	674
Cavalcante	550	373	—	—	—	923
Arraias	70	30	—	264[e]	—	364
Chapada	89	38	—	56	24	207
Carmo	43	21	—	54	39	157
Total, north	2,027	695	10	602	1,141	4,475
Sum total	4,817	920	966	2,473	5,830	15,006

Source: Mary Karasch, "Central Africans in Central Brazil, 1780–1835," in Heywood, Central Africans, table 4.12, p. 142. This table has been rearranged from the published version.
[a]Unknown place of employment.
[b]Includes house slaves.
[c]The 1,064 slaves in Traíras worked at occupations other than mining.
[d]The 10 slaves in São Félix worked on a cattle ranch.
[e]The 264 slaves in Arraias were used on roças, engenhos, and cattle ranches.

São José at 505. The next, at 420 each, were Meia Ponte and Pilar, followed by 320 in Anta, 250 in Cocal, 205 in Ouro Fino, 180 in Água Quente, and 80 in Vila Boa, where the fewest were devoted to mining. The total number of slaves employed by fifty slaveholders was 2,960.[50]

The almost 3,000 mining slaves who belonged to fifty slaveholders illustrates a decline from the 4,817 slaves employed either on lavras (mines) or as *faisqueiros* (prospectors) in 1783. But even in 1783 most slaves, 68 percent, had labored elsewhere than in the mines. Another official source also documents the shift to other places of work. The census of 1825 records only 41 mines, with 232 abandoned. Instead, most slaves labored on 249 sugar plantations, 667 cattle ranches, and 3,578 farms. There were also 1,581 looms.[51]

Descriptions of their actual labor are difficult to locate. It is also uncertain whether there were any occupations allocated to specific ethnic groups. Gender was more important in determining types of labor; for example, men mined, while women worked in the households at spinning, sewing, and weaving; sold foods and drinks; and did agricultural labor on the roças. Some slave women were also coerced into serving as prostitutes or concubines in the mining camps and towns. There was not an absolute division of labor by gender, however, because some women worked at the mines, washing gold and carrying ore-laden *gamelas* (wooden trays) on their heads, while some men labored in the households weaving cloth or in the fields.[52]

The mix of occupations among slaves is especially evident in the inventory of slaves from the estate of José Francisco Hutim, whose properties were confiscated in and near Vila Boa in 1805. He and his slaves were accused of stealing gold from the royal foundry house. The sequestration process reveals that Hutim had ten house slaves. Another group of twenty-eight slaves (eighteen males and ten females) had Miguel Angola as an overseer. Hutim also owned a small sugar plantation, where he employed twenty-two slaves with Caetano Angola as the master sugar technician. Hutim's third property was a small farm, where twenty-four slaves raised corn and other foodstuffs. Thus Hutim utilized his eighty-four slaves in a variety of occupations, only some of which gave them access to gold.[53]

While Hutim and his slaves apparently "mined for gold" at the foundry house, most slaves labored on lavras (mines) under direct supervision or went off prospecting on their own as faisqueiros, searching for gold in the rivers of the captaincy. If a master had many slaves, he set them to work using one of two techniques: in the first case, slaves perforated a hill or mountain, creating long galleries; in the second, they made perpendicular cuts into a mountain to locate veins of gold. This latter type of mining was used in Cocal and Natividade.[54] Digging and moving mountains of dirt under the direct supervision of a master or overseer were more hazardous and difficult than the labor of the faisqueiros, who could work on their own. Their slaveholders, however, required them to turn over a specific amount of gold on a weekly basis (the jornal). If they failed to do so, they faced a whipping; but whatever they found above that amount, they could keep for themselves. In 1766 the intendant of gold in São Félix reported that the gold brought to the royal foundry house was from miners who had received it as jornaes from their slaves.[55] When the mines were new and gold was plentiful, it was easier for slaves to pay the jornal, but as the alluvial gold gave out, it became more difficult. Furthermore, each man had to buy his own food and drinks, which he paid for in gold dust. Black women could accumulate gold by selling the men food and aguardente. Other blacks shared the gold they mined with slaves who cultivated foodstuffs.[56]

One of the more detailed descriptions of how blacks mined dates from the reign of Queen Maria (1777–1816). According to an anonymous author, those masters who lacked enough blacks to mine by digging in the mountains sent their few blacks to mine in the faisqueira style. He reported that each black went out separately to prospect for gold and made a pact with his master as to how much he was to give the master at the end of the week; anything above that amount he could keep for himself. He then went on to describe how the faiscadores of Traíras, Cocal, and Água Quente found the gold they had to turn over to their slaveholders. For the most part, they went to prospect in the Maranhão River, where they dove into the depths of the river. In one hand they carried a small *almocafre* (a sharp-pointed mining tool) and in the other a leather bag.[57] With their tool, they scraped up pebbles from the riverbed, placing them in the bag. They then rose to the surface of the water and unloaded the bag. After resting, they returned for another dive, repeating the process as many times as possible. Toward the end of the afternoon they sifted the gravel in the *bateia* (wooden bowl or pan), typically extracting one oitava or an oitava and a half of gold; sometimes they could collect two oitavas. In São José do Tocantins, however, slaves had to extract six oitavas of gold (fifteen grams) each day, or they would be punished with a "gross cord" called a *bacalhau*. Many must have been punished there, since the usual yield for Goiás by 1779–1822 was only half an oitava of gold each week. On the other hand, if a black had the good luck to find a leaf (folheta) of gold, he could fulfill the entire week's jornal and sometimes even a month's obligation.[58]

Technologies were unsophisticated: most miners apparently did all their labor with a bateia, a wooden or metal pan for washing gold; a gamela (wooden tray) for toting ore; and an almocafre, shovel, or hoe for digging earth. Leather bags were used to hold the gold dust and ore. The largest and most difficult labors recorded for the captaincy were the attempts to divert the Maranhão River from its riverbed and to build a sluice and aqueduct to the Morro do Clemente, which lacked water. Both projects ultimately failed, but they mostly involved the massive mobilization of enslaved workers, who dug great pits, toted what must have been tons of dirt, and sorted gold from gravel. When Cunha Matos saw the scale and size of the excavations and abandoned mines in the 1820s, he concluded that the massive earthworks must have been built by Cyclopes (mythical giants). But they were built by ordinary Africans, many of whom died due to accidents, hunger, disease, and heat prostration.[59]

Quilombos

The harshness of working conditions and the lack of food in the early years—popcorn and cornmeal (*fubá*) were the main diet—led enslaved Africans to run away.[60] Flight was easily the most common form of resistance to enslavement because it could be successful. If there were a number of fugitive slaves, they joined together in small mining camps or large settlements known as quilombos or *mocambos*.[61] Those who found refuge as quilombo dwellers (quilombolas) continued to mine; but unlike slaveholders, who ignored food production, they also raised foodstuffs. As they acquired women via persuasion or kidnapping, children became a part of the community. If the quilombo remained hidden and was never raided by bandeiras, the next generation of quilombolas came to evolve yet other identities as free blacks, but they often shared common cultural traits with those still enslaved. It is possible to locate many such quilombos in the former captaincy of Goiás and even to document the presence of the ancestors of the people of Kalunga near Cavalcante.[62]

The search for the free quilombolas of the captaincy of Goiás begins with an initial list compiled by Palacin and Salles, who identified the locales where many quilombos used to exist in the eighteenth century: Três Barras, with sixty blacks who "insulted" and caused the deaths of travelers; Tocantins; Arraias; Meia Ponte; Crixás; and Paracatú, on the road to Vila Rica, Minas Gerais. With reference to São Félix and Natividade, Captain-general Dom Marcos de Noronha (1749–1755) complained of the great number of Indians who had fled their aldeias and of the *aquilombados*. His fear and that of other colonial governors was that the inhabitants of quilombos would assault the convoys that conducted the quinto of gold and would interrupt mining by raiding mule teams and miners. His fear can easily be explained because near him in Vila Boa on the hill of São Gonçalo there were "various *cabanas* [small thatch-roofed dwellings] of quilombolas," who attacked neighboring fazendas, where they stole animals and raided fields for food.[63]

In addition to this basic list, the names of many other quilombos survive. To the north was the great quilombo at Pederneiras, above Alcobaça on the Tocantins River. When the anthropologist Curt Nimuendajú interviewed the Apinaje in the 1930s, they informed him that they had raided the quilombolas of Pederneiras for iron tools at the end of the eighteenth century. Their attacks on Pederneiras apparently forced its abandonment, thus ending "a great mocambo of fugitive slaves headed by a woman."[64] Other local traditions from the far north register the presence of at least one quilombo in the forested region of the Bico do Papagaio, the Parrot's Beak, between the Araguaia and Tocantins Rivers. Another was located along the Sono River, where the quilombo was known as Mumbuca, an indigenous name for a species of bee.[65]

To the north of the Sono River and east of the Tocantins River near the former Jesuit aldeia of Duro there are references to a quilombo of fugitive blacks. After the revolt of the Xacriabá and Akroá when they were being "pacified" near São Félix in 1761, sixty Indians were returned to the presídio, probably against their will. The sixty were those whom the Jesuits had loaned to a certain man "to go [and] give in a quilombo of fugitive blacks, which they did in reality with a political intent."[66] Perhaps this enigmatic reference suggests the existence of contacts between the Jesuits, Indians, and quilombolas living near São Félix or Duro.

South of Duro was located one of the richest mining regions of the captaincy, where thousands of Africans once labored. This was the "chapada [mesa] of the Negros," near the actual city of Arraias. Only great stone structures in the chapada remain to mark a once large settlement. Local traditions refer to "a revolt between whites and blacks." According to Rosalinda Batista de Abreu Cordeiro, "The black gave proof of his vocation for liberty: he rebelled against bad treatments and considered himself free." After the revolt, whites moved to a new site, which became the future mining town of Arraias in 1739–1740, while the chapada continued to shelter quilombolas. Although black descendants of quilombolas in the município of Arraias have preserved some African cultural traditions, they also adopted the Portuguese dance of the *roda de São Gonçalo*. Unfortunately, their long history living in a quilombo survives only in fragmented memories collected in oral interviews, some of which Wolfgang Teske recorded.[67]

In all of the northern comarca, possibly the region with the greatest number of quilombos was the valley of the Paranã River and nearby mountains, such as the Serra do Mocambo. Governor João Manuel de Mello (1759–1770) boasted of the success of one of the bandeiras that he had sent to the Paranã, because it had destroyed a quilombo, where there were banana trees and fields with "more than 200 fugitive blacks." The king of the quilombo had fought "valorously until he lost his life," but the queen was captured, together with other black women. Unlike quilombos composed only of African men, this one also had children. But that bandeira did not succeed in eradicating all the quilombos of the Paranã River region, since others continued to flourish near the mining towns of São Félix, Natividade, Arraias, and Cavalcante.[68]

Another important region of quilombos was near the mining towns of Pilar, São José do Tocantins, and Muquém. In Pilar and Muquém, bandeiras destroyed quilombos, imprisoned their inhabitants, and founded mining towns.[69] In 1741 João Godói Pinto Silveira encountered the quilombo of Papuão and "the mines of Papuã occupied by fugitive negros," which became the mining town of Pilar. As the miners introduced more enslaved Africans, quilombos grew in size around the town. They also came to threaten local miners and cattlemen, as they robbed for "money" (gold?) and cattle. In 1752 D. Marcos de Noronha (1749–1755) organized an expedition led by Sebastião José da Cunha Soares that demolished at least one quilombo, killing an "elevated number of blacks" and capturing others whom the expedition members divided among themselves. Perhaps anger at the destruction of that quilombo led others to plot an urban slave revolt. As would happen in Salvador, Bahia, in the nineteenth century, quilombolas conspired with slaves to plan a revolt in Pilar when slaveholders would be preoccupied with the rituals for the Holy Spirit during the Festa do Divino in 1755. The conspirators had obtained gunpowder and lead and were going to attack the local church when their plans were discovered. Informed of this, the authorities suspended the festival and suppressed the revolt.[70]

Near the mining town of São José do Tocantins (Niquelândia) there was also a quilombo. When Dulce Madalena Rios Pedroso collected oral testimonies in the region, she found references to "an agglomeration of mountain ranges, locales that were favored by quilombolas and autonomous Indians because they were of difficult access." A local rancher testified that the mountains formed a valley with fertile lands and a rocky river, the Acaba-vida River, which joins the Bagagem River. As Pedroso's interviews clarify, this rugged land protected not only quilombolas but also the Canoeiro.[71]

One of the more detailed descriptions of a quilombo comes from local traditions of the city of Muquém, which hosts a pilgrimage dedicated to Our Lady of Abadia on 15 August. According to José Chaves, there was once a quilombo of fugitive slaves in Muquém, which was located eight leagues from São José do Tocantins. On 20 December 1740, the day of St. Thomas, a company of free men headed by a captain of assault reached the mountainous region with "marble rocks" and "grottos," from whose height they saw the *choupanas* (thatched houses) of the blacks at the edge of the forest. Before they attacked the quilombo, they watched the blacks "set fire to some piles of firewood" and dance and sing around the bonfire to drum music. They then feasted on grilled meat, potatoes, and manioc, and drank aguardente. After they returned to their choupanas and went to sleep, the captain led his men down the mountain and attacked them. All were soon returned to their former masters, who undoubtedly punished them for their flight. In gratitude for the "victory" and for the gold they found there "in abundance," the captain had a church constructed, which was dedicated to St. Thomas; the settlement was thenceforth known as São Tomé do Muquém. Later an image of Our Lady of Abadia was imported from Portugal and placed in the church.[72] This statue of Our Lady soon became an object of veneration to the people of the sertão, including those who live in Kalunga.[73]

To the west of Pilar are Tesouras and Crixás. In 1757 a bush captain (*capitão do mato*) located the mines of the settlement of Tesouras, which were under the control of "fugitive captives in the creek of the Quilombo in whose area they [had] washed [gold] for some time." Apparently he had been sent to destroy the quilombo because its inhabitants were causing "as many damages as the Caiapó people." Since Crixás was then one of the richest mining towns with one of the largest forces of slave miners, it was usually on the lists of towns threatened by quilombos in its vicinity.[74]

In 1777 the pardos of the district of Crixás were ordered to destroy "a large quilombo of fugitive blacks" located on the banks of the Araguaia River. They were also sent there to open a new road to the presídio of Nova Beira. Farther west, on the other side of the Araguaia River in Mato Grosso, runs the Mortes River, an area reputed to be an asylum for quilombolas in the eighteenth century. Also in Mato Grosso, according to tradition, was the famous quilombo of Carlota that threatened Luso-Brazilians due to the number of fugitive miners who sought refuge there. It survived at least between 1770 and 1795, until it was repressed by Francisco de Mello Pereira e Cárceres. The quilombolas had maintained themselves by raising foodstuffs, tobacco, and cotton and attacking the Indians of the region, often stealing their women.[75]

Also impressive were the quilombos of the comarca of the Mortes River in Minas Gerais. According to Gilka Salles, "the first great quilombo listed [in Goiás] was situated near the Mortes River in 1746, in the vast fields and mountains that separate Minas from the Goiazes." In that region there was a large quilombo with more than six hundred fugitives. Not only did it have a king and queen, but it also possessed defensive fortifications and platoons of attack. When the quilombolas raided fazendas, they captured slaves and took them to the quilombo. Given the great threat that the quilombo represented to the mines of Minas Gerais, the captain-general Gomes Freire de Andrade organized an expedition that "decimated" it in 1751.[76]

Was this the famous quilombo of Ambrósio, which was destroyed by an expedition of three hundred men led by Antônio João de Oliveira? According to tradition, Jesuits had purchased the black Ambrósio in the slave market of the Valongo in Rio de Janeiro. They had then brought him to the aldeia of Tengotengo in the Triângulo Mineiro, where he received his freedom. He and his wife headed the aldeia of Tengotengo, which grew to more than a thousand inhabitants. Around 1746, Gomes Freire de Andrade referred to this settlement as a quilombo from which departed "parties of twenty to thirty blacks that executed robberies and very cruel deaths."[77] According to José Martins Pereira de Alencastre, the expeditionary force fought the quilombolas for many hours. With the death of their chief, Ambrósio, they were dispersed in groups throughout the sertão and reunited in other small quilombos. They then threatened the convoys and mines, leading to the formation of still other bandeiras against them.[78] Another reference to a quilombo in the comarca of the Mortes River comes from about 1767, when the authorities captured some blacks and punished them. The quilombo was then commanded by a king, "a daring black called the Batieiro," probably in reference to his skill with the bateia, the wooden bowl used in prospecting for gold. The king, however, governed "by mode of a Republic."[79]

There were still other quilombos in the south of the captaincy. The citizens of the village of Mesquita, a black community near Santa Luzia, descend from Africans originally from Ghana.[80] Perhaps they were related to the fugitives who "infested the roads of the arrayal of Bonfim" (actually Silvânia), extending their attacks to the roads in the proximity of Santa Luzia and Santa Cruz. In fact, a fugitive black discovered the mines of the Morro do Clemente in Santa

Cruz in 1772. Apparently the southern part of the captaincy of Goiás that extended to the Grande River was especially attractive to fugitives because it was so distant from the bandeiras sent out from Vila Boa or Vila Rica, Minas Gerais.[81]

In the far southeast of the captaincy there were still other quilombos. In 1733 a bandeira was sent with the mission of repelling the Indians and "destroying the great number of quilombos that had formed there with the fugitive slaves of the mines." Under the direction of Urbano do Couto, the bandeira crossed the São Francisco River and traveled to the São Marcos River in the actual frontier between Goiás and Minas Gerais.[82] In the eighteenth century the governors of Goiás frequently sent bandeiras to the other side of the Paranaíba River, another celebrated refuge of quilombolas, where they attacked quilombos in the region of the Araguari River or of the Velhas River, which is an affluent of the Paranaíba River, and they extended their military operations to Paracatú, where the quilombos were also said to be "abundant." To the east of the Velhas River was the Abaeté River, whose headwaters were not far from the Paranaíba. Perhaps that was the locale of the "quilombo of the headwaters of the Abaité."[83] In the extreme south of the captaincy runs the Grande River, which served as the colonial border between Goiás and Minas Gerais until Desemboque and Araxá became part of Minas Gerais. On one of its islands the Kayapó discovered "a great city of fugitive blacks," which had been there "since time immemorial." Presumably they were fugitives from Minas Gerais who "had propagated in peace" due to the "great distance" of their hidden quilombo from other settlements.[84]

This discovery calls attention to a long history of Kayapó and quilombo interactions in the south of the captaincy in the colonial period. Not only did the Kayapó attack quilombolas, but they also allied with them. In one case from 1760, documented by Marcel Mano, Indians even came to the defense of a quilombo when it was attacked by bush captains hunting fugitive slaves. On another occasion, in 1774, the Kayapó invaded a district in search of iron wares, but they also facilitated the flight of slaves.[85]

In contrast to the many references to quilombos in the late colonial period, the nineteenth century saw a decline of known quilombos. Although hidden quilombos, such as those in Kalunga, survived throughout the nineteenth century, the correspondence of provincial governors and police chiefs after 1835 is notably lacking in instructions to destroy quilombos. In the eighteenth century governors had written frequently about the problems that quilombos posed to the security of miners and the mining economy, but such concerns disappeared from the official correspondence of those most responsible for quilombo repression.[86] One reason for the decrease in the number of quilombos was due to the small number of enslaved African men in the captaincy. Furthermore, many of them were of advanced age, while more and more of the enslaved were crioulos, including women and children. As other studies on fugitive slaves have demonstrated, those most likely to run away were single African males.[87] Without new African men to fuel their numbers, quilombos also decreased in numbers, although hidden ones persisted in remote and rugged parts of the province.

In summary, therefore, censuses, tax records, and parish registers reveal that the enslaved population of the captaincy of Goiás ranged from indigenous captives to those defined as mulato, pardo, cabra, crioulo, Angola, Congo, Mina, and Guiné. This diverse population would play vital but ambiguous roles in the captaincy of Goiás in defending the captaincy from its enemies, mining gold, and providing foodstuffs. But at the same time, some Africans and their descendants would challenge Luso-Brazilian rule by revolting and running away to quilombos. Still others joined indigenous communities, becoming "Indian," in the view of the Portuguese, and leading their new people in battle against the Portuguese. Finally, a few, as we will see in the next chapter, lived in Christian missions and intermixed with the indigenous nations settled there. Not even the missions escaped the African presence on the frontier of Goiás.

PART THREE

Points of Contact and Culture Change

CHAPTER 8

People of the Holy Spirit

Christians and Their Sacred Spaces

On the night before the Feast of the Holy Spirit at Pentecost, processions of distinct groups enter the square before the Church of St. Ann: the king of Congo and his retinue, dressed in blue; the "civilized" caboclos, wearing green; and the Tapuios (Indians) with feathered headdresses.[1] In one way, the congada of the City of Goiás is a metaphor for past peaceful encounters of different peoples, separate in their identity yet united in their celebration of the Holy Spirit. In the late eighteenth and early nineteenth centuries, the introduction of diverse nations into the towns and villages of Central Brazil brought together Christians and non-Christians in the churches and squares to celebrate rituals significant to them; many others came to town simply to have a good time and frequent taverns and prostitution quarters.[2]

In the late colonial period, having one or more Catholic churches was fundamental to the social organization and identity of each community. Being Christian and having a church where they could attend Mass and receive the sacraments, as well as bury their dead, were fundamental values to Luso-Brazilians. After nearby gold mines gave out, a town or village often survived only because of a resident priest and one or more lay brotherhoods. As the official church weakened in the early nineteenth century, the lack of a priest even led to the abandonment of communities as people migrated to towns that still had priests and functioning churches. Since government funding for the missions also declined in the early nineteenth century, mission Indians also picked up and moved to places where they could baptize their children. Central themes of this period in the history of Christians in Goiás are the inadequacy of religious or secular support for churches and missions along with the evolution of a popular church that enabled laypeople to obtain the protection of a particular saint and practice religious rituals that they believed were vital to worshipping God, healing illnesses, and dying a good death, that is, saving

Figure 16. This depiction of a religious procession before Saint Ann's Church suggests the great popularity of these rituals in the City of Goiás. Source: Castelnau, Expédition. Courtesy of the Catholic University of America, Oliveira Lima Library, Washington, DC.

their souls.³ This chapter will begin, therefore, with the Catholic churches founded by bandeira leaders and lay brotherhoods and trace their decline by the 1830s with a severe shortage of priests outside of Vila Boa and Meia Ponte (Pirenópolis). Where possible, we will also describe popular religious practices of that period, including some linked with Africa. The last part of this chapter will survey a little of the life of the mission Indians who accepted Christianization; even though they had an identity as "Christian," their new beliefs were often in doubt, as they conducted ancient rituals and abandoned the missions at the first opportunity.

The early history of the church in Goiás begins with the chapels constructed by the leaders of bandeiras in gratitude for their "conquests." After discovering gold and securing captive Indians, the bandeira leaders had a chapel or church built in honor of the saint of their particular devotion. This focus on a popular saint continued throughout the colonial period with the construction of many private chapels. In Vila Boa one of the first such chapels was dedicated to St. Ann, and it became the parish church in 1729. Eventually it grew into the mother church of Santa Ana of Vila Boa, where the most powerful cleric in the captaincy resided, the vicar general. In the eighteenth century there was no cathedral due to the lack of a resident bishop. St. Ann's became a cathedral in 1815, its first resident bishop, D. Francisco Ferreira de Azevedo, took possession in 1824. Besides St. Ann's, there were eight affiliated chapels, which were built by private individuals or irmandades (lay brotherhoods) (appendix C).[4]

A second historic church in Vila Boa was that of Our Lady of the Rosary of the Blacks (1734), where the black irmandade of the same name was based. But in 1759 white irmandades moved there, after the roof of St. Ann's fell down; they remained at Our Lady's until 1762, when St. Ann's reopened, although still in ruins. Both the first St. Ann's Church, originally built as a chapel in 1727, and Our Lady of the Rosary did not survive. The first St. Ann's was demolished, and Our Lady of the Rosary was razed to be replaced by a nineteenth-century church built by the French Dominicans. The baroque chapel of Nossa Senhora da Boa Morte (Our Lady of the Good Death), built in 1779, served the pardo community in Vila Boa, but only its exterior and bell tower survived the fire that gutted its interior in 1921. A museum of sacred art has replaced the church's interior and houses many of the religious sculptures of José Joaquim da Veiga Valle (1806–1874), a nineteenth-century artist who worked in the baroque artistic styles of the eighteenth century.[5] A third significant church is São Francisco de Paula (1761), which is the location for the elite Irmandade do Senhor dos Passos, while Nossa Senhora da Abadia (Our Lady of the Abbey, 1790) is notable for its religious paintings and unusual shape. Three chapels, each dedicated to Our Lady, were Lapa (1749), Carmo of the Irmandade of S.t Benedict (1786), and the Barracas (1793). Santa Barbara (1780), on the road to the north, completes the number of chapels affiliated with St. Ann's in Vila Boa (appendix C).

As in other parts of the captaincy, Vila Boa was more notable for the number of small chapels than for one grandiose church, mainly because they were constructed by individuals or lay brotherhoods during the period of so-called decadence in the second half of the eighteenth century. A rich miner without heirs who was thinking of his own mortality and of saving his soul often preferred to donate gold to the building of churches rather than allow his estate to fall into the hands of the judge of orphans, which would only enrich the Portuguese bureaucracy and distant relatives.[6] Due to insufficient funding by church or state, most of Vila Boa's churches were small and without ornate exterior ornamentation. The Church of Boa Morte, for example, lacks an attached bell tower. The tower instead stands outside the church, and for this reason it survived the fire that gutted the church's interior. The current

St. Ann's Church, which is much larger than the original chapel, was erected in stages with many reforms that were completed only in 1998. In the 1870s an elegant façade had been planned for this church, but it was not constructed.[7]

The second important religious center in the south of the captaincy in terms of number of churches and priests was the parish of Meia Ponte (now Pirenópolis), which was founded in 1736. Its principal church was Our Lady of the Rosary, which was built on a square with a panoramic view of gardens and houses. The church itself was well built of adobe. According to Ana Maria Borges and Luís Palacin, it is "probably the most beautiful of all the colonial Goiana architecture." Its central altar with the image of Our Lady of the Rosary, the patroness of the city, was constructed in 1761 in a simple baroque style without excessive gold ornamentation. It also had four side altars that were richly decorated, including two dedicated to St. Francis de Paula and St. Michael, dating from 1733. Two other important churches in Meia Ponte are the Church of Our Lord of the Good Death (Senhor do Bonfim) and the Church of Our Lady of Carmo. The Church of Bonfim was built in the 1750s, and the statue of Our Lord of Bonfim was brought from Salvador by 260 slaves. The Church of Carmo was also built by private individuals, in 1750 on the right bank of the Almas River. Two other chapels in Meia Ponte were Our Lady of the Good Death of Lapa and São Francisco das Chagas, for a total of five chapels to serve the people of the parish. No other mining towns had as many chapels as Meia Ponte and Vila Boa, or as many priests and irmandades (appendix C). Both towns formed the Catholic religious center of the captaincy.[8]

To the northwest of Meia Ponte in Pilar, the Church of Our Lady of Pilar had three attached chapels: Our Lady of the Rosary, São Gonçalo, and Nossa Senhora das Mercês (Our Lady of Mercy). Particularly notable is the attached bell tower with three bells founded in Goiás. The mining town of Crixás had the Church of Our Lady of the [Immaculate] Conception and its affiliated Chapel of the Rosary and Chapel of Nossa Senhora da Abadia (Our Lady of the Abbey). Another church dedicated to Our Lady of the Rosary of the Blacks was built in Santa Luzia (Lusiânia) in 1763. Four hundred free and enslaved blacks constructed the church over three years. Some of them may have been skilled in colonial construction, since this church is one of the few in Goiás that preserves typical features of colonial churches, with two towers and two windows above a central doorway and an interior that is also similar to those built by brotherhoods.[9]

According to José Luiz de Castro, citing Eduardo Hoornaert, the central area of such churches was reserved for women without distinction of classes. On the spaces to the side of the center area stood the "good men" or free men; their posture and location symbolized their elevated status with reference to women and slaves. The space around the door in the back was reserved for peasants and slaves, who also stood, looking at the saints. The sacred space of a typical colonial church such as Santa Luzia, then, replicated the status values of local society, with each in their place by gender and class. Clerical space was also separated from that of the laity by an altar rail. Before the high altar with the image of the patron saint, the priest stood with his back to the laity when saying Mass in Latin.[10] Such rigid distinctions were not always observed in Goiás, however, since priests complained of women and men meeting together in church and of people dancing in the churches at night. One priest even protested against women dressing as men and men as women.[11]

A church was, of course, the sacred space designed for the living, but the churches also served as burial grounds for departed brothers and their families. After a costly and elaborate funeral with candles and music, the most privileged were buried in the church closest to the high altar, and the lowest in status (slaves) were buried outside the church if they did not belong to one of the black brotherhoods, which allowed them to be buried in its church. One's place in local society was thus reflected in where one was buried in consecrated ground to await the resurrection of the dead in Catholic belief. Although all good Catholics could expect burial in or near a church, slaveholders often denied such burials to their slaves. At best, deceased slaves were carried in a hammock or litter to the door of a church, where the priest received them and prayed for their soul. They were then taken to a burial ground where, as in Africa, offerings of food and drinks were later placed on the graves. At worst, they were abandoned and eaten by animals or secretly buried in a nearby forest.[12]

In the northern comarca the Irmandade of the Rosary of free and freed blacks of the mining town of Natividade tried to build the largest church in the captaincy of Goiás. They began construction on their church in 1786 but, according to local tradition, it was never completed and now stands roofless. According to Pohl, the blacks who raised the money for the church were determined to build this great church by themselves, and they refused to accept help from nonblacks in Natividade, so only half of the church was built. However, the artist William J. Burchell, who went to Natividade, depicted the Church of Our Lady of the Rosary with a roof. Although the ruins of this large church now stand vacant in Natividade, they have become a "national" symbol of the state of Tocantins.[13]

Figure 17. The ruins of the black church of Our Lady of the Rosary are in Natividade. Free blacks began its construction in 1786. Photograph courtesy of Mary C. Karasch.

In general, the churches in the north were even smaller than those in the south, although there were numerous chapels and some pilgrimage destinations, such as Muquém, where people came to honor Nossa Senhora da Abadia (Our Lady of the Abbey). But size seems to have had no correlation with religious significance. Although the bush captain João Crisostomo had built a small chapel in Muquém dedicated to Saint Thomas, widespread popular devotion to Nossa Senhora da Abadia began with a European (sometimes identified as Portuguese), Antônio Antunes, who lived near the chapel. Perhaps he had come from northern Portugal, where Nossa Senhora da Abadia was revered. Antunes had discovered rich gold mines, but he had hid his wealth in gold from authorities. Fearing that he would be punished, he appealed to Our Lady of the Abbey and promised to place an image of her in the chapel if he were freed of his "crime." According to one tradition, when a judge and a skilled miner arrived to determine whether he had gold on his property, they could find little of it. Therefore, Antunes traveled to Salvador and brought back a statue of Nossa Senhora da Abadia in 1748. Returning with him was a widowed mother of three sons and five daughters. After placing the image of Our Lady in the chapel, they began to celebrate her feast day on 15 August each year. From that time the feast day was organized and funded by the Irmandade of Nossa Senhora da Abadia. By 1812 the tiny community of Muquém was attracting pilgrims from various parts of Goiás and neighboring provinces, and a regional trading fair soon developed for the days of the pilgrimage, 6–15 August.[14]

Other northern towns did not equally attract the devout. In the early nineteenth century, northern churches included the following: Santo Antônio, Santa Ana, and the Chapel of Rosário in São Félix; Nossa Senhora da Natividade with the affiliated chapels Our Lady of the Rosary of the Blacks, Our Lady of the Terço (also Terceiros), and St. Benedict in Natividade; Nossa Senhora dos Remédios, Our Lady of the Rosary, and Our Lady of Conception of Arraias; Nossa Senhora das Mercês of Cocal; and Santa Ana, Our Lady of the Rosary, and Our Lord of Bonfim in Cavalcante. In Pontal were the Chapels of Santa Ana and Santo Antônio (appendix C).[15]

Thus we can document the existence of more than fifty churches and chapels built by individuals or brotherhoods in the captaincy of Goiás during the colonial period (appendix C).[16] Dedicated to Jesus Christ, his mother, Mary, and the saints, they reflected the devotion of laymen and laywomen, who were whites, blacks, and pardos, although Indians could also attend Mass and receive baptism for their children. Unlike the complex of churches constructed on the coast or in Minas Gerais, the gold of Goiás was not lavished on these churches. As Borges and Palacin explain, their "modest proportions" were due to their being constructed in the period of economic decadence as gold mining declined, allowing for enslaved labor to be shifted from mining to church construction.[17]

On the other hand, many of the elite preferred to erect a small chapel or oratorio where they could pray and hear Mass in their urban residence, as well as on their plantation or ranch. They had to receive permission to do so from the bishop in Rio de Janeiro, although not all knew that they needed his permission. In 1796, 1799, and 1805, the surgeon-mor Lourenço Antônio da Neiva was given permission to celebrate Mass on his small farm for two years. A widow, Dona Petronilha do Amor Divino, received permission to have Mass said in her private residence in 1800 because she had an altar, which was "decently ornamented and separated from domestic uses in the houses of her residence." One of the more lengthy justifications for hearing Masses in the oratorios of his private residence and on his sugar plantation is that of Surgeon-Mor Bartolomeu Lourenço da Silva. He argued for the right to have Mass said in his oratorios because he had a large family of children and slaves and it was gravely inconvenient to satisfy the requirement to attend Mass. He received a license for both oratorios in 1802 and 1805. A ranch chapel with elegant baroque paintings still survives on the fazenda Babilônia near Pirenópolis. Those without the resources to build their own private chapel often had recourse to praying before saints' images located throughout Vila Boa.[18]

Lay Brotherhoods

As official support weakened for the church in Goiás, at least as measured in funding, what allowed Christians and Christian identity to survive in Central Brazil were the lay brotherhoods that took care of their churches and chapels and arranged popular processions and festivals in honor of the Blessed Sacrament, Our Lady of the Rosary, and patron saints. As society was divided by color and status, so too were the brotherhoods of the captaincy, although there were exceptions where those of differing colors or ethnicities were admitted in violation of a brotherhood's charter. Furthermore, there were irmandades, such as Our Lady of the Good Death of Vila Boa and São José do Tocantins, whose charters welcomed "whites, blacks and freed pardos, and free crioulos" as members. The brotherhoods also had female associates who served on their boards. One exceptional brotherhood even petitioned the Crown to permit white women in Vila Boa "to govern and direct the affairs of" the Irmandade de Nossa Senhora da Lapa. In general, however, women served in support roles in the brotherhoods and, along with men, practiced acts of charity, raised alms, and celebrated feast days. They also joined together to honor "the saint of their devotion" and attend funerals and burials in their churches (appendix C).[19]

Claiming the highest status in the captaincy were the white brotherhoods, which excluded nonwhites and those of Jewish ancestry. The Irmandade do Senhor dos Passos, which organized processions for the Stations of the Cross during Lent and Holy Week, specifically refused to admit those with the "infamy" of being a *cristão novo* (new Christian of Jewish descent) or of an "infected nation or pardo." Their charters stressed that the brothers and their wives had to be white and married in the Catholic Church; if a white brother were discovered to have married a parda, he could be prohibited from exercising responsible offices in the brotherhood. But after he died, he would be treated like his other white brothers, except that his wife and the children born of that "infected matrimony" would not have the same rights as white spouses and children. A study of twenty-four members of the exclusive white brotherhoods of Santissimo Sacramento, Senhor dos Passos, and Santo Antônio in Vila Boa reveals that the majority of their brothers had been born in Portugal, in particular in the north.[20]

One of the earliest white brotherhoods in Santa Ana in Vila Boa was dedicated to the holy souls of purgatory, who were protected by St. Michael the archangel in popular belief. Those concerned with saving their souls often had a special devotion to St. Michael, and his statue was commonly found in churches throughout Goiás. In 1792 the Irmandade of São Miguel e Almas (St. Michael and Souls) was also based in Nossa Senhora da Conceição (Our Lady of the [Immaculate] Conception) in Crixás. Another white brotherhood, especially associated with the Portuguese troops stationed in Vila Boa, was the Brotherhood of Santo Antônio in Santa Ana. Its charter welcomed the military in Vila Boa, as well as those with a special devotion to Saint Anthony, that is, the Portuguese. In 1825 Cunha Matos reported that in 1750 all the troops of the First Line and public employees of the captaincy formed part of the Irmandade of Santo Antônio, whose protector was the governor of the captaincy. Its powerful men with ties to the governor gave this irmandade a high-status position in the captaincy, but in contrast its brothers often assisted the enslaved members of the black Brotherhood of the Rosary in Vila Boa. Yet another elite brotherhood, created in 1742, was the Confraria of the Republicans, who organized processions in honor of St. Sebastian. They were linked with the Senado da Camara of Vila Boa.[21]

The most important and widespread white brotherhood in the mining towns, however, was that of Santissimo Sacramento (the Blessed Sacrament), which was established in the Church of Santa Ana in Vila Boa before 1742. It was exclusive to whites, both men and women, and specifically excluded blacks. Its brothers were buried in Santa Ana. Besides taking Communion to the sick, one of its important religious responsibilities was to promote and organize the procession for the Body of God (Corpus Christi), which took place in May or June after Trinity Sunday. Every year they wrote to the bishop of Rio de Janeiro to receive permission to expose the Blessed Sacrament and walk in procession at Pentecost, which fell fifty days after Easter.[22]

Processions often reveal the status hierarchies in a particular city, and Vila Boa was no exception. Cristina Cássia P. Moraes has reconstructed the "customary order" in which white brotherhoods processed, followed by those of pardos and blacks. On Corpus Christi in the mid-eighteenth century, the procession left the main church with the statues of St. George and St. Sebastian, who were mounted on horses. After them came a parade of fifty cavalrymen. Flags preceded the irmandades of Vila Boa, who processed with their principal officers. First came the brothers of the Blessed Sacrament. They were followed by the Irmandades of St. Michael and Souls, the military of St. Anthony, Our Lady of Lapa of the merchants, and the martyr St. Sebastian of the Republicans. In a clear color hierarchy, the pardos came next with the Irmandade of Our Lady of the Good Death, followed by Our Lady of the Rosary of the black men and Santa Efigênia of the tailors. Ninth in line were the carpenters in the *confraria* (brotherhood of craftsmen) dedicated to São José (St. Joseph), with other artisans and craftsmen at the end.[23]

Of lower status than one of the white brotherhoods was that of the pardos, who restricted membership to free and freed pardos and excluded slaves. In Vila Boa the patroness of the pardos was Our Lady of the (Immaculate) Conception, whose image was honored in the Church of Boa Morte. The Irmandades of Our Lady of the Good Death and of the Martyr St. Gonçalo Garcia were also associated with that church. But in São José do Tocantins, the pardo irmandade was principally dedicated to São Gonçalo Garcia, who had been born in India of mixed parentage—his father was Portuguese and his mother Indian—and martyred in Japan in 1597. In other mining towns, such as Conceição, Our Lady of the (Immaculate) Conception was the patroness of the pardos. Churches dedicated to Our Lady of the Conception were also in Crixás, Traíras, and Arraias.[24]

The most popular brotherhoods, judging by the number of churches dedicated to the Virgin Mary, were the brotherhoods of Our Lady of the Rosary, built by whites or blacks. In most towns of the captaincy, the Church of Our Lady of the Rosary, built by blacks, was the second most important church after the mother church built by Luso-Brazilians. Free, freed, and enslaved blacks, both men and women, served on the board, engaged in fund-raising, and buried their dead in the churches dedicated to Our Lady. With their kings and queens presiding, they also celebrated her special feast days, such as the first Sunday of October, with a solemn high Mass, a sermon, and a procession afterward.[25]

Also significant was the black brotherhood devoted to the black saint Benedict, which celebrated his feast day of 16 July and that of the Three Kings on 6 January. It was the responsibility of the Irmandade of St. Benedict to celebrate the *folia* of the Three Kings, one of whom was the black "Lord of Ethiopia." Before 1786 St. Benedict had had a side altar in the Church of the Rosary in Vila Boa, but the brothers there were often in conflict. Therefore,

Governor Luis da Cunha Menezes (1778–1783) gave the Chapel of Our Lady of Carmo to the brothers of St. Benedict as a favor to a mulato musician of the irmandade, who had been his personal secretary. As of 1786 the confraria of St. Benedict was located in the Church of Our Lady of Carmo in Vila Boa, and it accepted brothers who were free crioulos, pardos, and whites. The largest church devoted to St. Benedict was built in Natividade, but many other small chapels named for St. Benedict have not survived.[26]

In São José do Tocantins there used to exist a brotherhood of crioulos dedicated to the African saint Santa Efigênia. According to Paulo Bertran, the substantial Church of Santa Efigênia in São José do Tocantins had been cared for by the brotherhood of the same name. On the feast days of 25–26 July that honored her and Our Lady of Carmo, the men of the brotherhood wore white suits and an *anágua* (short skirt) or red *avental* (cloth) ornamented with handkerchiefs and ribbons, as used in the congadas. On their heads they wore cockades of feathers. To the sound of tambourines, violas, the box, and the *bumba* (large drum), the faithful performed the dances of Congo and sang the praises of Santa Efigênia and Our Lady of Carmo. Not only did African traditions appear in their rituals, but they also painted the altar of Nosso Senhor dos Passos in an Afro-Portuguese style. The church itself was notable for a façade that included a square cross over the entrance, which could derive from both Portuguese and Kongo cross traditions. After two centuries of honoring Santa Efigênia, the brotherhood moved to the Church of São José in 1982.[27]

In nearby Traíras, free blacks, who had a chapel dedicated to Our Lady of the Rosary, also celebrated an annual festival in honor of Santa Efigênia. Before the feast day in June, Pohl observed "various blacks, dressed in Portuguese uniforms" galloping through the streets of Traíras and to the church, where they placed a flag with their saint's image on a tall pole. Accompanying the festivities were continual drum beats, rifle shots, and various instruments of Congo, which, to Pohl's displeasure, sounded all night. The next day whites gathered at the house of the empress, and then all of the participants proceeded to the church. At least twenty blacks accompanied them, dressed with feathers on their heads and suits of red velvet embroidered with gold. The black prince, in a Portuguese uniform, and the bejeweled princess, in a long white dress, carried flowers in one hand and in the other a staff with a silver head. After the royal couple came the black emperor and empress, both of whom wore crowns and carried scepters. Their court danced and sang as they walked to the church. Then followed a solemn high Mass with liturgical music, after which they announced the names of the new officials for the next year. At this point musicians entered the church, where they danced and sang to African music. After the dance, the "black monarch" ordered the festival of Santa Efigênia to begin with a drama about the saint and more dancing and singing that lasted until midnight.[28]

The use of the terms "emperor" and "empress" for the black monarchs may have been in imitation of the white emperor and empress who presided over festivities in honor of the Holy Spirit at Pentecost. Traditionally, prosperous whites, such as a rancher and his wife, were selected to be the royal couple, in part due to their high status but also because of the expenses they incurred. But in Traíras, Pohl reported that poorer inhabitants of the town acquired the necessary funding for the festival by begging for alms at nearby fazendas with a group of musicians and the flag of the Holy Spirit. Having secured the necessary alms, a poor man could become the new emperor, who would receive a crown and a wooden scepter. After Mass, the new emperor processed to his house with a crowd of people to the beat of drums and with the flag of the Holy Spirit, where he blessed all of the participants. Portuguese arms were then placed at the door of the house, and with this, the ritual ended. Although Pohl does not say so, one reason why the feast of the Holy Spirit customarily cost so much money was due to the food and drinks that were served afterward.[29]

One of the more unique black brotherhoods in the captaincy, however, was Our Lady of Mercies in the mining town of Cocal, where its members celebrated the Festival of Our Lady of Mercies each year during the eight days of Christmas. When the mines were rich, the brotherhood had required its members to donate one oitava of gold on a yearly basis, but as the wealth of the mines declined, they reduced it to one-half oitava. In the early years the black brotherhood had been more exclusive to Africans and crioulos, but when they reformed their charter in 1788, they admitted those of other colors. But their identity, as they proudly proclaimed in their charter, was "Ethiopian."[30]

Unlike the Spanish colonies that had *cofradías* of Indians, there do not appear to be any lay brotherhoods established specifically for the indigenous peoples of the captaincy, most likely because so few Indians lived in the mining towns. However, Moraes located documents that refer to "negros da terra" (blacks/slaves of the land) as members of the Irmandade do Rosário in Vila Boa. Furthermore, there is an image depicting the Bororo, who were enslaved by bandeiras, on one of the towers of Santa Ana in 1777. Historically, in colonial Brazil Christian Indians were expected to join enslaved Africans in churches dedicated to Our Lady of the Rosary, most likely because they too were enslaved. Otherwise, Christian Indians were housed in missions with churches funded by the secular Portuguese state during the period of the Directorate (1757–1798) and afterward.[31]

The Franciscans

Before the Directorate missions, however, the Franciscans and Jesuits had established another type of catechetical effort that relied on religious orders to Christianize the Indians. In the seventeenth century the Franciscans had worked along the Tocantins River, while the Jesuits established missions in the north at São Francisco Xavier and Duro, Natividade, and farther south at São José de Mossâmedes and around Rio das Velhas. The Franciscans reached the indigenous peoples of the Tocantins River in the early seventeenth century when Frei Cristovão Severin de Lisboa made his first missionary river trip on the Tocantins River. Accompanying him were other friars: Domingos, Christóvão de São José, and Sebastião de Coimbra, plus the layman Franciscano do Rosário. During the time they were contacting new groups along the river, they won the loyalty of the powerful cacique Tomagica. Friar Cristovão also "fought for the liberty of the Indians" by writing a pastoral letter protesting against their enslavement. When the Jesuit Padre Antônio Vieira traveled south on the Tocantins River in the 1650s, he encountered Christianized Indians, perhaps due to the eleven years of the friars' work on the Tocantins River.[32]

The other Franciscan presence in the captaincy was through the Esmolares da Terra Santa (Almsgivers for the Holy Land) that founded hospices in Meia Ponte and Traíras. In 1731 the two Franciscans who established hospices there were Friars João de Jesus e Maria and Domingos de Santiago. According to Saint-Hilaire, the hospice in Meia Ponte was "an asylum of the brothers of the Third Order of St. Francis." This order attracted laymen who requested burial in its habit. The role of the friars was to collect alms from the faithful for the maintenance of the Church of the Holy Sepulcher in Jerusalem, but Auguste de Saint-Hilaire wondered how much gold actually reached Jerusalem, because it had to pass through so many hands between Meia Ponte and Jerusalem.[33]

According to Cônego J. Trindade Fonseca e Silva, the following Franciscan friars raised alms for the Holy Land in the captaincy of Goiás: João de Jesus e Maria, who resided in Meia Ponte in 1731; Domingos de Santiago of both Meia Ponte (1731–1733) and Traíras, where he died of advanced age; José de Nossa Senhora dos Anjos, who lived in Meia Ponte but who obtained alms at the mines of the Tocantins between 1752 and 1791; João do Sacramento, who died in Traíras in 1783; and Francisco de Nossa Senhora do Monte do Carmo, who resided in the same region from 1805 to 1831. With the death of Friar Francisco, the Franciscan alms collectors ceased to collect donations; and their property went to build a charity hospital in Meia Ponte. In 1835 the Confraria of the Holy Land was officially declared extinct, and their property was auctioned off. Meia Ponte then built a public school in the same location as the early hospice.[34]

Before the Italian Capuchins arrived in Goiás in the 1840s, another friar who preached in the captaincy was an Italian Capuchin named Father Joseph, who stopped briefly in Vila Boa before continuing on to an aldeia in Mato Grosso. He preached to crowds of people who traveled for miles to hear him speak. He also heard their confessions and blessed their children. As he walked in the streets, the people kissed his hands and his habit. After a dinner with Father Joseph, Saint-Hilaire described him as a man of "austere customs, charitable, full of sweetness and patience, jovial, and of gentle temperament."[35]

Jesuit Missions

After the Franciscans, the religious order that received the official right to establish indigenous aldeias in the captaincy of Goiás was the Society of Jesus, known as the Jesuits. In the north of the captaincy their government-supported efforts in the mid-eighteenth century were the aldeias built for the Xacriabá and Akroá (São Francisco Xavier) and Akroá (São José do Duro), where they lived under the secular administrator Lieutenant Colonel Wenceslau Gomes da Silva. Four Jesuits served in the aldeias: Padres Bento Soares, José de Matos, José Vieira, and José Batista. Although the Jesuits attempted to Christianize the two indigenous nations, the exploitation of Gomes da Silva, who treated them like slaves, pushed them into rebellion and flight. After he was removed for corruption, the Akroá moved back to Duro, while some of the Xacriabá went to settle at the Jesuit-run aldeia of Santa Ana of Rio das Velhas. But they did not live long under the Jesuits because Padres Manuel da Cruz and Francisco José were forcibly arrested by soldiers from São Paulo as part of the general Jesuit expulsion from Brazil of 1759. Until this time, the Jesuits had also run eight cattle fazendas with seventeen slaves and two thousand head of cattle, some on the banks of the Santa Tereza and Maranhão Rivers; thenceforth the Canoeiro invaded and occupied former Jesuit lands.[36]

Even though the Jesuits had been exiled, some of their mission Indians did not abandon their lands. The aldeias of Duro and Santa Ana continued to house the Akroá and Xacriabá. In the 1770s the Akroá once again revolted and their chiefs were executed, but the survivors were sent to join the aldeia of São José de Mossâmedes along with the Kayapó, and later the Karajá and Javaé. According to Padre Silva e Souza, the aldeias of Duro and nearby Formiga had cost 84:490$249 réis, but in spite of all that expenditure, only 276 Indians still resided in Duro in 1832 (appendix B.13).[37]

The other Jesuit aldeia of São Francisco Xavier was then abandoned because the Xacriabá had been sent south to another aldeia. After visiting the governor in August 1775, some Xacriabá had their children baptized. Either this group or another of the Xacriabá continued on south to the aldeia of Santa Ana of Rio das Velhas. Previously this aldeia had housed the Bororo allies of Colonel Antônio Pires de Campos, but in 1775 the Bororo were moved to the aldeia of Lanhoso, which was twelve leagues away. Another aldeia inhabited by the Bororo was Rio das Pedras, also founded by Pires de Campos in 1741. Near there was Pissarrão, composed of those who had left the aldeia of Rio das Pedras. These four aldeias—Santa Ana, Lanhoso, Rio das Pedras, and Pissarrão—had been under the Jesuits until their expulsion. By 1810 the four missions, according to Padre Silva e Souza, had cost the Royal Treasury 19:534$224 réis; and secular priests then served the missions. In 1805–1808 Padre Gregorio Coelho de Moraes Castro lived briefly at Santa Ana. He was replaced by Bento Mariano de Castro in 1809 and Thomas Francisco da Fonseca in 1810. Finally the aldeias found a priest who stayed, from at least 1811 to 1817: Claudio José da Cunha. In 1816 these missions, which were then included in the parish of Araxá, passed to the control of the province of Minas Gerais.[38]

At the mission of Rio das Pedras, the people were speakers of the língua geral of the coastal Indians. To these and his Bororo allies, Pires de Campos had added some Karajá and Tapirapé, who mixed with the Bororo and in 1775 were replaced by a small number of the Xacriabá in 1783. The majority of the Xacriabá (two hundred people) lived in Santa Ana as of 1788. At Rio das Pedras, however, the mission Indians had intermarried with blacks, whites, and mulatos, and the Xacriabá seem to have had a minimal impact on the culture or language spoken there, since the people continued to speak the língua geral, as well as Portuguese.[39]

When Saint-Hilaire traveled to the aldeia of Santa Ana in 1816, he found that it had only thirty square houses with thatched roofs. Some houses were grouped around a rectangular square, one side of which had a small church, as depicted in the plan of 1775. Upon his arrival, only women dressed in skirts and blouses greeted him because the men were in the fields. They were then subject to the commander of the aldeia, who complained of his difficulty in getting them to work, presumably in cultivating the land, since the men preferred to hunt and fish. Although some still knew words of their original language, it was no longer spoken in the aldeia. In contrast to other missions, the people of Santa Ana seem to have experienced more assimilation than others, and they were treated like other poor Luso-Brazilians after troops left the region; that is, local whites invaded and seized their lands in 1821.[40]

Directorate Missions

In contrast to the Jesuit aldeias of the first half of the eighteenth century, the later aldeias formed part of the Directorate system (1757–1798); they were officially founded by the governors to Christianize and civilize "pacified Indians," who agreed to stop fighting and settle in missions as vassals of the Crown and under the protection of the governor of Goiás. These aldeias of the late colonial period were São José de Mossâmedes (1755; renovated 1775), Maria I (1780), Nova Beira (1775), and São José do Carretão (1788). The shortest-lived aldeia was Graciosa, which was established by Cunha Matos in 1824 and abandoned soon thereafter by the Xerente. In spite of government efforts, none of these aldeias flourished, and the following summary of conditions at the missions will help to explain why they declined in numbers in the late colonial period. On the other hand, Duro (now Dianópolis), Mossâmedes, and Carretão would evolve into Luso-Brazilian towns that endure to the present.[41]

The most famous aldeia of the captaincy of Goiás was São José de Mossâmedes, which was named for the governor general, the baron of Mossâmedes, who had it built in 1755; its church was not constructed until 1780. Destined to house the Akroá from Duro, as well as the Javaé and Karajá, the mission was chosen for its "agreeable" site near the Serra Dourada with "good waters" and "many forests." Governor José de Almeida Vasconcelos e Sobral e Carvalho (1772–1778) renovated the aldeia in 1775, and thenceforth it had a director, according to the norms of the Directorate. In that year the following nations built their malocas at São José: the Akroá, Xavante, Karajá, Javaé, Carijós, and Naúdoz. Since the aldeia was subject to the military, three dragoons were sent to it: one to inspect it, another to administer its fields, and

Figure 18. A drawing of the restored mission of São José de Mossâmedes, made by Joaquim Cardozo Xavier, alferes of the militia infantry of Vila Boa de Goiás, in 1804. Courtesy of the Biblioteca Mario de Andrade, São Paulo, Brazil.

a third to supervise its cattle fazenda. Although Governor Luiz da Cunha Menezes (1778–1783) transferred eight hundred Javaé and Karajá to São José, they did not remain there, and the Akroá also deserted, probably to return to Duro. Thus when the Kayapó entered São José, there had already been a long history of various nations inhabiting this aldeia.[42]

Our best descriptions of the aldeia begin with the Kayapó period of settlement in the mission. Both Saint-Hilaire and Pohl visited São José and provide good descriptions of its decadence in the early nineteenth century, which reveal how little success Catholic priests had had in converting the Kayapó. At least four priests had served the people of São José and the other mission of Maria I: Inácio Joaquim Moreira, Felipe Néri da Silva, and in 1805–1806, Padres José Maria de Santa Anna Fernandez and Manoel Rodrigues Jardim. After these two priests, Padre Innocencio Joaquim Moreira de Carvalho became the "missionary vicar" in 1807–1808. He was replaced by Padre Francisco José Xavier da Silva in 1809 and 1810 but returned to his position with the Kayapó from at least 1811 to 1817.[43]

According to its elaborate plan, the aldeia of São José formed a large "quadrilateral" in which there were small buildings on each side with a few two-story structures to lodge the officers who accompanied the governor on his visits to the aldeia. Saint-Hilaire measured the regular square, walking off 145 steps in length by 112 in width. Although the principal façade had had an upper story, it had been torn down. All that remained upon Pohl's visit was the ground level, which was divided up for housing for the Kayapó. On the west side was the "simple" but spacious church, whose exterior had been damaged by 1801.[44]

The governor also had his "very pleasing" house, where he could take a vacation from his duties in Vila Boa. Behind it was a large orchard, which was watered by a small stream that had been diverted from its course to serve the aldeia. Finally, one group of buildings was used as a granary for guarding the harvested crops of the community. In 1819 the rest of the buildings were inhabited not by the Kayapó but by poor mulatos that the government permitted to live with the Kayapó and plant their own crops on Kayapó lands.[45]

But where were the Kayapó in this mission community? As Saint-Hilaire and Pohl clarify, they preferred to live in their own small houses built of palm fronds and thatch. Therefore, only fifteen or sixteen soldiers occupied the actual aldeia, along with civilian mulatos. During the rainy season, the mission housing built with tiles was too cold for the Kayapó. Therefore, some constructed about ten thatch-roofed houses on the west side of the aldeia, while the rest lived among the trees a league away from the aldeia, where they planted fields of yams and potatoes. In front of the houses were large wooden logs they called *touros* (bulls), which were used on festive occasions, when they threw logs at each other or raced with them. Even women and children carried touros, but smaller ones.[46]

When Saint-Hilaire went to see their fields, he found some women collecting ears of corn under the supervision of two or three soldiers. He was unable to see the men at work; instead, they danced for him. Singing a "monotonous" slow song, the men formed a circle and marked the beat with their feet as they danced in a circle. In the dance of the *urubu* (vulture), one of the dancers entered the circle, bent down, extended three fingers held together, and hit the ground with them various times. He also pretended to hit the other dancers with his three fingers, thus imitating a vulture eating its carrion. This dance was followed with a new song and the dance of the jaguar. The same dancer went to the middle of the circle and danced with his back curved, his arms rigidly extended to the earth, and his fingers separated and curved like the claws of a cat. After repeating these gestures, he left the circle, took a child and placed him on his shoulders, and returned to the circle, still dancing, in imitation of a jaguar catching its prey and returning to its den.[47]

Observing these dances, Saint-Hilaire concluded that the Kayapó lived only in the present hour and "showed a contentment and happiness that are never seen among the melancholic Goianos." Yet Saint-Hilaire also recognized that their many flights from the mission were due to bad treatment by the soldiers. Only two hundred still lived at the aldeia, and he expected that it would soon be abandoned and the Kayapó subject to extermination, in part due to the venereal diseases they had contracted from the Portuguese.[48]

As for their religion, after years of contact and alleged Christianization, the Kayapó had only "a minimum idea of the Divinity." According to Saint-Hilaire, their word for God was *Puhanca*, but Pohl could not find anyone who knew how to say the "Our Father." At that time, all the Kayapó had been baptized, except for some of the elderly. When newborn infants were baptized, they received a Christian name from the priest and that of an animal from an elderly Kayapó.[49] The vicar also married them, and some even went to confession. Apparently, marriages combined both traditional and Christian elements. They were celebrated with a banquet and dancing, during which the bride held a cord that was fastened to the head of her husband.[50]

Saint-Hilaire helps to explain why their ideas about Christianity were rudimentary. The vicar only said Mass on Sundays. Instead of instructing, protecting, or "civilizing" the Kayapó, he raised sugar. Either he went to his brother's sugar plantation in Conceição, two leagues away, or he spent time on his own plantation at São Isidro, which was more distant. Pohl identified him as Padre Inocêncio and said that he had to be protected by armed guards during Mass because the Indians had killed another priest at the altar.[51]

On the other hand, the absence of the priest six days a week meant that the Kayapó could preserve more of their own beliefs and rituals, such as night dances that lasted until midnight, when they painted their bodies red with urucu and black with jenipapo, using long streaks of color. They also wore jewelry made of animal teeth, which were attached to cords and made noise with each movement of the feet. They sang loudly with a repeated "Ho! Ho! Ho!" to the music of instruments made from curved gourds or cattle horns.[52]

Another indication of the persistence of traditional beliefs and rituals was the ritual of *quebra-cabeça* (break-head). At the time of Lent, the chief, called the "coronel," went to the middle of a circle with a club. Then the others danced in a circle around him, during which time one man threw a log toward another, leaped in the direction of the chief, and knelt before him; he received a blow from a club on his forehead, which was just strong enough to make his blood flow. The women, dancing and singing, cleaned the blood from the wounded man. According to Pohl, all of them submitted to this ritual, but Pohl did not explain its meaning.[53]

Bloodletting also took place when a rich man died. In one ceremony they praised the deeds of the dead person, and on the next day they went to the chief's house to receive a club blow on the forehead. With blood flowing, they returned to the house of the dead person to spill this blood on his body. Notably, the dead person was not buried in the church but in a hole, in a seated position with his bow and arrow and food. Afterward there was a funeral banquet with dancing and singing.[54]

Under the direct supervision of the soldiers, the Kayapó cultivated the land, working five days a week. The harvest was stored in the granaries of the aldeia and subsequently distributed by the corporal commandant among the indigenous families, according to each one's needs. The excess was then sold to the towns or to the soldiers. The director general in Vila Boa then bought salt, tobacco, cotton cloth, and iron tools, which he sent to the corporal-commandant to distribute among the mission Indians.[55]

The Portuguese also introduced European technologies to the aldeia: a water mill that powered a grindstone to mill corn, a machine to deseed cotton, and twenty-four spinning wheels. According to Saint-Hilaire, a mulata woman was paid 50$000 réis per year to teach the Kayapó women how to spin and weave cotton, even though the Kayapó wore no clothing. The products of this labor also belonged to the community, as did the products of the fields. In an effort to develop the mission, the provincial government also tried new technologies at São José for producing charcoal, lumber, and iron.[56]

The two days that the Kayapó had off from their supervised work were Sunday and Monday, when they went hunting or cared for their own plots of land planted with yams and potatoes. This was probably the time when they made their bows and arrows and large burden baskets (*jucunus*). They also made small baskets, some of which Pohl took back to Vienna. During the Easter season, the men were permitted to do a race in which they hoisted a log to their shoulder and then ran with it in relay style, handing it over to other runners until the race was finished.[57]

Apparently the Portuguese allowed the Kayapó to retain some of their own traditional leaders and ways of ruling themselves. Traditionally they were governed by a cacique, who had various captains under his orders. In the aldeia, the Portuguese gave the titles of coronel, captain, and alferes (second lieutenant) to the most respected men in the community. The "Coronel of the Indians" used to go to Vila Boa and walk in processions, carrying a rifle. On those occasions, he wore short pants and a cotton shirt with a tricornered hat and a gold buckle.[58]

Saint-Hilaire also met the most famous person in the aldeia, Dona Damiana da Cunha. According to Saint-Hilaire, she spoke Portuguese correctly and was "amiable" and "jovial," with an "open and intelligent physiognomy." She was then preparing to go to the forests for three months to convince the Kayapó to return with her to São José because they would be "much happier there than in the middle of the forests." When Saint-Hilaire expressed doubt about her plans, she responded, "The respect that they have [for] me is too great for them not to do what I command." Her brother Manoel da Cunha served as the interim director of the aldeia until he was arrested and jailed in the City of Goiás, where he died. He was accused of being responsible for the flight of Indians from the mission.[59]

As these sources reveal, most Kayapó did not fully convert to Christianity or to a Luso-Brazilian lifestyle, even though the Portuguese government had expended large sums on the aldeia of São José. According to Padre Silva e Souza, the Portuguese had spent 67:346$066 réis on the construction and installation of the aldeia, but part of that expenditure went for two comfortable vacation houses for the governors in São José and Maria I, which were built for their occasional visits to the aldeias.[60]

Maria I was the second aldeia that sheltered the Kayapó, after 1780. Governor Luiz da Cunha Menezes (1778–1783) had the aldeia constructed in 1780 at a cost to the Royal Treasury of 13:684$021 réis and named it for the queen of Portugal.[61] According to both Saint-Hilaire and Pohl, the Kayapó who were transferred from Maria I to São José fondly remembered their first aldeia with *saudades* (longings) and always returned there for visits. Why the Kayapó did so is obvious from the aldeia's location. It was built on the banks of the Fartura River on a low hill behind which ran the Serra Dourada, and nearby were other rivers. The fertile region reputedly had good hunting and fishing grounds.[62]

The Kayapó who initially settled in Maria I were those whom José Luis Pereira had "pacified." Apparently the first two communities were led by Angraí-oxá (or Angraiochá) and Xaquenau (or Xaquenonau). Angraí-oxá and his wife, Xuinequá, were the grandparents of Dona Damiana da Cunha. The third community came later, on 27 September; its cacique was Cunã-puaxi (or Cananpuaxi). A year later a fourth cacique, Pupuarê, brought his people to the

Table 10. Population and deaths among the Kayapó of Maria I by age and sex, 1781–1783

Age	Males	Females	Total
Adults	112	151	263
8 or 10 years of age	51	61	112
6 or 7 years of age	56	62	118
Nursing infants	12	13	25
Total	231	287	518
Deaths			
Adults	11	14	25
Children	1[a]	2	3
Total	12	16	28

Source: AHU, Goiás, CD rom no. 4, Ofício do [governador e capitão-general de Goiás], Luiz da Cunha Menezes, ao [secretário de estado da Marinha e Ultramar], to Martinho de Melo e Castro, remetendo carta do sargento regente da aldeia Maria I, José Luis Pereira, e relação dos índios Caiapós da dita aldeia.
[a]Number is uncertain. It may be 10.

aldeia. Altogether there were 687 people, of whom 328 had been baptized, living in four separate villages. In May or June 1783 a group of Kayapó entered Maria I after a long journey from the area of the Grande River on the road to São Paulo. This information was attached to a list of the Kayapó who resided at Maria I from 15 July 1781 to 26 May 1783, which was compiled by José Luis Pereira (table 10).[63]

These Kayapó were notable for the number of women (151) and children (255) in the community. Of the 518 who settled in the aldeia, only 112 were adult men. Eventually the number of Kayapó in Maria I grew to an estimated 2,400.[64] In various years they were ravaged by epidemic diseases, while others were subjected to forced labor. Those who could flee did so. One of them was Captain Manuel, whom João Caetano da Silva of Meia Ponte met in Camapuã. Before his desertion, Captain Manuel had served as a pedestre (foot soldier) at Maria I and claimed that he had lived in the aldeia under Governor Tristão da Cunha Menezes (1783–1800). He had left the mission, however, along with another captain, Antônio, and made his way to Camapuã in traditional Kayapó territory. These captains were typical of many mission Indians who quit the aldeias to rejoin their people in their homelands. By 1813 only 129 residents remained at Maria I, and Governor Fernando Delgado Freire de Castilho (1809–1820) required them to move to São José de Mossâmedes.[65]

When Pohl visited Maria I, he found that the aldeia was already abandoned. Two houses built of wood and clay with tiled roofs were in ruins. One was the residence of the governor and the other of the administrator and his soldiers. The governor's residence was then inhabited by bats, mosquitoes, and a dead burro. According to a plan of 1782, there was to be a church dedicated to Our Lady of Glory, but Pohl did not describe one. Apparently one of the houses had served as the church.[66]

In front of the governor's residence there had been an area for dances for the Kayapó. A hundred steps toward the south was the large building in which they had guarded their harvested crops. Pohl also saw a forge and unfinished buildings, as well as the ruins of sugar and corn mills and an aguardente factory. The Kayapó houses had been built in a circle around the grain storage building, but they had long since burned down. There was also a small cattle fazenda, which seems to have functioned until at least 1821, when José Miguel reported on twenty-two head of cattle, one of which had died from a snake bite. According to Saint-Hilaire, four hundred cattle had once been raised there to provide meat for the governor and his men when they visited the aldeia. The impoverished condition of the aldeia combined with the Kayapó removal to Mato Grosso led to its official closure and final sale of its properties in 1833.[67]

In the case of Maria I, two conflicting images survive: one of the Kayapó fleeing the aldeia, but another of their choosing to return. Pohl partially explains why the mission Kayapó "esteemed" Maria I. When he entered the aldeia, he found it to be densely covered with wild vegetation that sheltered wild animals, and his men hunted down and killed a sloth. At Maria I the Kayapó had been able to hunt and fish and raise cattle, but at São José they could no longer do so and suffered from hunger.[68]

Between the initial founding of São José de Mossâmedes and Maria I, the Portuguese also attempted to establish another mission in 1778, on Bananal Island for the Karajá and Javaé. After their agreement to ally with the Portuguese, the Karajá accepted having an aldeia named Nova Beira and a presídio, São Pedro do Sul.[69] In fact, the cacique Abinarequê, along with a number of Javaé "princes," traveled to Vila Boa to ask for a priest. Apparently their request was not granted; instead, about eight hundred Karajá and Javaé were officially transferred from Bananal Island to São José de Mossâmedes in 1780. Later one thousand Javaé were sent to the aldeia of Carretão to live with the Xavante, where some remained into the 1820s. On the other hand,

180 Xavante from Carretão were ordered to move to a new aldeia in Salinas in Karajá territory in 1846. In general, official correspondence records the presence of the Karajá and Javaé in other aldeias of the captaincy rather than at Nova Beira. Padre Silva e Souza, however, reported that the Portuguese spent 4:582$196 réis on the aldeia of Nova Beira.[70] The more significant missions to the Karajá did not fully develop until the nineteenth century, with the establishment of aldeias such as São Joaquim (or São José) de Jamimbu, which was originally located in Salinas near the Araguaia River. Founded by Friar Taggia in 1845 for the Karajá, São Joaquim also came to house a group of Xavante, as of 1846, and later some Xerente.[71]

Most Xavante who entered a Directorate aldeia of the captaincy, however, went to the one designed for them at Pedro III do Carretão. According to tradition, this mission was named for the consort of Queen Maria I of Portugal, but it was also called Carretão for its large wagon cart. The aldeia was created in 1784, and two years later the guarda-mor João da Costa Lisboa gave thirty oitavas of gold to Commandant Domingos Gomes Albernós for works on the mission. According to Padre Silva e Souza, it actually cost 24:652$131 réis to build.[72] The Xavante did not arrive until 7 January 1788, when they made their dramatic dancing entrance and were welcomed by the vicar of Crixás, military officers, and José Pinto da Fonseca, who had "pacified" them. After their reception and the baptism of 412 children, a serious epidemic erupted, killing more than 100 hundred Xavante, who had been baptized "in their last moments."[73]

After the epidemic subsided, the Xavante returned to the aldeia and began work on the fields that the governor had set aside for them. The large number of Xavante (3,000 to 3,500), who had come from the Araguaia and Tocantins Rivers in the 1780s, did not remain at Carretão, and many died in a measles epidemic. The subsequent history of the aldeia was one of steadily diminishing numbers. When he visited the mission in 1819, Pohl counted only 227 Indians, and Cunha Matos found only 158 Xavante plus 15 other Indians in 1824 (table 11).[74]

According to Pohl, Carretão was twenty-two leagues distant from Vila Boa and was built on two hillsides. Between them ran the Carretão (also São Patricio) River of six to seven meters in width. On one side of the river were the sugar and corn mills plus the houses, aligned in a row, of the administrator and the soldiers. The priest also had a house. On the other side of the river and along a street were thirty clay "barracas" of the Indians, which were covered in grass (*ervas*). Thus the river divided the Luso-Brazilians from the indigenous community.[75]

An early list of the aldeia's buildings, possibly from the 1780s, recorded the following: one bell for prayer; two storage buildings for food; three mills for grinding cereals; a [storage?] box for manioc; a sugar mill house and a distillery for rum; 3 taxas (*tachas* used on engenhos?) and two ovens; three *tachos* (vases); one house for spinning and weaving cloth; one blacksmith's *tenda* (awning); one visitor's house; and three barracks for soldiers. The inventory reveals that the aldeia's inhabitants could process their own cereals and sugarcane and make aguardente and then safeguard their surplus in granaries or other storage places. The inclusion of buildings for weaving, a shelter for the blacksmith, and ovens for baking (manioc bread?) suggests that the aldeia was self-sufficient in food and clothing.[76]

From the beginning of its history, there was a military detachment based in the aldeia, with a commandant in place as early as 1786 along with a "missionary vicar." The government's religious objectives were initially fulfilled by the vicar of Pilar with the baptism of the Xavante, but later the aldeia acquired a permanent priest. In 1805–1806 the "missionary vicar" was Padre Filipe Néri da Silva; in 1806–1807, Padre Manoel Rodrigues Jardim; in 1808, Padre Thomas Francisco da Fonseca; and in 1809–1811, Padre Luis da Gama Mendonça. Finally, Reverend Rodrigo Coelho Furtado de Azevedo Lima was appointed "missionary vicar" in 1812 and he kept that post until 1824, when he was seventy years old. He had apparently lived there since at least 1795, when he paid the dízimo tax on his crops. Yet another priest, the vicar Francisco Xavier dos Guimarães Britto e Costa (a visitor?), reported on the clerical vestments and ritual objects being used in the aldeia's church in 1803.[77]

Although we lack illustrations of the mission church, two sources enable a reconstruction of the ritual items then in use in Catholic ceremonies. The central image on the main and only altar was that of Jesus Christ crucified. There were six candle holders made of painted wood and two smaller ones of brass; a chalice and small bell; small vases to hold water, wine, and holy oils; and numerous altar cloths used at Mass. The *Rituals of Paulo 5°* and a Roman missal with a stand made of wood were the only books. In 1803 there were two priestly vestments: one of purple and green, and the other of white and red, which were described as "old" in 1836. A baptistery was on the 1803 list but not listed in 1836, most likely because the 1836 list included those items that were to be sent to Salinas. Overall, the impression is one of the poverty of the church's ritual items in contrast to the inventories of white churches, with their gold and silver vessels. In Carretão, most metal objects were made of tin or brass, except for a silver paten and a cross with two "lanterns of leaf."[78]

Shortly after the Xavante settled in Carretão, officials were preoccupied with clothing them. In 1790 a royal official in Rio de Janeiro reported that two thousand hats and 6,383 *côvados* (a measurement equal to sixty-six centimeters) of *serafinas* (a wool cloth) could be sent to Carretão. They were to come from the military arsenal's warehouses in Rio de Janeiro. Although he recognized that the "Indians of Brazil" generally used cotton for clothing, he argued for sending them *baeta* (wool cloth) to cover themselves and use as coverlets for sleeping.[79]

Another problem for Portuguese officials was sustenance for the new arrivals in the mission. Although they allocated funds for food for the Xavante, they could not feed all of them. Therefore, the administrator of the aldeia and his soldiers forced them to work in the fields growing food crops. Those who resisted, according to tradition, were placed in the stocks, whipped, or given blows on the hand with the *palmatória*, a wooden paddle with holes. By 1795 the Xavante were planting a variety of crops in the large communal field: corn, beans, manioc, *alos* (*alho*, garlic?), peanuts, castor beans (mamona), cotton, and sugarcane. This list suggests that the Xavante had access to a variety of food crops—if they were not sold outside the aldeia or to the soldiers.[80]

Coerced labor, however, led most Xavante to flee the aldeia. According to Pohl, they were put to flight by "rough, imprudent, and bad treatment given them by its administrators."[81] In spite of what Pohl concluded, some Xavante still lived at the mission at the time of his visit in 1819, and he left a brief description of the aldeia when the "Indians" of Carretão had abandoned "all the uses and customs of the savage state." He was unable to find any informants willing or able to tell him how they used to live. Since they had been brought there as children, they spoke only Portuguese. The men had adopted the use of rifles, and they turned to bows and arrows only to hunt birds. All of them wore clothing, and when the women went to church, they dressed in blue mantles, as did Luso-Brazilian women. They followed the religious customs of Christianity, and many went to confession, which was rare in other missions.[82]

Before they were freed from colonial labor obligations in the 1820s, they used to work three days a week "for the king," from 8:00 to 11:00 a.m. Like enslaved Africans on a plantation, they assembled together before the house of the administrator, where they said prayers, including the Our Father, Hail Mary, Salve-Regina, and Confiteor. They also recited the Credo and Ten Commandments before going up to the administrator to receive his blessing. Unlike slaves, however, the men could take rifles to the fields where they labored cultivating corn, manioc, tobacco, cotton, and beans. At times women accompanied them, toting large burden baskets full of tools, "since no man carries any weight." Besides the basket, each woman also carried one or two children. Other women worked with cotton, especially as spinners, a common occupation for Luso-Brazilian women in Goiás. Only after they finished the day's fieldwork at about 2:00 p.m. were they given a meal of black beans and cornmeal from a large cauldron. Each person received his share in a gourd.[83]

After the official labor for the king, they were able to pursue their own activities. The men could hunt and fish or work on their own fields. Some also owned small herds of cattle, milk cows, chickens, and other domestic animals. They could sell the surplus from their fields, and, according to Pohl, they understood the value of money, with which they bought rifles, large knives, gunpowder, lead, cows, and blue mantles for the women.[84]

They also had the right to elect their chief, whom they called "captain," but both he and his people were under the authority of the administrator and his soldiers. The captain of Pohl's time privately complained to him of the bad treatment that they suffered in Carretão and of their heavy workload but, above all, of the frauds inflicted on them. He cited the example of an Indian who went to have his corn ground and received only half of it in return.[85]

Five years later, in 1824, Raimundo José da Cunha Matos visited Carretão. He found that the same priest still served as vicar. But he could count only 173 Indians: 158 Xavante, 3 Kayapó, 10 Javaé, and 2 of unknown nation still resident in the aldeia. He also reported that some Xerente had lived at Carretão, as some would do in the 1830s. Fortunately, Cunha Matos recorded those who lived in Carretão by household and ethnicity (table 11). First of all, there were twenty-five Luso-Brazilian houses made with tiles and thirty-three thatch-roofed houses. The non-Indians and married Xavante lived in the houses with tiles. Those who were described as single, even though they were part of a couple, were most likely to be Xavante in "grass" houses.[86] The household lists suggest a sharp distinction between Christians (white, pardo, and black) and the Xavante, Javaé, and Kayapó.

These documents also provide a glimpse of Christian social and political status. Heading the list was the white priest, age seventy. Also in his household was his elderly white agregada of sixty, the only white woman in the aldeia; his goddaughter, age seventeen; two female slaves—an Angola, age forty, and a cabra, age thirty-five; and two agregados—a crioulo freedman, age twenty, and a racially mixed woman, age seventeen. Also prominent was the commandant of the aldeia, the corporal João Lourenço de Oliveira, who was fifty-eight.

Table II. Inhabitants of Pedro III do Carretão, 1824

Color or nation	Males	Females	Total
Nonindigenous	16	12	28
Alvo (white)	2	1	3
Pardo	8	8	16
Cabra	2	1	3
Crioulo	4	1	5
Angola	–	1	1
Indigenous nations	85	88	173
Xavante	76	82	158
Married	19	22	41
Single	19	35	54
Children	38	25	63
Javaé	5	5	10
Married	1	3	4
Single	3	2	5
Children	1	–	1
Kayapó	3	–	3
Married	2	–	2
Single	1	–	1
Unknown, "Indian"	1	1	2
Sum total	101	100	201

Source: AHGDD, no. 68, Correspondência Dirigida do Comandante das Armas, Raimundo José da Cunha Matos, from João Lourenço de Oliveira, Carretão, 13 Novembro 1824, f. 217; Mapa de toda a gente que existe nesta aldeia de São Pedro Terceiro do Carretão, 12 December 1824, ff. 194–98; and Relação da população da aldea de S. Pedro Terceiro do Carretão, s. d., ff. 208–10.

Unlike the priest, he was a pardo. Also resident was Lourenço de Oliveira's female agregada Francisca da Silva, age thirty, and two pardo children, age ten and five, one of whom was the child of a Bazilio cabra, age sixteen or seventeen. Two crioulo men with the surname of Silva Cardozo, age forty and thirty-four, completed Lourenço de Oliveira's household of seven. A second military man was a pardo soldier of the pedestres, Manoel dos Santos Silva, age fifty. His household included his wife, the parda Antonia Moreira, age forty; his parda daughter, age ten; his son, age eight; and his eldest son, Antônio Joaquim, who was already married at age twenty-four to Maria Ciciaca (or Sereaca) of the Javaé nation, age twenty.

The administrator of the aldeia was Gonçalo Pereira da Silveira, age forty-six. Besides the priest, he was the only other white man in the aldeia. He was married to a Xavante woman, Potenciana Xavier de Barros, age twenty-four. Since he had only one crioulo slave, age fourteen, and a pardo agregado of eighteen, he was obviously not a wealthy man.

Besides the white and pardo men in the aldeia, the household lists also identify the indigenous leaders of the aldeia. The Xavante captain-mor was Vituriano Felippe de Ciqueira, age fifty. His wife, Dona Custodia, age sixty, was also a Xavante. The two others in the household were Brigida, Xavante, age twenty-five; and Lieutenant Januario, Xavante, nineteen. The next Xavante household was headed by Alferes Antônio Gonçalves, age forty; and his wife, Perpetua de Souza, age forty. Also in their household was Sergeant Roque, age thirty; and his wife, Francisca, age twenty. The corporal Felizardo, Xavante, age forty, was married to Damiana, age twenty-six, of the Javaé nation.

Some of the Xavante men without a military rank are of particular interest because the scribe recorded their occupations, such as Agostinho, carpenter, age forty, an Indian. Three of the Xavante men were weavers: Inocencio Rodrigues, age forty; Domingos, age forty; and Antônio, age sixteen. Also on the list were Miguel, age forty, an ox-cart guide (*carreiro*); Antônio José, age thirty, a mason/stonecutter; and Francisco Álvares, age forty, a blacksmith. Apparently, others of the Xavante worked in the fields.[87]

Those who cultivated crops had to pay the dízimo, a tax on agricultural production, and tax records of 1821 reveal that the aldeia was taxed on the following crops: 105 *alqueires* of corn, 99 of beans, 12 of castor beans, 6 of rice, and 30 of manioc, plus 5 arrobas of coffee and 3 of cotton, and 19 carts of sugarcane.[88] Before this time crops had been harvested under the colonial system that utilized communal labor on a large field, but by 1824 the mission's inhabitants had been set at liberty to labor for themselves, which must have affected food supply and distribution. Writing from Carretão on 28 October 1824, João Lourenço de Oliveira reported that the Indians were working for themselves and that there was no longer a large communal field. Therefore he no longer received food provisions to distribute to them. Again in 1829, the director Gonçalo Pereira da Silveira reiterated that the inhabitants of Carretão "worked for themselves" and did not do "any service in common."[89] The transition from communal to individual labor clearly took place in the 1820s and must have increased Xavante dissatisfaction with Carretão. By 1856 the Xavante had abandoned the aldeia, where they had suffered from the "palmatória, *tronco* [stocks], chain, *chicote* [whip], and collar," and they migrated to the Mortes River.[90]

When Father Gil Vilanova visited Carretão in the 1880s, he saw only stone bases for the mission church, although he easily located the governor's house due to its large backyard. A wooden bridge over the river and some houses in ruins were all that remained of the aldeia. Also surviving was the great wagon cart, the *carretão*, which he described as "the terror" of the Indians. Only one man and two women of the "Indian race" lived there, but some caboclos, or descendants of "Indian women" who had married black men, lived in its neighborhood. Although the forest had reclaimed the mission fields, here and there coffee trees were still growing.[91]

A century later, in 1980, Rita Heloísa de Almeida Lazarin interviewed local residents about Carretão. The land of the former mission then belonged to a rancher, and in 1979 a Javaé woman had gone to FUNAI on behalf of a community of seventy-five, seeking demarcation and protection of their lands. At that time they defined themselves as descendants of the Xavante, Javaé, and Kayapó, although outsiders called them "Tapuios." In 1980 one elderly man of ninety-seven proudly proclaimed that the mission (or lands?)] was "already ours. All [our] life." It was "given [to them] by Queen Maria I and D. Pedro I and the Queen [Maria II] with D. Pedro II." His father had been a fugitive slave from Pilar who had married an indigenous woman named Maria Raimunda. Along with other blacks and Indians in the community, the couple had a special devotion to Our Lady of the Rosary, and they used to go on pilgrimage to Retiro, which had a chapel dedicated to Our Lady of the Rosary.[92]

The last locations of Christian Indians were Graciosa, Carolina, and Porto Real (also Porto Imperial or Nacional) in the north. Twelve leagues from Porto Real on the left bank of the Tocantins River and the Tucuruçu (also Tacuarussú) River was the aldeia of Graciosa. It was created on 3 July 1824 upon the presentation of sixty-two "Cherentes Indians" to Cunha Matos. Eventually eight hundred Indians under as many as seventeen captains were settled there by the sergeant of pedestres Estevão Joaquim Pires, who was its first director. One of the Xerente captains who played an important role in their settlement at Graciosa was Francisco Xuathe. The last to settle there was Captain-Mor Acometh.[93]

In 1825 Cunha Matos left for Rio de Janeiro. Without his protection, the Xerente abandoned the aldeia because they had suffered "misery and privations" there. The mission's detachment of seven soldiers also deserted Graciosa. Three years later Graciosa had only sixty residents due to sezões (malaria) and lack of aid. In the end, most of those who had lived at Graciosa returned to raiding ranches in the vicinity of Carmo, Pontal, and Porto Real, and only twenty-five agreed to go to Carretão. In 1831 two Xerente, Bernardo de Siqueira and Victorino Caetano, "of Carretão," were given the task of carrying the mail from the north to the City of Goiás.[94]

In about the period that Graciosa was founded, a chapel with a thatched roof was built in São Pedro de Alcântara (now Carolina) that was dedicated to Our Lady of the (Immaculate) Conception. The governor of Goiás funded a missionary vicar in order to convert the Indians of the Tocantins River—but rather than convert or assist them, the priest entered into business dealings with slave dealers in Pará until he fled there in 1815, taking Indian captives with him. In spite of his betrayal, the church survived and attracted two hundred Christian "souls," including seventy-nine Christian Indians, by 1832. In that same year, there were also 53 of them in Porto Imperial, 33 in Palma, 25 in Natividade, and 13 in Cavalcante, São Félix, and Arraias combined. Thus in 1832 only 203 Christian Indians were living outside the aldeias in the northern comarca. But those who lived outside the missions in the south were counted in only three towns: 84 in the City of Goiás, 142 in Meia Ponte, and 72 in Crixás, for a total of 298 (table B.13).[95]

By the early nineteenth century, declining numbers of mission Indians suggest that none of the priests were notably successful at Christianization via the missions. Two censuses reveal how few Indians lived in Christian aldeias as of 1825 and 1832. The census takers of 1825 could find only 125 in São José, 198 in Carretão, and 300 in Duro, for a total "Indian" population of 623 for the province of Goiás. They were about equally divided by sex: 304 males to 319 females. In 1832 their numbers had dropped even further, to 216 males and 277 females (total of 493) who remained at the missions; thus the aldeia of São José had only 54 Indians; Carretão, 163; and Duro, 276. Even smaller numbers of Christian Indians were scattered among Luso-Brazilian towns. After more than a century of Christianization efforts, less than a thousand (994) Indians (459 males and 535 females) could be identified as Christians in the entire province of Goiás in 1832 (table B.13).[96]

In conclusion, the Catholic Church in Goiás was not only weak in its presence outside of Vila Boa and Meia Ponte but also remarkably unsuccessful in its efforts to convert the majority of the indigenous populations of Goiás in the late colonial period. The Portuguese system of imposing secular priests, administrators, and troops at the missions had usually led to resistance rather than conversion, except in the case of a small number of aldeia residents. After serving as a military officer in both Africa and Goiás, Cunha Matos regarded the hatred of the Xavante and other indigenous peoples toward "civilized people" as "most strange." But their hatred, he admitted, was due to the forced labor that was imposed on them and the robbery of their lands. It seems that any nation that spent time in a mission, such as the Xavante and the Kayapó, emerged from the experience embittered and ready for war, with European weaponry acquired at the missions. These allegedly Christian Indians were then the very ones who retaliated for what they had suffered in the aldeias by attacking Christian settlements and killing Christians.[97]

On the other hand, a popular church persisted because it was supported by lay Christians of every color who kept alive their favorite religious traditions in the absence of a priest and amid the threat of warfare. Even those who lived in quilombos honored Nossa Senhora da Abadia and São Gonçalo.[98] Their colorful rituals filled with music and songs dedicated to the Holy Spirit, the Virgin Mary, and other saints even brought disgruntled mission Indians to the Christian towns to participate in processions and prayers. Still others remained at the missions and intermarried with blacks and pardos stationed there, and, as we will see in the next chapter, some of the missions also contributed to the formation of Luso-Brazilian families of all colors in the region.

CHAPTER 9

Shadows in the Night

Women and Gender Relations

One of the common themes from the interior of Brazil is that of the hidden woman. Frontier violence led fathers and husbands to protect their daughters and wives in order to prevent any contact with strange men. Karajá men covered their women in canoes, while Luso-Brazilians cloistered them in their homes and did not permit them to talk to visiting men. Noting men's "great jealousy," Pohl reported that women were so well guarded that they proved the proverb "The woman ought to be taken to church only three times in her life: to baptism, for marriage and for burial." White women, in particular, were well hidden from view in the walled compounds of Vila Boa, where Saint-Hilaire found it difficult to meet women. During the heat of the day, they did not leave their households; only at night could he see groups of women, who were draped in woolen capes with scarves or hats over their heads, as they glided like "shadows" in the "silence of the night." Pohl also described their use of an overdress with a red mantle and fine muslin cloth that covered their heads. Even in the hot north, the women "all wore cloaks, either made of scotch tartan, or blue cloth, very similar to those worn by the factory girls of Glasgow in the winter season."[1] Only enslaved women and prostitutes could walk openly in the streets or meet men in the taverns. Needless to say, women's lives and relationships were strictly governed by men, not only to protect them from other men but also to coerce and control them, especially if they were captive indigenous women or enslaved Africans, who, at the first opportunity, might slip away into the forests.

This chapter, therefore, seeks to clarify points of contact that involved gender relations between Luso-Brazilian men and nonwhite women, out of which would emerge the free population of color of the nineteenth century. Major themes will include violence against women and children on the frontier, forced labor, coerced relationships involving white men and their nonwhite

Figure 19. These illustrations of an officer and a woman are from playing cards that depict styles of dress in Vila Boa de Goiás at the time that they were collected by Johann E. Pohl. Courtesy of the Museum für Völkerkunde, Vienna, Austria.

concubines, sexual exploitation via prostitution and sharing of women, and consensual unions or marriage that sometimes led to intermarriage across color lines.[2] A final theme is abandonment, either in Portugal or Goiás, since the impoverishment of women was also common.

Due to the remoteness of the captaincy of Goiás, men prone to violence were unfettered by social or religious institutions in what they chose to do with girls and women. Those who participated in bandeiras killed indigenous women and children as part of efforts to seize their lands and exterminate their nation; if they did not slaughter them, they brought them back to the towns as war captives. If women resisted, they were punished like enslaved African women with the whip and palmatória (wooden paddle). Among the first indigenous women taken captive by the bandeiras were those of the Araés and Karajá nations, but many of these women endured their captivity in São Paulo rather than in Goiás. Observing the golden jewelry of the Goiá, the bandeira leader Bartolomeu Bueno had their women kidnapped in order to make their husbands tell him where they had found gold. After the Goiá rebelled against such treatment, the men were taken to São Paulo as slaves, while captive women were kept in Vila Boa.³

On the other hand, most indigenous nations enslaved the women and children of their enemies, including Luso-Brazilians and Africans. Except for the Canoeiro, all groups involved in the frontier conflicts seized captive women and children. For example, the Xavante commonly raided the Karajá and kidnapped their women, while Vila Real documented the Karajá abduction of an Apinaje woman and her two small daughters. In the north, a woman captured by the Apinaje might have to serve as the village "wanton." Documentary evidence of indigenous sexual assaults is rare, except in the case of the Krahô who assisted a bandeira in attacking the Porekamekrã and raping their women and girls.⁴

Since indigenous women lived among their captors and learned their languages, they then became interpreters and go-betweens when warring groups sought to make peace. The most successful of these women was the Karajá Xuanam-piá, a former captive who played a significant role in the diplomacy of peacemaking and alliance between the Portuguese and the Karajá in 1775. A second skillful diplomat was a Macamecrã woman who assisted Francisco José Pinto as an "ambassador" and successfully negotiated a temporary peace between warring nations on the banks of the Tocantins River in the early nineteenth century.⁵

Most indigenous women, however, did not serve in such roles. In contrast, they went into battle with their husbands, and in the case of the Canoeiro, they fought as bravely as the men. Because women participated in combat, Luso-Brazilian bandeiras were merciless, treating them like their husbands, with violent deaths or enslavement. When they refused to give up their children to slavers, they were killed. Or they were captured and forced to leave their babies behind. Ribeiro personally saw captive women with milk-laden breasts weeping for their lost babies. Equally, their children were killed, sometimes brutally, in vengeance killings. Allied warriors used babies for target practice, shooting them with bows and arrows, or soldiers impaled them on bayonets as their mothers were forced to watch. In retaliation, indigenous warriors killed pregnant women, cutting the unborn child from the womb, leaving the corpses for the husband to find. In one notable case they burned a black woman alive, possibly in vengeance for the attacks of black militias in the area. According to Castelnau, the Canoeiro might even force a mother "to devour the brain of her own child," or they would tie a woman to the prow of a canoe, making her alternately plunge into the water and return to the surface, which could last for days.⁶ But there is little colonial evidence of cannibalism involving women, although some Kayapó men were accused of kidnapping and eating a girl in the nineteenth century.[7]

Nor is there much evidence of sexual violence on the part of indigenous or African men against white women. On the contrary, those who raped were Luso-Brazilian men, who assaulted both indigenous captives and enslaved black women. Since such men were not arrested for rape, little evidence of sexual assault survives in colonial documentation. Only the baptisms and deaths of mestizo children, also termed bastardos (bastards), after the arrival of a bandeira or the founding of a mining town may testify to coerced sexual relations with captive women. Presumably, male slaveholders treated captive and enslaved women as they did on the coast: they claimed sexual rights over all their slave women, sleeping with as many as they chose. If the enslaved woman belonged to another slaveholder, it might be a different matter. For the discharge of his conscience, Dionízio Furtado de Freitas admitted that he had deflowered Jozeva, the slave woman of Dona Maria Joana. As restitution, he willed ten head of cattle to her son, Basilio, but he did not compensate Jozeva in his will.[8]

Even masters who committed incest involving slaves could escape punishment. Coronel Manuel Lopes Chagas, a wealthy slaveholder, allegedly slept with both a mother and her daughter, Micaela crioula, by whom he had a pardo son, Lino Manuel Lopes Chagas. Although he recognized the pardo as his natural son in 1769, his son was unable to claim any inheritance because of the family incest involving his father, grandmother, and mother. Since the "law of the kingdom prohibited incestuous children from inheriting," the colonel willed his property to João Álvares Machado in 1780, which Lino Chagas contested because he had received a letter of legitimization in 1769. His birth status, however, was no hindrance to his military career, since he too became a colonel (chapter 10).[9]

A second case of incest, in 1784, involved two black women. Luiza, a black Mina freedwoman, was denounced for the offense of consenting to the "public concubinage" of her two children, Carlos Pinto, a cabra freedman, and his sister, Margarida crioula. The latter had been the slave woman of Lieutenant Colonel João Pinto Barboza Pimentel, who was deceased. Margarida was also accused of having an incestuous relationship with her brother Carlos Pinto, as well as having an abortion. Five years later Carlos Pinto, then described as a "pardo forro," signed a declaration that he would no longer live in the same house with his sister Margarida crioula. As in most such cases, we do not know what happened to his sister.[10]

Coerced Labor

Not only did newly enslaved women have to meet the sexual demands of their new masters, but they also had to work for them, in particular in providing typical domestic services such as preparing food, making clothing, doing laundry, and handling childcare. As slavery eroded in the nineteenth century, masters sold boys to Minas Gerais but retained enslaved women to continue to cook for them. The most common occupation that appears in nineteenth-century *matriculas* (registries) for black women is *cozinheira* (cook). Other documented occupations were spinning cotton into thread and sewing. According to Saint-Hilaire, women exchanged the cotton thread they spun for merchandise. In the village of Pontal six white women, fourteen pardas, and fifteen black women worked at spinning. White women were also listed as weavers on the household lists, especially of fine vegetable-dyed cotton coverlets, for which the women of Goiás are still known. After the cloth was made, sometimes by male weavers, women also worked as seamstresses. In Pontal two white women, three pardas, and one crioula woman were so identified. Childcare would obviously involve additional labor. Such domestic services would be expected of most women in the colonial period, but they would be fortunate if these were their only labors, for they also had to work in the fields. Domestic service and fieldwork were usually performed by the same enslaved women, and some men, in the late colonial period.[11]

Noncaptive indigenous women also performed this combination of labors in their villages. Since most indigenous people wore no clothing, women were free of the demands of making, washing, and caring for European styles of clothing. But their heaviest labors involved carrying burdens, as well as babies and toddlers, since their men allegedly would not do so. Other work involved gathering firewood and foods in the forests, as well as food processing, in particular of manioc meal, which was usually defined as women's work. They also made ceramics and wove baskets. While indigenous women could translate many skills learned in their village to life as captives, such as pottery making, one of their new challenges would be to master the care of Luso-Brazilian styles of dress.

Black women also did not escape the burden of toting heavy loads. Not only did they do fieldwork, but they also carried foodstuffs and other heavy loads on their heads. At times, some black women also worked at the mines. In the captaincy they were especially associated with gold washing, which gave them access to gold. Other black women toted foodstuffs and drinks to exchange for

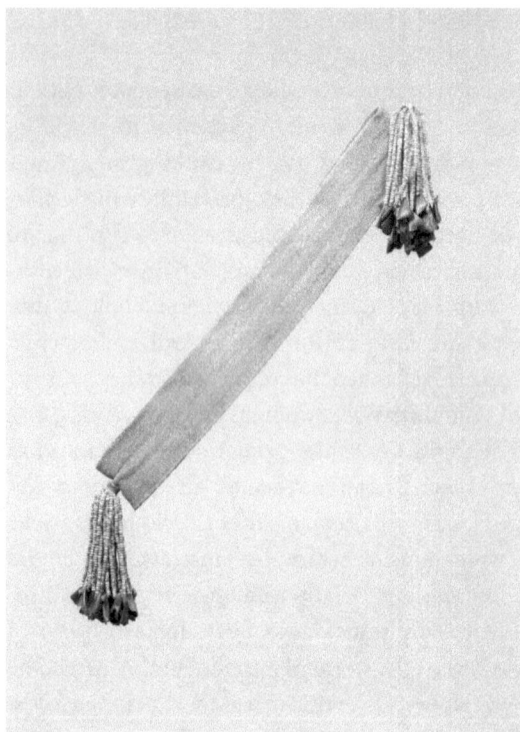

Figure 20. A baby-carrying sling from Cocal Grande. The Johann E. Pohl Ethnographic Collection. Courtesy of the Museum für Völkerkunde, Vienna, Austria.

gold dust with the miners. Their access to gold then made possible the purchase of their freedom or that of family members (chapter 10).

There are few good descriptions of the burdensome work that rural Goiano women did, but one comes from the 1880s, when the American traveler James W. Wells visited a ranch that shipped dried beef and hides to a port on the Tocantins River. He met with the workers on a small plot of land, where foodstuffs were being raised on the cattle ranch. After observing a dozen men who were sons or slaves of the captain, he complained that he "did not see any one man do a fair day's work." Instead, those who appeared "to do the most work" were the light-brown and black women. Unlike most travelers, he then went on to describe what they actually did, revealing the variety of their labors. After harvesting cotton, they cleaned it by hand and spun it into a "rough cloth." When necessary, they also worked in the fields. Furthermore, Wells enumerated such labor-intensive activities as "pounding maize or castor beans" as well as "making farinha" (manioc meal) and "rapadoura" (raw brown sugar).[12]

Elsewhere black women were also *alambiqueiros*, who distilled sugarcane as aguardente; others were licensed to sell it in taverns and vendas (market stalls), where such drinks were sold along with other goods. Women who entered the market selling fruits and vegetables as *quitandeiras* were also registered in the matriculas. One specific occupation of women, including white women, was that of making the famous *doces* (sugared sweets) out of fruits, such as the *marmelo* (quince). *Marmelada* was even an export from Goiás to other provinces in the nineteenth century, but most doces were consumed in the local households or sold in the markets.[13]

Since the range of occupations was so small and usually linked to the households and fields, women were often dependent on men for the sustenance of their families, especially white women, who were expected not to leave the seclusion of their households. While those of wealth and position could maintain their families through the labor of their agregados (household dependents) and slaves, others had only a husband, lover, or child as a means of support. Marriage and family life were notably unstable in the colonial period due to frontier warfare, the unbalanced sex ratio, and casual sexual relations, which left many women living and working alone with children to raise.

Concubinage

In the eighteenth century the captaincy of Goiás had a notable reputation among the Portuguese and foreign travelers for *libertinagem*, or sexual promiscuity. Not even the priests, it was claimed, lived celibate lives, and many tolerated concubinage among their parishioners. Portuguese governors and others nonnative to the region criticized the immoral and scandalous behavior of both priests and laypeople in the captaincy. In Vila Boa Saint-Hilaire concluded that "in no other city is the number of married persons so small," while Pohl accused the men of the captaincy of "habitual" infidelity. Missionary priests of the second half of the nineteenth century complained about the difficulties they encountered in finding married couples or of convincing indigenous men to abandon traditional patterns of sexuality and polygamy. Actually, one reason for the lack of marriage in the City of Goiás in the 1880s was the cost of a wedding dress, veil, and crown. Rather than appear in the church without appropriate clothing, couples preferred "to pass without the religious ceremony, and to be married as in the time of the patriarchs." A Dominican missionary, Frei Gil Vilanova, made a personal effort to visit unmarried couples in the City of Goiás to convince them to marry, but he had no luck in persuading them until he had a wedding dress made up that he provided to the women. Within three weeks, sixty or seventy couples of all ages and colors got married because the women handed the dress from one to another. Although these marriages took place in the 1880s, they suggest that status concerns and poverty discouraged many couples from marrying in the eighteenth and nineteenth centuries; instead they chose to live in long-term stable consensual unions, which outsiders stigmatized as concubinage.[14]

Typical of the foreign comments on reasons for concubinage in Goiás were those of Saint-Hilaire, who argued that the lack of marriage was due to the "immorality" of the early white men, who traveled to the region with black women but "their pride did not permit them to be united to them by marriage." Nor, he claimed, did they marry Indian women. Instead they had only "lovers" (*amantes*). In fact, he accused "all men, even to the most humble worker," of having "a lover . . . that they maintain in her own house." As a consequence, he concluded that "libertinagem" had become a "habit." Earlier, in 1778, a Catholic priest, João Antunes de Noronha, complained about similar attitudes held by the men of Vila Boa, who found the conjugal law to be "distasteful" and "destructive of the wealth of the Masters, and in the slaves, of the life." They also argued that concubinage is "desirous as useful to honor, and to wealth. And venereal use is [good for] health." Furthermore, Saint-Hilaire observed that "white men lead an unregulated life, in company of black and Indian women" and paid little attention to the children born of casual relationships. Therefore, "marriages are rare and always ridiculed." But even white men of high social status, including Portuguese bureaucrats and priests, lived in their houses with their lovers "as if they were their spouses."[15]

The most notable example of concubinage involved the Portuguese governors. According to Saint-Hilaire, "Among the captains-general that governed the province of Goiás until 1820, there was not one that was married, and all had amantes with whom they lived openly." Upon the arrival of each new governor, the men of Vila Boa knew that he would choose a woman to be his amante; until he did so, each man lived in fear that his woman would be chosen, while the women were "agitated." Nor did the "functionaries of the government" commonly marry, because "concubinage is generalized," and they easily adopted the local customs that they found so "comfortable." One of the governors who took an amante was Fernando Delgado Freire de Castilho (1809–1820), who lived in Vila Boa at the time of Saint-Hilaire's visit. When Saint-Hilaire met him, the governor impressed him as "a man of cold temperament" but with a "vivacity of spirit, some education [and] an honest character," who "knew the world" and wished to do well. On the occasion of a dinner with the governor at which they discussed "the strange customs of the place," the governor pointed to his two children, who were then seven and eight years of age, and said, "You think . . . that I could marry the mother of these children, with the daughter of a carpenter?" When the governor was recalled to Portugal in 1820, he took his amante and children with him as far as Rio de Janeiro. While waiting to embark for Lisbon, his mistress declared that she would go to Europe with him but only "in the quality of his legitimate spouse." Faced with "the dilemma" of either marrying "the daughter of a carpenter or of leaving her in Brasil," he committed suicide.[16]

Obviously the governor and the carpenter's daughter were an exceptional case, unique for his high social position and her demand for marriage. The more usual situation in Goiás was that of "passing unions" between white men and black, parda, mestiza, or indigenous women, especially with the women of their own households. In household lists from 1783, black and indigenous women appear in the households of single white men as agregadas, slaves, and obligated persons, sometimes with one or two pardo children. This pattern was especially common with single men with military titles. When troops were posted to frontier garrisons, wives—usually of high-ranking officers—and amantes, with their children, accompanied their men. In the absence of regular provisions for the troops, these women were essential to providing the agricultural labor for the cultivation of foodstuffs needed to feed their families at the garrisons. We can document these consensual unions between military officers and women of color through letters of legitimization in which the father recognized his natural children as legitimate heirs. In 1805, for example, Fernando José Leal, single, sergeant-mor of the Second Cavalry Regiment of Militias of Vila Boa, requested a letter of legitimization for the six children he had had with an unnamed "free, single woman." The number of children suggests that he had had a long-term consensual union with the children's mother. Also appearing in the wills of military officers were declarations of children by different women. In 1819, for example, the furriel of dragoons, José de Aguirra do Amaral, declared that he had two "natural daughters," one named Maria de Aguirra, who was the daughter of Luiza Barboza, freed black, single, and already deceased; and the other named Umbelina Maria Regina do Amaral, who was the daughter of Suzana, black of Guiné, who was also deceased.[17]

Additional evidence for concubinage comes from church records, since some priests were concerned about those who lived together without being married in the church. The Book of Denunciations from the archive of the curia in Goiânia records the statements of men who admitted to concubinage and sought to amend their lives. In the late eighteenth century priests denied the sacraments to those they believed were "living in sin" with an amante; thus the motivation for a person to sign a *termo* (declaration) was to be able to return to the church and receive the sacraments. In 1794 a married white man named José Rodriguez Xavier acknowledged his "public concubinage" with Maria Jozefa, a freed cabra of Vila Boa, while his white wife, Anna Ferreira de Queirós, resided in Meia Ponte. He had been living with Maria Jozefa on his sugar plantation for about two years. Apparently his motive for signing the document was to be readmitted to the church so that he could receive the sacraments. As the sign of his promise to amend his life, he was to "throw" Maria Jozefa out of his house within two months and to reunite with his wife and keep her company.[18] In 1784 a single white man signed a declaration to amend his life in the district of Anta. João Forquim lived in public concubinage with Catherina crioula, who was the slave of Dona Elena Cordeiro. But he was too poor to pay the fine, which suggests that they were unable to marry.[19]

Not only white men signed these termos; two pardos and a cabra man also admitted to public concubinage. In 1789 the pardo freedman Pedro Dias de Oliveira, who was a single resident of Ferreiro near Vila Boa, had been excommunicated for not satisfying the Lenten obligation of confessing and receiving Communion, which he could not do because of his public concubinage with Maria Roza Pinheiro, a single parda woman. After that he promised to amend his life.[20] Another pardo who declared his intention of amending his life was Aleixo José de Carvalho, a single freedman of Vila Boa who pledged to separate from Clara Maria Leite in 1791. He too had been excommunicated for publicly living in concubinage, but he also had not received permission from his parish priest when he had confessed and gone to Communion during Lent. In turn, Clara Maria Leite, a parda freedwoman of Vila Boa, also promised to amend her life in 1791. She too had been excommunicated and had gone to confession and Communion without the priest's permission. Since she was "an obedient daughter of the Church," she also agreed to separate herself from that "illicit friendship" and public concubinage so that she could fulfill her Lenten obligation; unlike Aleixo, she was unable to sign the document.[21]

Yet another term of separation and amendment of life suggests that a cabra freedman might have not one but two and possibly three women in his life. Manoel Ferreira Rebouça had been married in Santa Luzia but in 1794 he was living in Ouro Fino with Thomazia Aquina, a single parda freedwoman. In his declaration he agreed to separate from Thomazia within fifteen days and not to frequent the house of a black woman, Maria de Santa Anna.[22]

What happened to the women in these separations is unknown, but there were also women, as in the case of Clara Maria Leite, who agreed to leave their relationship. In her declaration, Joanna Rodriguez da Gama separated herself from the illicit relationship that she had had with Antônio de Souza Guimarães. In 1778 both of them were imprisoned in Vila Boa. Apparently she was the only one to sign the document, since Antônio did not also promise to amend his life, or his signed statement did not survive.[23] A second woman, however, agreed to return to her husband. In 1783 in Vila Boa, Rita Gonçalves da Silva, a black freedwoman, was separated from her husband, Joaquim Apolinario. She made a termo of confession and promised to live with him, facing the penalty of prison and payment of ten oitavas of gold for pious works if she did not do so. She was then to be united with her husband or to file an imminent cause of divorce.[24]

While the above sources point to the frequent practice of one white man living in concubinage with one or more women of color, conversely, one woman of color was often coerced into having sexual relations with more than one man. Obviously, prostitution was common in mining towns, and it usually involved the nonwhite women of the captaincy. It is difficult to document its prevalence, however, except for general references in official correspondence or the reports of travelers, such as Saint-Hilaire, who complained that "so many girls prostitute themselves." We rarely learn the names of the anonymous women who engaged in prostitution, except in the case of those who repented and agreed to leave the life of a prostitute. In 1783 two black women went to the vicar's residence to record their statement, promising "to leave and abandon, and repudiate the bad life" in which they were living as "public meretriz[es]," or those who received payment for sex. Since neither woman could read or write, Domingos Pires Maciel, a single pardo freedman, signed for them. Antonia Teixeira, a freed Mina black, and Domingas Gomes da Silva, a freed crioula, also repented and confessed their sin, giving up their former way of life, which may have been imposed on them by a former master. Notably, both women then enjoyed the freed status.[25]

Since slave prostitutes usually worked for gold dust, receiving payments that they had to turn over to their slaveholder, they could accumulate enough gold to purchase their freedom. But in the far north, captive indigenous women or women of color were required to have sexual relations with their slaveholder, such as a colonel, as well as with the loyal men around him, with no payment expected. This was also the fate of other free and enslaved women of color who lived as the sole woman among a gang of miners, river boatmen, or cowboys on isolated ranches. This tradition of having one woman who slept with all the colonel's men may have grown out of indigenous customs, such as those of the Apinaje, in which women were expected to exchange sexual favors for gifts with different men of their community. Those who refused to marry or have sex with men in the village could be gang raped for violating that norm of sexual behavior. It was also customary among the Apinaje to kidnap women of other nations to serve as the village "wanton," who was expected to sleep with the bachelors in the bachelors' house. The best documentation of the custom of men sharing one woman was recorded by Cunha Matos on one of his military expeditions to the north, where he described an indigenous woman who served as the sexual partner of the other men of the community.[26] A white woman, however, such as a colonel's wife, escaped that sexual abuse and reigned as the "queen" of a household, who demanded and received respect from everyone.[27]

When masters were involved with their enslaved women, jealous wives took vengeance on the slave concubines of their husbands. Pohl narrated infamous cases of sexual jealousy involving a Paulista woman who lived in the captaincy. When she observed that "the beauty of her two young daughters attracted attention and rivaled herself," she strangled both of them with a towel and buried them in a gold mine near Ouro Fino. The same "monster" in Pohl's narrative, but identified as another woman by Alencastre, was jealous of her husband's slave concubine, whose baby she killed in the belief that he was her husband's child. When her husband came to dinner, she presented him with the little boy's roasted body impaled on a spit. Another version, from the second half of the nineteenth century, involved the jealous wife of a fazenda owner, Dona Ana Paes, who prepared a fine table for her husband, whom she believed had fathered a child by his concubine. Clapping her hands, she had a slave bring in a large platter and place it in the center of the table. Dona Ana then removed the platter's covering to expose the body of the dead baby. Yet another woman, Dona Dina of Carmo, who was jealous of her husband's concubine, Ana Marina, took up a large needle and thread used in weaving and sewed the slave's clothing to her body. Dona Dina then sent the slave to gather firewood, but she never returned, and her body was found in a deep pool of water.[28]

Clerical Families

The contrast between cloistered women draped in long cloaks and sexual licentiousness suggests differing attitudes toward sexuality, consensual unions, and marriage in Central Brazil, even with reference to priests, who openly supported their own lovers and racially mixed children, including those by their slave women. George Gardner was among the foreign travelers who described the priests and their families in the north of Goiás. When Gardner arrived in Natividade, he found that the mining town had three priests, one of whom died while Gardner was there. As he reported, "These like most others I met with . . . were immoral to an extent almost past belief." The elderly priest, who was about seventy-four years of age when he died, was originally from Santos in São Paulo. Even though he was well educated and a cousin of José Bonifacio de Andrade, Gardner notes that he too had succumbed to the customs of the place. "A man of a very humane and benevolent disposition, . . . he left behind him a family of half a dozen children by his own slaves." Since he had not freed the children nor their mothers, most were sold to pay off his debts. The younger priest, who was about forty years of age, was the vicar general for the north, and Gardner called him a "half cast [sic]." Apparently he was a pardo, but he was also the largest cattle rancher in the district. About a month after Gardner had arrived in Natividade, he was called upon to help a sixteen-year-old slave girl who had just given birth to the priest's child. She died of puerperal fever a few days later. Gardner concluded that "this man was as much detested, as the old priest had been loved and esteemed."[29]

Saint-Hilaire gave less detailed information about the "immorality" of priests, but he too denounced their "bad behavior," reporting that their lovers lived with them and their children were raised around them.[30] Similar statements elsewhere lead to the problem of documenting further these types of clerical behaviors through other sources, which suggest that lack of celibacy was common, although not universal. For the town of Meia Ponte, Jarbas Jayme provides a genealogical history of the families of African descent. Along with a handsome photograph of the priest's son, who also became a priest, Jayme provides a brief biography of the family. The parents were Joana (a slave of Antônio Severiano da Luz) and Padre Marcelino Teixeira Chaves. Freed by his father at baptism, Bento Severiano da Luz was ordained a priest in Cuiabá and went on to study in Rome. He rose to be a monsignor and died in Cuiabá in 1917. Another enslaved woman, who once was owned by the same Antônio Severiano da Luz, was the parda Delfina, born in 1820, the daughter of Benedita, a parda slave. Delfina "passed under the dominion of Padre José Joaquim do Nascimento" and had five illegitimate children. In 1860 the priest freed her, as well as one of her sons, Pedro Tomaz do Nascimento. Although the genealogies do not record the name of the father of her children, three of the children adopted the priest's surname.[31]

Another example from Meia Ponte is also of interest. Padre Antônio da Costa Teixeira had a slave woman named Silvana, who bore two children whose father was not identified in the genealogical history. One of the children, Eufêmia, who was born in 1820, was described as "a beautiful morena," or light-brown woman. The priest did not free her but gave her to his nephew, Major Joaquim da Costa Teixeira, who freed her in 1838 because she was "his mistress" (*amásia*). The other daughter of Silvana, Carolina da Costa, did not marry but had three children.[32]

Also suggestive of the lack of clerical celibacy are the household lists of 1783 and the 1820s, which identify priests who lived in large households that included agregadas and slaves along with their pardo children. But even though there were women in the household, this did not necessarily indicate nonobservance of celibacy. Celibate priests often lived in a household of women who were related to them, that is, their mother, unmarried sisters, and nieces. Priests also gave refuge to poor women who sought refuge from abuse in their households; Padre Manuel da Silva Álvares even provided dowries to poor orphan girls so that they could marry. Another priest, the vicar of Santa Luzia, João Teixeira Álvarez, included his mother, sisters, nieces, and a disabled brother in his household. According to Saint-Hilaire, he planned to establish a house of retreat on his *chacara* for "girls of good family," where they could live a religious life, according to some rules, but without taking a nun's vows. In the absence of convents in Goiás, women who did not marry could follow the lifestyle of a beata, a laywoman who engaged in prayer and pursued charitable activities on behalf of the poor.[33]

Although Catholic priests may have scandalized visiting foreigners and Portuguese bureaucrats, the nonobservance of clerical celibacy was not socially stigmatized by the local people, which was also true in Bahia. For example, a priest's "woman" could openly accompany him to Mass in Vila Boa—to the great disapproval of Saint-Hilaire. Nor did it hinder a priest in his clerical and political career, as in the case of Padre Luiz Antônio da Silva e Souza, whose daughter lived with his sisters. Not only had he become the highest-ranking cleric in the captaincy as vicar general, but he also served as the assistant to the blind bishop of Goiás. For his many services, he was awarded the prestigious Order of Christ.[34]

Marriages

While the mother of a priest's children could not marry him and most people seem to have lived in consensual unions, we cannot conclude that no one married in Goiás. The censuses from 1783 to 1825, which were based on the reports of parish priests, who kept the marriage records in the colonial period, reveal that men and women of all colors and legal statuses did marry, some across color and ethnic boundaries. According to elite social mores of that time, marriage in the Catholic Church conferred an elevated social status on women and their legitimate children, and white women were especially concerned with getting married in the church. Therefore, whites usually had the highest number of marriages, but not in all cases, as table 12 clarifies.

The first census to provide insights into marriage patterns by color is the census of 1783 (table 12). Although single men outnumbered married men in most parishes in 1783, free and freed people of all colors did marry. Vila Boa and São Félix each had the largest number of married white men and women in their respective comarcas: Vila Boa had 559 and São Félix 56 couples. But pardo marriages were more numerous than those of whites in Pilar, Cocal, Amaro Leite, and Arraias. In Cocal there were even more married blacks than whites, but in general, black marriages did not number as many as white and pardo marriages.

Of particular interest in these official figures is that married men and women of color outnumbered married whites in the parishes in the north except in São Félix, which suggests that some people of color sought to marry in part to elevate their social status and legitimize their children but also for religious reasons, since marriage was also required for one to be in good standing with the church and irmandades.[35] Notably, in five parishes in the northern comarca there were more married pardo men than white men, in part because pardos were willing to marry women of color while white men were reluctant to do so. Only nine and sixteen racially mixed marriages were reported between white men and parda women in Crixás and Cavalcante, respectively.

Table 12. Number of married couples by color, 1783

	Whites	Pardos	Blacks	Total
COMARCA OF THE SOUTH				
Vila Boa	559	330[a]	295[a]	1,184
Santa Luzia	81	58	20	159
Santa Cruz	57	55	16[a]	128
Pilar	32	64[b]	39[a]	135
Crixás	7 (+9)[c]	16	—	32
COMARCA OF THE NORTH				
Conceição	18	27	13	58
Água Quente	14	12	14	40
Cocal	15	36	23	74
Cavalcante	14 (+16)[d]	22	4 or 6[a]	56 or 58
São José do Tocantins	40	38	23	101
Moquém	7	8	4	19
Amaro Leite	12	25	5	42
São Félix	56	14	21	91
Arraias	32	49	16	97

Source: RJBN, cod. 16, 3, 2, Notícia Geral da Capitania de Goiás, 1783. Table 1 does not include all couples in the captaincy, and some couples may not have been married.
[a] *Forros* (freedpersons).
[b] Includes some white men with *pardas*, plus 2 white men with *negras* (black women).
[c] 7 "houses" of white persons, plus 9 of white men with *pardas*.
[d] Plus 16 white men with *pardas*.

As might be anticipated in a slave society, blacks had the lowest incidence of marriage, in part due to the large number of black male slaves who were single. Moreover, slave marriages were apparently not recorded here.

More than fifteen years later, in 1799, the vicar of Vila Boa, João Pereira Pinto Bravo, reported that his parish had "near eight thousand souls," of which "six thousand are of Confession and of these almost three thousand are freed, and free." Furthermore, three hundred of these were married or couples; the rest were captives. In other words, only 10 percent of the free population was married in Vila Boa in 1799, and there had been a significant decline in the number of married couples since 1783.[36]

A more comprehensive survey of married couples in the captaincy of Goiás took place five years later, in 1804. As table 13 reveals, 1,710 whites were married, and the marriage rate was highest among this group, at 24.6 percent; the number of married mulatos was higher, at 3,123, although their rate of marriage was lower, at 20.2 percent. As usual in the captaincy, blacks were the least likely to be married, numbering only 1,122 and with a marriage rate of 14.1. In its breakdown by sex, table 13 also suggests that intermarriage across color lines took place, since more white males (901) than females (809) were married, while more mulato (1,605) and black (576) females were married than mulato (1,518) and black (546) males.

Therefore, the census of 1804 records the trend suggested in 1783, that more people of color married than whites, but the greater accuracy of the 1804 data allows for the calculation of marriage rates by color and sex. About one-fourth (25.7 percent) of white males were married in 1804, with a smaller percentage for white females (23.5 percent). As for free mulatos, about one-fifth of the males (20.6 percent) and females (19.9 percent) were married. Finally, the least married were the free blacks. Seventeen percent of black males were married, but only 12.2 percent of free black females, which in part reflected pervasive color prejudice against black women. In terms of the free population, blacks were the least likely to marry in 1804, as in 1783, but the racially mixed marriage rates had fallen behind the white rates by 1804, although more mulatos (3,123) than whites (1,710) married in the church. There were also 1,122 married blacks. Thus among those who were married, the 4,245 nonwhites outnumbered the 1,710 whites.

The next census, of 1825 also included marriages, providing insights into the marriages of whites, Indians, *ingênuos* (free people of color), and freedpersons (table 14). In particular, it documents the increasing number of marriages

Table 13. Percentage married by color and sex in the captaincy of Goiás, 1804

Sex	White		Mulatto		Black (Free)	
	Number married	% married	Number married	% married	Number married	% married
Males	901	25.7	1,518	20.6	546	17.0
Females	809	23.5	1,605	19.9	576	12.2
Total	1,710	24.6[a]	3,123	20.2[b]	1,122	14.1[c]

Source: AHU, cod. 2109, Reflexoens economicas sobre as tabellas statisticas da capitania de Goyaz pertencentes ao anno de 1804 e feitas no de 1806.
[a]Of total number of whites, 6,950 (3,508 males; 3,442 females).
[b]Of total number of mulattos, 15,452 (7,368 males; 8,084 females).
[c]Of total number of free blacks, 7,936 (3,208 males; 4,728 females).

among free people of color, at 8,728, while those among whites had almost doubled to 3, 264, but the number of black marriages had actually declined to 1,094.

The census of 1825 (table 14) also permits insights into the marriage rates of whites, mission Indians, free people of color, and freedpersons. In 1825, the groups with the highest share of married persons were freedmen (35.7 percent) and freedwomen (37.8 percent), followed by Indian men (35.5 percent) and women (34.8 percent), and white men (32.6 percent) and women (29.5 percent). Notably, in the north only 200 white women were married, as opposed to 1,319 in the south. Free women of color had the lowest rates of marriage, at 22.6 percent, compared to 23.4 percent for men of color. On the other hand, the 8,728 free persons of color who were married far outnumbered the 3,264 whites, 1,094 freedpersons, and 219 mission Indians. Of these, there were 4,486 free women of color, 1,519 white women, 544 freedwomen, and 111 Indian women. In other words, married women of color outnumbered married white women in 1825.

In addition to the general marriage statistics for 1825, there is a more detailed report from the mining town of Cavalcante (table 15). The priest's accounting of the marital status of 2,282 persons in 1828 duplicates percentages shown in the broader 1804 census. Furthermore, the priest distinguished between whites, Indians, and pardos, and identified free blacks as either Africans or Brazilian-born crioulos. The Cavalcante figures reveal that, as in the 1804 census, whites had the largest percentage married (31.3 percent). What is so notable about the Cavalcante data, however, is that they reveal that the next-highest percentage after that of whites was for the Africans (28.6 percent), followed by pardos (26.7 percent), Indians (20.8 percent), and crioulos (15.5 percent). This pattern was similar to the high rates of marriage for freed blacks in Vila Boa in 1783 and undoubtedly reflected the custom of freedpersons marrying after one or more of the spouses had achieved manumission. On the other hand, crioulos had the lowest marriage rate, followed by Indians.[37]

These census records challenge the observations of foreigners, who argued that few married in Goiás in the late colonial period. Men and women of all colors did marry, but black women appear to have been the group most prejudiced in their access to a church marriage, which would have elevated their status—and that of their children—in local society. They were more likely to appear in censuses as household dependents living in the homes of single men or married couples or living alone as *solteiras* (singles). White men and women had the highest marriage rates, although married pardos and blacks

Table 14. Percentage married by color, sex, and legal status in Goiás, 1825

Sex	White		Indian[a]		Ingênuo[b]		Freed[c]	
	Number married	% married	Number married	% married	Number married	% married	Number married	% married
Males	1,745	32.6	108	35.5	4,242	23.4	550	35.7
Females	1,519	29.5	111	34.8	4,486	22.6	544	37.8
Total	3,264[d]	31.1	219[e]	35.2	8,728[f]	23.0	1,094[g]	36.7

Source: RJBN, manuscript section, 11, 4, 2, Estatistica da provincia de Goyáz remettida á secretaria de estado dos negocios do imperio . . . , 1825.
[a] Mission Indians from São José, Carretão, and Duro.
[b] Free people of color.
[c] Libertos.
[d] Of a total number of 10,495 whites (5,351 males; 5,144 females).
[e] Of a total of 623 Indians (304 males; 319 females).
[f] Of a total of 37,985 ingênuos (18,105 males; 19,880 females).
[g] Of a total of 2,980 libertos (1,539 males; 1,441 females).

generally outnumbered them by the early nineteenth century. Even a small group of Indians married in the church by 1825. In other words, some priests had some success in counteracting customary concubinage and in convincing a certain proportion of each group to marry, but the majority of the people of the captaincy still lived in consensual unions, many of which had years of stability.

Table 15. Marital status by color in Cavalcante, 1828

COLOR	Married		Widowed		Single		Total
	N	%	N	%	N	%	N
Whites	81	31.3	12	4.6	166	64.1	259
Indians	5	20.8	—	—	19	79.2	24
Pardos	338	26.7	57	4.5	870	68.8	1,265
Crioulos	105	15.5	20	3.0	553	81.6	678
Africans	16	28.6	3	5.4	37	66.1	56
Sum total	545	23.9	92	4.0	1,645	72.1	2,282[a]

Source: AHG, Seção de Municípios, Cavalcante, Informação ... do julgado de Cavalcante, sua estastistica, ... satisfazendo-se a todos os quizitos expecificados na ordem de 14 de Abril 1828.
[a] This total includes 416 captives, 21 libertos, 48 servant boys (*moços de servir*), and 19 beggars. In the previous year 10 had married.

Marriages by Color and across Color Lines

On the whole, white men generally married white women, pardo men married pardas, black men married black women, and so forth. While racially prejudiced white men chose to marry women of their own color and quality, pardos did the same. One sample of marriages among sixty-three pardos in Meia Ponte between 1798 and 1805 suggests that pardo men preferred to marry parda women. In 1798 there were only four pardo couples, but the number rose to twelve in 1799 and twenty in 1800, then dropped to twelve in 1801, thirteen in 1802, none in 1803, and one each in 1804 and 1805. As of 1806, the priest stopped identifying pardo husbands and wives by color.[38]

Another sample of marriages by color in Vila Boa for the same period also reveals that pardo men tended to marry parda women (table 16). In the period 1796–1802, with one marriage in 1816, eleven pardo men married parda women, with another four choosing cabra women, who may have been darker in color. Only one pardo man elected to marry a black woman (crioula). As Pohl observed, white men who had children with mulata and black women did not want their pardo sons to marry them.[39] Five cabra men also did not marry black women, but instead chose a parda, three cabras, and one woman of unknown color. Even the one mestizo listed did not marry a black woman but instead a parda woman. Excluding two women of unknown color, twenty-three racially mixed men largely chose other racially mixed women as marriage partners; only one married a crioula. This small sample suggests that the racially mixed were also reluctant to marry black women.

Eleven African men were also able to marry, but only one chose an Angola and three chose Mina women; five other Africans married crioulas. One Angolan man and one Mina also each convinced a parda woman of higher social status to marry him. Possibly among the Africans were the three pretos who married two black women and one indigenous woman. As also occurred elsewhere in the captaincy, a black man and an indigenous woman married. No other Indian women were in this sample of marriages. Blacks born in Brazil, the crioulos, also faced prejudice. No pardas married them, although one cabra woman did so, but most cabras were regarded as darker in color than pardas. One crioulo man married an Angolan woman and another a Mina woman (in 1816). Five crioulos also found crioulas as marriage partners. Apparently, as pardos married each other, so too did crioulos. Finally, six men whose color was not recorded married two pardas, one cabra, one Angola, one crioula, and one woman of unknown color.

Table 16. Marriages of free people of color in Vila Boa and Meia Ponte, 1796–1816

Husbands				Wives					
	Parda	Cabra	Angola	Mina	Crioula	Preta[a]	India	Unknown	Total
MEN OF COLOR									
Pardo	11	4	—	—	1	—	—	1	17
Cabra	1	3	—	—	—	—	—	1	5
Mestizo	1	—	—	—	—	—	—	—	1
AFRICANS									
Mina	1	—	—	3	3	—	—	—	7
Angola[b]	1	—	1	—	2	—	—	—	4
Black[c]	—	1	1	1	5	2	1	—	11
Unknown	2	1	1	—	1	—	—	1[d]	6
Total	17	9	3	4	12	2	1	3	51

Sources: SGC, Século XVIII, Registros, Provisões [de casar-se], etc., Vila Boa, 1795–1805, f. 18; and SGC, Registro dos papeis que se passam na Comarca de Meiaponte, 1795–1816, ff. 10–80.
Note: 2 provisões are from Vila Boa, 1 is from a sitio, and the rest were registered for Meia Ponte.
[a] Black.
[b] Includes 1 Benguela man who married a crioula.
[c] Includes 2 pretos who married pretas and 1 preto who married an Indian woman. The rest of the husbands were crioulos.
[d] A slave married on a sitio. No names were given.

What these marriages reveal is that marriage across color lines did take place, but it was more likely to involve nonwhite men than white men, who continued to resist marrying below their "quality." Therefore, white men lived in concubinage with women of color without benefit of a Catholic marriage. When their period of service to the Crown ended or they made their fortune, they returned to Portugal, leaving behind their women and pardo children. The more generous freed their slave women and children, while others exacted payment in gold for their freedom. The former temporary "wife" might then move on with her life to a second or third consensual union, but too many faced the daunting challenge of raising pardo children alone in a society firmly prejudiced against their color. Few such women would achieve the status of the married *dona da casa* (lady of the house), who commanded a large household of slaves and agregados. One exception was the widow Catarina Fernandes of the Mina nation, who made a will in 1787 in which she recorded her ownership of fourteen slaves.[40]

Abandonment

Even marriage, however, might not bring lifetime security to women in Goiás. Yet another characteristic of women's lives in the captaincy was abandonment, or at least long-term separations while husbands lived and worked in distant mines, on riverboats, and in various military services to the Crown. We meet abandoned white women in the petitions of women "of quality" who appealed to the Crown for support due to their husband's service in Goiás. Impoverished single women of color can also be traced via censuses and death registries as beggars at the time of death, but unlike white women, they rarely had access to the petition process that reached Portuguese authorities in Lisbon.

One petition by a Portuguese woman was that of Dona Anna Flaminia Xavier Soares of Setubal, across the Tagus River from Lisbon. She was married to Captain Joaquim Theodoro da Roza, who had accompanied Governor Tristão da Cunha Menezes (1783–1800) to Goiás. At the time of her 1804 petition, he still had not returned to Portugal and had been gone for twenty-two years. She accused him of living in abundance as a wealthy man while she lived in "misery" with seven daughters to feed. The sense from her petition is that her husband provided no support for her, that he was in debt, and that she was being harassed by his creditors. Her situation must have been difficult, since the Overseas Council ordered the local ouvidor of her comarca to see that she and her daughters received food. Her local priest had testified in 1799 that she was one of the "noble persons of this parish" and lived with her daughters in much poverty, although with the honor appropriate to her quality. Two years later she had to petition again that her husband be required to send help or to return to Portugal.[41]

Also common were the men, including priests, who disappeared in the captaincy. Either they died of fevers, such as malaria, or from other health issues, such as heart disease, or they perished in the frontier warfare that claimed so many lives. Their untimely deaths left women of all colors with children to support. In 1790 Luiza de Souza Ferreira, the widow of Captain José Claro dos Santos of Vila Boa, had two minor sons and three daughters. Therefore she asked to be appointed their tutor and administrator of their persons and property. In such cases it was more common for powerful men to be appointed tutors.[42] In 1800 Dona Anna Francisca Xavier Leite of Meia Ponte, the widow of Lieutenant João Bonifacio, was left with five sons and two daughters. Her ranches, cattle, and slaves were then being sold to pay off her husband's debts connected to the contract for the dízimo tax.[43]

Another request to be the tutor and administrator of her property and six minor children (three sons and three daughters) was that of Joanna Vieira de Souza, the widow of João Ferreira Leite, who lived on the small farm of the Bacalhão in the parish of São José of the district of Traíras. When her husband died in São José, her oldest child was twelve and her youngest only four. According to an attached document dated 1791, she was a "woman of much capacity" who could govern her family and slaves by herself, without help from others. She was also a woman of some wealth, since she possessed mines, fields, and slaves, which she had inherited from her husband. Testifying on her behalf were a Portuguese businessman from Braga, another businessman from São José, and a Portuguese notary.[44]

Upon her husband's death, Dona Brittes Maria Leonor de Azeredo Coutinho, the widow of Captain João Leite Álvarez Fidalgo, both Paulistas and more than fifty years resident in Vila Boa, was left with seven children and one granddaughter. Although she claimed to live in poverty, three of her sons had careers. Antônio Leite had been serving for twenty years as a corporal in the dragoons. Another son, José Joaquim Leite, had received the position of scribe in Cavalcante. Her third son, Joaquim Leite de Azeredo, was studying at the University of Coimbra with a promising future ahead of him. A fourth son, Francisco Xavier Leite, already had a position in the Royal Treasury as a scribe. Her petition focused on getting support for her three daughters and one grandchild.[45]

In contrast to these high-status women, most free women whose husbands died or abandoned them were left in marginal circumstances. Even being white did not protect them from poverty. In fact, many were poorer than black women. According to Pohl, there were white women who were so poor in Vila Boa that they lacked the proper clothing to go to Mass on Sunday morning. Expressly created for them was a Mass said at 5:00 a.m. Those who came to the early morning Mass were impoverished white women, who arrived enveloped in mantles of "inferior quality" in order to avoid "the disdainful eyes" of black women, who attended a later Mass dressed in gold chains and lace.[46] Unless single or widowed white women owned slaves and property, they were in a most difficult circumstance because social norms did not permit them to work outside the household, whereas black women were expected to engage in work such as doing laundry and vending food and drinks. Free black women usually had the fewest slaves (one to three), and many had none. To support their families, all they had to offer was the thread they spun, which they bartered for merchandise. If unable to spin or raise food crops, abandoned and elderly women without protectors often ended their lives depending on the charity of others, or at least of their irmandades. The death registries of Natividade record the number of elderly black women who died on the steps of the churches after prolonged illnesses and lives as beggars.[47] Other women may have been forced into prostitution in order to feed their children.

In spite of enslavement and sexual abuse, concubinage, and prostitution, some women and their husbands, or their partners in consensual unions, managed to create families and raise children. These white, brown, and black families would grow in numbers in the nineteenth century as many indigenous families retreated to Mato Grosso, as in the case of the Xavante, where they could obtain lands and protect their children from the bandeiras. Other indigenous families would find refuge in new missions established for them in the nineteenth century. Basically, after the Portuguese left Goiás in the early nineteenth century, the free people of color kept some of the gender values of their former colonial masters but also evolved new ones, some based on indigenous and African gender norms. The image of the strong, commanding woman would become a stereotype on this frontier, from the indigenous women who went into battle or the black women who washed gold to the white women of "capacity" who took over and managed their large households and estates upon the death of a spouse. Many nonelite women, however, raised their children and farmed their fields alone because their men had to work so far from their homes. Others accompanied their men on military expeditions. The late colonial period was indeed not an easy one for Goiano women and their families, but in this period women of all ethnic backgrounds founded the large extended families of the region. Because of intermixture in the eighteenth century, however, many of these families can trace their ancestry back to indigenous or African women.[48]

CHAPTER 10

Defenders of the Conquest and Useful Vassals

The Free People of Color

In the view of the pardo men of the captaincy, they were the "vassals most useful to the state" because of their military services to stop attacks by indigenous nations and protect the missions. One foreign traveler also commented favorably on the "energetic race" made up of the racially mixed who were "admirably adapted to the fatigues of the desert."¹ These positive images are in sharp contrast to the prejudiced views of the city council of Vila Boa in the 1780s, which denigrated the pardos and blacks of the captaincy as "naturally lazy." How far pardos could rise, however, is documented by the case of the mulato colonel who became eligible to serve as interim governor of the captaincy in the event of the death of the governor. Both the city council of Vila Boa and officials in Portugal would not allow him to do so, for they refused to permit a pardo colonel to govern white men.²

Nonetheless, freeborn and freed men of color were essential to the functioning of colonial rule in the captaincy of Goiás. Without them, indigenous warriors would have ousted the Portuguese from Luso-Brazilian settlements, especially in the north. Perhaps for this reason Portuguese governors encouraged their social mobility and loyalty to the Crown by permitting pardos (but not blacks) to acquire military patents as officers in the pardo militia regiments, allegedly in exchange for gold. In turn, the pardos became significant allies of the governor against a city council dominated by white men, who challenged both the Portuguese and the pardos.

This chapter, therefore, will examine those who made up the last significant social group on this frontier, the freeborn and freed people of color (*gente de cor*). Not only did they support the Portuguese imperial system, but they also contributed to its whittling away, especially of the institution of slavery, as they purchased their freedom or fled to quilombos. The first part of the chapter will focus briefly on the process of manumission in the captaincy in order to document their own role in buying their freedom with gold, since few slaves received their freedom gratuitously. Next, through the censuses, we will examine the growing number of free/freed people of color. Since so many were the children of European men and African women, they may have had a genetic advantage inherited from their mother that enabled them to resist malarial parasites, while on their father's side they may have had greater resistance to European diseases. Hence they were often healthier than whites or indigenous peoples. Saint-Hilaire, for example, contrasted the ill health of whites in Vila Boa with the robustness of blacks and mulatos.[3]

Furthermore, the variety of their occupations clarifies how they were vital to the defense of the captaincy as well as to diverse productive activities in the economy, such as mining, transportation, the arts and crafts, and food production on farms and ranches. Some even engaged in the long-distance river trade to Belém do Pará or on overland routes to Bahia, where they sold cattle and other commodities. Thus this last chapter will also document what the pardos claimed in 1803: that they were "faithful" and "loyal vassals" of the Crown who were essential to its defense and prosperity. Although the captaincy of Goiás might not have survived indigenous attacks without their services, they were always in an ambiguous position: their very defense of the captaincy also led to their subordination to whites, who believed that they could never measure up to the good men of "quality" due to "the defect" of their color."[4]

Manumission

One reason why so many of the people of color reached free or freed legal status was due to the process of manumission, which functioned legally in the captaincy of Goiás, as it did elsewhere in Brazil.[5] As chapter 7 reveals, many people of color also secured the freedom of their children and descendants by running away to quilombos that were never destroyed, such as Kalunga near Cavalcante. Although many hid in remote mountains, others descended to the lowlands, where they formed villages and towns of free blacks. But these individuals were always at risk of re-enslavement, since only the process of manumission could legally secure the liberty of former slaves in a slaveholding society.

In the captaincy of Goiás, gold was central to enabling the enslaved to obtain their manumission. In the early years of the gold boom, enslaved and

Table 17. Manumitted slaves in the captaincy of Goiás, 1792–1824

	1792–1799 With letters of liberty			1810–1824 With taxes on letters of liberty		
	Male	Female	Total	Male	Female	Total
African	8	12	20	3	5	8
Mina	6	10	16[a]	2	4	6
Angola	—	1	1	1	1	2
Banguela	2	1	3	—	—	—
Brazilian	9	21	30	27	31	58
Mulato	2	5	7	3	9	12
Pardo	—	1	1	1	1	2
Crioulo	5	11	16	16	14	30
Cabra	2	4	6	5	5	10
Preto	—	—	—	2	2	4
Unknown	1	—	1	13	6	19
Total	18	33	51	43	42	85

Sources: City of Goiás, BFEG, Cartório do Primeiro Ofício, Vila Boa, 1792–1799; and AMB, Escravos, Sisas dos Escravos Ladinos, no. 167, Araxá, 1814–1820; and Arraias, 1811–1827, no. 1017, and 1824–1826; no. 172, Cavalcante, 1810–1822; no. 169, Conceição, 1810–1822, and Crixás, 1810–1821; no. 170, Flores, 1813–1824; no. 171, Meia Ponte, 1810–1822; no. 172, Natividade, 1811–1822, and Pilar, 1810–1822; no. 173, Santa Cruz, 1813–1822; no. 174, Santa Luzia, 1810–1822, and São João da Palma, 1815–1816; and no. 175, Traíras, 1811–1822.
[a] Includes 1 male Nagô.

fugitive prospectors went looking for new gold mines in the expectation they would be able to buy their freedom. But most of the enslaved failed to find a new mine and had to work at more prosaic occupations in order to buy their freedom, while others received it from another person who bought it for them, as in the case of children at the time of their baptism. In other cases, local officials required that the meia-sisa (sales tax) be paid upon the purchase of a *carta de liberdade* (letter of liberty). Thus one way to document who was freed through purchase is by means of the meia-sisas, which also reveals how much they had to pay for their freedom (table 17).[6]

This sample of meia-sisas from thirteen towns in the early nineteenth century reveals that adult men were manumitted as well as women and children. It also clarifies how many valued freedom, because they had to be willing to spend a fortune in gold to obtain it. In fact, half of those freed were males, and in some parishes more males than females purchased their freedom. In terms of ethnicity, few Africans were able to buy their freedom—only eight, of which six were Minas. Although some stereotypes about manumission stress the manumission of mulatos by their white fathers, table 17 records only twelve mulatos and two pardos manumitted; Brazilian-born blacks (crioulos) were the single largest group freed, at thirty. Another ten racially mixed cabras and four pretos (blacks) complete the list of known identities. Overall, fifty-eight Brazilian-born slaves secured their freedom via purchase in this sample of meia-sisas from the captaincy.

The tax records from 1810 to 1824 also reveal how much a letter of liberty cost in oitavas (an oitava equals an eighth ounce) of gold. Scribes recorded a sum as low as 10 oitavas, which was probably an installment payment, to as high as 160 and 192 oitavas of gold. On the whole, there was not a significant difference between the prices of males and females, although slightly more females than males were freed for lower amounts, ten to forty oitavas. These may have been children or elderly women, but the registries rarely permit an insight into the age of those freed.[7]

A smaller sample of manumissions from just one location, Vila Boa and its surrounding parish, also helps to document who secured their freedom from slave status in the 1790s. Elsewhere in Brazil, Minas were often more successful in the manumission process. The sample in table 17 suggests the same: ten Mina women and five Mina men plus one Nagô (Yoruba) man obtained letters of liberty. In contrast, only one Angolan woman and three Banguelas did so. Thus more Minas than other Africans succeeded in buying their freedom in the 1790s, as well as in the early nineteenth century. One possible explanation is that many Minas were imported into the captaincy when gold was more plentiful, but a second reason may be due to their prior mining experience in Africa. The Africans who achieved their manumission in Vila Boa may have known how to find gold and paid for their freedom using oitavas of gold. No Africans secured his or her manumission gratuitously, although some may have been manumitted after long years of service, combined with a payment in gold, as happened with two women of color. In one case, the mulata Francisca Borges was freed for the payment of fifty oitavas of gold, as well as her husband's fifty years of service. In a second case, Ana Maria parda received her freedom for eight oitavas plus thirty years of service, including raising her master's children, but she had little monetary value at the time of her manumission because she was so sick that she was at "death's door."[8]

Thirty Brazilian-born slaves also secured their freedom in the 1790s, although it was also common for a relative to buy the freedom of a child who was a crioulo or mulato. Thus sixteen crioulos, seven mulatos, and six cabras, but only one pardo, received a letter of liberty, among which only Antonia crioula, Manoel crioulo, and Francisco cabra bought their freedom. The others were purchased by a parent or relative. One example involved an uncle's purchase of his mulata niece because of their ties of "kinship," but more common was the purchase of a child's freedom by his or her mother or father. Thus Maria mulata, the legitimate daughter of Manuel de Candea and his wife, Anna Maria, both pardos, received her freedom because her father paid thirty-two oitavas on the occasion of her baptism. It took much longer, to the age of eighteen, for Maria crioula's mother to buy the freedom of her daughter via installments totaling one hundred oitavas, while Gervazio Martins Braga gave seventy oitavas for Hilaria, his mulata daughter.[9]

Maria mulata's manumission at the baptismal font suggests a common custom of freeing children upon the occasion of the child's baptism. Afterward, sometimes years later, the manumission would be registered in a notary's office, but not always, so the baptismal certificate might be the only record of a child being freed after birth. In 1784, Eugênio, the son of Joaquina Mina, a former slave, was baptized at Santa Ana and then freed, but his freedom was not registered until 13 July 1792. Other manumissions were recorded in wills and were not always notarized. In this sample, only three individuals received their full freedom upon the death of the slaveholder (table 18).[10]

Since crioulos were so numerous by the 1790s, it is not surprising that crioulo adults and children appear in Vila Boa's manumissions, as well as in those of the captaincy, but few adult mulatos—only one male and two females—were freed. Children who were racially mixed were also likely to be manumitted, such as four *mulatinhos* and four *cabrinhas*, but those who freed them were often black mothers or fathers. In 1793, for example, Felipa mulata, daughter of Anacleta crioula, received her letter of liberty upon payment of 128 oitavas of gold: 82 oitavas came from Anacleta and 46 from Felipa.[11]

The manumission registries also clarify how and why slaves were freed in Vila Boa. Table 18 illustrates that almost two-thirds of those freed were manumitted due to monetary compensation. Twelve of the freed men and women bought their own letters, while another nine were purchased by a third party, such as a parent. In a few cases, a slave exchanged another slave for his or her freedom. Salvador Nagô was freed by Francisca Rodrigues de Jesus because he gave her Manuel of the Angolan nation as his payment. Twelve slaves also

Table 18. Forms of manumission by number and gender, 1790s

	Males	Females	Total	%
Purchase by	11	27	38	64.4
Enslaved individual	6	6	12	—
Another	2	7	9	—
Exchange of slave	2	1	3	—
Installments	1	11	12	—
Gold and services	—	2	2	—
Will	2	1	3	5.1
Conditional	5	4	9	15.3
Unconditional	1	8	9	15.3
Total	19	40	59	—
%	32.2	67.8	—	—

Source: City of Goiás, BFEG, Cartório do Primeiro Ofício, Vila Boa, 1792–1799.

purchased their freedom via installments in the 1790s, sometimes supplemented by a gift in a slaveholder's will to complete the price of their evaluation. The length of time the installment method took is suggested in the letter passed to Anna Mina, who was freed for 160 oitavas of gold. The original installment agreement had been made in 1781, but she did not receive her letter of liberty until 1792. In other cases the slave received a contribution toward the payment of the letter of liberty upon the death of the slaveholder. For example, the crioulo Bonifacio Rodrigues Abade paid 32.25 oitavas toward his freedom, while his former mistress willed him 18.75 oitavas and 6 vinténs of gold to complete payments for his freedom.[12]

Another method of acquiring freedom was for a slave to accept an imposed condition. The conditional manumission, however, usually served a slaveholder's best interests in securing a slave's loyal services until death. In the case of three women and five men in the 1790s, they were required to serve until the death of each of their slaveholders. But a fourth woman, Esmeria crioula, was freed on the condition of never returning to the captaincy; if she did so, she would be returned to captivity. How long it might take to process a conditional manumission is suggested by the case of José Mina, who received his conditional manumission in 1763, but his final letter of liberty was not registered until 1792.[13]

Unless they were children, few slaves received unconditional freedom, gratuitously awarded by an allegedly "benevolent" master. As table 18 clarifies, only nine individuals (eight females and one male) without a purchase price or condition attached to their manumission can be identified. Some reasons for such manumissions included expressions of love for a child or gratitude for decades of good services. In 1792, for example, João Martins Pimenta "gratuitously" freed the cabrinhas Maria and Sebastiana because of his love for them. Carlos Pinto Barboza Pimentel manumitted José cabrinha because of his "great love" for him, while other slaveholders also freed beloved children or women because of their good services. In 1792 João de Bastos manumitted Roza crioula because of her good services and the "crias" (children) she had given him.[14]

Overall, fifty-one individuals were manumitted in Vila Boa, of which thirty-three, or 64.7 percent, were female (table 17). Even though enslaved males far outnumbered female slaves, females were clearly preferred in this manumission sample. Brazilian-born crioulos, mulatos, and pardos were also preferred over Africans; only 39.2 percent of those manumitted were African. Unfortunately, there is not enough data on age to determine whether children or the aged were commonly freed, since scribes only occasionally registered age data. In only one case, that of Ana Maria parda, did a master admit that a slave was sick and near death at the time of her manumission, in this case after thirty years of service.[15] In other words, this sample reveals that those who achieved their manumission in Vila Boa were likely to be females, but the captaincy-wide sample of 1810–1824 reveals that about half of those freed were males (table 17).

Numbers

That many in the captaincy secured their freedom via manumission or flight to quilombos led to the gradual expansion of the free and freed population of color. Censuses reveal their increasing numbers between 1804 and 1832. Late colonial censuses from 1779 to 1792 did not usually count the freeborn and freed population of color, although household lists for the 1783 census provide some insight into their numbers. Either the colonial censuses used the inclusive term "free" (*livre*) for those born free as well as those freed via the manumission process, or they simply recorded color: white, pardo (mulato in 1804), and preto (black), without attention to legal status. Another, incomplete census in 1798 did list the number of forros (freed) and free people of color for Vila Boa and São José do Tocantins. According to Vicar João Pereira Pinto Bravo, writing to the governor in May 1799, the parish of Vila Boa then had nearly 8,000 "souls," of which 6,000 were "of Confession." Of these, almost 3,000 were freed and free. While the vicar's number apparently includes whites, he also reported that 131 forros had been born in 1798, while 112 forros had died, as opposed to 82 captive births and 75 deaths.[16]

More detailed information on the free population of color survives for São José do Tocantins. In 1798 the parish priest counted 1,909 males: 116 whites, 647 pardos, 229 free blacks, and 917 captives, plus 50 newborn males. The female population included only 66 whites, who were far outnumbered by the 581 pardas, 264 free blacks, and 441 captives, for a total of 1,352, plus 42 female newborns. Thus the parish registry of São José documents that by 1798 the free population of color of 1,721 (1,228 pardos and 493 free blacks) outnumbered the 182 whites. More than half of the total population of São José (3,261) was composed of free pardos and blacks (52.8 percent). The captive population of 1,358 made up another 41.6 percent and the 182 whites only 5.6 percent. This pattern was replicated in other mining towns as the white population declined and the people of color grew in numbers.[17]

The next census, of 1804, clarifies how many free men and women of color remained in the captaincy (table B.14). Overall, 23,386 were defined in the census as free mulatos or blacks. The scribe also distinguished the mulatos and blacks by gender, thus revealing gender differences among the people of color. On the whole, male mulatos, at 7,368, were outnumbered by mulatas, with 8,084. In total, there were 15,452 free mulatos. Reflecting a native-born population, the mulatas outnumbered male mulatos in nine julgados, or they were notably close to them in number. In Vila Boa alone, the 1,603 mulatas exceeded 1,208 mulatos, although in Desemboque, Traíras, Cavalcante, Conceição, and Natividade mulato males were more numerous than mulatas

This mulato profile is contrary to the gender breakdown among the free black population, in which free black females outnumbered free black males, except in the far south in Desemboque, where there were 32 black males to 30 females. Overall, 4,726 black females enjoyed the free/freed status as opposed to 3,208 males. In Vila Boa the difference was especially marked since there were almost 600 black females as opposed to 413 males. Two other mining centers, Pilar and Traíras, also had sizeable proportions of free black females: 510 to 322 males in Pilar and 758 to 542 males in Traíras. Julgados in the northern comarca also reflected these differences, such as 214 free black females to 124 black males in Arraias or 524 black females to 130 black males in Natividade, or 234 black females to 195 black males in Carmo. What apparently accounted for the discrepancy between free black females and males in 1804 was the mining economy, which enabled black females to purchase their freedom with gold, while slaveholders did not permit their husbands or partners to do the same. As our brief sample of manumission for Vila Boa illustrates, and as studies on manumission from other parts of Brazil demonstrate, Brazilian slaveholders tended to free more females than males, in a proportion of three females to two males. In Arraias, for example, the free black population was 63.3 percent female, but the proportion was even higher in Natividade, at 80 percent female.[18]

The cumulative result of so many manumissions and subsequent births to free/freed black and mulata women appears in the census of 1825, the first of the empire (table B.15). Here the middle category of pardo/mulato was replaced by *ingênuo*, a term from Roman law for the freeborn, and *liberto*, another term for the manumitted.[19] Once again the free and freed were grouped together by census takers as an additional category besides whites and captives. By 1825 the 37,985 freeborn and freedpersons of color were the largest census group in the captaincy, forming 60.8 percent of the total population of 62,478. Numbering 8,366 in the City of Goiás, they also made up about the same percentage (59.1 percent) of the total population of the capital of 14,167.

Second in the size of the free/freed population was Meia Ponte, with 4,842 people, or 51.2 percent of the district's total of 9,451. Historically, Meia Ponte had had a larger white population, who were the descendants of Portuguese immigrants, and its 2,767 whites even outnumbered those in the City of Goiás. But it had a smaller enslaved population than the capital. The third-largest number of the free/freed were resident in Traíras, at 4,321, or 69.6 percent of the district's total of 6,209. Only 395 whites still resided there, and they were greatly surpassed by the free/freed people of color and the enslaved. Obviously, the district of Traíras was predominantly nonwhite, since only 6.4 percent of its residents were defined as white. Even a smaller percentage of whites hung on in São Félix: 5.1 percent, or 44 individuals out of 866. The rest of the people were free/freed, at 680, and captives, at 142. Porto Real (Nacional) then had only 35 whites (2.3 percent) but 1,137 free/freed and 376 slaves, for a total of 1,548. In other words, all but 2 percent of the population was nonwhite in Porto Real, and almost three-fourths (73.5 percent) enjoyed the free/freed status.

A survey of the population of the province of Goiás in 1825 reveals that those who populated Goiás were mostly free/freed people of color of African and indigenous descent. They ruled in numbers, if not in the government. Since the white elite in the province lived surrounded by nonwhites and autonomous indigenous nations, they were the ones who complained about the loss of population and of their inability to acquire and control enslaved Africans. Hence the decadence discourse actually obfuscates the population growth that occurred among the free population of color in the early nineteenth century. Although elderly enslaved Africans were dying, the descendants of Africans and indigenous captive women were having children, who survived to have their own children and descendants. Furthermore, free migrants of color entered the province of Goiás seeking land to farm and freedom from enslavement elsewhere in Brazil.

The census of 1825 also provides a gender breakdown by districts. As in 1804, *ingenuas* (freeborn females) were more numerous than the ingênuos (freeborn males) at 18,439 to 16,566. In twelve districts, excluding São João da Palma, Conceição, and Flores, free females of color were in the majority. Although the slight numerical edge given to the freeborn in most districts might be due to manumission, especially in Cavalcante, where there was such a difference in numbers, it is probable that men of color were undercounted in this period, because they were away on cattle drives, river boat trips, or manning the garrisons. After the National Guard was organized in the 1830s, many resisted being counted in order to avoid impressment in the nineteenth century.[20]

Besides providing a total for the ingênuo population of 35,005, the census takers of 1825 further divided the males and females by legal status into free or freed (table B.15). Thus the census reveals that there were 16,566 free males, while 18,439 females were also free, but there were more male freedmen (1,539) than freedwomen (1,441). The larger number of freedmen suggests that they had been able to buy their freedom from masters who needed gold in a period of economic decadence. Or the number of freedmen may simply reflect the higher proportion of male slaves to female slaves in the late colonial period.

The last census of this period, for 1832, provides even more data on the free population of color by recording their color (pardo) and birth in Brazil or Africa. Table B.16 reveals that the great majority of the free people of color were defined as pardo, that is, 32,711, or slightly over three-fourths (77 percent) of the free population of color of 42,481. The pardos were also well balanced by gender, with 16,421 males to 16,290 females, which may indicate that the census takers were more skilled at recording free men of color in 1832. Blacks, however, still included a majority of females among the free/freed population. There were 4,982 free black females to 4,788 free black males, which equals a total free black population of 9,770, or 23 percent of the total free population of color of 42,481.

Figure 21. These snakeskin boots, which were made from the skin of a very large snake, gun case, and straw hat were collected by Johann E. Pohl. Courtesy of the Museum für Völkerkunde, Vienna, Austria.

This census also reveals that most free blacks in 1832 had been born in Brazil; thus they were crioulos. In contrast to the 9,253 crioulos, there were only 517 free Africans, who were most likely freedmen and freedwomen rather than freeborn. Their low numbers suggest that most elderly enslaved Africans had already died and had not been replaced by newly imported Africans.[21] Once again, free crioula females were in the majority, numbering 4,771, but African men outnumbered African women, 306 to 211. As in 1825, freedmen were more numerous than freedwomen in this period, but the same generalization was true of the enslaved population.

Overall, what the censuses document is the growing number of free/freed men and women of color. They numbered 42,481 by 1832, almost two-thirds (62 percent) of the total population of 68,497. Their friends and relatives who were still enslaved added yet another 13,261 individuals (19.4 percent) to the nonwhite population of the province. Whites composed only 11,761, or 17.2 percent, of the population, while mission Indians numbered only 994 (1.5 percent), for a total of 68,497 (table B.17). In 1789 there had been 9,079 whites recorded, a number that had risen over more than forty years to 11,761 in 1832. In contrast, pardos had numbered 12,643 in 1789, a total that probably included slaves, but their population had more than doubled, to 32,711, by 1832.

Occupations

If the free people of color were in the majority by 1832, what did they do to support themselves and their families? First of all, some worked as sertanistas (frontier guides) and bandeira leaders, contacting or attacking indigenous communities and quilombos. Perhaps the most famous of the sertanistas was Tomás de Sousa Vila Real, who was commissioned by three merchants to explore the Araguaia River as a potential trade route in 1791–1792. He also commanded other state-sponsored canoe expeditions that contacted and established trade relations with the Karajá and other indigenous peoples. In 1848 an account of his explorations was published in the journal of the Historical and Geographical Institute in Rio de Janeiro. Thus his career profile was similar to that of European explorers of the late colonial period, but with one difference: he was a pardo.[22]

Another exceptional expedition leader was Commander Antônio Moreira da Silva, who was the son of a mulata woman and a black (negro). Although his father may have been a slave, his mother was probably freeborn or freed, since there is no reference to his being enslaved, even though he was a "very dark" mulato. At one point in his career he had worked as a capitão do mato (bush captain), which was an occupation pursued by free men of color. Notably, he had led small groups of men in pursuit of fugitive slaves, returning them to their slaveholders and to slavery. But he built his reputation as a bandeira leader by fighting in the bloody bandeiras of conquest, enslavement, and Indian removal in southern Maranhão before migrating with his family to the Tocantins River, where, in 1816, he founded the small settlement later known as Carolina (after 1823). He also served in the independence cause with men from Pastos Bons, Maranhão, when they defeated a royalist force led by Captain Francisco de Paula Ribeiro. Perhaps due to his participation in the proindependence cause, he was officially recognized as the commander of a Luso-Brazilian community in 1825, a post he may have held until his death from assassination six years later.[23]

Other men of color seldom became so prominent. In some cases they served as soldiers and guides in the pedestres, the paid foot soldiers composed of indigenous men and those of color, who guarded towns and missions from indigenous attacks, patrolled roads and guarded checkpoints (registros), and participated in bandeiras that contacted indigenous nations. Skilled in the ways of surviving in the forests, the racially diverse troops were on the front lines of penetration into the frontier. In the 1770s and 1780s the indigenous men who served in the pedestres of Vila Boa largely came from the Akroá and Kayapó nations, but there were also other Indians, such as one Xacriabá from the São Francisco River, one bastardo of the Paraci (Pareci) nation, and the son of Indians of Cuiabá. In other cases, officers and soldiers in the pedestres were quite diverse in color, ranging from a few men identified as whites or sons of white men to those of African descent: mulatos, pardos, cabras, and crioulos. The most common name for the racially mixed of indigenous descent in the pedestres was *bastardo* (bastard), but of particular interest is that they came from various towns and captaincies: São Paulo, Rio de Janeiro, Pernambuco, Bahia, and Cuiabá, as well as Goiás. One *mestiço* (mestizo) and four *castas da terra* (castes of the land) completed the sample of pedestres.[24]

Under the administration of Governor D. Luiz de Mascarenhas (1739–1748), the barefooted pedestres were organized into two companies that were sent throughout the captaincy on the governor's orders. Initially in 1743 they included forty mestizos who were commanded by Captain Antônio Lemos de Faria, originally from the Azores, until he was jailed for corruption in the 1760s. They were formed in order to resist indigenous attacks and to patrol the road to São Paulo against Kayapó raiders. By the 1770s and 1780s more than half of the pedestres were quartered in mission villages.[25]

An accounting of their numbers in 1784 permits a better understanding of how few men in the pedestres actually served in the captaincy. Of a total of 189 men, 82 lived at the aldeia Maria I, most likely guarding the Kayapó, with another group of 29 men in São José de Mossâmedes. At least two of the pedestres were so trusted that they accompanied the quinto shipments to the coast, while five others guarded the tax-collection points of the *contagens* and ten guarded the checkpoints. In 1777, for example, the pedestre Antônio José do Monte do Carmo served not only at the checkpoint of São Marcos but also in the conduct of the quinto to Rio de Janeiro in 1782. The latter may also have been the responsibility of the black Luis Bras, sergeant of the pedestres, who made a trip to Rio de Janeiro before being given the task of conducting Indian couples to the presídio of Manuel Alves Grande. Since there were cattle being raised at the aldeia Maria, the two in the pasture may have been guarding the cattle, but there was also a cattle ranch at Salinas where twenty-three pedestres were stationed. In addition, twelve pedestres were making rounds (i.e., going on patrols), two were protecting towns, ten were making official investigations, and two were serving in Cuiabá.[26]

By 1789 and 1806, however, the number of pedestres had declined to 104 and 110, respectively, while only 51 remained in the aldeias by 1789. Since they were often forcibly recruited, governors frequently complained about their desertions, especially when they were being sent to fight against a famously hostile nation, such as the Canoeiro, with bows and arrows or antiquated weapons, such as the arquebus.[27] Other grievances were little pay or none at all. Indigenous soldiers were paid half of what the other troops received; in the 1780s they received 75 réis per day as opposed to 150 réis for non-Indians.[28]

Pardo Regiments

In contrast to limited documentation on the pedestres, the most detailed sources on the men of color in the military concern the pardo militia regiments and the black Henriques. The men who were identified as the sons of Portuguese officers (and African mothers) served in separate regiments from their white fathers and the free/freed blacks. Unlike the Portuguese in the mounted dragoons and Luso-Brazilian white men in the ordenanças, mulatos had their own separate regiments in the auxiliary cavalry and the infantry. Here they were led by pardo officers, who received elegant patents of appointment approved by the governor of the captaincy and signed by the Crown in Portugal. Hence, petitions for patents reveal the individual names of pardo officers. Furthermore, they also sent petitions to Portugal in which they protested against the discrimination they endured in the captaincy due to their color, even though their father was a man of quality.[29]

When Portuguese governors collected data on the military in Goiás, they found some questionable information on the actual strength of pardo regiments, but there is one accounting of pardo companies in 1789 (table 19) that may be more accurate than later ones. Although this table suggests that the pardos were well organized, Governor Fernando Delgado Freire de Castilho (1809–1820) complained about the lack of military regimentation and record keeping of the militias in the captaincy. He reported that the militias had been regimented in 1783 by Governor Luiz da Cunha Menezes (1778–1783), who was succeeded by his brother Tristão da Cunha Menezes (1783–1800), but apparently nothing was altered from the original organization of 1783 until 1803 under Governor D. João Manoel de Menezes (1800–1804). He established two regiments of cavalry and one of infantry of pardo men, and since there were still more men for one or the other regiment, he created fourteen companies of cavalry that were annexed to the two regiments. In the same manner, he attached eighteen companies of mulatos to the infantry regiment and organized the many Henriques regiments in conformity to the same plan, passing patents of colonel and lieutenant colonel to their officers. Patents for black officers, however, were never confirmed in Lisbon, as were those for mulato officers.[30]

After further complaints about the lack of accurate record keeping in the militias, the governor concluded that there were only three regiments, with the attached companies noted above, that were located throughout the captaincy. As a result, each captain was "the absolute Chief of his company" and, "having only to respond to a Superior in [a] very great distance [away], he can do what he wishes to alter whatever superior order." Since many blacks and mulatos could not read, he argued, they could "counteract the orders of a distant Superior." There were, however, literate black and mulato officers who appear in the documentation. One sample of soldiers in the Henriques in São José do Tocantins reveals that twenty could read and eighteen could write, but only seven could count. Furthermore, an 1804 petition by the pardos of Vila Boa was signed by pardos, who were literate enough to write their names.[31]

This same petition by the pardos also documented many of their services to the Crown. When the Kayapó and Xavante attacked, they reported that they were "the first sent on the Bandeiras ... dispatched to conquer them." When the Javaé and Karajá first entered the aldeia of São José de Mossâmedes, the

Table 19. Number of *pardo* men in the auxiliary infantry regiment, 1789

Officers	5	Crixás	113
São José	112	Anta	113
Santa Luzia	112	Traíras	113
Vila Boa	112	*Agregada*, Vila Boa	97
Granadeiros, Vila Boa	102	*Quartel*, Vila Boa	103
Natividade	102	*Agregada*, Santa Cruz	92
Meia Ponte	113	Jaraguá	113
Pilar	113	*Agregados*	3

Source: Lisbon, AHU, Mappa em que Tristão da Cunha Menezes governador e capitão general da capitania de Goyaz aprezenta das tropas pagas, auxilliares da guarnição da mesma capitania, ... , 1789.
Note: The total was 1,515; these were the men who were actually available out of the required 1,605.

pardos served there, as well as in the aldeia Maria I when the Kayapó settled there. They were also stationed at Carretão upon the arrival of the Xavante, and they garrisoned that mission for four years afterward. They also claimed to have conquered the "ferocious Canoeiro." Furthermore, they were the ones who were armed and ready in the recruiting for the city of Grão Pará [Belém]. They also participated in the new navigation of the Oruú, Almas, and Maranhão Rivers and were even sent to help on the "frontier of Mato Grosso." They also cited their service in establishing the new tax register of São João das Duas Barras. Finally, they reminded the authorities that all this was done in addition to their regular duties that they performed in Vila Boa. In other words, they were "ready for everything." Their petition was signed by Colonel of Infantry Miguel Á. da Ora and eighty-one other men.[32]

Eight years later, in 1811, the two regiments of cavalry were without a colonel: one had died and the other was near death, being more than ninety years of age. According to Governor Fernando Delgado Freire de Castilho (1809–1820), the pardo regiment of infantry was then headed by a "very poor pardo," given to drunkenness. Since the leadership at the top of the pardo regiments was so ineffective, the governor had appointed his adjutant, José Manoel de Almeida, to regulate all the militias of the captaincy.[33]

Three years later there is yet more information on the pardo infantry regiment. In 1814 its colonel was still Miguel Á. da Ora, who was again described as poor and drinking too much, so Governor Freire de Castilho concluded that he was "totally incapable" of occupying his position. He recommended that Lieutenant Colonel Lino Manuel Lopes Chagas of the same regiment replace him. As of 1814, Lieutenant Colonel Lopes Chagas had served for thirty-one years and five months in various positions, including as lieutenant colonel for fourteen years. Thus his militia career must have begun in the 1780s. The third officer in the same regiment, Captain Thomé Joaquim Marques, had already occupied his posts for thirty-one years and five months, being captain for seven years. He commanded the four companies quartered in Vila Boa. Also attached to the pardo regiment was a dragoon, Antônio Francisco de Alexandria, the adjutant of the regiment. Since 1788, he had served twenty-six years and four months, and as adjutant for three years. He too held the rank of captain, earning eight mil-réis monthly from the Royal Treasury.[34]

In addition to the military and the militias, free pardos had other status and income sources, notably the priesthood and property ownership, including slaves. Even one exceptional mulato, Padre Antônio Alves da Rocha (1786–1791), was able to study at the University of Coimbra. His father was a rich mine owner and his mother was "Ana Nação Mina." Perhaps due to the shortage of priests in Goiás, the sons of African mothers and white fathers were ordained as priests, although the enslaved could not be ordained. As chapter 9 documents, at least two pardo priests served in Natividade. Saint-Hilaire met yet another mulato priest in Pilar and praised him for his courtesy, although he explained that the priest had "something of that servility in which Brazilian society maintains mestizo men, which they never forget when they are in the presence of whites." The son of an African woman from Guiné, the vicar Manuel da Silva Álvares, became one of the richest slaveholding priests in the captaincy, owning a sugar plantation as well as ninety-five slaves. Born in Traíras, he served there from 1812 to at least 1825. He also promoted trade between Pará and Traíras, for which he petitioned for the award of the Habit of Christ but was denied. The most successful of all of the priests of African descent in pursuing a clerical career was Monsenhor Bento Severiano da Luz (1855–1917). Born in Meia Ponte of a priest, who freed him at baptism, and the slave Joana, he studied in Rome and rose to be a monsenhor in Cuiabá, Mato Grosso, who was famous for his skills as an orator.[35]

Pardos often combined a military or clerical career with property ownership of land and slaves and merchant enterprises. Here they may have been influenced by their white fathers in combining multiple sources of wealth. As their fathers had done, they acquired land through inheritance or purchase, and a minority even owned large plantations and ranches where they raised sugar and cattle. Some also acquired wealth from gold mines. But these wealthy pardos were a minority; instead, the majority of them were small-scale farmers, raising food crops and animals on small plots of land (roças and *sitios*). They rarely owned more than twenty slaves, and most had only one to five slaves plus household dependents (agregados) by the 1820s. They clearly had a far different standard of living than the wealthiest whites with a hundred or more slaves.[36]

These propertied pardos can be traced through household lists that included slaves. In 1783 many had slaves at work at the mines or in agropastoral activities on fazendas and engenhos. For example, in the town of São Félix in 1783 pardo men owned a total of seventy-four slaves; they were also served by *pessoas de obrigação* (obligated persons). Their male slaves worked in mining (twenty-three), in agriculture (twenty-one), in the house (four), and in one unknown location, while all twenty-five of their female slaves were in their households, most likely as domestic servants. Although pardos did not possess as many slaves as white men, José Francisco da Conceição and his wife owned twenty slaves; João Barbosa and his wife, nine slaves; and Marcelina Gonçalves dos Santos, a widow, sixteen slaves. All other pardos held five or fewer slaves. These free pardos apparently lived off of the productivity of their obligated persons and enslaved miners and fieldworkers. Notably, no slave women owned by pardos did field labor. Other pardo men in São Félix pursued skilled trades as tailors (three), ironworkers (three), and cattle raisers (one).[37]

Additional pardos who owned lands and slaves can be documented through the household lists of the 1820s (table 20). In Água Quente, Captain Antônio da Silva was exceptional, with twenty-five male and four female slaves, whom he utilized in mining and on a cattle ranch. In fact, he possessed more enslaved workers than the white officer Ludovico Fernandes da Cunha, who had a cattle ranch, farm, and small mill but only ten slaves. But few on the household lists held even five slaves. The situation in Cocal was similar, with few slaveholders. Besides the vicar, Manuel da Silva Álvares, who owned a sugar plantation and small farm near Cocal with sixty-three slaves, a pardo furriel (third sergeant) in the infantry, Joaquim Cardozo de Souza, had fourteen slaves plus a farm and sugar plantation, while Maria de Souza's eleven slaves worked on a small farm. No whites owned as many slaves as these three pardos, but in Pontal two whites controlled the most slaves: the priest José da Franca Amaral, with thirty-four slaves, and the commander and adjutant Tristão Pinto Cerqueira, who raised cattle and horses on his ranch, with thirty-six slaves. In contrast, the pardo Manoel Lopes Chaves used only eleven slaves on his sugar plantation. All other pardos held fewer than seven slaves, and most none at all. In São José do Tocantins, the most prosperous pardo, with a sugar plantation, mining slaves, and a ranch, was Manuel Teixeira Chaves, then age sixty-four, with a wife and four children and nineteen slaves. As usual, most pardos owned few slaves or none at all. Finally, in Traíras another pardo, Lieutenant José Teixeira Chaves, had a sugar plantation and small farm as well as thirty-three slaves, a number almost matched by the thirty-two slaves of Vicar Manuel da Silva Álvarez. Apparently this priest was the wealthiest pardo slaveholder in these five districts, since he owned not only thirty-two slaves in Traíras but also another sixty-three slaves near Cocal, which made him competitive in slave ownership to the wealthiest whites in the captaincy.[38]

Besides providing insight into slave ownership in the 1820s, the household lists also clarify the many types of occupations that were open to pardos in these five communities. They ranged from the law to mechanical trades and farm labor. What is also illuminating is that the same types of occupations were pursued by blacks and pardos and many whites, although some types of

Table 20. *Pardo* occupations in five communities, 1820s

Occupation	Água Quente	Cocal	Pontal	São José	Traíras
Businessman	1[a]	—	1	5	5[a]
Lawyer, professor	—	—	—	—	2
Tavern keeper, grocer	—	—	1[a]	3	8[a]
Miner	8[a]	2[a]	1	1	—
Officer[b]	2	6	1	—	1
Pilot to Pará	—	—	1	—	—
Surgeon	1	—	—	—	1
Goldsmith	1	—	—	1	—
Tinsmith	—	—	—	2	1
Ironworker	2	—	1	1	1
Saddle maker	—	—	—	2	—
Carpenter	3	1	3	3	1
Potter, painter	—	—	1[a]	2[a]	—
Stonemason	—	—	—	—	1
Tailor, seamstress	2	—	5[c]	2	2
Shoemaker	3	1	6	5	7
Spinner, weaver[d]	4	3	40	2	5
Fazenda	1	1[a]	1	—	2[a]
Cattle raiser	—	—	10	5[a]	—
Butcher	—	—	2	—	—
Cowboy, carter	—	—	4	—	1
Sugar plantation	—	1	2	2[e]	3
Small farmer	9[f]	37[f]	—	3[a]	39[f]
Agricultural worker	22[g]	—	66[g]	38[g]	—

Source: AHGDD, no. 68, Correspondência Dirigida do comandante das Armas—Raimundo José da Cunha Matos, 1823–1824: Água Quente, ff. 112–21; Cocal, ff. 99–106; Pontal, ff. 175–85; São José do Tocantins, ff. 123–42; and Traíras, ff. 86–98.

[a]Includes 1 female, except in Traíras, where there were 7 women in *vendas* (stores).
[b]Officer of corporal rank and above without another occupation identified.
[c]Includes 4 seamstresses.
[d]Spinners or weavers were females, except for 2 male weavers in Pontal.
[e]Includes 1 overseer.
[f]Includes 4 women in Água Quente, 6 in Cocal, and 20 in Traíras.
[g]Includes 3 women in Água Quente, 5 in Pontal, and 4 in São José.

occupations attracted more pardos than blacks and vice versa. In general, it seems that pardos had more choice in occupations than blacks, although blacks had more access to gold and the wealth it could bring than pardos. Table 20 was compiled from the household lists and includes occupations listed by the scribe or a general term, such as *fazenda de gado* (cattle ranch). The table largely covers male occupations, but whenever women were listed, they are included. A brief description of female occupations follows.

Some pardos also engaged in long-distance trade via the Tocantins River to Belém or to Salvador, Bahia, or merely did business in the towns. Captain Vicente da Cunha Mendes, a pardo who was originally from Bahia, was a businessman in Natividade in 1804. Other towns with pardo businessmen were São José do Tocantins and Traíras, each of which had five pardos in business in the 1820s (table 20). What is unclear from the sources consulted, however, is the role of pardos in trade. Did they carry out all the same commercial functions as white merchants? Or did they merely transport goods from place to place? As chapter 5 reveals, pardos were the ones whom the Portuguese accused of being contrabandistas in gold. Since so many men of color served on the riverboats as crewmen or on the mule teams that carried cargo to Salvador, it was easy for them to hide contraband gold dust in the baggage, but most pardos and blacks were only petty traders in the sertão, dealing in trade goods that were not risky or not very profitable by the 1790s.[39]

In general, free men of color who did not pursue military or clerical careers and who were not large land and property owners had to pursue lower-status occupations that enabled them to support their families. In the towns pardos entered artisanal crafts such as tailoring and shoemaking, but in the countryside they often served as the trusted *camaradas*, or employees of wealthy ranchers and boat and mule-team owners. Some freedmen herded cattle as camaradas in the convoy trades between the north of the captaincy and Bahia. Others were agregados who farmed small plots of fazenda lands with the permission of the owner. Their lighter color, facility in Portuguese, and knowledge of Luso-Brazilian culture gave them an advantage over free/freed blacks, who usually had to pursue more menial crafts and rural occupations. Blacks, however, were more notably successful in finding gold, and gold mining was more closely associated with free blacks than pardos.[40]

On the other hand, there were many pardos and cabras who did not engage in productive occupations but instead joined the "vagabonds," thieves, and other criminal gangs of the captaincy. Also feared in Goiás were the gypsies (*ciganos*), who moved in family groups around the province in the nineteenth century. They and the criminal gangs were accused of animal thefts and other crimes. Reacting in fear, town councils petitioned the governors of Goiás for protection and for financial aid in building a jail to imprison alleged dangerous criminals—that is, the racially mixed men of the captaincy—while their women were denounced for prostitution.[41]

Militia Regiments of Free/Freed Black Men: The Henriques

That pardos usually enjoyed a more elevated status in regard to occupations than blacks can be further documented using the regimental lists of the Henriques between the 1780s and 1820s. Since these were militia registries, they also recorded individuals' full-time occupations in the mining towns. In contrast to the more numerous and more privileged pardo regiments, however, not as many men were enrolled in the black regiments in 1789, when there were only 752 freed black men in the Henriques. They were organized in seven companies, based in Vila Boa, Pilar, Traíras, São José, Crixás, Meia Ponte, and Santa Luzia. Twelve officers served in each company of one hundred soldiers, as well as one officer attached to the Henriques, an alferes (second lieutenant). Some towns, such as Vila Boa and Pilar, had 101 soldiers, while only São José had the mandated 100 soldiers. Those with fewer than 100 men were Crixás and Meia Ponte at 99, Traíras with 81, and Santa Luzia at 87. Thus the Henriques needed 39 men to bring the militia up to full strength in 1789, but by 1812 there were twelve companies of Henriques.[42]

Those who belonged to these companies of black men usually enjoyed the freeborn or freed status. In the eighteenth century they included Africans, but by the early nineteenth century they were mainly crioulos, who were the sons and grandsons of Africans. One list of blacks survives for the eighteenth century for the mining town of São José do Tocantins, which reveals that 115 men belonged to the Henriques regiment, which was headed by Captain Luis Gonçalves dos Santos. All of the men bore surnames without any indication of the slave status; furthermore, twenty-six of them were slaveholders. Thirty-nine of the men had been born in Africa (thirty-three Mina and six Guiné); but ninety-one fathers and ninety mothers of the troops had been born in Guiné or Mina. Thus the majority were in the second generation of those of African descent. A generation later, in the 1820s, a household list for São José reveals that the men were then crioulos, including their crioulo captain, Luis Gonçalves dos Santos, age seventy-eight, who was a tailor.[43]

Such detailed information on the Henriques in the 1790s is exceptional. Not until the 1820s militia registries is there similar information on those who served in the black troops, in particular with detailed information on their occupations (table 21).

Like their African fathers and grandfathers, seventy-one militiamen still worked in gold mining in the 1820s, especially in the City of Goiás and Santa Luzia. But by that time eleven were also in business, with some living by their own agency. One was a salesclerk and another a tavern keeper. Like the pardos, blacks also engaged in skilled occupations (*ofícios*). One was a goldsmith, another a tinsmith, and six others were ironworkers, but more worked as carpenters, tailors, and shoemakers. There was also one pilot (of riverboats), a musician, several saddle makers, and a carter. In the rural countryside they were small farmers, but some raised or herded animals, and three were ranchers in Cavalcante. Day laborers, household dependents, family members, and unknowns complete the list of occupations. Very few depended on slave labor to assist or sustain them.[44]

In contrast to the numerous occupations that free/freed men of color pursued, freeborn and freed parda and black women had fewer options.[45] If married or living in a consensual union, they had to perform the same household duties as enslaved women, such as cooking and childcare. But if they lived on a small farm, they had additional responsibilities in the care of food crops such as corn and manioc as well as care of small animals. Where cotton was raised, they must have been involved in planting and picking the cotton, cleaning the seeds, and carding and spinning it into thread, since so many were listed as spinners on the household lists. A minority of women were slaveholders. While a parda might possess as many as fifteen slaves, black women usually held only one to three, but there were exceptional free black women, often widows, who owned ten to fifteen slaves. Women of color also controlled "obligated persons" in the 1780s. How so many in Goiás acquired obligated persons is uncertain, but there is documentation of a free woman in Sabará, Minas Gerais, who exchanged a year of servitude for gold. It seems likely that this may also have occurred in Goiás. Exchanging gold for services would then have enabled women of color to expand their control over less expensive workers than enslaved Africans. At least in the 1780s, widowed and single women of color could acquire rights to the labor of slaves, obligated persons, and household dependents, but if they were married, such rights were limited by their husbands.

Women of color may have been able to acquire enough wealth to barter gold

Table 21. Occupations of black militiamen, 1820s

Parish	Mining	Farming[a]	Arts/Crafts	Business	Other	Total
Arraias	4	42	7	—	23[b]	76
Bonfim	1	15	8	2	—	26
Carmo	7	23	21	1	8[c]	60
Cavalcante	—	43[d]	5	—	5	53
City of Goiás	23	23	47[e]	2	15	110
Jaraguá	10	12	9	—	7	38
Meia Ponte	—	46	14	—	6	66
Natividade	1	69	19	2	—	91
Pilar	—	21	13	4	51[f]	89
Pontal	—	15	9[g]	—	6	30
Santa Cruz	—	18	5	—	4	27
Santa Luzia	24	35	7	—	7	73
São José	1[h]	21	37	—	10	69
Total	71	383	201	11	142	808

Source: AHGDD, no. 66, Relações do Regimento dos Henriques, Governo das Armas de Goiás, Regimento de Infantaria Miliciana de Henriques, 1823–1824.
[a] Includes those who cared for cattle.
[b] Includes 15 *agregados* and 8 family members.
[c] Includes 5 shepherds.
[d] Includes 3 *fazendeiros*.
[e] Includes 1 goldsmith, 16 carpenters, 6 ironworkers, 1 musician, 9 shoemakers, 1 stonemason, and 11 tailors.
[f] Includes 1 tavern keeper.
[g] Includes 1 pilot.
[h] There were also 53 who had *lavras*.

for services or buy slaves due to ownership of houses and small farms, which they purchased themselves or acquired via inheritance. Other sources of funds came from processing and selling aguardente (sugarcane liquor) in taverns and vendas (market stalls). Clothing production, then largely defined as women's work, also involved free women of color. Although a minority of them wove cloth, most labored as spinners, the single-largest occupation registered for women of color in the 1820s. White women were more likely to be recorded as weavers, while women of color sewed cloth together as seamstresses.

On the whole, freeborn and freed parda and black women occupied the lowest rungs of the social structure imposed by whites in late colonial Goiás, but through their ownership of gold, other property, and slaves, they could outrank poor white women in wealth and contribute to household incomes to the point at which they could free other family members who were still enslaved. They also could support religious irmandades.

In spite of what people of color could accomplish in terms of occupation and property ownership, they still faced prejudice and the possibility of enslavement if they wandered too far away from the protection of a powerful patron. In São Félix, according to an oral tradition recorded by Dulce Pedroso, there was such prejudice against blacks that they could not walk on certain streets.[46] But even worse, they could be enslaved. According to Portuguese law, legal authorities could seize stray animals as well as slaves, including runaways, who could not prove their status as a freeborn or freedperson and put them up for auction as "property of the wind" *(bens do vento* or *evento)*. In this case, an official would hold an auction, with the meia-sisa being imposed on the newly enslaved black. In 1810, for example, the crioulo Manoel was auctioned off as "bens do vento" by José Gabriel de Carvalho in Traíras for one hundred oitavas of gold, and the meia-sisa paid was five oitavas. Five years later the crioulo Severino, who had fled from the captaincy of Pará, was also captured in Traíras and auctioned off for eighty-five oitavas.[47] While such cases legally reduced a person to the status of property through the auction process and payment of the tax, far more people of color were illegally kidnapped into slavery and held by force of arms.

In brief, the discourse of decadence by Portuguese governors and elite Goianos suggests the abandonment of the captaincy of Goiás in the late colonial period, but the reality was otherwise. Goiás was by that time largely occupied by men and women of color, both free and enslaved. Of course, whites also remained there, but they were a small minority who were far outnumbered by those of color. This frontier had not evolved in the direction of equality for all but rather had become a society characterized by hierarchy and exclusion as whites protected their privileged position and pardos protested their lack of access to citizenship. The more people of color protested, the more local whites tried to put them in their place or, in the case of autonomous indigenous nations, to eliminate them and take their lands. The elite, however, did permit an exceptional few to rise in service occupations as priests and military officers and to own property and slaves, although usually not as many as white slaveholders. Otherwise, most pardos and blacks were limited to the difficult military chores of a violent frontier, such as fighting the Kayapó, guarding mission Indians, and going on patrols. Some were able to continue to use their mining skills, especially in Santa Luzia and the City of Goiás, but the rest were limited to the skilled occupations considered appropriate for men of color, such as shoemaking and farming small plots of land. Although free men and women of color had escaped slave status or were the descendants of slaves, their color and social origin left them invisible to those who composed the discourse of decadence. Exceptional for their many services to the Portuguese governors in the late colonial period, they would thenceforth be repressed in the new provincial government of the Empire of Brazil, as local white elites took over the government and carved out large ranches that left them in command of Goiás. But at the same time, the number of the people of color continued to grow as legal slavery was further eroded in the nineteenth century.

CONCLUSION

Reflections on Frontiers/Borderlands of Central Brazil

Colonial sources document that Central Brazil was violently contested from the establishment of the slaving frontier in the 1590s to the foundation of mining towns in the 1720s and the retreat of whites from the north in the early nineteenth century. On this frontier there was no inevitable progression from discovery to European settlement. Those on the forefront of penetration were often not even European by birth. Instead, we should stress the fluidity and mobility of populations, with an ebb and flow across borders leading to many disasters for those who would penetrate into the interior of Brazil, not to mention the decimation and disappearance of many small indigenous nations, such as the Crixá and Goiá. On the other hand, that very ability to pick up and move via land or river meant that other threatened communities could survive, such as the Xavante, who found refuge in Mato Grosso from the Goiano bandeiras.

The reason for the failure of complete conquest was that indigenous nations held so much territory in Central Brazil, and the Portuguese never could mount enough expeditions (bandeiras) that were skilled in the ways of the backlands to conquer them. As indigenous nations learned from the invaders and acquired European tools and weapons, they became more powerful in their own right and pushed would-be settlers back into towns or pockets of settlement. Thus Luso-Brazilians only controlled territory around mining towns in the center and to its northeast, while the indigenous established borders with them and other nations elsewhere in the region. What sometimes, but not always, separated populations were the mountains and rivers and even on occasion a road, which divided lands claimed by the Xavante and Canoeiro. In many cases, however, rivers marked the borderlands between peoples and served as arteries of trade and communication through the backlands of the sertão.

In colonial Brazil the most common term for the unexplored backlands was *sertão*, but this usage could indicate almost anywhere, from the rural hinterland of a small town to the vast interior of Brazil. Thus there were many sertões in Central Brazil. On occasion Luso-Brazilians used the Portuguese word *fronteira*, in the sense of a far-flung region at the border with another state, but there was no connotation of the frontier as a cradle of democracy in the mold of Frederick Jackson Turner. Unlike North American images of the frontier as a place of opportunity for Anglo settlers, the Brazilian sertão, as David McCreery summarizes, was viewed as "a dark, unknown, and dangerous space, without God, society, or the state."[1]

But the lands between the rivers—the Araguaia, Tocantins, and Rio Grande in the far south—were not vacant lands. They were already occupied with numerous nations, organized in towns and villages, who planted crops of corn and manioc and hunted and fished. Some of their largest towns rivaled Brazilian mining towns in size, and their fields fed hundreds and even thousands. The largest Kayapó and Apinaje towns comprised four thousand people, about the size of the capital of Vila Boa. Largely Gê-speaking, they often shared common cultural traditions that had evolved over centuries of interaction with each other. In Portuguese discourse, they were nomadic "wild animals" (feras) and barbarians, but in reality they had most sophisticated lifestyles, belief systems, and means of sustenance that enabled them to thrive in difficult environments. They also had the ability to mount coalitions of regiments that defeated invaders armed with muskets, rifles, and artillery.

Because there were dense indigenous populations in the seventeenth and eighteenth centuries, Franciscan and Jesuit missionaries attempted to establish missions among them. In the seventeenth century the Franciscans had a mission enterprise along the Tocantins River before the Jesuits set up missions in the north and south of the captaincy. With the expulsion of the Jesuits of 1759, there were few foreign missionaries in Goiás until the Italian Capuchins arrived in the 1840s. Under the Directorate system (1757–1798), local parish priests were to Christianize the Indians, but few of the converts agreed to settle in a mission aldeia under a secular administrator and the mulato and black troops who forced them to work. Thus the mission frontier was either very weak due to a severe shortage of priests or missing entirely for more than eighty years.

Another image from North America is that of vast numbers of land-hungry settlers sweeping into the Great Plains to settle them. Central Brazil also had immense lands to cross, but the difference was that so much of the landscape did not easily yield food crops or pasture for cattle. Settlers from Bahia had to cross arid backlands to reach the São Francisco River, and there were few inducements to stop and plant crops until they reached more fertile lands near the Tocantins River and its tributaries. Mountainous terrain also slowed their progression. If they migrated from Maranhão or Pará in the north, they also faced the daunting resistance of densely populated indigenous nations who controlled the rivers and claimed territory along each river's banks, where they planted their crops. Thus riverine borderlands were numerous, and they divided indigenous nations from one another—and from the Luso-Brazilians.

The captaincy of Goiás clearly does not fit the old Turnerian version of the frontier. The invading Portuguese did not inevitably conquer and settle this frontier. In fact, most of those who actually fought the invaders were men of color, while settlers were not whites bringing Christian civilization in the North American sense to the remote sertão but actually enslaved Africans and free/freed pardos and blacks, who often eliminated indigenous populations and practiced religions that Portuguese priests did not recognize. By the end of the colonial period the Portuguese were few in number, and free people of color composed two-thirds of the population by 1832.

Furthermore, indigenous populations did not welcome invading forces but instead fought to hold back the spread of an alien way of life and the seizure of their lands. Although the Portuguese declared their conquests of the indigenous populations, they did not actually succeed in occupying all of their territories. The situation in Goiás was more similar to a collection of borderland states, each one of which was autonomous, than one actually governed by an occupying military imported from Europe. Because each side could mobilize powerful forces, violence and conflict were continuing characteristics of this region throughout the colonial period. At times a fragile peace was negotiated between nations, oftentimes by cultural brokers, including women, but it usually fell apart due to local attacks on each other's villages or raids for cattle and corn. As the wars resumed, they were characterized by vicious cruelty against the women and children of the opposing side. The colonial period was thus marked by continual warfare, as Luso-Brazilians displaced peoples from their gold-rich lands and seized both lands and peoples for themselves.

But there was also another side to frontier life in Central Brazil. It was also marked by trade between enemies and allies. Trade flowed along the great rivers and across the mountains. In one sense, Central Brazil was like a "trading-post empire." Since gold was "the blood" of the mines, it circulated everywhere, even drawing indigenous nations and quilombolas into trade relations with Luso-Brazilians. If they would not trade, then indigenous nations and quilombolas acquired desired goods by raiding. The bandeirantes, however, were also great raiders, who expanded the slaving frontier into Central Brazil throughout the seventeenth and eighteenth centuries. While Luso-Brazilians lost their commodities to indigenous raiders, indigenous communities lost their people to the men of São Paulo, or, later, Indians took up guns to enslave their neighbors, as in the case of the Krahô.

After a century of warfare and occasional peaceful relations, Central Brazil did not have freedom and equality in the Turnerian sense. The bandeirantes began the process of coerced labor and sexual abuse by kidnapping and enslaving the Araés, Karajá, and Goiá. Captured women and children they kept for themselves and began the process of miscegenation that would lead to a large free population of color in the nineteenth century. During the early mining boom, Goiás was a male-dominated society with a shortage of women, except for the enslaved and sexually exploited. While white men of all social ranks took women of color as concubines and prostitutes, they rarely married them or recognized their children. Clearly, what emerged from the warfare and enslavement of the colonial period were very inequitable settler societies organized into color categories as eighteenth-century Luso-Brazilians transferred their notions of "good order" and "good men" to Goiás. Portuguese men of quality in service to the Portuguese Crown were deemed to be the rightful rulers of the imperial captaincy; all others were either enslaved or subjected to powerful whites. Everyone had their place in this hierarchical society, with whites at the top, the racially mixed in the middle, and enslaved blacks and captive Indians at the bottom. Those who resisted had to seek remote locations in which to escape enslavement, which lasted until 1888, although men and women of color continued to be illegally enslaved almost to the present. Upon independence, whites assumed the government of provincial Goiás, and powerful local potentates (the future coroneis) emerged to dominate local and provincial governments and exclude or manage the vote of the rest of the population. Neither social equality nor democracy would flourish in Central Brazil, although exceptional pardos and blacks did acquire wealth and practice occupations usually limited to white men.

What this frontier offered to ordinary people, however, was the opportunity to gain access to land, if not landownership, where they could plant their crops and raise small animals. Remoteness also enabled them to escape the strictures of church and state, allowing them to do as they pleased—as long as they could survive in the face of Indian attacks. Indigenous threats forced many to seek the protection of powerful men and their slave armies in the countryside or to move to small towns in which they could find militia forces to defend themselves and protect their families. As long as gold was plentiful, towns attracted merchants and craftsmen and sheltered one or more churches that provided essential religious rituals and brought people together to celebrate feast days. They also attracted less religious men to the town's taverns and brothels staffed by women of color.

In the eighteenth century this frontier had owed its settlement to gold, but after the decline of the mines in the 1770s the region began to deurbanize, with once rich mining towns, such as São Félix and Cocal, being abandoned. Without gold, as Goianos learned in the nineteenth century, there was little to encourage European immigrants to come. Therefore, indigenous nations, such as the Canoeiro, could rebuild or resettle new areas or launch new attacks on fragile towns. Instead, Luso-Brazilian settlers consolidated their control over large ranches and populated their territories with cattle and horses. Throughout Goiás, cattle increasingly replaced indigenous peoples, and a trade in smuggled cattle brought riches to the cattle barons of Central Brazil. In the nineteenth century, therefore, provincial Goiás seems similar to the cattle frontiers of Texas, where cattle were raised and then driven over long distances to markets.

In summary, Central Brazil went through many frontiers: a slaving frontier as in Angola, a mission frontier under the Franciscans and Jesuits, a mining frontier that led to Indian removal and even genocide, a trading and raiding frontier as in Araucanian Chile, a farming frontier as land-hungry settlers invaded areas in the north and west, and a cattle frontier in the nineteenth century. In the twenty-first century, the current frontier is the soybean frontier, in which highly capitalized agribusinesses are invading savannas and forests and transforming them into immense fields of soybeans for export to global markets. Indigenous populations, such as the Xerente and Apinaje, now live on reserves established by the federal government.

While we may use the concept of frontier from other historical studies, most do not fully capture the complexity of social interactions in Central Brazil over centuries. As David McCreery concludes, "Goiás does not easily fit standard frontier patterns."[2] Furthermore, most isolated towns and settlements, especially in the nineteenth century, had their own "frontiers"; they were like a series of islands (an archipelago) in a sea of grass or green forests surrounded by "the other," who held their own autonomous territories. Other settlers occupied river ports that were connected by river traders. Since there were many borderlands, with each town having its own sertão, Luso-Brazilians held only small portions of the vast territory of Central Brazil. Indigenous nations and quilombolas, as well as the free people of color, occupied territories and governed themselves unless a bandeira invaded their lands and enslaved them. Clearly the frontier did not close in the colonial period, and the many frontiers of Goiás continued well into the twentieth century without resolution in favor of an imperial state.

APPENDIX A: Indigenous Nations of Central Brazil

Table A.1

Name	Modern name	Location	Dates
Acarayá	Karaja[a]	Tocantins River, east of	1782
Acroá	Akroá	Tocantins River, east of	18th–19th c.
Acroá-Assú	Akroá	Tocantins River, east of	—
Acroâ-Mirim	Akroá	Tocantins River, east of	—
Acurúa, Acoroá	Akroá	banks of the Mearim River	1740s
Affotigês, Afotigés	Apinaje	Araguaia, Tocantins Rivers	1824
Agurujá	—	Tocantins River, east of	1782
Amadús	—	Near Bananal Island	—
Amanayós	—	Tocantins River, east of	1782
Anicu	—	Neighbors of Guayã	1783–1800
Apiaca, Apiaká[b]	Tupi language	Mato Grosso	1840s
Apinagés, Apinayé	Apinaje	Tocantins River, north	1812
Apuatiaras,	Kayapó	Paraúpava *sertão*	1613, 1616
Aputiaras	—	—	—
Arachás, Araxãs	Araxá	Triangulo Mineiro, Minas Gerais	1636
Araés, Aracis	—	Araguaia, Maranhão, and Mortes Rivers	1590s–1770s
Arauerê[c]	Related to Javaé	Araguaia River	1792
Arauqueres	—	Araguaia/Tocantins Rivers	1670–1674
Arcoro-á	Akroá	Tocantins River, east of	1757
Aricobés	Arikobé	Tocantins River, north	1820s
Aripoconé, Coxiponé	—	Mato Grosso	1716
Aroaquins	Lingua geral	Araguaia/Tocantins Rivers	1670–1674
Aroaquiz, Aruaque, Aruaquis	Arawak (Aruak)[d]	Araguaia/Tocantins Rivers	1670s, 1792
Assus	—	Tocantins River, east	—
Augútê, Augutgé	—	Tocantins River	1815
Avá-Canoeiro	Tupi language	Maranhão River	18th–20th c.
Bacaerís	Bakairi[e]	Mato Grosso	1799
Bilreiros	Kayapó do Sul	Claro, Pilões Rivers	1590s–17th c.
Biobebas	—	captives of Araujo	1618
Bororo	Bororo	Rio das Velhas	1741
Caatingas, Cátinga	—	Tocantins River, east of	1613–1614
Caiapó, Cayapó	Kayapó do Sul	Paranaíba, Grande Rivers	18th c.
Cakamekra	—	Tocantins River	1815
Canacatagé, Canaquetgê	Timbira group	Farinha River	1814
Canella fina	Canela[f]	Maranhão	1816–1821
Canoeiros	Tupi language	Maranhão River	18th c.
Capepuxis	Krahô[g]	see Pépuxis	1812–1819
Capiécrá, Capiecran	Kapiekran (Canela)	Maranhão	1815–1817
Caracategé	Timbira group	—	—
Caracaty, Krikati	Krikati, Krikateye	Tocantins River	1844

305

Table A.I (continued)

Name	Modern name	Location	Dates
Caracutás	—	São João do Araguaia	1884
Carahôs	Krahô	Tocantins River	1820
Carajá	Karajá	Araguaia River	1671
Carajai, Carajais, Carajáz, Carajahîs	Karajá	Araguaia River	17th c.–1792
Carajaúna, Carajaputanga, Carajaupivana	Karajá	Araguaia River	1611–1644
Caraôs, Carahó	Krahô	Tocantins River, east of	1820s
Carauadû[h]	Karajá name	Araguaia River	1792
Carauau	Karajá name	Araguaia River	1792
Carcabas	Karajá name	north	1814
Carijós	captives, São Paulo	*sertão*, Paraúpava	1616–1618
Chacriabás	Xacriabá	Tocantins River, east of, and Rio das Velhas	18th c., 19th c.
Chambioá	Karajá	Araguaia River	1840s
Chavantes, Shavante	Xavante	Araguaia/Tocantins Rivers and Mato Grasso	18th–19th c., 19th–21st c.
Cherentes, Sherente	Xerente	Tocantins River	1780s–21st c.
Chicriabá, Chikriabá, Chyquiriabás	Xacriabá	Tocantins River, east of	18th–19th c.
Comacariz	—	Araguaia River	1770s
Comarcaôns	—	Tocantins River	1815
Copejé	—	Araguaia River	1782
Copé-poly	—	Tocantins River, east of	1782
Copinharó, Cupinharó, Cupinharóz	Porécamekrã	Tocantins River	1816?
Copinheiro	Porécamekrã?	Tocantins River/Maranhão	1816?
Coròa	Xavante	Araguaia River (raids)	1775
Coroá, Coroamerim	Akroá	Tocantins River, east of	18th c.
Coroados	Akroá	Peixe River	1820s
Coroá, Coroados	Akroá	Tocantins River, east of	18th c.
Cororû	—	—	1757
Cortís[i]	Apinaje	Tocantins River	1820s
Corumbarê, Curimbarés	Karajá person	Araguaia River	18th c.
Corvetijes?	—	Tocantins River, west bank	1823
Coxiponé	Coxiponé	Mato Grosso	1716
Craós	Krahô	Tocantins River	1819
Crayaz	Canoe people	—	1757
Crixá, Crixás	—	town in Goiás	1730s
Cupelobos	Kupe-rob[j]	Vermelho Lake	—
Curemecrãs[k]	Timbira	—	1819
Curuá-merim	Akroá	Tocantins River, east of	1782
Curuá-vacú	Akroá	Tocantins River, east of	1782

Indigenous Nations of Central Brazil

Name	Modern name	Location	Dates
Curumaré[1]	Karajá	Bananal Island	1750s
Gabião, Gaveão	Gavião	Tocantins River, east bank	1816–1830
Gamelas	—	Mearim River, Maranhão	1740s
Goiás, Goiases	Goiá	Vila Boa region	1720s
Gradaús, Gradahú	Kayapó do Norte	Tocantins/Araguaia Rivers	1819–1840s
Grajará	—	Araguaia/Tocantins Rivers	1674
Grajaú	—	Tocantins River	1650s
Guaicurú, Guaiaguçus, Guayagussús	Guaikuru	Pantanal, Mato Grosso	1740s
Guajará	—	Araguaia/Tocantins Rivers	1674
Guajurá	Guajajara	Tocantins River, west of	1782
Gualachos	—	on the way to Paraúpava	1616
Guapindayez	—	—	1757
Guarajós	—	Tocantins River	1670s
Guarajú	—	Tocantins River, east bank	1673
Guayã	Goiá?	Vila Boa region	1720s
Guegêz, Gueguêz	Guegué, Guenguen	Tocantins River, east of	18th c.
Guerengua	Guerén, Gren, Kren	Tocantins until São Féliz and Bahia	1757
Inhajurupés	Xavante?	Graciosa, Tocantins River	1820s
Inheiguará, Inheyguará, Neiguará	—	Tocantins River	1659
Iparanim	—	Araguaia River	1792
Iricoxés	—	Tocantins River	1819
Jacaribás	Xacriabá	—	18th c.
Jacudá	Jacundá?	Araguaia River	1792
Jacundá, Jacundás	Jacundá	Araguaia River, east of	1793–1844
Jaguari	—	Tocantins River	1721–1722
Jandariz	—	Araguaia River	1770s
Janquirage	—	Araguaia River	1770s
Javaés	Javaé	Araguaia River	1775
Jundiahy	—	Itaboca Falls, Tocantins R.	1830
Jundiá-is	—	Tocantins River	1844
Kapiekran	Canela	Neves River	—
Karajá	Karajá, Macro-Gê	Araguaia River	17th c.
Kayapó	Kayapó do Sul	southern Goiás	18th c.
Kayapó do Norte	Mebengokre	Araguaia River, west of	—
Kradaú-ya	Gradahú	Araguaia River	1819
Krahô	Krahô	Tocantins River, east bank of	19th c.
Kupe-rob	Kupe-rob	Vermelho Lake	—
Lauecrayues	—	Araguaia River	1770s
Macamecrã	Krahô	Tocantins River	1815–1819

Table A.I (continued)

Name	Modern name	Location	Dates
Macamecrans, Macamekrans, Mākamekra, Maquemecranz	—	—	—
Mucú[m]	Myky	Tocantins River, east of	1782
Mucúru[n]	Myky or Mucura	Tocantins River, west of	1782
Mudrucû[o]	Munduruku	Tocantins River	1792
Naúdoz	—	São José de Mossâmedes	1775
Neiguarás	see Inheiguarás	Tocantins River	1658/1659
Nhyrykwaye	Kayapó do Norte	Araguaia-Tocantins Rivers	1810
Norocoagê	Xerente	Tocantins River	1824
Noroguagês, Noroguajés	—	—	—
Othogês, Otogês, Otajé	Apinaje	Tocantins River	1824
Otoeporaz	—	Tocantins River	—
Pacajá	Pacajá River	Tocantins River, west of	1656
Pachiguirás	—	Tocantins River	1658/1659
Paiaguá	—	Mato Grosso	1733
Pânaca	Akroá	Tocantins River, Piauí	18th c.
Panajé	Apinaje	Tocantins River, east bank	1782
Panarás	Kayapó	Grande River/Paranaíba	1911
Panavi	—	Tocantins River, east of	1782
Paraci,[p] Paresi	Pareci	Mato Grosso	18th c.
Pépuxis, Pepuchy, Capepuxis[q]	Krahô	Tocantins River/Maranhão	1819
Pinajé, Pinagés	Apinaje	Araguaia River, north	1820s
Pinaré	Apinaje?	Araguaia River	1792
Pindaré	—	Tocantins River	1740
Pinoré	Apinaje	Araguaia River, north	1753
Piócóbgez[r]	Gavião	Tocantins River	1815
Pirapés	Tapirapés	Araguaia River, west	1656
Pitanga	—	Tocantins River, east of	1782
Pivoca[s]	Gavião	Colégio Isabel	1877
Pochiguará, Potyguará, Poquiguará, Poquiguirá	—	Tocantins River, north	1650s
Poquins	—	Tocantins River	1659
Poquis, Poquizes	—	Tocantins River	1668–1669
Porecamecrãs, Purécamekrans	Porekamekrã,[t]	Cocal Grande, Tocantins River	1808–1819
Póxeti, Poxety,[u] Puxiti	Xavante (branch of)	mountains west of Xavante, Tocantins River	1813–1819
Pukóbye, Pukopye[v]	"Timbira tribe"	Tocantins River, east of	1804, 1930s
Pururá	—	Tocantins River, east of	1782

Indigenous Nations of Central Brazil

Name	Modern name	Location	Dates
Quirixás	Crixás	Region of Crixás, Goiás	1720s
Sirinquique	—	Araguaia River	1770s
Sony	—	Tocantins River, east of	1782
Tacuayuna	—	Araguaia River	1792
Tamimbós, Tamembós, Temembõ, Temenbós	Krahô	Tocantins River, east of	1815–1819
Tapacoâ, Tapacuá	Xavante	slopes of the Serra Negra	1774
Tápe	Acroâ-mirim?	Meia Ponte *agregado*	1775
Tapirapéz	Tapirapé	Araguaia River, west of	1750s
Tapirasse	—	Araguaia River	1792
Tapucura	—	Araguaia River	1770s
Tapuyrapé	Tapirapé	Araguaia River, west of	1757
Taquanhina (Tacayuna)	—	Tocantins River	1721
Tecemadú, Tessemedús	—	Araguaia River	1794, 1819
Tembéassu[w]	Tembé	Tocantins River	1738
Tembemeri?	—	Tocantins River	1738
Tembira	Tembé or Timbira	Tocantins River, east of	1782
Temiminós	—	captives of Araujo	1618
Timbira	Timbira	Maranhão	1816
Tocaíuna	—	Tocantins River	1721–1722
Tupinambá	Tupinambá	Tocantins River	1658
Turiuara	—	Araguaia River	1792
Turiurá[x]	—	Tocantins River, west of	1782
Uacuruhá	Akroá?	Araguaia River	1792
Uajá[y]	Wauja	Tocantins River, west of	1782
Uitixés	—	Carolina, Tocantins R.	1819
Xacriabá	Xacriabá	Formiga River, Rio das Velhas	1750s, 19th c.
Xambioá	Karajá	Araguaia River, north	1844
Xavante, Chavante	Akwê-Xavante	Araguaia/Tocantins Rivers	18th–19th c.
Xavante de canoa	Avá-Canoeiro	Maranhão River	1773
Xavante de Quá	—	Mato Grosso	19th–21st c.
Xerente, Sherente	Xerente	Tocantins River	18th–21st c.
Xerentediquá[z]	Xerente	Tocantins River	1782
Xocamekran	—	—	—

Note: The first column lists names as they appear in source documents. The second column lists the modern name or linguistic group. The location and specific dates are from the historic sources.
[a] This seems to be the Karajá of the region of the falls of the Araguaia River and perhaps parts of the Tocantins River, but, according to Odair Giraldin, "it is little probable" that they were east of the Tocantins River, as recorded by Braun in 1782. This identification, as well as others noted below, are by Odair Giraldin.
[b] See figure 4, portraits of Karajá and Apiaká, from Francis de Castelnau's expedition in the 1840s. Both Odair Giraldin and Andrés Salanova identify the Apiaca as the Apiaká. In an email of 3 October 2015, Salanova describes them as Tupi, but he notes that "very little is known about the language."

Table A.I (continued)

^c^ This name recalls the name of one of the peoples who gave rise to the actual Javaé. According to their history, various peoples left the subterranean or subaquatic world in which they lived. One of them was the Weré, which is pronounced as "Ueré."
^d^ Aruak is a linguistic trunk with a widespread distribution of speakers, but the Aruak people closest to the Araguaia River are the Mehinaku, who live in the Xingu.
^e^ The Bakairi actually live in the southeast of Mato Grosso and speak a language of the Karib trunk.
^f^ Also actually known as Ram-Ko'kamekra.
^g^ The word "Pepuxis" is more a proper name among various Timbira groups.
^h^ This name and the two following ones are more like personal Karajá names or positions of leadership, such as Wedu or Deriodu.
^i^ The name of one of the ceremonial halves of the Apinaje: Koo-ti.
^j^ These Cupe rop who were known for having many glass beads could be the Wauja, of the Xingu River, also known as the Juruna.
^k^ This name also appears similar to that of the Carecateje or Carekamekra, or one of the Timbira peoples.
^l^ Kurumaré is a personal name of the Karajá, which is still used.
^m^ The Mucú are the same as the group named Myky, who are a people who actually live in lands demarcated in the *município* of Brasnorte in Mato Grosso, which is very distant from the Tocantins River.
^n^ Mucuru recalls Myky, but it could also be Mucura, because there was a Timbira people who were known as Mucura, but their region was near Piauí.
^o^ This name appears to be the Munduruku, who have always lived in the southwest of Pará.
^p^ This may be the Pareci, a people who lived in Mato Grosso.
^q^ These may be personal names.
^r^ This name is similar to Pyrcohp catiji, which is the way in which the Gavião of Maranhão self-define themselves; also written as Pucob-jê.
^s^ One of the Timbira peoples who join with the Pyrcohp catiji to form the actual Gaviões.
^t^ "Põ" is the Timbira word for the open *cerrado* with lots of grass. "Ré" is the diminutive. "Kamekra" is a suffix that indicates a "person, group, family" of a specific place. Actually, the Krikati are called Põcateje by the Gavião Pyrcohp catiji, who are called Irõm coteje (people of the forest) by the Krikati.
^u^ "Xeti" in the Timbira languages signifies the smell of something grilled. Then "Poxeti" would be the smell of grilled or roasted deer.
^v^ See note s.
^w^ This must refer to the Tembé, a Tupi-Guarani group, very near to the Guajajara.
^x^ In the region east of the lower Tocantins River there is a river called Turiaçu. This may be a reference to some people of that region.
^y^ This name is like that of the Waujá, who lived (and live) in the Xingu. But it also could refer to the Awa-Guajá, a nomadic people who lived to the east of the lower Tocantins River.
^z^ The suffix "Tdekwa" signifies "the proper," "owners of."

APPENDIX B: Censuses

Table B.I. Whites in the Comarca of the South, 1779–1832

Year	Vila Boa	Meia Ponte	Santa Luzia	Santa Cruz	Pilar	Crixás	Velhas	Other[a]	Total
1779	1,460	1,809	490	562	576	219	—	602	5,718
1781	2,310	1,809	623	562	576	219	35	—	6,134
1782	2,289	1,840	625	438	576	241	34	—	6,043
1783	2,289	1,727	625	483	576	270	35	—	6,005
1784	2,267	1,716	423	479	567	269	35	—	5,756
1785	2,287	1,719	322	479	568	379	44	—	5,798
1789	2,293	1,772	617	459	619	353	53	—	6,166
1791	2,279	1,766	553	454	623	320	52	—	6,047
1792	2,233	1,725	560	427	581	371	558	—	6,455
1804	1,219	1,268	530	878	365	79	—	1,203	5,542
1825	2,527	2,767	1,113	2,083	380	270	—	—	9,140
1832	2,527	2,441	1,113	3,330	549	40	—	1	10,001

Sources: RJIHGB, Arq 1.2.7, Estatística, Ofício de Luis da Cunha Menezes á Martinho de Mello e Castro, remetendo o Mapa da população da Capitania de Goiás, com distinção de classes, Vila Boa, 8 July 1780, f. 246; Mappa em que Luis da Cunha Menezes... aprezenta ao Real Ministerio,... Relaçõens dos Parrochos..., 1781, Projeto Resgate, CD rom, vol. 4; Mappa em que Luis da Cunha Menezes... aprezenta ao Real Ministerio... o numero existente dos habitantes,1782, Projeto Resgate, CD rom, vol. 4; RJBN, Manuscript Section, Cod. 16.3.2, Notícia Geral da Capitania de Goiás, 1783; Mappa em que Tristão da Cunha Menezes... aprezenta ao Real Ministerio... o numero existente dos habitantes..., 1784, Projeto Resgate, CD rom, vol. 4; Mappa em que Tristam da Cunha Menezes... aprezenta ao Real Ministerio... o numero dos habitantes..., 1785, Projeto Resgate, CD rom, vol. 4; AHU, Goiás, caixa 35, Mappa em que Tristão da Cunha Menezes... apresenta ao Real Ministerio... o numero existente dos habitantes..., 1789, Vila Boa, 19 October 1790; RJIHGB, Arq. 1.2.8., vol. 37, Relação em que Tristão da Cunha Menezes... aprezenta ao Real Ministerio..., 1791, f. 7; AHU, Goiás, caixa 35, Mappa em que... Tristão da Cunha Menezes aprezenta ao Real Ministerio..., 1792, Vila Boa, 29 July 1792; AHU, Cod. 2109, Reflexoens economicas sobre as tabellas statisticas da capitania de Goyaz pertencentes ao anno de 1804 e feitas no de 1806; RJBN, 11,4,2, Estatística da provincia de Goyáz remetida á secretaria de estado dos negocios do imperio..., 1825; and RJAN, Cod. 808, vol. 1, Goiás, Censo da População da Provincia de Goyaz, 30 May 1832, f. 96.
[a]In 1779, "other" included Anta with 602; in 1804 Desemboque had 1,203; and in 1832 only one at the mission of Carretão.

Table B.2. Whites in the Comarca of the North, 1779–1832

Year	Traíras	Cavalcante	São Félix	Arraias	Conceição	Natividade	Other[a]	Total
1779	679	142	387	156	—	555	1,293	3,212
1781	955	142	387	274	490	690	—	2,938
1782	960	143	382	274	484	677	—	2,920
1783	967	145	379	277	497	628	—	2,893
1784	904	145	376	297	496	528	—	2,746
1785	843	160	374	304	495	589	—	2,765
1789	914	171	385	311	489	643	—	2,913
1791	906	187	400	307	491	623	—	2,914
1792	808	149	362	309	459	630	—	2,717
1804	372[b]	338	78	139	199	201	81	1,036
1825	395	163	44	267	50	157	279	1,355
1832	517	182	6	415	19	128	493	1,760

Sources: See table B.1.
[a] "Other" includes, in 1779, Tocantins with 276 whites; Carmo, 84; Barra da Palma, 530; São Domingos, 118; Pontal, 87; and Paraná de Cima, 198. In 1804 there were 81 whites in Carmo. In 1825, Palma, S.J., had 34 whites, Flores 210, and Porto Real 35. In 1832 Palma had 27 whites, Flores 291, Porto Imperial 73, Carolina 100, and Duro 2.
[b] In 1804 Traíras was counted with the Comarca of the South.

Table B.3. Whites in the captaincy of Goiás, 1779–1832

Year	Comarca of the South	Comarca of the North	Total
1779	5,718	3,212	8,930
1781	6,134	2,938	9,072
1782	6,043	2,920	8,963
1783	6,005	2,893	8,898
1784	5,756	2,746	8,502
1785	5,798	2,765	8,563
1789	6,166	2,913	9,079
1791	6,047	2,914	8,961
1792	6,455	2,717	9,172
1804	5,542	1,036	6,578
1825	9,140	1,355	10,495
1832	10,001	1,760	11,761

Sources: Tables B.1 and B.2.

Table B.4. Whites and slaves by sex, 1804

Location	White males	White females	Total whites	Slave males	Slave females	Total slaves
SOUTH						
City of Goiás	610	609	1,219	2,637	1,795	4,432
Meia Ponte	586	682	1,268	1,356	926	2,282
Santa Cruz	426	452	878	617	380	997
Santa Luzia	254	276	530	768	496	1,264
Pilar	206	159	365	1,037	538	1,575
Crixás	48	31	79	422	212	634
Desemboque	610	593	1,203	413	247	660
Traíras	198	174	372	1,624	1,183	2,807
Total, south	2,938	2,976	5,914	8,874	5,777	14,651
NORTH						
Cavalcante	194	144	338	753	456	1,209
São Félix	39	39	78	331	310	641
Arraias	74	65	139	282	187	469
Conceição	97	102	199	304	380	684
Natividade	116	85	201	925	604	1,529
Carmo	50	31	81	625	219	844
Total, north	570	466	1,036	3,220	2,156	5,376
Sum total	3,508	3,442	6,950	12,094	7,933	20,027

Source: RJAN, cod. 808, vol. 1, Goiás, Censo da População de Goiás, 1832, f. 96.

Table B.5. Whites and slaves by sex, 1825

Location	White males	White females	Total whites	Slave males	Slave females	Total slaves
SOUTH						
City of Goiás	1,423	1,104	2,527	1,793	1,481	3,274
Meia Ponte	1,360	1,407	2,767	969	873	1,842
Santa Cruz	936	1,147	2,083	494	393	887
Santa Luzia	553	560	1,113	390	351	741
Pilar	196	184	380	494	475	969
Crixás	147	123	270	398	301	699
Total, south	4,615	4,525	9,140	4,538	3,874	8,412
NORTH						
São João	16	18	34	46	32	78
Traíras	189	206	395	788	705	1,493
Conceição	24	26	50	179	92	271
Natividade	88	69	157	519	385	904
Porto Real	25	10	35	217	159	376
Flores	133	77	210	293	185	478
Arraias	161	106	267	412	353	765
São Félix	22	22	44	95	47	142
Cavalcante	78	85	163	242	214	456
Total, north	736	619	1,355	2,791	2,172	4,963
Sum total	5,351	5,144	10,495	7,329	6,046	13,375

Source: RJBN, manuscript section, 11, 4, 2, Estatistica da provincia de Goyáz remettida á secretaria de estado dos negocios do imperio . . . , "Censo da População," 1825.

Table B.6. Whites and slaves by sex, 1832

Location	White males	White females	Total whites	Slave[a] males	Slave females	Total slaves
SOUTH						
City of Goiás	1,423	1,104	2,527	1,675	1,398	3,073
Meia Ponte	1,159	1,282	2,441	960	840	1,800
Santa Luzia	553	560	1,113	390	351	741
Santa Cruz	1,733	1,597	3,330	605	489	1,094
Pilar	389	160	549	650	383	1,033
Crixás	26	14	40	192	192	384
Carretão, aldeia	—	1	1	2	3	5
Total, south	5,283	4,718	10,001	4,474	3,656	8,130
NORTH						
Vila da Palma	13	14	27	100	128	228
Traíras	269	248	517	771	670	1,441
São Félix	6	—	6	119	112	231
Cavalcante	93	89	182	254	220	474
Flores	169	122	291	342	219	561
Arraias	200	215	415	428	364	792
Conceição	12	7	19	90	66	156
Natividade	60	68	128	440	439	879
Duro, aldeia	1	1	2	3	2	5
Porto Imperial	32	41	73	177	148	325
Carolina	48	52	100	22	17	39
Total, north	903	857	1,760	2,746	2,385	5,131
Sum total	6,186	5,575	11,761	7,220	6,041	13,261

Source: RJAN, cod. 808, v. 1, Goyaz, Censo da População da Provincia de Goyaz, f. 96.
[a] The census categories were *pardos, pardas, pretos, pretas do Brasil* (blacks of Brazil) and Africanos/Africanas.

Table B.7. Enslaved population in the south, 1736–1750

Year	Santa Anna	Meia Ponte	Crixás	Others[a]	Total
1736	4,021[b]	—	1,366	3,682	9,069[c]
1737	4,474	—	1,735	—	6,209[d]
1738	7,604[e]	—	—	—	7,370
1739	—	—	—	—	7,346
1740	2,378	1,334	1,076	267	5,055
1741	4,252	1,336	2,736	—	8,324
1742	4,461	1,316	2,559	330	8,666[f]
1748	4,836	1,086	1,292	780[g]	7,994
1749	4,720	1,086	1,432	3,652[h]	10,890[i]

Sources: AHU, Goiás, caixa 4, Mapa geral ... 1736, 1737 (6 September 1738); 1738–1749: Salles, Economia e escravidão, 231–33, 275–76 (anexo 13); and Palacin, Goiás, 40–42.
[a] Others are those who were not identified by name in 1736—they arrived during the year—or who were identified only by sertão, in 1740, 1742, and 1748.
[b] All the mines of the south.
[c] An alternate figure is 9,142, from AHU, 1738. Salles, Economia e escravidão, 275, has 7,330 for 1736; and Palacin, Goiás, 40, has 10,263.
[d] An alternate figure is 7,191, from Salles, Economia e escravidão, 275.
[e] Statistics after 1738 are from Salles, Economia e escravidão, 275. Her total for the south is 7,370.
[f] Palacin, Goiás, 41, gives a total of 8,082.
[g] Salles, Economia e escravidão, gives 780 for the sertão of Desemboque.
[h] Includes 2,762 for Pilar, 422 for the sertão, 262 for Santa Luzia, and 206 for Santa Cruz.
[i] This is my total. Salles, Economia e escravidão, 276, gives 17,154 as a total for the enslaved of the captaincy.

Table B.8. Enslaved population in the north, 1736–1749

Year	Tocantins	São Félix	Natividade	Arraias and others	Total
1736	1,196[a]	—	—	—	2,933
1737	4,382	—	—	1,998[b]	6,380[c]
1738	6,202[d]	—	—	—	6,202
1741	2,666	432	730	3,169	6,997
1742	3,817	1,165	1,010	970	6,962[e]
1748	2,936	926[f]	701	293	4,856
1749	3,191	1,017	1,820	229	6,264

Sources: See table B.7.
[a] Palacin, Goiás, 40, lists 1,196 for Tocantins. Salles, Economia e escravidão, 275, records 2,933 for 1736.
[b] From the Conquista do Descoberta.
[c] Salles, Economia e escravidão, 275, has 5,960.
[d] Palacin, Goiás, 41, gives a total of 6,202. Salles, Economia e escravidão, 275, lists 5,128 for 1738.
[e] Palacin, Goiás, 41, has 6,248.
[f] Salles, Economia e escravidão, 232, lists 1,721 slaves for São Félix.

Table B.9. Enslaved population of the captaincy of Goiás, 1782–1832[a]

Location	1782	1789	1792	1804	1825	1832
SOUTH						
Vila Boa	8,988	9,200	8,568	4,432	3,274	3,073
Meia Ponte	4,545	4,777	4,855	2,282	1,842	1,800
Santa Luzia	2,543	2,960	2,491	1,264	741	741
Santa Cruz	1,169	1,223	1,153	997	887	1,094
Pilar	3,772	1,967	3,839	1,575	969	1,033
Crixás	2,100	2,444	2,045	634	699	384
Rio das Velhas	148	277	2,261	—	—	—
Traíras[b]	—	—	—	2,807	—	—
Others	—	—	—	660[c]	—	5
Total, south	23,265	22,848	25,212	14,651	8,412	8,130
NORTH						
Vila de São João[d]	—	—	—	—	78	—
Traíras	6,080	6,245	5,328	—	1,493	1,441
Cavalcante	921	993	950	1,209	456	474
São Félix	2,681	2,707	2,599	641	142	231
Arraias	1,085	1,198	1,198	469	765	792
Conceição	760	986	908	684	271	156
Natividade	3,398	2,332	2,338	1,529	904	879
Others	—	—	—	844[e]	854[f]	1,158[g]
Total, north	14,925	14,461	13,321	5,376	4,963	5,131
Sum total	38,190	37,309	38,533	20,027	13,375	13,261

Sources: See table B.1; and Mary C. Karasch, "Central Africans in Central Brazil, 1780–1835," in Heywood, Central Africans and Cultural Transformations, table 4.1, 120.
[a] Unlike other censuses that listed "blacks," these statistics are only for slaves.
[b] Traíras was counted as part of the southern comarca in 1804, but I have kept it with the northern comarca on this table.
[c] Desemboque.
[d] Seat of the Comarca of the North.
[e] Carmo.
[f] Two others were Porto Real, with 376, and Flores, with 478.
[g] Includes Palma, with 228; Flores, with 561; Porto Imperial, with 325; Carolina, with 39; and Duro, with 5.

Table B.10. Enslaved Africans, blacks of Brazil, and *pardos*, 1832

Location	Africans	Blacks of Brazil	Pardos	Total	% African
SOUTH					
City of Goiás	523	1,666	884	3,073	17.0
Meia Ponte	304	976	520	1,800	16.9
Santa Cruz	195	769	130	1,094	17.8
Santa Luzia	106	491	144	741	14.3
Pilar	208	825	—	1,033	20.1
Crixás	75	309	—	384	19.5
Carretão	1	4	—	5	20.0
Total, south	1,412	5,040	1,678	8,130	17.4
NORTH					
Palma	—	228	—	228	0.0
Traíras	132	1,309	—	1,441	9.2
Cavalcante	56	418	—	474	11.8
Flores	16	545	—	561	2.9
São Félix	10	221	—	231	4.3
Arraias	111	681	—	792	14.0
Conceição	—	156	—	156	0.0
Natividade	180	699	—	879	20.5
Porto Imperial	—	325	—	325	0.0
Carolina	5	26	8	39	12.8
Duro	1	4	—	5	20.0
Total, north	511	4,612	8	5,131	10.0
Sum total	1,923	9,652	1,686	13,261	14.5

Source: RJAN, cod. 808, vol. 1, Goiás, Censo da População de Goiás, 1832, f. 96.

Table B.II. Blacks in the Comarca of the South, 1779–1832

Year	Vila Boa[a]	Meia Pont	Santa Luzia	Santa Cruz	Pilar	Crixás	Other	Total
1779	4,491	4,495	2,177	704	3,650	2,247	1,377[b]	19,141
1781	7,826	4,495	2,563	704	3,650	2,247	84[c]	21,569
1782	7,705	4,528	2,562	933	3,648	2,269	82	21,727
1783	7,734	4,389	2,613	1,063	3,651	2,370	82[d]	21,902
1784	7,864	4,378	2,640	1,050	3,644	2,329	80	21,985
1785	7,872	4,378	2,619	1,056	3,647	2,330	92	21,994
1789	7,857	4,433	2,638	1,067	3,663	2,401	122	22,181
1791	7,848	4,435	2,641	1,070	3,696	2,398	125	22,213
1792	8,029	4,472	2,737	1,047	3,561	2,388	2,644	24,878
1804	5,444	2,991	1,757	1,216	2,407	1,077	722[e]	15,614
1825	3,274	1,842	741	887	969	699	—	8,412
1832[f]	3,309	1,939	1,064	1,408	2,808	635	14[g]	11,177

Sources: See table B.1.
Note: Blacks encompass free, freed, and enslaved blacks. Figures for 1804 include free blacks and slaves, which may include *pardos*. In 1825 the total is only for slaves.
[a] Some totals for Vila Boa appear to be for the town, while others are for the parish or district. In 1783 Salles, *Economia e escravidão*, 275, counted only 4,689 for Vila Boa.
[b] Anta.
[c] Rio das Velhas, 1781–1792.
[d] Captives only, Rio das Velhas, 1783.
[e] Desemboque.
[f] The total in 1832 is for free and enslaved blacks and excludes *pardos*.
[g] Aldeia do Carretão.

Table B.12. Blacks in the Comarca of the North, 1779–1832

Year	Traíras	Cavalcante	São Félix	Arraias	Conceição	Natividade	Others	Total
1779	3,176	974	2,681	762	—	1,980	6,162[a]	15,735
1781	6,220	974	2,645	1,043	716	3,536	—	15,134
1782	6,208	977	2,645	1,039	724	3,521	—	15,114
1783	6,208	976	2,692	938	724	3,608	—	15,146
1784	5,302	957	2,676	1,029	622	3,588	—	14,174
1785	5,301	981	2,685	1,027	724	3,598	—	14,316
1789	5,302	1,011	2,697	981	760	2,312	—	13,063
1791	5,305	1,017	2,683	988	770	2,279	—	13,042
1792	5,243	991	2,696	1,000	741	2,296	—	12,967
1804	4,107	1,725	1,003	807	1,251	2,183	1,273[b]	12,349[c]
1825	1,493	456	142	765	271	904	932[d]	4,963
1832	3,076	832	412	1,589	457	1,367	2,435[e]	10,168

Sources: See table B.1.
Note: Blacks include free, freed, and enslaved blacks. Figures for 1804 include free blacks and slaves, which may include *pardos*, but in 1832, blacks included both free and enslaved. In 1825 the total is only for slaves and does not include freed or free blacks.
[a] In 1779 the other locations were Tocantins, 3,042; Carmo, 885; Palma, 716; São Domingos, 281; Pontal, 653; and Paraná de cima, 585.
[b] In 1804 Carmo had 1,273 slaves.
[c] In 1804 scribes listed only 8,242 for the north because they moved Traíras to the south. This total includes Traíras.
[d] In 1825 this total includes Palma, 78; Flores, 478; and Porto Real, 376.
[e] In 1832 this total includes Palma, 403; Flores, 1,136; Porto Imperial, 787; Carolina, 60; and Duro, 49.

Table B.I3. Indians, 1832

Location	Males	Females	Total
SOUTH			
City of Goiás	50	34	84
Meia Ponte	71	71	142
Crixás	34	38	72
São José de Mossâmedes	23	31	54
Pedro III do Carretão	59	104	163
Total, south	237	278	515
NORTH			
Villa da Palma	16	17	33
São Félix	2	—	2
Cavalcante	3	—	3
Arraias	4	4	8
Natividade	10	15	25
Aldeia do Duro	134	142	276
Porto Imperial	23	30	53
Carolina	30	49	79
Total, north	222	257	479
Sum total	459	535	994

Source: RJAN, cod. 808, vol. 1, Censo da População da Província de Goiás, Cidade de Goiás, 30 May 1832, f. 96. Comparative statistics from the 1825 census are cited in chapter 8.

Table B.14. Free people of color, 1804

Location	Mulatto males	Mulatto females	Total mulattoes	Black males	Black females	Total black	Total free people of color
SOUTH							
Vila Boa	1,208	1,603	2,811	413	599	1,012	3,823
Meia Ponte	918	996	1,914	305	404	709	2,623
Crixás	199	248	447	168	275	443	890
Pilar	413	444	857	322	510	832	1,689
Santa Luzia	603	767	1,370	192	301	493	1,863
Santa Cruz	403	407	810	88	131	219	1,029
Desemboque	246	202	448	32	30	62	510
Traíras[a]	1,055	1,052	2,107	542	758	1,300	3,407
Total, south	5,045	5,719	10,764	2,062	3,008	5,070	15,834
NORTH							
Cavalcante	573	561	1,134	251	265	516	1,650
São Félix	303	370	673	167	193	360	1,033
Arraias	338	367	705	124	214	338	1,043
Conceição	368	276	644	279	288	567	1,211
Natividade	509	504	1,013	130	524	654	1,667
Carmo	232	287	519	195	234	429	948
Total, north	2,323	2,365	4,688	1,146	1,718	2,864	7,552
Sum total	7,368	8,084	15,452	3,208	4,726	7,934	23,386

Source: AHU, cod. 2109, Reflexoens economicas sobre as tabellas statisticas da capitania de Goyaz pertencentes ao anno de 1804 e feitas no de 1806.
[a] Traíras was included in the totals for the Comarca do Sul in 1804.

Table B.15. Free people of color, 1825

Location	Ingênuos (freeborn) males	Ingênuas (freeborn) females	Total ingênuos	Libertos (freed) males	Libertas (freed) females	Total libertos	Sum total
SOUTH							
City of Goiás	3,595	3,997	7,592	453	321	774	8,366
Meia Ponte	2,153	2,370	4,523	169	150	319	4,842
Santa Cruz	1,301	1,348	2,649	109	137	246	2,895
Santa Luzia	1,219	1,485	2,704	35	38	73	2,777
Pilar	816	923	1,739	109	190	299	2,038
Crixás	452	477	929	48	54	102	1,031
Total, south	9,536	10,600	20,136	923	890	1,813	21,949
NORTH							
São João	141	129	270	10	8	18	288
Traíras	1,840	2,151	3,991	163	167	330	4,321
Conceição	504	441	945	28	6	34	979
Natividade	860	995	1,855	75	47	122	1,977
Porto Real	520	570	1,090	27	20	47	1,137
Flores	1,324	1,261	2,585	52	64	116	2,701
Arraias	1,104	1,309	2,413	50	42	92	2,505
São Félix	291	351	642	23	15	38	680
Cavalcante	446	632	1,078	188	182	370	1,448
Total, north	7,030	7,839	14,869	616	551	1,167	16,036
Sum total	16,566	18,439	35,005	1,539	1,441	2,980	37,985

Source: RJBN, manuscript section, 11, 4, 2, Estatistica da provincia de Goyáz remettida á secretaria de estado dos negocios do imperio ..., "Censo da População," 1825.

Table B.l6. Free people of color, 1832

Location	Pardo males	Preto males	African males	Total males	Parda females	Preta females	African females	Total females	Sum total
SOUTH									
City of Goiás	3,659	403	104	4,166	3,788	563	50	4,401	8,567
Meia Ponte	2,095	231	60	2,386	2,275	338	30	2,643	5,029
Santa Luzia	1,037	182	35	1,254	1,273	212	38	1,523	2,777
Santa Cruz	1,407	199	9	1,615	1,361	221	15	1,597	3,212
Pilar	1,382	1,020	40	2,442	318	700	15	1,033	3,475
Crixás	222	98	10	330	190	134	9	333	663
Carretão, aldeia[a]	12	6	—	18	16	3	—	19	37
Total, south	9,814	2,139	258	12,211	9,221	2,171	157	11,549	23,760
NORTH									
Vila da Palma	500	70	7	577	510	90	8	608	1,185
Traíras	1,222	673	—	1,895	1,385	962	—	2,347	4,242
São Félix	152	65	—	217	320	116	—	436	653
Cavalcante	596	190	—	786	669	168	—	837	1,623
Flores	1,153	326	—	1,479	1,001	249	—	1,250	2,729
Arraias	900	447	—	1,347	924	350	—	1,274	2,621
Conceição	400	120	12	532	413	155	14	582	1,114
Natividade	1,100	200	20	1,320	1,193	240	28	1,461	2,781
Duro, aldeia	84	23	4	111	85	16	1	102	213
Porto Imperial	403	219	—	622	489	243	—	732	1,354
Carolina	97	10	5	112	80	11	3	94	206
Total, north	6,607	2,343	48	8,998	7,069	2,600	54	9,723	18,721
Sum total	16,421	4,482	306	21,209	16,290	4,771	211	21,272	42,481

Source: RJAN, cod. 808, v. 1, Goyaz, Censo da População da Província de Goyaz, f. 96.

Note: The census categories were *pardos, pardas, pretos, pretas, pretos do Brasil* (blacks of Brazil), and *Africanos/Africanas*. The census also included 994 "Indios," but they are not a part of this table. See table B.13, Indians in 1832.

[a] The census also included 994 "Indios," but they are not a part of this table.

Table B.17. Population of the captaincy of Goiás, 1779–1832

Year	Comarca of the South	Comarca of the North	Total
1779	30,395	24,094	54,489
1781	35,473	23,356	58,829
1782	36,476	23,311	59,787
1783	35,768	22,889	58,657[a]
1784	35,423	21,663	58,494[b]
1785	35,561	21,787	58,871[c]
1789	36,992	21,512	58,504[d]
1791	35,972	20,932	56,904
1792	39,807	20,621	60,428
1804	36,399	13,966	50,365
1825	39,824	22,654	62,478
1832	42,406	26,091	68,497

Sources: See table B.1; and IHGB, arq. 1.2.7, Ofício of Luiz da Cunha Menezes to Martinho de Mello e Castro, Vila Boa, 15 February 1783.
[a] The governor reported the total population of the captaincy as 59,287. The total here is my total for the captive and free population based on the census of 1783.
[b] This total is my calculation for whites, *pardos*, blacks, and 1,408 newborns. The scribe's total is 58,703.
[c] This total is my calculation for whites, *pardos*, blacks, and 1,523 newborns. The scribe's total is 58,669.
[d] This is the scribe's total. My calculation is 58,499.

APPENDIX C: Colonial Churches and Lay Brotherhoods in the Captaincy of Goiás

Table C.1

Town or village	Church or chapel[a]	Lay brotherhood	Members[b]
COMARCA OF THE SOUTH			
Vila Boa	Santa Ana	São Miguel e Almas	whites
		Santa Ana	
		Santo Antônio	Military, public officials
		Santissimo Sacramento	whites
		Senhor dos Passos[c]	"noble officials"
	Nossa Senhora do Rosário dos pretos	Our Lady of the Rosary	blacks, *negros da terra*
		Patriarca São José	carpenters, craftsmen
	Nossa Senhora da Boa Morte	Our Lady of the Good Death	*pardos, forros* (freed)
		Martyr São Gonçalo Garcia	*pardos*
	Nossa Senhora da Lapa	Nossa Senhora da Lapa	whites, merchants
	Nossa Senhora do Carmo	São Benedito	free *crioulos, pardos*, whites
	São Francisco de Paula	Senhor dos Passos	whites
	Santa Barbara		
	Nossa Senhora da Abadia		
	Nossa Senhora das Barracas		
		Santa Efigênia	tailors
		St. Sebastian	Republicans
Anicuns*	São Francisco de Assis		
Barra*	Nossa Senhora do Rosário		
Ferreiro*	São João Batista		
Anta	Senhor Bom Jesus		
Mossâmedes	São José	Mission	Kayapó
Meia Ponte	Nossa Senhora do Rosário	Santissimo Sacramento	whites
		Nossa Senhora do Rosário does pretos	blacks
		São Benedito	blacks?
	Nossa Senhora da Boa Morte da Lapa		
	São Francisco das Chagas		
	Nosso Senhor do Bonfim		
	Nossa Senhora do Carmo		
Jaraguá*	Nossa Senhora do Rosário		
	Nossa Senhora da Penha	Santissimo Sacramento	whites
Corumbá*	Nossa Senhora da Penha		

Table C.1 (continued)

Town or village	Church or chapel[a]	Lay brotherhood	Members[b]
Santa Luzia	Nossa Senhora do Rosário	Nossa Senhora do Rosário	blacks
	Nossa Senhora da Abadia		
		Santissimo Sacramento	
		São Miguel e Almas	
Santa Cruz	Nossa Senhora da Conceição		
	Nossa Senhora do Rosário		
Rio das Velhas	Nossa Senhora do Desterro		
Araxá	São Domingos		
Pilar	Nossa Senhora do Pilar	Senhor dos Passos	whites
		Santissimo Sacramento	
	Nossa Senhora do Rosário		
	Nossa Senhora das Mercês		
	São Gonçalo		
Crixás	Nossa Senhora do Conceição	São Miguel e Almas	
	Nossa Senhora da Abadia		
	Nossa Senhora do Rosário dos Pretos	Nossa Senhora do Rosário	blacks
	Santa Efigênia		
Traíras	Nossa Senhora da Conceição	Santissimo Sacramento	
	Nossa Senhora do Rosário		free blacks
	Senhor Bom Jesus		
São José do Tocantins	Senhor dos Passos*	Senhor dos Passos	
	Nossa Senhora da Boa Morte	Senhora da Boa Morte	
	Nossa Senhora do Rosário	São Gonçalo Garcia	
	Santa Efigênia*	Santa Efigênia	crioulos
		São Miguel e Almas	
Salinas or Boa Vista		Mission	Xavante, Javaé
Carretão	Pedro III do Carretão	Mission	Xavante
Rio das Velhas	Santa Ana	Mission	Xacriabá
Tesouras	São Miguel		

COMARCA OF THE NORTH
Pontal	Santa Ana		
	Santo Antônio		
Porto Real*	Nossa Senhora das Mercês		
Carmo	Nossa Senhora do Carmo		
	Nossa Senhora do Rosário		

Table C.1 (continued)

Town or village	Church or chapel[a]	Lay brotherhood	Members[b]
Chapada*	Nossa Senhora do Rosário		
Conceição	Nossa Senhora da Conceição		
	Nossa Senhora do Rosário		
São Domingos	São Domingos		
São Félix	Santo Antônio		
	Capela do Rosário		
	Abadia e Santa Ana*		
São Miguel e Almas	São Miguel e Almas		
Natividade	Nossa Senhora da Natividade	Santissimo Sacramento	
	Nossa Senhora do Rosário	Our Lady of the Rosary	free and freed blacks
	Nossa Senhora do Terço		
	St. Benedict		blacks
Arraias	Nossa Senhora dos Remédios		
	Nossa Senhora do Rosário		
	Nossa Senhora da Conceição		
Muquém*	São Tomé	Nossa Senhora da Abadia	all free, 1857
Cavalcante*	Santa Ana	Santissimo Sacramento	
	Nossa Senhora do Rosário		
	Senhor do Bonfim		
São Joaquim do Cocal*	Nossa Senhora das Mercês	Nossa Senhora das Mercês	Africans, *crioulos*
Água Quente*	Nossa Senhora das Mercês	Nossa Senhora do Livramento	blacks
	São Sebastião		
Flores	Nossa Senhora do Rosário		
	Nossa Senhora do Rosário dos Pretos		blacks
Duro	São José	Mission	Akroá, Xacriabá
São João da Palma			

Sources: RJBN, 9, 2, 10, Silva e Souza, Memória, f. 35; Moraes, "Corpo místico"; Castro, *Organização*, quadros 1–2, pp. 136, 139; and Cunha Matos, *Corografia histórica*, 27–44, 110–129.
[a] This table follows the order used in Castro, with some additions, indicated with asterisks. Notably, it is incomplete and does not include many small or ruined chapels and churches.
[b] Members as identified in the *compromissos* (charters) or other *irmandade* sources.
[c] The *irmandade* dos Passos was based in Vila Boa and also in Nossa Senhora la Lapa.

Glossary

agregado: Household dependent
aldeia: Village, mission village
arroba: Unit of weight, about fifteen kilos or thirty-three pounds
bandeira: Armed expedition that enslaved indigenous populations and found gold
bandeirante: Expedition participant
bastardo: Colonial term for a mestizo
cabra: Dark-skinned person of African descent
capitação: Portuguese tax on a slave, before 1750
captaincy: Territorial division of the Portuguese Empire
cerrado: Savanna, grasslands
comarca: Judicial district
crioulo: Black born in Brazil
engenho: Mill; by extension, a sugar plantation
engenhoca: Small sugarcane or manioc mill
entrada: Exploratory expedition into the interior, sometimes led by a Jesuit priest
faisqueiro: Prospector, gold miner
farinha: Manioc meal
fazenda: Large estate
forro: Freedperson
goiano: Person from the state or province of Goiás
henriques: Black militia force
ingênuo: Freeborn person of color
irmandade: Lay brotherhood in the Catholic Church
jornal: Sum of gold to be delivered to a slaveholder on a weekly basis
julgado: Judicial district
lavra: Mine
lavrador: Farmer, agricultural worker
liberto: Freed slave
loja: Store
mata: Forest
meia sisa: Tax on the sale or manumission of a slave

mestizo: Person of indigenous and European descent
mulato: Person of European and African descent
oitava: One-eighth ounce of gold
ordenança: White militia force
ouvidor: Judge of the comarca
pardo: Brown-skinned person of European, African, or indigenous descent
pedestre: Paid infantry man, often indigenous by birth
pessoa de obrigação: Obligated person, temporarily subject to another person
presídio: Small fort or garrison
quilombo, quilombola: Community of fugitive slaves; inhabitant of a quilombo
quinto: "Fifth"; tax of a fifth or a tenth on gold production
rapadura: Raw brown sugar in brick shape
real, pl. réis: Colonial currency
registo, registro: Checkpoint to collect import duties and stop export of contraband gold
roça, roceiro: Small farm for food crops; small farmer
sertanista: Explorer, frontiersman
sertão: Hinterland of a town; backlands; the interior of Brazil
sesmaria: Land grant
sítio: Small plot of land

Notes

Introduction

1. On the making of the film, see Cowell, *Tribe that Hides*, 17–18.
2. Kreen-Akarore notice of first contact: Howe, "Amazon Tribe Takes a Step Out." As a branch of the Kayapó do Sul, who once lived in São José de Mossâmedes in Goiás: see Aryon Dall'Igna Rodrigues, "Apresentação," in Giraldin, *Cayapó e Panará*, 16. Rodrigues also notes that after contact in the 1970s, the Kreen-Akarore were decimated, their population shrinking from seven hundred persons to less than one hundred, who were transferred to Xingu National Park. See also Terence Turner, "Os Mebengokre Kayapó: História e mudança social," in Cunha, *História dos índios no Brasil*, 311–12; and Mead, "Caiapó do Sul," 16–25.
3. Wooden looms and textiles: M. Garcia, *Tecelagem artesenal*.
4. Karasch, Damiana da Cunha."
5. Darnton, *Great Cat Massacre*, 78.
6. Karasch, "Catequese e cativeiro."
7. Giraldin, *Cayapó e Panará*. He continues to work closely with indigenous peoples of the state of Tocantins and teaches at the Federal University of Tocantins.
8. Both Natividade and the City of Goiás are registered for historic preservation and restoration. Photographs of both towns are in A. Borges and Palacin, *Patrimônio histórico de Goiás*, 7–22, 53–60. I would like to thank Ana Maria Borges for a copy of this book.
9. Frontiers: Hemming, *Amazon Frontier*, chap. 10, "The Tocantins-Araguaia Frontier"; White, *Middle Ground*; Weber and Rausch, *Where Cultures Meet*; Cayton and Teute, *Contact Points*; Guy and Sheridan, *Contested Ground*; and Metcalf, *Go-Betweens*.
10. African diaspora: Heywood, *Central Africans and Cultural Transformations*; and Curto and Lovejoy, *Enslaving Connections*.
11. Gender: Gaspar and Hine, *Beyond Bondage*; Silva, *Sexualidade, família e religião*; and Gaspar and Hine, *More Than Chattel*.
12. Atlantic World: Daniels and Kennedy, *Negotiated Empires*.
13. Identity/culture/nation: Karasch, "Minha Nação"; and Karasch, "Quality, Nation, and Color."
14. Environment/health: Tucker and Russell, *Natural Enemy, Natural Ally*; and Freitas, *Saúde e doenças em Goiás*.

15. José Ribamar Bessa Freire, personal communication, Palmas, Tocantins, May 30, 2004. Among his many publications is *Rio babel: A história das linguas na Amazônia*.
16. The concept of the slaving frontier is from Miller, *Way of Death*, 140–42.
17. [Vila Real, Tomás de Sousa], "Viagem de Thomaz de Souza Villa Real"; Pohl, *Viagem*; Saint-Hilaire, *Viagem*; Castelnau, *Expédition*; [Burchell], *Brasil do primeiro reinado*; and Cunha Matos, *Chorographia historica*.
18. Congadas: Karasch, "Central Africans," 149–51; and Kiddy, *Blacks of the Rosary*, chaps. 6–7.
19. Espirito Santo: personal observation, Natividade, May 2004; C. Pereira and Ferretti, *Divino toque do Maranhão*; M. Abreu, *O império do divino*; and Britto, Prado, and Rosa, *Os sentidos da devoção*.
20. *Carta regia* that authorized enslavement: Karasch, "Catequese e cativeiro," 402.
21. McCreery, *Frontier Goiás*.

Chapter One

1. The captaincy of Goiás as the heart of Brazil: RJIHGB, arq. 1.2.7., vol. 36, Ofício de João Manoel de Mello to the Conde d'Oeiras, Vila Boa, 29 May 1760.
2. This focus on landscapes follows the insights of environmental historians, who see landscapes as historical constructions of those who viewed the environment and nature. As much as possible, we will try to reconstruct how late colonial observers saw the captaincy of Goiás in the late colonial period. Rarely can we also include indigenous or African perspectives. Influences on this chapter include McEnroe, "Sites of Diplomacy, Violence, and Refuge"; and Rogers, "Laboring Landscapes." See also Rogers, *Deepest Wounds*, 6–8. Landscape themes are also developed in L. Garcia, *Goyaz*.
3. Vila Boa and Goiás: Karasch, "Periphery of the Periphery?"; Gomes, Neto, and Barbosa, *Geografia: Goiás/Tocantins*, 41; and Gallais, *Apostolo do Araguaia*, 68.
4. Area of the captaincy of Goiás: Gomes, Neto, and Barbosa, *Geografia: Goiás/Tocantins*, 52–53 (map); and Chaim, *Aldeamentos indígenas*, 15–17.
5. Trade: "Goiás no Sistema Colonial" (map), in Mendes Rocha, *Atlas histórico*, 39. I am grateful to Cristina de Cássia Pereira Moraes for a copy of this useful atlas. See also Karasch, "Periphery of the Periphery?," 158–65; Chaul, *Caminhos de Goiás*, with maps; and RJIHGB, arq. 1.5.16, Goiás, Ribeiro, "Viagem ao Rio do Tucantins [sic] em 1815, pelos sertoens do Maranham. Divizão de lemites [sic] entre as Capitanias de Maranham e Goiaz em 1816. Observações gerais relatives aos sertoens da mesma capitania, propriedade dos seus terrenos. Discripção [sic] dos seus rios e estado dos seus habitantes, indios colonnos; pelo Major Francisco de Paulo Ribeiro," 1818, f. 264. Citations are to the manuscript copy rather than the version printed as [Ribeiro], "Roteiro da viagem."

6. Merchants: Davidson, "Rivers and Empire," 135–37; and RJBN, I-31, 21, 9, Goiás (Capitania), "Copia da Memoria oferecida pelo Capitam d'Ordenanças Francisco José Pinto de Mangalhens [Magalhães] em 3 de Janeiro [January] de 1813." Magalhães had made six trips from Porto Real to the city of Grão Pará (Belém) with goods that he brought from Goiás, and from there he returned with his small commerce, which he disposed of in the mines, most likely in Natividade, which was his homeland.
7. Tocantins River: RJBN, II-31, 19, 13, Goiás—Limites, "Voto do Comiçario Francisco José Pinto de Magalhães . . . ," 12 August 1815; Alfredo Taunay, *Goyaz*, 37–38; Doles, *Comunicações fluviais*, 17–23; Rodrigues, *Roteiro do Tocantins*, maps; Oliveira, *Portos do sertão*; and KEW, William John Burchell to Dr. Hooker, Fulham, 1 November 1830, f. 19.
8. Canoes: RJIHGB, lata 281, pasta 4, doc. 2, "Ofício (cópia antiga) asinado por Feliciano José Gonçalves . . . apresentando . . . o Diário . . . de Tomás de Sousa Vila Real . . . ," Pará, 1/3/1793; RJIHGB, arq. 1.5.16, Ribeiro, "Viagem," f. 263; Castelnau, *Expédition*. This edition's original lithographs are at the Oliveira Lima Library in Washington, DC. I would like to thank Asunción Lavrin for the reference to these lithographs. For a drawing of an ajôjo with crew and covered portions of the canoe, see [Burchell], *Brasil do primeiro reinado*, 151, 153. For ubás and igarités, see Delson, "Inland Navigation," 9, 12–13. My thanks to Roberta M. Delson for a copy of this illustrated article. Apinaje use of ubá: Nimuendajú, *Apinayé*, 4.
9. Difficulties on Tocantins River: KEW, Burchell to Hooker, 1 November 1830, f. 19; [Burchell], *Brasil do primeiro reinado*, 140, 152; RJAN, cod. 807, v. 10, Francisco Joze Roiz Barata, "Memoria sobre a agricultura e commercio da capitania de Goyaz," Lisbon, 1806, f. 69; and RJBN, 22, 1, 22; Berford, *Roteiro e mapa*, 19. For locations of falls on the Tocantins River, see maps in Rodrigues, *Roteiro do Tocantins*, 97–100, 111–13, 127–29, 141–44, 170–73.
10. Alcobaça and other towns: RJIHGB, arq. 1.5.16, Ribeiro, "Viagem," ff. 258–59, 261; and fugitives: Nimuendajú, *Apinayé*, 2–3 and map (1938).
11. São Pedro de Alcântara: RJIHGB, arq. 1.5.16, Ribeiro, "Viagem," ff. 261, 271; RJBN, I-31, 21, 9, Magalhães, "Memoria," 1813; and maps in "Principais Caminhos Coloniais, Século XVIII," in Mendes Rocha, *Atlas histórico*, 51; and in Burchell, *Brasil do primeiro reinado*, 140.
12. Araguaia River and Karajá: RJIHGB, lata 281, pasta 4, doc. 3, "Diario da Navegação, que fez Thomáz de Souza Villa Real pellos Rios Tocantins, Araguaia, e Vermelho desde Villa Boa . . . até a Cidade do Pará," 1792–1793; RJIHGB, lata 281, pasta 4, doc. 5, "Diário da viagem que se fez pelos rios Tocantins e Araguari [Araguaia] a transporter os índios silvestres de nação Carajás às suas nações [habitações]," 1792; and Karasch, "Rethinking the Conquest," 473–80.
13. Quirixá: see chapter 3, note 12.

14. Serra dos Caiapó: Giraldin, *Cayapó e Panará*, 57–59; and Library of Congress, Geography and Map Division, "Carta da provincia de Goyaz organizada em 1874 . . . ," gravada por C. Lomelino de Carvalho, Rio de Janeiro, 1875.
15. Tocantins nations: Nimuendajú, *Apinayé*, 1–8 and map; RJBN, I-31, 21, 9, Magalhães, "Memoria," 1813, n53; and Berford, *Roteiro e mapa*, 20–21.
16. Gentile nations: Berford, *Roteiro e mapa*, 20–22. See maps of Timbira in Nimuendajú, *Eastern Timbira*.
17. Giraldin, "Pontal e Porto Real," 131–33. The remnants of the mining town of Pontal are located on a bluff with a commanding view of the countryside below. Professor Odair Giraldin and I visited the site of Pontal. Only piles of stone rubble from the mining operations and the floor stones of houses and a small chapel where the Jesuits said Mass survive. Professor Giraldin has had a video record made of the site. Estrada do Norte: RJBN 9, 2, 10, Padre Luiz Antônio da Silva e Souza, "Memoria sobre o descobrimento, governo, população e cousas [*sic*] mais notaveis da capitania de Goyaz," Vila Boa, 30 Setembro 1812, f. 49; first published in *Patriota* 12 (July–August 1814): 429, and reprinted in *Revista Trimensal de História e Geographia do IHGB*, no. 16 (4o Trimestre de 1849): 71–139. My citations are to the manuscript copy.
18. Maranhão and Almas Rivers: Pohl, *Viagem*, 191; Cruls, *Planalto central*, map, "Districto Federal," 334, and the Rio das Almas (photo), 125.
19. Manuel Alves and Santa Teresa rivers: Adonias, *Cartografia da Região Amazônica*, map facing p. 640.
20. Paranã River and Paraúpaba: RJBN, II-31, 19, 13, Goiás—Limites, Pinto de Magalhães, 1815; and Cruls, *Planalto central*, map, "Districto Federal," 334, and 233, "perfectly healthy" in the Paranã River valley (1890s). Bandeiras to the sertão of Paraúpava: F. Franco, *Dicionário*, 177, 186, 198, 263, 274, 278.
21. Trade routes, captaincy of Maranhão: RJBN, 11, 2, 4, [no author], Roteiro do Maranhão à Goyaz pela capitania do Piauhy, 1800, copy, ff. 7, 12, note 40; and RJBN, I-31, 21, 9, Magalhães, "Memoria," 1813. See also "Mappa Geographico da Capitania do Maranhão e de Parte das Capitanias Circundantes," in Berford, *Roteiro e mappa*.
22. Overland routes: chapter 5; Chaul, *Caminhos de Goiás*, 41–42, 45, 48–49, 52, 59 (maps); and drawn on the printed map in "Mappa Geographico da Capitania do Maranhão e de Parte das Capitanias Circundantes," in Berford, *Roteiro e mappa*, 21. According to Magalhães, RJBN, I-31, 21, 9, "Memoria," 1813, the journey from Porto Real do Pontal to the city of G. Pará with cargo animals took "32 days of march."
23. Mearim route: ANTT, maço 500, "Copia da informação e resposta da d.a ao Ex. mo General do Estado José Telles da Silva ao seu officio de 5 Janeiro 1785," signed Antonio Correa Furtado de Mendonça [?], Maranhão, 15 February 1785; and RJBN 11, 2, 4, Roteiro do Maranhão, f. 12. Map of the "Miarim," Itapicuru, and Parnaíba Rivers with aldeias (1750) is attached to a letter from Francisco

Pedro de [?] to Padre Gaspar da Encarnação, Pará, 14 September 1750, at ANTT, Ministério do Reino, Negocios do Ultramar, maço 597, caixa 700, pasta 1.
24. Itapicuru, Parnaíba routes: Berford, *Roteiro e mappa*, 25–41, 93. His route ran via the Itapicuru River to Caxias, Pastos Bons, and overland parallel to the Balsas River to the Mirador ranch on the Manuel Alves Grande River. It took him from 29 September 1809 to 2–3 December 1809, with eighteen days of "march." See also RJBN 11, 2, 4, Roteiro do Maranhão, ff. 5, 7, 12. Location of Akroá: Apolinário, *Os Akroá*, 47 (map).
25. Xerente migration: see chap. 2, note 47.
26. Piauí routes: RJBN 11, 2, 4, Roteiro do Maranhão, notes 104, 108.
27. Cattle routes to Goiás: Gardner, *Travels*, 305–6; and McCreery, *Frontier Goias*, 130.
28. Gueguê, Guenguen: see chapter 8 on Duro; as allies with the Akroá and Timbira in fighting settlers and in the aldeia near Oeiras: Apolinário, *Os Akroá*, 79–80, 83.
29. Jesuit routes to Goiás: see chapter 3, notes 40–48.
30. Pernambuco: my personal observations of the road between Oeiras and Carolina in 2000. Buritis: KEW, William J. Burchell to Dr. Hooker, Fulham, 11 December 1830; and Karasch, "Periphery of the Periphery?," 159–60.
31. Salvador: Karasch, "Periphery of the Periphery?," 159, 162; and AHU, caixa 25, letter of Governor Luis da Cunha Menezes [to the Queen], Vila Boa, 22 October 1778. He reached Vila Boa on 16 October 1778 after "37 days of march," as well as some days for rest or other activities.
32. Contraband gold, Bahia: ATC, no. 4076, Contadoria Geral do Rio de Janeiro, 9 August 1787, ff. 45–54. Salt trade: McCreery, *Frontier Goiás*, 137. By 1780 the captaincy was importing nine thousand to twelve thousand surrões (one *surão* = thirty to forty pounds) of salt a year from the São Francisco River.
33. Bahian sertão routes: Karasch, "Periphery of the Periphery?," 159; and trade via Couros: Jacintho, *Esboço histórico*, 6, 9–10.
34. Rio-Minas trade: Karasch, "Periphery of the Periphery?," 160–61.
35. Conde de São Miguel (1755–1759): AHU, caixa 15, Cartas do Conde de São Miguel to Minister Sebastião José de Carvalho Mello, Rio de Janeiro, 28 May 1755 and 25 September 1755. I would like to thank Waldinice Nascimento for typed copies of these documents.
36. Dragoons made the trip between Rio de Janeiro and Vila Rica in nineteen days in 1751 and thirteen days in 1752. RJIHGB, lata 772, pasta 52, Raimundo José da Cunha Matos, "Etapas do itinerário Rio/Minas: Do brigadeiro Cunha Matos (1823) e anteriores, de Daniel Pimentel e Inácio de Noronha Câmara (1751/52), de Luiz de Melo Pereira e Cáceres (1772) e do Colonel Sebastião Gomes Berford (1809) . . ." Return trips took sixteen days in 1751 and thirteen days in 1752. Missions on the road: RJBN, 9, 2, 10, Silva e Souza, "Memoria," f. 49.

37. Routes from São Paulo: RJBN 9, 2, 10, Silva e Souza, "Memoria," f. 49. In 1613 it took 120 days for a Paulista bandeira to reach the Ilha do Bananal, where they encountered the Carajaúna and the Caatinga. Monteiro, *Negros da terra*, 79–80.
38. São Paulo routes: AHU, no. 1001, caixa 2, Capm. Mor Antonio de Souza Telles Menezes, "Negociante," letters regarding trade with São Paulo in salt, 12 April 1794; trade with Rio and São Paulo, 2 May 1794; and ironware brought from Rio, 12 April 1794. He also identified those in the petty trade of the sertão as pardos (mulatos) and pretos (blacks). Goiás and Cuiabá: Davidson, "Rivers and Empire," 37; Giraldin, *Cayapó e Panará*, 58–59 (map); and Monteiro, *Negros da terra*, 79–80.
39. "Routes of the 'Monsoons' ca. 1736" (map), in Boxer, *Golden Age of Brazil*, 262; Holanda, *Monções*, 126; and Mead, "Caiapó do Sul," 35–36.
40. Western river routes: Davidson, "Rivers and Empire," xxi–xxii, 37, 109–10, 198–99, and map, x–xi. Trade in "herva de Paraguai" to Desemboque: RJBN, 9, 2, 10, Silva e Souza, "Memoria," f. 48.
41. Goiano gold and Mato Grosso: Davidson, "Rivers and Empire," 105–6, 362–64 (table B, "Annual Gold Subsidy Remitted from Goiás to Mato Grosso, 1759–1821").
42. Vila Boa to Cuiabá in twenty-five days: AHU, No. 1001, caixa 2, letter of 5 December 1750 to the Conde dos Arcos. Cuiabá to Mearim trip by Indian: ANTT, maço 500, Ministerio do Reino, Negocios do Brazil e Ultramar, 1730–1823, Copia da informação e resposta da D.a ao Ex.mo General do Estado José Telles da Silva ao seu officio de 5 Janeiro 1785, Antônio Correa Furtado de Mendonça, Maranhão, 15 February 1785. Fazenda do Leda: RJIHGB, lata 281, pasta 4, doc. 2, Ofício (cópia antiga) assinado por Feliciano José Gonçalves, et al., Belém, 1 March 1793; and Giraldin, *Cayapó e Panará*, 61.
43. Rainy season: RJIHGB, arq. 1.2.7, Ofício de João Manoel de Mello to Paulo de Carvalho e Mendonça, Vila Boa, 29 May 1760, vol. 36, f. 51. Very rigorous *estação das aguas* in 1791: AHU, caixa 35, letter to Martinho de Mello e Castro from Governor Tristão da Cunha Menezes, Vila Boa, 28 July 1792.
44. Pohl, *Viagem*, 249; and Kayapó: see chapter 8, note 46. Pohl actually observed how they kept warm during the rainy season.
45. Dry season, temperatures at night and burnings, Cruls, *Planalto central*, 215–17. Dry season and drystorms: RJIHGB, arq. 1.5.16, Ribeiro, "Viagem," ff. 212–13. Kayapó burnings: Mead, "Caiapó do Sul," 99. Canoeiro raids: AHG, Doc. Div., no. 18, Correspondência Ofício to João Gomes da Silveira Mendonça from Cunha Matos, Cavalcante, 6 January 1824, ff. 48–51.
46. Heavy rains and thunder: Pohl, *Viagem*, 124; RJIHGB, arq. 1.2.7, Ofício, Manoel de Mello to Paulo de Carvalho e Mendonça, 29 May 1760, v. 36, f. 51; and RJIHGB, arq. 1.5.16, Ribeiro, "Viagem," ff. 212–13.
47. Floods and hunger: Karasch, "História," 40–41; AHG, caixa 27, Avisos, pacote 5, aviso no. 41, Francisco de Paula de [?] to the president of the province

of Goiás, Palacio do Rio de Janeiro, 7 May 1839; and AHG, Municipios, Porto Nacional, caixa 1, Manoel Ferreira da Cruz [?], Delegado de Polícia, to Doutor Estevão Ribeiro de Rezende, Chefe de Polícia desta Provincia, Porto Imperial, 1 November 1846.

48. Maranhão River fevers, 1730s: Karasch, "História," 21–22.
49. Fevers: AHG, Doc. Div. no. 70, Cunha Matos, Registro de Correspondência Militares ao Governo Civil da Província, 1823–1826, ff. 72, 214–15.
50. Sezões and maleitas: Karasch, "História," 21–22; Wells, *Exploring and Travelling*, 188; and RJIHGB, lata 281, pasta 4, doc. 3, Diario, Souza Villa Real, 26 January 1793.
51. Xavante refusal to move to Salinas: Karasch, "Rethinking the Conquest," 483–84. Maleitas death of Antonio João: RJIHGB, lata 281, pasta 4, doc. 3, Diario, Souza Villa Real, 26 January 1793.
52. Fevers in north: Karasch, "História," 22–23. McCreery, *Frontier Goiás*, 132, clarifies that annual flooding of the Paranã River left many pools of stagnant water, which most likely contributed to plagues of mosquitoes and fevers.
53. Putrid fever: Pohl, *Viagem*, 124; Karasch, "História," 23; and Sigaud, *Du climat*, 168, on intermittent fevers in the district of Águaquente.
54. Apoplexy: Karasch, "História," 38–39. On cerebral malaria, see Kiple, *Cambridge World History*, 859.
55. Indigenous deaths: RJAN, cod. 807, v. 10, Francisco José Rodrigues Barata, "Memoria sobre a Agricultura e Commercio [sic] da Capitania de Goyaz," Lisbon, 1806, ff. 78–79; and violent epidemics: Karasch, "História," 25.
56. Blacks in the basin of the Paranã River: G. Moura, *História do povo Kalunga*, 23, 27–29, 32, 36. Santo Antônio: Jacintho, *Esboço histórico*, 9–10. With reference to Salinas, a bandeira discovered a quilombo near the Araguaia River where blacks extracted salt for their use. AHU, cod. 1657, Instruçõens respectivas ao exame das Salinas, Vila Boa, 28 June 1774, ff. 78–79.
57. Fevers, south: Karasch, "História," 23–24.
58. Araguaia fevers: ibid., 24–25; AHU, no. 1013, caixa 7, Goiás, copy of letter of Manoel Gomes Rebello to Dr. Pedro Bernardino de Souza Brandão, Vila Boa, 10 October 1778; and healthiness: RJIHGB, lata 281, pasta 4, doc. 5, Vila Real, Diário, 1792–1793.
59. Paranaíba River: Karasch, "História," 25; Sigaud, *Du climat*, 169; and quilombo na ilha do Rio Grande: Karasch, "Os quilombos do ouro," 252–53.
60. Maps (1893) with location of future capital: Cruls, *Planalto central*, 45; maps of Formosa: Cruls, *Planalto central*, 334; Couros: RJBN, 9, 2, 10, Silva e Souza, "Memoria," f. 38; and Jacintho, *Esboço histórico*, 9–11.
61. Caldas Novas: RJBN, 9, 2, 10, Silva e Souza, "Memoria," f. 45; Sigaud, *Du climat*, 507–9; Oriente, org., *Fabulosas águas*; Cruls, *Planalto central*, 194–203; and Jacintho, *Esboço histórico*, 9–10.

62. Cerrado: Gardner, *Travels*, 294–95; Leal, *Viagem ás terras Goyanas*, 98; Alfredo Taunay, *Goyaz*, 49–54; illustrations of the *tatu*, *ariranha*, and *guará*: Adonias, *Fauna e flora brasileira*, 175, 169, 167.
63. Forests: Cruls, *Planalto central*, 187–94; KEW, Burchell to Dr. Hooker, Fulham, 11 December 1830; sesmarias defined: McCreery, *Frontier Goiás*, 155–57; Timbira da Matta: Berford, *Roteiro e mappa*, 21.
64. Location of the Pireneus mountains, between the Corumbá and Almas Rivers: Cruls, *Planalto central*, 85 (map), 77–82 (altitude of). A drawing of a bridge and the Almas River is in Burchell, *Brasil do primeiro reinado*, 117.
65. Serra Dourada and Kalunga: Cruls, *Planalto central*, 205; G. Moura, *História do povo Kalunga*, 24; and Karasch, "Os quilombos do ouro," 245.
66. Vampire bats: McCreery, *Frontier Goiás*, 138.
67. Chapada das Mangabeiras: LC, Geography and Map Division, "Carta da Provincia de Goyaz Organizada em 1874 . . . ," gravada por C Lomelino de Carvalho, Rio de Janeiro, 1875.
68. The Serra Geral de Goiás was formerly called the "Expinhaço do Brazil." RJBN II-31, 19, 13, "Voto do Comiçario Francisco Jozé Pinto de Magalhaens Cap.am d'Ordenanças . . . ," São Pedro de Alcântara, 11 August 1815; and RJIHGB, arq. 1.2.7., vol. 36, Ofício de José de Almeida de Vasconcelos to Martinho de Mello e Castro, Vila Boa, January 1774, ff. 169–70. "Brazil, Bolivia & Peru," a map in Bradford, *Comprehensive Atlas*, illustrates the mountains to the east of the Tocantins River.
69. Chapada dos Veadeiros: G. Moura, *História do povo Kalunga*, 23–24; Cruls, *Planalto central*, 93–96; and RJBN, I-31, 21, 9, Magalhães, "Memoria," 1813.
70. Other serras: LC, Carta da Provincia de Goyaz, 1874; and Spix and Martius, *Viagem pelo Brasil* (1968), attached map.
71. Southern mountains: Gallais, *Apostolo do Araguaia*, 93–94; Giraldin, *Cayapó e Panará*, 57–61, with map; and locations of Kayapó villages: Mead, "Caiapó do Sul," 91.
72. Chagas disease: Karasch, "História," 32–33, 37 (photo); Stepan, *Picturing Tropical Nature*, 185–97, 206–7; and ANTT, maço 500, Ministério do Reino, Negócios do Brasil e Ultramar, 1730–1823, 10 Novembro 1810.
73. Goiter: Saint-Hilaire, *Viagem*, 51; Karasch, "História," 33–35, 36 (photo); and still common in the 1890s: Cruls, *Planalto central*, 234–35; and salt shortages: McCreery, *Frontier Goiás*, 136–37. In the 1820s, Cunha Matos, *Itinerario*, 2:10, recorded that an alqueire of salt from Rio de Janeiro cost sixteen oitavas of gold. An alqueire is about 13.8 liters; an oitava is one-eighth of an ounce: McCreery, *Frontier Goiás*, 217–18.
74. Smallpox, rarity: Karasch, "História," 25; and Pohl, *Viagem*, 124.
75. Smallpox virus: Kiple, *Cambridge World History*, 1008–9; in Goiás: Karasch, "História," 52–54; in Meia Ponte: RJBN 9, 2, 10, Memoria, f. 31; self-inoculation by black slaves: AHU, caixa 43, Goiás, Francisco de Assis Mascarenhas to the

Visconde de Anadia, Vila Boa, 29 June 1806. By 1806, 3,230 had been vaccinated: AHU, caixa 43, Goiás, Bartolomeu Locer.a da Silva to Francisco de Assis Mascarenhas, Vila Boa, 22 June 1806.

76. Three epidemics and Meia Ponte: Karasch, "História," 26; and RJBN, 9, 2, 10, Silva e Souza, "Memoria," f. 31. According to Giraldin, *Cayapó e Panará*, 98, another epidemic of smallpox attacked the Kayapó and the south of the captaincy in 1811. There were also severe epidemics of smallpox and measles in the north in the 1740s, which reduced the population of Belém by half in 1749. See Davidson, "Rivers and Empire," 143–44.

77. Smallpox, 1817: Karasch, "História," 25–26; and Hoornaert, *História* 244–45. According to Nimuendajú, *Apinayé*, 6, smallpox was spread to the Apinaje and others by fugitive Capiecran (Ramko'kamekra or Canela) from Caxias, Maranhão. See also Crocker, *Canela*, 69; Hemming, *Amazon Frontier*, 186, 189; and RJIHGB, arq. 1.5.16, Ribeiro, "Viagem," f. 169. Sigaud, *Du climat*, 169, reported that smallpox was epidemic in Maranhão and Pará, thus suggesting that one route of the disease into Goiás had come from the north. Sick slaves: Karasch, "História," 26.

78. Smallpox, 1873: Karasch, "História," 26.

79. Measles: Karasch, "História," 26–27; V. Franco, *Viagens*, 40; among the Kayapó: Saint-Hilaire, *Viagem*, 69; and Giraldin, *Caiapó e Panará*, 98; epidemic of 1753: see chapter 2, note 8.

80. Filariasis: Karasch, "História," 27–28; and Cristina de Cássia Pereira Moraes, "O Hospital de Caridade São Pedro de Alcântara e os trabalhadores na cidade de Goiás (1830–1860)," in Freitas, *Saúde e doençãs*, 138–39. For a description of elephantiasis in Minas Gerais, see Spix and Martius, *Viagem pelo Brasil* (1938), 2:135.

81. Leprosy: Sigaud, *Du climat*, 507–9 (treatment for it at Caldas Novas); Karasch, "História," 27–29; and Cristina de Cássia Pereira Moraes, "O Hospital de Caridade São Pedro de Alcântara e os trabalhadores na cidade de Goiás (1830–1860)," in Freitas, *Saúde e doençãs*, 138–39. On pellagra, see Kiple, *Cambridge World History*, 919–20.

82. Syphilis: Karasch, "História," 29–30; Gardner, *Travels*, 340; and Gilka Vasconcelos Ferreira de Salles, "Saúde e doenças em Goiás (1826–1930)," in Freitas, *Saúde e doençãs*, 89. Still a serious problem in the 1890s: Cruls, *Planalto central*, 228–29.

83. Additional health problems are discussed in Karasch, "História" and other essays in Freitas, *Saúde e doençãs*, as well as by Dr. Antônio Pimental in Cruls, *Planalto central*, 227–35. See also the list of illnesses in Gilka Vasconcelos Ferreira de Salles, "Saúde e doenças em Goiás (1826–1930)," in Freitas, *Saúde e doençãs*, 88–90.

Chapter Two

1. The concept of nation as used in the eighteenth and nineteenth centuries is explored in Karasch, "Minha Nação."
2. There are no accurate statistics on the total indigenous population of the captaincy of Goiás in the colonial period. Pohl, *Viagem*, 125, guessed at more than fifty thousand, but he probably did not include many peoples of the far north or far south. In 1819 Francisco de Paula Ribeiro believed that there were eighty thousand indigenous people in the region of the Tocantins. See the introduction to his "Memória sobre as nações gentias que presentemente habitam o continente do Maranhão" by João Renôr F. de Carvalho, in [Ribeiro], *Francisco de Paula Ribeiro*, 198–99. Such a population density explains why so many people migrated into Goiás, especially when pushed by the advancing settler frontier.
3. Sereburã et al., *Wamrêmé Za'ra*.
4. Akroá and Xacriabá: Greg Urban, "A história da cultura brasileira segundo as línguas nativas," trans. Beatriz Perrone-Moisés, in Cunha, *História dos índios no Brasil*, 88, 90–91; Chaim, *Aldeamentos indígenas*, 43, 53; and Apolinário, *Os Akroá*, esp. 45–49, 77–79, and maps on 47, 96, 116. On their experiences in the mission aldeias, see Apolinário, *Os Akroá*; and chapter 8 herein. Chyquiriabás: ANTT, maço 598, José dos Santos Pereira to Pedro Barboza Cannaes, São Félix, 5 October 1761, attached with a letter from the bishop of Pará to Francisco Xavier de Mendonça Furtado, 26 May 1762; and Xacriabá: Apolinário, *Os Akroá*, 112.
5. Bandeiras and Gueguê: Hemming, *Amazon Frontier*, 62–66; in Piauí, see Galindo Lima, *O governo das almas*, 279; Alencastre, *Anais*, 120–21; Chaim, *Aldeamentos indígenas*, 114; and Apolinário, *Os Akroá*, 55, 64, 78, 102 (in Natividade).
6. Gomes da Silva: AHU, 995, caixa 17, Ultima Carta de Venceslao Gomes da Silva, administrador temporal do gentio da Natividade, presídio de São José, 12 February 1758, signed Venceslao Gomes da Sylva (copy). Also see AHU, 995, caixa 17, Cartas de Venceslao Gomes da Silva, administrador contratado pelo Conde dos Arcos, Vila Boa, 1 February 1757, Wenceslao Gomes da Sylva to the Conde de São Miguel; Chaim, *Aldeamentos indígenas*, 114–15; and Apolinário, *Os Akroá*, 109–10, 119, 130–48. This bandeira leader had used "practices of extermination" since age fifteen.
7. Two aldeias: AHU, caixa 4, *Provizão* (copy), 17 July 1747, with correspondence of 12 October 1764; Chaim, *Aldeamentos indígenas*, 117; Hemming, *Amazon Frontier*, 65–66; and Apolinário, *Os Akroá*, 114–16, and map.
8. Hemming, *Amazon Frontier*, 62–64; measles: Chaim, *Aldeamentos indígenas*, 151; and Apolinário, *Os Akroá*, 123–25.
9. Jesuits: Apolinário, *Os Akroá*, 114–15. See also Saint-Hilaire, *Viagem*, 62n9.

10. Duro and Cunha Matos: AHGDD, João Manoel de Menezes, Cadete, Quartel do Duro, 4 February 1824, ff. 50–51, 199–200; Cunha Matos, *Itinerario* 2:163; and Hemming, *Amazon Frontier*, 66.
11. Xacriabá: ANTT, maço 600, Ministerio do Reino, letra D, to the Marques do Pombal from José d'Almeida Vasconcelos, Vila Boa, 26 August 1775.
12. Jesuits at Rio das Velhas: [Caeiro], *Primeira publicação*, 261; former Jesuit aldeias and Xacriabá: Saint-Hilaire, *Viagem*, 128–47.
13. I have adopted the spelling *Apinaje*, as used by Odair Giraldin in his dissertation, "AXPÊN PYRÀK"; LBN, Rare Books, Cod. 568, "Da viagem que se faz da cidade de Bellem [*sic*] do Grão Pará, athe ás ultimas colonias dos dominios portuguezes nos rios Amazonas, e Negro Pelo tenente Colonel de Engenharia João Vasco Manoel de Braun," 1782, f. 41; and RJBN, 9, 2, 10, Silva e Souza, "Memoria."
14. Nimuendajú, *Apinayé*, 1–10.
15. Hemming, *Amazon Frontier*, 188–89. My thanks to Heather Roller for her notes on letters by Hilário de Morais Betancourt from the Engenho do Carmelo, which are held at the Arquivo Público do Pará, Correspondência de Diversos com o Governo, 447.33, 22 July 1790; and 447.34, 8 [?] August 1790.
16. Karajá comparisons and ubás: Nimuendajú, *Apinayé*, 3–4.
17. Attack of soldiers: ibid., 5; and [Ribeiro], "Roteiro da viagem," 37; and coalition: see chapter 4, note 31.
18. Smallpox and crafts: Nimuendajú, *Apinayé*, 6–7; and Pohl, *Viagem*, 248–49.
19. Apinaje as allies: Hemming, *Amazon Frontier*, 189; AHGDD, no. 69, Xavier de Barros to Cunha Mattos, Natividade, 26 May 1824; AHGDD, no. 70, Registro de Correspondências Militares, Cunha Matos to the president and deputies of the Junta of the Provisional Government, Natividade, 17 June 1824, f. 99; and ibid., City of Goiás, 22 August 1824, f. 104.
20. AHGDD, no. 68, Correspondência Dirigida do Comandante da Armas—Raymundo José da Cunha Mattos, 1823–1824, Rellação das Aldeyas do Apinayé, ff. 201–2; and fugitive black: Hemming, *Amazon Frontier*, 189.
21. Nimuendajú, *Apinayé*, 7.
22. Krahô: Greg Urban, "A história da cultura brasileira segundo as línguas nativas," trans. Beatriz Perrone-Moisés, in Cunha, *História dos índios no Brasil*, 88, 90; Hemming, *Amazon Frontier*, 190; Nimuendajú, *Eastern Timbira*, 22–27. Location on the east bank of the Tocantins: Nimuendajú, *Eastern Timbira*, 25–26. Nimuendajú argues that the Pépuxis were "unlikely" to be Krahô (23).
23. Apúicrît: Hemming, *Amazon Frontier*, 191; and Nimuendajú, *Eastern Timbira*, 22.
24. Pŏrekamekrã and Moreira da Silva: Pohl, *Viagem*, 249–50; Hemming, *Amazon Frontier*, 192; Nimuendajú, *Eastern Timbira*, 27–28; [Ribeiro], "Memória sobre as nações gentias," 316–18; and Karasch, "Antônio Moreira da Silva."

25. Three thousand Krahô: RJBN, I-31, 21, 9, Magalhães, "Memoria," 1813; and visit to Krahô: [Ribeiro], "Memória sobre as nações gentias," 320–21. See also Pohl, *Viagem*, 245.
26. Krahô as allies: RJBN, I-31, 21, 9, Magalhães, "Memoria," 1813. He requested assistance from the Royal Treasury in giving his allies (the cacique plus seven captains) cotton cloth, hats, knives, and other goods. Faithful allies of Magalhães: Nimuendajú, *Eastern Timbira*, 24.
27. Later aldeia experiences: Karasch, "Catechese e cativeiro," in Cunha, *História dos Índios no Brazil*, 408–9; and Nimuendajú, *Eastern Timbira*, 25.
28. Karajá defined: Toral, "Cosmologia e sociedade Karajá," 14–16; map in Chaim, *Aldeamentos indigenas*, 43; M. Borges, "Diferenças entre as falas feminina e masculina"; and more than one thousand years: Gomes, Neto, and Barbosa, *Geografia Goiás-Tocantins*, 49.
29. Seventeenth-century Karajá: E. Abreu, "Contatos interetnicos," 122–28; Ferreira, *Bandeiras*, 112; and chapter 3 herein.
30. Karajá, 1644: Ferreira, *Bandeiras*, 195–97; and 1650s: see chapter 3, notes 43–44.
31. Karajá contact with the bandeiras of 1755 and 1775 is narrated at greater length in Karasch, "Rethinking the Conquest," 472–80. The original document on which this is based is in LBA, 54-XIII-16n.0, "Relação de uma bandeira aos índios Carajás e Javaís, que terminou com o estabelecimento da Aldeia de S. Pedro do Sul e de outra mais pequena, a que puseram o nome de Aldeia da Lapa, Ilha de Santa Ana," 2 August 1775, f. 138.
32. This list of nations "who drink in the river [Araguaia]" was omitted from the published version of the narrative about the bandeira in *Revista do Instituto Histórico e Geographico Brasileiro* 7 (1846). See LBA, 54-XIII-16n.0, "Relação de uma bandeira," 2 August 1775, f. 138.
33. Three villages: Cunha Matos, *Chorographia histórica*, 134–35.
34. Karajá history in the aldeias: Karasch, "Catequese e cativeiro," 403–9; and Karajá trade with Pará merchants: AHG, Niquelandia, letter of Souza Von Araujo J. to Santos e Sousa, 1776; five ubás: Arquivo Público do Pará, Correspondência de Diversos, 447.5, Betancourt to Governor Albuquerque, Carmelo, 6 May 1787, as noted by Heather Roller.
35. Xambioá Karajá: Castelnau, *Expedição*, 177–91. A French edition with full colored pictures of the Karajá is available at the Oliveira Lima Library in Washington, DC. As of 2015, one of the Karajá masks collected in the 1930s is on display at the Smithsonian National Museum of the American Indian in New York City.
36. Baldus, *Tapirapé*, 20–42; Tapirapéz and Araés: RJBN 9, 2, 10, Silva e Souza, "Memoria," ff. 43–44; chapter 3, on bandeiras sent to the Araés; and Araés and the Xingu River: Castelnau, *Expedição*, 194.
37. Xavante origin at the sea in Rio de Janeiro and first contacts: Graham, *Performing Dreams*, 27; Aracy Lopes da Silva, "Dois séculos e meio de história

Xavante," in Cunha, *História dos Índios no Brasil*, 362–64. Map, 1751: Chaim, *Aldeamentos indígenas*, 43; Nimuendajú, *Serente*, 1–7; and map with Xavante warrior: Apolinário, *Os Akroá*, 231.

38. Carretão: Lazarin, "Aldeamento do Carretão." A longer version of the history of Xavante settlement at Carretão is in Karasch, "Rethinking the Conquest," 481–85. See also chapter 8 on the mission.
39. According to Odair Giraldin in an email of 27 April 2013, "Xavante de Quá" or "Xerente de Quá" was the term used to refer to the proper Xavante or Xerente. Carretão, 1819: Pohl, *Viagem*, 237–38; and Karasch, "Catequese e cativeiro," 403.
40. Xavante, 1814–1819: Ravagnani, "A experiência Xavante," 91–92; RJIHGB, arq. 1.5.16, Ribeiro, "Viagem," f. 262; and Pohl, *Viagem*, 236–42.
41. Photographs of Xavante with red and black body paint, white cords, and sticks: Sereburã et al., *Wamrêmé Za'ra*, 15, 109.
42. Photographs of bows and arrows: ibid., 111.
43. Divisions: Aracy Lopes da Silva, "Dois séculos e meio de história Xavante," in Cunha, *História dos Índios no Brasil*, 364–65; and separation by 1820: Graham, *Performing Dreams*, 25–26. See Graham's maps for locations of contemporary Xavante.
44. Xerente language: Nimuendajú, *Serente*, 1–2, 4; Greg Urban, "A história da cultura brasileira segundo as línguas nativas," trans. Beatriz Perrone-Moisés, in Cunha, *História dos Indios no Brasil*, 88; and AHGG, pasta 2, doc. 51, Governor Miguel Lino de Moraes to José Clemente Pereira, City of Goiás, 25 August 1829, f. 17. Balsas River village: Pohl, *Viagem*, 272.
45. SGC, Vicente Ayres Silva, Itinerario, photocopy, 399. In September 1850 Ayres Silva traveled on the Sono River to the Balsas River and found two aldeias of the Cherente. One had twenty-eight large houses with a population of eight hundred Indians and thirteen large fields of corn. Xerentediquá: LBN, Braun, "Da Viagem," 1782, f. 41; Cherentes: IHGG, pasta 002, doc. 51, no. 34, Miguel Lino de Moraes to José Clemente Pereira, City of Goiás, 25 August 1829, f. 17–18; Nimuendajú, *Serente*, 5; RJBN, Silva e Souza, "Memoria," ff. 31, 43–44; RJBN, I-31, 2 1, 9, Magalhães, "Memoria," 1813; and Pohl, *Viagem*, 272.
46. Two Chavante: AHGDD, no. 69, Pacifico Antônio Xavier de Barros to Cunha Matos, Porto Real, 18 April 1824, ff. 182–85; and AHGDD, no. 69, Felizardo de Nazareth Bitancourth, Cabo de Esquadra de Dragoens to Xavier de Barros, Porto Real, 7 May 1824, ff. 213–17.
47. Enemies: AHGDD, no. 69, Estevão Joaquim Pires to Cunha Matos, Graciosa, 1 September 1824, ff. 237–38; Noroguajés/Noroguagés: AHGDD, no. 69, João Manoel de Meneses, Cadete, to Cunha Matos, 18 August 1824, f. 236; and AHGDD, Cunha Matos, no. 18, no. 77, Ofício a Secretaria de Estado sobre o ataque dos Noraguajés, Traíras, 4 November 1824, ff. 114–15. See also Nimuendajú, *Eastern Timbira*, 36, for debates on their identity and variant

spellings. Maybury-Lewis, *Savage and the Innocent*, 39, translates *gurgulho* as "gurgle."
48. Pacifico (Indian) and Xerente captains: AHGDD, no. 69, 1823–1825, Origenais dos Comandantes dos Registros e Presidios da Província, Estevão Joaquim Pires, Pacifico Antônio Xavier de Barros, to Cunha Matos, Porto Real, 7 May 1824, 207, 216. The location of Graciosa, north of Porto Nacional, is shown on the map in Nimuendajú, *Serente*.
49. Abandonment of Graciosa: IHGG, pasta 2, doc. 51, Lino de Moraes to Pereira, City of Goiás, 25 August 1829, f. 18; and AHG, cod. 136, Luiz Gonzaga de Camargo Fleury to the juíz de paz of Porto Imperial, 1 April 1837.
50. Pedroso, "Avá-Canoeiro: A história do povo invisível"; Pedroso et al., *Avá-Canoeiro*; Dulce Madalena Rios Pedroso, "Avá-Canoeiro," in M. Moura, *Índios de Goiás*, 91–133; Toral, "Os índios negros"; and Karasch, "Rethinking the Conquest," 485–92.
51. Tupi-speakers: Rivet, "Les indiens Canoeiros," 172; Nimuendajú, *Serente*, 4; and Pedroso, "Avá-Canoeiro," in M. Moura, *Índios de Goiás*, 91–92.
52. Canoeiro as similar to Payaguás: AHGDD, no. 18, Correspondência Dirigida ao Comandante das Armas, Raimundo José da Cunha Matos, 1823–1825, from João Gomes da Silveira Mendonça, Cavalcante, 6 January 1824, f. 50; and occupation of Jesuit fazendas: Pedroso, "Avá-Canoeiro," in M. Moura, *Índios de Goiás*, 93.
53. Pedroso, "Avá-Canoeiro: A história do povo invisível," 144–48, argues that the Canoeiro lived in the lower Tocantins River region before the seventeenth century. On Tupinambás recorded in Duro, see Cunha Matos, *Itinerario*, 2:163.
54. Pedroso, "Avá-Canoeiro," in M. Moura, *Índios de Goiás*, 91.
55. This paragraph is based on Pedroso, "Avá-Canoeiro," in M. Moura, *Índios de Goiás*, 120–22.
56. Locations of villages: IHGG, Documentos, pasta 002, doc. 51, livro 4, Miguel Lino de Moraes to the Marquez de Caravellas, 28 September 1830, f. 59; Pedroso, "Avá-Canoeiro," in M. Moura, *Índios de Goiás*, 100–103, and maps, 129–30; and Rivet, "Les indiens Canoeiros," map, 171.
57. Canoeiro attacks on Amaro Leite, Descoberto, and all the inhabitants of the road of Porto Real to Pilar by the "ferocious, barbarous, and very cruel Gentiles denominated Canoeiro": RJIHGB, lata 72, pasta 6, Ofício no. 18, Goiás, "Registro dos ofícios do deputado do governo Luiz Gonzaga de Camargo Fleuri . . . ," 14 June 1823, Natividade, f. 24; and São Félix: Pedroso, "Avá-Canoeiro: A história do povo invisível," 123, 125. See also chapter 4, note 62.
58. RJBN, 9, 2, 10, Silva e Souza, "Memoria," f. 28, 43. An English version of this description of the Canoeiro is in Southey, *History of Brazil*, 677–78. Lances and arrows with barbs: Pohl, *Viagem*, 214.
59. AHGDD, no. 18, Cunha Matos, Cavalcante, 6 January 1824, f. 50.
60. Violence against them, 1773–1803: see chapter 3, notes 71–72; Karasch, "Rethinking the Conquest," 486–87; and Southey, *History of Brazil*, 678.

61. Massacre, 1819: see chapter 3; Karasch, "Rethinking the Conquest," 488; and Pohl, *Viagem*, 214–15.
62. Karasch, "Rethinking the Conquest," 489–90; and Cunha Matos: see chapter 3, notes 73–74.
63. Castelnau, *Expedição*, 230 (torture of victims), 245–46.
64. Karasch and McCreery, "Indigenous Resistance," 242–43.
65. Terence Turner, "Os Mebengokre Kayapó: História e mudança social, de comunidades autônomas para a coexistência interétnica," in Cunha, *História dos índios no Brasil*, 311–38; Ataídes, *Sob o signo da violência*, 66–68; and Mead, "Caiapó do Sul," 59n9.
66. First contact: Giraldin, *Cayapó e Panará*, 55; and Mead, "Caiapó do Sul," 16.
67. Bilreiros (clubbers): Giraldin, *Cayapó e Panará*, 55; and Mead, "Caiapó do Sul," 33.
68. Nhyrykwaye: Terence Turner, "Os Mebengokre Kayapó: História e mudança social, de comunidades autônomas para a coexistência interétnica," in Cunha, *História dos índios no Brasil*, 313–14; and Nyurukwayé on the west bank of the Tocantins River: Nimuendajú, *Eastern Timbira*, 36 and map. For the Gradaús: Mead, "Caiapó do Sul," 59n9; and for the Northern Kayapó also being called the Coroás or Coroados, see Mead, "Caiapó do Sul," 59n12.
69. Early Kayapó history and territory: see chapter 3; Giraldin, *Cayapó e Panará*, 55–81, and map, 58–59; and Mead, "Caiapó do Sul," 91.
70. Translated descriptions of Kayapó villages and fields: Mead, "Caiapó do Sul," 95–99.
71. Kayapó in Vila Boa: RJIHGB, lata 397, doc. 2, Goiás, Redução dos índios da Capitania de Goiás, [no author, no date], but from the archive of Dr. Ernesto Ferreira. See also Karasch, "Damiana da Cunha," 103–5.
72. Saint-Hilaire visited the abandoned aldeia of Maria I and admired its location. Saint-Hilaire, *Viagem*, 75. Two thousand four hundred inhabitants: Giraldin, *Cayapó e Panará*, 95.
73. Aldeia fugitives and removal to Mato Grosso: see chapter 8; and Mead, "Caiapó do Sul," 316–22.
74. Postmission Kayapó: Mead, "Caiapó do Sul," 330–404, 409–10; route of their migration to Peixoto de Azevedo: Giraldin, *Cayapó e Panará*, 133–36.

Chapter Three

1. Short biographies of those who led or participated in bandeiras are in F. Franco, *Dicionário*. One study of Paulista bandeiras is Affonso Taunay, *História*. See also Langfur, *Forbidden Lands*, 165–67; and Russell-Wood, "New Directions."

2. Priests: Hemming, *Amazon Frontier*, 191; Alencastre, *Anais*, 144; Padre Luiz Antônio da Silva e Souza, "Memoria sobre o descobrimento, governo, população, e cousas mais notaveis da Capitania de Goyaz [1812]," *Revista do Instituto Histórico e Geographico Brasileiro*, no. 16 (4o Trimestre de 1849): 90; and Castro, *Organização*, 77.
3. I have drawn the concept of the slaving frontier from Miller, *Way of Death*, 140–42.
4. Bandeiras of the 1590s and Araés: Affonso Taunay, *História*, 2:183; *atas da Camara da Vila de São Paulo*: Salles, *Economia e escravidão*, 53–54; "on the region of the Araguaia-Tocantins" as the sertão do Paraúpava: Monteiro, *Negros da terra*, 79. There was also a river, once known as the Araés, but later as the "rio dos Pilões." See Varnhagen, *História geral*, 4:124.
5. On the Apuatiaras as Kayapó, see Toral, "Cosmologia e sociedade Karajá," 14–23; and Monteiro, *Negros da terra*, 82.
6. André Fernandes, 1613–1614: Ferreira, *Bandeiras*, 117–27; Affonso Taunay, *História*, 2:183–84; and Salles, *Economia e escravidão*, 54–55. The Caatingas were a people of the língua geral and were visited by Padre Araújo in 1632. Taunay also refers to an expedition of thirty sertanistas in 1813, led by Pero Domingues.
7. Alvarenga, 1615: F. Franco, *Dicionário*, 30–31; and Ferreira, *Bandeiras*, 132–37, 136 (map). Monteiro, *Negros da terra*, 70, identifies the Gualachos as Kaingang.
8. 1613–1618: Silva e Souza, "Memoria," *Revista do Instituto Histórico e Geographico Brasileiro*, no. 16 (4o Trimestre de 1849): 73; and Alencastre, *Anais*, 26–28, who notes the uncertainties regarding the dates of his bandeiras.
9. Lopes Benavides and Paulo Bueno, 1664–1665: F. Franco, *Dicionário*, 69, 91.
10. First Anhangüera: Alencastre, *Anais*, 28, 30, 78 (with Pires de Campos); and Hemming, *Red Gold*, 377–78.
11. Bandeira of 1722: Silva e Souza, "Memoria," *Revista do Instituto Histórico e Geographico Brasileiro*, no. 16 (4o Trimestre de 1849): 76–77; F. Franco, *Dicionário*, 372–76; route of the bandeira: Varnhagen, *História geral*, 4:122–24; Affonso Taunay, *História*, 2:189–99; Alencastre, *Anais*, 32–40; account by Ensign José Peixoto da Silva Braga: Hemming, *Red Gold*, 381–84; and map of his route: Mendes Rocha, *Atlas histórico*, 29.
12. Salles, *Economia e escravidão*, 70, identifies the two principal associates of Bueno as Domingos Rodrigues do Prado and João Leite da Silva Ortiz. The latter sold rich mines in Rio das Velhas to finance the expedition. Bueno's bandeira also reached the Claro River, fought with the Kayapó, and acquired five "indígenas," one of whom was the "India Thereza," who resided in Anta in 1781. Ibid., 70–71. Lordelo brothers: F. Franco, *Dicionário*, 228; list of those who left for Belém: Affonso Taunay, *Relatos sertanistas*, 131–33. On the Quirixás as the extinct nation known as the Crixás, see Varnhagen, *História geral*, 4:123.

13. Bueno's discoveries: Alencastre, *Anais*, 32–47; Salles, *Economia e escravidão*, 70–72; Silva e Souza, "Memoria," *Revista do Instituto Histórico e Geographico Brasileiro*, no. 16 (40 Trimestre de 1849): 77–78; and Affonso Taunay, *História*, 2:201–2. On Cañamares, see F. Franco, *Dicionário*, 105.
14. According to Affonso Taunay, *História*, 2:201, Sergeant-mor Manoel de Barros, an engineer with knowledge of mining, accompanied Bueno in 1726. Also cited in Salles, *Economia e escravidão*, 62. From this gold, which was about thirty *quilos*, the first quintos were "possibly" sent to the Crown. Ibid., 71. Seizure of women and leaves of gold: Alencastre, *Anais*, 29; and Silva e Souza, "Memoria," *Revista do Instituto Histórico e Geographico Brasileiro*, no. 16 (40 Trimestre de 1849): 78.
15. Bueno's *mercê*, death, and son: Taunry, *História*, 2:211–12; and Silva e Souza, "Memoria," *Revista do Instituto Histórico e Geographico Brasileiro*, no. 16 (40 Trimestre de 1849): 82–83.
16. Pires de Campos, senior: Affonso Taunay, *História*, 2:245; and Ataídes, *Sob o signo da violência*, 72.
17. Campos Bicudo, senior, and twenty-four entradas into the sertão: Ataídes, *Sob o signo da violência*, 72. See also Affonso Taunay, *História*, 2:245.
18. Pires de Campos, senior, 1716–1746: Affonso Taunay, *História*, 2:245; Affonso Taunay, "Os dois Antônio Pires de Campos," 509–17; and Ataídes, *Sob o signo da violência*, 72.
19. Bilreiros: Mead, "Caiapó do Sul," 33–34, 63–86; Giraldin, *Cayapó e Panará*, 55–56; and Ferreira, *Bandeiras*, 113 (map).
20. Early bandeiras to the Kayapó: Mead, "Caiapó do Sul," 73–75; Giraldin, *Cayapó e Panará*, 55–56; and Ferreira, *Bandeiras*, 105–10, 116.
21. 1608–1611: Karasch, "Rethinking the Conquest," 472; Salles, *Economia e escravidão*, 314n7, recorded three Carajaúna plus "índios Teminimós" in the inventory. See also Ferreira, *Bandeiras*, 112. According to Toral, "Cosmologia e sociedade Karajá," 17, Carajaúna is a Tupi designation for the Karajá.
22. Mascarenhas, 1742: Ataídes, *Sob o signo da violência*, 24.
23. Pais de Oliveira, 1742: Affonso Taunay, *História*, 2:240, 246; and F. Franco, *Dicionário*, 275.
24. Pires de Campos: Affonso Taunay, *História*, 2:246–49; Ataídes, *Sob o signo da violência*, 25–26, 72–74; Mead, "Caiapó do Sul," 146–62, 149 (contract); Giraldin, *Caiapó e Panará*, 70, 73–77; and Hemming, *Red Gold*, 407. An arroba of gold would weigh about fifteen kilos or thirty-three pounds, according to McCreery, *Frontier Goiás*, 217.
25. Bororo, reasons for their alliance: Mead, "Caiapó do Sul," 147–62.
26. Bandeira, 1742: Alencastre, *Anais*, 74–75; Giraldin, *Caiapó e Panará*, 70; Ataídes, *Sob o signo da violência*, 24–25, 72–73; and Mead, "Caiapó do Sul," 149.
27. "Ultimate excess": Alencastre, *Anais*, 75.
28. Model: ibid., 76–77.

29. Share in Indian hunting: ibid., 77.
30. Bororo families sent to aldeias: RJBN 9, 2, 10, Silva e Souza, "Memoria," ff. 42–43; and Mead, "Caiapó do Sul," 151–52.
31. Bororo as allies and slaves: Ataídes, *Sob o signo da violência*, 25; Hemming, *Red Gold*, 405–6; Giraldin, *Caiapó e Panará*, 70; Mead, "Caiapó do Sul," 147–49; Affonso Taunay, *História*, 2:247; and AHU, no. 995, caixa 17, Dom Luis Mascarenhas, Praça de Santos, 15 July 1748.
32. Pires de Campos, 1748: Hemming, *Red Gold*, 407–8; and Giraldin, *Cayapó e Panará*, 75–76.
33. Karajá: Alencastre, *Anais*, 198; Hemming, *Amazon Frontier*, 68; Mead, "Caiapó do Sul," 161–62; and Karasch, "Rethinking the Conquest," 473.
34. Kayapó and his death, 1751: AHU, 1001, caixa 2, Goiás, Conde D. Marcos de Noronha, Vila Boa, 25 January 1752; Ataídes, *Sob o signo da violência*, 74; Hemming, *Red Gold*, 68; Affonso Taunay, "Os dois Antônio Pires de Campos," 537–39; and Mead, "Caiapó do Sul," 156–62.
35. Campos Bicudo and Pinto da Silveira: AHU 995, caixa 17, Conde D'Arcos de Noronha, Vila Boa, 11 April 1755. See also F. Franco, *Dicionário*, 388; Giraldin, *Cayapó e Panará*, 77; and Mead, "Caiapó do Sul," 164–5.
36. Pinto da Silveira's bandeiras: Alencastre, *Anais*, 75; Mead, "Caiapó do Sul," 165–72; and F. Franco, *Dicionário*, 388. Some Cururû accompanied the bandeira to Vila Boa.
37. Gold of Araés: Alencastre, *Anais*, 77–78; and guided by Araés: Salles, *Economia e escravidão*, 62.
38. Amaro Leite: RJBN, 9, 2, 10, Silva e Souza, "Memoria," f. 40; F. Franco, *Dicionário*, 263; Alencastre, *Anais*, 77–78; and Mead, "Caiapó do Sul," 159–60.
39. Sertão do Amaro Leite: F. Franco, *Dicionário*, 263; and Alencastre, *Anais*, 78.
40. SGC, Documentos Históricos de Goiás: Diversos, Arquivo José Mendonça Teles, Odorico Costa, "Os Jesuítas em Goiaz," *Oeste*, 5; and Leite, *Suma histórica*, 99. On the Indians who descended on the Tocantins River, see Roller, *Amazonian Routes*, 94–102; and Sommer, "Colony of the Sertão," 4–15.
41. Vieira's entrada: Leite, *Suma histórica*, 100; J. Silva, *Lugares e pessoas*, 44–46; and Hemming, *Red Gold*, 321–22.
42. Sotomaior, 1656: Leite, *Suma histórica*, 96–97.
43. Veloso and Ribeiro, 1655: ibid., 100; J. Silva, *Lugares e pessoas*, 47; Ferreira, *Bandeiras*, 202; and Hemming, *Red Gold*, 324–25. On Tupinambá in the aldeias of the Tocantins River, see R. Almeida, *O diretório dos índios*, 278–80.
44. Nunes, 1658/59: J. Silva, *Lugares e pessoas*, 46–48; and Ferreira, *Bandeiras*, 205–7.
45. Pirapés, 1661: Vieira, carta no. 91, as cited in J. Silva, *Lugares e pessoas*, 48.
46. Ribeiro and Carew, 1658: Leite, *Suma histórica*, 100; J. Silva, *Lugares e pessoas*, 51; and Ferreira, *Bandeiras*, 203, 207.

47. Misch and Almeida, 1668: Leite, *Suma histórica*, 100; 1671 entrada: J. Silva, *Lugares e pessoas*, 51; and Ferreira, *Bandeiras*, 208–9.
48. Jesuit gold mines: SGC, Documentos Históricos de Goiás: Diversos, Arquivo José Mendonça Teles, Odorico Costa, "Os Jesuítas em Goiaz," *Oeste*, 5–6.
49. Bandeiras, 1669: see "Pires, Almeida Freire," in F. Franco, *Dicionário*, 171, 309.
50. Mota Falcão, Barros, Raposo, Mota, and da Gama: ibid., 41, 150; Ferreira, *Bandeiras*, 209–10; Mead, "Caiapó do Sul," 76–77; and Ataídes, *Sob o signo da violência*, 28. Affonso Taunay, *História*, 2:261, records the enslaved Indians as the Guarajós.
51. F. Franco, *Dicionário*, 346 (Costa Romero), 134 (Pacheco do Couto), 107 (Cardoso), 41 (Araujo), 421 (Tomar), and 362 (Sanches). See also Palacin, *Goiás*, 34; and chapter 7 herein.
52. Gamela Bandeira: F. Franco, *Dicionário*, 395; and ANTT, maço 598, Ministerio do Reino—Negocios do Ultramar, letra B, 1753–1763, Adjutant João Pereira Brandão, et al., Arraial de S. José do Rio Mearim, 18 September 1754.
53. Conquest of Akroá and Xacriabá: see chapter 2. Accord to pacify Akroá: AHU, 995, caixa 17, Lisbon, 31 May 1753; and choice of Wenceslau Gomes da Silva: AHU, 995, caixa 17, Vila Boa, 11 April 1755, Conde de D'Arcos de Noronha. Conditions for conquest: AHU, 995, caixa 17, letter of Venceslao Gomes da Sylva, Arrayal de S. Antonio, Minas de S. Félix, 14 June 1754. For additional correspondence on his bandeiras, see Apolinário, *Os Akroá*, 130–48; and Hemming, *Amazon Frontier*, 65–66; for Duro and his death, see Cunha Matos, *Itinerário*, 2:163–65.
54. Karasch, "Rethinking the Conquest of Goiás," *Americas*, 61: 463–92, provides more complete narratives of the pacification expeditions of the period 1775–1819; see also Karasch, "Interethnic Conflict and Resistance on the Brazilian Frontier of Goiás, 1750–1890," in Guy and Sheridan, *Contested Ground*, 124–25. For correspondence on bandeiras of the 1770s, see AHU, cod. 1657, "Livro primeiro para registo de portarias, bandos, edictães, instrucções, e regimentos para as bandeiras, . . . da Capitania de Goyaz, e Minas."
55. Karajá conquest: Karasch, "Rethinking the Conquest," 473–77. Fonseca later petitioned for the honor of the Habit of Christ. See table 3.
56. For Pereira's bandeira, see table 10 herein; Karasch, "Rethinking the Conquest," 469; and Mead, "Caiapó do Sul," 222.
57. This and subsequent paragraphs are based in part on Karasch, "Damiana da Cunha." Additional sources will be cited in subsequent notes in this chapter. See also "Damiana and Manoel da Cunha," in Mead, "Caiapó do Sul," chap. 7, 285–329. Mead is especially insightful on Dona Damiana's brother's role in the aldeia.
58. Title of captain-mor: AHG, Doc. Diversa, Registro de Correspondências Militares ao Governo Civil da Província, no. 70, Ofício de Luiz da Costa Freire de Freitas to the Ex.mo Senhor Presidente, Goiás, 12 July 1825, f. 188. See also

Mead, "Caiapó do Sul," 294–95, 300–302, 307, 310; Ataídes, *Sob o signo da violência*, 81–85; and Raimundo José da Cunha Matos, "Corographia histórica da Província de Goyaz," *Revista do Instituto Histórico e Geographico Brasileiro* 37 (1874): 305.

59. Da Cunha, 1819–1821: Mead, "Caiapó do Sul," 302–6.
60. Da Cunha, 1827–1829: ibid., 310–11; petition for the *meio soldo* (soldier's pay) of her husband: AHG, caixa 11, Assuntos Militares, João Vieira de Carvalho, Rio de Janeiro, 7 April 1823; Dona Damiana's pension as the widow of José Luiz Pereira, with the salary of 150 reis per diem, 54$750: RJAN, IG1 218, Ministerio da Guerra, Correspondência, Goiás, pacote 1826, Pensions, "Tabella dos vencimentos da Corporação Militar no estado actual," Goyaz, 27 September 1826.
61. Last expedition and death: IHGG, pasta 002, doc. 51, livro 4, Miguel Lino de Moraes para o Imperio, Estrangeiros, e Marinha, Ofício to the Marquez de Caravellas, City of Goiás, 1 October 1830, ff. 61–62; IHGG, pasta 002, doc. 51, livro 4, Ofício to José Antônio da Silva Maia, City of Goiás, 24 January 1831, ff. 68–69; pension of nine mil-réis given to Dona Damiana: AMB, 1676, Ministerio da Agricultura, Catequese, Aldeias, order of Miguel Lino de Moraes, City of Goiás, 15 May 1830; denial of compensation for services to Manoel Pereira da Cruz: IHGG, pasta 002, doc. 51, livro 4, Ofício of Miguel Lino de Moraes to José Clemente Pereira, City of Goiás, 24 November 1829, ff. 26–27; Mead, "Caiapó do Sul," 312–15; and Ataídes, *Sob o signo da violência*, 92.
62. Manoel da Cunha and postmission conflicts: Mead, "Caiapó do Sul," 289, 316–77; Ataídes, *Sob o signo da violência*, 50, 55–56, 92; and Giraldin, *Caiapó e Panará*, 121–36.
63. Xavante "conquest": Karasch, "Rethinking the Conquest," 481–85.
64. Freire's bandeira: ibid., 481–82.
65. Kayapó chief: Karasch, "Rethinking the Conquest," 483.
66. Carretão entrance: ibid., 484–85. On Carretão, see also chapter 8.
67. Warfare resumed: Karasch and McCreery, "Indigenous Resistance," 238–39.
68. Karasch, "Antônio Moreira da Silva."
69. Martins dos Reys: Karasch, "Rethinking the Conquest," 485; and Amaro Leite: V. Franco, *Viagens*, 62–63. On Canoeiro resistance, see Karasch and McCreery, "Indigenous Resistance," 239–43.
70. Canoeiro bandeiras, 1773–1796: Karasch, "Rethinking the Conquest," 486–87; to Tocantins islands: Ataídes, *Sob o signo da violência*, 42.
71. Pereira's bandeira: Karasch, "Rethinking the Conquest," 487. See also Southey, *History of Brazil*, 677–78.
72. Segurado's bandeira: Karasch, "Rethinking the Conquest," 488.
73. Cunha Matos's expeditions, 1823–1825: ibid, 489–90.
74. Pereira and Cunha Matos, 1824: ibid.
75. Continued warfare: Karasch and McCreery, "Indigenous Resistance," 242–43; and V. Franco, *Viagens*, 120–26.

76. On Xavante pacifications, 1941–1966, see Garfield, *Indigenous Struggle*, 45–65; and on the contact of Orlando and Claudio Villas Boas with the Kreen-Akarore/Panará: Cowell, *Tribe That Hides*; and Mead, "Caiapó do Sul," 16–25.

Chapter Four

1. Karasch, "Catequese e cativeiro."
2. "Homens brancos, esses cristãos": Pohl, *Viagem*, 255; and Karasch, "Rethinking the Conquest," 463–64.
3. ANTT, Reino, maço 598, to Conde de Oeyras from Frei João, Bispo do Pará, Pará, 8 November 1760 (copy).
4. Apinaje: AHGDD, no. 18, Correspondência Dirigida ao Comandante das Armas, Raimundo José da Cunha Matos, 1823–1825; and no. 48, "Ofício a Secretaria d'Estado a respeito dos Barbaros Indios . . . ," to João Gomes da Silveira Mendonça, from José Raimundo da Cunha Mattos, Cavalcante, 23 February 1824. Karajá as enemies of Apinaje: RJIHGB, lata 281, pasta 4, doc. 3, Diary of Thomaz de Souza Villa Real, 1 and 8 February 1793. Kupe-rob: Nimuendajú, *Apinayé*, map and 121.
5. War and raiding: Nimuendajú, *Apinayé*, 3, 120; LBN, Rare Books, cod. 568, "Da viagem que se faz da cidade de Bellem do Grão Pará, athé ás ultimas colonias dos Dominios Portugezes nos Rios Amazonas, e Negro Pelo Tenente Colonel de Engenharia João Vasco Manoel de Braun," 1782; and RJIHGB, lata 281, pasta 4, doc. 3, diary, Villa Real, 1 February 1793.
6. Attacks on quilombos: Nimuendajú, *Apinayé*, 3; and AHU, no. 995, caixa 17, Goiás, 1756–1799 [1779?].
7. Apinaje weapons: LBN, cod. 568, "Da Viagem," Braun, 1782.
8. Clubs: Nimuendajú, *Apinayé*, 124–25.
9. Tactics: ibid., 2–3; ANTT, Ministério do Reino, Negocios do Ultramar, letra B, 1753–1763, maço 598, 1760; and Hemming, *Amazon Frontier*, 187.
10. Pohl, *Viagem*, 2:168, as cited in Nimuendajú, *Apinayé*, 5; Santa Maria: RJIHGB, arq. 1.5.16, Ribeiro, "Viagem"; and Hemming, *Amazon Frontier*, 188–89.
11. Alliances: Hemming, *Amazon Frontier*, 188–89; and AHGDD, no. 18, no. 48, Silveira Mendonça, from Cunha Mattos, Ofício, f. 62.
12. Porekamekrã: Pohl, *Viagem*, 247–48; Carvalho: Hemming, *Amazon Frontier*, 190–91; and Nimuendajú, *Eastern Timbira*, 28. Nimuendajú argues that Pohl must have met the Xerente, not the Porekamekrã, given the number of inhabitants Pohl described. The Xerente also had a village named Cocal on the Tocantins River. In Portuguese, *cocal* means a grove of palm trees. However, Pohl reported that the people he met spoke a different language than the Xavante. See Pohl, *Viagem*, 250.

13. Porekamekrã, 1808–1813: Nimuendajú, *Eastern Timbira*, 27–28; Hemming, *Amazon Frontier*, 190–92; and RJIHGB, arq. 1.5.16, Ribeiro, "Viagem," f. 268.
14. Warfare at Cocal: Pohl, *Viagem*, 255–56, 251 (axe).
15. Pictures of semilunar axe: Mendes Rocha, *Atlas histórico*, 21; Berta G. Ribeiro and Lucia H. van Velthem, "Coleções etnográficas," in Cunha, *História dos índios no Brasil*, 105; and photograph of Porecramecan anchor-axe: Augustat, *Beyond Brazil*, 162.
16. Tacape, sixteenth century: Ribeiro and van Velthem, "Coleções," in Cunha, *História dos índios no Brasil*, 106 (picture).
17. Alliance, Porekamekrã: [Ribeiro], "Roteiro da viagem," 45–46; RJBN, I-31, 21, 9, Magalhães, "Memoria," 1813; and Hemming, *Amazon Frontier*, 184–85.
18. Second village: RJIHGB, arq. 1.5.16, Ribeiro, "Viagem," ff. 278–79; and Hemming, *Amazon Frontier*, 184–85.
19. Baby: RJIHGB, arq. 1.5.16, Ribeiro, "Viagem," f. 277.
20. Cocrît, Carolina: Nimuendajú, *Eastern Timbira*, 27–28.
21. Krahô: Pohl, *Viagem*, 257; RJBN I-31, 21, 9, Magalhães, "Memoria," 1813; and RJIHGB, arq. 1.5.16, Ribeiro, "Viagem," ff. 268–69.
22. Krahô as allies: Hemming, *Amazon Frontier*, 190; RJIHGB, arq. 1.5.16, Ribeiro, "Viagem," ff. 271–72; and Nimuendajú, *Eastern Timbira*, 4.
23. Alliance with Magalhães: RJIHGB, arq. 1.5.16, Ribeiro, "Viagem," f. 271; and Hemming, *Amazon Frontier*, 190–91.
24. Trade goods, prices for slaves: AHGDD, no. 18, Correspondência, Cunha Matos, 1823–1825, f. 50; Nimuendajú, *Eastern Timbira*, 4; and RJIHGB, arq. 1.5.16, Ribeiro, "Viagem," f. 276.
25. Petition of five nations: ANTT, maço 500, Ministério do Reino, Negocios do Brasil e Ultramar, 1730–1823.
26. Krahô, 1820s: Hemming, *Amazon Frontier*, 191; and Nimuendajú, *Serente*, 74.
27. Karajá enemies: Karasch, "Rethinking the Conquest," 474; and Apinaje: RJIHGB, lata 281, pasta 4, doc. 1, D. Francisco de Souza Coutinho to Martinho de Mello e Castro, Pará, 8 March 1793.
28. Karajá raid: RJIHGB, lata 281, pasta 4, doc. 3, 8 February 1793.
29. Visit to Pará: RJIHGB, lata 281, pasta 4, doc. 1, Souza Coutinho to Mello e Castro, Pará, 8 March 1793; RJIHGB, lata 281, pasta 4, doc. 3, 17–28 January 1793; and theft of guns: RJBN, I-31, 21, 9, Magalhães, "Memoria," 1813.
30. Karasch, "Rethinking the Conquest," 475, 478.
31. Ibid., 480. For a dramatic narrative of the attack on the presídio, see Alencastre, *Anais*, 331–36.
32. Xavante raids, eighteenth century: RJIHGB, arq. 1.2.7, v. 36, Ofício of Tristão da Cunha Menezes to Martinho de Mello e Castro, Vila Boa, 17 July 1784, f. 283; and Lazarin, "Aldeamento do Carretão," 133.
33. Xavante anger at whites: Pohl, *Viagem*, 237–39.
34. Xavante women: Pohl, *Viagem*, 240; and desire for iron: Pohl, *Viagem*, 180, 240.

35. Xavante enemies and slaves: Spix and Martius, *Viagem pelo Brasil* (1938), 2:229; and of Krahô: Ravagnani, "A experiência Xavante," 91–92. The Macamecran as enemies of Xerente and Xavante: RJBN, I-31, 21, 9, Magalhães, "Memoria," 1813; and Karasch, "Rethinking the Conquest," 481–85.
36. Goiânia, IHGG, pasta 002, doc. 51, Livro 4 para o Imperio, 1829–1831, ff. 17–18, no. 34, Miguel Lino de Moraes to José Clemente Pereira, City of Goiás, 25 August 1829; and Xerente associated with Xavante who fled Carretão: RJBN, I-31, 21, 9, Magalhães, "Memoria," 1813. Akroá and Xavante: Pohl, *Viagem*, 239.
37. Antiblack: Pohl, *Viagem*, 238.
38. Raids and rafts: AHGDD, no. 18, Correspondência, Cunha Matos, 1823–1825, f. 48.
39. Raids, 1830s: Karasch and McCreery, "Indigenous Resistance," 238–39.
40. Conduct of war and weapons: Pohl: *Viagem*, 181 (firearms at Carretão), 240; and Sereburã et al., *Wamrêmé Za'ra*, 111, 119, 153 (photos).
41. Tactics: Pohl, *Viagem*, 232, 260; raids, 1830: Karasch and McCreery, "Indigenous Resistance," 238.
42. Carretão: Pohl, *Viagem*, 180–82; and ANTT, maço 600, Governador e Capitão General de Goyazes, [no place], [no date, but after 1786].
43. Hemming, *Amazon Frontier*, 72–74; and Karasch, "Rethinking the Conquest," 481–85.
44. Xavante in Pontal: Palacin, Garcia, and Amado, *História*, 1:32; and Karasch, "Rethinking the Conquest," 483.
45. Giraldin, "Pontal e Porto Real," 134–35.
46. Xerente warfare: ibid., 134–41; and Nimuendajú, *Serente*, 75–76.
47. Xerente enemies: Nimuendajú, *Serente*, 9, 75–76; Pohl, *Viagem*, 238; Hemming, *Amazon Town*, 194; chapter 4, note 56, herein; RJBN, I-31, 21, 9, Magalhães, "Memoria," 1813; Karasch and McCreery, "Indigenous Resistance," 236–37; Giraldin, "Pontal e Porto Real," 139; Southern Kayapó: Spix and Martius, *Viagem pelo Brasil* (1938), 2:229; and killing of juíz de paz: *Relatorio* of the president of Goiás, José Rodrigues Jardim, 1835, "Relatorios dos governos," 37.
48. Weapons: Nimuendajú, *Serente*, 75–76; clava: Spix and Martius, *Viagem pelo Brasil* (1938), 2:229; use of firearms: IHGG, pasta 002, doc. 51, livro 4, 29 October 1829, ff. 24–25; Cherente-dequá: Cunha Mattos, *Itinerario*, 2:249.
49. Strategies: Nimuendajú, *Serente*, 76–77; and Spix and Martius, *Viagem pelo Brasil* (1938), 2:229.
50. Nimuendajú, *Serente*, 77.
51. Xerente use of fire: Nimuendajú, *Serente*, 77.
52. Padre Jardim, who was the informant for Spix and Martius, accused the Xerente of being an "anthropophagous nation," who ate their dead relatives. Spix and Martius, *Viagem pelo Brasil* (1938), 2:229. Castelnau, as cited in Nimuendajú, *Serente*, 78, also accused the Chavante of consuming the bodies of their aged parents.

53. This narrative of peaceful contact is based on AHGDD, no. 70, Registro de Correspondências Militares ao Governo Civil da Província, 1823–1826, ff. 167–69; AHGDD, no. 70, Ofício ao conselho da Província, from Cunha Matos, Trahiras, 26 February 1825; AHGDD, no. 69, Pacifico Antônio Xavier de Barros to Cunha Matos, Porto Real, 18 April 1824, ff. 182–185; AHGDD, no. 69, Felizardo de Nazareth Bitancourth, Cabo de Esquadra de Dragoens to Xavier de Barros, Porto Real, 7 May 1824, ff. 213–217; AHGDD, no. 69, Xavier de Barros to Felizardo de Nazareth, Porto Real, 23 April 1824, f. 198; and AHGDD, no. 69, Xavier de Barros to Cunha Mattos, Porto Real, 25 April 1824, f. 193; AHGDD, no. 69, Felizardo de Nazareth Bitancourth to Xavier de Barros, Porto Real, 7 May 1824, ff. 213–217, and 8 May 1824, f. 212. The location of Graciosa, north of Porto Nacional, is on the map in Nimuendajú, *Serente*.
54. Xerentediquá: LBN, Braun, "Da Viagem," 1782, f. 41; 249; RJBN, 9, 2, 10, Silva e Souza, "Memoria," ff. 31, 43–44; Cunha Matos, *Itinerario*, 2:249; and Nimuendajú, *Serente*, 5.
55. "Noroguaje habitantes na praia de Gorgulho"/Noroguagé/Noraguajé: AHGDD, no. 69, João Manoel de Meneses, Cadete, to Cunha Mattos, 18 August 1824, f. 236; and AHG, Cunha Mattos, no. 18, no. 77, Ofício a Secretaria de Estado sobre o ataque dos Noraguajés, Traíras, 4 November 1824, ff. 114–15. See also Nimuendajú, *Eastern Timbira*, 36, for debates on their identity and variant spellings.
56. Threats to Xerente and their response: AHGDD, no. 69, Estevão Joaquim Pires to Cunha Mattos, Graciosa, 1 September 1824, ff. 237–238; and Maybury-Lewis, *Savage and the Innocent*, 39. He translates *gurgulho* as "gurgle."
57. Abandonment of Graciosa: IHGG, pasta 2, doc. 51, Lino de Moraes to Pereira, City of Goiás, 25 August 1829, f. 18; and bandeira of 1836: AHG, cod. 136, Luiz Gonzaga de Camargo Fleury to the juíz de paz de Porto Imperial, 1 April 1837; Karasch and McCreery, "Indigenous Resistance," 238–39; and Giraldin, "Pontal e Porto Real," 140–41.
58. Canoeiro warfare: Hemming, *Amazon Frontier*, 193; V. Franco, *Viagens*, 124, 151; and AHGDD, no. 18, no. 48, Ofício, to Silveira Mendonça from Cunha Mattos, f. 62. For a summary of the territory in which the Canoeiro lived and attacked, see Pedroso, "Avá-Canoeiro," in Moura, *Índios de Goiás*, 100–103, and maps, 130–31.
59. Road as boundary: Castelnau, *Expedição*, 245–46.
60. Blacks and Canoeiro: Pedroso, "Avá-Canoeiro: A história do povo invisivel," 132–36; and opposition to being slaves: RJBN, I-28, 31, 26, Goiás (Província), "Ofício de Miguel Lino de Moraes . . . , expondo o estado econômico [e político] da província de Goiaz" (cópia), Goiaz, 1 December 1830.
61. RJBN, 9, 2, 10, Silva e Souza, "Memoria," ff. 28, 43; and Dr. José Vieira Couto de Magalhães: Hemming, *Amazon Frontier*, 193, 198.

62. One thousand arcos: AHGDD, no. 18, Correspondência, Ofício a Secretaria do Estado sobre varios acontecimentos na Comarca do Norte, Cunha Mattos, f. 24; and Karasch, "Rethinking the Conquest," 488.
63. Canoeiro tactics: AHGDD, no. 18, Correspondência, Ofício a Secretaria do Estado sobre varios acontecimentos na Comarca do Norte, Cunha Mattos, f. 25 (use of fire); hiding canoes: Pohl, *Viagem*, 213; and retreat to mountains: AHGDD, no. 18, Correspondência, Ofício to João Gomes da Silveira Mendonça, from Cunha Mattos, Cavalcante, 6 January 1824, ff. 48–51.
64. Berthet, "Uma viagem de missão," 1:145.
65. Towns and fazendas destroyed: AHGDD, no. 18, Correspondência, Ofício, to Silveira Mendonça from Cunha Mattos, Cavalcante, 6 January 1824, ff. 48–49, 62.
66. Canoeiro weapons: ibid., f. 49 *(macana* or *caxeira* and arrows); RJBN, 9, 2, 10, Silva e Souza, "Memoria," ff. 28, 43; and barbed arrows and lances: Pohl, *Viagem*, 214; flaming arrows: Pedroso, "Avá-Canoeiro" in Moura, *Índios de Goias*, 102.
67. Pacification, 1980s: Toral, "Os índios negros"; and summary of twentieth-century contacts: Pedroso, "Avá-Canoeiro," in Moura, *Índios de Goiás*, 104–17.
68. Karasch, "Damiana da Cunha"; hostility to whites: Giraldin, *Cayapó e Panará*, 46; and warfare: Mead, "Caiapó do Sul," 99–127.
69. Giraldin, *Cayapó e Panará*, 55–56, 80–81, 94, 49 (vengeance motive); and Mead, "Caiapó do Sul," 113–14.
70. Attacks along roads: Giraldin, *Cayapó e Panará*, 81–85; Ataídes, "A chegada do colonizador," 67; on road to Mato Grosso: RJBN, I-28, 31, 26, Ofício de Lino de Moraes, 1 December 1830. Mead, "Caiapó do Sul," 436–37, also explains the cultural context of their raids for "plunder."
71. RJIHGB, lata 397, doc. 2, Goiás, Redução dos índios da Capitania de Goiás, do Arquivo do Dr. Ernesto Ferreira França Filho, [no date].
72. Captain Julio: RJAN, IJJ9-493, Ministério do Reino, Goiás, Ofícios dos Presidentes, pacote 1813, doc. 1 (copy).
73. Removal to Arinos and new wars: Karasch, "Interethnic Conflict," in Guy and Sheridan, *Contested Ground*, 131; and Karasch and McCreery, "Indigenous Resistance," 231–33.
74. Bororo: Alencastre, *Anais*, 74–75; and Goiá and Crixá: Mead, "Caiapó do Sul," 109–11, 114.
75. Quilombo, Rio Grande: RJIHGB, lata 397, doc. 2, "Redução dos índios"; and capture of fugitive slaves: Mead, "Caiapó do Sul," 124.
76. Kayapó tactics: AHU 995, Goiás, caixa 17, Senado da Camara de Vila Boa, 11 June 1757; night assaults: Spix and Martius, *Viagem pelo Brasil* (1938), 2:229; and as "incendiary Indians": Ataídes, *Sob o signo da violência*, 68.
77. Use of fire: Giraldin, *Cayapó e Panará*, 81.
78. São Paulo attacks and burning of houses: ibid., 47, 83–84.

79. Slaves killed: RJIHGB, lata 397, doc. 2, Redução de índios; and Giraldin, *Cayapó e Panará*, 79–81.
80. Weapons: Mead, "Caiapó do Sul," 95; Giraldin, *Cayapó e Panará*, 55; and accusations of cannibalism: AHU, 995, caixa 17, Senado da Camara de Vila Boa, 11 June 1757.
81. Cannibalism and offensive war: Giraldin, *Cayapó e Panará*, 51, 69; Mead, "Caiapó do Sul," 95; and Ataídes, "A chegada do colonizador," 80–81. The Poxeti were also accused of cannibalism, not only of Christians but also of neighboring nations. RJBN, I-31, 21, 9, Magalhães, "Memoria," 1813.
82. Warfare and migration route: Giraldin, *Cayapó e Panará*, 121–28, 133–36.

Chapter Five

1. "*Boa Ordem*" (Good Order): Russell-Wood, "New Directions," 359.
2. "Homens bons" (good men): A. J. R. Russell-Wood, "Centers and Peripheries in the Luso-Brazilian World, 1500–1808," in Daniels and Kennedy, *Negotiated Empires*, 117. Many themes in this chapter were first developed in Karasch, "Periphery of the Periphery?"
3. Gomes, Neto, and Barbosa, *Geografia Goiás-Tocantins*, 52–55; and map in Mendes Rocha, *Atlas histórico*, 1:56.
4. Governors of São Paulo: Mendes Rocha, *Atlas histórico*, 1:71.
5. Early administration: Alencastre, *Anais*, 32–47; and Palacin, *Goiás*, 23–26.
6. In the late colonial period, the king of Portugal was José I (1750–1777), followed by Queen Maria I (1777–1816). In early 1792 the queen suffered from a mental illness that left her unable to rule. Thereafter her son Dom João VI governed as regent (1792–1816) and then as king, 1816–1826. He lived in Rio de Janeiro from 1808 to 1821, when he returned to Portugal. His son Dom Pedro I assumed the throne of Brazil in 1822 (until 1831). For a general analysis of the Portuguese imperial system, see A. J. R. Russell-Wood, "Centers and Peripheries in the Luso-Brazilian World, 1500–1808," in Daniels and Kennedy, *Negotiated Empires*, 105–42.
7. Fifth-richest captaincy: ANTT, Conselho de Guerra, Secretaria de Estado da Guerra, Relação das freguesias de Portugal, 1798, livro 1, numero de ordem 279, copy of Thomas Bastos, 1801.
8. Governors: Palacin, *Goiás*, 140–44; and suicide of governor: Saint-Hilaire, *Viagem*, 55–56.
9. Élis, *Chegou o governador*; Karasch, "Catequese e cativeiro"; and Karasch, "Os quilombos do ouro," 253–54.
10. Confiscation of José Francisco Hutim's properties and slaves: Karasch, "Central Africans," 141–42.

11. Governor's palace: A. Borges and Palacin, *Patrimônio histórico de Goiás*, 7; and Saint-Hilaire, *Viagem*, 55–56.
12. Eschwege, *Pluto brasiliensis*, 2:12, 279n245.
13. Corruption: Eschwege, *Pluto brasiliensis*, 2:261; Conde de São Miguel: Alencastre, *Anais*, 125–58; and RJBN, manuscript section, 3, 1, 25, Goiás (Capitania), "Prospecto da Capitania de Goyáz no anno de mil outocentos [sic] e trez [1803], em que tomou pósse de Secretario do Governo della o Bacharel Manoel Joaquim da Silveira Felis."
14. The casa de fundição, which is variously translated as "foundry" or "smelting house," is described in Boxer, *Golden Age of Brazil*, 56. The mint was in Rio de Janeiro in the late colonial period.
15. Intendants: Eschwege, *Pluto brasiliensis*, 1:61. The conflict between Intendant of Gold Manuel Pinto Coelho and Governor Dom Manuel de Meneses is narrated in Hernani Cidade, "Um dramático episódio," 417–28. A list of the twelve intendants who served in Goiás is in F. Azevedo, *Annuario histórico*, 102.
16. Comarcas, judges, and slowness of justice: Casal, *Corografia brasílica*, 150–51; Palacin, *Goiás*, 147–52; Alden, *Royal Government*, 423–24; Schwartz, *Sovereignty and Society*, 25–26, 149–50; and list of colonial ouvidores: F. Azevedo, *Annuario histórico*, 101.
17. Devassas: Schwartz, *Sovereignty and Society*, 164.
18. J. Segurado, "Memória econômica e política," 34.
19. Juízes de fóra, ordinários: Casal, *Corografia brasílica*, 150–52; lists of the juízes de fora are in F. Azevedo, *Annuario histórico*, 101. See also Palacin, *Goiás*, 149; and Alden, *Royal Government*, 430–31.
20. Julgados: Mendes Rocha, *Atlas histórico*, 58.
21. A photograph of the Casa da Câmara is in A. Borges and Palacin, *Patrimônio histórico de Goiás*, 20.
22. Weak jails, nineteenth century: McCreery, *Frontier Goiás*, 34.
23. Real fazenda: Casal, *Corografia brasílica*, 153; Palacin, *Goiás*, 152–53; and *provedor-mór da fazenda*: Schwartz, *Sovereignty and Society*, 399.
24. Quinto: Palacin, *Goiás*, 152–53 (table of income); and Salles, *Economia e escravidão*, 184–89 (tables).
25. False gold: AHU, 1003, caixa 11, Intendant of Gold Manuel Gomez da Costa, São Félix, 15 March 1766; and Saint-Hilaire, *Viagem*, 54.
26. Quinto expeditions: see chapter 1, note 36.
27. Taxes: Alden, *Royal Government*, 303–4; Palacin, *Goiás*, 153–56; Salles, *Economia e escravidão*, 207 (table of income from entradas); and McCreery, *Frontier Goiás*, 53–54.
28. Passagens: Alden, *Royal Government*, 304.
29. Information about the collection of donations in Goiás is from a letter written to the ouvidor da comarca from the provincial Francisco of the observance of Portugal regarding Friar José de Nossa Senhora dos Anjos, who had gone to

Goiás ten years earlier to ask for alms to rebuild the Convent of Belém in Lisbon. The problem was that he had not yet sent any money back, and his provincial asked the ouvidor's assistance in finding the gold and sending it via a coastal seaport for export to Lisbon. See AHU, caixa 2, 11 September 1755.
30. ANTT, Conselho de Guerra, Relação das freguesias, 1798, numero 279; and Karasch, "Periphery of the Periphery?," 152. In the colonial period, currency figures in the millions of *réis* (plural of *real*) were written with a colon and a dollar sign before the last three digits.
31. Culture of evasion: A. J. R. Russell-Wood, "Centers and Peripheries in the Luso-Brazilian World, 1500–1808," in Daniels and Kennedy, *Negotiated Empires*, 119. One example of successful smuggling was that of the Carmelite friar Ignacio de Santa Teresa, who took three hundred oitavas of gold through the register of São Domingos. He hid the gold in a statue of Our Lady and passed undetected. The Portuguese learned of what he had done only because he confessed his "sin" on his deathbed. AHU, cod. 1657, "Livro primeiro para registo de Portarias . . . , Capitania de Goyaz, e Minas . . . ," f. 17.
32. Kristine L. Jones, "Comparative Raiding Economies," in Guy and Sheridan, *Contested Ground*, 97–114; and chapter 3 herein.
33. Old mining cores: AHU, no. 1013, caixa 7, Petição da Câmara, copy, Bernardo Miguel de Souza Magalhaens, Lisbon, 22 October 1788.
34. Hunger: See Karasch, "História," 40–41.
35. Sesmarias: McCreery, *Frontier Goiás*, 155–57.
36. For example, José da Rocha Couta, resident of Santa Luzia and lavrador with an engenho de canas (cane mill) and roças with more than twenty slaves, received a sesmaria confirmation on 5 November 1804 that was expedited 6 December 1804. AHU, caixa 42, Goiás. Sesmaria confirmations may be found at the AHU in Lisbon and the AHG in Goiânia.
37. McCreery, *Frontier Goiás*, 161; and AHG, document in restoration, carta de sesmaria, passed to Manoel José dos Santos (who had a fazenda with cattle and horses), Vila Boa, 17 November 1808.
38. The cattle frontier, nineteenth century: McCreery, *Frontier Goiás*, chap. 5, "Stock Raising."
39. Retail: See table 5.
40. Textiles: Cunha Matos, *Chorographia histórica*, 68–69; and Cunha Matos, *Itinerario* 2:316.
41. Gold as blood: RJIHGB, arquivo, lata 356, Goiás, "Que utilidades pode dar a campanha vedada de Pilões, se se facultar," doc. 15, ponto 1, "Fazer circular oiro [sic], evitando os monopolies," [no author], [no date, but after 1785].
42. Salvador–Vila Boa trade: AHU, caixa 35, Vila Boa em Câmara, 28 July 1792 (concerns the decline in trade in slaves and foodstuffs); RJBN, manuscript section, 11, 2, 4, Roteiro do Maranhão á Goyaz pela Capitania do Piauhy, [no date, but with copy dated 1800].

43. Mato Grosso trade: Davidson, "Rivers and Empire," xxii, 37 (opening of the Goiás-Cuiabá route in 1736), and 48 (Moxos). On the amount of gold sent from Goiás to Mato Grosso, see Davidson, "Rivers and Empire," 105–6 and 362–64 (table). The overland route between Vila Boa and Cuiabá is traced on a map in the collection of the Library of Congress, Geography and Map Division, "Mappa geographico da capitania de Mato Grosso formado no anno de 1802. . . ."
44. Maranhão, Piauí, and Pernambuco trades: AHU, cod. 1657, "Livro primeiro para registo de Portarias . . . ," f. 29 (contraband gold via Bocaina); commodities traded: AHU, caixa 2, letters of Captain Major Antônio de Souza Telles Menezes, 16 November 1793 and 24 December 1793; AHGDD, doc. div., no. 69, Origenais dos Comandantes dos Registros e Présidios da Província, 1823–1825, ff. 58, 60, 62–63, 255, 317–18; Salles, *Economia e escravidão*, 161–62; and gold trade: AHU, caixa 11, Manuel Gomez da Costa, intendant of gold, São Félix, 15 March 1766.
45. Trade routes in Maranhão: RJBN 11, 2, 4, Roteiro do Maranhão, ff. 7, 12n40.
46. Tocantins-Belém trade: Doles, *Comunicações fluviais*, 17–21, 27–30, 39–44, 47–50; gold smuggling due to the opening of the Tocantins River: ATC, no. 4076, Contadoria Geral, 21 April 1801, ff. 139–41. Other documents on trade are in RJAN, cod. 807, vol. 10, Joaquim Teotonio Segurado, Memoria sobre o commercio da Capitania de Goyaz, 1806, ff. 11–14; RJBN, 11, 2, 4, Roteiro do Maranhão á Goyaz pela Capitania do Piauhy; and RJBN, I-31, 21, 9, Magalhães, "Memoria," 1813; and Oliveira, *Portos do sertão*, 41–45.
47. Araguaia trades: Doles, *Comunicações fluviais*, 21–23, 44–47; RJIHGB, lata 281, pasta 4, doc. 2, "Ofício (cópia antiga) assinado por Feliciano José Gonçalves; Manuel José da Cunha; e Ambrosio Henriques; apresentando ao Governador . . . o Diário . . . de Tomás de Sousa Vila Real . . . ," Pará, 1 March 1793; AHG, Seção de Municípios, Niquelândia, letter of Alexandre de Souza Von Ar.o J., São José do Tocantins, 5 February 1776, to Vigario José Pires dos Santos e Sousa; RJIHGB, lata 281, pasta 4, doc. 10, Ofício de Francisco de Souza Coutinho to Dom Rodrigo de Souza Coutinho, Pará, 24 June 1797; and RJAN, cod. 807, vol. 10, Segurado, Memoria, 1806, ff. 13–14.
48. Enslaved Africans to Belém: Davidson, "Rivers and Empire," 477–84. Indigenous captives, Belém: RJBN, I-31, 21, 9, Magalhães, "Memória," 1813; and Nimuendajú, *Eastern Timbira*, 24.
49. Vila Boa–Minas Gerais–Rio de Janeiro trade: AHU, caixa 43, letter of José de Aguirre do Amaral, cabo de esquadra da companhia de dragões, Desemboque, 19 April 1806. In 1791–1799, 1,208 new slaves were brought to Goiás, mostly from Rio de Janeiro. See Salles, *Economia e escravidão*, 162.
50. São Paulo to Vila Boa trade: RJIHGB, lata 48, doc. 3, "Digressão que fez João Caetano da Silva, natural de Meia Ponte, em 1817, para descobrir como com eff.o descobrio, a nova Navegação entre a Capitania de Goiáz, e a de São Paulo,

pelo Rio dos Bois até ao Rio Grande, . . ." On the attached map Silva shows that the traditional overland route ran from Vila Boa to Meia Ponte, Bonfim, and Santa Cruz, then across the rivers Corumbá, Parnaíba, Rio Grande, Rio Pardo, and Rio Jagua-rimirim to Vila de Mojimirim, Vila de São Carlos, Vila de Jundiahy, and finally São Paulo. On the salt trade from São Paulo, see AHU, Goiás, Relatorio de Antônio Luis de Souza Leal sobre o estado geral da capitania, Vila Boa, 2 March 1805; and Arquivo do Estado de São Paulo, no. 334, lata 88, 1802–1803, petition of Dona Anna Rita Mascarenhas e Silva with attached document dated 1 June 1803, Vila Boa, regarding the trade goods her husband imported into Vila Boa from São Paulo, via Rio das Velhas. Alida C. Metcalf, in *Family and Frontier*, 57–60, describes the links between wealthy families in Santana and Goiás.

51. Silver trade: Davidson, "Rivers and Empire," 198–200.
52. Contraband: Palacin, *Goiás*, 65; Eschwege, *Pluto brasiliensis*, 2:155–60 (by comboieiros and tavern owners); AHU, caixa 2, 16 November 1793; and ATC, no. 4076, Contadoria Geral do Rio de Janeiro, 9 August 1787 (by nonwhites).
53. João Botelho da Cunha: Mott, "Inquisição, 70–72; and City of Goiás, BFEG, unclassified Paracatú documents attached to *escrituras* of July 1781, which record the sale of four slaves of the Mina nation for nine hundred oitavas of gold. They had been brought to the captaincy by a comboieiro from the city of Bahia. Merchants who traded large convoys of slaves and dry goods from Bahia are identified in Mott, "Inquisição," 170.
54. Francisco José Barretto: AHU, 1003, caixa 11, June 14, 1766–28 May 1768. In an attached document dated 18 June 1763, São Félix, Antônio Luis Lisboa identified him as an inhabitant of Natividade who delivered gold to the foundry house between 1757 and 1763.
55. Antônio de Souza Telles e Menezes: AHU, caixa 2, 16 November 1793; 24 December 1793, 12 April 1794, 2 May 1794, and 10 May 1794. A protest signed by him is in caixa 44, 28 December 1800. Entradas defined: Alden, *Royal Government*, 303.
56. Manoel José Tavares da Cunha: AHU, caixa 43, Requerimento of 22 December 1807; and AHU, caixa 36, Ouvedoria Geral, Auto Civeis, Vila Boa, 1800.
57. Antônio Navarro de Abreu: RJAN, IJJ9-493, Ministério do Reino, Goiás, doc. 2, Fernando Delgado Freire de Castilho, Vila Boa, 31 May 1816.
58. Cattle contraband: AHU, caixa 4, Manoel Joaquim de Aguiar Mourão, Meia Ponte, 29 December 1800. David J. McCreery continues the history of the contraband trade in cattle in his *Frontier Goiás*.
59. AHU, Goiás, 1805, Relatorio de Antônio Luis de Souza Leal sobre o estado geral da capitania, Vila Boa, 2 March 1805.
60. Paid troops: AHU, Goiás, caixa 43, Dom Francisco de Assis Mascarenhas, "Mappa das companhias de dragoens, e pedestres da capitania de Goiaz," Vila Boa de Goiás, 15 April 1806; Palacin, *Goiás*, 156–58; Karasch, "Periphery of the

Periphery?," 167n32, and map of military forces, 1780, which illustrates concentration of dragoons in the mining towns; only two dragoons were in the north in Natividade. See Mendes Rocha, *Atlas histórico*, 1:59.

61. Pedestres: Mendes Rocha, *Atlas histórico*, 1:59. On racial mixture, see RJIHGB, arq. 1.2.7, vol. 36, Ofício of João Manuel de Mello to Francisco Xavier de Mendonça Furtado, Vila Boa, 4 July 1766, f. 147; ATC, Livro de registo das representações da Capitania de Goyaz . . . , no. 4076, 3 Prejuizo, 26 April 1785, f. 8 (*índios mansos*); and City of Goiás, AMB, no. 444, Praça de Militares, Pedestres [lists of troops], 1777–1794.

62. Ordenanças, number of 3,311: AHU, Goiás, caixa 43, D. Francisco de Assis Mascarenhas, "Mappa das companhias de ordenanças da capitania de Goyaz," Vila Boa, 19 June 1806; Palacin, *Goiás*, 129; Silva e Souza, "Memoria," *Revista do Instituto Histórico e Geographico Brasileiro*, no. 16 (4o Trimestre de 1849): 94; and AHGDD, no. 68, 1823–1824, Correspondencia dirigida do Comandante das Armas—Raimundo José da Cunha Mattos, "Lista da companhia das ordenanças do distrito do Arrayal de Santa Cruz da provincia de Goiás creada no anno de 1773 . . . ," ff. 18–24. One man was eighty years old, others seventy and sixty-five, while many others were in their forties and fifties. Most were from Goiás or Minas Gerais, and most were lavradores (farmers).

63. Pardos: AHU, caixa 41, "Os homens pardos nacionais e habitantes da Capitania de Vila Boa de Goyaz . . . ," 5 February 1803 and 7 January 1804. See also AHU, caixa 25, letter of the Câmara of Vila Boa, 31 September 1785; letter of Governor Tristão da Cunha, 20 May 1789; and his note of 5 July 1790 that "mulatos" who had the patent of a colonel did not have any right to be interim governor. The original copies of the signed patents for the pardos of Goiás are at the AHU in Lisbon. See also chapter 10.

64. Henriques: AHU, caixa 7, Ofício de Luis da Cunha Meneses, Vila Boa, 16 May 1783; Goiânia, Archive of the Cúria, Capitão Luis Gonçalves dos Santos and his men. This regimental list is a part of a Boa Morte *sepultamento* (burial) dated 1799. For the number of men, see chapter 10, note 42.

65. Weak church due to economic decadence: AHU, Goiás, letter of Filippe Neri Monteiro e Mendonça to Bispo de Titopoli, 5 June 1805. Two of the best studies of the Catholic Church in Goiás are J. Silva, *Lugares e pessoas*; and Castro, *Organização*.

66. Friar Francisco de Mosanvito arrived in Rio de Janeiro in 1841 and a year later was working among the Apinaje. See J. Silva, *Lugares e pessoas*, 415–16, and 418–21 (on the Dominicans from Toulouse).

67. Four bishops: Teles, *Vida e obra*, 57–58.

68. Blind bishop: F. Azevedo, *Annuario histórico*, 123; Teles, *Vida e obra*, 58–61; and P. Azevedo, *D. Francisco*.

69. Mott, "Inquisição," identifies those who worked for the Inquisition in Goiás, as well as victims who were deported to Portugal. The *visitas pastorais* for Goiás

that I consulted are in Goiânia at the Instituto de Pesquisas e Estudos Históricos do Brasil Central (IPEHBC), which houses the archive of the Curia. Other copies may survive at the Arquivo Metropolitana da Curia, Bispado do Rio de Janeiro.

70. Moreyra, *Vida sertaneja*, 149; and Rio de Janeiro, Arquivo da Cúria Metropolitana, livro 2, Ordens, Relação das igrejas aqui se aderão os 50 Ecclezasticos que se admittirão a ordens em virtude do avizo de 16 de 7bro de 1780, 27 August 1782, f. 104. Description of a vicar general of the north: see chapter 9, note 29; and seminary: J. Silva, *Lugares e pessoas*, 216.

71. The *amantes* of priests openly accompanied them to Mass, according to Saint-Hilaire, *Viagem*, 53. See also chapter 9, note 33.

72. Padre Manoel da Silva Alvares: AHG, document in restoration, Ofício of Governor Fernando Delgado Freire de Castilho, to the Marquez d'Aguiar, no. 3, Vila Boa, 31 May 1816, f. 132, regarding his petition for the Habit of Christ; further information about his clerical career is in RJAN, caixa 315, pacote 2, doc. 7, Trahiras, 13 December 1821; RJAN, IJJ9-493, Ministério do Reino, Goiás, Ofícios dos Presidentes, 1816, doc. 3.

73. Padre Silva e Souza (1764–1840) was born in Tejuco, Minas Gerais, and arrived in Goiás in 1790 at the age of twenty-six. He had studied in Rome and was an erudite professor of Latin and a poet as well as an early historian of Goiás. His principal clerical office was as vicar of Santa Anna and assistant to the first bishop of Goiás. Although elected as a deputy to the Cortes in Lisbon, he did not travel there. In his final will he recognized his daughter, Maria Luiza da Silva e Souza, who resided with his sisters. See Teles, *Vida e obra*; F. Azevedo, *Annuario historico*, 130–31; and Moreyra, *Vida sertaneja*, 121.

74. Secular duties: AHG, Ofício of Governor Freire de Castilho to the Marquez d'Aguiar, Vila Boa, 31 May 1816, f. 132; and complaint against the priest Joaquim Liandro da Silva for nonperformance of his religious duties: RJAN, caixa 315, pacote 2, doc. 7, queixas, Goiás, [no date but attached to documents dated 1821].

75. Quiteria was *recolhida* in the convent. See AHU, Goiás, caixa 35, 30 August 1794. On the life of recolhidas, see Myscofski, *Amazons, Wives, Nuns, and Witches*, 159–67.

76. Various charters of the brotherhoods for Goiás are archived in Lisbon at the AHU, in the City of Goiás at the BFEG, and in Goiânia at the SCG. See Moraes, "corpo místico," chap. 8, table 1.

77. Brandão, *O divino*.

Chapter Six

1. This chapter discusses only a sampling of the wealthy white elites of the late colonial period. It seeks to identify some of the wealthiest whites based on slave

ownership. Included in this category of whites are those born in Portugal, Spain, the Azores Islands, and other captaincies of Brazil, such as São Paulo, Minas Gerais, Rio de Janeiro, Bahia, and Pará. Unfortunately, birthplaces or specific identities were usually not noted in the census data, and not all sources include both color and occupation. Even parish registers did not always report the birthplace of a Portuguese immigrant.

2. Decline of easily located gold: RJBN, manuscript section, 3, 1, 25, Goiás Capitania, "Prospecto da Capitania de Goyáz no anno de mil outocentos [sic] e trez, em que tomou posse de Secretario do Governo della o Bacharel Manoel Joaquim da Silveira Felis," 8 February 1803. To follow the agropastoral elites into the nineteenth century, see McCreery, *Frontier Goiás*.
3. Decadence and end of abundant gold in 1778: Palacin, *Goiás*, 91.
4. Quality: Karasch, "Quality, Nation, and Color."
5. The term *alvo* appears on household lists. AHGDD, no. 68, Correspondência Dirigida ao Comandante das Armas, Raimundo José da Cunha Matos, Mappa da População do Destrito do Pontal, Pontal, 16 December 1793.
6. Jayme, *Famílias Pirenopolinas*, chap. 115, "Famílias de origem africana," 5:393–447.
7. Bertran, *Notícia geral* 1:159. Subsequent citations to the *Notícia geral* of 1783 are to the manuscript copy rather than this edited edition with notes by Bertran. The published version has many errors in numbers, perhaps due to difficulty in reading the manuscript, but it is also indispensable for clarifying many topics.
8. Lavra defined: Palacin, *Goiás*, 81–84; faisqueira by slaves: RJIHGB, lata 356, doc.15, Goiás, "Que utilidades pode dar a campanha vedada de Pilões, se se facultar," [no author], [no date, but after 1785, while Queen Maria (1777–1816) governed].
9. Francisco José Barretto, Comboieiro de Fazendas Secas e Escravos da Bahia, AHU 1003, Goiás, caixa 11, 1750–1807. According to Boxer, *Golden Age of Brazil*, 356, the marco equaled eight *onças*, or 4,608 *grãos*; the onça equaled eight oitavas (drams), and the oitava equaled seventy-two grãos (grains). McCreery, *Frontier Goiás*, 218, defines the oitava as one-eighth of an ounce and an arroba as a unit of weight of approximately fifteen kilos, or thirty-three pounds.
10. Exhausted mines: AHU, no. 1013, caixa 7, Petição da Camara (copy), Bernardo Miguel de Souza Magalhaens, Lisbon, 22 October 1788.
11. Household lists: RJBN, manuscript section, cod. 16.3.2, Notícia geral da capitania de Goiás, 1783.
12. AHU, caixa 35, "Auto de conferencia com os livros do registo das Barras do oiro, e suas guias entradas na caza da Moeda desta Cidade e todo o precedente anno de 1786" (copia), Bahia, 12 February 1787. The total was 513 *cartas de guias* of foundry houses.
13. IHGG, doc. 142, pasta 8, "Lembrança dos mineiros de que tenho noticia, e dos escravos que tem pouco mais ou menos," [no author], [no date, but possibly compiled during the great drought of 1780–1782].

14. List of gold mines: RJBN, I-47, 26, 21, "Abaixo-assinado de José Rodrigues Jardim e outros a José Feliciano Fernandes Pinheiro, sobre as despesas da Companhia Inglesa exploradora de minas na província de Goiás," City of Goiás, 30 May 1826 (cópia). The *parecer* dated 30 May 1826 of Luís Antônio de Silva e Sousa accompanies this document with the list of mining sites.
15. See chapter 6, note 5. See also Cunha Matos, *Chorographia histórica*, which has summaries of population statistics.
16. Stores: Saint-Hilaire, *Viagem*, 52.
17. Ibid.
18. Carvalho: Pohl, *Viagem*, 247–48; and Hemming, *Amazon Frontier*, 190–91.
19. AHU, Goiás, no. 1013, caixa 7, 12 January 1791.
20. Cattle ranches: RJBN, manuscript section, cod. 16, 3, 2, Notícia Geral da capitania de Goiás, 1783; AHGDD, Registro de Correspondências Militares ao Governo Civil da Província, no. 19, to the president of the province from Raimundo José da Cunha Matos, Traíras, 25 October 1825, f. 115, and 13 November 1824, ff. 131–32.
21. Small farmers, Cavalcante: AHG, Municípios, Cavalcante, População, 1828. In 1828 the julgado of Cavalcante had 123 lavouras, where they cultivated wheat, manioc, corn, rice, beans, sugarcane, coffee, tobacco, cotton, and mamona; twenty-four cattle fazendas; twenty-three abandoned lavras; and eight engenhos.
22. Alvos: AHGDD, no. 68, Mappa da população do destrito do Pontal, 16 December 1824, ff. 175–85. Alvos with roças, fazendas, and engenhos were also listed for Água Quente, Cocal, Crixás, district of Gongome, Porto Real, and Santa Cruz.
23. Pilar: RJBN, cod. 16, 3, 2, Notícia geral da capitania de Goiás, 1783.
24. AHGDD, no. 68, mappa da população do destrito do Pontal, 16 December 1824, ff. 175–85.
25. Wealthy priests: the first Vicar in Vila Boa accumulated a fortune of four hundred thousand cruzados in five years. His successor, Dr. Gonçalo José da Silva, acquired eighty thousand cruzados in gold in four years. At that time an oitava was valued at 1$200 to 1$500 réis. Alencastre, *Anais*, 163. See also chapter 5, note 74; Saint-Hilaire, *Viagem*, 70; and priest of Anta: RJBN, cod. 16, 3, 2, Notícia geral da capitania de Goiás, 1783.
26. Slaveholding priests: RJBN, cod. 16, 3, 2, Notícia geral da capitania de Goiás, 1783.
27. Military officers and guards at the registros: Palacin, *Goiás*, 65. The use of some military titles may actually indicate their position within the militia of the ordenança.
28. Elderly officers: see chapter 5, note 63.
29. José Rodrigues Freire: Karasch, "Os quilombos do ouro," 254.

30. Corruption: RJIHGB, lata 356, doc. 15; RJBN, 3, 1, 25, Prospecto da Capitania de Goyáz, 8 February 1803; and Palacin, *Goiás*, 62–65.
31. Costa Mattos (1754–1758), *bacharel em leis*: Moreyra, *Vida sertaneja*, 39, 42; lack of doctors and list of surgeons: Karasch, "História," 42–44.
32. Moreyra, *Vida sertaneja*, 42.

Chapter Seven

1. Salles, *Economia e escravidão*, 288; and Karasch, "Central Africans," 149–51. "Masters of the Dance," is from Saint-Hilaire, *Viagem*, 47.
2. Monteiro, *Negros da terra*, 165.
3. Karajá: Salles, *Economia e escravidão*, 314n4, 314n7. In the same inventories were the Tamoio and Temiminó. In the colonial period, to call a person "negro" was to name the individual as a slave. Thus *negro da terra* could also be translated as "slave of the land."
4. São Paulo inventories: Salles, *Economia e escravidão*, 56.
5. Bueno's slaves: see chapter 3, note 11.
6. Goiá men on São Paulo baptismal registries: John Monteiro, personal communication, Londrina, Paraná, July 2005. On Bueno's bandeiras, see chapter 3, notes 11–14, herein.
7. Salles, *Economia e escravidão*, 61; see also 57–60 and 59 (map), for the geology of the region where alluvial gold was found.
8. Bandos: Salles, *Economia e escravidão*, 227–28.
9. Santa Cruz: ibid., 61. Water had to come from the Peixe River, over fifty kilometers distant. Artiaga, *Geologia*, 193–94.
10. Palacin, *Goiás*, 34–35; and Salles, *Economia e escravidão*, 229.
11. Jaraguá, Claro, and Pilões Rivers: Salles, *Economia e escravidão*, 81, 290; and diamonds: Palacin, *Goiás*, 35; and Salles, *Economia e escravidão*, 99. For the mines of Corumbá, see Artiaga, *Geologia*, 194.
12. Gold: Silva e Souza, "Memoria," *Revista do Instituto Histórico e Geographico Brasileiro*, no. 16 (40 Trimestre de 1849): 96; Palacin, *Goiás*, 35; and Salles, *Economia e escravidão*, 61. Forty-three pounds of gold from Água Quente alone was sent to a museum in Lisbon; the gold was stolen by the French army when they invaded Lisbon. See Henderson, *History of Brazil*, 251.
13. Maranhão River: Silva e Souza, "Memoria," *Revista do Instituto Histórico e Geographico Brasileiro*, no. 16 (40 Trimestre de 1849): 96; and RJBN, 9, 2, 10, Silva e Souza, "Memoria," f. 40; and Salles, *Economia e escravidão*, 75–76.
14. Crixás: Salles, *Economia e escravidão*, 76–77. Crixás in 1779: RJIHGB, arq. 1.2.7, Estatística, Ofício de Luiz da Cunha Menezes à Martinho de Mello e Castro, remetendo o mapa da população da capitania de Goiáz, com distinção de

classes, Vila Boa, 8 July 1780, ff. 245–47. The total for Crixás was 2,814, of which 2,247 were blacks.
15. Other strikes, north: Salles, *Economia e escravidão*, 78; Palacin, *Goiás*, 35–36; and M. Silva, *Quilombos*, 453.
16. Arraias, Cavalcante, Pilar, Conceiçao: Palacin, *Goiás*, 36; Apolinário, *Escravidão negra*, 57–59; and M. Silva, *Quilombos*, 186.
17. Pilar and Tesouras: Salles, *Economia e escravidão*, 290–91; and Palacin, *Goiás*, 36.
18. Cocal, Santa Luzia, Carmo: Palacin, *Goiás*, 36. Artiaga, *Geologia*, 188–89, claimed that thirty-four thousand slaves and many *garimpeiros* (prospectors) had once worked at Cocal. See also Bertran, *Memória de Niquelândia*, 39–40.
19. *Capitação*: Salles, *Economia e escravidão*, 229–33; and Palacin, *Goiás*, 35.
20. First convoy, 1752: Salles, *Economia e escravidão*, 229.
21. Meia Ponte convoy: M. Silva, *Quilombos*, 78, and n109.
22. Entry of slaves, 1760–1767: Salles, *Economia e escravidão*, 233; and total of 1,123: AHU, caixa 21, Mappa das Contagens . . . , 1767, 24 June 1768. My thanks to Marivone Chaim for a copy of this mappa.
23. Total of 1,208 new slaves: Salles, *Economia e escravidão*, 236.
24. Michaela Xavier: Karasch, "Central Africans," 127, and n15.
25. 10,263 slaves: Palacin, *Goiás*, 40. My total is 10,265. Note that Palacin's figures do not always agree with mine on tables 1–2 or with Salles's.
26. Forty thousand slaves: Cunha Matos, as cited by Palacin, *Goiás*, 40, 42 (ten thousand in mining).
27. Higher capitação tax in the north: Palacin, *Goiás*, 35.
28. 17,154 slaves: Salles, *Economia e escravidão*, anexo 13, 275; and 14,437: Palacin, *Goiás*, 41.
29. Foundry houses: Palacin, *Goiás*, 88–90; and census of 1779: RJIHGB, arq. 1.2.7, Estatística, Ofício de Luiz da Cunha Menezes, 8 July 1780, ff. 245–47. On this census the scribe's total is 34,882 blacks, or 62.8 percent of the population. This total disagrees with the sum total by comarca of 15,735 for the south and 19,141 for the north, or 34,876.
30. As far as I was able to determine, government officials in the City of Goiás received the order to burn the documents regarding slavery at the time of abolition, but only a small number of documents were burned in the governor's office.
31. An explanation of the meia-sisa is in Karasch, "Guiné," 169. Apolinário, *Escravidão negra*, 66–67, located eighty Minas, ten Nagôs, and forty-nine Central Africans in the colonial inventories held at the Cartório of Arraias. See also Karasch, "Central Africans," table 4.8, 136.
32. Henriques: ibid., 171, 173. On Guiné, see Hawthorne, *From Africa to Brazil*, 16–19.
33. Joaquim Angola: Hemming, *Amazon Frontier*, 189.

NOTES TO PAGES 196–204　　　　　　　　　　367

34. The complete table of Africans taxed in the City of Goiás, 1837–1838, is in Karasch, "Central Africans," table 4.6, 133.
35. Lack of African baptisms: Salles, *Economia e escravidão*, 228.
36. According to John Hemming, in *Red Gold*, 276, the "euphemism" for the holding of Indian slaves in colonial São Paulo was an "administration." Hence those held in such a manner became administrados in official records. Baptisms, Santa Luzia: SGC, Archive of the Curia, Livro de Batismos de Santa Luzia (Luziânia), 1749–1754.
37. St. Ann's: Karasch, "Central Africans," table 4.4, 131. For a published reproduction of a Mina slave's baptismal registry from 1782, see C. Brito, *A Mulher*, 38. Rosa Mina lived to be more than one hundred years of age (Brito, *A Mulher*, 45).
38. Goiânia, AHG, caixa 10, letter regarding "Representação inclusa dos moradores da capitania de Goiás, Paço," Thomas Antônio de Villanova, Portugal, 24 March 1820.
39. See also M. Silva, *Quilombos*, 134, on Minas baptized in Meia Ponte.
40. Angolan mothers: Karasch, "Central Africans," table 4.14, 147.
41. Jaraguá baptisms: SGC, Archive of the Curia, Registro de Batizados, Jaraguá, 1824 à 1832; and ages of new Africans: Karasch, *Slave Life*, table 2.4, 34.
42. Picture of Nossa Senhora do Monte do Carmo: A. Borges and Palacin, *Patrimônio histórico de Goiás*, 71–73. Location of Carmo on a map: Mendes Rocha, *Atlas histórico*, 62.
43. Nation: Karasch, "Minha Nação," 128.
44. Cabra: M. Silva, *Quilombos*, 135. Citing Bertran, *Memória de Niquelândia*, 46, Silva identifies the cabras of São José do Tocantins as coming from Cabo Verde via Bahia. These cabras were noted for their "fidelity, intelligence, astuteness, and ferocity." See also Karasch, "Guiné," 174.
45. Sale of indigenous captives: Hemming, *Amazon Frontier*, 183–85.
46. Census of 1779: RJIHGB, arq. 1.2.7, Estatística, Ofício de Luiz da Cunha Menezes, 8 July 1780, ff. 245–47.
47. Census of 1832: 1,923 Africans (1,297 males and 626 females); RJAN, codice 808, vol. 1, Goiás, Censo da População da Provincia de Goyaz, 30 May 1832, f. 96.
48. Census of 1783: RJBN, manuscript section, cod. 16.3.2, Notícia geral da Capitania de Goiás, 1783; and Bertran, *Notícia geral*. I have used the manuscript copy of the census for the statistics and the published version to verify names.
49. Sesmarias: McCreery, *Frontier Goiás*, 155–57. In 1779 the captain-general reported that more than a thousand sesmarias had been given, but few were confirmed in Lisbon. Requests for sesmarias in colonial Goiás are at the Arquivo Histórico Ultramarino.
50. Mining Slaves: IHGG, doc. 142, pasta 8, Lenbrança [*sic*] dos Mineiros de que tenho noticia, e dos escravos que tem pouco mais ou menos, [no date]. Number of slaveholders: Vila Boa, Água Quente, and Cocal, two each; Ouro Fino and

Anta, five each; Meia Ponte and Pilar, nine each; Santa Luzia, six; and Traíras and São José, ten.
51. Census of 1825: RJBN, 11, 4, 2, Estatistica da Provincia de Goyáz remettida á Secretaria de Estado dos Negocios do Imperio por Caetano Maria Lopes Gama, Presidente da mesma Provincia, 1825.
52. Prostitution: SGC, Livro de Denuncias, Termo que faz Antonia Teixeira preta Mina forra, e Meretrix [prostitute] . . . , Vila Boa, 8 March 1783; and Domingas Gomes da Sylva, crioula forra, 8 March 1783, f. 88. Both signed a document promising to abandon their life as a "public meretriz." Enslaved women and work: see chapter 9 and Karasch, "Slave Women," 85–89.
53. Hutim: Karasch, "Central Africans," 141–42.
54. Mining techniques: M. Silva, *Quilombos*, 184–85, 453 (working conditions).
55. Jornal, plural jornaes: AHU, 1003, caixa 11, Manoel Gomez da Costa, O Intendente de ouro, São Félix, 15 March 1766; and RJIHGB, arquivo, lata 356, doc. 15, Goiás, Que utilidades pode dar a campanha vedada de Pilões, se se facultar; anônimo, sem lugar, sem data. It also includes a proposal to improve mining in the Maranhão River, but it is incomplete.
56. Black women venders and sharing gold: Karasch, "Slave Women," 87; and AHU, Goiás, caixa 42 or 43, Antônio Luis de Souza Leal, 2 March 1805. He reported that a society of sixty freedmen included forty who mined and twenty others who worked in agriculture to sustain the others. Afterward they divided up the gold equally among themselves.
57. Work with the almocafre: RJIHGB, lata 356, doc. 15, Que utilidades, sem data. A drawing of an almocafre by Aluane de Sá da Silva from São Félix, Cavalcante, Goiás, is archived at the Laboratório de Arqueologia, Universidade Federal de Goiás, www.museu.ufg.br/labarq/legislac/foto2.htm. In Minas Gerais, Richard Burton defined the almocafre as "the iron hoe which turns up the pebbles, and it appears in four shapes, the rounded-conical, the square, the lozenge, and the triangle." Burton, *Explorations*, 438.
58. Six oitavas required: Bertran, *Memória de Niquelândia*, 44; and half oitava: Russell-Wood, *Black Man*, 121.
59. Slaves with gamelas: Chaul, *Caminhos de Goiás*, 28; and cyclopes: Cunha Matos, as cited by Palacin, *Goiás*, 39. In the 1940s, Artiaga, *Geologia*, 185, observed the great pits left at Santa Luzia. On how slaves died, see M. Silva, *Quilombos*, 453.
60. Fubá, *pipocas*, and *guariroba*: Karasch, "História," 40. In Minas Gerais, the sale of fubá was prohibited in 1733 because when it was uncooked it "lay in the stomach in a congealed mass." Russell-Wood, *Black Man*, 118.
61. Both terms for communities of runaways were used in the captaincy of Goiás. M. Silva, *Quilombos*, 28–33. In 1740 the Overseas Council in Lisbon defined any habitation of more than five fugitive blacks as a quilombo. Ibid., 33. Map of quilombos: Mendes Rocha, *Atlas histórico*, 46.

62. Kalunga: Baiocchi, *Kalunga*, 27–41, 36–37 (maps); and M. Silva, *Quilombos*, 373–94. Both books include photographs of Kalunga.
63. Karasch, "Os quilombos do ouro," 246.
64. Pederneiras: ibid., 246–47.
65. Bico: ibid., 247.
66. Duro: ibid., 247.
67. Arraias: Cordeiro, *Arraias*, 14; and Teske, *A roda de São Gonçalo*.
68. Paranã River and Serra do Mocambo: Baiocchi, *Kalunga*, 22–26; and Karasch, "Os quilombos do ouro," 247, 249, 261–62n51.
69. Pilar and Muquém: Artiaga, *Geologia*, 191–92. Artiaga also reported on gold deposits throughout the valley of the Bagagem River, with vestiges of intense mining in Muquém.
70. Pilar: Karasch, "Os quilombos do ouro," 249; and Costa, "A escravidão." My thanks to José Mendonça Teles for the reference to this article from his personal archive at the SGC, Documentos Históricos de Goiás: Diversos.
71. São José: Karasch, "Os quilombos do ouro," 249–50.
72. Muquém: Karasch, "Os quilombos do ouro," 250.
73. Nossa Senhora da Abadia: "Dos quilombos fez-se kalunga."
74. Tesouras and Crixás: Karasch, "Os quilombos do ouro," 250–51.
75. Araguaia quilombo: AHU, cod. 1657, "Livro primeiro para registo de Portarias, ... para as Bandeiras, no Governo do ... José de Almeida de Vasconcelos de Sobral e Carvalho ... Portaria," Vila Boa, 1 September 1777. Quilombo of Carlota: Karasch, "Os quilombos do ouro," 252; Salles, *Economia e escravidão*, 290; and M. Silva *Quilombos*, 300–301. According to Silva, there was no quilombo of Carlota. It was actually a planned community. Upon the quilombo of Quariterê or of the Piolho being destroyed in 1795, a captain general transferred his ex-slaves to that location. They had been freed due to their advanced age. The community in Mato Grosso came to be called Carlota in honor of D. João VI's wife.
76. Mortes River: Karasch, "Os quilombos do ouro," 251; and Salles, *Economia e escravidão*, 288–89.
77. Ambrosio: Karasch, "Os quilombos do ouro," 251–52. A map of the quilombo of Ambrosio is in Mano, "Índios e negros," 536. According to Mano (535), "quilombos were located near rivers, half way between the waters and the forest," and their houses were built "around a *praça central*" (central square).
78. Death of Ambrosio: Karasch, "Os quilombos do ouro," 251–52; and Alencastre, *Anais*, 117.
79. Batieiro: Karasch, "Os quilombos do ouro," 252.
80. Mesquita: ibid. Russell-Wood, *Black Man*, 123, describes the skills of African gold miners in the Akan states of Ghana. Had these villagers also mined gold?
81. Santa Cruz: Salles, *Economia e escravidão*, 290.
82. Bandeira, 1733: ibid., 252.

83. Abaité: ibid., 252, 256.
84. Kayapó discovery: Karasch, "Os quilombos do ouro," 252–53.
85. Mano, "Índios e negros," 524, 539–42.
86. Decline of quilombos: McCreery, *Frontier Goiás*, 58–60.
87. Older slaves: ibid., 59–60. Typical runaways in Rio (1826–1837) were Central Africans and males (85 percent). Karasch, *Slave Life*, 305.

Chapter Eight

1. Congada: Karasch, "Central Africans," 149–51; Assunção, *A guerra dos Bem-te-vis*, 163, helped me to understand how diverse communities could celebrate a feast day while maintaining separate identities based on their dedication to a particular saint.
2. Religious obligations ignored: AHU 1003, caixa 11, letter of Vicar João Antunes de Noronha, Vila Boa, 1 October 1778.
3. Eduardo Hoornaert explores the dichotomy between the official hierarchy and popular lay religious practices in colonial Brazil in *A igreja no Brasil-Colônia (1550–1800)*. Two essential books on the history of the church in Goiás are J. Silva, *Lugares e pessoas*; and Castro, *Organização*. My thanks to Waldinice M. Nascimento for an initial copy of Castro's thesis.
4. Early chapels and Vila Boa's churches: Castro, *Organização*, 134, 143–47. On the first bishop, see chapter 5 herein. See also A. Borges and Palacin, *Patrimônio histórico de Goiás*, 7–21; and Coelho, *Guia dos bens*, with photographs and plans.
5. St. Ann's, 1759: Rosa and Britto, *Nos Passos da Paixão*, 70. Veiga Valle: A. Borges and Palacin, *Patrimônio histórico de Goiás*, 21 (statue of São Miguel). Churches: RJBN, manuscript section, 9, 2, 10, Silva e Souza, "Memoria," f. 35. See also Coelho, *Guia dos bens*, 40–43 (Boa Morte), 74–76 (São Francisco de Paula), 90–93 (Abadia), 86–89 (Carmo), and 94–97 (Santa Barbara). Coelho, *Guia dos bens*, 102–5, also includes São João Batista (1761) in Ferreiro. See Unes, *Veiga Valle*, for the museum and his sculptures.
6. Donations to avoid judge and reasons for small chapels: A. Borges and Palacin, *Patrimonio histórico de Goiás*, 14.
7. Santa Ana: Coelho, *Guia dos bens*, 52–55; and RJAN, IJJ9–501, doc. 25, Plano para reconstrucção do frontispicio e corpo da Cathedral pelo Capm. d'Engenheiros Joaquim Rodrigues de M. Jardim, 1874. Ruins of Santa Ana: AHG, Municípios, Goiás, caixa 1, "Exame a que se-procedeu com assistencia do Ex.mo Conselho sobre as ruinas da Igreja Cathedral de Santa Anna," Secretaria do Governo de Goyaz, Antônio Ferreira dos Santos Azevedo, 2 April 1833, and attached letter of José Rodrigues Jardim, 2 April 1833.

8. Meia Ponte's churches: A. Borges and Palacin, *Patrimônio histórico de Goiás*, 81–87; Saint-Hilaire, *Viagem*, 36.
9. Pilar, Crixás, Santa Luzia: A. Borges and Palacin, *Patrimônio histórico de Goiás*, 25–26, 23–24, 95–96; and Rosário, Santa Luzia: Castro, *Organização*, 155–56.
10. Santa Luzia: A. Borges and Palacin, *Patrimônio histórico de Goiás*, 95–96; and Castro, *Organização*, 155–56.
11. Dancing: SGC, Edital, Vicar João Antunes de Noronha, Vila Boa, 4 May 1773, ff. 64–65; and women dressing as men: Edital, Visitador José Correa Leitão, Vila Boa, 23 June 1784 (copy), ff. 98–99.
12. Burials in churches: SGC, Archive of the Curia, Compromisso da Irmandade de Nossa Senhora das Mercês dos Captivos do Arrayal de São Joaquim do Cocal anno de 1772, cap. 18; and use of hammock in taking slaves to burial area: Moraes, "Corpo místico," chap. 9, 25–27. Henceforth, citations to Moraes's dissertation, a copy of which Dr. Moraes kindly gave me, are by chapter and page number. Abandoned slaves: AHU, 1003, caixa 11, letter of Vicar João Antunes de Noronha, Vila Boa, 1 October 1778; and hidden burials of slaves: Moraes, "Corpo místico," chap. 4, 42.
13. Natividade: A. Borges and Palacin, *Patrimônio histórico de Goiás*, 53–60; and Nossa Senhora do Rosário dos Pretos: Pohl, *Viagem*, 271; and [Burchell], *Brasil do primeiro reinado*, 144.
14. Muquém: Bertran, *Memória de Niquelandia*, 46, 89–93. He quotes Padre Silva e Souza regarding the small chapel of Our Lady of Abadia, to which there was a pilgrimage each 15 August. Thus the pilgrimage tradition can be documented from 1812 on, but it was already practiced in the eighteenth century.
15. Northern churches: Castro, *Organização*, 183–84. For Traíras and São José do Tocantins, see Bertran, *Memoria de Niquelândia*, 30–31 (photos of Rosário and Conceição), and 40–43 (photos of Santa Efigênia).
16. In 1783 there had been twenty-one churches with sixteen affiliated chapels: RJIHGB, arq. 1.2.7, vol. 36, Ofício of Luiz da Cunha Menezes, Vila Boa, 15 February 1783, f. 267.
17. Modest churches: A. Borges and Palacin, *Patrimônio histórico de Goiás*, 7–9.
18. Oratorios: SGC, Século XVIII, Registros, Provisões, Vila Boa, 1795–1805: Provizão registered for Lourenço Antônio da Neiva, December of 1799, f. 22; and for Bartolomeu Lourenço da Silva, 12 March 1805, ff. 63, 80; and SGC, Pastorais, Editais . . . , 1771–1859, Meiaponte, provizão for Dona Petronilha do Amor Divino, registered 31 December 1804, ff. 77–78. Photograph of Fazenda Babilônia: A. Borges and Palacin, *Patrimônio histórico de Goiás*, 92.
19. The most comprehensive study of the colonial irmandades of Goiás is Moraes, "Corpo místico." On race mixture in brotherhoods, see Moraes, "Corpo místico," chap. 6, 7, and chap. 4, 24 (Nossa Senhora da Lapa).

20. Exclusion of those of Jewish descent and of pardos in the irmandade do Senhor dos Passos in Pilar: Moraes, "Corpo místico," chap. 4, 52–53, and chap. 4, 59–61 (list of white brothers). See also her study "Os passos dos irmãos," on the excluded in the irmandade, in Rosa and Britto, *Nos Passos da Paixão*, 34–45.
21. The Irmandade de São Miguel e Almas in Vila Boa required its members to be white persons, men as well as women. SGC, Archive of the Curia, Compromisso que ha de server na irmandade das Santas Almas . . . da Senhora Santa Anna . . . , 1736, with attached notes of 1733, 1735, and 1742–1743; and AHU, 1003, caixa 11, Irmandade do Gloriozo São Miguel e Almas of Crixás, 23 March 1792. See also Moraes, "Corpo místico," chap. 4, 10–15, and chap. 4, 18–23 (Santo Antônio). Military officers (alferes) who served as treasurers and procuradors for the Irmandade do Rosário: BFEG, Livro dos Termos de Mesa, City of Goiás, 14 May 1837, f. 44. The Confraria of the Republicans is in Lemes, "Na arena do sagrado."
22. Santissimo Sacramento: A. Borges and Palacin, *Patrimônio histórico de Goiás*, 18; Castro, *Organização*, 162–63, 167–69; and Moraes, "Corpo místico," chap. 4, 29–49. For petitions for processions, see SGC, Registro de Provisões, Portarias, Pastorais, etc., 1782–1868, Santa Luzia, 11 June 1821 and 25 May 1822, f. 85.
23. Procession order: Moraes, "Corpo místico," chap. 8, 33; and Lemes, "Na arena do sagrado."
24. Irmandades dos pardos: Moraes, "Corpo místico," chap. 6, 8–21; and São Gonçalo Garcia: Karasch, "Construindo comunidades."
25. Nossa Senhora do Rosário: Castro, *Organização*, 163; Moraes, "Corpo místico," chap. 7, 10; church in Traíras: Bertran, *Memória de Niquelândia*, 30; and in Meia Ponte in the chapel of the rosary of the pretos: Moraes, "Corpo místico," chap. 7, 4–14.
26. St. Benedict in Carmo: A. Borges and Palacin, *Patrimônio histórico de Goiás*, 15 and 58 (church in Natividade); Moraes, "Corpo místico," chap. 6, 21–32 (devotion and charter), and chap. 8, 6–7 (Three Kings).
27. Santa Efigênia: Bertran, *Memória de Niquelândia*, 41–43, including photo. He also has a photograph of a congada from the 1940s on page 35. See Moraes, "Corpo místico," chap. 7, 14–18, for a brief discussion of the devotion to her and its charter. This irmandade of crioulos also accepted "senhores e senhoras brancos."
28. Santa Efigênia, Traíras: Pohl, *Viagem*, 203–5, who reports that whites participated in the procession of blacks that celebrated Santa Efigênia's feast day. Photograph of church with cross: A. Borges and Palacin, *Patrimônio histórico de Goiás*, 34.
29. Holy Spirit: Pohl, *Viagem*, 202–3. For the Festa do Divino in Pirenópolis, see Brandão, *O divino*, 15–29; in Arraias: Cunha Matos, *Itinerario*, 1:240–44; and in the City of Goiás: Britto, Prado, and Rosa, *Os sentidos da devoção*.
30. Our Lady of Mercy, Cocal: Karasch, "Rainhas e juízas," 61–64.

31. Bororo: Moraes, "Corpo místico," chap. 5, 29; and Directorate: R. Almeida, *O diretório dos índios*, chap. 5, 149–225.
32. Franciscans and Vieira: J. Silva, *Lugares e pessoas*, 39–43; and Castro, *Organização*, 103–10.
33. Esmolares: J. Silva, *Lugares e pessoas*, 42; and Third Order of St. Francis in Meia Ponte: Saint-Hilaire, *Viagem*, 37.
34. J. Silva, *Lugares e pessoas*, 42.
35. Father Joseph: Saint-Hilaire, *Viagem*, 57.
36. Jesuit missions: J. Silva, *Lugares e pessoas*, 44–51; Castro, *Organização*, 105–10; and Apolinário, *Os Akroá*, 116 (map), 120–28; cattle fazendas: J. Silva, *Lugares e pessoas*, 49–50; and Cunha Matos, *Itinerario*, 2:147.
37. Akroá and Xacriabá: Saint-Hilaire *Viagem*, 62; Apolinário, *Os Akroá*, chap. 2, 91–158; Alencastre, *Anais*, 120–23; Chaim, *Aldeamentos indigenas*, 61–63, 100–101, 111–12; Tupinambá in Duro: Cunha Mattos, *Itinerario*, 2:163; AHGDD, no. 68, Correspondência Dirigida do Comandante das Armas, Raymundo José da Cunha Mattos, Mappa dos Indios Amigos . . . na Aldeia de S. José do Duro, Cadete João Manoel de Meneses, 29 December 1823, ff. 211–12; and RJBN, 9, 2, 10, Silva e Souza, "Memoria," f. 43.
38. A basic plan of the aldeia of Santa Ana in 1775 is reproduced in N. Reis, *Imagens de vilas*, 243. See also AHU, Ordens que deve executar . . . Jozé Rodrigues Freire na Commandancia do distrito do Rio das Velhas, Governor José de Almeida Vasconcelos e Sobral e Carvalho, Vila Boa, 27 January 1776; and AHG, document in restoration, letter of Governor Fernando Delgado Freire de Castilho, Vila Boa, 12 November 1816. Cost of four missions: RJBN, 9, 2, 10, Silva e Souza, "Memoria," ff. 42–43. Priests: SGC, Archive of the Curia, Matricula das Freguezias, Sacerdotes, e mais pessoas sugeitas á Jurisdicção Ecclez.a da Prelazia de Goyaz no anno de 1805–1817.
39. Rio das Pedras and Santa Ana: Saint-Hilaire, *Viagem*, 128–34, 142–47; RJBN, manuscript section, cod. 16.3.2, Notícia geral da capitania de Goiás, 1783; 200 Xacriabá: AHU, Goiás, Luis José de Brito, 17 October 1788; and Chaim, *Aldeamentos indigenas*, 101.
40. Santa Ana: Saint-Hilaire, *Viagem*, 142–47.
41. Portuguese Indian policy: Karasch, "Catequese e cativeiro"; Chaim, *Aldeamentos indígenas*, 78–98; and Hemming, *Amazon Frontier*, 62–80.
42. São José: Cost: RJBN, 9, 2, 10, Silva e Souza, "Memoria," f. 43. Plans of the mission are in Reis, *Imagens de vilas*, 241. Various nations and early history: Saint-Hilaire, *Viagem*, 63, 66 (self-identity as Panariá to distinguish themselves from blacks and whites); and Mead, "Caiapó do Sul," chap. 6, 226–84.
43. Priests at São José: SGC, Archive of the Curia, Matricula das Freguezias, Sacerdotes, 1805–1817. Padre Innocencio Joaquim Moreira de Carvalho, who was at São José from 1811 to 1817, is likely the priest mentioned by Saint-Hilaire

and Pohl. See chap. 8, note 51. According to Castro, *Organização*, 106–7, the Jesuits had also been at São José.
44. Location: Pohl, *Viagem*, 152; Saint-Hilaire, *Viagem*, 64.
45. Governor's house and mulatos: Saint-Hilaire, *Viagem*, 64.
46. Housing: Pohl, *Viagem*, 152–53; and Saint-Hilaire, *Viagem*, 64, 66; touros: RJBN, 9, 2, 10, Silva e Souza, "Memoria," f. 43; and Saint-Hilaire, *Viagem*, 71; and *jiraus* and mats for sleeping: Saint-Hilaire, *Viagem*, 66, 70; traditional housing: Ataídes, "A chegada do colonizador," 77.
47. Women and dances: Saint-Hilaire, *Viagem*, 66. In 1964 Maybury-Lewis recorded singing and dancing "in homage to the jaguar and to give a name to women." Cited in Ataídes, *Sob o signo da violência*, 118–19.
48. Contentment and diseases: Saint-Hilaire, *Viagem*, 66, 69.
49. Puhanca and baptism: Saint-Hilaire, *Viagem*, 67, 71; and Pohl, *Viagem*, 152.
50. Marriage: Saint-Hilaire, *Viagem*, 71; and at eight years: Pohl, *Viagem*, 153.
51. Absent priests: Saint-Hilaire, *Viagem*, 70. Pohl, *Viagem*, 152, 156–57, met a Padre Inocêncio at his plantation.
52. Night dancing: RJBN, 9, 2, 10, Silva e Souza, "Memoria," f. 43; and Pohl, *Viagem*, 152–53.
53. Bloodletting: Pohl, *Viagem*, 153; and Saint-Hilaire, *Viagem*, 71.
54. Burials: RJBN, 9, 2, 10, Silva e Souza, "Memoria," f. 43, also called attention to dancing for the dead. Burials by status in Cocal: Karasch, "Rainhas e juízas," 63; and Pohl, *Viagem*, 153.
55. Workdays, food redistribution: Saint-Hilaire, *Viagem*, 64–65.
56. Technologies: Saint-Hilaire, *Viagem*, 65; RJBN, 17, 2, 12, Goiás (Província de), 1835, Resolution of the Provincial Legislative Assembly, José Rodrigues Jardim (president), 23 July 1835; and charcoal and iron factory: Ataídes, *Sob o signo da violência*, 91–92. In 1835 Anna Luiza do Sacramento, who had taught spinning and weaving, retired with a pension of sixty thousand réis.
57. Days off, log races, and baskets: Saint-Hilaire, *Viagem*, 65–66. The *tora do buriti* race still occurs among the Jê. See Ataídes, "A chegada do colonizador," 79.
58. Leaders: Saint-Hilaire, *Viagem*, 64–65, 70–71; and Pohl, *Viagem*, 152, 154. The Kayapó were subject to a colonel in Vila Boa, who directed São José and other aldeias. Below him was the military officer resident in São José, who was a corporal and, according to Pohl, a cavalryman. He headed the local military detachment, including a soldier of the dragoons, both of whom belonged to the Company of Vila Boa, and fifteen pedestres, including two officers. The corporal had the authority to punish the Kayapó, putting the men in stocks (the tronco) and subjecting women and children to the palmatória, a wooden paddle with holes.
59. Dona Damiana: Saint-Hilaire, *Viagem*, 71–72; and Karasch, "Damiana da Cunha." See also Ataídes, "A chegada do colonizador," 72; and Mead, "Cayapó do Sul," chap. 7, 285–329.

60. São José, cost: RJBN, 9, 2, 10, Silva e Souza, "Memoria," f. 43; and governor's house at Maria I and São José: Pohl, *Viagem*, 156; and Saint-Hilaire, *Viagem*, 64.
61. Founding of Maria I: Pohl, *Viagem*, 156; and RJBN, 9, 2, 10, Silva e Souza, "Memoria," f. 43. The plan of Maria I in 1782 is in R. Almeida, *O diretório dos índios*, pl. 23, following 208, and 191–92. A more extended treatment of the Kayapó at Maria I is in Mead, "Cayapó do Sul," chap. 6, 226–84.
62. Kayapó visits and saudades: Saint-Hilaire, *Viagem*, 75; and Pohl, *Viagem*, 155–56.
63. Four communities: Giraldin, *Cayapó e Panará*, 92, and 99 (Damiana's grandparents).
64. Estimate of 2,400: Giraldin, *Cayapó e Panará*, 95.
65. Smallpox in 1811 and measles in 1819: ibid., 98; Manuel: RJIHGB, lata 48, doc. 3, Digressão q.e fez João Caetano da Silva natural de Meia Ponte, em 1817, para descobrir, como com eff.o descobrio, a nova Navegação entre a Capitania de Goiáz, e a de S. Paulo . . .; and removal to São José and 129 Indians: Chaim, *Aldeamentos indígenas*, 151–52.
66. Maria I: Pohl, *Viagem*, 156; plan of 1782 with Our Lady of Gloria: Reis, *Imagens de vilas*, 242.
67. Pohl, *Viagem*, 156; cattle: AMB, vol. 338, III-Bens, letter to Raymundo Nonnato Hyasinto from José Miguel, Aldeia Maria, 21 September 1821; and Saint-Hilaire, *Viagem*, 74; removal to Arinos in 1833–1834: Mead, "Caiapó do Sul," 322.
68. Sloth: Pohl, *Viagem*, 155–56; and hunger at São José: Pohl, *Viagem*, 152.
69. Nova Beira: RJBN, 9, 2, 10, Silva e Souza, "Memoria," f. 43; Chaim, *Aldeamentos indígenas*, 123–25; and Karasch, "Catequese e cativeiro," 400. It was extinguished under Governor Luiz da Cunha Meneses (1779–1783). See Chaim, *Aldeamentos indígenas*, 153.
70. Karajá and Javaé, in missions: Ataídes, *Sob o signo da violencia*; and Karasch, "Catequese e cativeiro," 403–9.
71. São Joaquim: Karasch, "Catequese e cativeiro," 409.
72. Carretão: Pohl, *Viagem*, 180–82; AMB, III-Bens, 4, Aldeia de São Pedro III do Carretão, O Comandante Domingos Gomes Albernós, Carretão, 13 May 1786; and RJBN, 9, 2, 10, Silva e Souza, "Memoria," f. 43. See also Ataídes, *Documenta indigena*, 172–83.
73. Xavante arrival and epidemics: a more complete description of the pacification and arrival of the Xavante is in Karasch, "Rethinking the Conquest," 481–85.
74. Population numbers: three thousand: AHU, no. 1002, caixa 4, Consulta do Conselho Ultramarino, 17 October 1788; and 3,500: RJBN, 9, 2, 10, Silva e Souza, "Memoria," f. 28. See also Pohl, *Viagem*, 181; and AHGDD, no. 68, Correspondência, Cunha Matos, de João Lourenço Oliveira, Carretão, 13 November 1824, f. 217; AHGDD, no. 68, Mapa de Toda a Gente q.e existe nesta Aldeia de São Pedro Terceiro da Carretão, 12 December 1824, ff. 194–98;

and AHGDD, no. 68, Relação da População da Aldeia de S. Pedro Terceiro do Carretão, sem data, ff. 208-10.
75. Description: Pohl, *Viagem*, 180; and measles: Cunha Matos, *Chorographia histórica*, 42-43.
76. Carretão's buildings: Ataídes, *Documenta indigena*, 176.
77. Priests: SGC, Archive of the Curia, Matricula das Freguezias, Sacerdotes, 1805-1817; and AHG, caixa 53, Relação de paramentos, que achei pertencentes ao Altar portatil . . . de Pedro 30 do Carretão, Francisco Xavier dos Guimarães Britto e Costa, Carretão, 18 July 1803.
78. Ritual goods: AHG, caixa 53, Britto e Costa, 1803; and AMB, 1676, Ministerio da Agricultura, Pedro III do Carretão, Relação dos Paramentos pertencentes ao culto Divino, que tem nesta Aldêa de Pedro 30 do Carretão . . . Gonçalo Pereira da Silveira, 6 June 1836.
79. Hats and wool cloth: ATC, livro 4076, Contadoria Geral do Rio de Janeiro, 4 August 1790, ff. 106-7.
80. Communal field: AMB, v. 338, III-Bens, Pedro 30—Carretão, Ralação [sic] dos mantimentos da Rossa Grande, do Comun plantada nesta Aldea de P. 30 no anno de 1795.
81. Flights and warfare: Pohl, *Viagem*, 237-38.
82. Confession: ibid., 181.
83. Daily work: ibid.
84. Use of money: ibid., 182.
85. Captain's complaint: ibid., 181.
86. *Casas de telha* and *capim*: AHGDD, no. 68, to General and Governador das Armas [Cunha Matos] from João Lourenço de Oliveira, Carretão, 13 November 1824, f. 217; and Xerente at Carretão: IHGG, pasta 002, doc. 51, Miguel Lino de Moraes, Livro 40 para o Imperio, Estrangeiros, e Marinha 1829 a 1831, no. 34, to José Clemente Pereira, from Miguel Lino de Moraes, City of Goiás, 25 August 1829.
87. Xavante craftsmen: AHGDD, no. 68, Relação da População da Aldeia de S. Pedro Terceiro do Carretão, ff. 208-10.
88. Dízimo: AMB, v. 338, III-Bens, Rendimento dos Dízimos da Aldeya de Pedro Terceiro do Carretão, 1821.
89. Individual work, 1824: AHGDD, no. 68, João Lourenço de Oliveira, Carretão, 28 October 1824; and AMB, 1676, Ministerio da Agricultura, Gonçalo Pereira da Silveira to João Gomes Machado Corumbá, Aldeia Carretão, 17 April 1829.
90. Forced labor and punishments: Karasch, "Catequese e cativeiro," 408; and flight to Rio das Mortes: Lazarin, "Aldeamento do carretão," 60.
91. Carretão, 1880s: Gallais, *Apóstolo do Araguaia*, 74-75.
92. Carretão, 1980s: Lazarin, "Aldeamento do Carretão," 52, 66-67; and update with photographs: Marlene Castro Ossami de Moura, "Os Tapuios do Carretão," in M. Moura, *Índios de Goiás*, 153-219, 368-73.

93. Graciosa, location: "Map of Historic Locations of Savánte-Serénte in East Central Brazil," in Nimuendajú, *Serente*, inside back cover; number of Xerente, Graciosa: Ataídes, *Sob o signo da violência*, 46–47. For contact, see chapter 2 herein.
94. Xerente desertion of Graciosa: IHGG, pasta 002, doc. 51, no. 34, to José Clemente Pereira from Miguel Lino de Moraes, City of Goiás, 25 August 1829, f. 17; mail: AMB, 1676, Min. Agricultura, Aldeia Carretão, Miguel Lino de Moraes, City of Goiás, 25 May 1831; and chapter 4 herein.
95. Christians in north, Aldeia Carolina: Cunha Matos, *Chorographia histórica*, 131–32; and census of 1832: RJAN, cod. 808, vol. 1, Censo da População da Província de Goiás, Cidade de Goiás, 30 May 1832, f. 96.
96. Numbers of mission Indians: RJBN, 11, 4, 2, Estatistica da Provincia de Goyáz remetida á Secretaria de Estado dos Negocios do Imperio . . . , 1825; and RJAN, cod. 808, vol. 1, Goiás, Censo da População, 30 May 1832, f. 96.
97. Hatred and resistance: AHGDD, no. 18, Correspondências Dirigida ao Comandante das Armas, Raimundo José da Cunha Matos, f. 49; and Araújo, *Memórias*, 212. As early as 1813, Xavante who had lived at Carretão were using "our arms," which made them very effective in their attacks. RJBN, I-31, 21, 9, Mangalhães, "Memoria," 1813. A Xavante attack near Salinas was also made by those formerly resident in Carretão. See Lazarin, "Aldeamento do Carretão," 151–52.
98. Nossa Senhora da Abadia, Kalunga: see chapter 7, note 73; and São Gonçalo: Teske, *A roda de São Gonçalo*. It is uncertain exactly when devotion to Our Lady and São Gonçalo began in the quilombos.

Chapter Nine

1. Secluded women: Pohl, *Viagem*, 194; Saint-Hilaire, *Viagem*, 42, 54; Gardner, *Travels*, 338; and Myscofski, *Amazons, Wives, Nuns, and Witches*, 76–79.
2. Concubines, defined: Myscofski, *Amazons, Wives, Nuns, and Witches*, 122–26.
3. Captive women: Salles, *Economia e escravidão*, 314n4, 314n7 (1611–1612); and Karasch, "Rethinking the Conquest," 473–76. See also chapter 3 herein. Useful for insights on the impact of conquest on indigenous women is Powers, *Women in the Crucible of Conquest*, in particular chapters 4–5.
4. Indigenous captive women: Nimuendajú, *Apinayé*, 120; Karasch, "Rethinking the Conquest," 473–74; on Xavante raids for Karajá women: see chapter 4, note 27; Karajá capture of Apinaje woman: RJIHGB, archive, lata 281, pasta 4, doc. 3, Diário, Thomaz de Souza Villa Real, 8 February 1793; and Krahô rapes: RJIHGB, arq. 1.5.16, Ribeiro, "Viagem," ff. 278–79; and Hemming, *Amazon Frontier*, 184–85.

5. On go-betweens, see Metcalf, *Go-Betweens*; and interpreters: Karasch, "Rethinking the Conquest," 472–77; and Pohl, *Viagem*, 248.
6. Violence against women: Alencastre, *Anais*, 110–12; RJIHGB, arq. 1.5.16, Ribeiro, "Viagem," f. 274; and Castelnau, *Expedição*, 230.
7. Cannibalism, Kayapó: Gallais, *Apóstolo do Araguaia*, 80–81. This was the only case the missionaries had encountered in the 1880s. For bloodletting, see Pohl, *Viagem*, 153.
8. Escrava Jozeva: Parente, *O avesso do silêncio*, 129.
9. Incest: AHU, Goiás, caixa 30, requerimento with attached documents of Manoel Lopes Chagas, "filho natural do Coronel Manoel Lopes Chagas, que este o legitimou [in 1769] por Provizão regia . . . ," 1785–1787. In 1783 the colonel was one of the captaincy's largest slaveholders, with eighty slaves. See Bertran, *Notícia geral*, 2:104.
10. Carlos Pinto: SGC, Prelazia de Goiás, Rol dos Culpados, 1800–1805, letra L, ff. 19 and 21; and SGC, Livro de Registro dos Denuncias, 1753–1794, "Termo de obrigação que asigna Carlos Pinto pardo forro de viver separado de sua Irmãa Margarida . . . ," Vila Boa, 22 November 1789, ff. 89v–90.
11. Women's work: Karasch, "Slave Women," 85–89; spinners and weavers: AHGDD, no. 68, Correspondência Dirigida do Comandante da Armas, Raimundo José da Cunha Matos, Relação da População do Arraial de Água Quente, ff. 112–21; the laundress Rosa Mina: C. Brito, *A mulher*; Saint-Hilaire, *Viagem*, 33; and Karasch, "Mujeres negras," 815–29.
12. Rural work: Karasch, "Slave Women," 85–87; and Wells, *Exploring and Travelling*, 187.
13. Retail trades and doces: Karasch, "Slave Women," 86–88.
14. Concubinage and lack of marriage: Myscofski, *Amazons, Wives, Nuns, and Witches*, 123–26; Saint-Hilaire, *Viagem*, 53; Pohl, *Viagem*, 194; and Gallais, *Apóstolo do Araguaia*, 107–9. Kathleen J. Higgins documents similar patterns of "libertinagem" in *"Licentious Liberty."*
15. Saint-Hilaire, *Viagem*, 53, 56, 125; and AHU, caixa 11, Vila Boa, 1 October 1778.
16. Saint-Hilaire, *Viagem*, 55–56. Note that the son of Fernando Delgado died in Paris while still young, when he was serving as an attaché to the Brazilian legation. Bernardo Élis, in the novel *Chegou o governador*, depicted a romance between D. Francisco de Assis Mascarenhas (governor 1804–1809) and Ángela Ludovico.
17. Military and women of color, Fernando José Leal: AHU, caixa 42, 11 March 1805.
18. SGC, Livro de Registro dos Denuncias, 1753–1794, Termo que faz o asigna José Rodriguez Xavier, homem branco, cazado de emenda de vida do publico concubinato . . . , Vila Boa, 22 January 1794, f. 93.
19. Ibid., Termo que faz, e asigna João Forquim, homem solteiro . . . , Vila Boa, 5 October 1784, f. 89.

20. Ibid., Termo de Obrigação que faz e asigna Pedro Dias, pardo forro de emenda da vida do publico concubinato..., Vila Boa, 30 December 1789, f. 90.
21. Ibid., Termo que faz, e asigna Aleixo José de Carvalho de emenda de vida do publico concubinato..., Vila Boa, 13 October 1791, f. 92; and Termo que faz Clara Maria Leite parda liberta de emenda de vida do publico concubinato, Vila Boa, 14 October 1791, f. 92.
22. Ibid., Termo de Separação e emenda de vida que faz Manoel Ferreira Rebouça [also Reboussa], homem cabra liberto..., Vila Boa, 6 March 1794, ff. 93–94.
23. Ibid., Termo que fas Joanna Rodrigues da Gama para se separar do ilicito trato que tem com Antônio de Souza Guimaraes presos nas Cadeias..., Vila Boa, 7 December 1778, f. 87.
24. Ibid., Termo [de confisão] que faz Ritta Gonçalvez da Silva preta liberta separada de seu marido..., Vila Boa, 16 March 1783, f. 88.
25. Prostitution: Saint-Hilaire, *Viagem*, 42. The two cases of freedwomen who abandoned the life of a public meretriz in Vila Boa are in SGC, Livro de Registro de Denuncias, 1753–1794, f. 88. See also Higgins, *"Licentious Liberty,"* 197–200, on slave women who sold food and drinks to miners in Sabará and also "exchanged sexual favors" for gold; and Luciano Figueiredo, *O avesso da memória*, 75–110, on freedwomen who were meretrizes. The most comprehensive portrait of an African woman who left the life of a prostitute to become a spiritual leader is Mott, *Rosa Egipcíaca*.
26. Village wanton: Nimuendajú, *Apinayé*, 120; and AHGDD, Correspondência, n. 35, Cunha Mattos, Cavalcante, 6 January 1824, ff. 48–51.
27. One description of this custom is in the historical novel by Bernardo Élis, *O tronco*, 25. Élis based his novels on the oral traditions of the region. After describing the multiple tasks of a colonel's servants, the descendants of slaves still maintained in slavery (1917–1918), he reported that the young girls of the household "prostituted themselves with the patrons, with the relatives of the patrons, with the camaradas." In other words, young servant women were "shared" by the men in the household.
28. Pohl, *Viagem*, 129; and Alencastre, *Anais*, 110. The violence of women against slave women and children is also addressed in M. Silva, *Quilombos*, 249–54.
29. On the "Vida Moral do Clero," or rather lack thereof, see Castro, *Organização*, 85–93; and priests in Natividade: Gardner, *Travels*, 338–39.
30. Amantes: Saint-Hilaire, *Viagem*, 53.
31. Jayme, *Famílias Pirenopolinas*, 5:411–13, and photos of those of African descent.
32. Ibid., 5:414.
33. Priest's women: see chapter 5, note 72; poor women: RJAN, caixa 315, pacote 2, document 7. Padre Manuel da Silva Álvares of Traíras, said to be the son of a Guiné woman, sheltered the poor and gave dowries to orphan women. Vicar of Santa Luzia: Saint-Hilaire, *Viagem*, 28. Was this a type of *recolhimento*? See Myscofski, *Amazons, Wives, Nuns, and Witches*, 159–67 and 162 (beatas); see

also Hoornaert, *A igreja no Brasil-Colônia*, 22, on beatas as "poor women who opted for virginity" outside of recolhimentos or convents.

34. Mattoso, in "Splendors and Improprieties," also found that local people were tolerant of their priests who had families. My thanks to David Higgs for a copy of Mattoso's paper. See also Saint-Hilaire, *Viagem*, 53; chapter 5, notes 72, 74.
35. A Dona da Casa who demanded respect because she was married: Saint-Hilaire, *Viagem*, 101. On the marriage requirement in the charters of irmandades, such as the Irmandade do Senhor dos Passos, see chapter 8.
36. Vila Boa couples, 1799: AMB, Vários Assuntos, vol. 353, no. 15, Freguesias, letter of the Vigario João Pereira Pinto Bravo to Governor Tristão da Cunha Menezes, Vila Boa, 22 May 1799.
37. More than half of the people of color who requested a *provisão de casar-se* were freedpersons. See table 16 for sources of these *provisões*.
38. Pardo marriages, Meia Ponte: SGC, Registro dos Papeis, 20 February 1798–February 1805, ff. 13–40.
39. Pohl, *Viagem*, 142.
40. Catarina: Karasch, "Slave Women," 87 and 95n23.
41. Dona Anna, requerimentos: AHU, Goiás, caixa 38, Lisbon, 19 September 1804; caixa 41, 10 December 1804, with attached document, Setubal, 9 June 1799; and caixa 43, 30 May 1806.
42. Women as tutors: AHU, no. 1013, caixa 7, 24 September 1790.
43. Dona Anna Francisca: AHU, Goiás, caixa 36, 22 January 1800.
44. Joanna Vieira de Souza: AHU, no. 1001, caixa 2, Traíras, 30 September 1791 and 17 April 1792.
45. Dona Brittes: AHG, no. 35, Documentos Diversos, 1799; and Director's Armário, 1799, Instruções-Portarias e outras da Corte ao Governador da Capitania de Goiás, ff. 62–64. She signed this document.
46. Pohl, *Viagem*, 141–42.
47. Blacks as beggars: BFEG, Livro de Obitos, Natividade, 1809–1859.
48. Large families: Jayme Jarbas, in his five-volume *Famílias Pirenopolinas*, organizes his genealogical history according to the major families of Meia Ponte. Among elite families there were numerous legitimate marriages with many children.

Chapter Ten

1. Useful vassals, requerimento of pardos (copy): AHU, Goiás, no. 1002, caixa 4, 7 January 1804, pacote, with attached testimony of Governor Tristão da Cunha Menezes, Vila Boa, 4 February 1803; and Castelnau, *Expedição*, 168.
2. Prejudice against pardos: ANTT, maço 600, Ministerio do Reino, Letra D, Camara da Vila Boa, 1 January 1783, signed Custodio Barrozo Basto, Antônio

Joze de Artiaga, Joze de Papoz [?] de Silva, and Joaquim Pereira Gayo [?] Peçanha. In 1785 the Camara of Vila Boa also asked that the mulato colonel be excluded from the interim government. According to the Camara, the oldest patent belonged to the mulato colonel, "who by his quality ought not to be admitted to the interim government." They also described the mulatos as "proud" by nature. AHU, caixa 25, Goiás, 1765–1799, Camara of Vila Boa, 31 December 1785; and Tristão da Cunha, 20 May 1789, with attached note of 5 July 1790, declaring that the patent of colonels does not give a mulato any right to be interim governor. Furthermore, they should "voluntarily" subject themselves to the "exclusion."

3. Saint-Hilaire, *Viagem*, 51, and n12.
4. Defect of color: AHU, Goiás, caixa 41, 1800–1807, requerimento of pardos with signatures, Vila Boa, 5 February 1803.
5. Higgins, *"Licentious Liberty,"* chap. 5, 145–74, provides a useful comparative study on manumission in another gold-mining region, especially with reference to "family-motivated manumissions of children" and women. As a result, two-thirds of the free population was made up of nonwhites in Minas Gerais (39–40).
6. Prospectors: Salles, *Economia e escravidão*, 290; the meia-sisa, or sisa, defined: Karasch, "Central Africans," 136–40; letter of liberty explained: Karasch, *Slave Life*, 335.
7. See table 17. Number of those who paid oitavas in gold: two paid 130–140s; eight, 110–120s; seven, 90–100s; four, 70–80s; six, 50–60s; fourteen, 30–40s; and seven, 10–20s. Those who paid in mil-réis are not included here. Anna Mina was freed for 160 oitavas of gold, paid in installments. The first agreement was made in 1781 and registered upon the final payment on 4 October 1792 (ff. 37–38). The largest amount was the 192 oitavas that Josefa Mina paid for her letter. The initial agreement was 14 April 1784; the letter was registered by João Ferreira, 2 March 1793, f. 57.
8. These letters of liberty were registered in the City of Goiás; BFEG, Cartório do Primeiro Ofício, 1792–1799. For the mulata Francisca Borges, see 26 September 1790, with registration on 18 June 1792, f. 10; and for Ana Maria, see 6 June 1792, with registration on 26 July 1793, f. 101.
9. José da Costa de Oliveira freed his niece Maria mulatinha, the daughter of Luiza. Cartório do Primeiro Ofício, 26 October 1793, f. 123. See also Maria crioula, 3 April 1793, ff. 84–85; Maria mulata, 30 July 1792, f. 23; and Hilaria, June 1792, ff. 6–7.
10. The use of baptism to record the liberty of a child is suggested in a "declaration of liberty" by Sebastião de Candea de Abreo and his wife, Marianna Pinta de Jesus, for Maria mulata, the legitimate daughter of Manuel de Candea and his wife, Anna Maria, pardos. Her father had paid thirty-two oitavas for her liberty at the time of baptism. The couple made this declaration due to the lack of a

baptismal certificate. The original letter was dated 27 January 1782; it was registered on 30 July 1792; Cartório do Primeiro Ofício, f. 23. Also freed at baptism were Thomazia mulata, 23 November 1792, f. 45; and Eugênio, 13 July 1792, f. 19. Eugênio's godmother, Antonia Maria Álvares, had paid a fourth of gold for his freedom. "Testamentary manumissions" were not always recorded in a notary's office. Higgins, *"Licentious Liberty,"* 148.

11. Felipa mulata's letter given by Antônio de Melo e Vazconcelos: Cartório do Primeiro Ofício, 1 April 1793, f. 83.
12. Salvador Nagô: Cartório do Primeiro Ofício, 24 December 1792, f. 48; and Anna Mina: 4 October 1792, ff. 37–38. Installments: the payment was fifty oitavas in 1789, followed by twenty oitavas in two payments in 1790; eleven oitavas in two payments in 1791, and nineteen oitavas in 1792, for a total of one hundred oitavas of gold. Cartório do Primeiro Ofício, 1792–1799, ff. 33–34; and Bonifacio crioulo, Cartório do Primeiro Ofício, 1792–1799, f. 13.
13. Esmeria: RJAN IJJ9, 535, Ministerio do Reino e Império, Goiás, Ofícios de diversas autoridades (1808–1829), to Manoel Ignacio de Sampaio from Joaquim Álvares de Oliveira, Meia Ponte, 28 October 1820; and José Mina: Cartório do Primeiro Ofício, 24 August 1763, registered 18 August 1792, f. 29.
14. João Martins Pimenta, Cartório do Primeiro Ofício, 20 June 1792, f. 12; José cabrinha, 4 October 1792, f. 38; and Roza crioula, 6 September 1792, f. 84.
15. Ana Maria parda: Cartório do Primeiro Ofício, 6 June 1792, registered 26 July 1793, f. 101. Women were also freed in Sabará; Higgins, *"Licentious Liberty,"* 219.
16. AMB, Documentos, Mapas Diversos, v. 342, Mappa das pessoas que contem a freguezia de São José do Tocantins no anno de 1798; and AMB, no. 353, Vários Assuntos, no. 15, João Pereira Pinto Bravo Vigario to Tristão da Cunha Menezes, Vila Boa, 22 May 1799.
17. AMB, Documentos, v. 342, Mappa das pessoas, São José do Tocantins, 1798.
18. Females freed in Brazil: Karasch, *Slave Life*, 345; and Higgins, *"Licentious Liberty,"* 152–54.
19. In Roman law an ingênuo (ingénua) was a freeborn person. "Liberto" defined a person who had been liberated. Apparently the census taker was familiar with Roman law when he used "ingênuo" in the census of 1825. See Conrad, *Children of God's Fire*, 491.
20. Resistance to conscription: McCreery, *Frontier Goiás*, 34–40.
21. In 1832 there were only 1,923 enslaved Africans. See appendix B, table B.10.
22. Karasch, "Tomás de Sousa Vila Real."
23. Karasch, "Antônio Moreira da Silva." Another black (crioulo) who served as a capitão do mato was Apolinario Ferreira, age forty, married, with a parda wife and three crioulo children. They lived in Traíras. AHGDD, no. 68, Correspondência Dirigida do Comandante da Armas—Raymundo José da Cunha Mattos, 1823–1824, Relação da População do Destrito de Traíras, f. 95.

24. Color, ethnicities, pedestres: AHU, caixa 30, correspondence regarding Antônio Lemos de Faria, captain of the pedestres of Goiás, 26 March 1773, who petitioned to return to the city of Angra on Terceira Island [the Azores], his homeland. In a letter of 27 March 1773 that denied his request, Manoel da Fonseca Brandão quoted a description of the pedestres as "Mestiços, cabras, vermelhos [reds], and Mulatos, who were continuously deserting." The alferes and captain were whites. See also AMB, 444, Praça de Militares, Pedestres, 1760–1783 [and 1790s].
25. AHU, caixa 30, correspondence regarding Antônio Lemos de Faria, captain of the pedestres of Goiás, 26 March 1773. Forty mestizos: ATC, 4076, Livro de registo das representações da Capitania de Goyaz . . . [1784–1805], 3.0 Prejuizo [to the Royal Fazenda], 26 April, 1785, f. 8. The places they guarded included São José de Mossâmedes, Aldeia Maria, Nova Beira, and Rio das Velhas. Of interest is that the Kayapó in the pedestres of Vila Boa were sent to guard the Kayapó in the missions.
26. AHU, Mappa da Companhia de Pedestres que guarnece a Capitania de Goyaz, Alferes Commandante, José da Silva Maldonado d'Heça (?), Quartel General d'Villa Boa, 14 January 1784, E:/043/003/0537, TIF, Goiás, CD-rom no. 4; AMB, 444, Pedestres, 1760–1783, also records their duties and locations where they served in the captaincy of Goiás. Luis Bras: AHG, document in restoration, Livro dos Ofícios, no. 16, Fernando Delgado Freire de Castilho to the Conde de Linhares, Vila Boa, 6 June 1811, f. 70. Discussion on using a pedestre to carry mail between provinces: ATC, 4078, Informaçõens da Capitania de Goyaz . . . [1784–1810], Contadoria Geral do Rio de Janeiro, f. 17.
27. Desertions of pedestres: AHU, caixa 30, Brandão, letter of 27 March 1773. Miguel de Souza Cabra, who had guarded the Kayapó, deserted the Aldeia Maria because he did not want to obey the sergeant commandant. RJIHGB, lata 48, doc. 3, Digressão que fez João Caetano da Silva, natural de Meia Ponte, em 1817, para descobrir, como com effeito descobrio, a nova Navegação entre a Capitania de Goiás, e a de São Paulo . . . , recounts the meeting with the Indians Captain Manuel and Captain Antônio. Manuel had been a pedestre in the time of Governor Tristão da Cunha Menezes (1783–1800) and had served in the Aldeia Maria when he deserted with Captain Antônio. By 1817 he was a chief of his people, as was Captain Antônio. Arquebuses used against the Canoeiro: AHGDD, no. 69, Origenais dos Comandantes dos Registros e Presídios da Província, 1823–1825, f. 114. In the aldeia do Duro were twelve "Arcabuses do Padrão velho, ja arruinados." AHGDD, no. 69, Origenais dos Comandantes, to Cunha Matos from João Manoel de Meneses, Cadete, Quartel de Duro, 4 February 1824, f. 41.
28. In contrast, Sergeant José Luis Pereira, who served in the bandeira that "conquered" the Kayapó and guarded them in the early 1780s, earned 375 réis per

day. AMB, 444, Pedestres, 1782 and 1780s. Other salaries for non-Indians are listed in Palacin, *Goiás*, 158.

29. Pardo regiments: see chapter 5. Patents of the pardos are at the AHU in Lisbon.
30. AHG, in restoration, Livro Ofícios, no. 15, to Conde de Linhares from Fernando Delgado Freire de Castilho, Vila Boa, 11 May 1811, ff. 67–70.
31. Ibid., f. 69; Henriques signatures: SGC, Archive of the Curia, Diocese de Goyaz, Registros, Vila Boa, 8 March–18 February 1805, Capitão Luis Gonçalves dos Santos, part of a Boa Morte burial, 1799. A copy of the requerimento of the pardos is archived in AHU, Goiás, no. 1002, caixa 4, 7 January 1804. Part of their petition is in Palacin, Garcia, and Amado, *História*, 188–89. Luís Palacin also wrote a short article, "Os homens pardos de Goiás à procura da cidadania," which carries no publication data. I would like to thank Geraldo da Silva Gomes of Araguaina for a copy of it.
32. Pardo services to crown: AHU, caixa 41, Goiás, 1800–1807, Minas de Goyaz, Vila Boa de Santa Anna, 5 February 1803, with attached signatures beginning with Miguel Álvarez da Ora with the response of the Overseas Council of 7 January 1804 that their requerimento would not have any progress (forward) and "their papers suppressed for now in the secretary of this Tribunal."
33. Poor pardo: AHG, Livro Ofícios, no. 15, to Linhares from Freire de Castilho, 11 May 1811, f. 69.
34. Ora and Chagas: AHG, in restoration, Ofícios, 1812, Ofício of Fernando Delgado Freire de Castilho, "Proposta dos Postos vagos da Capitania de Goyaz . . . ," Vila Boa, 14 November 1814, ff. 96–99. Governor João Manoel de Menezes reported that Captain Chagas of the infantry regiment of the pardos was the son of a colonel and was well established. AHU, Goiás, 1801–1803, caixa 44, Relação dos Postos, que provi por Patentes afim de ter os Corpos de Milicias completos na conformidade das Reais Ordens, Vila Boa, 20 April 1802.
35. Ana Mina's son: Moreyra, *Vida sertaneja*, 40; mulato priest, Jaraguá: Saint-Hilaire, *Viagem*, as cited in Palacin, Garcia, and Amado, *História*, 188. Álvares's wealth is suggested by the sisas for Traíras. In 1815 he bought ten slaves—two Minas, four cabras, three crioulos, and one mulato—for 493 oitavas of gold. AMB, Traíras, no. 175, 1815. On his being a son of a "pretta [sic] de Guine" and owning "slaves, cattle ranches, engenho, and all sorts of businesses," see RJAN, caixa 315, pacote 2, doc. 7, Queixas, Goiás, Traíras, 13 December 1821. Attached is a letter from Bishop Francisco dated 26 January 1825, attesting that he was still in Traíras and exemplarily fulfilling his duties. Registered with thirty-two slaves on the household list for Traíras: AHGDD, no. 69, Origenais dos Comandantes dos Registros e Présidios da Província, 1823–1825. His petition for the Order of Christ is in AHG, in restoration, Ofício of Fernando Delgado Freire de Castilho to the Marquez d'Aguiar via the Secretary of State, Negocios do Reino, no. 3, Vila Boa, 31 May 1816. Another copy is at RJAN, IJJ9-493, Ministério do Reino, Goiás, Ofícios dos Presidentes, 1808–1818, doc. 3, Vila

Boa, 31 May 1816. The official reason for the denial was that he had already received the exemption for the entrada of all commodities exported from the captaincy for ten years. For how the interior customs duties (entradas) functioned in Minas Gerais, see Alden, *Royal Government*, 303–4. Photograph of Bento Severiano da Luz: Jayme, *Famílias Pirenopolinas*, documentação fotográfica, following 5:450.

36. Pardo property owners: AHGDD, no. 68, Correspondência, Cunha Matos, 1823–1824, which includes household lists by name, color, occupation, and slave ownership (table 4).
37. RJBN, manuscript section, cod. 16.3.2, Notícia geral da capitania de Goiás, "Abitadores [sic] do Arraial de Santo Antônio, e Minas de São Félix de Carlos Marinho, e de toda a Freguezia, Repartidos em três classes de Brancos, Pardos, e Pretos," 1783, f. 155.
38. Small slaveholders, 1820s: AHG, Doc. Diversa, no. 68, Correspondência, Cunha Mattos, Mappas, Aguaquente, ff. 112–21v; Cocal, ff. 99–106; Pontal, ff. 175–85; São José, ff. 123–42; and Traíras, ff. 86–98.
39. Pardos, contraband trade to Salvador: ATC, no. 4076, Livro de registro das representações da capitania de Goyaz, Contadoria Geral do Rio de Janeiro, 9 August 1787, ff. 45–54. As petty traders: AHU, no. 1001, caixa 2, Goiás, 1734–1832, correspondence of Capitão Mor Antônio de Souza Telles e Menezes, 16 November 1793 and 14 April 1794; and AHGDD, no. 69, Origenais dos Comandantes dos Registros e Presídios da Província, 1823–1825.
40. AHU, no. 1002, caixa 4, Goiás, 1736–1825, copy of Devassa da morte accontecida a José Joaquim da Silva Prado, principiada atirar pelo Juis Ordinario da Natividade..., Vila Boa, 10 December 1804. In addition to a tailor and two shoemakers, a lawyer, a musician, and the businessman Cunha Mendes testified at the devassa. All were pardos. Lists of camaradas, who included freedmen: AHGDD, no. 69, Origenais dos Comandantes, 1823–1825; on camaradas and agregados: McCreery, *Frontier Goiás*, 198–202.
41. Vagabonds, gypsies, and criminals: McCreery, *Frontier Goiás*, 68–69, 196–97, 205 (disorderly conduct by women). Complaint of Judge José Joaquim Leite Pereira to Governor Fernando Delgado Freire de Castilho, regarding the "scandalous liberty" with which freedmen and captives openly carried knives, being the cause of many repeated crimes: RJAN, IJJ9, 535, Ministerio do Reino, Ofícios, Meia Ponte, 18 September 1818.
42. Henriques, 1789: AHU, Mappa em que Tristão da Cunha Menezes... apresenta das Tropas..., 1789. Each company also had a captain, lieutenant, alferes, sergeant, flag bearer, furriel, drummer, and five corporals. See also chapter 5, note 65; and Karasch, "Guiné," 176–82.
43. Henriques of São José do Tocantins and Captain Luis Gonçalves dos Santos: SGC, Archive of the Curia, part of a Boa Morte burial, 1799; and 1805: SGC, Archive of the Curia, attached to Diocese de Goyaz, Registros, Vila Boa,

8 March 1805, Lista da Companhia de Infantaria Auxiliar do Arraial de S. José, formada dos Crioulos e Pretos Minas forros . . .; and AHGDD, no. 68, Correspondência Dirigida do Comandante da Armas—Raimundo José da Cunha Matos, Relação da População do Arraial de São José do Tocantins, 1823-1824, f. 134v.

44. Henriques occupations, 1820s: table 21 herein, which is based on AHGDD, no. 66, Relações do Regimento dos Henriques, Governo das Armas de Goiás, Regimento de Infantaria Miliciana de Henriques, 1823-1824. A copy is also in Karasch, "Guine," 179-80. Salles, *Economia e escravidão*, 292, lists occupations of black freedmen as overseers on the fazendas, *chefes* of sugar mills, and administrators of slaves. In 1783 one freedman directed the work of twelve slaves on a mine. But their best opportunities were in the pastoral industry. A freedman could raise a given quota of young animals and eventually become a property owner after years of services. McCreery, *Frontier Goiás*, 201-2, explains how a cowboy could build up his own herd by keeping one-quarter of the calves.

45. A longer survey of the occupations of freeborn and freed women of color is in Karasch, "Free Women of Color," 249-52. A fine description of the workday of rural women in Goiás is in McCreery, *Frontier Goiás*, 204. Photographs of a spinning wheel and spindles are in Parente, *O avesso do silêncio*, 62.

46. Pedroso, "Avá-Canoeiro: A história do povo invisível," 123.

47. Bens do vento: AMB, Goiás, no. 175, Escravos, Traíras (1810-1822), 1810, f. 1 [?]; and 1815, ff. 2-3. For a further explanation, see Conrad, *Children of God's Fire*, 322-30.

Conclusion

1. McCreery, *Frontier Goiás*, 15.
2. Ibid., 21.

Bibliography

Archives and Manuscript Collections

Lisbon, Portugal

AHM	Arquivo Histórico Militar
AHU	Arquivo Histórico Ultramarino
ANTT	Arquivo Nacional da Torre do Tombo
ATC	Arquivo Histórico do Tribunal de Contas
GEAEM	Gabinete de Estudos Arqueológicos de Engenharia Militar, Arquivo do Desenho (and maps)
LBA	Biblioteca da Ajuda
LBN	Biblioteca Nacional

London, England

KEW	Kew Archives, Directors' Correspondence, vol. 66, South American letters, William John Burchell, 1828–1831

Vienna, Austria

VMV	Museum für Völkerkunde

Brasília, D.F.

BCD	Camara dos Deputados, Seção das Obras Raras da
CENAGRI	Centro Nacional de Informação Documental Agricola; formerly the Biblioteca Nacional de Agricultura
FUNAI	Fundação Nacional do Indio, documents section and library
Senado	Library of the Senate

Goiás, City of

AMB	Museu das Bandeiras
BFEG	Biblioteca da Fundação Educacional da Cidade de Goiás (Arquivo Frei Simão Dorvi)
DGAG	Diocese de Goiás, Arquivo Geral, Orfenato de São José

Goiânia

AHG	Arquivo Histórico do Estado de Goiás
AHGDD	Arquivo Histórico do Estado de Goiás, Documentação Diversa

IHGG	Instituto Histórico e Geográfico de Goiás
SGC	Sociedade Goiana de Cultura, Instituto de Pesquisas e Estudos Históricos do Brasil-Central

Rio de Janeiro

RJAMC	Arquivo Metropolitana da Curia, Bispado do Rio de Janeiro
RJAN	Arquivo Nacional
RJBN	Biblioteca Nacional do Brasil
RJCOC	Casa Oswaldo Cruz
RJIHGB	Instituto Histórico e Geográfico do Brasil
RJMI	Museu do Indio

São Paulo

SPBM	Biblioteca Mario de Andrade, Seção de Obras Raras e Especiais
SPIHG	Instituto Histórico e Geográfico de São Paulo

Washington, DC

LC	Library of Congress
OL	Oliveira Lima Library, Catholic University of America

Printed Primary Sources and Travel Narratives

Alincourt, Luiz d'. *Memória sobre a viagem do porto de Santos à cidade de Cuiabá*. 1818. Reprint, Belo Horizonte: Ed. Itatiaia, 1975.

Audrin, Frei José M. *Os sertanejos que eu conheci*. Rio de Janeiro: José Olympio, 1963.

Baena, Antônio L. Monteiro. *Ensaio corográfico sôbre a Provincia do Pará*. Pará: Typ. a de Santos & Menor, 1839.

Barata, Francisco José Rodrigues. "Memoria em que se mostram algumas providencias tendentes ao melhoramento da agricultura e commercio da capitania de Goyaz." *Revista do Instituto Histórico e Geographico Brasileiro* 11, 2nd ed. (Rio de Janeiro, 1871): 336–65.

Berford, Sebastião Gomes da Silva. *Roteiro e mapa da viagem da cidade de S. Luiz do Maranhão até a corte do Rio de Janeiro feita por ordem do governador, e capitão general daquella capitania*. Rio de Janeiro: Impressão Regia, 1810.

[Berthet, Frei Michel Laurent Berthet]. "Uma viagem de Missão, escrita por Frei Michel Laurent Berthet, em 1883." (1890). Translated by Laura Chaer. In *Memórias Goianas*, 1:109–70. Goiânia: Editora Centauro, 1982.

Bertran, Paulo, ed. *Notícia geral da capitania de Goiás*. 2 vols. Goiânia: Ed. da

Universidade Católica de Goiás and Universidade Federal de Goiás; Brasília: Solo Editores, 1997.
"Breve reflexão sobre o meio eficaz de se remediar a decadência da Capitania de Goiáz." *Revista do Instituto Histórico e Geographico Brasileiro* 55, pt. 1 (1892): 399-402.
Brotero, Frederico de Barros. "Uma viagem a Goiaz em 1867." *Revista do Instituto Histórico e Geográfico de São Paulo* 38 (1940): 21-51.
[Burchell, William John]. *O Brasil do primeiro reinado visto pelo botânico William John Burchell, 1825/1829.* Ed. Gilberto Ferrez. Rio de Janeiro: Fundação João Moreira Salles, Fundação Nacional Pró-Memória, 1981.
Burton, Richard F. *Explorations of the Highlands of Brazil; with a Full Account of the Gold and Diamond Mines . . .* Vol. 1. London: Tinsley Brothers, 1869.
Caiado, Leolídio di Ramos. *Dramas do oeste: História de uma excursão nas regiões da Ilha do Bananal, em 1950.* Goiânia: Oriente, 1974.
Carneiro, João Roberto Ayres. "Itinerário da viagem da expedição exploradora e colonisadora ao Tocantins em 1849." *Anais da Biblioteca e Archivo Publico do Pará* 7 (1910): 5-197.
Casal, Manuel Aires de. *Corografia Brasílica ou relação histórico-geográfica do reino do Brasil.* Rio de Janeiro: Impressão Regia, 1817. Reprint, Belo Horizonte: Ed. Itatiaia, 1976.
Castelnau, Francis de. *Expedição às regiões centrais da América do Sul.* Translated by Olivério M. de Oliveira Pinto. Belo Horizonte: Itatiaia, 2000.
———. *Expédition dans les parties centrals de l'Amérique du Sud, de Rio de Janeiro a Lima, et de Lima au Para; . . . Pt. 2, Vues et scènes.* Les planches lithographiés par Champin. Paris, 1852-1853.
Cook, William Azel. *Through the Wildernesses of Brazil by Horse, Canoe, and Float.* London: T. Fisher Unwin, 1911.
Coudreau, Henri [Anatole]. *Voyage au Tocantins-Araguaya, 31 décembre 1896-23 mai 1897.* Paris: A. Lahure, 1897.
Couto de Magalhães, José Vieira. *Viagem ao Araguaya.* 3rd ed. São Paulo: Companhia Editora Nacional, 1934.
Cruls, L., and Brasil, Comissão Exploradora do Planalto Central. *Relatorio apresentado a o ex. o sr. ministro da industria, viação e obras publicas por L. Cruls . . .* Rio de Janeiro: H. Lombaorts, 1894.
Cruls, Luiz. *Planalto central do Brasil.* 3rd ed. Rio de Janeiro: Livraria José Olympio Editôra, 1957. First ed. published 1894.
Cunha Matos, Raimundo José da. *Chorographia histórica da província de Goyaz.* 1874. Goiânia: Gráfica Editora Líder, 1979.
———. *Itinerario do Rio de Janeiro ao Pará & Maranhão, pelas provincias de Minas Gerais e Goiaz.* 2 vols. Rio de Janeiro: Typ. Imperial, 1836.
Debret, Jean Baptiste. *Voyage pittoresque et historique au Brésil: Séjour d'un artiste*

français au Brésil, depuis 1816 jusqu'én 1831. 3 vols. Paris: Firmin Didot Frères, 1834–1839.
Dodt, Gustavo Luiz G. *Descripção dos rios Parnahyba e Gurupy*. São Paulo: Companhia Editora Nacional, 1939.
Eschwege, Wilhelm Ludwig von. *Pluto brasiliensis*. Translated by Domício de Figueiredo Murta. 2 vols. Belo Horizonte: Ed. Itatiaia, 1979.
Fleming, Peter. *Brazilian Adventure*. New York: Charles Scribner's Sons, 1934.
Fonseca, João Severiano. *Viagem ao redor do Brasil, 1875–1878*. 2 vols. Rio de Janeiro: Biblioteca do Exército Editora, 1986.
Franco, Vírgilio Martins de Mello. *Viagens pelo interior de Minas Geraes e Goyaz*. Rio de Janeiro: Imprensa Nacional, 1888.
Gardner, George. *Travels in the Interior of Brazil, Principally Through the Northern Provinces, and the Gold and Diamond Districts, During the Years 1836–1841*. London, 1846. Reprint, New York: AMS Press, 1970.
Gomes, Dr. Vicente Ferreira. "Itinerario da Cidade da Palma, Em Goyaz, á Cidade de Belem no Pará, pelo Rio Tocantins, e breve noticia do norte da provincia de Goyaz." *Revista do Instituto Histórico e Geographico Brasileiro* 25 (1862): 485–513.
Henderson, James. *A History of Brazil: Comprising its Geography, Commerce, Colonization, Aboriginal Inhabitants, &c. &c. &c.* London: Longman, Hurst, Rees, Orme, and Brown, 1821.
Jardim, Joaquim Rodrigues de Moraes. *O Rio Araguaya: Relatorio de sua exploração pelo Major D'Engenheiros Joaquim R. de Moraes Jardim precedido de um resumo historico sobre sua navegação . . . e seguido de um estudo sobre os indios que habitam suas margens pelo Dr. Aristides de Souza Spinola Presidente de Goyaz*. Rio de Janeiro: Typ. Nacional, 1880.
Krause, Fritz. "A viagem do Dr. Fritz Krause ao Araguaya [1909]." *Revista do Instituto Histórico e Geographico Brasileiro* 73, pt. 1 (1910): 259–75.
Lago, Antônio Florencio Pereira do. *Relatorio dos estudos da commissão exploradora dos rios Tocantins e Araguaia apresentado pelo major do Corpo de estado maior de 1a classe . . . agosto de 1875*. Rio de Janeiro: Typographia Nacional, 1876.
Leal, Oscar. *Viagem ao centro do Brazil: Impressões*. Lisboa: Typ. Largo do Pelourinho, 188?.
———. *Viagem ás terras Goyanas (Brasil Central)*. Edição facsimile. Lisbon: Typ. Minerva Central, 1892. Reprint, Goiânia: Editora UFG, 1980.
———. *Viagem a um país de selvagens*. Lisbon: Antonio Maria Pereira, 1895.
Lelong, [Father] Maurice Hyacinthe. *Symphonie brésilienne*. Paris: Frédéric Chambriand, 1951.
Macintyre, Archie. *Down the Araguaya: Travels in the Heart of Brazil*. London: Religious Tract Society, n.d.

Magalhães, Amilcar A. Botelho de. *Pelos sertões do Brasil*. Porto Alegre: Edição da Livraria do Globo, 1930.

Magalhães, José Vieira Couto de. *O selvagem*. São Paulo: Livraria Magalhães, ca. 1913.

———. *Viagem ao Araguaia*. 7th ed. São Paulo: Editora Nacional, 1975. First edition published 1934.

Menezes, José Pedro Cesar de. "Topographia: Roteiro para seguir a melhor Estrada do Maranhão para a Côrte do Rio de Janeiro [1810]." *Revista do Instituto Histórico e Geographico Brasileiro* 3, no. 12 (1841): 512–14.

Moura, Ignacio Baptista de. *De Belém a S. João do Araguaya: Valle do rio Tocantins*. Rio de Janeiro: H. Garnier, 1910.

Neiva, Artur, and Belisário Pena. *Viagem científica pelo norte da Bahia, sudoeste de Pernambuco, Sul do Piauí e de norte a sul de Goiás*. Brasília: Academia Brasiliense de Letras, 1984.

Peregrino, Umberto. *Imagens do Tocantins e da Amazônia*. Rio de Janeiro: Companhia Editora Americana, 1942.

Pimentel, Antônio Martins de Azevedo. "O Brazil Central." *Revista do Instituto Histórico e Geographico Brasileiro* 68, pt. 2 (1907): 253–376.

[Pires de Campos, Antônio]. "Breve noticia que dá o Capitão Antonio Pires de Campos do gentio barbaro que ha na derrota da viagem das minas do Cuyabá e seu reconcavo, . . . até o dia 20 de Maio de 1723." *Revista do Instituto Histórico e Geographico Brasileiro* 25 (1a trimestre de 1862): 437–49.

Pohl, Johann Emanuel. *Viagem no interior do Brasil*. Translated by Milton Amado and Eugênio Amado. Belo Horizonte: Itatiaia, 1976.

"Regimento pelo qual o governador Bernardo Pereira de Berredo mandou descobrir o curso do rio Tocantins 1719." *Revista do Instituto Histórico e Geographico Brasileiro* 46, pt. 1 (1883): 177–81.

"Relatorios dos governos da província de Goiás, 1835–1843." In *Memórias Goianas*, no. 3. Goiânia: UCG, 1986.

Rendu, Alphonse. *Etudes topographiques, médicales et agronomiques sur le Brésil*. Paris: J. B. Baillière, 1848.

[Ribeiro, Francisco de Paula]. "Descripção do territorio de Pastos Bons, nos sertões do Maranhão: Propriedades dos seus terrenos, suas producções, caracter dos seus habitantes colonos, e estado actual dos seus estabelecimentos . . . 29 março 1819." *Revista do Instituto Histórico e Geographico Brasileiro* 12 (1849; 2nd ed., 1874): 41–86.

———. *Francisco de Paula Ribeiro: Desbravador dos sertões de Pastos Bons: A base geográfica e humana do Sul do Maranhão*. Edited by Adalberto Franklin and João Renôr F. de Carvalho. Imperatriz, MA: Ética, 2007.

———. "Memória sobre as nações gentias que presentemente habitam o continente do Maranhão; Analyse de algumas tribus mais conhecidas; Processo de suas hostilidades sobre os habitantes: Causas que lhes tem difficultado a reducção, e unico methodo que seriamente poderá reduzil-as . . . [1819]."

  Revista do Instituto Histórico e Geographico Brasileiro 3 (1841; reprinted 1860), no. 10, 184–97; no. 11, 297–322; no. 12, 442–56.

———. "Roteiro da viagem que fez o Capitão Francisco de Paula Ribeiro a's [sic] fronteiras da capitania do Maranhão e da de Goyaz no anno de 1815 em serviço de S. M. Fidelissima." *Revista do Instituto Histórico e Geographico Brasileiro* 10, 12 (1848; 2nd ed., 1870): 5–80.

Rimini, P. Savino da. *Tra i selvaggi dell'Araguaya: Memorie illustrate dei miei 29 anni di missione.* Ancona: Scuola Tipografica Francescana, 1925.

Rodrigues, Lysias. *O rio dos Tocantins.* 2nd ed. Palmas, Tocantins: Alexandre Acampora, 2001.

———. *Roteiro do Tocantins.* 4th ed. Palmas, Tocantins: Alexandre Acampora, 2001.

Rugendas, Johann M. *Rugendas e a viagem pitoresca através do Brasil.* Translated by Sérgio Milliet. Rio de Janeiro: A Casa do Livro, 1972.

Saint-Hilaire, Auguste de. *Viagem à provincia de Goiás.* Translated by Regina Regis Junqueira. Belo Horizonte: Ed. Itatiaia, 1975.

Segurado, Joaquim Theotônio. "Memória econômica e política sobre o comércio ativo da capitania de Goiás [1806]." In *Memórias Goianas*, vol. 1. Goiânia: Centauro, 1982.

Segurado, Rufino Theotonio. "Viagem de Goyaz ao Pará [27 March 1848]." *Revista do Instituto Histórico e Geographico Brasileiro* 10 (1848; 2nd ed., 1870): 178–212.

Silva, Hermano Ribeiro da. *Nos sertões do Araguaia.* São Paulo: Edições Cultura Brasileira, 1935.

Silva, J. Norberto de Souza e. "Biographia Damiana da Cunha." *Revista do Instituto Histórico e Geographico Brasileiro* 24 (1861): 525–38.

Silva e Souza, Padre Luiz Antônio da. "Memoria sobre o descobrimento, governo, população, e cousas [sic] mais notaveis da capitania de Goyaz [1812]." *Revista Trimensal de Historia e Geographia do IHGB*, no. 16 (40 trimestre de 1849): 71–139.

Spix, Johann Baptiste von, and Karl Friedrich Philipp von Martius. *Viagem pelo Brasil.* Translated by Lucia Furquim Lahmeyer. 2 vols. Rio de Janeiro: Imprensa Nacional, 1938.

———. *Viagem pelo Brasil, 1817–1820: Excertos e ilustrações.* São Paulo: Edições Melhoramentos, 1968.

Tapie, Père Marie Hilaire. *Chevauchées à travers déserts et forêts vierges du Brésil inconnu.* Paris: Librairie Plon, 1928.

———. *Chez les Peaux-Rouges: Feuilles de route d'un missionnaire dans le Brésil inconnu.* Paris: Librairie Plon, 1926.

[Vila Real, Tomás de Sousa]. "Viagem de Thomaz de Souza Villa Real pelos rios Tocantins, Araguaya e Vermelho." *Revista do Instituto Histórico e Geographico Brasileiro* 11 (1848) [2nd ser., 4 (Rio de Janeiro, 1891)]: 401–44.

Waibel, Lee. *Uma viagem de reconhecimento ao sul de Goiás . . .* Rio de Janeiro:

Conselho Nacional de Geografia, 1949; separated from the *Revista Brasileira da Geografia*, no. 3, ano 9.

Walle, Paul. *Au Brésil: Etats de Goyaz et de Matto Grosso*. Paris: E. Guilmoto, 1912.

Wells, James W. *Exploring and Travelling Three Thousand Miles through Brazil from Rio de Janeiro to Maranhão* . . . 2 vols. Philadelphia: J. B. Lippincott, 1886.

Published and Unpublished Secondary Sources

Abreu, Euripedes Balsanulfo de Freitas e. "Contatos interetnicos em Goiás colonial." Master's thesis, Federal University of Goiás, 1992.

Abreu, Martha. *O império do divino: Festas religiosas e cultura popular no Rio de Janeiro, 1830–1900*. Rio de Janeiro: Nova Fronteira, 1999.

Adonias, Isa. *A cartografia da Região Amazônica—Catálogo descritivo (1500–1961)*. Vol. 2. Rio de Janeiro: Conselho Nacional de Pesquisas, Instituto Nacional de Pesquisas da Amazônia, 1963.

———. *Fauna e flora brasileira, séculos XVIII*. Rio de Janeiro: Spala Editora, 1986.

Aguiar, Luciana. *Olhos d'Água: A tradição artisanal da tecelagem*. Olhos d'Água: ACORDE, Associação Comunitária de Desenvolvimento Sustentável de Olhos d'Água [2000?].

Alden, Dauril. *Royal Government in Colonial Brazil*. Berkeley: University of California Press, 1968.

Alencastre, José Martins Pereira de. *Anais da provincia de Goiás*. 1863. Reprint, Brasília: Ed. Gráfica Ipiranga, 1979. First published in *Revista do Instituto Histórico e Geographico Brasileiro*, 1864.

Almeida, Rita Heloísa de. *O diretório dos índios*. Brasília: Ed. UnB, 1997.

Almeida, Victor Coelho de. *Goiaz: Usos, costumes, riquezas naturais*. São Paulo: Empresa gráfica da "Revista dos tribunais," 1944.

Amantino, Marcia. *O mundo das feras: Os moradores do sertão oeste de Minas Gerais—século XVIII*. São Paulo: Annablume, 2008.

Apolinário, Juciene Ricarte. *Escravidão negra no Tocantins colonial: Vivências escravistas em Arraias (1739–1800)*. Goiânia: Editora Kelps, 2000.

———. *Os Akroá e outros povos indigenas nas fronteiras do sertão*. Goiânia: Editora Kelps, 2006.

Araújo, José de Sousa Azevedo Pizarro e. *Memórias históricas do Rio de Janeiro*. Vol. 9. Rio de Janeiro: Imprensa Nacional, 1948.

Artiaga, Zoroastro. *Contribuição para a história de Goiaz*. Goiânia: Departamento Estadual de Cultura, 1947.

———. *Dos indios do Brasil Central*. Uberaba: Gráfico Triangulo, 1948?.

———. *Geografia econômica, histórica e descritiva do estado de Goiaz*. 2 vols. Goiânia: Tip. Triangulo, 1951.

———. *Geologia económica de Goiaz*. Uberaba: Estabelecimento Gráfico Triangulo, 1947.
Assis, Wilson Rocha. *Estudos de história de Goiás*. Goiânia: Editora Vieira, 2005.
Assunção, Matthias Röhrig. *A guerra dos Bem-te-vis: A balaiada na memória oral*. São Luís, MA: SIOGE, 1988.
Ataídes, Jézus Marco de. "A chegada do colonizador e os Kayapó do sul." In *Índios de Goiás: Uma perspectiva histórico-cultural*, edited by Marlene Castro Ossami de Moura, 51–88. Goiânia: UCG, Editora Kelps, Editora Vieira, 2006.
———. *Documenta indígena do Brasil Central*. Goiânia: Editora UCG, 2001.
———. *Sob o signo da violência: Colonizadores e Kayapó do sul no Brasil Central*. Goiânia: Editora UCG, 1998.
Audrin, Frei José M. *Entre sertanejos e indios do norte, o bispo-missionário Dom Domingos Carrérot, O. P.* Rio de Janeiro: AGIR Editora, 1946.
Augustat, Claudia, ed. *Beyond Brazil: Johann Natterer and the Ethnographic Collections from the Austrian Expedition to Brazil (1817–1835)*. Vienna: Museum für Völkerkunde, 2013.
———. "In the Shadow of Johann Natterer: Johann Emanuel Pohl's Ethnographic Collection." Copy of article or chapter, pp. 59–66, given to me at the Museum für Völkerkunde, 2013.
Azevedo, Francisco Ferreira dos Santos. *Annuario historico, geographico e descriptivo do estado de Goyaz para 1910*. Uberaba-Araguary-Goyaz: Livraria Século XX, 1910. Reprint, Brasília: SPHAN/8a DR, 1987.
Azevedo, Pedro Cordolino Ferreira de Azevedo. *D. Francisco: O bispo cego*. Rio de Janeiro: Ministério da Educação e Cultura, Serviço de Documentação, 1954.
Baiocchi, Mari de Nasaré. *Kalunga: Povo da terra*. Brasília: Ministério da Justiça, Secretaria dos Direitos Humanos, 1999.
———. *Negros de Cedro: Estudo antropologico de um bairro rural de negros em Goiás*. São Paulo: Editora Atica, 1983.
Baldus, Herbert. *Tapirapé: Tribo Tupí no Brasil Central*. São Paulo: Companhia Editora Nacional, 1970.
Bertran, Paulo. *Cidade de Goiás, patrimônio da humanidade: Origens*. Brasília: Editora Verano; Sáo Paulo: Editora Takano, c. 2001.
———. *Formação econômica de Goiás*. Goiânia: Oriente, 1978.
———. *História da terra e do homem no planalto central: Eco-história do Distrito Federal do indigena ao colonizador*. Brasília: Editora UnB, 2011.
———. *Memória de Niquelândia*. Brasília: Fundação Nacional Pró-Memória, 1985.
Blomberg, Rolf. *Chavante: An Expedition to the Tribes of the Mato Grosso*. London: Allen & Unwin, 1960.
Borges, Ana Maria, and Luís Palacin. *Patrimônio histórico de Goiás*. 2nd ed. Brasília: SPHAN/Pró-Memória, 1987.

Borges, Mônica Veloso. "Diferenças entre as falas feminina e masculina no Karajá e em outras linguas brasileiras: Aspectos tipológicos." *Liames* 4 (Spring 2004): 103-13.
Boschi, Caio César. *Os leigos e o poder: Irmandades leigas e política colonizadora em Minas Gerais*. São Paulo: Editora Ática, 1986.
Boxer, C. R. *The Golden Age of Brazil: Growing Pains of a Colonial Society, 1695-1750*. New York: St. Martins Press, 1995.
Bradford, Thomas G. *A Comprehensive Atlas Geographical, Historical and Commercial*. Boston: W. D. Ticknor, ca. 1835-1836.
Brandão, Carlos Rodrigues. *Cavalhadas de Pirenópolis*. Goiânia: Oriente, 1974.
———. *O divino, o santo e a senhora*. Rio de Janeiro: Campanha de Defesa do Folclore Brasileiro, 1978.
———. *A Festa do Santo de Preto*. Rio de Janeiro: FUNARTE/Insituto Nacional do Folclore; Goiânia: Universidade Federal de Goiás, 1985.
———. *Peões, pretos e congos: Trabalho e identidade étnica em Goiás*. Brasília: UnB, 1977.
Brasil, Antônio Americano do. "Cunha Mattos em Goiaz, 1823-1826." *Revista do Instituto Histórico e Geographico Brasileiro* 96, vol. 150 (1924): 183-251.
———. *Súmula de história de Goiás*. 2nd ed. Goiânia: Departamento Estadual de Cultura, 1961. First edition published 1932.
Brito, Célia Coutinho Seixo de. *A mulher, a história e Goiás*. Goiânia: Departamento Estadual de Cultura, Editora Cultura Goiana, 1974.
Brito, Walter Gualberto de. *Memórias de uma família negra brasileira*. Brasília: Thesaurus, 2006.
Britto, Clovis Carvalho, Paulo Brito do Prado, and Rafael Lino Rosa, orgs. *Os sentidos da devoção: O império do divino na cidade de Goiás (séculos XIX e XX)*. Goiânia: Editora Espaço Acadêmico, 2015.
Bruno, Ernani Silva. *História do Brasil: Geral e regional. Vol. 6, Grande oeste: Goiás, Matto Grosso*. São Paulo: Ed. Cultrix, 1967.
[Caeiro, José]. *Primeira publicação após anos do manuscrito inédito de José Caeiro sobre os Jesuitas do Brasil e da india na perseguição do Marquês do Pombal (século XVIII)*. Bahia: Escola Tipografica Salesiana, 1936.
Câmara, Jaime. *Nos tempos de Frei Germano*. Goiânia: Editora Cultura Goiana, 1974.
Canesin, Maria Tereza, and Telma Camargo da Silva, orgs. *A Folia de Reis de Jaraguá*. Goiânia: Centro de Estudos da Cultura Popular, 1983.
Carvalho, Adelmo de, org. *Pirenópolis: Coletânea, 1727-2000: História, turismo e curiosidades*. Goiânia: Kelps, 2000 [?].
Casal, Manuel Aires de. *Corografia brasílica*. 1817. Reprint, Belo Horizonte: Editora Itatiaia, 1976.
Castro, José Luiz de. *A organização da Igreja Católica na capitania de Goiás (1726-1824)*. Goiânia: Ed. da UCG, 2006.
Catálogo de verbetes dos documentos manuscritos avulsos da capitania de Goiás

existentes no Arquivo Histórico Ultramarino, Lisboa-Portugal (1731–1822). Brasília: Ministério da Cultura; Goiânia: Sociedade Goiana de Cultura, Instituto de Pesquisas e Estudos Históricos do Brasil-Central, 2001.
Cayton, Andrew R. L., and Fredrika J. Teute, eds. *Contact Points: American Frontiers from the Mohawk Valley to the Mississippi, 1750–1830.* Chapel Hill: University of North Carolina Press, 1998.
Chaim, Marivone Matos. *Os aldeamentos indigenas na capitania de Goiás: Sua importância na política de povoamento (1749–1811).* Goiânia: Oriente, 1974.
Chaul, Nasr N. Fayad. *Caminhos de Goiás: Da construção da decadência aos limites da modernidade.* Goiânia: Ed. UCG, 1997.
Chaul, Nasr N. Fayad, and Paulo Bertran. *Goias: 1722–2002.* Goiás: Governo de Goiás, Agência Goiana de Cultura, 2002.
Chaul, Nasr N. Fayad, and Luís Sérgio Duarte da Silva, orgs. *As cidades dos sonhos: Desenvolvimento urbano em Goiâs.* Goiânia: Ed. da UFG, 2004.
Chaul, Nasr N. Fayad, and Paulo Rodrigues Ribeiro. *Goiás: Identidade, paisagem e tradição.* Goiânia: Editora da UCG, 2001.
Chauvet, Gustavo. *Brasília e Formosa: 4,500 anos de história.* Goiânia: Kelps, 2005.
Cidade, Hernani. "Um dramático episódio da história de Goiás." In *Anais do Congresso Comemorativo,* IHGB (1963). Vol. 1. Rio de Janeiro: Imprensa Nacional, 1967.
Coelho, Gustavo Neiva. *Guia dos bens imóveis tombados em Goiás: Vila Boa.* Vol. 1. Goiânia: Trilhas Urbanas, 2001.
Conrad, Robert E. *Children of God's Fire: A Documentary History of Black Slavery in Brazil.* 2nd ed. University Park: Pennsylvania State University Press, 1994.
Cordeiro, Rosalinda Batista de Abreu. *Arraias: Suas raízes e sua gente.* Goiânia: Sem Editora, 1991.
Costa, Odorico. "A escravidão nas Minas de Goiaz." *Oeste: Revista Mensal,* 7–8. Journal published 1942–1945.
———."Os Jesuitas em Goiaz." *Oeste: Revista Mensal,* 5–7. Journal published 1942–1945.
Cowell, Adrian. *The Tribe That Hides from Man.* New York: Stein and Day, 1974.
Crocker, William H. *The Canela (Eastern Timbira), I: An Ethnographic Introduction.* Washington, DC: Smithsonian Institution Press, 1990.
Cunha, Manuela Carneiro da, ed. *História dos índios no Brasil.* São Paulo: Companhia das Letras, 1992.
Curto, José C., and Paul E. Lovejoy. *Enslaving Connections: Changing Cultures of Africa and Brazil During the Era of Slavery.* New York: Humanity Books, 2004.
Daniels, Christine, and Michael V. Kennedy, eds. *Negotiated Empires: Centers and Peripheries in the Americas, 1500–1820.* New York: Routledge, 2002.
Darnton, Robert. *The Great Cat Massacre and Other Episodes in French Cultural History.* New York: Vintage Books, 1984.
Davidson, David Michael. "Rivers and Empire: The Madeira Route and the

Incorporation of the Brazilian Far West, 1737–1808." PhD diss., Yale University, 1970.

Delson, Roberta Marx. "Inland Navigation in Colonial Brazil: Using Canoes on the Amazon." *International Journal of Maritime History* 7, no. 1 (June 1995): 1–28.

Deus, Maria Socorro de, and Mônica Martins da Silva. *História das festas e religiosidades em Goiás*. Goiânia: Editora Alternativa, 2003.

Doles, Dalísia Elizabeth Martins. *As comunicações fluviais pelo Tocantins e Araguaia no século XIX*. Goiânia: Ed. Oriente, 1973.

"Dos quilombos fez-se kalunga." In *Goianidade*, edição especial, Goiânia (dezembro de 1992), documentários 12–13.

Élis, Bernardo. *Chegou o governador*. Rio de Janeiro: José Olympio Editora, 1987.

———. *O tronco*. Rio de Janeiro: José Olympio, 1979.

Expedição Langsdorff ao Brasil, 1821–1829. 3 vols. Rio de Janeiro: Edições Alumbramento, Livroarte Editora, 1988.

Ferguson, R. Brian, and Neil L. Whitehead, eds. *War in the Tribal Zone: Expanding States and Indigenous Warfare*. Santa Fe, NM: School of American Research Press, 1992.

Ferreira, Manoel Rodrigues. *As bandeiras do Paraupava*. São Paulo: Prefeitura Municipal de São Paulo, 1977.

Figueiredo, Luciano. *O avesso da memória: Cotidiano e trabalho da mulher em Minas Gerais no século XVIII*. Rio de Janeiro: José Olympio, 1993.

Franco, Francisco de Assis Carvalho. *Dicionário de bandeirantes e sertanisas do Brasil: Século XVI, XVII, XVIII*. Belo Horizonte: Ed. Itatiaia, 1989.

Freire, José Ribamar Bessa. *Rio babel: A história das línguas na Amazônia*. Rio de Janeiro: Atlântica, 2004.

Freitas, Lena Castello Branco Ferreira de, ed. *Saúde e doenças em Goiás: A medicina possível*. Goiânia: Ed. da UFG, 1999.

Galindo Lima, Marcos. *O governo das almas: A expansão colonial no país dos tapuia, 1651–1798*. Leiden, the Netherlands: Universiteit Leiden, 2004.

Gallais, P. Estevão Maria. *O apóstolo do Araguaia: Frei Gil Vilanova, misionário dominicano*. Translated by Pedro Secondy and Soares de Azevedo. N.p.: Conceição do Araguaia, 1942.

Galli, Ubirajara. *A história da mineração em Goiás: Das primeiras lavras aos dias de hoje*. Goiânia: Ed. da UCG, 2005.

Garcia, Ledonias Franco. *Goyaz: Uma província do sertão*. Goiânia: Cânone Editorial, 2010.

Garcia, Marcolina Martins. *Tecelagem artesenal: Estudo etnográfico em Hidrolândia-Goiás*. Goiânia: Ed. da UFG, 1981.

Garfield, Seth. *Indigenous Struggle at the Heart of Brazil: State Policy, Frontier Expansion, and the Xavante Indians, 1937–1988*. Durham, NC: Duke University Press, 2001.

Gaspar, David Barry, and Darlene Clark Hine, eds. *Beyond Bondage: Free Women of Color in the Americas.* Urbana: University of Illinois Press, 2004.

———. *More Than Chattel: Black Women and Slavery in the Americas.* Bloomington: Indiana University Press, 1996.

Giraldin, Odair. "AXPÊN PRYÀK: História, cosmologia, onomástica e amizade formal Apinaje." PhD diss., Universidade Estadual de Campinas, 2000.

———. *Cayapó e Panará: Luta e sobrevivência de um povo Jê no Brasil Central.* Campinas: Ed. da UNICAMP, 1997.

———. "Pontal e Porto Real: Dois arraiais do norte de Goiás e os conflitos com os Xerente nos séculos XVIII e XIX." *Revista Amazonense de História* (Universidade Federal do Amazonas) 1, no. 1 (January/December 2002).

Gomes, Horieste, Antônio Teixeira Neto, and Altair Sales Barbosa. *Geografia: Goiás-Tocantins.* 2nd ed., revised and amplified. Goiânia: Editora UFG, 2005.

Graham, Laura R. *Performing Dreams: Discourses of Immortality Among the Xavante of Central Brazil.* 2nd ed. Tucson: Fenestra Books, 2003.

Guy, Donna J., and Thomas E. Sheridan, eds. *Contested Ground: Comparative Frontiers on the Northern and Southern Edges of the Spanish Empire.* Tucson: University of Arizona Press, 1998.

Hawthorne, Walter. *From Africa to Brazil: Culture, Identity, and an Atlantic Slave Trade, 1600–1830.* Cambridge: Cambridge University Press, 2010.

Hemming, John. *Amazon Frontier: The Defeat of the Brazilian Indians.* Cambridge, MA: Harvard University Press, 1987.

———. *Red Gold: The Conquest of the Brazilian Indians, 1500–1760.* Cambridge, MA: Harvard University Press, 1978.

Heywood, Linda M., ed. *Central Africans and Cultural Transformations in the American Diaspora.* Cambridge: Cambridge University Press, 2002.

Higgins, Kathleen J. *"Licentious Liberty" in a Brazilian Gold-Mining Region: Slavery, Gender, and Social Control in Eighteenth-Century Sabará, Minas Gerais.* University Park: Pennsylvania State University Press, 1999.

Holanda, Sérgio Buarque de. *Monções.* Rio de Janeiro: Livraria-Editora da Casa do Estudante do Brasil, 1945.

Hoornaert, Eduardo, org. *História da Igreja na Amazônia.* Petrópolis: Vozes, 1992.

———. *A igreja no Brasil-Colônia (1550–1800).* São Paulo: Ed. Brasiliense, 1982.

Howe, Marvine. "An Amazon Tribe Takes a Step Out: Kranhacarore Indians Make Contact with Brazilians." *New York Times,* 11 February 1973.

Jacintho, Olympio. *Esboço histórico de Formosa.* Brasília: Independência, 1979.

Jayme, Jarbas. *Famílias Pirenopolinas (Ensaios genealógicos).* 5 vols. Goiânia: Editora Rio Bonito, 1973.

Kaiser, Gloria, and Robert Wagner. *Thomas Ender: Brasilien expedition/expedição ao Brasil 1817: Aquarelas do cabinete de gravuras da Academia de Artes Viena.* Graz, Austria: Akademische Druck-u. Verlagsanstalt, ca. 1994.

Karasch, Mary C. "Antônio Moreira da Silva." In *Dictionary of Caribbean and*

Afro-Latin American Biography, edited by Henry Louis Gates Jr. and Franklin K. Knight. New York: Oxford University Press, 2016.

———. "Catequese e cativeiro: Politica indigenista em Goiás, 1780–1889." Translated by Beatriz Perrone-Moisés. In *História dos índios no Brasil*, edited by Manuela Carneiro da Cunha, 397–412. São Paulo: Companhia das Letras, 1992.

———. "Central Africans in Central Brazil, 1780–1835." In *Central Africans and Cultural Transformations in the American Diaspora*, edited by Linda M. Heywood, 117–52. Cambridge: Cambridge University Press, 2002.

———. "Construindo comunidades: As irmandades dos pretos e pardos no Brasil colonial e em Goiás." *História Revista* 15, no. 2 (July/December 2010): 257–83.

———. "Damiana da Cunha: Catechist and Sertanista." In *Struggle and Survival in Colonial America*, edited by David G. Sweet and Gary B. Nash, 102–20. Berkeley: University of California Press, 1981.

———. "Free Women of Color in Central Brazil, 1779–1832." In *Beyond Bondage: Free Women of Color in the Americas*, edited by David Barry Gaspar and Darlene Clark Hine, 237–70. Urbana: University of Illinois Press, 2004.

———. "Guiné, Mina, Angola, and Benguela: African and Crioulo Nations in Central Brazil, 1780–1835." In *Enslaving Connections*, edited by José C. Curto and Paul E. Lovejoy, 163–84. Amherst, NY: Humanity Books, 2004.

———. "História das doenças e dos cuidados médicos na capitania de Goiás." In *Saúde e doenças em Goiás: A medicina possível*, edited by Lena Castello Branco Ferreira de Freitas, 19–62. Goiânia: Ed. da UFG, 1999.

———. "'Minha Nação': Identidades escravas no fim do Brazil colonial." Translated by Ângela Domingues. In *Brasil: Colonização e escravidão*, edited by Maria Beatriz Nizza da Silva, 127–41. Rio de Janeiro: Nova Fronteira, 2000.

———. "Mujeres negras y trabajo en Brasil." In *Historia de las mujeres en España y América Latina*, edited by Isabel Morant, 815–34. Madrid: Editorial Cátedra, 2006.

———. "The Periphery of the Periphery? Vila Boa de Goiás, 1780–1835." In *Negotiated Empires: Centers and Peripheries in the Americas, 1500–1820*, edited by Christine Daniels and Michael V. Kennedy, 143–69. New York: Routledge, 2002.

———. "Quality, Nation, and Color: Constructing Identities in Central Brazil, 1775–1835." *Estudios Interdisciplinarios de América Latina y el Caribe* 19, no. 1 (January–June 2008): 1–12.

———. "Os quilombos do ouro na capitania de Goiás." Translated by João José Reis. In *Liberdade por um fio: História dos quilombos no Brasil*, edited by João José Reis and Flávio dos Santos Gomes, 240–62. São Paulo: Companhia das Letras, 1996.

———. "Rainhas e juízas: As negras nas irmandades dos pretos no Brasil central

(1722–1860)." In *Mulheres negras no Brasil escravista e do pós-emancipação*, edited by Giovana Xavier, Juliana Barreto Farias, and Flávio Gomes, 52–66. São Paulo: Selo Negro, 2012.

———. "Rethinking the Conquest of Goias, 1775–1819." *The Americas* 61, no. 3 (January 2005): 463–92.

———. *Slave Life in Rio de Janeiro, 1808–1850*. Princeton, NJ: Princeton University Press, 1987.

———. "Slave Women on the Brazilian Frontier in the Nineteenth Century." In *More Than Chattel: Black Women and Slavery in the Americas*, edited by David Barry Gaspar and Darlene Clark Hine, 79–96. Bloomington: Indiana University Press, 1996.

———. "Tomás de Sousa Vila Real." In *Dictionary of Caribbean and Afro-Latin American Biography*, edited by Henry Louis Gates Jr. and Franklin K. Knight. New York: Oxford University Press, 2016.

Karasch, Mary C., and David McCreery. "Indigenous Resistance in Central Brazil, 1770–1890." In *Native Brazil: Beyond the Convert and the Cannibal, 1500–1900*, edited by Hal Langfur, 225–49. Albuquerque: University of New Mexico Press, 2014.

Kiddy, Elizabeth W. *Blacks of the Rosary: Memory and History in Minas Gerais, Brazil*. University Park: Pennsylvania State University Press, 2005.

Kiple, Kenneth F., ed. *Cambridge World History of Human Disease*. Cambridge: Cambridge University Press, 1996.

Langfur, Hal. *The Forbidden Lands: Colonial Identity, Frontier Violence, and the Persistence of Brazil's Eastern Indians, 1750–1830*. Stanford, CA: Stanford University Press, 2006.

———, ed. *Native Brazil: Beyond the Convert and the Cannibal, 1500–1900*. Albuquerque: University of New Mexico Press, 2014.

Lazarin, Rita Heloísa de Almeida. "O aldeamento do Carretão: Duas histórias." Master's thesis, University of Brasília, 1985.

Leite, Serafim. *Suma histórica da Companhia de Jesus no Brasil (assistência de Portugal), 1549–1760*. Lisbon: Junta de Investigações do Ultramar, 1965.

Lemes, Fernando Lobo. "Na arena do sagrado: Poder político e vida religiosa nas minas de Goiás." *Revista Brasileira de Historia* (São Paulo; online) 32, no. 63 (2012): 59–81.

———. "Poder local e rede urbana nas minas de Goias." *História* (São Paulo, Franca), 28, no. 1 (2009): 1–14.

Maia, Tom. *Vila Boa de Goiás*. São Paulo: Companhia Editora Nacional, 1979.

Mano, Marcel. "Índios e negros nos sertões das minas: Contatos e identidades." *Varia Historia* (Belo Horizonte) 31, no. 56 (May/August 2015): 511–46.

Mapa etno-histórico de Curt Nimuendajú. Fundação Instituto Brasileiro de Geografia e Estatística em colaboração com a Fundação Nacional Pró-Memória. Rio de Janeiro: IBGE, 1981.

Mattoso, Katia M. de Queirós. "Splendors and Improprieties among the Bahian Clergy at the End of the Colonial Period, 1800–1822." Unpublished paper.
Maybury-Lewis, David. *The Savage and the Innocent*. Boston: Beacon Press, 1965.
McCreery, David. *Frontier Goiás, 1822–1889*. Stanford, CA: Stanford University Press, 2006.
McEnroe, Sean F. "Sites of Diplomacy, Violence, and Refuge: Topography and Negotiation in the Mountains of New Spain." *The Americas* 69, no. 2 (October 2012): 179–202.
Mead, David L. "Os Caiapó do Sul: An Ethnohistory (1610–1920)." PhD diss., University of Florida, 2010.
Meirelles, Evangelino, and Gelmires Reis. *Almanach de Santa Luzia*. Santa Luzia: Typ. d'O Planalto, 1920.
Melatti, Júlio Cezar. *Indios e criadores: A situação dos Krahô na area pastoril do Tocantins*. Rio de Janeiro: Instituto de Ciências Sociais, 1967.
Mendes Rocha, Leandro, ed. *Atlas histórico: Goiás pré-colonial e colonial*. Vol. 1. Goiânia: Ed. CECAB, 2001.
Metcalf, Alida C. *Family and Frontier in Colonial Brazil: Santana de Parnaíba, 1580–1822*. Berkeley: University of California Press, 1992.
———. *Go-Betweens and the Colonization of Brazil, 1500–1600*. Austin: University of Texas Press, 2005.
Miller, Joseph C. *Way of Death: Merchant Capitalism and the Angolan Slave Trade, 1730–1830*. Madison: University of Wisconsin Press, 1988.
Monteiro, John Manuel. *Negros da terra: Índios e bandeirantes nas origens de São Paulo*. São Paulo: Companhia das Letras, 1994.
Moraes, Cristina de Cássia Pereira. "Do corpo místico de Cristo: Irmandades e confrarias na capitania de Goiás, 1736–1808." PhD diss., Universidade Nova de Lisboa, 2006.
Moreyra, Sérgio Paulo. *Vida sertaneja: Aspirações metropolitanas: Alunos da Universidade de Coimbra nascidos em Goiás*. Goiânia: Editora da UFG, 2015.
Mott, Luiz R. B. "A Inquisição em Goiás—Fontes e pistas." *Revista do Instituto Histórico e Geográphico de Goiás*, no. 13 (1993): 33–76.
———. *Rosa Egipcíaca: Uma santa africana no Brasil*. Rio de Janeiro: Editora Bertrand Brasil, 1993.
Moura, Denise A. Soares de. *Saindo das sombras: Homens livres no declinio do escravismo*. Campinas, SP: Centro de Memória-UNICAMP, 1998.
Moura, Gloria, coord. *Uma história do povo Kalunga*. Brasília: Ministério da Educação, Secretaria de Educação Fundamental—MEC, SEF, 2001.
Moura, Marlene Castro Ossami de, ed. *Índios de Goiás: Uma perspectiva histórico-cultural*. Goiânia: UCG, Editora Kelps, Editora Vieira, 2006.
Mulvey, Patricia A. "Slave Confraternities in Brazil: Their Role in Colonial Society." *The Americas* 39, no. 1 (July 1982): 39–68.

Myscofski, Carole A. *Amazons, Wives, Nuns, and Witches*. Austin: University of Texas Press, 2013.
Neiva, Artur e Belisário Pena. *Viagem científica pelo norte da Bahia, sudoeste de Pernambuco, sul do Piauí e do norte a sul de Goiás*. Brasília: Academia Brasiliense de Letras, 1984.
Nimuendajú, Curt. *The Apinayé*. Translated by Robert H. Lowie. Edited by Robert H. Lowie and John M. Cooper. New York: Humanities Press, 1967.
———. *The Eastern Timbira*. Translated and edited by Robert H. Lowie. Berkeley: University of California Press, 1946.
———. *The Serente*. Translated by Robert H. Lowie 1942. Reprint, New York: AMS Press, 1979.
Oliveira, Maria de Fátima. *Portos do sertão: Cidades ribeirinhas do rio Tocantins*. Goiânia: Ed. da PUC Goiás, 2010.
Oriente, T., org. *As fabulosas águas quentes de caldas novas*. Goiânia: Ed. Irmãos Oriente, 1971.
Palacin, Luís. *Goiás, 1722–1822: Estrutura e conjuntura numa capitania de Minas*. 2nd ed. Goiânia: Oriente, 1976.
———. *Quatro tempos de ideologia em Goiás*. Goiânia: Cerne, 1986.
———. *Subversão e corrupção: Um estudo da administração Pombalina em Goiás*. Goiânia: UFG Editora, 1983.
Palacin, Luís, Ledonias Franco Garcia, and Janaína Amado. *História de Goiás em documentos*. Vol. 1, *Colônia*. Goiânia: Editora da UFG, 1995.
Palacin, Luís, and Maria Augusta de Sant'Anna Moraes. *História de Goiás (1722–1972)*. 3rd ed. Goiânia: Livraria e Editora Cultura Goiania, 1981.
Parente, Temis Gomes. *O avesso do silêncio: Vivências cotidianas das mulheres do século XIX*. Goiânia: Editora UFG, 2005.
Pedroso, Dulce Madalena Rios. "Avá-Canoeiro: A história do povo invisível—séculos XVIII e XIX," Master's thesis, Federal University of Goiás, 1992.
Pedroso, Dulce Madalena Rios, et al. *Avá-Canoeiro: A terra, o homem, a luta*. Goiânia: Editora UCG, 1990.
Pereira, Carla Rocha, and Sergio F. Ferretti. *Divino toque do Maranhão*. Rio de Janeiro: Instituto do Patrimônio Histórico e Artístico Nacional, CNFCP, 2005.
Pereira, Niomar de Souza. *Cavalhadas no Brasil: De cortejo a cavalo a lutas de Mouros e Cristãos*. São Paulo: Escola de Folclore, 1984.
Powers, Karen Vieira. *Women in the Crucible of Conquest: The Gendered Genesis of Spanish American Society, 1500–1600*. Albuquerque: University of New Mexico Press, 2005.
Queiroz, Jerônimo Geraldo de. *Evolução cultural de Goiás (estudo)*. Goiânia: Oriente, 1969.
Radding, Cynthia, and Danna A. Levin Rojo, eds. *Borderlands of the Iberian World*. New York: Oxford University Press, forthcoming.

Ravagnani, Oswaldo Martins. "A experiência Xavante com o mundo dos Brancos." PhD diss., Escola de Sociologia e Política de São Paulo, 1978.
Reis, João José, and Flávio dos Santos Gomes, eds. *Liberdade por um fio*. São Paulo: Companhia das Letras, 1996.
Reis, Nestor Goulart. *Imagens de vilas e cidades do Brasil colonial*. São Paulo: Universidade de São Paulo, 2000.
Rivet, Paul. "Les indiens Canoeiros," *Journal de la Sociéte des Américanistes de Paris*, n.s., 16 (1924): 169–75.
Rodrigues, Lysias. *Roteiro do Tocantins*. 4th ed. Palmas, TO: Alexandre Acampora, 2001.
Rogers, Thomas D. *The Deepest Wounds: A Labor and Environmental History of Sugar in Northeast Brazil*. Chapel Hill: University of North Carolina Press, 2010.
———. "Laboring Landscapes: The Environmental, Racial, and Class Worldview of the Brazilian Northeast's Sugar Elite, 1880s-1930s." *Luso-Brazilian Review* 46, no. 2 (2009): 22–53.
Roller, Heather F. *Amazonian Routes: Indigenous Mobility and Colonial Communities in Northern Brazil*. Stanford, CA: Stanford University Press, 2014.
Rosa, Rafael Lino, and Clovis Carvalho Britto, orgs. *Nos Passos da Paixão: A irmandade do senhor Bom Jesus dos Passos em Goiás*. Goiânia: Ed. PUC-GO/Kelps, 2011.
Russell-Wood, A. J. R. *The Black Man in Slavery and Freedom in Colonial Brazil*. New York: St. Martin's Press, 1982.
———. "New Directions in *Bandeirismo* Studies in Colonial Brazil." *The Americas* 61, no. 3 (January 2005): 353–71.
———. *Society and Government in Colonial Brazil, 1500-1822*. Bookfield, VT: Variorum, 1992.
Salles, Gilka V. F. de. *Economia e escravidão na capitania de Goiás*. Goiânia: CEGRAF/UFG, 1992.
Sandes, Noé Freire, ed. *Memória e região*. Brasília: Ministério da Integração Nacional, UFG, 2002.
Schwartz, Stuart B. *Sovereignty and Society in Colonial Brazil*. Berkeley: University of California Press, 1973.
Sereburã, Hipru, Rupawê, Serezabdi, and Sereñimirãmi. *Wamrêmé za'ra: Mito e história do Povo Xavante: Nossa palavra* [Wamrêmé za'ra: Myth and History of the Xavante People: Our Word]. São Paulo: Editora Senac, 1998.
Sigaud, J. F. X. *Du climat et des maladies du Brésil ou statistique médicale de cet empire*. Paris: Chez Fortin, Masson et Cie Libraires, 1844.
Silva, J. Trindade da Fonseca e. *Lugares e pessoas: Subídios eclesiásticos para a história de Goiás*. São Paulo: Escolas Profissionais Salesianas, 1948. Reprint, Goiânia: Ed. da UCG, 2006.

Silva, Maria Beatriz Nizza da, ed. *Brasil: Colonização e escravidão*. Rio de Janeiro: Nova Fronteira, 2000.
———. *Sexualidade, familia e religião na colonização do Brasil*. Lisbon: Livros Horizonte, 2001.
Silva, Martiniano J. *Quilombos do Brasil Central: Violência e resistência escrava, 1719–1888*. Goiânia: Kelps, 2003.
———. *Sombra dos quilombos: Introdução ao estudo do negro em Goiás*. Goiânia: Livraria e Editora Cultura Goiana, 1974.
Silva, Valtuir Moreira da. *História agrária em Goiás*. Goiânia: AGEPEL/UEG, 2002.
Sommer, Barbara A. "A Colony of the Sertão: Expeditions in the Brazilian North, 1650–1750." Paper presented at the American Historical Association and the Conference of Latin American History, Washington, DC, January 2004.
Southey, Robert. *History of Brazil*. Vol. 3. 1822. Reprint, New York: Burt Franklin, 1970.
Stepan, Nancy Leys. *Picturing Tropical Nature*. Ithaca, NY: Cornell University Press, 2001.
Steward, Julian H., ed. *Handbook of South American Indians*. Vol. 3, *The Tropical Forest Tribes*. Washington, DC: Government Printing Office, 1948.
Sweet, David G., and Gary B. Nash, eds. *Struggle and Survival in Colonial America*. Berkeley: University of California Press, 1981.
Taubaté, P. Fr. Modesto Rezende de, and P. Fr. Fidelis Motta de Primerio. *Os missionarios capuchinhos no Brasil: Esboço historico prefaciado pelo Dr. Affonso de E. Taunay*. São Paulo: Convento da Immaculada Conceição, 1931.
Taunay, Affonso de E. "Os dois Antônio Pires de Campos: A campanha dos Caiapós." In *Anais do IV Congresso de História Nacional*, 509–42. Rio de Janeiro: Imprensa Nacional, 1950.
———. *História das bandeiras paulistas*. 3rd ed. 3 vols. São Paulo: Edições Melhoramentos, 1975.
———. *Relatos sertanistas*. Belo Horizonte: Ed. Itatiaia, 1981.
Taunay, Alfredo e'Escragnolle. *Goyaz*. Edited by Wolney Unes. Goiânia: Instituto Centro-Brasileiro de Cultura, 2004.
Teles, José Mendonça. *Vida e obra de Silva e Souza*. Goiânia: Oriente, 1978.
Teske, Wolfgang. *A roda de São Gonçalo na comunidade quilombola da Lagoa da Pedra em Arraiais (TO): Um estudo de caso de processo folkcomunicacional*. Goiânia: Kelps, 2008.
Toral, André Amaral de. "Cosmologia e sociedade Karajá." Master's thesis, Universidade Federal do Rio de Janeiro, 1992.
———. "Os índios negros ou os Carijó de Goiás: A história dos Avá-Canoeiro," *Revista de Antropologia* 27/28 (1984–1985): 287–326.
Tucker, Richard P., and Edmund Russell, eds. *Natural Enemy, Natural Ally: Toward an Environmental History of War*. Corvallis: Oregon State University Press, 2004.

Unes, Wolney, org. *Veiga Valle*. Goiânia: Instituto Brasil de Cultura, 2011.
Valdez, Diane. *História da infância em Goiás: Séculos XVIII e XIX*. Goiânia: AGEPEL/
 UEG, 2002.
Varnhagen, Francisco Adolfo de. *História geral do Brasil*. 5 vols. São Paulo: Edições
 Melhoramentos, n.d.
Weber, David J. *Bárbaros: Spaniards and Their Savages in the Age of Enlightenment*.
 New Haven, CT: Yale University Press, 2005.
Weber, David J., and Jane M. Rausch, eds. *Where Cultures Meet: Frontiers in Latin
 American History*. Wilmington, DE: Scholarly Resources, 1994.
White, Richard. *The Middle Ground: Indians, Empires, and Republics in the Great Lakes
 Region, 1650–1815*. Cambridge: Cambridge University Press, 1991.

Index

Page numbers in italic text indicate illustrations.

Abade, Bonifacio Rodrigues, 278
abandonment, 268–71
administrados, 367n36
Africa, African Nations, 185, 195–201; Angola, 7, 15, 196–99, 200, 204, 267, 276–77; Azores, 15, 173, 383n24; Benguela, 196; Cape Verde, 15, 201, 367n44; Central Africans, 366n31; Congo, 7, 15, 186, 196–99, 200; Dances of, 225; Ghana, 210, 369n80; Guiné, 7, 15, 196, 255, 289, 379n33; Mina, 15, 190, 196–99, 200, 250, 267–68, 276–78, 289, 293, 360n53, 366n31, 367n37, 378n11, 381n7, 382n12–13; Mozambique, 7, 198; Nagô, 196, 198–99, 276–77, 366n31, 382n12; São Tomé, 15
agregado (household dependent), 151, 161, 242, 329; command of, 268; farming, 292; labor of, 253; ownership of, 175; *pardo*, 243, 289; priests and, 260; white, 172, 241, 255
agropastoral economy, 120, 136–38, 149, 159, 289
Agua Quente, 19, 21–22
Aguiar, Alferes Mathias de Crasto, 169, 181
Aguiar, Antônio Rodrigues de, 154
Aires de Casal, Manuel, 20, 73
ajôjos (long canoes), 8
Akroá, 11, 13; *bandeiras* against, 36, 83; *bandeiras* with, 86; Cunha Matos on, 37; indigenous nation, 35–38; interpreter, 90, 111; measles among, 30, 36; mission settlements, 35–38, 228–31; in Natividade, 36; pacification, 83; in *pedestres*, 150; raids, 14; Silva e Souza on, 51; transfer of, 36–37; warriors, 36–37; Xacriabá as enemy, 36; Xavante, and, 50–51, 108

Alarcão, Baltazar Gomes, 78
Albernós, Domingos Gomes, 238
Alcobaça, 9, 106
Aldeas Altas, 12, 14
aldeia (village), 329; of Bororo, 229; Carretão, 230, 238–40, 242–44; directorate missions, 230–38; Duro, São José do, 228–29; Graciosa, 54–55, 114–18; Maria I, 230, 235–37; military in, 239, 383n25; Pedro Affonso, 44; Rio das Pedras, 229; Saint-Hilaire on, 229–30; Santa Ana do Rio das Velhas, 37, 228–29; São Francisco Xavier, 228–29; São José de Mossâmedes, 37, 48, 62, 229–32, 237, 373n42; Silva e Souza on, 229
Alencastre, José Martins Pereira de, 73–74, 210, 258
Alexandria, Antônio Francisco de, 288, 346n8
Almas River, 11, 21, 25
Almeida, Jacinto de, 72
Almeida, João de, 81
Almeida, José Manoel de, 288
Almeida, Manuel José de, 90, 111
Almeida, Rita Heloísa de, 80
Almeida de Vasconcelos, José de, 26
Almeida Freire, João de, 82
Almeida Lazarin, Rita Heloísa de, 244
Almeida Vasconcelos, José de, 58
almocafre, 368, n57
Alvares, José, 169
Alvares, Manuel da Silva, 155, 260, 289, 290, 379n33, 384n35
Alvares de Oliveira, Dr. Ignacio José, 182
Alvarez, Francisco da Cruz, 180

Alvarez, João Teixeira, 260
Alves, Francisco, 180
Alves, Francisco da Cruz, 180
Alves, Gabriel, 83
Alves, Manoel, 83
Alves da Rocha, Antônio, 288
Alves dos Santos, Francisco, 105
Amado, José de Oliveira, 181
Amaral, Joaquim José do, 175
Amaral, José da Franca, 179–80, 290
Amaral, José de Aguirra do, 255
Amazon region, 7
Amorim, Miguel Pereira de, 181
Amurim, José da Costa, 172
Ana Maria parda, 276, 279
Ana Mina, 278
anchor-axe, 98, 100
Andrade, Gomes Freire de, 210
Andrade, José Bonifacio de, 259
Angraí-oxá, 61, 86, 235
Anhangúera, 69. *See also* Bueno da Silva, Bartolomeu
Antunes, Antônio, 220
Apiaká, 47
Apinaje, 29, 38–42; attack on Karajá, 105–6; autonomy, 42; baskets, 40, 41; blood-revenge, 96; canoe raiders, 38–42; Cunha Matos assisted by, 96; Cunha Matos on, 41; Gê language, 38; great house, 39; indigenous nation, 38–42; ironwares, 7; Nimuendajú on, 38, 41, 96, 98, 207; peace interlude, 98; Pohl on, 98; Reserve, 303; revolt, 40–41; smallpox among, 41; subject to Moreira da Silva, 91; towns, 300; trading with Karajá, 40; warfare, 96–99; warrior, 40–41, 97; weapons, 98; women, 258
Apollinario, João, 103
apoplexy, 22
Aquino, Paulo José de, 164
Araés, 33, 47–49, 66–69, 78, 248, 302

Araés river, 346n4
Araguaia River, 9, 23, 27; *bandeira* to, 71–78; explorations, 68; indigenous nations dwelling on, 44–49; *sertanistas* on, 284; villages, 44
Araujo, Bartholomeu Ferreira, 173
Araujo, João Carvalho de, 169
Araujo, José Antônio de, 179–80
Araujo, Manoel de, 104–5
Araujo, Monteiro de, 179
Araujo, Padre, 346n6, 1632
Araujo, Pedro Monteiro de, 168, 170, 180
Aricobés, 37
armed expedition. *See bandeira*
Arraias, 15, 21, 26, 28
arroba (fifteen kilos), 147–48, 164, 181, 329, 347n24, 363n9
Arruda e Sá, Miguel de, 89, 92, 111
Ataíde, Bartolomeu Barreiros de, 44
Ataídes, Jézus Marco de, 60, 71
Azevedo, Francisco Ferreira, 154, 217
Azevedo, Manoel Francisco de, 167
Azevedo Lima, Rodrigo Coelho Furtado de, 239

Babilônia, fazenda, 222
baby-carrying sling, 252
Bahia, 5, 15, 27
Balsas River, 10, 12
Bananal Island, 9, 20, 23
bandeira (armed expedition), xxi, 329; against Akroá, 36, 83; Bororo accompanying, 86; by Bueno da Silva, 69–71; against Canoeiro, 91–94; captives, 72, 82; chaplain, 65, 74; desertions, 70; *entrada*, 65–67; expanding slavery, xxi, 63; for gold, 73, 83; Indians with, 86, 91, 187; invasions, 304; to Karajá, 69; to Kayapó and Araguaia River, 71–78; local, 65; map, 64; Mato Grosso, 71, 88, 121–23; mestizo and, 82; model for, 74; in North,

78–84; overview, 63–67; pacification, xvii, 84–94; Paraúpava slaving frontier, 67–69; Paulistas, 5, 60, 67–68, 72, 78, 186–87; *pedestre* in, 66; of Pires de Campos, 71; predatory corsairs, 63, 65; priests and, 66–67; São Paulo, 17–18, 49, 63, 67–69; *sertanistas*, 83; state-funded, 65; twentieth-century, 94; against Xacriabá, 83
Bandeira, Pedro Rodrigues, 173
bandeirante (expedition participant), 88, 159, 302, 329
baptisms, 381n10; enslaved Africans, 198–201; manumission and, 381n10–382n10; mestizo, 250
Barata, Francisco José Rodrigues, 22
Barboza, Agostinho, 20
Barboza, João, 290
barracas (thatch-roofed shelters), 39, 46, 238
Barreiros de Ataíde, Bartolomeu, 44–45
Barretto, Francisco José, 147
Barros, Elias Ferreira de, 11
Barros, Manoel de, 347n14
bastardo (mestizo), 74, 76, 150, 250, 285, 329
Basto, Antônio Barrozo, 170
Bastos, João de, 279
Batista, José, 228
Belém, 5, 7
bens do vento, 296
Berford, Sebastião Gomes da Silva, 10–12
Berthet, Frei, 118
Bertran, Paulo, 163, 225
Bilreiros, 59–60, 72, 82, 121
black born in Brazil. See *crioulo*
black militia force (*Henriques*), 286–87, 293–97, 329, 385n42
black miners society, 149, 368n56
blacks. See Africans
bloodletting, 234
blood-revenge, 96

Bonfim, Our Lord of, 167, 190, 218
Borges, Ana Maria, 218, 221
Borges, Francisca, 276
Bororo: accompanying *bandeira*, 86; baptism of, 198; descendants, 37; families, 75; Kayapó enemy, 61, 73, 123; Mato Grosso, 61, 75; Pires de Campos and, 75–77, 229; at Santa Ana, 37; slaves, 85, 105, 198, 226; warriors, 75
Botelho da Cunha, João, 146–47
Braga, Francisco da Silva, 168, 181
Braga, Gervazio Martins, 277
Bragança, José Rodriguez, 177, 181
Bras, Luis, 285
Brasília, xix, 3, 24
Braun, João Vasco Manuel de, 53, 97
Brazil, 4
Brazil nuts, 82
Britto e Costa, Francisco Xavier dos Guimarães, 239
brown-skinned person. See *pardo*
Bueno, Paulo, 68
Bueno da Silva, Bartolomeu, 68, 82, 187, 248–49, 346n12; *bandeiras*, 69–71; father and son, 69–71; seeking gold, 69–70; Silva e Souza on, 70
Bueno e Gusmão, Balthezar de Godoy, 124
Burchell, John, xxii, 7, 219
Buriti palm trees, 14–15
Burton, Richard, 368n57

Caatingas, 68, 80–81, 346n6
cabra (dark-brown person), 200–202, 256, 266–67, 276–77, 279, 292, 329, 367n44
Caldas Novas, 24, 30–31
Camargo Fleury, Luiz Gonzaga de, 55
Campos, Antônio José de, 190
Campos Bicudo, Manuel de, 71, 77
Candea, Manuel de, 277
Canela, 29

cannibalism, 249–50, 353n52, 356n81, 378n7; Kayapó accused of, 71, 125
Canoeiro, 55–59; Avá-Canoeiro, 56; *bandeiras* against, 91, 94; Castelnau on, 249; Christians and, 55; Cunha Matos and, 56, 58, 59, 93–94, 119; enemies, 119; enslavement of, 58; indigenous nation, 55–59; Jesuits and, 56; lands of, 299, 344n53; Luso-Brazilians on, 119; Massacres of, 58; Pohl on, 120; raids, 19, 56–57, 118, 344n57; resistance, 58–59, 91, 93, 119; Silva e Souza on, 57; on Tocantins River, 56–57; Tupi language and, 55–59; villages, 56–57; as violent, 57–58, 344n57; warfare, 118–21; weapons, 58, 120; women, 57–58, 118, 249; Xavante enemy, 55, 58, 119
canoes (*ubás*), 8; Apinaje raiding, 38–42; Karajá and, 45
capitaçao (tax on slave), 189–92, 329
capitão do mato (bush captain), 209, 211, 284, 382n23
captaincy (territorial division), 3, 5, 16, 129, *143*, 329. See also Goiás, captaincy of; Mato Grosso; São Paulo
captains, in directorate missions, 241, 243
Capuchins, 60, 153
Cardoso, Agostinho Alvarez, 169, 179, 180, 181
Cardoso, Domingos Antônio, 169, 181
Cardoso, Gaspar Gonçalves, 79
Cardozo, Agostinho Alvarez, 169
Cardozo de Souza, Joaquim, 290
Carew, Ricardo, 81
Carijós, 68
Carlota, 209, 369n75
Carmo, 11, 13
Carneiro, Belchior Dias, 72
Carolina, 9, 14, 244–45
carrapato, 24–25

Carretão, 238–40, 242–44; Cunha Matos in, 241; residents, 244; Xavante, 48, 50, 55, 90, 92–93, 108, 111; Xerente, 53
carta de liberdade (letter of liberty), 275–76
Carvalho, Aleixo José de, 256
Carvalho, Henrique Manoel de, 173
Carvalho, José Francisco de, 169, 181
Carvalho, José Gabriel de, 296
Carvalho, Plácido Moreira de, 176
Castelnau, Francis, xxii, 48, 59; on Canoeiro, 59, 249; on Kayapó, 60; on Xambioá Karajá, 48
Castilho, Fernando Delgado Freire de, 28, 53, 237, 254, 286, 288, 378n16
Castro, Bento Mariano de, 229
Castro, Gregorio Coelho de Moraes, 229
Castro, José de Mello e, 111
Castro, José Luiz de, 218–19
Catholic Church: bishops, 153–54; Christianization and, xxiii; circuit riders, 155; commercial ventures, 155–56; convents and nuns, 156; Dominicans, 153, 217; imperial system of Portugal and, 153–57; Inquisition, 154–55; lay brotherhoods (*irmandades*), 156; priests, 155–56; seminary, 155; slaves and, 155. See also Christians
cattle, 14, *160*; *cerrado* supporting, 25; contraband in, 149; drives, 142; *fazenda*, 228, 231, 237; frontier, 303; Krahô raiding, 42–44; ranches, 139; ranch hands (*camaradas*), 292
Cavalcante, 15, 21, 364n21
Cavalhadas, 95
Caxias, 12–13
Cerqueira, Tristão Pinto, 179, 290
cerrado (savanna), xvii, 3, 329; animals, birds, reptiles, 25; cattle-raising, 25; disease and, 27; flourishing, 24; hunting, 25; occupation, 60
César de Meneses, Rodrigo, 69

Chagas, Coronel Manuel Lopes, 250
Chagas, Lino Manuel Lopes, 250, 288
Chagas, Manoel Lopes, 169, 180, 181
Chagas disease, 27, 31
Chapada dos Veadeiros, 12, 26–27
chapadas (tablelands), 14–15; in Goiás captaincy, 24–28
Chaves, José, 209
Chaves, José Teixeira, 290
Chaves, Manoel Lopes, 290
Chaves, Manuel Teixeira, 290
Chaves, Marcelino Teixeira, 260
checkpoint. *See registo, registro*
Cherentes, 53–55, 117–18, 244, 343n45
Chiotay, 53
Christianization: accepting, 216; Catholic Church and, xxiii; centers, 74; Kayapó, 233; lack of success, 245; Luso-Brazilian goal, 84; pride in, 131; priests' focus, 46; resistance to, 41
Christians: Canoeiro and, 55; conquests by, 95; directorate missions, 230–46, 300; Franciscan catechetical efforts, 227–28; gentiles and, 95; Indians, 81, 226–27, 244–46; Inheiguarás killing, 80; Jesuit missions, 228–30; lay brotherhood, 222–27, 329; overview, 215–22; retrieving, 112; role of churches, 219; white propertied elites, 184; Xavante and, 108
Churches: Church of Our Lady of Carmo, 218; Church of Our Lady of Mercy, 218; Church of Our Lady of Monte do Carmo, 200; Church of our Lady of Pilar, 218; Church of Our Lady of the Abbey, 217–18, 371n14; Church of Our Lady of the Good Death, 217; Church of Our Lady of the Immaculate Conception, 218; Church of Our Lady of the Rosary, 217, 218, 219, 220; Church of Our Lord of the Good Death, 218, 222; Church of Santa Efigênia, xviii, 225; Church of São Francisco de Paula, 217; Church of St. Ann, 215–17; Church of St. Benedict, 225; funerals and burials in, 219; in Goiás captaincy, 326–28; Indians and, 221; in Natividade, 221 225; in Pontal, 221
Claro dos Santos, José, 269
Cocal: marriages in, 261; mining, 168, *171*, 172, 189, 204–5, 226, 290, 303, 366n18; peace in, 103; slaves in, 170, 290, 368n50; violence, 57, 120; warfare and, 99–100; Xerente in, 351n12
Cocal Grande, 18, 43, 99, 176
Cocrît, 102–3
Coelho, Manuel Pinto, 132
coerced labor, 62, 185, 302; fleeing from, 240; in Pontal, 251; women, 251–53
Coimbra, Sebastião de, 227
Coimbra, University of, 133–34, 147, 183, 269, 288
colonial currency (*real, réis*), 76–77, 136, *138, 143*, 286, 330
colonial order, xxiii
comarca (judicial district), 5, 133–35, 329; of North, 143, *143*, 145, 161, 192, 195–96, 208, 219, 245, 261, 262, 280, *312*, 320, 325, *327*; orphans, 148; of South, *143*, 145–46, 161, 192, 194–96, 202, 262, *311, 312, 319, 325, 326*
comboios, comboieiros, 15, 141, 144, 173, 360n53
community of fugitive slaves. *See quilombo*
Conceição (town), 28
Conceiçao, José Francisco da, 289–90
Conceiçao, Quiteria Rodrigues da, 156
concubinage, 253–58
congada (theatrical dance), xxii–xxiii, 185, *186*, 215, 225, 370n1, 372
contrabandistas (smugglers), 12, 15, 146, 292

Conumo, Jozê, 41
Cordeiro, Elena, 256
Correia, José Antônio, 175
Correia, Sorocabano Manuel, 68
Costa, Pedro, 79–80
Costa Portella, Manoel da, 124
Costa Romero, Manuel de, 82
Couros (Formosa), 15, 22–24
Coutinho, Brittes Maria Leonor de Azeredo, 269
Coutinho, Francisco de Souza, 144
Coutinho Gentil, José Nicolau de Azevedo, 153
Couto, José da Rocha, 358n36
Couto, Urbano, 211
Couto de Magalhaes, José Vieira, 54, 56, 119
cowboys, 160, 178, 258, 386n44; in Northeast region, 14
Cowell, Adrian, xvii
crioulo (black born in Brazil), 24, 152, 200, 276–77, 279, 293, 329; census of 1832, 202; lay brotherhood, 24; location in 1832, *318*; nations, 195, 201–2; in North, 1779–1832, *320*; overview, 186; in South, 1779–1832, *319*
Crisostomo, João, 220
crixá and *crixás* (town), 9, 70, 188, 299
Cruz, Manuel da, 228
Cuiabá, 17
culture of evasion, 149
Cunha, Claudio José da, 229
Cunha, Damiana da, xviii–xix, 86–89, 121, 235, 350n60–61
Cunha, Manoel da, 86–88, 235
Cunha, Manuela Carneiro da, xix
Cunha e Roza, André Vilella da, 182
Cunha Matos, Raimundo José da, xxii, 20–21, 23, 87, 170, 191, 223, 245–46, 258; on abandoned mines, 206; on Akroá, 37; on Apinaje, 41; Apinaje assisting, 96, 99; on buying Indians, 104; Canoeiro and, 56, 58, 59, 93–94, 119; in Carretão, 238, 241; on Graciosa, 244; on Karajá villages, 47–48; on Kayapó, 37; on Krahô, 43; on leprosy, 30; seeking assistance from, 55; on small pox, 29; on syphilis, 31; on Xavante, 109; Xerente and, 113–17; Xuathe and, 115–16
Cunha Menezes, Luis da, 22, 225, 231. *See also* Menezes, Luiz da Cunha
Cunha Menezes, Tristão da, 57, 89, 110–11, 151, 268. *See also* Menezes, Tristão da Cunha

da Gama, Jerônimo, 82
dark-brown person (*cabra*), 200–202, 256, 266–67, 276–77, 292, 329
Darnton, Robert, xviii–xix
decadence period, 134, 137, 159, 167–68
Desemboque, 17
desertion, 26, 70, 122, 151, 286, 383n24, 383n27
devassa (judicial inquiry), 133
diamonds and mines, 10, 27, 73, 137, 188
Dias, Lourenço, 172
Dias d'Aguiar, João, 177
Dias de Mattos, José, 41
directorate missions, 227, 300; *aldeia*, 230–38; captains in, 241, 243; declining numbers, 245; forced labor, 240, 245; Kayapó and, 231–37; for pacified Indians, 230–46; Pedro III inhabitants, 242; status in, 241–42; sustenance in, 240; women in, 241; Xavante and, 238–41, 243; Xerente and, 244. *See also aldeia*
disease: *cerrado* and, 27; Chagas disease, 27, 31; Kayapó, 61; in Natividade, 22, 28, 31; nutritional diseases, 19, 30, 139; Tapirapé, 49, 77. *See also* epidemic diseases
Divine Holy Spirit Festival, xxiii, 208, 226

dízimo (tax), 135–36, 243
Domingues, Pêro, 68, 346n6
Dominicans, 153, 217
Dorvi, Frei Simao, xviii, xxii
dragoons, 86, 89, 111, 135, 150, 255, 335n36, 361n60; gold and, 16, 150; in imperial system of Portugal, 149–53; in Vila Boa de Goiás, 151
droughts, 13–14, 19, 52
dry season, 18–20, 23–25
Duro, 11, 14–15, 83

elephantiasis, 30–31
engenho (mill), 176–77, 178, 329; imperial system of Portugal and, 139; of military officers, 181–82; of slave masters, 203
engenhoca (sugar cane mill), 176, 177, *177*, 180, 329
enslaved population: arrival in Salvador, 141; baptisms, 198–201; burials of, 371, n12; censuses of 1782–1832, 317; census of 1779, 192; census of 1780, 193; census of 1782, 194; census of 1783, 192; census of 1789, 193; census of 1792, 193; census of 1804, 193–94, *313*; census of 1825, 194–95, *314*; census of 1832, 194–95, *315*, *318*; centers of, 192; convoys, 190; early arrivals and gold discoveries, 185–89; estimated populations, 1730s–1740s, 189–91; foods of, 368n60; in Goiás captaincy, 5, 7; in Goiás captaincy, 1782–1832, *317*; Guiné, 7, 186, 196; location in 1832, *318*; marriages, 200; nations, 195–201; in North, 1736-1749, *316*, *320*; numbers, 1736-1750, 316; overview, 186; populations after 1750, 192–95; *quilombo* and, 206–12; sales, 1810-1824, *197*; in São Paulo, 186; in South, 1736-1750, *316*, *319*; taxes, 196–97; work of, 202–6

entrada (expedition), 329; *bandeira*, 65–67; for gold, 79–82; Jesuit-led, 65–67, 78–81; in North, 78–84; on Tocantins River, 79–80
entrada (tax), 135–36
epidemic diseases: among Araés, 71; at Carretão, 50, 90; fevers, 19–20; filariasis, 30; in Goiás captaincy, 28–32; leprosy, 30–31; measles, 28–30, 36, 339n76; self-inoculation, 28–29; smallpox, 28–29, 41, 339n76, 339n77; syphilis, 30–31; vaccinations, 29
Eschwege, Wilhelm Ludwig von, 132
expedition. See *entrada*
expedition participant (*bandeirante*), 88, 159, 302, 329
explorer. See *sertanista*

faiscador, faisqueiro (prospector), 164, 168–69, 204–5, 329
Faria, Antônio Lemos de, 383n24
farinha (manioc meal), 17, 43, 116, 179, 251, 329
farmer (*lavrador*), 178, 329, 361n62
Faustino, José da Gama, 167
fazenda (large estate), 42, *165*, 329; attacks on, 206, 210; cash crops, 139; cattle, 228, 231, 237; farming, 292; on fertile soil, 163; overseers, 386n44; ownership, 181; of *pardos*, 289
feiticeiros, 154
Fernandes, André, 68
Fernandes, Catarina, 268
Fernandes da Cunha, Ludovico, 290
Fernandez, José Maria de Santa Anna, 231
Ferraz Cardoso, Francisco, 82
Ferraz de Araujo, Manuel, 82
Ferreira, Apolinario, 382n23
Ferreira, Dr. José Pinto, 182
Ferreira, Luiza de Souza, 269
Ferreira da Costa, Serafim, 167

Ferreira da Cruz, Manoel, 172
Ferreira da Cruz, Severino, 54, 114
Ferreira de Freitas, Lena Castello Branco, xx
festivals, xxii–xxiii, 52, 208, 222, 225–26. See also *congada*; rituals
Fiçao, Francisco Gomes, 182
fifteen kilos (*arroba*), 73, 147–48, 164, 173, 181, 329
Figueira, Luis, 79
filariasis, 30
floods, 19, 337n52
Fonçeca, José Ribeiro da, 182
Fonseca, José Pinto da, 84–85, 90, 181, 238
Fonseca, Thomaz Francisco da, 229, 239
Fonseca Brandao, Manoel da, 383n24
Fonseca e Silva, Cônego J. Trindade, 227
Fontes, Antônio Barradas, 177
forest (*mata*), 25, 329
Formosa, 12, 24
Forquim, João, 256
forro (freedperson), 200, 279–80, 326, 329
fort. See *presídio*
foundry houses, 11, 132, 182–83, 192, 204–5
Franciscans, 79, 227, 300; alms collectors, 227–28; Amazon region expeditions, 7, 78–79; catechetical efforts, 227–28; hospice and hospital, 227–28; Third Order of St. Francis, 227
Francisco José, Padre, 228
Franco, Virgílio Martins de Mello, 30
freeborn and freed people of color (*gente de cor*): census of 1783, 279–80; census of 1798, 279–80; census of 1804, 280, 322; census of 1825, 281–82, 323; census of 1832, 282–83, 324; criminals and vagrants, 292–93, 385n41; governance, 304; Henriques, 293–97; manumission, 274–79; marriages, 380n37; mulato profile, 280; numbers, 279–84; occupations, 284–86, 290–92, 294–95; overview, 273–74; *pardo* regiments, 286–93; *pedestres*, 285–86; prejudices against, 273–74, 296; property ownership, 289–90; two-thirds of population in 1832, 301; as vassals, 273; women, 282, 294
freeborn person (*ingênuo*), 263, 281–82, 329
freedperson (*forro*), 149, 200, 279–80, 326, 329
freed slave (*liberto*), 281, 323, 329
Freire, José Ribamar Bessa, xx
Freire, José Rodrigues, 89, 181
Freire de Castilho, Fernando Delgado, 28–29, 53, 87, 131, 237, 286, 288
Freitas, Dionízio Furtado de, 250
frontier, xxiii–xxiv, 300; Mato Grosso, 288; mining, 303; mission settlements, 303; Paraúpava slaving, 67–69; slavery, xxi, 303
fugitive slaves, 9, 11, 41, 97, 296; and discovery of gold, 188–89

Gallais, Estevao-Maria, 4
Gama, Jerônimo da, 82
Gama, Lucianno da, 172
Gamela, 83
Gardner, George, 21–22, 259; on goiter, 28
Garro, Paulo Martins, 80
Gê language, 36; Apinaje, 38; Karajá, 44; Kayapó, 59–60; Krahô, 42; among nomads, 62; Xavante, 49; Xerente, 52
gente de cor. See freeborn and freed people of color
gentiles, 92; barbarous, 344n57; Christians and, 95; converting, 156; fighting with, 83; nations, 10, 66; peace with, 39; pursuit of, 71; stealing by, 107; as threatening, 78, 97; wild, 68

Giraldin, Odair, xix, xxiii, 121, 334n17, 341n13, 343n39
Goiá, 4, 70, 186–87, 248–49, 299, 302
Goiânia, 4, 24
goiano (person from Goiás), 131, 134–35, 138, 149, 303, 329; elite, 159, 296; melancholic, 233; white, 160; women, 156–57, 252, 271
Goiás, xxi, 329; derivation, 4; slavery in, xx, xxiii; touring, xvii–xviii
Goiás, captaincy of, xxi, 4; Chagas disease in, 27, 31; churches, 326–28; City of Goiás, xviii, 3–4; early inhabitants, 4–5; enslaved Africans imported to, 5, 7; epidemic diseases, 28–32, 36, 41; goiter in, 27–28; gold in, 5; as heart of Brazil, 3; landscapes, 332n2; lay brotherhoods, 326–28; manumitted slaves, 1792-1824, 275, 275–76; map of, 112; *matas*, 25; Northeast region, 12–18; northern region, 7–12; overview, 3–7; plateaus, *chapadas*, and mountains, 24–28; population, 1779-1832, 325; season of the waters, 18–24; settlers, 301; Southeast and West region, 16–18; subject to São Paulo, 130; white propertied elites, 1779-1832, 312
goiter, 27–28
gold: *bandeira* for, 73, 83; Bueno da Silva seeking, 69–70; circulation of, 301–2; contraband, 137, 143, 146; discoveries, 82–83, 186–89; dragoons and, 16, 150; *entrada* for, 79–80; in Goiás captaincy, 5, 167–68; imperial system of Portugal and, 131–32; Jesuits and, 81; legends of Araés and Martírios, 69; locations, 1826, 171; *oitava*, 69–70, 205, 226, 276–78, 296, 330, 363n9; of Paulistas, 145; Pires de Campos traveling with, 135; to Salvador, 169;

Southeast and West region mines, 16–17; subsidy to Mato Grosso, 142; theft by French, 365n12; on Tocantins River, 82–83; trading posts and, 141, 143; white propertied elites and, 159
Gomes, Malaquias, 172
Gomes da Silva, Domingas, 257
Gomes da Silva, Wenceslau, 36, 83–84, 228
Gomes Leite, Antônio, 36, 83
Gomes Ruxaque, Lourenço, 44
Gonçalves da Silva, Rita, 257
Gonçalves dos Santos, Marcelina, 290
Gonçalves Lima, Balthazar, 83
good order, 129, 156–57, 302
governors, 130–32. See also *specific governors*
Grande River, 16–17, 23–24
The Great Cat Massacre (Darnton), xviii–xix
Gueguê: *bandeiras* against, 36; disappearance, 37; at missions, 14
Guimaraens, Manoel Antunes, 92
Guimaraes, Antônio de Souza, 257
Guimaraes, Felippe Gomes, 175
Guimaraes, João Pereira, 169
Guimarens, João Pereira, 170
gypsies (*ciganos*), 292–93

Habit of Christ, 147. See also Order of Christ
Hemming, John, 80
Henriques (black militia force), 150, 196, 286–87, 293–97, 329, 385n42, 386n44
hinterland. See *sertao*
Hoornaert, Eduardo, 218–19, 370n4
hospices, 227
household dependent. See *agregado*
human settlement, xx
hunting, 25, 45, 51, 57, 122, 137, 235
Hutim, José Francisco, 204

imperial system of Portugal: administrative structures, 129–36; agropastoral wealth, 138–39; captaincy of Goiás, 4, 129; Catholic Church and, 153–57; cattle ranches, 139; dragoons, *pedestres*, militias, 149–53; *engenho* and, 139; extractive economy and, 136–41; financial system, 134–35; good order, 129, 156–57, 302; governors, 130–32; intendants of gold, 132; judicial system, 133–34; manufacturing, 139, 141; mining camps in, 137–39; overview, 129–36; raiding economy, 137; taxes, 135–36; trade networks and commodities, 141–46; trade routes and towns, *140*; Vila Boa de Goiás founding, 129, *130*
incest, 250
Indians, 97, 101, 116, 176; *administrados*, 198; autonomous, 208; with *bandeira*, 86, 91, 187; baptizing, 80, 200; bellicose, 96; buying, 104; canoe, 45, 55, 118; captive, 49, 66, 71–72, 79, 207, 216, 302; census of, 321; Christian, 81, 226–27, 244–46; churches and, 221; clothing of, 240; converting, 245, 300; enslaved, 7, 67–69; epidemics among, 22–23, 28–29; locations, 1832, *321*; mission, 33, 35–38, 150–51, 215–16, 229, 234–38, 244, 264, 283, 296; pacified, 230; priests and, 65; rebelling, 157; sylvan, 25, 91–92; trade in, 43; warfare and, 73, 124, 210; workers, 141. See *also* indigenous nations
India Thereza, 346n12
indigenous and European descent, person of. See mestizo
indigenous nations: Akroá and Xacriabá, 35–38; Apinaje, 38–42; on Araguaia River, 44–49; Canoeiro, 55–59; captivity, *66*, 186; governance, 304; informants, xix; Karajá, Javaé, Xambioá, 44–49; Kayapó, 59–62; Krahô, 42–44; Luso-Brazilians moving, 31; map, *34*; names, locations, dates, 305–10; nine nations, 11; numbers of, 33, 340n2; oral traditions and, 33; overview, 33–35; resettlement of, 22; resistance of, 301; sociopolitical organization, 35; territory of, 299; trade of, 176; women in, 249; Xavante and Xerente, 49–55
indigenous person (*bastardo*), 74, 76, 150, 250, 285, 329
infected matrimony, 222
ingênuo (freeborn person), 263, 281–82, 323, 329, 382n19
inhabitant of a quilombo. See *quilombola*
Inhajurupés, 117–18
Inheiguarás, 80–81
Inquisition, 147, 154–55
Instituto Histórico e Geographico de Goiás, 169
irmandade: do Rosário in Vila Boa, 226, 372n21; do Senhor dos Passos, 222–23; in Natividade, 219; of Nossa Senhora da Abadia, 220; of Santa Efigênia, 372n27–28; of São Miguel, 372n21. See *also* lay brotherhood
Italian Capuchins, xxii, 33, 60, 153, 228, 300

Jardim Padre, 112, 123
Javaé, 9; illnesses, 23; indigenous nation on Araguaia River, 44–49; at missions, 48, 230–31, 237, 244; Pinto da Fonseca on, 106; warfare, 105–6; weapons, 106
Jayme, Jarbas, 259
Jesuits, xxii, 300; Canoeiro and, 56; cattle *fazendas*, 228–29; *entradas*, 65–67, 78–81; expulsion, 33, 37, 153, 228; gold and, 81; on Karajá, 105; missions, 16,

30, 74, 83, 227, 228–30; Northeast region mission villages, 13–14; northern expeditions, 7; on Tocantins River, 81, 82; Xavante and, 52

Jesus e Maria, Friar João de, 227

Jews, 154, 222, 372n20

Jezus do Bomfim, 167

João VI, 131, 356n6

jornal (payment to slaveholder), 168, 205, 329

José da Motta, Fernando, 180

José I, 356n6

Joseph, Friar, 228

judge of the comarca (*ouvidor*), 77, 92, 130, 133, 160, 330

judges and bureaucrats: in São Félix, 1783, 183, *183*; slaveholders, 182; white propertied elites, 182–84

judicial district. See *comarca*; *julgado*

judicial inquiry (*devassa*), 133

judicial system, 133–34

julgado (judicial district), 177, 192, 329; judges, 133; *mulatos*, 280; Natividade, 134; of North, 134, 161, 163, 194–95; slaves in, 192–94; of South, 133; white, 161

Juxum, Marcelino, 41

Kalunga, 26, 206, 209, 211, 274

Karajá, 44–48; agriculture, 46; alliance with Portuguese, 106; and Apinaje, 105; canoes, 45; as captives, 72; Carajaúna, 347n21; catechizing attempts, 81; coalition with Xerente and Xavante, 106; contact with Luso-Brazilians, 44–45, 80–81; driven inland by river, 9; enslavement, 186, 302; firearms, 48, 106; first contact, xvii; Gê language, 44; gift giving, 46–47; illnesses, 23; indigenous nation on Araguaia River, 9, 44–49; mask, 1930s, 342n35; in missions, 37, 229–31, 237–38; pacification *bandeira* against, 84–85; Pinto da Fonseca on, 84–85, 106; pottery, 46; principal chiefs, 47, 106; relations with Apinaje, 96; trade, 10, 144; trading with Apinaje, 40; Vila Real and, 47, 105–6; villages, 47–48; warfare, 105–6; warrior, 47, 106, *107*; weapons, 45–46, 48; women hiding, 45

Kayapó, xviii, 18, 59–62; aid to *bandeira*, 111; attacks, 10; *bandeira* to, 60, 71–78, 121; as Bilreiros, 59–60, 72, 121; Bororo as enemy, 61, 73, 123; cannibalism accusation, 61, 71, 125; Castelnau on, 60; Christianization, 233; Cunha Matos on, 37; dances, 374n47, 374n52, 374n54; directorate missions and, 232–37, 244; diseases, 29–30, 61; ethnohistory, xix; expeditions to, xviii–xix; fire used by, 60, 124; Gê language, 59–60; interpreter, 90; Maria I, 61; measles among, 30; as Mebengokre in North, 60; in missions, 61–62, 231–37, 374n58; pacification *bandeira* against, 85–89; as Panará, 59–60, 125; *pedestres*, and, 151, 285; Pinto da Silveira, on, 61; Pires de Campos and, 73, 76, 124–25; polities, 35; *quilombo* and, 123, 211; raids, 18, 27, 85, 89, 122–23, 125; raids for captives, 123; removal from São José de Mossâmedes, 122–23; Saint-Hilaire on, 234; São José de Mossâmedes, 62; smallpox among, 29; territory, 17; towns, 300; vengeance by, 75, 121–23; villages, 10, 19, 27, 60–61; violence against, 87; visit to Vila Boa, 61; warfare, 121–26; warriors, 72; weapons, 61, 124–25; Xerente enemy, 112

king of Congo, *186*, 215

Krahô, 10–11, 13, 91, 99, 302; as allies, 342n26; Cunha Matos on, 43; enemies

Krahô (*continued*)
  of Xavante, 104; Gê language, 42; herdsmen, 42–44, 44; Luso-Brazilians as ally, 44, 103, 105; Luso-Brazilians vengeance on, 104; Magalhaes and, 43, 103–4; in missions, 44, 103; peace agreement, 104–5; Porekamekra merging, 43; raids, 13–14, 42–44, 104; Ribeiro on, 42, 43; sexual assault, 249; warfare, 99–105
Kreen-Akarore: contact with, xvii, 94; decimation of, 331n2; descendants, 60

land grant. See *sesmaria*
landscapes, 332n2
language: changing, 62; in missions, 230. See also Gê language; Tupi language
large estate. See *fazenda*
lavra (mine), 164, 168–70, *171*, 180, 329; Mato Grosso, 17; slaves in, 168–70, 204–5
lavrador (farmer), 178, 329, 361n62
lay brotherhood (*irmandade*), 329; black, 224–26; Blessed Sacrament, 222; *crioulo*, 24; in Goiás captaincy, *326–28*; Irmandade do Senhor dos Passos, 222–23; Our Lady of Lapa, 222; Our Lady of Mercies, 226; Our Lady of the (Immaculate) Conception, 224; Our Lady of the Good Death, 222; Our Lady of the Rosary, 222, 223, 224, 226, 372n21; *pardo*, 224; Pohl on festivities, 225–26; Republicans, 223; Santa Efigênia, 224–26, 372n27–28; Santo Antônio, 223; São Gonçalo Garcia, 224; São Miguel e Almas, 223, 372n21; St. Benedict, 224–25; white, 222–23
Lazarin, Rita Heloísa de Almeida, 244
Leal, Antônio Luis de Souza, 149
Leal, Fernando José, 255
Leao, Pedro Barbosa, 168
Leite, Anna Francisca Xavier, 269
Leite, Antônio da Silva, 172
Leite, Antônio Gomes, 36
Leite, Clara Maria, 256–57
Leite, Francisco Xavier, 181
Leite, João Ferreira, 269
Leite, Serafim, 79, 82
Leite Álvarez Fidalgo, João, 269
Leite brothers, 269
Leme, João, 76
Lemos de Faria, Antônio de, 72, 285, 383n24
leprosy, 24, 30–31
Levin-Rojo, Danna, xx
liberto (freed slave), 281, 323, 329, 382n19
Lima, Rodrigo Coelho Furtado de Azevedo, 239
Lima, Salvador de, 72
Língua geral, 37, 79–80
Lino de Moraes, Miguel, 21, 53, 87–88
Lisboa, Antônio da Silva, 173
Lisboa, Antônio Luiz Tavares, 38
Lisboa, Cristovão Severin de, 227
Lisboa, Francisco da Silva, 173
Lisboa, Gaspar José, 190
Lisboa, João da Costa, 238
Lisboa, José Pedroso, 182
Lisboa, José Pereira, 169, 170
Lisbon, 5, 136
Lobo, Antônio de Meirelles, 169
local *bandeira*, 65
loja (store), 173–74, *175*, 329
Lopes, João, 172
Lopes Benavides, Francisco, 68
Lopes de Miranda, Diogo, 83
Lordelo, Francisco Carvalho de, 70
Lordelo, José Alves de, 70
Lourenço da Silva, Bartolomeu, 221
Ludovico, Ángela, 378n16
Luís Grau, Domingos, 67
Luso-Brazilians: attacks and wars, 40–42; on Canoeiro, 119; Christianization goal, 84; contact

with, 36; culture, 38; expansion and rule, 121; hunters, 25; Karajá contact with, 44–45; Krahô as ally, 44; landgrabs, 122; massacres, 58; merchants, 48; moving indigenous nations, 31; priests defended by, 65; refuge from, 26; settlements, 11, 27; sources, 56; territory controlled by, 299; traders, 9, 16; vengeance on Krahô, 104; warfare view, 95; working for, 84; Xavante as enemy, 108. *See also* white propertied elites

Macamecra, 103
Macedo, Antônio de, 67
Machado, Antônio, 83
Machado, João Álvares, 250
Machado de Miranda, João, 173
Maciel, Domingos Pires, 257
Magalhaes, 10, 12–13, 43, 104
malaria, 20–21, 22–24
mameluco (mestizo), 82
manioc meal (*farinha*), 17, 43, 116, 179, 251, 329
Mano, Marcel, 211
Manoel de Mello, João, 3
Manuel, Kayapó (captain), 17
Manuel Alves Grande Rivers, 10–13
Manuel Correia, Sorocabano, 68
manumission: achieving, 190, 264; at baptism, 381–82n10; "family-motivated," 381n5; forms of in 1790s, 277–79, *278*; in Goiás captaincy, 1792–1824, 275, 275–76; of people of color, 274–79; prices paid for, 381 n7; records, 196
Maranhão, captaincy, 4–5, 10, 12–14, 26–27
Maranhão River, 11–12, 19–20, 145, 188, 205–6
Maria I, *aldeia*, 230, 235–37
Maria I, (Queen), 86, 90, 131, 238, 244, 356n6

Marinho, Sebastiao, 67
Marques, Thomé Joaquim, 288
marriage: in Cavalcante, 264, *266*; census of 1783, 261, 262; census of 1804, 262–63, *263*; census of 1825, 263–64, 264–65, *265*; in Cocal, 261; by color, 1828, 265–66; of elite, 380n48; enslaved Africans, 200; of free people of color, 1796–1816, 267; and *irmandades*, 380n35; women across color lines, 266–68; women and, 261–66
Martins, Diogo, 72
Martins, Manoel Ferreira, 169
Martins des Reys, Francisco, 91
Mascarenhas, Francisco de Assis, 378n16
Mascarenhas, Luís de, 72, 74, 76, 83, 285
mata (forest), 25, 329
Mato Grosso, 5, 17–18, 27, *140*; Apiaká, 47; *bandeiras*, 71, 88, 121–23; Bororo, 61, *75*; Carlota, 209, 369n75; culture, 56; frontier, 288; guards, 29; Kayapó raids, 18, 85, 89; mines, 17; Pinto da Silveira explorations, 77; retreating to, 270; trade, 142, 144, 146, 148; Xavante in, 299
Matos, Gregorio da Costa, 182–83
Matos, José de, 228
matriculas (slave registries), 251
Mattos, José Dias de, 41
Maybury-Lewis, David, 54, 118
McCreery, David, 300, 303, 337n52
Mead, David L., 60
Mearim River, 13, 18
measles, 28–30, 36, 339n76
Mebengokre, 60
Meia Ponte, 15–16, 24, 187; Church of Our Lady of Carmo, 218; Church of Our Lord of the Good Death, 218; Our Lady of the Rosary church, 218
meia sisa (tax, slave sale), 195–96, 201, 275–76, 296, 329
Meirelles Lobo, Antônio de, 169

Mello, João Manuel de, 3, 208
Mendes, Vicente da Cunha, 292
Mendonça, Luis da Gama, 239
Menezes, João Manoel de, 22, 178, 286–87
Menezes, Luiz da Cunha, 15, 86, 235, 286, 375n69
Menezes, Tristão da Cunha, 20–21, 89, 111, 151, 236, 286
men of backlands (*sertanejos*), 12, 17
merchants and businessmen: Amazon region, 7, 144; identities, 146–49; retail centers, 174, *175*; tavern owners, 174; white propertied elites, 173–76
mestizo (person of indigenous-European descent), xxii, 201–2, 267, 285, 330; adventurous, 74; *bandeira*, 82; baptisms, 250; gang leader, 65; *pedestres*, 150, 285; sale of, 202; servility and, 289
methodologies, xx–xxiv
military officers: *engenho* and, 181–82; slaves of, 180–82; uniform, *248*; white propertied elites, 180–82. See also dragoons
militias: captives in, 150; characteristics, 151, 153; in imperial system of Portugal, 149–53; local, 65; occupations, 1820s, 295; Palacin on, 151; role of, 123. See also *Henriques*; *ordenança*
mill. See *engenho*
Minas Gerais, captaincy, 16
mine. See *lavra*
mine owners, 165–66; decadence period, 134, 137, 159, 167–68, 171; mine locations, *171*, 172; priests as, 66, 132, 166–67; slaves of, 164, 168–70, 171–72, 367–68n50; wealth of, 169–70; white propertied elites, 164–72
mining: camps, 130, 137–39; Cocal, 168, *171*, 172, 189, 204–5, 226, 303; frontier, 303; Maranhão River, 188;

Natividade, xxi, 7, 11–13, 15, 26, 82–83, 138, 141, 162–63, 167, 188, 191, 205–6, 208, 219, 259, 280–81; Pilar, 189, 191; Pontal, 7, 11, 13–14, 57, 82–83, 112, 138, 141, 167, 172, 188, 251, 334n17; São José do Tocantins, 188–89; work of, 204–6
miscegenation, 302
Misch, Gaspar, 81
missionaries, xxii, 33, 105, 153. See also baptisms; Catholic Church; Dominicans; Franciscans; Italian Capuchins; Jesuits; priests
mission settlements: Akroá, 35–38, 228–29; frontier, 303; Gueguê at, 14; Indians, 33, 35–38, 150–51, 215–16, 229, 234–38, 244, 264, 283, 296; Jesuit, 228–30; Kayapó in, 61–62; language in, 230; Maria I, 25; Natividade, 14, 66, 227; Northeast region, 13–14; Pedro Afonso, 103; Pires de Campos and, 74–75; Pontal, 66; relocations to, 22–23; São Francisco Xavier, 36–37; São José de Mossâmedes, *231*; São José do Duro, 36–37; Tocantins River, 80; Xacriabá, 35–38, 228–29; Xavante and Xerente in, 107. See also directorate missions
mocambo, 27, 206. See also *quilombo*
monsoon expeditions, 17
Monte do Carmo, Antônio José do, 285
Monteiro, John, xix, 346n7
Monteiro Guimaraes, José, 83
Moraes, Cristina Cássia P., 223, 226
Moraes, Miguel Lino de, 53 88
Morais Betancourt, Hilário de, 39
Moreira, Amaro Leite, 77
Moreira, Inácio Joaquim, 231
Moreira da Silva, Antônio, 43, 91, 98–99, 284; *bandeira* against Porekamekra, 102–3
Moreira de Carvalho, Innocencio Joaquim, 231

Moreira de Carvalho, Plácido, 41, 99, 176
Moreira de Paiva, Barnabé, 177, 181
Mortes River, 5, 10
mosquitoes, 19–21, 23, 337n52
Mota, Manuel da, 82
Mota Falcao, Francisco da, 82
Mott, Luiz, 154
Motta, Fernando José da, 180
mountains: Chapada dos Veadeiros, 26–27; in Goiás captaincy, 24–28; Pireneus range, 25–26; Serra Dourada, 26, 27; Serra Geral de Goiás, 26; *sertao*, 15
mulato (person of European and African descent), 23, 201–2, 276–77, 280–84, 286, 288–89, 330, 381n2
mule teams, 17–18, 142
Muquém, 209, 220–21, 369n69

Nascimento, José Joaquim do, 260
Nascimento, Pedro Tomaz do, 260
nation, concept of, 33
Natividade, xix; Akroá, 36; churches in, 221, 225; disease in, 22, 28, 31; *julgado*, 134; mining, xxi, 7, 11–13, 15, 26, 82–83, 138, 141, 162–63, 167, 188, 191, 205–6, 208, 219, 259, 280–81; mission settlement, 14, 66, 227; *mulatos*, 280; priests in, 289; slaves in, 193–95; trade, 142–44, 146–47; white propertied elites in, 162–63; women, 270; Xavante and, 107
Navarro de Abreu, Antônio, 148
Nazareth, Felizardo, 116
negro, 44, 69, 186, 190, 207–8
negro da terra, 186, 226, 365n3
Neiva, Lourenço Antônio da, 221
Néri da Silva, Felipe, 231, 239
Nhyrykwaye, 60
Nimuendajú, Curt: on Apinaje, 38, 41, 96, 98, 207; on Canoeiro, 56; fieldwork, 33, 35; on Krahô, 44, 341n22; on victimization, 104; on Xavante and Xerente, 52; on Xerente, 52, 112–13, 351n12
Nogueira, Catherina, 172
Nogueira, Francisco Rodrigues, 175
Noroguagé, 54, 117–18
Noronha, João Antunes de, 254
Noronha, Marcos de, 16, 49, 83, 130, 191, 206–7, 208
North American settlers, 300–301
Northeast region: Bahian routes through, 15; *chapadas*, 14–15; cowboys in, 14; of Goiás captaincy, 12–18; Jesuit mission villages, 13–14; river travel, 13; São Luis port, 12–13; slave trade, 15
Northern region: Araguaia route, 9–10; Franciscan and Jesuit expeditions, 7; of Goiás captaincy, 7–12; indigenous nations, 10–11; Maranhão River, 11–12; Paranã River, 12; *registros*, 9; Tocantins River trips, 8, 8–11; travel to Belém do Pará at delta, 7–8
Nossa Senhora do Monte do Carmo, Friar Francisco de, 228
Nossa Senhora dos Anjos, Friar José de, 227–28, 357–58n29
Nova Beira, 20, 23, 48, 237–38
Nunes, Antônio, 72
Nunes, Manuel, 45, 80–81

obligated person (*pessoa de obrigaçao*), 289, 294, 330
occupations: black militiamen, 1820s, 295; freeborn and freed people of color, 284–86; *pardo*, 1820s, 291; of slaves, 1783, 203
oitava (one-eighth ounce of gold), 69–70, 205, 226, 276–78, 296, 330
Oliveira, Antônio João de, 210
Oliveira, Bento Pais de, 72–73
Oliveira, João de Souza de, 180

Oliveira, João Lourenço de, 241–43
Oliveira, Pedro Dias de, 256
one-eighth ounce of gold (*oitava*), 69–70, 205, 226, 276–78, 296, 330
Ora, Miguel A. da, 288
oral traditions, xxii, 33, 49, 60, 296
ordenança (white militia force), 147, 151, 181, 286, 330, 361n62
Order of Christ, 147–48, 155, 164, 167, 181–82, 261
orphans, 148, 268, 379n33
Ortiz, João Leite da Silva, 346n12
Our Lady of Abadia, 209, 220, 371n14
Our Lady of Carmo, 225
Our Lady of Mercies, 226
Our Lady of the Rosary church, 218
Our Lady of the Rosary feastday, 185
Our Lady of the Rosary of the Blacks, 217, 221
ouvidor (judge of the comarca), 77, 92, 130, 133, 160, 330

Pacheco do Couto, João, 82
pacification: accepting, xvii; Akroá and Xacriabá, 83; leading, xviii, 65; permanent, 125; resistance, 56; Xavante, 111
pacification *bandeira*, xvii; against Karajá, 84–85; against Kayapó, 85–89; success, 94; against Xavante, 89–94
paid infantry man. See *pedestre*
Pais de Abreu, Bartolomeu, 69
Pais de Araujo, Pascoal, 82
Pais de Barros, Sebastiao, 82
Palacin, Luis, 146, 187, 191, 218, 220; on militia, 151; on *quilombo*, 206
palmatória, 240, 249, 374n58
Panará, 59–62, 94; Panariá, 373n42
Pará, captaincy and state of, 5, 14
Paracatú, 5, 16, 24
Paranaíba River, 13, 17, 23, 27
Paraná River, 12, 16–17, 27, 208

Paranã River, 12, 15, 21, 24
Paraúpava, sertão do, 67–68, 346n4
Paraúpava River, 44, 67–69
pardo (brown-skinned person), xxii, 152, 201–2, 224, 280, 282, 284, 289–90, 292, 330; *agregado*, 243, 289; in auxiliary regiment, 151–52, 287; *fazenda*, 289; freeborn and freed people of color regiments, 286–93; location in 1832, *318*; long-distance trade, 292; occupations, 1820s, *291*; prejudice and discrimination against, 152, 361n63, 381n2; Xavante and, 288
Parnaíba, port city, 14
passagens (taxes), 70
Pastos Bons, Maranhão, 12–13
Paulistas, 269; *bandeira*, 5, 60, 67–68, 72, 78, 186–87; explorations, 73; gold of, 145; predatory, 67; *sertanistas*, 77, 81; slaving, 81; in Vila Boa de Goiás, 145; women, 258
payment to slaveholder (*jornal*), 168, 205, 329
peace, 302; Apinaje interlude, 98; in Cocal Grande, 102–3; fragile, 301; with gentiles, 39; Krahô agreement, 104; Xavante making, 110–11
Pecobo, Francisco, 41
pedestre (paid infantry man), 37, 87, 92–93, 122, 330; in *bandeira*, 66; desertions, 383n27; freeborn and freed people of color, 150, 284–86, 383n24; in imperial system of Portugal, 149–53; in missions, 62, 285; services, 152; soldiers, 62; in Vila Boa de Goiás, 150–51, 285
Pedro I, 244, 356n6
Pedro II, 244
Pedro III, 50, 90, 238, 242
Pedroso, Dulce Madalena Rios, 56–57, 208, 296
Pedroso de Alvarenga, Antônio, 68

Pereira, Antônio Rodrigues, 169, 182
Pereira, Joaquim, 93, 94
Pereira, José Godoi, 73
Pereira, José Luis, 58, 86, 87, 92, 236, 350n60, 384n28
Pereira Brandao, João, 83
Pereira da Cruz, Manuel, 88, 350n61
Pereira do Lago, Francisco, 169
Pereira e Cárceres, Francisco de Mello, 210
Pereyra, José dos Santos, 167
Pernambuco, 5, 14
person from Goiás. See *goiano*
person of European and African descent (*mulato*), 201, 280, 284, 286, 330, 381n2
pessoa de obrigação (obligated person), 289, 330
Piauí, captaincy and state of, 5, 12–13, 26–27
Pilar, 57, 66, 120; assaults on, 54; Church of our Lady of Pilar, 218; mining, 189, 191; *roças*, 179; slaves in, 168, 193–94; vicar of, 90, 154
pilgrimages, 209, 220–21, 244, 371n14
Pimenta, João Martins, 279
Pimentel, Antônio de Camargo, 169
Pimentel, Carlos Pinto Barboza, 279
Pimentel, João Pinto Barboza, 250
Pindarê, 83
Pinheiro, Maria Roza, 256
Pinto, Manoel Cardozo, 173
Pinto Bravo, João Pereira, 262, 279–80
Pinto da Fonseca, José, 45–47, 85, 90, 148; on Javaé, 106; on Karajá, 106
Pinto da Silveira, João Godói, 49, 61, 73–74, 77, 189, 208, 348n36; Mato Grosso explorations, 77
Pinto de Aguiar, Paulo de Souza, 168, 179–80
Pinto de Magalhaes, Francisco José, 10, 13, 42, 99, 102, 333n6

Pinto dos Santos, Jacinto José, 177
Pinto e Aguiar, Paulo de Souza, 180
Pinto Magalhaes, Francisco José de, 99, 104, 145, 249. See also Magalhaes.
Pireneus range, 25–26
Pires, Domingos, 169
Pires, Estevão Joaquim, 54, 117, 244
Pires, Gonçalo, 82
Pires de Campos, Antônio, 37, 45, 61, 69, 78; allies, 229; *bandeira*, 71, 73–74; Bororo and, 37, 73, 75–77, 229; captives of, 73–74, 77, 84; death of, 86; excesses, 73–74; father and son, 71, 73; Karajá, 76; Kayapó and, 61, 71, 73, 76, 124–25; massacre of Araés, 49; mission settlements and, 74–75; skill and experience, 74; traveling with gold, 135
Pizarro e Araújo, José de Sousa Azevedo, 20
planters and ranchers: predators and, 178; slaves of, 177, 177–79; white propertied elites, 176–79
plateaus, 24–28
Pohl, Johann Emanuel, xxii, 21, 22–23, 219, 231–35, 238, 240–41, 253, 336n44, 374n58; on Apinaje, 41, 98; on Canoeiro, 120; on Carretão, 50, 238; on Carvalho, P., house, 176; on lay brotherhood festivities, 225–26; on Maria I, 237; meeting Macamecra, 103; on Porekamekra, 42–43; on Porekamekras warfare, 99–102, 108; on poverty of women, 270; on São José de Mossâmedes, 230; on sexual jealousy, 258; on smallpox, 28; on syphilis, 31; on warfare, 99–101; on women, 247; on Xavante, 50–52, 108–10; on Xerente, 54, 112, 351n12
Pontal: Canoeiro raiding, 57; churches, 221; coerced labor in, 251; mining, 7, 11, 13–14, 82–83, 112, 138, 141, 167, 172,

Pontal (*continued*)
188, 334n17; mission settlement, 66; slaves in, 179, 290; trade, 146; Xavante in, 111
Poquiguirá, 79–81
Poquis, Poquizes, 81–82
Porekamekra, 18, 42–43, 91, 99; anchoraxe, *100*; *bandeira* of Moreira da Silva, 91, 102–3; Pohl on warfare, 99–102, 109; warfare, 99–105, 108; weapons, 101–2
Porto, Alferes José Francisco, 182
Porto Real, Porto Nacional, 7, 11, 21
predatory *bandeira*, 63, 65
presídio (fort), 20, 23, 122, 330; attacks on, 40, 48, 98, 106; construction, 23, 48; soldiers, 30, 40, 98
priests, 15; *agregado* and, 260; *bandeira* chaplain, 74; *bandeira* leaders, 66–67; Catholic Church, 155–56; Christianization focus, 46; Indians and, 65; Luso-Brazilians defending, 65; as mine owners, 66, 132, 166–67; in Natividade, 289; Saint-Hilaire on, 259, 289; shortage of, 216; tolerance of clerical families, 34, 380; wealth of, 364n25; white propertied elites, 179–80; women in clerical families, 259–61
prospector (*faisqueiro*), 204–5, 329
prostitution, 204, 247–48, 257, 270, 302, 379n25, 379n27
protest, of five nations, 104–5
protest against Indian slavery, 227

Queirós, Anna Ferreira de, 256
quilombo (community of fugitive slaves), xxi, 23, 26, 123, 330, 337n56, 368–69n61, 369n77; Ambrosio, 210; Apinaje attacks on, 96–97; Carlota, 209–10, 369n75; decrease in, 212; descendants of, 210–11; destruction of, 209, 211; enslaved Africans and, 206–12; governance, 210, 304; Kalunga, 26, 206, 209, 211, 274; Kayapó and, 123, 211; locations, 189, 206–9, 369n77; Palacin on, 206; at Paraná River, 208; raids on, 207–10; revolt by, 208; running away to, 274; saints of, 246; Salles on, 206
quilombola (inhabitant of a quilombo), 92, 330; assaults on, 96, 211; danger from, 39; raids, 207, 210, 302; refuge of, 206, 211; revolting, 208; territory, 304; trade with, 302
quinine, 17, 21, 142
quinto (tax of a fifth), 74, 77, 130, 135, 330; annual income, 1752–1805, 137, *138*; capturing, 202; decline, 149; decline in annual income, 1752–1805, 135, *135*; first *quintos*, 347n14; paid for Habit of Christ, 135–36; Vila Boa de Goiás collection, 136
Quirixá, 70, 346n12. See also *crixá* and *crixás*
quitandeiras, 253

Radding, Cynthia, xx
raids: Apinaje, 38–42; Canoeiro, 19, 57; cattle, 42–44; Kayapó, 27, 85, 89; Krahô, 13–14, 42–43; *quilombo*, 207–10; *quilombola*, 207, 210; Xavante, 10, 13; Xerente, 55
rapadura (raw brown sugar), 143, 149, 177–78, 330
Raposo, Antônio, 82
raw brown sugar (*rapadura*), 143, 149, 177–78, 330
real, *réis* (colonial currency), 76–77, 136, *138*, *143*, 286, 330
Rebello, Manoel Gomes, 23
Rebello, Simão da Silva, 173
Rebouça, Manoel Ferreira, 256–57
registo, *registro* (checkpoint), 330; Duro, Taguatinga, São Domingos, 12, 15, 26;

Lagoa Feia, 15, 24; northern region, 9; patrolling, 285; Rio das Velhas, 16; taxes paid at, 135–36
Reis, José Alves dos, 173
Ribeiro, Antônio, 79
Ribeiro, Francisco de Paula, 9, 29, 50, 79, 249, 284; on Krahô, 42, 43; as leader of royalist force, 91, 105; on Porekamekra, 42, 102–3; Ribeiro, Mamedes Mendes, 170, 180
Ribeiro, João Nepumuceno, 172
Ribeiro, Tomé, 80–81
Ribeiro da Costa, Manoel, 173
Ribeiro da Silva, Manuel, 169, 170
Rio de Janeiro, capital and captaincy, 5, 16; role in trade, 145
rituals, xxii, 156, 181, 208, 215–16, 233, 303
Rituals of Paulo 5, 239
Roballo, Manoel Nunes, 105
roça (small farm), 107, 178–79, 203, 330
roceiro (small farmer), 19, 330
Rocha, José da Silva, 181
Rodrigues, Domingos, 186
Rodrigues, Garcia, 72
Rodrigues, Martins, 186
Rodrigues de Jesus, Francisca, 277
Rodrigues do Prado, Domingos, 346n12
Rodrigues Jardim, José, 170
Rodrigues Jardim, Manoel, 231, 239
Rodrigues Jardim, Silvestre, 168, 181
Rodrigues Pereira, Antônio, 169, 182
Rodrigues Vilares, Antônio, 68
Rodriguez da Gama, Joanna, 257
Rodriguez de Sá, João de Oliveira, 182
Rodriguez Xavier, José, 256
Romexi, 86
Rosário, Franciscano do, 227
Royal Word, 103
Roza, Joaquim Theodoro da, 268
Ruxaque, Lourenço Gomes, 72

Saint Anne's Church, 216, 216–17

Saint-Hilaire, Auguste de, xxii, 23, 174, 227–28, 231–33, 235, 247, 251, 257, 260, 274; on *aldeia*, 229–30; on concubinage, 254–55; on Cunha, Damiana da, 87, 235; on filariasis, 30; on goiter, 28; on hospices, 227; on Kayapó, 234; on leprosy, 30; on Maria I, 237; on measles, 30; on priests, 179, 259, 289; on Santa Ana, 37, 229–30; on São José de Mossâmedes, 230, 232; on Vila Boa de Goiás, 132; on Xacriabá, 37–38
Salinas, 23, 48, 238–39
Salles, Gilka, 186, 188, 191; on *quilombo*, 206, 210
salt, 5, 15, 28, 136, 141–44, 234, 337n56, 338n73
Salvador, Bahia, 5, 15, 141
Salvamento, Manoel do, 167
Sanches, Antônio, 82–83
Santa Ana do Rio das Velhas, 37
Santa Cruz, 16–17
Santa Efigênia festival, 225–26
Santa Luzia, 24
Santa Teresa, Ignacio de, 358n31
Santa Teresa River, 11, 26
Santiago, Friar Domingos de, 227
Santos, José Claro dos, 269
Santos, Luis Gonçalves dos, 293
São Félix, 7, 11–12, 14–15, 303
São Francisco de Paula church, 217
São Francisco River, 15–16, 26
São Gonçalo, chapel, 218; dance 207
São João da Palma, 21
São João das Duas Barras, 9, 40
São José, Christóvao, 227
São José de Mossâmedes, 230–32, 231, 237
São José do Carretão, 230
São José do Tocantins, 11
São Luis port, 12–13
São Miguel, Conde de, 16, 132
São Paulo: *bandeiras*, 17–18, 49, 63, 67–69; captaincy and town, 5, 16–17;

São Paulo (*continued*)
  slavery, 44; town, 17. *See also*
  Paulistas
São Pedro de Alcântara: hospital, 30;
  town, 9, 14, 99, 102–3, 245
savanna. *See cerrado*
season of the waters: apoplexy during,
  22; destruction during, 18–19; dry
  season during, 19; in Goiás captaincy,
  18–24; malaria, 20–21, 23–24; mosquitoes breeding, 19–21; relocations
  to Christian missions, 22–23;
  unhealthiness, 23
Segurado, Joaquim Theotonio, 58, 92–93,
  133, 144
Senado da Câmara, 133–34, 184
Serras, 12, 27; Serra dos Caiapó, 10; Serra
  Dourada, 11, 26–27; Serra Geral de
  Goiás, 26
sertanejos (men of backlands), 12, 17
sertanista (explorer), 36, 65, 72, 284, 330;
  on Araguaia River, 284; *bandeira*, 83;
  experienced, 84; Paulista, 77, 81; on
  Tocantins River, 82; women, 88; work
  of, 284
sertão (hinterland), xxi, 300, 330; backlands, 299; crossing, 13–15; do Amaro
  Leite, 78; droughts, 14; drugs of, 142;
  entering, 69–71; high, 91–92; mountains, 15; remote, 301; rivers, 67–68;
  trade, 146, 292, 336n38; wilderness, 65
sesmaria (land grant), 25, 63, 70, 139, 330,
  358n36, 367n49; petitions, 138–39, 203
Severiano da Luz, Antônio, 259–60
Severiano da Luz, Bento, 259, 289
Severin de Lisboa, Cristovao, 79, 227
sexual assault, 250, 302
sexual jealousy, 258
Silva, Antônio da, 290
Silva, Dr. Gonçalo José da, 364n215
Silva, Francisco José Xavier da, 231
Silva, João Caetano da, 17, 236

Silva Braga, José Peixoto da, 70
Silva e Souza, Luiz Antônio da, 16, 41, 49,
  51, 53–54, 74, 170, 188, 260–61; on
  aldeia, 229, 235, 238; on Bueno da
  Silva, 70; on Canoeiro, 57, 119; clerical
  office and cortês, 154–55, 362n73; on
  Xerente, 53–55
Silveira, Gonçalo Pereira da, 242–43
Silveira, João Godói Pinto da, 208
silver, 17
sítio (small land plot), 289, 330
slave revolt, 208. *See also quilombo*
slavery: *bandeira* expanding, 63; Bororo
  slaves, 85, 105, 198, 226; captivity, 66,
  81; Catholic Church and, 155; in
  Cocal, 170, 290, 368n50; documents
  burned, 366n30; by *entradas*,
  Tocantins River, 79–80; frontier, xxi,
  302; in Goiás, xvii, xx, xxiii; judges
  and bureaucrats, 182; in *julgado*, 192–
  94; military officers and, 180–82;
  mine owners and, 164, 168–70, 171–72;
  in mines, 168–70, 204; in Natividade,
  193–95; Northeast region trade, 15;
  Paraúpava River frontier, 67–69; by
  Paulistas, 72, 81; in Pilar, 168, 193–94;
  planters and ranchers, 177, 177–79; in
  Pontal, 179, 290; São Paulo, 44; trading post trade, 145; Xavante, 108. *See
  also crioulo*
slaves, 74, 313–15
slave trades, 145, 147; in Africans, 190,
  199, 359n49; in Indians, 43, 58, 102,
  104, 245
slaving frontier, xxi, 63, 302
small farm (*roça*), 107, 178–79, 203, 330
small farmer (*roceiro*), 19, 330
small land plot (*sítio*), 289, 330
smallpox, 28–29, 41, 339n76
smugglers (*contrabandistas*), 12, 15, 292
smuggling, 12, 15, 292, 358n31
snakeskin hat, boots, gun case, 283

Soares, Anna Flaminia Xavier, 268
Soares, Bento, 228
Soares, Sebastião José da Cunha, 208
sociopolitical organization, 35
Sono River, 10, 13
Sotomaior, João de, 79–80
Sousa Botafogo, João Pereira de, 67
Sousa Henriques, Luís de, 67–68
Sousa Vila Real, Tomás de, 284
Southeast and West region, 16–18; of Goiás captaincy, 16–18; monsoon expeditions, 17; mule teams, 17–18; routes to gold mine, 16–17
Souza, Joanna Vieira de, 269
Souza, Manoel de, 79
Souza, Maria de, 290
Souza, Miguel de, 383n27
Souza, Simão de, 117
Souza de Oliveira, João de, 180
Souza Leal, Antônio Luis de, 149
Spix, Johann B. and Carl Friedrich P. von, 27
state-funded *bandeira*, 65
store (*loja*), 173–74, *175*, 329
sugar cane mill (*engenhoca*), 176, 177, *177*, 180, 329
Sweet, David J., xviii
syphilis, 30–31

tablelands (*chapadas*), 14–15, 24–28
Taggia, Rafael, 105, 238
Tapirapé, 37, 47–49, 80–81, 229
Tapuios, 215, 244
Tavares, Manoel José, 147–48
Tavares, Valentim, 167
Tavares da Cunha, Manoel José, 147–48
Tavares Lisboa, Antônio Luiz, 38, 98
tax evasion, 191
tax of a fifth. *See quinto*
tax on slave (*capitaçao*), 189–92, 329
tax slave sale (*meia sisa*), 195–96, 201, 275–76, 296, 329

Teixeira, Antonia, 257
Teixeira, Antônio, 260
Teixeira, Francisco Alves, 180
Teixeira, Franco Alves, 169
Teixeira, Joaquim da Costa, 260
Teixeira, Sebastiao, 81
Teixeira de Souza, João, 173
Telles e Menezes, Antônio de Souza, 27, 147
Tenório de Aguilar, Martim Rodrigues, 72
Terceiro, Pedro, 90
territorial division (*captaincy*), 3, 5, 16, *143*, 329
Teske, Wolfgang, 208
thatch-roofed shelters (*barracas*), 39, 46, 238
theatrical dance (*congada*), xxii–xxiii, 185, *186*, 215, 225, 370n1
Tietê River, 17
Timbira, 13, 25, 38, 41, 83, 103, 105
time of waters, 18–24
Tocantins River, 8, 26; Canoeiro on, 56–57; *entrada* on, 79–80; exploration, 82; gold on, 82–83; Jesuits on, 81, 82; juncture, 68, 81; mission settlements, 80; *sertanistas* on, 82; trade forbidden, 144; trade routes, 144; trips on, 8, 8–9, 13; Xavante hiding on, 110
Tocantins state, 5
Tomás, Manuel Rodrigues, 82, 187
Tovar, Vicente Alexandre de, 154
trade: with Bahia, 24; between enemies and allies, 301–2; exports of captaincy, 5, 24; with Karajá, 10; Luso-Brazilians, 9, 16; Mato Grosso, 142, 144, 146, 148; Natividade, 142–44, 146–47; *pardo*, 292; routes and towns, *140*, 144; slave, 15
trade in imperial system of Portugal, 141–49; cattle drives, 142; empire of,

trade in imperial system of Portugal (*continued*)
301; gold and, 141, 143; legal and contraband, 143, 146; long-distance traders, 146–47; mule teams, 142; river routes, 144–45, 146; roles of merchants, 148; slave trade, 145; trade value, 1804, *143*; Vila Real on, 144

Traíras, 11, 192–93

triatomines, 27

The Tribe That Hides from Man (film), xvii

Tucker, Richard, xx

Tupi language, 55–59

Tupinambá, 37, 80–81

Turner, Frederick Jackson, 300

Turner, Terry, 60

typhoid fever, 21

ubás (long canoes), 8, 38–42, 45

United Indian Nations, 104

vaccinations, 29

Valadares, Francisco, 81

Vallée, Ernesto, 23

vampire bats, 26

Vansina, Jan, xvii

Vasconcelos, José de, 84, 89

Vasconcelos, José de Almeida de, 26, 58, 91, 230

Veiga, Custodio Pereira da, 28

Veiga Bueno, João da, 78

Veiga Valle, José Joaquim da, 217

Veloso, Francisco, 79–80

vengeance, 75, 104, 121–23

Veras, Gonçalo de, 81

Vermelho River, 5, 9–10, 18, 23, 70

Vianna, Antônio Gonçalvez, 173

Vianna, José Mauricio, 173

Vieira, Antônio, 79, 81, 227

Vieira, José, 228

Vieira, José da Costa, 177

Vila Bela, 17

Vila Boa de Goiás, *130*; administrative inefficiency, 149; chapels, 217–18; dragoons in, 151; founding, 3, 129, 130; Irmandade do Rosário in Vila Boa, 226; judicial system, 133–34; Junta of the Treasury, 134–35; mining camps, 130; Our Lady of the Rosary of the Blacks, 217, 221; Paulistas in, 145; *pedestre*, 150–51; *quinto* collection, 136; Saint Ann's Church, *216*, 216–17; Saint-Hilaire on, 132; São Francisco de Paula church, 217; taxes, 135–36; white propertied elites in, 162; women, *248*

Vilanova, Gil, 243–44, 253–54

Vila Real, Tomás de Sousa, xxii, 7, 21, 23, 249; on Apinaje, 96, 105–6; Araguaia route and trade, 9–10, 144, 284; Karajá and, 47, 105–6, 284; on trading posts, 144

Vila Rica, 16

village. *See* aldeia

Villas Boas, Claudio, xvii, 94

Villas Boas, Orlando, xvii, 94

violence: Canoeiro and, 57; Cocal, 57, 120; against women, 248. *See also* warfare; warriors; weapons

warfare, 301; Apinaje, 96–99; Canoeiro, 118–21; Cocal and, 99–100; episodic, 125; Indians and, 73, 124, 210; Javaé, 105–6; Karajá, 105–6; Kayapó, 121–26; Krahô, 99–105; Luso-Brazilian view, 95; overview, 95–96; Pohl on, 99–101, 109; Porekamekra, 99–105, 108; weapons and skill, 101, 126; Xavante and Xerente, 107–18

warriors: Akroá, 35–38; Apinaje, *97*; Bororo, 75; Karajá, *107*; Kayapó, 72; Xavante, 49–50

weapons: Apinaje, 98; Canoeiro, 120;

European, 73; Javaé, 106; Karajá, 45–46, 48; Kayapó, 61, 124–25; Porekamekra, 101–2; warfare, 126; Xavante, 109–10; Xerente, 112
Wells, James, 20, 252
white militia force (*ordenança*), 147, 151, 181, 286, 330
white propertied elites, 159, 362–63n11; census of 1779, 161; census of 1781, 162; census of 1782, 162; census of 1783, 162; census of 1789, 162; census of 1791, 162; census of 1792, 163; census of 1798, 162; census of 1804, 162–63, *313*; census of 1825, 163, *314*; census of 1832, 163, *315*; chapels, 221; Christians, 184; in Goiás captaincy, 1779–1832, *311–12*; gold and, 159, 165–66; inbreeding, 161; in isolation, 184; judges and bureaucrats, 182–84; merchants and businessmen, 173–76; military officers, 180–82; mine owners, 164–72, 180; in Natividade, 162–63; in North, 1779–1832, *312*; overview, 159–64; planters and ranchers, 176–80; priests, 179–80; quality, 160–61; and slaves, 313–15; in South, 1779–1832, *311*; in Vila Boa de Goiás, 162; whites defined, 160–61
women: abandonment of, 268–71; Apinaje, 96, 249, 258; Araés, 248; in battle, 249; *beatas*, 156, 260, 380n33; Canoeiro, 249; captives, 66; in clerical families, 259–61; coerced labor, 251–53; concubinage, 253–58; in directorate missions, 241; freeborn and freed people of color, 282; *goiano*, 156–57, 252, 271; healers, 156; incest, 250; in indigenous nations, 249; interpreters, 249; Karajá, 45, 84–85, 248–49; Kayapó, 87; marriages, 261–66; marriages across color lines, 266–68; Natividade, 270; occupations, 251–53; overview, 247–50; Paulista, 258; Pohl on, 247, 270; poverty, 170, 270; *sertanistas*, 88; sexual assault, 102, 249–50; sexual relations, 258–569; slave labor of, 204; Vila Boa de Goiás, *248*; violence against, 70, 248–50; violence against babies, 103, 249, 258; Xavante, 105, 108
work: of enslaved Africans, 202–6; identity and, 202; mining, 204–6; occupations of slaves, 1783, *203*

Xacriabá, 11, 35–38; Akroá as enemy, 36; *bandeira* against, 83; indigenous nation, 35–38; measles among, 30, 36; mission settlements, 35–38, 228–29; pacification, 83; in *pedestre*, 285; Saint-Hilaire on, 37–38
Xambioá, 40, 44–49, 96
Xavante, xviii, 49–52; baskets, *x*viii, *40*; battle horn, 109–10, *110*; Canoeiro enemy, 52, 55; at Carretão, 50, 55, 90, 92–93, 108, 238–44; chiefs, 51; Christians and, 108; coalition, 40; Cunha Matos and, 93; directorate missions and, 238–41, 243; enemy of Karajá, 44–45, 105, 108; enemy of Krahô, 42, 104; expanding territory, 110; Gê language, 49; hiding on Tocantins River, 110; incorporation of Akroá and Xerente, 108; indigenous nation, 49–55; Jesuits and, 52; lands of, 299; Luso-Brazilian enemy, 108; in Mato Grosso, 299; in mission settlements, 107, 230, 237–38; move, refusal to, 20–21; Natividade and, 107; Nimuendajú on, 52; pacification, 111; pacification *bandeira* against, 89–94; *pardo* and, 288; peacemaking, 110–11; Pohl on, 50–52, 108–9; in Pontal, 111; raids, 10, 13, 85, 107–9, 249; religion, 52; Salinas, and, 48; settled life, 51; slaves, 108; Tristão da Cunha, 89–90,

Xavante (continued)
    111; warfare, 49, 107–18; warriors, 49–50; weapons, 108–10, 377n97; women, 108; written history, 33; Xerente split from, 52–55, 109; Xerente united with, 50–51
Xavante split from, 52–55, 109
Xavante united with, 50–51, 108
Xavier, Joaquim Cardoso (artist), 130, 231
Xavier de Aguirre, Michaela, 190
Xavier de Barros, Pacifico Antônio, 114–15, 154
Xerente, 10–11, 52–55; Balsas River *aldeias*, 343n45; *bandeira*, 1836, 118; In Carretão, 53; chiefs (captains), 55, 116; Chiotay, chief, 53; Cocal, 351n12; Cunha Matos and, 113–17; directorate missions and, 244; enemies of, 54, 112; Gê language, 52; at Graciosa, 54–55, 114–18; indigenous nation, 49–55; Kayapó as enemy, 112; leadership, 55; in mission settlements, 107, 114, 244; Nimuendajú on, 52, 112–13; Pohl on, 112; raids, 13, 55, 112; reserve, 303; savage reputation, 113–14; seeking refuge and peace, 13, 95; Silva e Souza on, 55; warfare, 107–18; weapons, 112
Xuanam-piá, 45, 84–85, 2249
Xuathe, 54, 114–15
Xuathe, Francisco, 54–55, *114*, 114–16, 244

Zouro, Antônio, 67

www.ingramcontent.com/pod-product-compliance
Lightning Source LLC
Chambersburg PA
CBHW030515230426
43665CB00010B/624